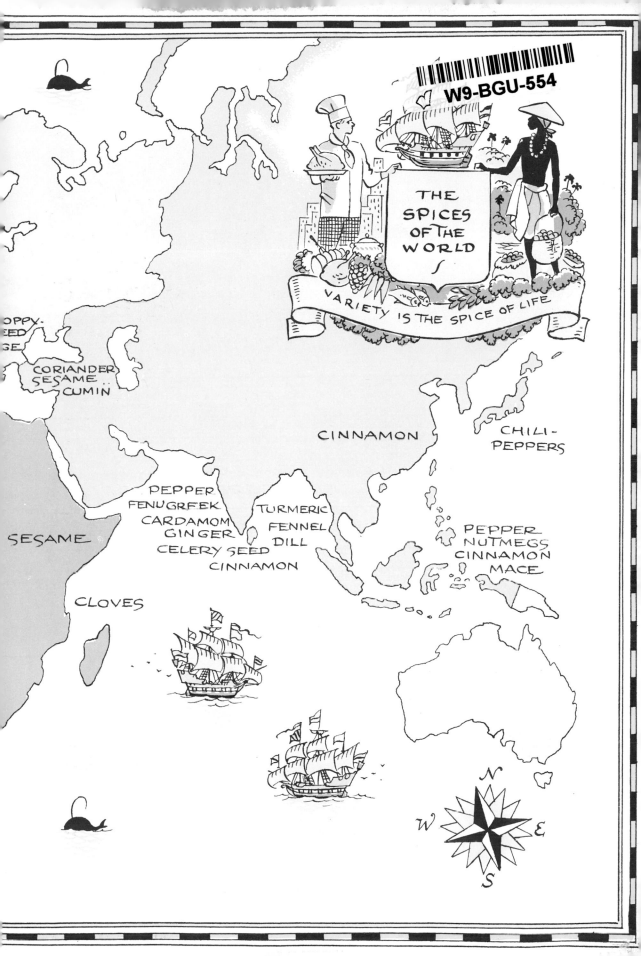

THE
SPICES
OF THE
WORLD
∫

VARIETY IS THE SPICE OF LIFE

W9-BGU-554

OPPY·
EED
GE

CORIANDER
SESAME
CUMIN

CINNAMON

CHILI-
PEPPERS

PEPPER
FENUGREEK
CARDAMOM
GINGER
CELERY SEED
CINNAMON

TURMERIC
FENNEL
DILL

PEPPER
NUTMEGS
CINNAMON
MACE

SESAME

CLOVES

N
W   E
S

THE SPICE
COOKBOOK

THE SPICE COOKBOOK

BY AVANELLE DAY AND LILLIE STUCKEY

ILLUSTRATED BY JO SPIER

DAVID WHITE COMPANY, NEW YORK

COPYRIGHT © 1964 BY AVANELLE S. DAY
AND LILLIE M. STUCKEY

ALL RIGHTS RESERVED

NO PART OF THIS BOOK MAY BE REPRODUCED IN ANY MANNER WITHOUT
PERMISSION IN WRITING FROM THE PUBLISHER, EXCEPT IN THE CASE OF
A REVIEWER WHO MAY QUOTE A SINGLE RECIPE AND BRIEF PASSAGES IN A
REVIEW FOR A NEWSPAPER OR MAGAZINE.

DAVID WHITE COMPANY
60 EAST 55TH STREET, NEW YORK, NEW YORK

PRINTED IN THE UNITED STATES OF AMERICA BY RAE LITHOGRAPHERS

COOKERY

"What does cookery mean? It means the knowledge of Medea, and of Circe, and of Calypso, and of Helen, and of Rebekah, and of the Queen of Sheba. It means knowledge of all herbs, and fruits, and balms, and spices, and of all that is healing and sweet in groves, and savory in meat. It means carefulness and inventiveness, watchfulness, willingness, and readiness of appliances. It means the economy of your great-grandmother, and the science of modern chemistry, and French art and Arabian hospitality. It means, in fine, that you are to see imperatively that everyone has something nice to eat."

—JOHN RUSKIN

ACKNOWLEDGMENTS

We owe a great debt of gratitude to the many people who have been so materially helpful in preparing this book.

First of all, to Lester Day for having served as guinea pig for lo, these many years of married life; for the right phrases, the critical comment, and the many long hours of speedy and accurate typing.

To Dr. Helen Judy Bond for having been a favorite and inspiring professor and a life-long friend; and for her gratifying foreword to this book.

To Dr. John C. Zimmer for his critical reading of certain sections requiring his specialized knowledge of chemistry.

Our sincerest thanks, too, go to the staff of the New York Public Library —especially the librarians in the Rare Book Room; to the staff of the Library of the Horticultural Society of New York; to the staff of the Bronx Botanical Garden Library; and to James R. Jackson for the use of source material in his private collection.

We are greatly indebted to Evelyn H. Van Horne for her interest and encouragement, her critical reading of the manuscript, and for her many excellent suggestions.

We thank Luz Serrano, formerly of Bogota, Colombia, who contributed some of her country's wonderful recipes, and was most helpful in the preparation of this book.

And, for all these years, we have been owing a debt of gratitude to our mothers, Daisy Salmon and Wilhelmina Stuckey, for having us underfoot in the kitchen, for letting us look—and sometimes lick—and for answering so patiently our many, many questions. In short, for having let us learn, at an early age, that cooking is fun.

A. S. D.
L. M. S.

CONTENTS

FOREWORD

SUGAR and spice and all things nice. That and much more is what this book is made of. *The Spice Cookbook* is not "just another cook book." It is a significant contribution to the important literature on the art of cooking.

And more, it is a work of art. Each drawing is fascinating and uniquely authentic. The artist, Jo Spier, has traveled to many parts of the world—and much of the artwork in this lovely book is based on sketches made by Mr. Spier in the Spice Islands, in India, in the Middle and Near East, in Europe—and, indeed, across the length and breadth of the United States.

The Spice Cookbook is a world atlas that carries the reader to far-flung islands and to remote areas of many continents. It reveals the world of trade from the earliest system of barter to the highly competitive market of today. It captures all of the romance of the spice industry, from its earliest beginnings to the present where, in this country alone, we consume more than 200,000,000 pounds of spices annually.

But above all, *The Spice Cookbook* is a superb cookbook. In it culinary art has reached a high peak of perfection. The more than 1400 recipes have been thoroughly tested in the home and in the home economics laboratory. They can be used with assurance by the most inexperienced cook or by the home-maker whose greatest joy is the production of prize-winning dishes.

The Spice Cookbook is the product of world travel, international acquaintances, educational and professional experience, and the rare combination of the personal talents of Avanelle Salmon Day, a home economist, food writer Lillie Stuckey, and Jo Spier, the artist. These professionals have made this a beautiful and interesting book as well as a connoisseur's collection of spice recipes.

The Spice Cookbook will be treasured by every family and it will be handed down from generation to generation. In years to come, Grandmother's *Spice Cookbook* will not be found stored away in the attic. With well-worn pages between dog-eared covers, it will be used by the fortunate granddaughter who inherited it. There will be cherished memories of the wonderful spicy odors that came from grandmother's kitchen and of the delicious meals served at her bountiful table.

Both authors learned to cook in childhood. Avanelle Day received her bachelor's degree in Home Economics from Women's College of Georgia, and later, her master's degree from Columbia University. Several years of teaching in junior and senior high schools and in cafeteria management have been followed by almost two decades in recipe research with the emphasis on spice cookery. During this time she has tested and perfected thousands of recipes, using all known varieties of spices.

Lillie Stuckey is a graduate of the University of the City of Toledo in Ohio, where she majored in Journalism. Her insatiable curiosity has proved priceless in her research and writing in the field of foods. This, added to her natural food sense and her unusual ability to unearth little-known and fascinating facts about foods, particularly spices, has made her contribution to this volume most valuable.

To these rare talents was added the interest, and very real assistance, of Mrs. Day's husband. Lester Day has accompanied the author on many of her trips to spice-producing countries and, as a chemist, has given advice on many technical matters and made valuable contributions from his own professional field.

As a home economist of long standing, it is gratifying to see a member of our profession contribute a book with such high standards and of such great value to the literature of our field. But with even greater pride I have watched one of my former students, Avanelle Salmon, grow in professional stature and demonstrate all that is best in home economics—so well-evidenced by this practical and artistic contribution to the art, science and joy of home and family living.

HELEN JUDY BOND
Professor Emeritus
Columbia University

THE SPICE
COOKBOOK

SPICE ISLAND
'PERKENIERS' HOUSE

A History of the Spice Trade

L IKE rivers of fragrance, all the spices of the East—pepper, poppy seed, ginger, cloves, and sesame; nutmeg, mace, turmeric, cinnamon, and basil—have poured forth to bring their bounty. For thousands of years these insignificant curls of bark and shriveled seeds, these dried leaves and gnarled roots have flowed along the curving trade routes of antiquity into man's legend and history. From the perfumed ritual of the bath and the aromatic goodness of the hearth to the sacred worship of the gods, spices have added their magic. This was so, in whole or in part, when man was prehistoric; it was thus with the ancient Babylonians and Assyrians and Hebrews. Today the routes are buried by time, but time's tradition remains.

Eighteen centuries before Christ, Joseph was sold by his brothers to "a company of Ishmaelites come from Gilead, with their camels bearing spicery and balm and myrrh, going to carry it down to Egypt." These were the Arabs of the spice trade, already, more than three thousand years ago, monopolists. Their products came from the Indians, and from the Chinese and Javanese who put into Indian ports. But for centuries the Arabs would not give away the secret of their sources of supply, only telling dark stories to their would-be rivals of dangers in distant lands. Meanwhile their caravans, with as many as four thousand camels laden with spices and silks and the rich treasures of the East, made their way from Goa, Calicut, and the Orient to the hungry markets of Nineveh and Babylon; of Carthage, Alexandria, and Rome. And in this trade the Arabs grew rich as their perfumed nights.

3

If they knew any rivals, they were the Phoenicians who, besides being famous for their purple dyes and fabrics, their metalwork and colored glass, were renowned navigators and traders. In their ships they carried a vast array of merchandise; at Tyre, their richest and busiest port, the Bible tells us, they traded, "of all spices, and with all precious stones and gold." It is thought that King Solomon, around 1000 B.C., richer as well as wiser than all the kings of the earth, made some of his great wealth from spices. By his agreement with the Phoenician king, Hiram, Solomon built the ships in which the Phoenicians and Israelites sailed in search of them. And when the Queen of Sheba visited the illustrious king, she brought to him as a gift "a very great train, with camels that bare spices." She must have had them to give, of course, for Sheba, or Saba, ancient name for today's Yemen, was that region of Arabia Felix that the Greeks and Romans believed to be the spices' happy homeland.

Due to the secretive Arabs, the spice buyers of Greece and Rome knew as little about the actual whereabouts of the spicelands as they knew of the Western Hemisphere. But they did have a vague notion that there were countries, farther even than India, which produced spices, gold, and tin. Finally, Pliny tells us, Augustus, the first Roman emperor, sent an expedition to Arabia to find their sources and routes. The Arabs, forced by the Romans to give directions, set them on a path that took them the long way round, through vast regions desolate and waterless, so that they were lucky to return with their lives. They had learned little of what they had set out to find.

If the Romans knew that the overland route was endless and treacherous, the water route, closely following the Arabian and Indian shore line, had only greater speed to recommend it. In their little ships intrepid sailors fought storm and shipwreck and pirate alike; those who reached port counted luck not the least of their good fortune.

Then, in the days of Tiberius Caesar, spanning the beginnings of the Christian Era, seafaring men discovered how to make use of the monsoons— those seasonal winds of the Indian Ocean that blow east in summer and west in winter. Now, pushed by these kindly forces, spice ships could reach the great markets of Europe in record time.

Europe's markets were great indeed. For Rome, during Christianity's early centuries, was profligate with wealth. Not only did she use spices to crown her emperors; she also used spices to bury them. And after Nero kicked his wife Poppaea to death in A.D. 65, he used, Tacitus tells us, an entire year of Rome's cinnamon supply to bury her.

Then, one day in 410, Alaric and his Visigoth hordes swarmed through Rome's gates. Gone were the happy days of banquets, debaucheries, and circuses. Gone was a ransom of gold and silver, silken robes and fine scarlet cloth, and "three thousand pounds weight of pepper."

With Rome's defeat, religion, law, art, and science virtually stood still. So, too, did navigation and commerce among nations. By the end of the seventh century papyrus from Egypt had disappeared, and with it, spices. For these two concomitants of mind and body traveled in the same vessels. Now only kings and high dignitaries of the Church could afford those rare packets that reached the West.

Meanwhile, while darkness covered much of western Europe, there lived in Mecca, on the eastern shore of the Red Sea, a young camel driver named Mohammed. His marriage to the widow of a wealthy Arabian spice trader was a happy wedding of religion and trade. For while Europe lay stagnant, his missionaries took his new religion of Islam throughout Asia; and as they gathered believers and spread Mohammed's word, they gathered spices and spread their use. When the Mohammedan Moors, strong in their beliefs, landed in Spain in 711 and conquered the Visigoths, they brought with them the East's learning and luxury—and their own appetite for spices.

By the tenth century the winds of trade were once more touching Europe's shores. Venice, that jeweled cluster of small mud islands at the head of the Adriatic Sea, had been founded five hundred years earlier as a refuge from invading barbarians from the North. Her great merchant fleet, defended by her many warships, now kept a tight hold on the commerce of Western waters. From Alexandria, to which spiceloads had been shipped or taken by overland caravan from Cairo, Venetian merchants sailed their galleys laden with spice sacks worth 200,000 ducats.

This was rich fare: during the Middle Ages in Europe a pound of ginger bought a sheep; a pound of mace, three sheep or half a cow. Pepper was almost priceless, counted out berry by berry; and worth taxes, tributes, dowries, rents. In medieval France a pound of it could buy a serf his freedom.

But Europe still did not know the sources of this wealth. During the Crusades feudal lords and rich merchants, who carried the Cross to win the Holy Land from the Moslems and find new markets on the way, looked for a paradise by the River Ganges, from which, they believed, precious spices and gems were washed down. They thought this Eden was far to the northeast

of Jerusalem, many months of travel beyond it; the march to the Holy Land was a first long step.

Nine Crusades brought East and West together in the rich trading centers of Constantinople, Cairo, and Baghdad. Here, amid the haggle-babble of a hundred tongues, excited traders exchanged Western woolens and linens for Eastern spices and silks. From the East, the spoils poured into Venice, the proudest city of the Western world, that lay upon her lagoons "like a sea bird's nest afloat on the shallow waves." Halfway between East and West, her harbor drew silks and spices, camphor and ivory, jewels and perfumes and carpets, by way of Egypt's Nile and overland to Alexandria, or through the fertile lands of Persia, or across the highlands of Central Asia. From Venice horses carried them across the Alps to Germany and France, or by galleys through Gibraltar to Brugge and Southampton and London, where close sewing guarded dock guards' pockets against dock guards' pilfering.

But the Crusaders returned with as little knowledge of the spicelands themselves as had their Roman ancestors so long before.

The year that saw the start of the last Crusade saw the beginning of another, perhaps more momentous, journey. In 1271, while thousands carried the Cross once more toward the Holy Land, two Venetian jewel merchants, Nicolo and Maffeo Polo, took off in the same direction. Their goal was not Palestine, though they had to touch on her along the way. They headed for China, which they called Cathay, thousands of miles farther away. This was a large undertaking, but not new to these experienced travelers. Not only had they sailed on buying and selling trips throughout the eastern Mediterranean and traded in Constantinople, but they had already been overland to China. It was only two years since their return.

This time Nicolo was taking his seventeen-year-old son, Marco, with him. Marco was forty-one when the Polos came home to Venice.

For seventeen of those twenty-four years they journeyed all over Asia— to China, Indochina, Burma, India. They served the Mongol conqueror Kublai Khan in his court in Peking and on missions to many parts of the Orient. They were rewarded with rich gifts of silk and jewels of rare value.

Three years after his return Marco, in command of a galley in one of Venice's incessant battles with her ancient rival Genoa, was captured. The fortunes of war swung fairly evenly between these two great cities, but there was one permanent consequence to this conflict: Marco Polo told his endlessly fascinating tales of his travels not only to the Genoese who flocked to hear them, but to another prisoner, Rusticiano of Pisa, who wrote them down. His story was to become the first link in a chain of great events: the downfall of Venice as a rich market; the end of the Arabian spice monopoly; the discovery of the New World; and the opening of direct trade with the Orient.

The Book of Marco Polo was an eyewitness and accurate account of sights and sounds and smells almost beyond belief, in lands so far away they were themselves almost unbelievable (some of the places Marco visited were not to be seen again until the twentieth century). It revealed China in all her vastness and wealth, and the nations on her borders with their strange manners and religions. It spoke of cannibal races and obscene ascetics, of diamonds and sea beds of pearls; of dog sledges and white bears—and of spices.

Marco Polo had seen them growing:

In Java: "From thence also is obtained the greatest part of the spices that are distributed throughout the world."

At Ormus, the gateway to India: "Whose port is frequented by traders from all parts of India, who bring spices and drugs. . . . These they dispose

of to a different set of traders, by whom they are dispersed throughout the world."

In the kingdom of Dely, that "produced large quantities of pepper and ginger, with many other articles of spicery."

Now Marco Polo's wondrous adventures spurred missionaries and merchants alike to go by land or sea to Cathay—Franciscan friars like John of Monte Corvino, who became Archbishop of Peking; and so many merchants that one of them, Francis Balducci Pegolotti, could write in 1340, "The road you travel from Tana to Cathay is perfectly safe, whether by day or night, according to what merchants say who have used it."

Then, in the middle of the fourteenth century, the Tartar dynasty fell and China's new rulers turned their backs to the West as Islam spread its conquests all over Central Asia. A new wall of darkness, more impregnable than China's great wall of stone, stood between the Far East and the Occident. Marco's millions were memory now.

But the book of Marco's travels was being read in Latin by a young Genoese sea captain. How to reach these marvels of Cathay now? On over seventy pages of *The Book of Marco Polo* he made notes; and he decided to sail west. And so, with three small ships, a crew mostly of convicts, and the inspiration of the Venetian traveler, Columbus discovered America.

With the new land came Europe's new chance, in which "the calamity of our time" gave way to a revival of the human spirit, where the concept of the golden age lay not in the pagan past, but in what was ahead. So long as the main trade routes to the East were overland, Venice and Genoa had held their keys. But now, ahead, lay drama and daring and the quick pulse of a new race.

Spain had the Italian-born Columbus and the Portuguese-born Magellan, who began his trip around the world with five ships and a crew of two hundred forty. Magellan himself died on the way home, as did two hundred twenty-two of his men. Four of the original five ships were lost. The one surviving ship, the *Victoria,* carried only eighteen men into her home port in Spain almost three years later. But sparse as was her crew, her holds burgeoned with enough spices to pay the cost of the entire expedition. Later, Spain's king Charles V sold his discovery rights to the Moluccas (Spice Islands) to his brother-in-law, Portugal's John III.

The little kingdom of Portugal had for some time been mastering navigation skills and, beyond the Mediterranean's gates, now rivaled her Italian tutors. Prince Henry the Navigator, a younger son of John I, had in 1418 established his naval college, to which he called to service the finest scientists of the time, and had begun his systematic explorations. The next year Madeira was discovered, then Cape Bojador and Cape Verde. In 1448 settlements were

established on the Azores, and in 1486 Diaz rounded the Cape of Good Hope. Five and a half years after Columbus's first voyage, Vasco da Gama sailed the Indian Ocean and reached the coast of Malabar. Thus, steadily did Portugal make her way down the western coast of Africa and open the seaway to China and Japan, always with the hope of finding safer passage to those great markets.

By the next century the Dutch were giving Portugal formidable competition by taking Malacca, the Malay Peninsula, and northern Sumatra. By 1658 they controlled the cinnamon trade in Ceylon, and in 1663 the richest pepper ports of the Indian Malabar coast were theirs. So, too, before the century's end, were the spices of Celebes and Java.

To challenge the Dutch was England, the little isle that as early as the twelfth century had formed a Guild of Pepperers which, in 1345, became the Worshipful Company of Grocers. (One of its rules: "All merchandise shall

be weighed fairly so that the weigher shall remove his hands therefrom.")
More and more English ships crossed the oceans to distant lands as greater
and greater tonnage filled her teeming ports. By 1600 her trade with the
Eastern Hemisphere was so heavy that she chartered the East India Company
to handle it.

Two years later the Dutch formed their own company to counter the
threat. For two hundred years these two great establishments vied with each
other in peace and war to monopolize trade.

Across another ocean, colonials were coping with a new land. The soil
and climate of the New World were harsh; but her timber stood magnificent,
her harbors kind, and the offshore fishing banks were fertile with riches. From
every harbor of New England's coast—Falmouth and Portsmouth and New-
buryport, Salem and Marblehead and Boston, New Bedford and Providence
and New London and Bridgeport—hundreds of little schooners, sloops, and
ketches put forth each year for ports near and far from home. And in every
harbor were men rich from the wealth the sea brought them, wealth that gave
them power in the social structure. Elias Haskett Derby, America's first mil-
lionaire, made much of his fortune in pepper, but he was far from unique. The
voyage of the one hundred-ton brig *Cadet,* sailing out of Salem one sunny
April morning in 1788 in search of Sumatra's pepper, was but the first of
almost a thousand "pepper voyages" that Americans undertook in the next
eighty-five years. Such 24,000-mile journeys meant two and three years of
danger and hardship, but New England's seamen were veteran fishermen on
the Grand Banks, and the most expert whalers in the world. With them
sailed a singular blend of daring, enterprise, and toughness.

Salem sings the song of spice romance. Almost half of those pepper voyages logged her as their starting point. "India" in Salem meant all the exotic lands on the other side of the Cape of Good Hope, and almost every family had someone who had gone "to the farthest port of the rich East." When they came back they brought heavy cargo, and curious and beautiful objects, and sometimes even a strangely beautiful woman dressed in the fabulous finery of the East, with coral hairpins in her fine dark hair.

So great was the pepper trade in the early nineteenth century, that the import duties in this little seaport were enough to pay five per cent of the expenses of the entire United States Government, and a large portion of the pepper itself—too much for Americans to consume—had to be re-exported to Europe.

Even though the pepper trade was so very lucrative, pirates finally put America out of the Oriental trade. Our merchant ships were raided and destroyed time and again. United States Navy frigates, ones with names as impressive as the *Potomac,* the *Columbia,* and the *Constitution,* were sent to protect the pepper trade along the west coast of Sumatra. Finally, however, our young government felt it should no longer back the spice trade with naval protection in foreign waters, and the ships were withdrawn.

In the late eighteenth and early nineteenth centuries, immigrants from all over the world poured into the United States, bringing with them their own eating habits, their particular national dishes, and the spices and herbs which flavored them. And today, it requires the various forms and blends of almost one hundred of these spices and herbs to season the dishes of our land.

No longer do the spicy tendrils wend with camel slowness or the river's lazy flow. Nor do the glorious galleys or the clippers of the lofty rig fight the sea's strength. Now some six hundred deep-water ships dock at United States ports alone to bring their spice cargoes. And within each curl of bark and shriveled seed and dried leaf and gnarled root is something of what the world has been. It is here for you, within the pages of this book.

ALLSPICE
The Spice Columbus Missed

IT is one of the ironies of history that, in an age of frantic exploration for spices and gold, Christopher Columbus should have sailed past one of the richest spice treasures in the Western Hemisphere. Twice, as he made way through the Caribbean Islands, he viewed "trees of a thousand kinds, all laden with fruit which the Admiral believed to be spiceries and nutmeg—but they were not ripe and he did not recognize them." Had Columbus been a botanist, he undoubtedly would have recognized them as allspice trees, bearers of one of the most valued among all true spices.

Today, as when Columbus sailed so blithely past them, allspice trees grow wild in dark, shiny-foliaged forests. From late April into October the trees are covered with berries in various stages of ripeness. And it was probably at this stage, when the trees were fragrant with fruit, that allspice was eventually discovered by other, later Spaniards. Apparently they thought them to be pepper, since the dried allspice berry looks exactly like an oversized peppercorn. The Spaniards named the spice "pimento" and the botanists called the tree *Pimenta officinalis,* which is still its scientific name. In Jamaica, where allspice grows most lavishly, the name "pimento" still clings to it, and this is how the U.S. Customs Department lists it in its records.

Allspice played an important part in the era of melodramatic cloak-and-dagger derring-do. During the days when such swashbuckling seventeenth-century pirates as Henry Morgan and Calico Jack Rackham left a trail of dark deeds along the Spanish Main, they used allspice to preserve meats—mostly that of wild pigs—with which they stocked their galleys. Meat cured (smoked and seasoned) with allspice was called "boucan." Stemming from the pirates' dependence upon "boucan," they were labeled "boucaneers," from which eventually evolved the word now familiar to us, "buccaneers."

Many people think that allspice derives its name from being a blend of spices. This isn't the case, of course, but within the allspice berry itself is the mingled fragrance of cinnamon, cloves, and nutmeg; hence its simple if somewhat misleading name.

Allspice is used both whole and in ground form. The latter makes a delicious baking spice, adding a zestful aroma to fruit pies and cakes, spice cakes, and spiced fruit compotes. It is indispensable in making mince meat and plum puddings, steamed puddings, and similar dishes.

From the island of Jamaica comes the practice of seasoning chicken stock with allspice—approximately ¼ teaspoonful of whole allspice with what, when finished, will become 7 or 8 cups of stock. At the start of the cooking period, add the *whole* allspice; at the end, if you have some on hand, *ground* allspice may be added.

ANISE
Favorite of the Ancient Romans

IF you have had the pleasure of visiting the Roman Forum, the "main street" of Julius Caesar's day, you may have observed, here and there, straggly herbs—growing waist-high—covered with seeds.

Should you pick a seed, no one will object, since anise is nothing but a weed that grows along the fence beyond which is accelerated modern Rome. Nibbling the comma-shaped seed, you will be reminded of the taste of the pungent, shoestring licorice candy sold in your neighborhood grocery store; or, on a more sophisticated level, of the aromatic liqueur that seems so innocuous at first sip, but is so unexpectedly potent!

It is not at all unlikely that these wild and untended anise plants are direct descendants—1900 generations later!—of anise which by chance fell to the ground from Roman banquet tables. It was believed that anise could prevent indigestion. It was, too, a useful antidote for scorpion bite. Throughout the great sweep of the ages, anise has also been endowed with magic powers: keep a bit in your pocket and you would be safeguarded against an evil eye; tucked under a pillow, your sleep would be free of nightmares. It has been cherished as a perfume as well. Edward IV of England (fifteenth century) ordered that his bed linen be scented with small sachet bags of anise seeds and, in Oriental countries, anise is still used as a breath sweetener.

Anise, a small annual plant, stems from the parsley family. It originated, in prehistoric times, from that part of the eastern Mediterranean which historians call the Fertile Crescent, probably because so many of our useful plants seem to have been born there.

Anise was found in Egypt in 1500 B.C., according to records, and is mentioned in the Bible. With the passing of years, it made its way to India, sections of northern Europe and, more recently, to the Americas. When the settlers of Virginia were making their laws, anise was considered so valuable that every newcomer was required to plant six anise seeds.

Anise seeds, sold whole, are an appetizing addition to cookies, cakes, and sweet rolls. A pinch of anise used with fruits adds to their deliciousness, too. Cook ¼ to ½ teaspoonful of anise seeds with each cup of sugar syrup used to sweeten a fruit cup, fruit compote, or fruit beverages; or, sprinkle ¼ teaspoonful anise seeds over a fruit and cabbage slaw.

Occasionally we receive a letter from a housewife who has been trying to buy "star anise." This is a star-shaped seed having an anise flavor, but one which comes from an entirely different plant—a small evergreen tree of the magnolia family. Since this is a native of southeastern Asia and is cultivated in China, it is not readily available in the United States today, though certain Chinese groceries in the larger American cities occasionally keep some in stock.

BASIL Cut with a Golden Sickle

COOKS gifted with a flair for seasoning have ever treasured basil as one of the most savory of culinary herbs. More delicate than some of the lustier herbs, like oregano, it may be used generously in a variety of vegetables to lend a subtle, if entirely distinctive, flavor.

The word basil stems from two possible origins. One is from the Greek for "royal" or "kingly"; the other, from a tongue-twister, also Greek, meaning "lizard." In Greek mythology this was indeed a very special lizard, a basilisk, which needed only to look at or breathe upon his victim to kill him.

The Greeks believed that only the sovereign himself should be allowed to cut the basil, using a golden sickle. Yet, according to history, basil was a symbol of hate; why this was so is open to conjecture.

On the other hand, in Italy, basil has always been a token of love, and is called "kiss-me-Nicholas" in some of its regions. Any girl who wears a sprig of basil is suggesting to her beau, and not too subtly, that there is no need for him to keep his distance. In Romania, however, things are somewhat more definite: when a boy accepts a sprig of basil from his girl, it means he is engaged!

In its native India, basil, called *tulasi,* is considered a holy herb and grown in pots near every temple and dwelling of devout Hindus. Though especially sacred to Vishnu, Krishna, and Lakshmi, all the other gods esteem it, too.

Throughout the ages, doctors and herbalists have used basil in medicine and magic, although there seems to have been a happy lack of agreement as to its merits for either. "This is the herb which all authors are to-gether by the ears about, and rail at one another like lawyers," wrote herbalist Nicholas Culpeper in 1652. "Galen and Dioscorides hold it not fit to be taken inwardly, and Chrysippus rails at it with downright Billingsgate rhetoric. Pliny and the Arabian Physicians defend it."

That this fragrant herb aroused controversy adds to its interest. John Gerard, Shakespeare's contemporary, was enthusiastic, saying: "A smell of Basil is good for the heart and head—cureth the infirmities of the heart, taketh away sorrowfulness which cometh of melancholia and maketh a man merry and glad."

Whatever its merits or failures may be as a remedy for physical ailments, basil is a delightful contribution to a variety of dishes. Since, as mentioned earlier, it is one of the most delicate herbs, it may be used more generously than lustier ones. Basil blends tastily with tomatoes, but also enhances vegetables such as eggplant, green beans, zucchini, peas, or cooked cucumber dishes. Basil is often used with, or as a substitute for, oregano in pizza topping, spaghetti sauce, or a macaroni and cheese casserole.

BAY LEAF To Win One's Laurels

IN Rome's Borghese Museum, preserved forever in a Bernini marble is the most romantic of all spice legends. It was inspired by Ovid's *Metamorphoses*, the story of Daphne transformed into a laurel tree to escape the advances of Apollo.

In a rare malicious mood, the otherwise mischievous Cupid caused the change. Cupid was angry with Apollo for having dubbed him a mere boy and, in revenge, he shot the arrow of desire into the heart of this god of youth and manly beauty. But with a second arrow he wounded the lovely nymph Daphne, which made her flee from all love, most especially from Apollo's. The more swiftly he pursued her, the more desperate was Daphne's flight.

Finally, she could run no longer. As Apollo's hand touched her, she prayed to the gods to camouflage the beauty which had been so pleasing.

At once, her feet took root, her arms became boughs and leaves sprouted from her finger tips. Before Apollo's unbelieving eyes stood a beautiful tree. As he stared in wonder at its green and shining leaves, he vowed that since she could not be his bride, she would be his tree, honored and renowned. Poets would ever crown it with their songs, and Roman festivals it would adorn. No prize was great enough for his love, transformed though she was. She would be the sacred guardian at Caesar's gate, safe from thunder and never-fading. He willed her branches ever to be green.

The laurel became what Apollo vowed it would. Laurel boughs decorated the palace gates of the Caesars, and the Caesars themselves wore laurel or stayed close to where it grew. This custom had multiple reasons: Julius Caesar, for example, clung to his laurel wreath because it helped to hide his baldness. On the other hand, the Emperor Tiberius, terrified of lightning, set a crown of laurel leaves on his head as protection at the onset of a Roman thunderstorm. It is also related that, to insure his safety, he would hide under his bed as well. Since laurel was supposed to purify the air, the Emperor Claudius, during an epidemic, fled to Laurentum—so named because of its many laurel trees. As if anticipating the death of Nero, legend tells us, laurel trees withered just before he died.

For centuries the laurel wreath has been the symbol of the triumphant leader, the celebrated athlete, the distinguished scholar. Thus our modern expression, "To win one's laurels."

The bough of the laurel was also endowed with magical qualities, giving prophets the gift of seeing the unknown and the future. Placing a laurel leaf beneath the pillow would induce future events to appear in a dream. The priestess of Apollo, at Delphi, shook a laurel tree and sometimes chewed the leaves before offering oracles from the sacred pedestal.

Ancient Greek physicians held laurel in great esteem as a promoter of good health. When a Greek said that he carried a branch of laurel, it meant that he feared neither poison nor sorcery. During grave illness a laurel branch was hung on the door, to drive away death and evil spirits. Because of these associations with physical health and welfare, young doctors were crowned with laurel berries, *Bacca Lauri,* and called baccalaureates, or bachelors.

There seems no end to the magic powers attributed to laurel. For in-

SPICE ISLAND

stance, young girls would burn laurel leaves to win back errant lovers. In one part of Italy the success or failure of local crops could be predicted by the burning of laurel leaves. If the leaves crackled while burning, the crops would be good; if they burned silently, hard times were ahead.

So far as the cook is concerned, it may be well to heed this advice from a culinary editor of a nineteenth-century magazine: "To win a laurel wreath for your brow, put a laurel leaf in the stew pot now."

Though "laurel leaf" is more poetic, you will, when scanning the tantalizing array of spice jars at the grocer's, find it labeled "bay leaf."

Bay leaf lends a provocative aroma to meats, fish, fowl, stews, and soups of all kinds. Make frequent use of the bay leaf, but not too much at a time. Usually, 1 medium-size leaf is adequate for 6 portions.

CAPSICUM PEPPERS Gift of the New World

ALL during the many centuries when caravans were wending westward toward Egypt, Greece, and Rome with the spices of the Orient, there flourished in tropical America the almost endlessly varied *capsicum,* or pod-pepper genus. From the first, these capsicums were misnamed "peppers," although they are not even remotely related to the classical peppercorn which commanded such a fortune in ancient and medieval times.

Today there are hundreds—if not thousands—of capsicum varieties. Some are large; some tiny. Some are long and cone-shaped, others squat and button-shaped. They may be violet, white, green, yellow, and red. Their pungency ranges from "warm" to *wow*. On the American spice shelf you can find mild paprika, sweet pepper flakes, chili peppers, red peppers, and cayenne, as well as blends such as chili powder, curry powder, mixed pickling spice, barbecue spice, and seafood seasoning.

Paprika is the brilliantly red "garnish spice." In America we prefer mild paprika, but it is possible to buy paprika with considerable zip. This kind is traditionally used in Hungarian dishes, such as *paprikash*. If you want an extra nip in your paprika, add a bit of red pepper or cayenne.

Next in importance on our spice shelf is chili powder which, of course, starts out as chili pepper. Legend has it that chili powder was dreamed up by an Englishman living in Texas about a century ago. In his attempt to approximate the curry powder he had known in India, he hit upon the chili powder blend.

Barbecue spice is a variation of chili powder. Ground or crushed red pepper comes from capsicums grown in the Carolinas, California, Louisiana, and in Turkey. Crushed red pepper is an essential ingredient in many Mexican and Italian dishes, and is often called "pepperoni rosso" or "pizza peppers."

Cayenne is always a ground product made from the small, very hot varieties of capsicums. Often more than one variety of hot pepper is used in making cayenne. Today some manufacturers have dropped the term "cayenne" and simply call their hottest product "red pepper."

CARAWAY The Ancient Spice

IT is generally believed that caraway came originally from Asia Minor, and that its migrations began thousands of years ago. Caraway seeds were among the 5000-year-old debris left by the primitive lake dwellers of Switzerland. Puzzled as to how so tiny a seed could be preserved over such a great span of time, we asked the American Museum of Natural History for an explanation.

One of their archaeologists said this had been made possible by the caraway seeds having been completely and constantly submerged in a peaty wetness. Even something as perishable as a seed can survive indefinitely under such conditions.

Roman soldiers, no doubt, scattered or planted caraway seeds throughout most of the known world. Northern Europeans, especially the English

and Germans, seem to have used caraway at least a thousand years past. One of Shakespeare's characters offered a guest, "Pippin of my own graffing, with a dish of caraways." The devotion of the Germans to caraway had been recorded by Pierre Pomet, chief druggist to Louis XIV of France, as follows: "The Germans have such regard for it, they always put it into the Pye-Crust, mix it in their Bread, and in great Measure in all their Sauces."

For the past hundred years the Netherlands—halfway between England and Germany—have been growing caraway on the heavy clay land that they managed to wrest from the inundation of the North Sea. Since the ripe seed heads shatter so easily when dry, all caraway seeds must be harvested during the dewy hours of the night and early morning, before the hot sun reaches the fields.

While our acquaintance with caraway may be confined to rye bread, to which it lends a savory aroma, there are many other delightful uses for these seeds. As an example, the Germans prefer pork generously flavored with caraway, especially when it is served with sauerkraut or boiled cabbage. The Austrians use it in beef stews, while the Hungarians create a caraway soup by boiling seeds in stock or water, then thickening the soup with bread crumbs. (Such a soup is believed to be very strengthening for new mothers.) In Italy, street vendors sell hot chestnuts that have been boiled with caraway seeds. And it is the caraway seed, along with cumin and anise, that gives Kümmel, the popular liqueur, its distinctive flavor. Then, too, candy-covered caraway seeds, called "comfits," are sold in various parts of the United States. Less politely they are known as "whisky-killers," since they can also serve to mask an alcoholic breath.

CARDAMOM A Delicate Treasure

W E might well wonder why cardamom is so popular in India, where it grows, almost equally in demand in far-off Scandinavian countries—and yet used rarely throughout the several thousand miles which separate these contrasting regions.

The Vikings, who were superb seafarers, went on expeditions more than a thousand years ago that took them as far as Constantinople, one of the major spice-trading centers of the Middle East. Cardamom soon proved to be their favorite spice. Centuries past, cardamom was used in the festival cakes of the Vikings and is said to have been mentioned in the *Eddas,* the great sagas of the north countries.

Cardamom, a member of the ginger family, is the world's second most valued spice, yielding top honors only to saffron. Native to India and south-eastern Asia, it thrives in the warm, moist tropics, growing upon the partially shaded areas that exist in the middle of mountain slopes. Though the fruits ripen throughout the year, they are harvested—snipped off with sharp scissors

—when about three-quarters ripe. Each straw-colored pod, about the size of a cranberry, holds from 17 to 20 tiny, black, sharply aromatic seeds.

Cardamoms were used in ancient Greece and Rome 2000 years ago. Historians and medical writers inform us that cardamom was used not only in foods, but made an important ingredient for medicines and perfumes.

The Indians themselves use up most of the cardamoms grown in their own country, since it is a favorite seasoning for curries, desserts, and after-dinner tidbits. In Scandinavian countries it lends its special aroma to what has become known as "Danish pastry," as well as serving as a delightful alternate to cinnamon in many sweet dishes.

Cardamom is available in ground or whole form. Scandinavian cooks mix approximately ½ teaspoonful of ground cardamom with 1 cup of sugar, using it much the same way as we use cinnamon sugar.

CELERY SEED T'is Smallage

THE classification of celery seed—the spice—reminds us of the story of an old cook who had made several varieties of two-crust Thanksgiving pies. Each pie, regardless of the filling, had the letters "TS" pricked in the upper crust. This, she explained, signified simply, "T'is mince" and "T'aint mince."

And so with celery seeds. The labels say *t'is* celery, but American seedmen say *t'aint* celery. The celery stalks we munch on have little connection with the celery seeds on our spice shelves. The latter, or the "spice" known as celery seed, is actually a wild variety of celery, commonly called *smallage*.

Smallage has been known for centuries around the Mediterranean. Indeed, its history can be traced to the time of Homer, in the ninth century B.C. Apparently, it was considered an excellent medicine. A contemporary poet-doctor wrote: "The disease then to celery yields, conquered by the remedy."

Celery seed is a delightful seasoning for sauces, salads, pickles, soups, vegetables, and many other dishes. Whole celery seeds are available at every spice counter; or you can use celery salt, which is a combination of ground celery seeds and ordinary table salt.

CHERVIL Delighteth the Taste

CHERVIL, like a virtuous young lady, has a minimum of personal history. Legend has it that it makes one merry, sharpens a dull wit, prods the memory, and gives the aged the *élan* of youth. But, unlike so many herbs, chervil never made a name for itself as a remedy for the bites of serpents or mad dogs; young ladies never depended on it to produce dreams of future husbands; and it had absolutely no value in witchcraft.

However, chervil has always been greatly admired for its beautiful, fern-like leaves, and its flavor, "so like in taste unto Anis seede," as seventeenth-century John Parkinson observed, "that it much delighteth the taste among other herbs in a sallet."

De Candolle, nineteenth-century author of *The Origin of Cultivated Plants,* believed that chervil was native to southeastern Russia. It probably reached the northern shores of the Mediterranean about 300 B.C. The Romans took chervil to northern Europe and England.

Today chervil is a great favorite in French kitchens, where it is used as an alternate to parsley in soups; salads, particularly potato salad; and very often in the classic *fines herbes* combination. It is available only in whole form.

CINNAMON The Fabulous Spice

THE birth of the cinnamon varieties coincides with the beginning of botanical history in primeval fields and forests. This, of course, makes it most difficult to separate fact from fable regarding this fabulous spice.

First, let us distinguish between the two kinds of cinnamon, which share a place of honor on the world's spice shelf: *Cinnamomum cassia* and *Cinnamomum zeylanicum.* Cassia cinnamon is the reddish-brown, pungently sweet variety which we prefer in the United States. Beyond the spice trade, the term cassia is rarely heard these days. It is labeled as well as specified in recipes as, simply, cinnamon.

Cinnamomum zeylanicum, or Ceylon cinnamon, is buff-colored, quite mild, and popular in many parts of the world, especially in Mexico, but not often seen in this country. Most of what we import is then exported to Mexico.

We know that cassia cinnamon is native to southern China, having been described by a Chinese writer of the third century A.D., but knowledge of cassia goes back centuries before that time.

Ancient religious belief in China regarded the cassia tree as the Tree of

Life, flourishing since time's beginning in Paradise, an exquisite garden at the headwaters of the Yellow River. Whoever entered Paradise, it was believed, and ate the fruit of this tree would win immortality and eternal bliss.

Both cinnamon and cassia are mentioned in the Bible in several instances. The Lord told Moses on Mount Sinai to make an anointing oil, which was to include not only sweet cinnamon, but "of cassia five hundred shekels. . . ." In the Forty-fifth Psalm, we read: "All thy garments smell of myrrh, and aloes, and cassia. . . ." Speaking of the wealth of the great city of Tyre in Phoenicia, we find in Ezekiel 27:19: "Bright iron, cassia and calamus, were in thy market. . . ." And, in Proverbs, chapter 7, there is the account of a woman planning—and achieving—the seduction of a young man by promising him that her couch had been scented with "myrrh, aloes, and cinnamon."

If ever we could collect all the knowledge relating to the history of cinnamon, we would simultaneously know the history of transportation, of caravan routes, of the first ocean voyages, of battles won and lost, and the risks and skulduggery involved in trading as men from the earliest days wandered from place to place. The Phoenicians, too (the Canaanites of the Old Testament), and the Arabs would become familiar, since these two peoples for so many centuries controlled East-West trade.

Not only were the Phoenicians bold navigators and shrewd businessmen, as is evident from their trade alliance with King Solomon of Israel in 1000 B.C., but they understood human nature. This is made clear by the rumors they spread among their potential rivals of the dangers in the cinnamon country. This was calculated, of course, to arouse fear. Herodotus, in his history written in the fourth century B.C., speaks of very fierce bats, menacing birds, and inaccessible precipices—all of which constituted a threat to those who would collect cinnamon.

Today, cinnamon grows in very much the same way as it grew 3000 years past. In Indonesia and South Vietnam, our two principal sources, the trees are moderate-sized evergreens. Cinnamon is harvested during the rainy season, since the wet atmosphere makes the bark more manageable. After the bark is stripped off it is rolled into long, slender quills, which we call cinnamon sticks.

Cinnamon, whole or ground, may be used in hundreds of ways. The Pennsylvania Dutch, for example, sprinkle cinnamon sugar over ripe tomato slices, and serve them as a relish. Greeks use a cinnamon stick in beef stews. North Indians include cinnamon in their curries. Mexicans are fond of using it in chocolate.

Cinnamon has a universal appeal, and it contributes happily to all kinds of baked dishes and desserts, as a garnish or an integral part of a dish's original ingredients.

CLOVES
A Forest of Flowers

IN *Colloquies on the Simples and Drugs of India,* by Dr. Garcia da Orta, published in India in 1563, the author wrote: "The scent of the clove is said to be the most fragrant in the world. I experienced this coming from Cochin to Goa, with the wind from the shore, and at night it was calm when we were a league from the land. The scent was so strong and delicious that I thought there must be a forest of flowers. On enquiring I found that we were near a ship coming from Maluco with cloves and then I understood the truth. Afterwards, men from Maluco told me that when the clove is dry it gives out a strong scent extending far from where it is."

To this eulogy can be added that of botanist Rumphius, who wrote from the Moluccas early in the seventeenth century: "The most beautiful, the most elegant, the most precious of all trees."

A forerunner of these two admirers of the clove tree was Dr. Pigafetta, the physician who accompanied Magellan around the world. In his book, published not long after his return in 1522, he said: "I went to see how the clove grows. The clove tree is tall and thick as a man's body . . . its leaves resemble those of the laurel and the bark is of a dark color. . . . The cloves grow at the end of the twigs, ten or twenty in a cluster. . . . When the cloves sprout they are white, when ripe, red, and when dried, black. They are gathered twice a year, once at the Nativity of our Savior and the other at the nativity of St. John the Baptist. . . . These cloves grow only in the mountains, and if any of them are planted in the lowlands near the mountains, they do not live. . . . Almost every day we saw a mist descend and circle now one and now another of these mountains on account of which those cloves become perfect."

Cloves grew so happily in the Moluccas that it was believed that "by no human industry can they be propagated or perfectly cultivated elsewhere." These early spice traders did not reckon with the plans of a young French adventurer, Pierre Poivre, who "liberated" young clove seedlings from Dutch plantations in the Far East and took them to mountainous Mauritius in the Indian Ocean. From Mauritius they migrated, early in the nineteenth century, to Zanzibar, Pemba, and Madagascar off the east coast of Africa. With its 5,000,000 clove trees this region has now become clove grower to the world.

A forest of clove trees all in bloom would be breath-takingly lovely but, alas, this cannot be—we need the unopened clove buds for pickling, for pomanders, and for poking into hams. Buds are picked in clusters from a main stem composed of 10 to 15 heads. Each tree carries from 30,000 to 50,000 buds, which make about 7 pounds when dried.

Cloves, whole or ground, are among the most pungent of spices. Use 3 or 4 whole cloves per 2 quarts of water when making stock. Use a pinch of ground cloves to season any of the sweet yellow vegetables.

CORIANDER
For Good Boys and Girls

THOUGH your current spice shelf may not include coriander, it may soon become part of your repertory of spices. If you are devoted to frankfurters, real Indian curry, or like a nip of gin now and then, you are already acquainted—if unknowingly—with coriander seeds. For generations, coriander has been known to good boys and girls who have been rewarded with old-fashioned pink or white candies, known as "comfits." To reach the coriander seed at the center of these comfits requires a great deal of sucking and tumbling between teeth and tongue. But once the hard sugar shell is penetrated, there is the treasured seed.

Coriander is another of those timeless meat-magic-and-medicine, good-for-man-or-beast spices whose history stems from earliest times. With the rise of civilization the coriander plant, native to the Mediterranean, developed into a product of world-wide trade. It grew in the Hanging Gardens of Babylon; it was among the medicinal plants mentioned in the Medical

Papyrus of Thebes—written in 1552 B.C.—and it was placed in Egyptian tombs some 3000 years ago.

All Sunday-school students will recall that the Children of Israel, on their long trek to the Promised Land, were nourished by manna, . . . "which was as coriander seed. . . . And the people went about, and gathered it, and ground it in mills, or beat it in a mortar, and baked it in pans and made cakes of it; and the taste of it was as the taste of fresh oil."

Coriander is a small seed, ranging in color from white to yellowish brown. The seeds are almost round, having alternating straight and curving ridges, and vary in size from ⅛ to ³⁄₁₆ of an inch in diameter. Coriander has a pleasing aromatic taste, suggesting to some a combination of lemon peel and sage, and to others a mixture of caraway and cumin.

CUMIN To Keep Husbands from Straying

THIS is a spice which should always be kept handy by wives whose husbands are apt to wander away just when the cheese soufflé reaches its proudest moment. Cumin can be relied upon to discourage such disloyalty to the art of cookery, judging by old wives' tales of long ago. (It can also serve to stop chickens and pigeons from straying—if this has been a problem lately.)

Folklore fails to inform us precisely how this works. Should the wife eat the seeds, carry them in her apron pocket, or deposit them in the pocket of her husband's trousers? Upon the subject of medieval weddings in Germany the literature, however, is specific. Both the bride and groom carried cumin, dill, and salt in their pockets during the marriage ceremony, to ensure faithfulness, forsaking all others so long as they both lived. In parts of Europe, a young man leaving home to become a soldier would carry along a loaf of cumin bread baked by his sweetheart. Or she might share his farewell glass of wine, in which powdered cumin had been mixed.

Cumin seeds originated in Egypt and were used with meats, fish, and stews. Cleopatra's cooks could have put a pinch of cumin in the rich sauces Antony ate. We can guess this from a line in Shakespeare's *Antony and Cleopatra:* "Epicurean cooks sharpen with cloyless sauce his appetite." Cumin seems, in this instance, to have helped bind the lovers long enough to produce three children. When Octavian, later Emperor Augustus, defeated them in battle, suicide seemed the only answer for both.

Among ancient Greeks cumin was the symbol of greed, while in Rome misers were said to have eaten cumin. Antoninus Pius, one of the few good Roman emperors (A.D. 86-161), was simple in his tastes, and devoted to his subjects' welfare. In order to provide money for his good works' projects, he practiced the most rigid economy in his social life. Scornful politicians nicknamed him "the cumin splitter," a sobriquet by which he is still known.

The seeds of this annual herb have been used as flavoring and medicine for thousands of years. Even the Bible mentions it in Matthew 23:23: "For ye pay tithe of mint and anise and cumin."

There is a distinct difference in the flavor of cumin and its caraway cousin (both members of the parsley family), as those familiar with both seeds know. Yet the Germans call both seeds *kümmel;* the French use the same word for cumin, having named caraway *cumin de pres* or *carvi.* The Spanish, however, call cumin *comino,* to distinguish it from *carvi,* their word for caraway.

By the time cumin seeds reached India, cumin became *jiraka*. It is an essential ingredient in curries of all kinds. Brought west by Spanish explorers, cumin reached Latin America several centuries ago and is now used almost everywhere south of the Rio Grande. Our ever-popular chili powder, regardless of who manufactures it, contains a certain amount of ground cumin.

Whole or ground cumin is used commercially in the preparation of meats, pickles, cheese, sausages, soups, and stews. It makes an excellent addition to such foods as rice, potatoes, and bread. Dust cumin over rice at serving time. Latin-American cooks use approximately ½ teaspoonful cumin for 6 servings of a delicious stew that combines chicken, corn, zucchini, and tomatoes.

CURRY
POWDER A Timeless Spice Blend

THE present-day cook upon discovering the extraordinary and pervasive aroma of curry powder may assume that this, like many convenient foods, must surely be a modern creation.

To the contrary, it has been known for generations. Although American grocers of fifty years ago sold relatively little curry powder, it was not an unfamiliar spice blend a century or more ago. Curry powder was one of the exotic treasures that many sailors in the past brought home to wives or mothers.

Cook books yellowed by time included recipes which called for curry powder. The recipe for "Currey of Chicken," appearing in a rare cook book printed in Philadelphia in 1792, instructs: "Get a bottle of currey powder. Strew it over the chicken when frying . . . if it is not seasoned high enough, put in a little Cayan [cayenne]."

India was the original home of the multiple-spiced curry. The Greek Athenaeus, author of *Deipnosophistai* ("Specialists in Dining"), as early as the third century A.D. described what surely must have been an Indian curry: "Among the Indians, at a banquet, a table is set before each individual . . . and on the table is placed a golden dish on which they throw first . . . boiled rice . . . then they add many sorts of meats *dressed* [author's italics] after the Indian fashion." As far back as 1500 years ago an Indian tale records that rice was ". . . dressed in butter, with its full accompaniment of curries."

Such curries, of course, would not have been created with ready-to-use curry powder. In India, even today, whole spices are ground freshly or pounded for each day's cooking. Even more important, had curries been prepared before Columbus's discovery of America, they would have lacked what is one of modern Indian curry's most essential ingredients—capsicum or red pepper. These pod peppers were not to reach India for many years. Thus, the ancient curry dishes would have been sorely lacking the degree of pungency that is so desirable in hot-weather countries.

The curry powders on our own American spice shelves usually contain coriander, cumin, fenugreek, cayenne pepper, and turmeric. Typical also are: allspice, cassia, cardamom, cloves, fennel, ginger, mace, mustard, and black or white pepper.

These spices create a fabulous flavor, good not only in exotic dishes of the East, but as a delightful fillip to such popular American dishes as pea soup, meat loaf, buttered zucchini, potato salad, and corn custard, among others. Amounts used can be varied to taste, but generally ½ to 1 teaspoonful per 6 servings delicately flavors a dish. Should a hotter flavor of curry powder be desired, use more cayenne pepper.

Consult the index for menus for typical Indian dinners and recipes for curries, kormas, and related dishes.

CURRIES AND THE INDIAN CUISINE

There must be hundreds, if not thousands, of variations of Indian curry, perhaps as many as there are cooks in India. The word "curry" means a richly spiced sauce. This lends itself to infinite possibilities, allowing each cook to re-create the sauce to suit his special taste.

In Bombay, for example, we might be served a delicious concoction of meats, lentils, vegetables, and nuts in a sauce seasoned with a dozen or more spices. Amusingly, this is known as "wide-mouthed curry."

Korma is a "dry curry." The sauce clings to the cooked meat in very much the same way as barbecue sauce. Meats used in a *korma* are marinated in yogurt before cooking. Some cooks thicken the sauce by adding desiccated coconut or poppy seeds.

Kebab curries, as might be anticipated, are pieces of meat, onions, ginger, garlic, etc., threaded on short skewers, then fried and allowed to simmer in a spiced gravy. *Kofta* curries consist of finely ground chicken or mutton molded into balls, then cooked slowly in a curry sauce.

Vindaloo is a "sour curry," meaning that meats are marinated in well-spiced vinegar for several hours before they are cooked.

Among the most delicious of Indian dishes is a prawn *malai* curry: spiced prawns baked in a whole, almost mature coconut until the delicate coconut meat has dissolved and mingled with the spices.

An American or European traveler who has just returned from India may say authoritatively that curries are "hot" or not "hot," depending upon the region he has visited and the dishes he has sampled. In Bombay, foods are quite highly spiced and many red chilis are used. In Madras, in the southern part of India, they also use generous amounts of red peppers. Not only do Indians enjoy the sharp taste, but the hot seasoning causes them to perspire more freely—a cooling effect most welcome when living only 10 degrees from the Equator.

There is one rule, however, for the cooking of curry that applies in all of India. The dish's freshly ground or whole spices must initially be heated in fat, which process is needed to develop the characteristic flavor. The Indian housewife has a "curry stone" on which she pulverizes the spices daily. Indians away from home confess to a nostalgia for the familiar sound in their homeland of the thump-thump-thump of spices being pounded.

Rice is a food consumed daily in southern and eastern India. Wheat and its products, though, are preferred in the north. But all of India eats *dal,* which is a purée made of lentils. Though Indian eating habits are in the process of change, there are still millions of Indians who do not eat either meat, fish, or eggs. These vegetarians, however, use milk products quite freely. "Curds" or yogurt are served daily. The finely chopped vegetables and yogurt that accompany curries furnish a pleasantly cool contrast.

American curry enthusiasts have adopted the practice of serving a variety of condiments with their curries. It is not an authentic Indian practice, but it is a popular one in this country. Because these accompaniments are very tasty and add a colorful touch to the meal, we have included the following list for your consideration. Serve as many as you like in small bowls and let the family or guests choose those which appeal to them most. Sprinkle a variety of these accompaniments right on the curry and white rice, and experiment to find your favorites:

raisins, chopped or whole
almonds, toasted and slivered
grapes, seedless green
peanuts, salted and chopped
egg, hard-cooked and chopped
pineapple tidbits
onion, grated or thinly sliced
tomato, fresh, chopped

pickle relish
bacon, crisp, crumbled
apple, fresh, diced
radishes, diced
green pepper, finely chopped
celery, finely chopped
stuffed olives, chopped
chutney, mango, or other fruit

coconut, fresh or canned, shredded

DILL To Avert the Evil Eye

DILL beds must surely have been weeded and watered anxiously by medieval gardeners. Not only did this herb bring an intriguing aroma to foods, but it was considered a powerful ingredient in magic potions, as well as in those that were antimagic! It could work either way. When sorcerers gathered together to stir up a pot of trouble for someone, they included dill to make their concoction more potent. If, however, the intended victim got an inkling that he was being hexed, he too hastened to his dill patch. "Here holy Vervain and here Dill," says the old rhyme, "Gainst witchcraft much availing." No record seems available as to whether dill magic or dill antimagic was stronger, so the partisans of both sides must have relied on "getting there fustest with the mostest."

Even when there was no witchcraft afoot, there still might be the Evil Eye. To make oneself invulnerable against it, nothing was considered better than carrying a bag of dried dill over the heart. The Evil Eye—as encyclopedias explain—was, supposedly, the art of "fascination," which gave some people the power to bewitch, injure, or kill merely with a glance. Since the

Evil Eye has always been most malevolent in the lands around the Mediterranean, it is fortunate, indeed, that dill grows wild (and abundantly) there and in parts of Asia Minor.

Dill—*Anethum graveolens*—is an annual plant of the parsley family. Though both the seeds and dried leaves are used, the seeds are more commonly made use of.

In modern times dill has been most famous for perking up pickles. Some 250 years ago, essayist Addison wrote: "I am always pleased with that particular time of year when it is proper for the pickling of dill and cucumbers."

Dill comes in whole form only. It is a delicious addition to sour-cream sauces, green beans, cabbage, cucumbers, broccoli, cauliflower, potato salad, or a macaroni and cheese casserole. Since dill is a moderately aromatic herb, use about ¼ to ½ teaspoonful seed per pound of green beans, or for 6 servings of potato salad, or in a small casserole of macaroni and cheese.

FENNEL Venerable Panacea

THIS aromatic seed, whose smell is very much like that of anise, was believed by ancient scholars to be among the nine sacred herbs that could cure the nine causes of disease. It was considered a rejuvenator, an aphrodisiac, a fortifier, and an aid to slenderness. It restored and sharpened the eyesight, stopped the hiccups, freed one from "loathings," cured wheezing, and improved "the ill colour in the face after sickness," according to Culpeper, who added that "Both leaves, seeds and roots thereof, are much used in drink or broth, to make people lean that are too fat." On the other hand, the very poor of the seventeenth century, who could seldom eat enough to grow fat, drank fennel tea to allay the pangs of hunger!

Very few herbs can boast of having had their varied virtues eulogized by a poet as famous as Longfellow. The following is from his "The Goblet of Life":

> Above the lowly plants it towers,
> The fennel, with its yellow flowers,
> And, in an earlier age than ours
> Was gifted with the wondrous powers
> Lost vision to restore.
> It gave new strength and fearless mood;
> And gladiators fierce and rude,
> Mingled it with their daily food;
> And he who battled and subdued,
> A wreath of fennel wore.

We use the seeds of this perennial herb of the parsley family. Only whole seeds are sold nationally and there are many delightful uses for them. Shower them over the apples in a pie or scatter generously over the crumb topping of a seafood casserole. Italian bakers stud bread and rolls with whole fennel seeds. The seeds are also excellent in roast duck or duck pilaf, chicken and fish dishes.

GARLIC
An Old Favorite with New Status

GARLIC at last has won appreciation from people all over the United States. It has not always been savored by Americans, especially in sections of the country where immigrants from northern Europe had settled. In cook books used a half century past we occasionally find a rare recipe calling rather timidly for a "bean" or clove of garlic.

But newcomers from southern Europe and Latin countries appreciated the effluvium of garlic, and used it freely. Cooks of French, Italian, Spanish, Mexican, or Jewish backgrounds required garlic to create their traditional dishes. But foreign dishes were rarely adapted to American usage. Often the daughters and granddaughters of the cooks who had used garlic generously

lost interest in old-world cookery. Following World War II the hobby cook came upon the scene. Usually he was a former G.I. who was attempting to re-create some of the exciting dishes he had eaten in various parts of the world. Garlic began playing its proper role, especially since it had become possible to buy dehydrated garlic—garlic salt, garlic powder, and the instant minced variety.

Garlic has been used for many, many centuries and appears to have originated in western Asia. Eastern legend tells us that when Satan made his way out of the Garden of Eden after the fall of man, onions sprang up from the place left by his right footprint, garlic from the left.

So highly did the Egyptians regard garlic—both as food and medicine —they used it to swear by when offering some solemn vow.

The Israelites developed a taste for garlic during their stay in Egypt and, after the Exodus, yearned for it on their exhausting trek to the Promised Land. The Greeks, curiously, disliked garlic, although modern Greek cooks use it in special dishes. Roman legions freely consumed this potent little bulb in the belief that it would make them better and fiercer fighters.

Garlic was a respected medication and charm from Roman times all through the Middle Ages. The Roman Pliny claimed that sixty-one ailments could be cured with garlic. Medieval doctors, visiting the sick, brought along a few cloves of garlic to serve as a combined charm and disinfectant. In early England anxious parents inserted cloves of garlic into the stockings of any child suffering from whooping cough. Not only was garlic an unusually effective charm against the wicked deeds of witches but, on the positive side, everyone who purchased garlic on St. John's Day believed that he would be safe from poverty during the coming year.

Garlic lends an appetizing aroma to meats, fish, fowl, salads and salad dressings, and many varieties of vegetables. However, when using garlic, be discreet. Because a little is good does not necessarily mean that a larger quantity is better. Garlic powder is more potent than garlic salt, since the latter is a mixture of pure garlic with ordinary table salt. A bit of garlic powder—1/16 teaspoonful—is an adequate starting point when experimenting with some dish of 4 to 6 portions. About twice as much garlic salt may be used. Instant minced garlic is ideal for use in cooked dishes.

GINGER As in Gingerbread

ANYONE who has affectionately fashioned a gingerbread man for a favorite child may not be aware that this is the most ancient of sweetmeat treats. It has been said that though Egyptians were eating gingerbread when the great pyramid of Cheops was young, the first recipe originated in Greece, where it was discovered by a baker on the island of Rhodes, about 2400 B.C. These unleavened, honey-sweetened cakes were famous, and for years many a ship sailed into Rhodes, between the straddled feet of the Colossus, bound for the bake shops of the port, where the taste for gingerbread could be indulged.

Many things originated by the Greeks were eventually copied by the Romans, and this was true of gingerbread. Roman legions carried the gingerbread recipes to all parts of their vast empire. During the Dark Ages, directions for making gingerbread had been preserved in the monasteries. Since the monks then were among the few who could read and write, there was a long period in which the common man almost forgot how ginger or other Oriental spices tasted.

By the thirteenth century ginger and gingerbread were well known and appreciated in England. In the fourteenth century Chaucer, who seems to have been food-conscious, records: "They sette hym Roiall spicerye and Gyngerbreed." Throughout the sixteenth, seventeenth, and eighteenth centuries gingerbread grew ever more elaborate. Queen Elizabeth I of England, never one to deny a sweet tooth, knew that her guests were fond of gingerbread, especially if the cake was molded in the image of the guest to whom it was offered. A gingerbread likeness proved to be so successful a conversation piece, Elizabeth I hired a special artist-baker, whose sole work was the creation of gingerbread lords and ladies to amuse and flatter her courtiers.

Not only were gingerbread "honours" popular in England, but in other parts of Europe, too. When Peter the Great of Russia was born, his father's friends sent him dozens of huge gingerbread creations. Among the largest were the coat of arms of Moscow, with the Kremlin—turrets and all.

Ginger was among the first authentic Oriental spices to make its way to Alexandria, and from that great harbor city to Greece and Rome. This must have occurred before the first century A.D., since Dioscorides and Pliny mention it, and ginger appears often in the Roman recipe book of Apicius, published at the height of Rome's most luxurious days.

For many years, ginger—then often worth its weight in gold—was a rich man's spice. Known by its Sanskrit name, *singabera,* this root was grown in India and southern China in remotest times. It is said to have been introduced into the Western Hemisphere, to "New Spain," by Francisco de Mendoca at least four centuries ago, as there are records of ginger shipments from San Domingo as far back as 1585. Today, the island of Jamaica, British West Indies, is our largest supplier.

It is the root, of course, which is used as a spice. The lilylike plant is a perennial one. When about a year old, the roots are dug up, washed, and dried in the sun. Ginger is available whole and ground. (Crystallized and preserved gingers are considered confections rather than spices.) Whole ginger root is preferred when making flavored syrups and pickling vinegars. About half an hour of cooking is required to release the flavor. A half-inch of whole ginger lends a delicious aroma to chicken or beef stock, or tongue. Ground ginger may be used in all baked dishes, or as a last-minute seasoning for soup or sauce.

MARJORAM
Herb of Honor and Happiness

WHEN the first chords of the Lohengrin "March" are heard, wedding guests crane to see the colorful procession, led by a dainty little moppet who scatters rose petals along the path of the bride on her way to the altar. This charming custom is not at all new. Such a shower of fragrant herbs and blossoms can be traced back hundreds of years.

In England, at the twelfth-century court of King Stephen, the knights were more numerous than chairs—and so most of them, if they wanted to sit at all, used the floor. To save their clothing from being soiled, King Stephen ordered the court to be strewn with fresh straw in winter and fragrant greens in summer.

Marjoram was among the most prized of sweet herbs used for this purpose, since it also served as an air sweetener. The person chosen to scatter these herbs on the floor was called "Strewer of Herbs in Ordinary to His Majesty." At the coronation of James II of England—in mid-seventeenth century—the sweet fragrance must have been overwhelming, as the Strewer of Herbs in Ordinary was assisted by six women; they scattered eighteen bushels of marjoram and sweet herbs!

Marjoram is a perennial herb of the mint family, a cousin of the increasingly popular oregano. (Marjoram is sweeter, more delicate; oregano much lustier, pleasantly bitter and assertive.) Oregano was, until quite recently, called "wild marjoram," while older botany books spoke of marjoram as *Origanum majorana;* this, of course, created confusion. (In modern botany books it appears as *Majorana hortensis Moench.*)

From western Asia and the Mediterranean region originally, the scent of marjoram has always been very highly prized, and in some countries the plant is the symbol of honor and happiness. Both Greeks and Romans used sweet marjoram in creating the crowns worn by happy young couples. Marjoram was also planted on graves, to delight the souls of loved ones. Once the Romans had carried marjoram as far as England and Germany, it became a charm against witchcraft, for they believed that he who had sold his soul to the devil could not endure the fragrance of this happy herb.

In the modern kitchen marjoram is the herb of a thousand uses. Distinctively aromatic, ¼ or ½ teaspoonful of marjoram lends piquant flavor to about 6 servings of meats, fish, eggs, or any one in a long list of vegetables, such as lima beans, peas, snap beans, spinach, and Swiss chard. It is good, too, in most salads and stuffing.

MINT Symbol of Hospitality

ONE of Ovid's tales of gods and goddesses, written 2000 years ago, was inspired by mint—the symbol of hospitality. Philemon and Baucis, man and wife, were living in Phrygia, a country in Asia Minor. The land was so poor, this couple had scarcely sufficient food to keep them alive. One day two strangers knocked at their door, asking to be fed. Despite their poverty, Philemon and Baucis were delighted to have guests, and prepared the best meal possible from their meager supplies. Wanting to fill their humble home with an inviting fragrance, they rubbed their table with mint leaves. At that point their anxieties were past—the guests proved to be Zeus and Hermes, incognito. The hovel was soon transformed into a temple, and priests ministered to all the needs of Philemon and Baucis for the duration of their lives.

Mint, plant historians claim, came originally from the Mediterranean shores. Mythology offers a far more romantic story: mint was once the nymph Mentha, unfortunate to have attracted the eye of Pluto. Persephone, his jealous wife, pursued Mentha, and trod her ferociously underfoot. Pluto, unable to control his wife's fury, changed Mentha into a delightful herb, ever after sacred to this god of the underworld.

Mint was well known and highly esteemed in the ancient world. We read in the Bible that the Pharisees paid tithes of mint, anise, and cumin. In Greece, crushed mint leaves were used as perfume for the arms and to scent the bath.

Naturalist Pliny had the highest regard for mint as a medicine. "The very smell of it reanimates the spirit," he wrote, considering mint to possess many virtues. It could, for example, stop hiccups, provide an antidote for the stings of sea serpents and, if consumed just before an oration, clear the voice.

Roman legions carried mint plants to all parts of the Empire. It had been mentioned in the early medieval lists of plants, and could be found in all monastery gardens a thousand years past.

Though there are numerous varieties of mint, only spearmint (*Mentha spicata*) and peppermint (*Mentha piperita*) have a place on the spice shelf. For many centuries, mint has been used with lamb, being one of the "bitter herbs" eaten with the Paschal lamb. Syrian cooks include a bit of dried mint in leafy salad greens. Minted sugar syrup is a delicious sweetener for fruits, especially pears, pineapple, and melon balls. To steep mint flakes, add 1 to 2 teaspoonfuls of mint to about ¼ cup of boiling water. Let mint "tea" stand covered for about 6 or 7 minutes. Then strain the mint leaves and use the mint water.

MUSTARD Unique Among Spices

MUSTARD is truly unique on the spice shelf. Unlike other aromatic spices, powdered mustard, so long as it is dry, has no more redolence than cornstarch. Its tingling pungency invades our senses only after the flavor has been freed by an enzyme activity that is initiated as soon as mustard is mixed with cold water. After about 10 to 15 minutes the mustard flavor is at its best. The aroma fades quickly, however, with exposure to air and room temperature. In homes or restaurants where powdered mustard and water are mixed freshly for each serving, any that remains is discarded at the completion of the meal.

Mustard, of Asiatic origin, has been known to man since prehistoric times. The Chinese used mustard many thousands of years past. Indeed, even today, our pleasure in eating a Chinese egg roll is enhanced by the freshly mixed, sharp mustard that accompanies it. This Chinese-restaurant mustard is nothing more than brown Oriental mustard combined with cold water and stirred to a paste.

Two thousand years ago mustard was called *sinapis* by the Greeks and Romans. The Roman legions carried mustard seeds everywhere, including England. We have inherited several recipes for making variations of mustard sauce from as far back as the first and fourth centuries A.D. However, it was not called mustard until the French began mixing the crushed seeds with *must* (unfermented wine). Mustard-mixing became one of the culinary arts. In eighteenth-century France, they experimented with caper mustard, rose-water mustard, anchovy mustard, and truffle mustard. They even tried mixing it with vanilla!

Dumas's *Dictionary of Cuisine* contains references to mustard consumption in ancient days. When, in medieval France, King Philip VI entertained the Duke of Burgundy, one hundred gallons of mustard were said to have been consumed. King Louis XI of France—no doubt fearful his hosts would serve no mustard—always carried the royal mustard pot with him when he was invited to dinner.

There are two basic types of mustard seeds: *Brassica alba,* which are white or yellow seeds, and *Brassica juncea,* dark brown seeds also called "Oriental" mustard. Mustard comes in three forms: whole seeds, powder, and the now familiar prepared mustard.

Mustard is not only appetizing in itself, but it enhances other flavors. The Mustard Gingerbread* tastes deliciously spicy, though not at all "mustardy." Add ¼ to ½ teaspoonful mustard (which has already been mixed with a teaspoonful of water and allowed to stand for 10 minutes) to 6 servings of cheese soufflé, or macaroni and cheese. Add it to mayonnaise, too, a little if it is to be used with fruits and vegetables; more, to taste, if it is to be added to meat, fish, and poultry salads.

In France, at one time, they served both "gentlemen's mustard" and "ladies' mustard." As might be anticipated the "ladies' mustard" was on the mild side. The more powerful "gentlemen's mustard" can be concocted by blending 1 tablespoonful of powdered mustard, 1 tablespoonful of cold water, and ⅛ teaspoonful of salt into a smooth paste. Then, after setting it aside to steep for 10 minutes, spread on sliced cold beef, frankfurters, or other foods.

*An asterisk after the name of a dish indicates that the recipe for this dish appears in the book. Consult the Index for the page number.

NUTMEG and
MACE Sister Spices

NUTMEG and mace are sister spices; they come from the same peachlike fruit, *Myristica fragrans*. In the tropics, the home of this evergreen tree, the natives eat the pulp of the fruit. In commercial use the seed of the fruit is known as nutmeg, and the lacy red membrane surrounding the seed as mace. The nutmeg itself weighs a great deal more than the mace which envelopes it . . . 10 to 400 times as much, depending upon its particular variety.

The nutmeg tree grew in what is now Indonesia for thousands of years before its two spice products became known in Europe. In early times the radius of spice traders was limited, and spices of the Far East moved westward in relays; from the Moluccas, a thousand miles west to Java; from Java to India; from India west to Constantinople or Alexandria; and finally, from these great spice-trading centers to Europe. Since the Indians grew nutmeg of an inferior variety, there was little interest in the spice in the West. Better varieties of nutmeg and mace did begin to reach Europe some time in the sixth century A.D., however, and by the end of the twelfth century, these spices were in great demand. Records reveal that a pound of mace was worth three sheep or half a cow.

If you are looking for an interesting hobby, you may enjoy collecting nutmeg graters. There are hundreds of varieties, ranging in price from five cents to astronomical sums. Most of these are antiques, of course. There are so many types of graters because tinsmiths or tinkers used to make the pierced-tin kind in their spare time. Older graters, usually English or European, were made of sterling silver. There were also folding types, small enough to be carried in a gentleman's waistcoat. At his club or a grog shop he was then able to grate a bit of nutmeg into his hot punch. In the distant past nutmeg and other spices were so costly, wealthy men carried their own supply of nutmeg as the modern man carries a cigarette case. Ladies, too, had portable graters that could be folded to the size of a lipstick. They used grated nutmeg as a sachet. Sometimes they even carried a whole nutmeg in a filigreed silver case, suspended by a silver chain, which made everything within close range smell delightfully spicy!

It has often been said that nutmegs must be able to smell the sea, growing best on tropical islands, approximately 1000 feet above the pounding surf. The *Myristica fragrans* is an evergreen tree, and grows to about 25 feet in height. The first fruits are born when the tree is 6 or 7 years old. This continues for another 60 years before the tree's yield diminishes. A large tree will produce about 1000 nutmegs yearly.

The flavor of nutmeg is sweet, with a warm and spicy undertone. It has a thousand and one uses, and is mentioned almost more than any other spice in the recipe books of early America. Great-grandmother liked to mix it with rose water as a flavoring for all kinds of delicate desserts. Nutmeg is not only a delicious spice for baked dishes, but contributes flavor to the main course. It is excellent with vegetables such as spinach, green beans, and succotash. The Scandinavians use nutmeg in meat balls; the Germans include it in potato dumplings.

Mace resembles nutmeg, but is more pungent. It is the traditional spice for pound cake, but it also enhances the taste of cherry pie, chocolate dishes, and whipped cream. It is very good, indeed, in seafood and fish sauces, or in chicken fricassées. But since it is on the potent side start—as with all spices—with a pinch when experimenting, adding more if a fuller flavor is desired.

ONION "Rose Among Roots"

HAD Robert Louis Stevenson been a modern advertising man, and been offered a fee to glorify the onion, he couldn't have done better than in his poem on salad making:

> First let the onion flourish there,
> Rose among roots, the maiden-fair
> Wine-scented and poetic soul
> Of the capacious salad bowl!

Then there was the eighteenth-century clergyman and wit, the Reverend Sydney Smith, who initiated a salad with a bit of minced onion. His rhymed recipe prescribed:

> Let onion's atoms lurk within the bowl,
> And scarce suspected, animate the whole.

The early nineteenth century seems to have produced a quantity of recipes written in rhyme, or what seemed to have passed for rhyme in those days. There was one recipe for roast stuffed swan which reads, in part, ". . . an onion, will heighten the flavor in gourmand's opinion."

Another near miss went:

> All cooks agree with this opinion—
> No savoury dish without an onion.

The onion has been used for so many centuries by so many people throughout the world it is hardly possible to determine its origin. Most likely it was in Asia Minor, the home of so many Old World vegetables. We know that the Egyptians ate onions in great quantities. Even the pyramids seem to be indebted to the onion. For the manpower that built them was fortified with onions, according to history as recorded by Herodotus. He noted that in his time there was an inscription on the Great Pyramid of Cheops saying that 1600 talents of silver had been spent on onions, garlic, and radishes for the workmen in 2900 B.C.

Efficiency-oriented twentieth-century cooks now have available to them dehydrated onions in various forms: instant minced (or chopped); onion powder (or granulated), and onion salt. The onion powder is more purely onion than the onion salt, since the latter is a blend of onion and table salt. Use about ¼ to ⅓ as much instant minced onion as you would freshly chopped onion. If the instant minced onion is to be included in a soup, sauce, or cooked mixture, add without further ado. On the other hand, if it is to be added, uncooked, to. a salad or sandwich filling, or to be sautéed, mix the instant minced onion with an equal quantity of cold water and let it stand for 3 minutes.

OREGANO The Pizza Herb

BEFORE World War II few Americans were familiar with oregano. It had been grouped with certain lesser spices and herbs, and was never mentioned by name in the records of the United States Customs. When the war ended, American G.I.s, returning from Italy, praised a fabulous pielike concoction called "pizza." Wives and mothers initiated the demand for the lusty herb, which had to be sprinkled lightly over the finished pizza to give just the right taste. Within a decade every good cook had mastered the correct pronunciation of "oregano"—accenting the second syllable—and sales had jumped 5000 per cent!

At the turn of the century, American cook books seemed never to have called it oregano—the Spanish name for marjoram. At various times in the past it has been called wild marjoram, winter sweet, organy, and origan.

Oregano was brought to the New World at an early date. Latin American and Mexican cooks used it frequently. It grew luxuriously wild in Mexico, and became known as Mexican sage. Botanists and herb growers are still trying to classify the "pizza herb" to everyone's satisfaction; the American Spice Trade Association continues to list it as unclassified.

Oregano is native to the hillsides of the Mediterranean region, and is a perennial of the mint family. The name *origanum,* derived from the Greek *orus,* meaning mountain, and *ganus,* meaning joy, thus signified "joy of the mountain" to the Greeks 2000 years ago. It grew easily then, as it still does in Greece, Italy, and Spain.

In ancient times oregano was valued as much for its medicinal qualities as its savory flavor. The Roman naturalist, Pliny the Elder, prescribed it as a cure for indigestion and first aid for spider and scorpion stings. In the Middle Ages physicians used a mixture of oregano and other herbs to "cleanse the brain" and improve sight. While Culpeper thought highly of oregano as a digestive, soothing to jittery nerves, and as a treatment for "the bites of venomous beasts," he was in accord with modern cooks when he wrote, "There is scarcely a better herb growing for relieving loss of appetite."

Oregano is among the more potent herbs. It can be used in all tomato dishes. In cheese and egg mixtures a pinch of oregano may be added. Add ¼ teaspoonful of oregano to 2 cups of soft bread crumbs when stuffing a fish. It is excellent, too, in clear, vegetable, and beef broths.

PARSLEY The Ubiquitous Herb

DESPITE such flippant rhymes as "Parsley is garsely" and

> Parsley, parsley everywhere!
> Damn, I like my victuals bare!

this remains one of our most popular herbs—and with good reason.

French cooks are devoted to parsley, using it both as a *bouquet garni* or whenever a dish is prepared *aux fines herbes*. If the difference between these flavoring techniques has been confusing to you, the following might be enlightening: when a dish is prepared *aux fines herbes,* the finely chopped herbs are stirred into the mixture and served with it (as in parsley-scrambled eggs). The *bouquet garni* is, quite literally, a bouquet composed of parsley and other culinary herbs that are tied with string and lowered into a simmering soup or stew. When the dish is done, the *bouquet* is removed and discarded. To modern French cooks *aux fines herbes* usually implies the use of parsley by itself, although the classic *fines herbes* may include tarragon, chives, or chervil. The simplest *bouquet garni* also consists of parsley, though bay leaf, thyme, basil, celery, chervil, tarragon, rosemary, or savory may be added, depending upon the dish being prepared. (Dehydrated parsley flakes should be tied in a small piece of cheesecloth when used as a *bouquet garni*.)

Parsley has been cultivated for thousands of years. Its early history is lost in Greek mythology. Hercules supposedly wore a garland of parsley. Juno's horses were said to have accelerated their speed after nipping parsley, as did the chargers of Homer's heroes.

In imperial Rome parsley was also fashioned into crowns for banquet guests. This, the host hoped, would prevent drunkenness and raucousness at the table. Roman legions carried parsley to northern Europe and England, where the English used it to make parsley pies.

And when English youngsters ask the inevitable "Where did I come from, Mommy?"—the answer is likely to be, "From the parsley bed, my dear." According to the Oxford Dictionary, this reply seems to have been used for centuries. One philosophical nine-year-old, the younger son of a noble family, mentioned his parsley-bed origin in this charming poem:

> This day from parsley-bed I'm sure
> Was dug my elder brother, Moore,
> Had papa dug me up before him,
> So many would not now adore him,
> But, hang it! He's but only one,
> If he trips off, then I'm Sir John.

PEPPER The Master Spice

IF you happened to drop your container of peppercorns, would you hunt each black berry as if it were an heirloom pearl? Most surely not, since today it is possible to buy pepper in quantity for only a few pennies. But this was not true a thousand or more years past, when peppercorns were so costly they were often used in trading as a substitute for money!

Pepper, black or white, is frequently called "the master spice." During all ages people have found its aroma to be provocative, irresistible. The history of the spice trade is, above all, the history of pepper; legends lead us to believe that pepper was already moving westward from India 4000 years ago.

The ancient Greeks and Romans used both black and white pepper. Judging by the varied names pepper had in ancient days, we realize how well

pepper was already known as far back as 2000 and 3000 years ago. Our word *pepper* originates from the Latin *piper* which, in turn, comes from the Sanskrit *pippali.* *Pippali* became *biber* or *pilpil* in Persian, *filfil* in Arabic, *peperi* in Greek. And the Latin *piper* not only gave us our *pepper,* but *poivre, pfeffer, pepe, pimienta,* and *peppar* in French, German, Italian, Spanish, and Swedish, respectively.

Pepper is native to the hot jungle lands that are never farther than 20 degrees from the Equator. The names associated with pepper sound like a globe-trotter's itinerary of India and the Far East. Tellicherry, Alleppey, and Pandjang, for example, have been pepper ports for hundreds, if not thousands, of years.

Piper nigrum, believed to be native to Malabar—on the western coast of India, extending from a little above Mangalore down to a little below Alleppey—is the tropical vine that produces both black and white pepper. At present, the world's pepper supply comes from India, southeast Sumatra, Sarawak, Ceylon, and—most recently—from equatorial Brazil.

Though both berries are born of the same vine, there is a difference between black and white pepper. Pepper berries to be used for black pepper are picked just before they are fully ripe. Those which are to be sold as white peppercorns are allowed to ripen completely; this makes the removal of the dark outer covering easier, leaving only the inner, straw-colored kernel. Black peppercorns, of course, are used by leaving the dark outer covering intact. This causes black pepper to be somewhat more pungent than white pepper. In the United States we use eleven or twelve times as much black pepper as white; in Europe the reverse is true.

Black pepper is available in three forms: whole peppercorns, regular or "table" grind, and coarse grind. White pepper is available nationally in medium grind. Pepper is good in almost anything, from soup to nuts. Here is a valuable spice cake or pumpkin pie secret that proves it: ⅛ teaspoonful of finely ground black pepper lends the other sweet spices a mystifying and delectable bouquet. Try the recipe for Old Fashioned Pumpkin Pie* and see.

AND THE QUEEN OF SHEBA
CAME TO JERUSALEM WITH
A VERY GREAT TRAIN WITH
CAMELS THAT BARE SPICES
AND VERY MUCH GOLD AND
PRECIOUS STONES ....
1. KINGS 10·3

seeds become the filling for the Jewish Hamentashen* or Purim (festive holiday) cakes.

Magic has often been attributed to poppy seeds. Long ago anyone wishing to escape his creditors had only to scatter poppy seeds in his shoes, which allowed him to pass among them unseen.

When poppy seeds are to be used in a butter sauce, to achieve the best flavor the seeds should be cooked with the butter until the butter turns golden. Poppy-seed butter is superb over noodles and fish, and lends a nutlike flavor to cooked vegetables such as green beans, cabbage, new potatoes, spinach, carrots, white onions, zucchini, and summer squash.

ROSEMARY For Remembrance

THE small flower that is part of rosemary—an evergreen of the mint family—once was white. Legend recounts that one night the Virgin Mary—fleeing with the Christ Child from Herod's soldiers—hung her sky-blue cloak on a rosemary bush. From that day on the color of rosemary blossoms was transformed to blue.

The mention of rosemary will call to mind an ancient symbol of remembrance and fidelity. Shakespeare made this sentiment famous in *Hamlet*, when the tragic Ophelia speaks the immortal line: "There's rosemary, that's for remembrance."

One seventeenth-century preacher urged at a wedding: "Let this Rosemarinus, this flower of men, ensigne of your wisdom, love and loyaltie, be carried not only in your hands, but in your heads and hearts." It was the custom then for bridesmaids to present the bridegroom with "a bunch of Rosemary, bound with ribands" on the morning of his wedding.

Despite this herb having been a symbol of fidelity for lovers since Roman

POPPY SEEDS

The Only "Blue" Spice

ANY gardener who can readily translate the Latin names of plants knows that *Papaver somniferum* means "sleep-bearing poppy." If he is an expert botanist as well, he is aware that the fluid in the bud—which becomes opium—is present only before the seed forms. By the time the seed is harvested the fluid has dried completely, leaving the seeds wholly free of any narcotic elements.

While spices and herbs appear in many attractive shades of red, off-white, warm brown, and gold, poppy seeds are usually slate-blue, though there is a white variety.

Today the poppy that gives us flavoring seeds is grown in so many parts of the world it is difficult to ascertain its original habitat—probably southern Europe and western Asia. At any rate, the poppy has been known to us for centuries. Homer referred to it as a garden plant. The Greek physician Galen, in the second century A.D., recommended poppy seeds as a flavoring for bread. Mohammed's missionaries, on pilgrimage to India during the seventh century, seeking converts to Islam, also introduced poppy seeds to that country. Indian cooks ingeniously combined poppy seeds with the juice of the native sugar cane in the creation of sweetmeats.

Poppy seeds are used freely in many parts of Europe—both in varied baked dishes and as topping for them. Many homes have a small poppy-seed grinder for crushing the seeds. Mixed with sweetening, the crushed times, it seems to have lost its magic in the marriage of Anne of Cleves to Henry VIII. She had gone to the altar wearing a rosemary wreath, yet this marriage ended in divorce several months later. And many bridegrooms may have doubted the binding powers of rosemary, believing it hardly conducive to their happiness, judging by an English superstition: "Where rosemary flourisheth, the woman ruleth."

Rosemary has had many other uses, too, in the course of time. The varying regions where it grew dictated its uses. Rosemary decorated churches and banquet halls; was used as incense in religious ceremonies, as an amulet against the Evil Eye, and as a hair-restorer! It was the custom, as a New Year's gift, to give a sprig of the herb together with a pomander. Herbalist Culpeper mentioned that rosemary sprigs in the seventeenth-century English courts were used to "expel the contagion of the pestilence from which poor prisoners often suffered."

In some European countries, even today, pillows are stuffed with rosemary; and often its delightful, refreshing fragrance can be detected in the bouquet of soaps and modern cosmetics. Were you to trace the ancestry of today's toilet waters, you would discover that in the fourteenth century there was a rosemary-scented branch of the family tree known as Hungary Water. It was a hardy branch, too, immortalized by folklorist Charles Perrault some 300 years past in *The Sleeping Beauty;* the heroine's temples were massaged with Hungary Water to revive her after she had pricked her finger.

If used sparingly, rosemary is one of the most pleasing herbs. It is excellent with lamb and chicken, as well as with salads of these meats, and with seafood. It also adds to one's relish when used on green beans, asparagus, zucchini, tomatoes, and mashed potatoes.

SAFFRON World's Costliest Spice

SAFFRON is today the world's most costly aromatic, for it takes the stigmas (pistil tips) of 75,000 *Crocus sativus* blossoms to make a single pound when dried.

Saffron has been treasured from remotest times as a culinary spice, a coloring for foodstuffs, a cosmetic, a fabric dye, and as a medicine. Homer was acquainted with its golden hue when he wrote a "saffron-robed morning." Saffron may have come originally from the Holy Land; from the Songs of Solomon we have learned that it was among the "chief spices": "Thy plants are an orchard of Pomegranates, with pleasant fruits, Camphire with

Spikenard, and Saffron, Calamus and Cinnamon, with all trees of Frankincense, Myrrh and Aloes."

In nearby Egypt, in the days of the Pharaohs, kings were anointed with oils perfumed with saffron, myrrh, frankincense, cassia, and cinnamon. In ancient Syria one of the kings named Antiochus was addicted to entertaining lavishly. This included having his guests sprinkled with perfumes of saffron, cinnamon, or lilies. So numerous was the throng, 200 beautiful women were required to serve as perfume dispensers. Later, during the prodigal days of imperial Rome, saffron was strewn through the Forum, and used to scent the luxurious baths.

The Greeks and Romans called saffron *Krokus,* and the little bulb followed the Roman legions all over Europe. Then came the fall of Rome, and the beginning of the Dark Ages. The golden days were past; luxuries, among them saffron, were relegated to memory.

In the course of several centuries many of the plants the Romans had introduced, including saffron, disappeared from gardens in England and northern Europe. But when the Moors conquered Spain, one of the treasures they brought with them was the spice *zafran,* meaning "yellow." That is why, for the past 12 centuries, so many of Spain's best dishes have been redolent of this golden spice.

In England, long after the saffron bulb had died of neglect in the remnants of what had once been Roman gardens, saffron was once more to make its way to that island. This time one single bulb had been transported secretly in the hollow knob of a pilgrim's staff. This solitary bulb was to become the ancestor of the many thousands whose yield was to suggest the name of Saffron Walden, just north of London, and Saffron Hill in that great metropolis. "And so he brought this roote into this realme," the sixteenth-century account records, "with venture of his life: for if he had been taken, by the law of the country from whence it came [Barbary], he had died for the fact."

"It makes the English sprightly," declared Francis Bacon. Whatever its influence was, the English loved it, and the saffron bulb loved England. That explains, no doubt, why in the fourteenth-century cook book, *The Forme of Cury,* almost half of the recipes called for saffron.

Saffron is among those spices often used too lavishly. Just a few strands are adequate to give excellent color and aroma to a pot of rice; or, see recipes for Saffron Rice Pilaf* and Saffron-Lemon Tea Bread.*

SAGE Herb of Many Virtues

SAGE has had an honored place on the American spice shelf for many generations. Some of its numerous virtues were summed up by Susannah Carter in her 1802 book, *The Frugal Housewife.* "There is no herbe, almost of more use in the houses of high and low, rich and poor, for inward and outward occasions; outwardly for bathings and among other herbs for strawings; inwardly for most sorts of broths, with rosemary, also to make a sauce for divers sorts both of fish and flesh as to stuff a goose to be roasted." (Frugal or not, lives there a housewife in the twentieth century who would prepare stuffing for the Thanksgiving turkey without sage?)

There is a superstition, centuries old, that the sage plant will thrive when all is well with its owner, and droop when misfortune threatens. Another is that the sage plant grows most lustily where the wife rules the home!

"How can a man die who grows sage in his garden?" asked the doctors of the Salerno, Italy, school in medieval times. Its botanical name, *Salvia*

officinalis, means to save or heal, and in Italy, Spain, and Germany it is called *salvia* or *salbei* even today. In England it became known as "sage" because sage decoctions, sipped regularly, supposedly made men prudent and strengthened the memory. In short, according to seventeenth-century John Evelyn, " 'Tis a plant, indeed, with so many and wonderful properties as that the assiduous use of it is said to render men immortal."

Not only was it said that sage might render men immortal, but romantic young ladies could envisage—with the aid of sage sprigs—their future husbands, provided this custom was followed on Midsummer's Eve, just after sunset. A group of three, five, or seven maidens would visit a lonely garden, where each would gather a sprig of sage. Other weird rites were involved, but if pursued correctly, precisely at midnight each prospective husband would appear, and use the sage sprig to sprinkle rose water on the smock of his bride-to-be.

The hardy sage plant came originally from the northern shores of the Mediterranean. While many varieties of sage are grown throughout the world, *Salvia officinalis* is the finest for seasoning purposes. We import most of our sage supply from the Dalmatian coast of Yugoslavia and Albania. It can be purchased in whole, rubbed, or ground form.

Sage's odor is strong and fragrant. It is a perfect seasoning for pork dishes of all kinds, and the most important ingredient in poultry seasoning. Use sage in stuffing, seafood, chicken, and cheese dishes generally. A little sage gives delightful aroma to breads. Such breads are especially good for making sandwiches with pork, turkey, or chicken.

SAVORY
Summer and Winter Varieties

SAVORY, of Mediterranean origin, was popular in Greek and Roman cookery and medicine. The Romans introduced this herb to England, as they did so many other plants, almost 2000 years ago.

From Pliny we learn that the pantheistic Druids, the learned men of the Celts, used large numbers of medicinal herbs, gathering them with superstitious ceremony, since they considered many plants holy. Surely they must have revered the fragrant savory—but we shall never know; when the Vikings plundered England in the 800's, they destroyed the libraries in the monasteries. Obviously, there had once been books on herbs, judging by the eighth-century

English missionary, St. Boniface, who records that he had been asked for books on "simples," meaning medicinal herbs.

A thousand years ago in England, vegetable gardens, as we now know them, did not exist. The Anglo-Saxons of that day planted only herb gardens —not only the culinary herbs held in esteem today, but flowers such as roses, violets, and marigolds, which were also eaten.

There are two kinds of savory, a summer one, usually found on spice shelves, and a winter savory, which has a somewhat more potent flavor. Germans have always called both of these "bean herbs," because they add such a delicious aroma either to green or dried beans. Savory is among the ingredients used in poultry seasoning. From this it is clear that savory is also an excellent flavoring for meats, meat dressings, chicken soups, salads, sauces, and scrambled eggs.

SESAME Symbol of Good Luck

THREE or four centuries ago, many herbalists believed in what was then called "The Doctrine of Signatures." The substance of this doctrine was that each plant could somehow offer man a hint as to its proper use. A dandelion, for example, being golden, could cure jaundice. And Solomon's Seal, with its seal-like markings, must surely, it was supposed, close wounds and heal broken bones. Every plant, in short, possessed an appearance, an environment, and habits that served as their labels.

Since sesame seeds pop from the hull as soon as ripe, scattering in all directions, this seemed to be a plant which could not only free itself from all barriers, but could serve to open any lock, and discover any secret place. When Queen Scheherazade—telling the story of Sinbad the Sailor—needed a

password to open the robbers' treasure trove, she chose, "Open, Sesame!"

Sesame is among the world's oldest spice and oil-seed crops. In fact, it is so old that folklore relates that the gods of the ancient Assyrians refreshed themselves with sesame wine before they began the arduous task of creating the world. A drawing in an Egyptian tomb, dating back 4000 years, depicts a baker adding sesame seeds to a dough. As revealed in the Old Testament, sesame was well known in those times, and was an important food source in the days of Cleopatra. (We now know that it is fabulously high in protein.) Greek soldiers, too, carried a supply of sesame seeds for emergency rations.

When plantation owners in the Western Hemisphere first imported slave labor from Africa in the early seventeenth century, the Africans brought with them not only many of their own folkways, but sesame seeds—to them a symbol of good luck. "Benne seeds," they called them. Here, as in their homeland, sesame was used not only as a food, but as a soothing oil and medicine, and even as an oil for lighting their homes. Even today in the South, sesame seeds are often called "benne."

Since toasted sesame seeds have a delicate, almondlike flavor, they can be used, more or less in unmeasured amounts, in any dish in which chopped nutmeats would be included. Untoasted when purchased, they can be used without preliminary heating if scattered on top of dishes about to be baked, as crumb-topped casseroles, or on any surface that will brown during the course of cooking.

But if sesame seeds are to be stirred into batters and doughs or sprinkled on salad greens or (cooked) buttered noodles, they must first be toasted. To toast, scatter sesame seeds thinly in a baking dish and bake 20 to 22 minutes in a moderate oven (350° F.) or until they are pale brown and of full flavor.

TARRAGON The Little Dragon

ANYONE who has imagined Siberia as a vast, frosty wasteland, where mad wolves pursue droshkies across the tundra, may indeed be surprised to learn that this arctic region is the native home of tarragon—the treasured herb of the sophisticated salad-tosser and sauce-maker.

Tarragon was completely unknown to the ancients who lived near the Mediterranean—to the Egyptians, the Greeks, and the Romans. It was first mentioned in the thirteenth century by a famous Arab doctor, El-beithar, who called it *tarkhum,* Arabic for "dragon," and prescribed it as a purifier in times of pestilence.

By the sixteenth century it had reached European kitchens. The French seem to have held it in higher esteem than other nations have; they, too, called it "little dragon" or *estragon,* since the roots grow in serpentine fashion.

Tarragon is a delightful herb, having a distinctive aroma, with just a touch of licorice flavor. For this reason it cannot be used as experimentally as most herbs and it should be used lightly in a *fines herbes* mixture. It makes an ideal herb for leafy green salads; for use in mayonnaise, fish sauce, and in an especially tasty Béarnaise sauce.

THYME Symbol of Activity

AMONG the attractive accomplishments of proper young ladies of the past was a knowledge of the language of flowers. From a book devoted to this lore, which appeared in 1836, they learned that thyme "is a symbol of activity."

"Beetles of all hues, light butterflies, and vigilant bees, for ever surround the flowery tufts of Thyme," the author noted. "It may be that to these cheerful inhabitants of the air, whose life is a long spring, these little tufts appear like an immense tree, old as the earth and covered with eternal verdure, begemmed with myriads of flowery vases, filled with honey for their express enjoyment," the author continued.

It is true that bees have never been able to resist the fragrance of thyme. The ancient Greeks relished the honey made by the bees buzzing over Mount Hymettus, near Athens, where thyme grew abundantly. So highly esteemed was the delicate fragrance of thyme that "to smell of thyme" was one of the most desirable compliments one Athenian could offer another.

Ladies of the Middle Ages also observed the attraction thyme held for bees. A favorite design that a lady embroidered on the scarf of her knight-errant was composed of a bee hovering over a sprig of thyme—which mingled the sweet and amiable with high courage and martial action. To enhance their own charms these ladies included thyme sprigs in the "tussie-mussies" they fashioned. A tussie-mussie was a demure bouquet of very fragrant flowers and sweet-scented leaves. It was always held tightly by a lady so that the warmth of her hand could release the scent of the lovely bouquet.

Thyme was among the many herbs used widely in incantations and charms. To conjure the fairy folk, one had only to gather some thyme on a hillside where fairies were known to frolic. It was in *A Midsummer Night's Dream* that Oberon suggested seeking Titania and her court on "a bank where the wild thyme blows."

Thyme has been a popular herb in the United States for many years. New England clam chowder would not be complete without its proper measure of fragrant thyme. Thyme is one of the traditional herbs of the Creole cuisine in New Orleans. In the Middle West thyme is used in a tempting poultry stuffing and, further west, it is among the many aromatic plants grown in California.

Thyme can be purchased either in whole or ground form. Since it is

one of the moderately potent herbs, you might use between ¼ and ½ teaspoonful of ground or whole thyme in a concoction to serve 6. In the stuffing for a 3-pound fish, for example, you would use ½ teaspoonful of thyme; in a quart of creamy oyster stew, no more than ¼ teaspoonful.

Whenever possible, delay adding thyme or any other herb to a mixture that requires a long time to cook until within 10 minutes before the end of the cooking period.

TURMERIC Oriental Amulet

IF you are an average American cook, you most likely have only a superficial knowledge of turmeric. You might have heard it called "tumeric" (without the first "r" being uttered), as our great-grandmothers pronounced it. Turmeric is the deep yellow spice so dear to the relish-maker and those devoted to home-pickling of foods. Often it is added to prepared mustard, and is always among the ingredients in curry powder. These, in the past, have covered the use of this golden powder in the United States.

Turmeric, however, has been used for a very long time throughout Asia, not only as a culinary spice, but it has served as a dye, a medicine, a ceremonial color, and an amulet. It is the root of this lilylike plant of the ginger family that is used. A native of Asia, turmeric is now also grown in the Caribbean and wherever ginger thrives. Because of its brilliant golden color, it has been most closely identified with saffron throughout the centuries and, in medieval times, turmeric was called "Indian saffron," or *Crocus indicus.*

In addition to its many uses as a spice, turmeric has long been a valued dyestuff; but as with saffron, it has largely been replaced by coal-tar dyes. Turmeric is probably the "sweet calamus," along with sweet cinnamon and myrrh described as "the principal spices" which the Children of Israel carried with them on their flight from Egypt.

Sun-worshipers, speaking an Aryan language, made of the saffron crocus a sacred flower, and its yellow became a holy color. The demand for it was so great, alternates had to be found. Thus turmeric soon began to be used for ceremonial purposes, too. Hindu brides, for example, are painted with it, while married women in regions of India rinse their hands in turmeric water, and rub it lightly over their cheeks when they wish to look their best. Lending a golden glow to the skin, it is used as a general cosmetic in many parts of Asia.

In many parts of the Orient turmeric is regarded highly as a charm. A bit of turmeric root is suspended around the neck of a newborn baby, or turmeric water is dabbed on the child's head daily, until it is old enough to walk. In Bengal, should anyone become possessed by a tree spirit, an exorcist is summoned; he waves a piece of burning turmeric root slowly and hypnotically before the face of the victim. This, it is said, causes the ghost to depart at once—for ghosts cannot endure the smell of charred turmeric!

The taste of turmeric is related to mustard, since many prepared mustards have been blended with ground turmeric. This furnishes a clue to the use of this venerable spice in modern foods. It can be used in very much the same way that saffron is: with chicken, fish, and pork; also in rice concoctions; creamed eggs; in spiced butters for corn, snap beans, and steamed green cabbage. If you are bored preparing potatoes in the old, familiar way, dress them with turmeric butter, a speck of cayenne, and some chopped chives.

How much turmeric is to be used depends on the type of dish you are making. A good rule is to start with ¼ or ½ teaspoonful in a recipe to serve 4, then taste and add more as needed.

How to Cook with Spices

SPICES are the main flavor source of the world's greatest cookery. Used imaginatively and judiciously, they can transform the most pedestrian dish into a triumph of *haute cuisine*.

Happily, there are no real "mysteries" about spice cooking. But what does seem to puzzle many of our friends is the difference between spices and herbs. There is a difference, of course, but in the vernacular of cooking the word "spice" has come to mean all those spices, seeds, herbs, and vegetable seasonings used to flavor food.

But if you have literal-minded friends who demand the facts, then you can tell them true spices are parts of plants that usually grow in the tropics; herbs are always leaves of plants that grow in temperate zones; seeds, such as mustard, caraway, and poppy, are actually seeds, or sometimes the fruits of plants that grow either in tropical or temperate zones; and dehydrated vegetable seasonings are the powdered or flaked forms of garlic, onion, green peppers, and other vegetables.

Here are a few suggestions that should help you get the most out of your spices.

First, don't confuse the word *spice* with the word *hot*. Very few spices are hot. In fact, the majority are quite mild and used sparingly will add only the most subtle flavor to a dish.

Second, overcome the urge to use too much spice flavoring (or too little, for that matter) unless the recipe calls for a certain predominant flavor. When you first use spices, it is perhaps natural to expect flavor miracles in direct proportion to the amount used. Miraculous cookery is the result of delicacy and restraint.

63

Third, feel free to experiment. Remember that spices do not change the chemistry of cookery. You may use spices according to the dictates of your own imagination by altering the quantities called for in an existing recipe— *so long as you do not tamper with the basic ingredients.*

Fourth, become familiar with the flavors of numerous spices, just as an artist knows his pigments. The top ten spices, according to their popularity in American cooking are: black pepper; cinnamon; nutmeg; garlic (minced, salt, or powder); paprika; chili powder; oregano; celery (salt or seeds); onion (minced, flakes, salt, or powder) and parsley flakes. Start with these when building up your spice shelf.

Then, buy a different spice each week and familiarize yourself with its particular aroma and flavor. Consult the Spice Charts in the section that follows and try your new spice in a dish with compatible flavor. For example, anise can be used to flavor cookies, lend aroma to Figs in Anise-Rum Sauce,* give distinction to French dressing for fruit salads and cole slaw, and complement Roast Duck, Chinese Style.*

Once you have acquired a well-stocked spice shelf, take pride in keeping your spices at their best. Store them in the coolest part of the kitchen—away from either direct sunlight or the heat of the stove. After using, always close the spice containers carefully. (The aroma of spices can rise from an opened container just as easily as from some well-seasoned concoction.) Check your spices every season and discard those that have lost their verve. The best thing to do, of course, is to make constant use of them, brightening every meal with their heady scents.

SPICE AND
HERB CHARTS

SPICE CHART

	APPETIZERS	BREAD	CHEESE	DESSERTS	EGGS

ALLSPICE	Cranberry juice
	Tomato juice
		Coffee cake
		Sweet rolls
		Tea bread
				Fruit compotes
				Cakes, cookies
				Gingerbread
				Pumpkin pie
				Mince pie
				Baked and
				  steamed
				  puddings	

ANISE	Fruit juice
	Fruit cup
	Cheese canapés
	Shellfish
	  canapés
		Coffee cake
		Sweet rolls
		Tea bread
			Cottage cheese
			  and other
			  mild-flavored
			  cheese
				Cakes and
				  cookies
				Apple pie
				Fruit compotes
				Baked apple	

CARAWAY
SEED
	Canapé
	  spreads
	Tomato juice
		Rye bread
		Pumpernickel
		Coffee cakes
		Onion bread
		Rolls and buns
			Cheese spreads
			Cottage cheese
			Cheese omelets
				Cakes and
				  cookies
				Apple pie
					Omelet
					Sandwich
					  spreads

CARDA-
MOM
SEED
	All melons
	  except
	  watermelon
		Danish pastry
		Lucia buns
		Sweet yeast
		  bread
		Coffee cake
				Cakes, cookies
				Apple pie
				Pumpkin pie
				Fruit compotes
				Baked apple	

CAYENNE	Guacamole	Cheese wafers
		  and straws
			Dips
			Fondue,
			  macaroni,
			  and cheese
			Soufflé
			Welsh rarebit
					Omelet
					Soufflé
					Deviled eggs

CELERY SEED	Tomato juice Clam juice	Cheese wafers and straws	Cheese spreads		Omelet Scrambled Soufflé

CHILI
POWDER
	Tomato juice
	Guacamole
		French bread
		Biscuits
			Cottage cheese
			Dips and
			  spreads
			Fondue
			Welsh rarebit
					Deviled
					Omelet
					Scrambled
					Sandwich
					  spreads

MEATS	POULTRY	SALADS	SAUCES	SEAFOOD	SOUPS	VEGETABLES
Beef, lamb, and veal pot roasts and stews Meat balls and loaf Ham patties Ham glaze	Chicken and turkey fricassee Chicken and turkey pie Braised chicken Duck stew	Fruit Cabbage	Dessert Chili Tomato catsup Tomato Meat	Poached fish	Chicken Consommé Fish chowder Potato Tomato Turtle Vegetable	Beets Carrots Parsnips Sweet potatoes Turnips Spinach Winter squash
Beef and veal stew	Braised chicken Roast duck Chicken and duck pilaf	Fruit Cabbage French dressing	Dessert Whipped cream		Fruit	
Beef roasts and stews Pork roast Sauerbraten	Roast goose	Cole slaw Cottage cheese Cucumber Tomato French dressing Sour cream dressing	Butter sauce for noodles, spaghetti, and vegetables Cucumber Sour cream	Broiled fish crab, and lobster Poached fish Stuffed fish	Cabbage Potato	Cabbage Carrots Celery Cucumbers Onions Potatoes Turnips
Curried beef, lamb, veal, and pork	Curried poultry dishes		Hard sauce Lemon Orange	Curried seafood dishes		Carrots Sweet potatoes Pumpkin Winter squash
Ham croquettes Ham soufflé Pork sausage Paprikash Curried meats	Broiled chicken Barbecued poultry Paprikash Curried chicken	Cheese Egg Macaroni Seafood Red kidney beans	Barbecue Spaghetti Tomato Cheese	Boiled shrimp Broiled shrimp, lobster, and crabmeat	Brunswick stew Vegetable	Cabbage Collard greens Turnip greens Kale
Meat roasts and stews Meat loaf	Chicken fricassee	Cole slaw French dressing	Celery Tomato sauce	Fish chowder	Chowders Bisques	Beets Braised lettuce Cabbage Cucumbers
Chili con carne Beef stew Meat balls Meat loaf Hamburgers Tamale pie	Barbecued chicken Broiled chicken Poultry casseroles Fried chicken	Egg Mixed vegetable Potato Seafood Salad dressing	Barbecue Cocktail Spaghetti Tomato Cheese	Shrimp Fish Lobster	Black bean Bean bisque Pea Tomato	Lima beans Corn Eggplant Onions Tomatoes

SPICE CHART

 N W E S	APPETIZERS	BREAD	CHEESE	DESSERTS	EGGS

CINNAMON	Tomato juice
	Cranberry juice
		Biscuits
		Coffee cake
		Sweet rolls
		  and buns
		Pumpkin bread
		Tea loaf
		Toast
				Apple desserts
				Cakes, cookies
				Chocolate
				  desserts
				Rice pudding
				Gingerbread
				Fruit compotes	

CLOVES	Tomato juice
	Cranberry juice
		Coffee cakes
		Sweet rolls
		Sweet yeast
		  bread
		Tea loaf
				Cakes, cookies
				Fruit compotes
				Baked, steamed
				  puddings
				Chocolate
				  desserts
				Gingerbread	

CORIANDER		Biscuits and
		  buns
				Apple desserts
				Cakes and
				  cookies
				Gingerbread
					Omelet
					Curried
					Scrambled
					Sandwich
					  spreads

CUMIN SEED	Cheese and egg
	  canapés
			Cheese spreads	Cakes and
				  cookies
					Curried eggs
					Stuffed

CURRY POWDER		French bread	Cottage cheese Cream cheese Fondue Cheese noodles	Apple pie	Curried Scrambled Deviled Sandwich spreads

DILL SEED	Tomato juice
	Vegetable juice
		Yeast loaf
		Dill-onion
		  bread and
		  rolls
			Cottage cheese
			Cream cheese
				Green apple
				  pie
					Deviled
					Sandwich
					  spreads

FENNEL SEED		Yeast loaf Muffins		Apple desserts Cakes Cookies	

GINGER	Apple juice
	Prune juice
	Cantaloupe
		Tea bread
		Pumpkin bread
		Sweet rolls
			Macaroni and
			  cheese
			Other cheese
			  dishes
				Fruit desserts
				Cakes
				Cookies
				Gingerbread
				Steamed, baked
				  puddings
				Indian pudding	

MEATS	POULTRY	SALADS	SAUCES	SEAFOOD	SOUPS	VEGETABLES

Beef stew
Sauerbraten
		Spiced fruit
		Spiced jellied
		  fruit
			Applesauce
			Raisin
			Chocolate
			Cranberry
			Lemon and
			  orange
					Fruit	Beets
						Carrots
						Onions
						Pumpkin
						Sweet potatoes
						Winter squash
						Tomatoes

Corned beef
Ham
Pork
Stews
Tongue
		Spiced fruit
		Spiced jellied
		  fruit
			Applesauce
			Raisin sauce
			Tomato catsup
			Tomato sauce
			Chili
			Chocolate
					Chicken and
					  meat stocks
					Onion
						Beets
						Carrots
						Onions
						Pumpkin
						Sweet potatoes
						Winter squash

All kinds of
  meat curries
Pork sausage
Meat balls
	Curried
	  chicken
	Stuffing
		Mixed greens
		Salad dressings
					Pea
					Soup stocks
						Cauliflower
						Onions
						Spinach
						Tomatoes

Curried meat
Meat balls
Meat loaf
	Curried poultry
	  dishes
	Stuffing
		Salad dressing
		  for fruit or
		  chicken
			Curried seafood
			  and poultry
			  sauces
				Shrimp
				Lobster
				Fish		

Pork and lamb
Meat balls
Meat loaf
Curried meat
  dishes
	Curried
	  chicken and
	  duck
	Stuffing
		Chicken
		Fruit
		Seafood
		Salad dressings
			Butter
			Egg
			Cheese
			Onion
			Celery
				Crabmeat
				Fish
				Lobster
				Shrimp
				Stuffing
					Chicken
					Consommé
					Pea
					Tomato
					Turtle
					Vegetable
						Beets
						Carrots
						Parsnips
						Sweet potatoes
						Turnips
						Winter squash

Lamb chops
Lamb roast
Lamb stew
	Chicken and
	  rice
	Creamed
	  chicken
		Cabbage,
		  potato,
		  vegetable,
		  cucumber,
		  tomato
		French dressing
			Gravy
			Sour cream
			Fish
			Butter
				Seafood and
				  rice
				Fish loaf
				Broiled
				Fish balls
					Fruit	

Italian sausage
Beef
Lamb
Pork
	Chicken and
	  duck pilafs
		Seafood
		Green
		  vegetable
			Sauces for
			  ham, pork,
			  and tongue
			Dessert
				Seafood pilaf
				Baked fish and
				  shellfish
				Poached fish
					Cabbage
					Potato
						Cabbage
						Onions
						Cucumbers
						Potatoes

Meats
(roasts,
  chops, and
  stews)
Oriental meat
  dishes
	Fried chicken
	Roast chicken
	Baked duck
	Chicken and
	  duck
	  casseroles
		French dressing	Sauces for
			  ham, pork,
			  and tongue
			Dessert
						Carrots
						Sweet potatoes
						Winter squash

SPICE CHART

 N W E S	APPETIZERS	BREAD	CHEESE	DESSERTS	EGGS

MACE		Banana bread
		Tea bread
		Doughnuts
		Sweet yeast
		  rolls and
		  bread
			Welsh rarebit	Pound, other
				  spice cakes
				Cookies; Choc-
				  olate dishes
				Lemon, lime,
				  and orange
				  desserts	

MUSTARD	Shrimp
	  cocktail
		Cheese yeast
		  bread
			All cheese
			  dishes
				Spice cake
				Gingerbread
				Molasses
				  cookies
					Deviled
					Sandwich
					  spreads

NUTMEG		Banana bread
		Tea bread
		Sweet yeast
		  bread and
		  rolls
				Custard
				Puddings
				Apple desserts
				Cakes, cookies
				Doughnuts
				Apple and
				  pumpkin pies
					Eggnog

PAPRIKA	Garnish		Garnish		Garnish

**PEPPER,
BLACK**
	Fish and
	  shellfish
	  appetizers
	All vegetable
	  juices
	Pâtés
		Italian yeast
		Easter bread
		Crackling
		  bread
		Spice tea loaf
			All cheese
			  dishes
				Spice cake
				  and cookies
				Gingerbread
					All egg dishes

**PEPPER,
WHITE**
	Same as above
	  (where black
	  specks are
	  not desirable)
		Same as above	Same as above	Same as above	Same as above

SESAME SEED	Garnish	Quick bread Tea bread Coffee cake Rolls	Fondue, omelet Spreads Garnish	Cakes, cookies Pies	Scrambled Garnish
TURMERIC					Sandwich spreads Deviled Creamed

MEATS	POULTRY	SALADS	SAUCES	SEAFOOD	SOUPS	VEGETABLES

Meat loaf
Veal chops
	Chicken
	  fricassee
	Sauces for
	  chicken
			Fish
			Chicken
			Desserts
			Whipped
			  cream
				Clam bisque
				Oyster stew
					Brunswick stew
					Vegetable
						Broccoli
						Brussels
						  sprouts
						Cabbage
						Snap beans

Ham and pork
Hamburgers
  and meat
  balls
Meat loaf
		Ham and other
		  meat and egg
		  salads
		Boiled and
		  French
		  dressings
			Cheese
			Egg
			Meat
			Vegetable
					Chowders
					Bisques
						Beets
						Braised lettuce
						Cabbage
						Cucumbers

Swedish meat
  balls
Meat pie
  pastry
Meat loaf
			Fruit
			Foamy
			Hard
			Butter
			Whipped
			  cream
					Black bean
					Pea
					Tomato
					Potato
						Tomatoes
						Beans
						Corn
						Eggplant
						Onions

Beef and veal
  paprikash
Garnish
	Chicken
	  paprikash
	Garnish
		Salad dressings
		Garnish
			Barbecue
			Butter
			Cucumber
				Stuffings for
				  fish
				Garnish
					Pea	Cauliflower
						Corn
						Spinach

All meat dishes	All poultry
	  dishes
		All vegetable
		All meat
		All seafood
		Egg
			Barbecue
			Butter
			Marinades
			Cheese
			Egg
			Cream
				All seafood
				  dishes
					Fruit	Beets
						Carrots
						Onions
						Rutabagas
						Sweet potatoes
						Tomatoes

Same as above
  (where black
  specks are
  not desired)
	Same as above	Same as above	Same as above	Same as above	Chicken and
					  veal stock
					Vegetable
						Beets
						Carrots
						Onions
						Sweet potatoes
						Winter squash

	Stuffing
	Fried chicken
	Broiled chicken
	Baked chicken
	  and duck
		Fruit
		Chicken
		Tomato
		Salad dressings
			Butter	Broiled fish
				Crabmeat
				Lobster
				Shrimp
				Stuffing
						Corn
						Summer and
						  zucchini
						  squash

Curried meats	Curried
	  chicken,
	  duck or
	  turkey
	Duck or
	  chicken pilaf
		Deviled egg
		Potato
		Chicken
			Sauces for
			  eggs, chicken,
			  fish, or
			  shellfish
				Pilafs, fish,
				  lobster, and
				  shrimp		

HERB CHART

	APPETIZERS	BREAD	CHEESE	EGGS	MEATS

BASIL	Tomato juice
	Vegetable juice
	Seafood
	  cocktail
		Yeast loaf	Pizza pie
			Rarebits
				Scrambled
				Deviled
				Sandwich
				  spreads
					Beef, lamb, an
					  veal roasts
					  and stews
					Hamburgers
					Meat balls
					Meat pies
					Lamb chops

BAY LEAF	Tomato juice				Beef, lamb,
					  and veal
					  stews and
					  pot roasts
					Tongue

CHERVIL		Herb bread	Cottage cheese Cream cheese	Omelet Scrambled Shirred	

ITALIAN SEASONING	Clam juice
	Tomato juice
	Vegetable juice
		Herb bread	Soufflé
			Omelet
			Macaroni and
			  cheese
				Omelet
				Scrambled
					Beef, lamb an
					  veal stews
					  and pot
					  roasts
					Pork chops

MARJORAM	Chopped liver
	  and onion
	Liver pâté
	Tomato juice
		Herb bread	Sharp cheese
			  spreads
				Omelet
				Scrambled
					Pot roast
					Stews, stuffin
					Meat loaf

MINT	Fruit cup Fruit juice Melon balls		Cream cheese spreads		Lamb stew

OREGANO	Guacamole
	Tomato juice
	Vegetable juice
			Pizza pie
			Cheese spreads
				Deviled
				Omelet
				Sandwich
				  spreads
					Chili con car
					Hamburgers
					Beef and lan
					  roasts and
					  stews
					Pork dishes

...OULTRY	SALADS	SAUCES	SEAFOOD	SOUPS	VEGETABLES
...d chicken	Tomato Vegetable Seafood Aspic French dressing	Tomato Cheese Butter Spaghetti	Fish Shrimp Crabmeat Lobster	Minestrone Pea Potato Spinach Turtle Vegetable	Asparagus Beets; Broccoli Cabbage; Car- rots; Celery Cucumbers Eggplant; Peas Tomatoes; Tur- nip; Spinach

...ken stew
...d fricassee
...son
...it
	Aspic
	Molded
	  vegetable
		Spaghetti
		Meat
		Tomato
			Poached fish
			Pickled fish
			Court bouillon
			Shrimp and
			  lobster
				Bouillabaisse
				Consommé
				Chicken
				Vegetable	

...d
...cken
	Egg
	Vegetable
	Chicken
	Salad dressing
		Béarnaise
		Tomato
		Vinaigrette
			Shellfish	Cream of
				  potato
				Cream of
				  spinach
					Beets
					Celery
					Cucumbers
					Lettuce
					Potatoes
					Tomatoes

...en ...asse ...en and ...cy pie ...g	Vegetable Seafood French dressing	Cheese Gravy Spaghetti Tomato	Baked fish Broiled fish Stuffing	Fish chowder Potato Vegetable	Eggplant Tomatoes

...chicken
...en
...assee
...duck
...turkey
...g
	Chicken
	Egg
	Seafood
	French
	  dressing
		Gravy
		Seafood
		Butter
		Tomato
			Crabmeat
			Fish
			Shrimp
			Stuffing
				Cream of
				  celery
				Cream of
				  chicken
				Onion
				Potato
				Spinach
					Celery
					Collard greens
					Turnip greens
					Onions
					Peas
					Potatoes

	Cole slaw Fruit	Lamb Dessert Whipped cream		Cream of pea	Carrots Peas
...hen ...nt	Egg Kidney bean Vegetable Tomato Meat Shrimp Salad dressing	Butter Spaghetti Tomato Shrimp	Fish stuffing Broiled fish Broiled shrimp	Bean Minestrone Tomato	Broccoli Eggplant Cabbage Tomatoes Lentils Dried beans

HERB CHART

 W ⊕ E (compass)	APPETIZERS	BREAD	CHEESE	EGGS	MEATS
PARSLEY	Clam juice Tomato juice Aspic	Biscuits Herb loaf	Cottage cheese Cream cheese Cheese dips Soufflé	Deviled Creamed Scrambled Omelet	Beef, lamb, and veal stew Meat pies Meat loaf
POULTRY SEASONING		In biscuits to serve with poultry and fish dishes			Croquettes All meat stews Meat casserole Stuffings
ROSEMARY	Fruit cups	Yeast loaf		Omelet Scrambled Soufflé Shirred	Lamb roast and stew Shish kebab Liver loaf Pot roasts
SAFFRON		Tea bread Yeast rolls and bread	Cream cheese	Scrambled	
SAGE	Tomato juice Clam juice	Corn bread and biscuits to serve with poultry and seafood	Cheddar cheese spreads Omelet Fondue		Pork dishes Veal dishes Sausage Stuffing
SAVORY	Tomato juice Vegetable juice Liver pâté			Deviled Omelet Scrambled	Roast beef, lamb, pork, or veal Meat pies Hamburgers
TARRAGON	Tomato juice Fruit juice Liver pâté			All egg dishes	Lamb dishes Veal dishes
THYME	Tomato juice Fish cocktail spreads Aspic Liver pâté	Corn bread and biscuits served with poultry and fish dishes Yeast loaf	Cottage cheese	Deviled Scrambled Shirred	All roasts and stews Meat loaf and balls Croquettes Liver loaf

...OULTRY	SALADS	SAUCES	SEAFOOD	SOUPS	VEGETABLES
...icken ...ricasse ...cken and ...urkey pie ...ffing	Chicken Egg Potato Seafood Vegetable	Butter Tartar Bordelaise Remoulade Spaghetti	Fish and shellfish Lobster thermidor Paella Stuffing	Court bouillon Chicken and meat stocks All vegetable soups	Beets; Cabbage Carrots; Cauliflower; Celery Onions; Potatoes; Turnip Eggplant
...chicken ...d turkey ...shes ...k and ...tabaga ...ew ...ing	Egg Chicken or turkey Seafood	Gravy Cream sauce for seafood or poultry	Broiled fish Seafood casseroles Stuffings	Chicken Fish chowder Potato chowder or soup	Onions Potatoes
...chicken and ...rkey dishes ...fings	Chicken and turkey salad Seafood Lamb French dressing	Lamb gravy Cream sauce for chicken, seafood, or lamb Butter	Fish Scallops Croquettes Tuna loaf Stuffing	Chicken Lamb broth Tomato Fish chowder	Cauliflower Potatoes Turnips
...ken ...k ...ey ...z con pollo			Fish Paella Shrimp Seafood pilafs		
...ken, ...rkey, and ...ck ...sseroles ...uettes ...d chicken ...ng	Chicken Turkey Salad dressing	Chicken and turkey gravy Butter for fish Cream sauce for poultry	Stuffing Baked fish Chowder	Chicken and turkey	Beets Celery Onions Summer and zucchini squash Tomatoes
...ken and ...key dishes	Green salads Tomato Salad dressing	Sauces for fish and poultry dishes	Broiled fish Stuffing	Chicken Cucumber Potato Tomato Meat broth	Beans Cucumbers Potatoes Tomatoes Carrots
...ken ...ey	Chicken Green salads Tomato Potato	Sauces for lamb and chicken	Fish Shrimp	Chicken Mushroom Pea Tomato	Beets Carrots Summer and zucchini squash String beans Onions
...icken ...d turkey ...seroles ...pies ...chicken ...duck ...ng	Chicken Ham Tuna fish Egg Beet Tomato	Sauces for poultry and seafood dishes Creoles Tomato Gravy	Tuna Scallops Crabmeat Fish Lobster Shrimp Stuffing	Clam chowder Clam bisque Fish chowder Chicken and mushroom Tomato Vegetable	Beets Carrots Onions Potatoes Mushrooms Summer and zucchini squash

POIVRE, ADMINISTRATOR OF
THE FRENCH ISLANDS REUNION
AND MAURITIUS BREAKS THE
DUTCH „SPICE MONOPOLY"
BIJ STARTING A NUTMEG –
PLANTATION ON MAURITIUS

Preface to the Recipes

IN an age of constant change in ingredients and cookery methods, we must tell you briefly what kinds of materials, techniques, and equipment were used in testing and perfecting these recipes—and how you should best use the recipes themselves.

First, read the recipe carefully—every word, from beginning to end.

Next, check your supplies to see that you have all the ingredients called for. Make sure your mixing equipment and cooking pans are of the correct size. This is very important, since a recipe can fail if it is mixed or cooked in a bowl or pan too large or too small for the mixture.

Grease baking pans well and flour lightly, when required, before starting to mix the ingredients. Paper liners are necessary only when baking cakes containing fruit. When a preheated oven is called for, allow it to warm up while you are mixing the ingredients.

Be accurate when measuring your ingredients. Use standard measuring spoons and cups and make all measurements level. When measuring small quantities, use a set of 4 spoons having capacities of ¼, ½, and 1 teaspoon and 1 tablespoon. To measure ⅛ teaspoon, fill and level off the ¼ teaspoon measure, cut the contents in half lengthwise with a knife or spatula and use ½.

When measuring dry ingredients, use a set of 4 measuring "cups" having capacities of ¼, ⅓, ½, and 1 standard cup. This set of cups is sometimes known as the "Mary Ann" set. When measuring liquids, use a 1-cup measuring cup whose rim is above the 1-cup line and which has a pouring lip to prevent spilling. Fractions of a cup can be measured in it by filling to the lower graduation lines. If the cup is made of glass or other transparent material, the intermediate lines can be read more accurately. The 2-cup and 1-quart sizes also are convenient.

Sift all flour before measuring, except when 2 or 3 tablespoons are required for gravy, etc., or when the recipe specifically calls for measuring without sifting. Then spoon it lightly into the measuring cup, without packing or shaking, and level it off with the edge of a metal spatula or straight-edged knife. In recipes calling for brown sugar, use the light brown unless otherwise specified. If it is lumpy, place the package in a warm oven (250° F.) for 10 minutes and then roll out the lumps with a rolling pin, or press them out with a spoon or fingers. Spoon into the measuring cup and pack it only firmly enough so that it will hold the shape of the cup when turned out. If packed too tightly, too much will be measured and used.

Unless otherwise stated, all recipes in this book that call for eggs were tested with *large* eggs.

In recipes calling for butter or margarine, do not use the whipped types because they contain less fat per cup. Do not substitute lard or vegetable shortening for butter or margarine in a recipe, since the fat contents of these shortenings differ. For instance, the fat content of 1 cup lard is 220 grams; 1 cup vegetable shortening is 200 grams; 1 cup butter or margarine 181.4 grams fat. Vegetable shortening was used in all recipes specifying shortening. Wherever *melted* butter, margarine, or shortening is specified in a recipe, it should be measured *before* melting.

Never alter the basic ingredients of a recipe. However, ingredients such as spices and flavoring extracts which do not change the chemistry of a recipe may be varied. And never double a recipe. It is better to make the recipe a second time. Larger portions usually require different cooking times and temperatures and may require other changes. The recipes in this book give the number of servings each yields. This means an average-size serving per person and does not allow for second helpings.

Those little lines (———) you see between ingredients in almost every recipe are there to help you keep score. They are inserted at logical breaks between one step in the recipe and the next, and are usually keyed to a specific number of ingredients that are to be used, in some fashion, all at the same time.

An asterisk after the name of a dish that is capitalized (Example: Spiced Pumpkin Raisin Bread*) indicates that the recipe is included in the book. Consult the Index for the page number.

Glossary of Terms

A LA   In the fashion of.

A LA MODE   (a) Topped with ice cream (as pie or cake).
(b) Marinated and braised with carrots, mushrooms, onions, etc. (roast beef à la mode).

APERITIF   A beverage served as an appetizer before a meal.

ASPIC   A savory meat jelly, with or without added gelatine, containing bits of meat, fowl, fish, game, egg, or vegetables.

AU GRATIN   Baked with bread crumbs, cheese, or both.

AU JUS   Served in its natural juices (roast prime ribs of beef au jus).

AU LAIT   Made and served with milk (café au lait).

BAKE   To cook by dry heat in an oven or oven-type appliance in a covered or uncovered container.

BAR-LE-DUC   A special type of fruit preserve made from currants.

BARBECUE   To roast slowly on a spit or grid over slow-burning coals or under a broiler, usually basting with a highly seasoned sauce.

BASTE   To moisten (meat or other foods) while cooking to prevent drying and to add flavor. The liquid may be pan drippings, melted fat, butter, margarine, oil, fruit juice, sauce, or even salt water.

BATTER   Flour or meal mixture containing sufficient liquid so that it can be poured or dropped from a spoon before baking.

BEAT   To agitate with rapid, regular strokes that lift and turn the mixture, thereby incorporating air and making it smooth. The tool may be a spoon or wire whisk, a hand-operated rotary beater, or an electric beater of the air-incorporating type.

79

BLANCH   To preheat in boiling water or steam 1 to 5 minutes, followed by draining and rinsing in cold water. Uses: (1) To remove skins from some fruits, vegetables, and nuts. (2) To inactivate enzymes and shrink food for canning, freezing, and drying.

BLEND   To combine thoroughly two or more ingredients.

BOIL   To cook food in boiling liquid, usually water. A liquid is boiling when bubbles of its vapor continuously rise to the surface and break. The boiling temperature of pure water at sea level is 212° F. (100° C.).

BOUILLON   A clear soup made from a brown beef stock, delicately seasoned. (Clam bouillon is an exception.)

BRAISE   To brown (meat or vegetable) in a small amount of hot fat and then to cover and cook slowly in the food's own juices, with or without the addition of a small amount of other liquid.

BREAD   To cover or coat with bread crumbs alone, or to coat first with bread crumbs, then with beaten egg diluted with milk or water, and then again with bread crumbs.

BROCHETTE   Cut-up pieces (meat, tomatoes, onions, etc.) threaded on skewers and cooked over an open fire.

BROIL   To cook directly under the heating unit or over an open fire.

BRUSH   To coat the surface with melted butter, oil, milk, cream, or beaten egg white, using a pastry brush.

CANDY   (a) To cook (fruit) in heavy sugar syrup until transparent, then drain and dry (candied orange or grapefruit peel).

(b) To cook (vegetables. or fruits, such as sweet potatoes or apple slices) with sugar or syrup to give a glaze.

CARAMELIZE   To melt sugar slowly over medium-low heat until it develops its characteristic caramel flavor and golden-brown color.

CHOP   To cut into small pieces with a sharp knife.

COAT   To roll food in flour, crumbs, sugar, chopped nuts, etc., until uniformly covered; or to dip in bread crumbs, in egg and milk, and again in crumbs.

CODDLE   To cook slowly in water just below boiling point (coddled egg).

COMPOTE   Two or more fruits in sugar syrup.

CONSERVE   Fruit preserve made with two or more fruits plus nuts or raisins.

CONSOMME   A clear soup usually made from a combination of meat stocks.

COURT BOUILLON   A well-seasoned stock made from fish.

CRACKLINGS   The crisp pieces left after rendering the fat from pork.

CREAM   To mix shortening until it is smooth and creamy by rubbing it against the side of the bowl with a spoon. This term is usually applied to mixing sugar with shortening in making cake.

CREPE   A thin, rich pancake rolled with a filling and served with a sauce for the main dish or dessert. Crêpes Suzettes are made with grated orange rind and various liqueurs. Crêpes Gruyère have a cheese filling.

CROUTONS   Small cubes of fried or toasted bread served with soup.

CUBE   To cut in small (½-inch square) pieces.

CUT   (a) To divide food into pieces with a knife or scissors.

    (b) To combine shortening with dry ingredients with two knives, a fork, or a pastry blender.

DEMITASSE   A small cup of strong black coffee, usually served after dinner.

DEVEIN   To remove the veins (as from shrimp).

DEVIL   To mix with hot seasonings, as pepper or mustard (deviled eggs).

DICE   To cut into cubes ¼ inch in size.

DOT   To scatter bits of butter, nuts, chocolate, etc., over the surface of food.

DOUGH   A mixture of flour, liquid, etc., stiff enough so that it can be kneaded or handled.

DREDGE   To coat with seasoned flour or other dry ingredients.

DRIPPINGS   Fat or juice that cooks out of meat or poultry and falls into the roasting pan.

DUST   To sprinkle or coat lightly with sugar or flour.

EGGS, LIGHTLY BEATEN   Beat only enough to blend yolks and whites.

EGGS, WELL BEATEN   Beat eggs until light and frothy.

EGG WHITES, BEATEN IN SOFT, STIFF PEAKS   Whites are beaten until stiff but not dry. They stand in moist, glossy peaks that droop over a bit when the beater is lifted from the eggs.

EGG WHITES, BEATEN VERY STIFF   Points of peaks stand upright without drooping when beater is removed. Surface should look dry.

EGG YOLKS, WELL BEATEN   Beat until yolks are thick and lemon-colored.

FILLET   Boneless strips of meat or fish.

FLAKE   To break into small pieces.

FLAMBE   To cover warm food with warmed brandy, rum, or liqueur of high alcohol content, to ignite and serve flaming (plum pudding, cherries jubilee).

FLAN   Custard baked in caramel-coated cups or casserole.

FOLD   To combine ingredients by cutting vertically through the mixture and gently turning it under and over until thoroughly blended, using a rubber spatula, wire whip, or spoon.

FONDUE   (a) A baked dish similar to cheese soufflé with bread crumbs added.

(b) Swiss cheese melted with wine in a chafing dish.

FORCEMEAT   Finely chopped meat or fish.

FRICASSEE   To cook meat or fowl, cut into pieces, by braising.

FRY, SHALLOW FAT   To cook in a small amount of fat on top of stove. (Also called sauté or pan-fry.)

FRY, DEEP FAT   To cook in a deep layer of fat preheated to the desired temperature. The results should be food with a golden, crisp crust and a thoroughly cooked center that has not absorbed too much fat.

GARNISH   To decorate a dish with parsley, fruit slices, etc.

GLACE   To coat with a sugar syrup cooked to the crack stage.

GLAZE   To make a smooth glossy surface by coating with a thin layer of aspic, melted jelly, sugar syrup, icing, or fruit juice sweetened and thickened with a little cornstarch.

GOULASH   A thick meat stew with vegetables and paprika.

GRILL   *See* BROIL.

JULIENNE   To cut into thin strips.

KNEAD   To work or press dough into a smooth mass with the heel of your hand so the dough becomes stretched and elastic. This usually is necessary for yeast breads.

LARD   To insert strips of fat, known as lardoons, in gashes in lean meat; to thread fat into meat by means of a larding needle, or to place strips of fat on top of meat or fish before cooking. This gives flavor and prevents the surface from becoming dry.

THE
SPICE STORE

LYONNAISE   Cooked with chopped onion.

MACEDOINE   A cut-up mixture of fruits or vegetables.

MARINATE   To let food stand several hours in a seasoned oil-acid mixture to improve flavor and tenderness.

PLANK   To broil or bake meat or fish on a wooden plank.

POT ROAST   To cook by braising (moist heat).

PRECOOK   To partially cook food in liquid below the boiling point.

PREHEAT   To heat the oven to a given temperature before the food is inserted.

RENDER   To free fat from connective tissue by melting over low heat.

RISSOLE   Minced meat, fish, or potatoes, covered in pastry and fried in deep fat.

ROAST   To cook by dry heat in an oven (*see* BAKE).

ROUX   Cooked mixture of flour and butter used to thicken soups and sauces.

SAUTE   To fry food in a small amount of fat.

SCALD   (a) To heat milk or other food just below boiling point.
(b) To dip certain foods in boiling water (*see* BLANCH).

SCALLOP   To arrange foods in layers in a casserole with sauce.

SCORE   To cut shallow gashes or slits in fat of meat before cooking (as in steaks) to prevent curling, or crisscross lines in ham before glazing.

SEAR   To brown surface (of meat) over high heat or in very hot oven.

SHIRR   To break eggs into a dish with cream and crumbs and bake.

SIMMER   To cook in liquid just below boiling point.

SKEWER   Metal or wooden rods to hold meat, poultry, fish, or vegetables in place while barbecuing or broiling.

SLIVER   To cut (meat, vegetables, or cheese) into thin, narrow strips.

SNIP   To cut with scissors with short, quick strokes (snipped parsley).

STEEP   To extract the essence by standing in liquid.

STEW   To cook in a small quantity of liquid over gentle heat.

STOCK   Liquid in which meat, poultry, fish, or vegetables have been cooked (*see* BROTH).

TORTE   A rich cake, usually in layers, topped with fruit and whipped cream. It usually is rich in eggs and may contain crumbs, nuts, and fruit.

TOSS   To mix with a light, quick motion without crushing or tearing the ingredients.

WHIP   To beat rapidly to incorporate air and to increase volume, as in eggs, cream, and gelatine dishes.

APPETIZERS

APPETIZERS are purely for fun. *Hors d'oeuvres* the French call them: "outside of the works." They are likely to have a wicked lot of calories but most people have come to expect them with cocktails. The French picked up the habit of pre-dinner snacking from the Russians, who call such tidbits *zakuskis*. Italians have their little plates of *antipasto*, while Scandinavians serve all manner of spicy, pickly things at a *smorgasbord* and make a complete meal of them.

Because appetizers must be nicely spiced, we have naturally included a wide selection. Some are complicated, many quite simple. When you entertain you may want to serve two or three kinds, preferably a few that can be made well in advance, or that require a minimum of attention just at serving time.

Hot hors d'oeuvres are always a treat. You may have to spend a few last minutes with them, but they are worth whatever confusion they create. Some, such as tiny cream puffs, turnovers, and meat balls can be completely cooked well in advance, then popped into the oven just before the first guests arrive.

Do keep appetizers bite-size. Their function is to titillate the appetite, not satisfy it.

ANCHOVY ABBADABBAS

We discovered this handwritten recipe in a century-old, family "receipt" book in Mystic, Connecticut.

1 cup sifted all-purpose flour
½ teaspoon salt
¾ teaspoon powdered mustard
¼ teaspoon garlic powder
¹⁄₁₆ teaspoon cayenne

⅓ cup (⅔ stick) butter *or* margarine
3 tablespoons water
2 tablespoons melted butter *or* margarine
Anchovy paste
¼ cup grated Cheddar cheese

Sift together the first 5 ingredients. Add butter or margarine and cut it in with a pastry blender or 2 knives until mixture is the consistency of corn meal. Sprinkle in cold water. Mix to form dough.

Chill 2 hours or until dough is stiff enough to roll. Roll into two 9 x 7 x ⅛-inch rectangles on a lightly floured board. Brush surface with melted butter or margarine. Spread thinly with anchovy paste and sprinkle with grated cheese. Roll up in jelly-roll fashion. Wrap in waxed paper. Chill until firm enough to slice. Cut into slices ¼ inch thick. Place on lightly greased baking sheets. Bake in a preheated hot oven (400° F.) 12 to 14 minutes or until lightly browned. Serve as a canapé or as an accompaniment to salads.

YIELD: 3 dozen canapés

CHILI PECAN ROLL

"A huge success with the ladies of the missionary society," wrote one of our friends from the South. It can be made the day before, then sliced for serving on crackers. It has a good lively chili flavor.

½ pound processed American cheese
3-ounce package cream cheese

½ teaspoon salt
½ teaspoon instant minced onion
¼ teaspoon instant minced garlic
¹⁄₁₆ teaspoon ground red pepper
2 teaspoons lemon juice
¾ cup finely chopped pecans

3 tablespoons chili powder

Have cheeses at room temperature and mix together until well blended. Add next 6 ingredients. Mix well. Shape into rolls 4 inches long and 1½ inches in diameter. Chill 30 minutes. Roll each in chili powder and wrap in foil. Chill until firm. Cut into slices ⅛ inch thick and serve on round crackers.

YIELD: About 3 dozen canapés

CHOPPED CHICKEN LIVERS

¼ cup instant minced onion
¼ cup water
6 tablespoons chicken fat, butter, *or* margarine
1 pound chicken livers
2 hard-cooked eggs
1¼ teaspoons salt

⅛ teaspoon ground black pepper
⅛ teaspoon garlic powder
½ teaspoon parsley flakes

Soften instant minced onion in water and sauté in 3 tablespoons of the chicken fat, butter, or margarine until lightly browned. Trim membranes from liver and cut each in half. Place liver in a pan, broil for 6 minutes, 4 inches from the source of heat. Turn liver and broil 1 minute longer. Grind broiled liver and eggs in a food chopper using the fine blade, or chop very fine in a chopping bowl. Add sautéed onion, remaining chicken fat, butter, or margarine, and the 3 seasonings. Mix thoroughly. Serve on rounds of rye bread. Garnish with sieved hard-cooked egg yolk and parsley, if desired.

YIELD: 2 cups

CURRY TOMATO CANAPES

Cut small tomatoes (1½ to 2 inches in diameter) into slices ¼ inch thick. Cut rounds of bread the same size and spread with soft butter. Top each with a slice of tomato and sprinkle lightly with salt and ground black pepper. Garnish center with a little Curry Mayonnaise.*

YIELD: 6 slices from each tomato

*An asterisk after the name of a dish indicates that the recipe for this dish appears in the book. Consult the Index for the page number.

ENGLISH RABBIT CANAPES
The corruption of "rabbit" is "rarebit."

6 slices firm textured bread
2 to 3 tablespoons butter *or* margarine

1 cup grated sharp American cheese
⅛ teaspoon ground black pepper
¼ teaspoon ground ginger
4 teaspoons dry sherry wine

Parsley flakes

Trim crusts from bread and cut bread into ½-inch squares. Sauté one side in butter or margarine and toast the other side. Combine the next 4 ingredients and spread on the buttered side of the bread squares. Place under broiler (oven control set to broil) ½ to 1 minute to melt and brown cheese. Garnish with parsley flakes. Serve at once.

YIELD: 2 dozen canapés

1 teaspoon ground cumin seed
¾ teaspoon salt
½ teaspoon powdered mustard
¹⁄₁₆ teaspoon garlic salt
¼ teaspoon instant minced onion

3 dozen 2-inch bread rounds, toasted
Parsley

Sauté chicken livers in butter or margarine. When done, turn them into a wooden chopping bowl and chop very fine. Add next 6 ingredients. Mix well. Spread on lightly toasted rounds of bread, buttered. Place under broiler to brown and puff. Garnish with parsley.

YIELD: 3 dozen canapés

LIVERWURST PATE

If you have champagne tastes and a beer income, here is an approximation of the famous French pâtés. This will keep for several days under refrigeration in a covered jar.

½ pound liverwurst

¼ teaspoon ground cloves
½ teaspoon celery salt
1 teaspoon Dijon-type mustard
Dash cayenne
1 teaspoon lemon juice
¼ cup heavy cream *or* undiluted
  evaporated milk

Mix liverwurst with a fork until smooth. Add remaining ingredients. Stir until well mixed. Serve as a sandwich spread, a dip, or use for making canapés. The pâté will keep for several days under refrigeration in a covered jar.

YIELD: 1 cup

LIVER PATE CANAPES

½ pound chicken livers
2 tablespoons butter *or* margarine

¼ cup sour cream

NEAPOLITAN APPETIZER

6 slices firm-textured bread
Mozzarella cheese
Salt
Ground black pepper
Crumbled oregano leaves
6 anchovy fillets
2 to 3 tablespoons butter *or* margarine

Remove crusts from bread and cut each slice in half. Toast on one side only. Cut slices of cheese to fit and place on the toasted sides of half of the bread slices. Sprinkle lightly with salt, black pepper, and oregano. Top each with an anchovy fillet and a slice of remaining bread, untoasted-side up. Melt butter or margarine in a skillet and fry sandwiches 3 to 4 minutes, turning to brown both sides. Cut each into 3 smaller sandwiches. Serve as a hot hors d'oeuvre.

YIELD: 18 hors d'oeuvres

ROQUEFORT CHEESE
AND LIVER CANAPES

¼ pound chicken livers
1 tablespoon butter *or* margarine

3 tablespoons (1 ounce) crumbled
  Roquefort cheese
¼ teaspoon salt
¼ teaspoon onion powder
¹⁄₁₆ teaspoon ground black pepper
Dash cayenne
Sliced bread

Sauté chicken livers in butter or margarine. Put them through a food chopper, using the fine blade, or chop very fine with knives. Mash cheese and add to liver along with salt and spices. Trim crust from bread and sauté one side of each slice in butter or margarine. Toast the other side until golden. Spread the sautéed side with cheese-liver mixture. Cut each into 4 squares.

YIELD: About 16 canapés

SESAME SEED CHEESE FINGERS

These can be prepared ahead of time and popped into the oven just before serving.

1 cup sifted all-purpose flour
½ teaspoon salt
¹⁄₁₆ teaspoon cayenne
½ teaspoon powdered mustard
½ teaspoon ground ginger
½ teaspoon sugar
½ cup grated sharp American cheese
⅓ cup Toasted Sesame Seed (see
  below)
1 large egg yolk, lightly beaten
⅓ cup (⅔ stick) butter or margarine,
  melted
1 tablespoon water

Sift first 6 ingredients together. Stir in the cheese and sesame seed. Combine remaining ingredients. Add to first mixture and stir, forming a ball. Wrap in waxed paper and chill. Pat to ⅛-inch thickness on a lightly floured board. Cut

in 1 x 2-inch strips. Place on ungreased baking sheet. Bake in moderate oven (350° F.) 15 minutes, or until done. Cool.

TOASTED SESAME SEED
Place sesame seeds in a shallow baking pan and heat in a preheated moderate oven (350° F.) 20 to 22 minutes, stirring 2 or 3 times to obtain uniform toasting.

YIELD: 40 fingers

SMOKED SALMON CANAPES

3-ounce package cream cheese
3 tablespoons heavy cream
¾ to 1 teaspoon curry powder
1 teaspoon instant minced onion
———
4 thin slices smoked salmon
24 rounds toast *or* crackers
24 thin slices unpeeled cucumber
24 slices pimiento-stuffed olives

Combine the first 4 ingredients. Spread over the salmon slices, carrying the mixture to the edges. Roll up in jelly-roll fashion. Chill overnight or several hours. Place thin slices of scored, unpeeled cucumber on crackers or toast. Top each with a ⅛-inch slice of salmon roll and a slice of stuffed olive. Serve as an appetizer or as a tea accompaniment.

YIELD: 24 canapés

SPICY HAM CANAPES

1 cup ground, cooked ham
½ cup sour cream
1 tablespoon mayonnaise
1 teaspoon curry powder
¼ teaspoon salt
¼ teaspoon powdered mustard
¹⁄₁₆ teaspoon garlic powder
¹⁄₁₆ teaspoon onion powder
¹⁄₁₆ teaspoon ground red pepper
———
About 4 dozen toasted, buttered 2-inch
  bread rounds

Combine first 9 ingredients. Mix well. Spread on toasted bread rounds. Place under the broiler to puff and brown.

YIELD: 4 dozen

TOASTED PAPRIKA FROMAGE LOGS

¼ cup (½ stick) butter *or* margarine
¼ cup grated mild American cheese
¼ teaspoon salt
¼ teaspoon powdered mustard
Dash cayenne
1 teaspoon paprika

8 thin slices of white bread

Soften butter or margarine and blend with next 5 ingredients. Trim crust from bread and spread with the mixture. Roll each and hold edges in place with toothpicks. Toast under the broiler. Cut into crosswise halves, if desired. Serve with cocktails or as salad accompaniment.

PIQUANT CHEESE CRACKERS
Spread the Paprika Fromage mixture on unsweetened crackers. Dust with additional paprika. Place under broiler to melt cheese. Serve hot with soup or cocktails.

YIELD: 16 servings

BLEU CHEESE ONION DIP

3-ounce package cream cheese
3-ounce package Bleu cheese

¾ cup mayonnaise
½ teaspoon salt
1 tablespoon instant minced onion
¹⁄₁₆ teaspoon garlic powder
¹⁄₁₆ teaspoon ground black pepper

Combine cheeses and mash well. Add remaining ingredients and mix well. Serve in the center of a platter surrounded with fresh vegetable sticks, potato chips, and crackers.

YIELD: 1¼ cups

CHILI BEAN COCKTAIL DIP

1 cup canned red kidney beans, drained

1 tablespoon lemon juice
1 tablespoon mayonnaise
½ teaspoon instant minced onion
½ teaspoon salt
½ teaspoon chili powder
⅛ teaspoon garlic powder
¼ cup finely chopped tomatoes

Chopped parsley

Mash beans and put through a sieve. Add next 7 ingredients and mix until thoroughly blended. Or put first 8 ingredients in an electric blender and blend until smooth. Turn into a serving bowl and garnish with chopped parsley. Serve as a dip with potato chips, crackers, or raw vegetable sticks.

YIELD: 1 cup

COTTAGE CHEESE AND BACON DIP

A very good dip if you're counting calories.

8-ounce package creamy cottage cheese
3 slices crisp bacon, crumbled
⅛ to ¼ teaspoon garlic powder
½ teaspoon onion salt
2 tablespoons mayonnaise
1 teaspoon fresh lemon juice
1½ tablespoons milk
Paprika

Combine all ingredients except paprika. Turn into a 1-cup sauce dish. Garnish with paprika. Serve as a dip with potato chips, crackers, or fresh vegetable sticks.

YIELD: 1 cup

GUACAMOLE MEXICANO

1¼ cups avocado purée (made from 1 large avocado)
½ cup finely chopped peeled and seeded tomato
1½ teaspoons salt
1 teaspoon onion powder
½ teaspoon garlic powder
½ teaspoon chili powder
Dash cayenne
1 teaspoon olive oil
1 tablespoon fresh lemon juice

Combine all ingredients and mix well. Serve as a dip.

YIELD: 1½ cups

GREEN GODDESS AVOCADO DIP

1 medium-size ripe avocado
2 teaspoons fresh lemon juice
———
3-ounce package cream cheese
2 tablespoons mayonnaise
2 teaspoons finely chopped chives *or* green onion tops
1 tablespoon finely chopped parsley
¾ teaspoon salt (or to taste)
1⁄16 teaspoon garlic powder
Dash cayenne
———
Pimiento, finely diced

Cut avocado in half, remove seed, scoop out meat and place it in a bowl with the lemon juice. Mash and mix well. Blend in next 7 ingredients. Scatter with pimiento dice. Serve in avocado shells or in a small bowl surrounded with raw vegetable sticks, potato chips, or crackers.

YIELD: 2 cups

ONION SOUR CREAM DIP

1 cup sour cream
¼ teaspoon lemon juice
2 teaspoons instant minced onion
⅛ teaspoon ground black pepper
½ teaspoon salt

Blend all ingredients together. Serve in a bowl on a tray surrounded by crisp crackers or fresh vegetable sticks.

YIELD: 1 cup

COCKTAIL DIP FOR SHRIMP

½ cup catsup
2 teaspoons fresh lemon juice
2 teaspoons horseradish
½ teaspoon salt
½ teaspoon chili powder
⅛ teaspoon cayenne
⅛ teaspoon garlic powder

½ pound cold, cooked, deveined
    shrimp
Hearts of lettuce

Combine the first 7 ingredients and turn
into a small serving dish. Place dish in
the center of an hors d'oeuvre tray and
surround with shrimp in lettuce cups.

YIELD: ⅔ cup sauce

SOUR CREAM CLAM DIP

½ cup sour cream
¼ cup minced, canned clams,
    well drained
¼ teaspoon garlic powder
¼ teaspoon onion powder
Dash ground black pepper
Dash cayenne
¼ teaspoon ground basil leaves
¼ teaspoon salt
———
Paprika

Combine the first 8 ingredients and mix
well. Turn into an attractive small bowl.
Garnish with a dash of paprika. Place on
a large plate and surround with carrot and
celery sticks, potato chips, and small crisp
crackers. Serve with cocktails or vegetable juice.

YIELD: ¾ cup

TOMATO CLAM DIP

3-ounce package cream cheese
2 tablespoons finely diced tomatoes
2 tablespoons minced clams
1 tablespoon clam juice
1 teaspoon parsley flakes
¾ teaspoon salt
⅛ teaspoon ground black pepper
¹⁄₁₆ teaspoon garlic powder

Soften cream cheese. Add remaining ingredients and beat until fluffy. Use as a
dip.

YIELD: 1 cup

CARAWAY SEED SNAPS

*A delicious little snap which can be made
the day before the party.*

1 cup sifted all-purpose flour
1 teaspoon celery salt
1 teaspoon powdered mustard
⅛ teaspoon cayenne
———
⅓ cup (⅔ stick) butter *or* margarine
3 ounces Snappy cheese
Caraway seeds

Sift first 4 ingredients together. Add butter or margarine and cheese and blend
with pastry blender or 2 knives until the
mixture forms a dough that can be handled. Shape into 2 rolls, each 8 x 1½
inches. Wrap in waxed paper or foil.
Chill overnight or until dough is stiff
enough to slice.

Cut into crosswise slices ⅛ inch thick.
Place on ungreased baking sheets. Sprinkle with caraway seeds and pat them
lightly into the dough. Bake in a preheated moderate oven (350° F.) for 15
minutes or until lightly browned around
the edges. Cool on baking sheets ½
minute. Remove to wire rack to finish

cooling. Serve with cocktails, tomato or vegetable juice, or with salads. Store airtight.

YIELD: 2½ dozen

PAPRIKA CHEESE FINGERS

½ cup (1 stick) soft butter *or* margarine
3 ounces Snappy cheese
1 cup sifted all-purpose flour
Paprika

Combine butter or margarine and cheese. Add flour and mix well. Shape into a 1-inch diameter roll on a lightly floured board. Wrap in waxed paper and chill until firm enough to slice. Then, slice ⅛ inch thick. Place fingers on ungreased cooky sheets. Sprinkle paprika over the tops. Bake 5 minutes in a preheated very hot oven (450° F.). Cool slightly before removing from the cooky sheet. Store airtight.

YIELD: 4 dozen

WILLIAMSBURG CHEESE STRAWS

1 cup sifted all-purpose flour
½ teaspoon salt
¼ teaspoon powdered mustard
⅛ teaspoon cayenne

⅓ cup (⅔ stick) butter *or* margarine
1 cup grated sharp Cheddar cheese
1½ tablespoons water
1 teaspoon celery seed

Sift the first 4 ingredients into a mixing bowl. Add butter or margarine and ½ cup of the grated cheese and cut into a coarse crumb consistency. Add water and toss lightly.

Shape into a ball. Roll to ⅛-inch thickness. Sprinkle 1 side of the dough with ¼ cup of the cheese. Fold dough over and sprinkle on the remaining ¼ cup grated cheese. Roll to ⅛-inch thickness. Cut into 4-inch strips ½ inch wide. Sprinkle with celery seed. Bake on a cooky sheet in a preheated moderate oven (350° F.) 12 to 15 minutes.

YIELD: 5 dozen straws

INDIAN POTATO STRAWS
(ALU KE LACHCHE)

Indian Potato Straws are a tea-time food in India. They are as delicious as they are easy to make and certainly new to the American cuisine.

2 medium-size potatoes
½ teaspoon salt
¾ teaspoon ground caraway
¹⁄₁₆ teaspoon ground red pepper

Peel and cut or shred potatoes to size of wooden match sticks. Drain and dry. Fry in hot deep fat (375° F.) 3 to 5 minutes, or until brown. Drain. Mix seasonings and sprinkle over potato straws, mixing carefully. Good cocktail accompaniment.

YIELD: About 2 cups

CORN AND SAUSAGE FRITTERS

1 cup sifted all-purpose flour
1 teaspoon double-acting
  baking powder
1 teaspoon salt
¼ teaspoon onion powder
½ teaspoon paprika
⅛ teaspoon ground black pepper

1 cup cooked sausage meat
1 cup fresh corn, cut from the cob
2 large eggs, separated
½ cup milk

Sift together the first 6 ingredients. Break sausage into small pieces and mix with corn, beaten egg yolks, and milk. Add to dry mixture. Mix well. Fold in stiffly beaten egg whites.

Drop the batter, a teaspoonful at a time, into deep hot fat preheated to 350° F. Cook until browned on all sides, turning as necessary. Drain on paper towels. Serve as a hot hors d'oeuvre.

YIELD: 3 dozen fritters

CURRIED OYSTER FRITTERS

This delicious recipe was discovered in an old cook book in the library of the American Antiquarian Society in Worcester, Massachusetts.

2 cups sifted all-purpose flour
2 teaspoons double-acting
  baking powder
2 teaspoons salt
1½ teaspoons curry powder
¼ teaspoon garlic powder
1/16 teaspoon cayenne
1/16 teaspoon ground black pepper

½ teaspoon instant minced onion
2 eggs, lightly beaten

½ cup milk
½ cup oyster liquor

1 cup drained fresh *or* frozen oysters
Celery salt

Sift first 7 ingredients into a mixing bowl. Combine next 4 ingredients and stir into the dry ingredients. Chop oysters coarsely and blend with the mixture. Drop one teaspoon batter at a time into deep fat, preheated to 375° F. Cook for 3 minutes or until brown on all sides. Sprinkle with celery salt. Serve on toothpicks as a hot hors d'oeuvre.

YIELD: About 50

MOCK OYSTERS

Serve these as an appetizer or as a fritter with a main course.

1 cup frozen corn *or* fresh corn, cut
  from the cob
1 tablespoon melted butter *or*
  margarine
2 large eggs, separated
½ teaspoon salt
⅛ teaspoon ground black pepper
Dash cayenne
¼ teaspoon ground marjoram
½ cup sifted all-purpose flour
Celery salt

Combine corn, butter or margarine, egg yolks, seasonings, and flour. Beat egg whites until they stand in soft, stiff peaks and fold into the mixture. Drop from teaspoon into deep fat preheated to 350° F. Fry until golden. Drain on paper towels. Sprinkle lightly with celery salt.

YIELD: 5 dozen

GINGERED MELON

Combine 1 tablespoon confectioners' sugar with ¼ teaspoon ground ginger. Sprinkle to taste over chilled wedges of honeydew melon or cantaloupe. Serve as an appetizer.

YIELD: 6 wedges

CURRIED CASHEW NUTS

2 tablespoons butter *or* margarine
1 cup unsalted cashew nuts
1 teaspoon curry powder
Salt (to taste)

Melt butter or margarine in a frying pan. Add nuts and curry powder and fry until lightly browned. Drain on paper towels. Sprinkle with salt to taste.

YIELD: 1 cup

SPICED CEREAL TIDBITS

2 tablespoons butter *or* margarine
½ teaspoon celery salt
½ teaspoon onion salt
⅛ teaspoon garlic salt
1 cup Cheerios
1 cup Wheat Chex

Melt butter or margarine and add celery, onion and garlic salts. Toss Cheerios and Wheat Chex in mixture until all the butter or margarine is absorbed.

YIELD: 2 cups

DEVILED CASHEW NUTS

2 cups cashew nuts
1½ tablespoons butter *or* margarine
1 teaspoon salt
¼ teaspoon cayenne
½ teaspoon ground cumin seed
½ teaspoon ground coriander seed

Fry cashew nuts in butter or margarine until golden, about 3 minutes. Drain. Combine salt and spices and mix with nuts. Serve cold with cocktails or as a tea-time savory.

YIELD: 2 cups

HUNGARIAN LAYER PANCAKES

1 cup sifted all-purpose flour
½ teaspoon salt
½ teaspoon sugar
⅛ teaspoon soda
_____
1 large egg, separated
1½ cups milk
Ham Filling *(see below)*

Sift the first 4 ingredients into a mixing bowl. Combine egg yolk and milk and stir gradually into the dry ingredients. Beat egg white until it stands in soft peaks. Fold into the mixture. Pour tablespoons of batter onto a hot, greased griddle. Cook on one side until brown, about 1 minute. Turn and cook on other side 1 minute or until brown. As pancakes are cooked, turn out onto a lightly buttered baking sheet. Spread with a layer of Ham Filling. Top with another pancake. Repeat until you have as many layers as desired.

Brush the top layer with melted butter. Bake in a preheated moderate oven (350° F.) until filling is set, about 20 minutes. Cut into 4 wedges and serve as a hot hors d'oeuvre. For a luncheon or supper dish, *double* the recipe and make 8-inch pancakes. Serve a wedge to each person.

HAM FILLING FOR PANCAKES
½ pound chopped boiled ham
1 egg yolk
¼ cup sour cream
½ teaspoon powdered mustard ·
½ teaspoon paprika
½ teaspoon salt
¹⁄₁₆ teaspoon ground black pepper

Combine all ingredients and mix well. Spread between layers of pancakes.

YIELD: 32 pancakes

BEATEN BISCUIT AND HAM PUFFS
2 cups sifted all-purpose flour
½ teaspoon salt
⅓ cup shortening
½ cup water
Ham Filling *(see below)*

Sift flour and salt together. Cut in shortening until the mixture resembles coarse meal. Stir in water. Knead dough ½ minute. Then put through a food chopper 8 times, using the medium blade. Roll dough to ¼-inch thickness. Fold in half. Roll again to ¼-inch thickness. Shape with a 1½-inch round biscuit cutter.

Bake 25 to 30 minutes, or until lightly browned, in a preheated moderate oven (350° F.). These biscuits will puff and the centers will be hollow. When cold, split and fill with the Ham Filling. Serve as canapés.

HAM FILLING FOR PUFFS
1 cup ground cooked ham
2 teaspoons instant minced onion
¼ teaspoon powdered mustard
Dash of ground black pepper
¼ cup sour cream

Mix all ingredients well and fill biscuits.

YIELD: 30 puffs

CHILI CHEESE PUFFS
1 pound sharp Cheddar cheese spread
¼ cup (½ stick) butter *or* margarine
1 teaspoon chili powder
1 teaspoon salt
_____
1 cup sifted all-purpose flour
Small pimiento-stuffed olives *or*
    pecan halves
Paprika

Combine the first 4 ingredients. Stir in flour. Shape dough around stuffed olives or pecan halves; cut in half. Dust with paprika. Bake in a preheated hot oven (400° F.) 10 minutes or until lightly browned. Serve hot.

YIELD: 3 dozen

CRABMEAT BOUCHEES
½ cup finely chopped celery
2 tablespoons butter *or* margarine
2 tablespoons all-purpose flour
½ cup milk
6½-ounce can crabmeat
_____
1 large egg, beaten
1 teaspoon celery salt

¼ teaspoon ground mace
½ teaspoon parsley flakes
¼ teaspoon ground black pepper
⅛ teaspoon cayenne
2 teaspoons instant minced onion
2 teaspoons chopped pimiento
2 teaspoons fresh lemon juice
1 tablespoon chopped sautéed
  mushrooms

1 large egg, beaten
Fine, dry bread crumbs

Sauté celery in butter or margarine 7 minutes or until tender. Remove from heat. Blend in flour. Stir in milk. Stir and cook until thickened (DO NOT BOIL). Put crabmeat through a food chopper, using fine blade, and stir into the mixture along with next 10 ingredients. Chill 4 or 5 hours or overnight.

Shape into ½-inch balls. Dip each into beaten egg and then into bread crumbs. Fry until golden brown in deep fat pre-

heated to 375° F. Drain on paper towels. Serve warm, on toothpicks.

YIELD: About 5 dozen bouchées

CURRIED SHRIMP AND CRABMEAT BALLS

These should be chilled overnight before cooking. Serve either as an hors d'oeuvre, or make larger balls and serve as a main dish.

¾ cup minced canned shrimp
½ cup minced canned crabmeat
½ teaspoon curry powder
¼ teaspoon celery salt
⅛ teaspoon ground black pepper
2 large egg yolks
2 tablespoons heavy cream

¼ cup fine, dry bread crumbs
3 tablespoons untoasted sesame seeds

Combine first 7 ingredients. Chill overnight (10 to 12 hours). Shape into 1-inch balls. Roll the balls in combined bread crumbs and sesame seeds.

Fry until golden brown in 1 inch of hot fat. Serve warm on toothpicks as a hot hors d'oeuvre.

YIELD: Thirty 1-inch balls

FRIED CHEESE BALLS

These can be made several hours before serving, then reheated in a moderate oven. Delicious and inexpensive.

1½ cups grated mild cheese
3 tablespoons all-purpose flour
¼ teaspoon salt
Dash cayenne
¼ teaspoon powdered mustard
½ teaspoon paprika

3 large egg whites
⅓ cup very fine cracker crumbs
Paprika

Combine first 6 ingredients. Beat egg whites until stiff and fold into the cheese mixture. Allow to stand 5 minutes to stiffen slightly. Drop by rounded teaspoonful into bread crumbs. Lift out with fork and drop into hot fat. Fry until golden in hot deep fat preheated to 375° F. Drain on paper towels and sprinkle with paprika. Serve as a hot hors d'oeuvre or as a salad accompaniment.

YIELD: About 2 dozen

PETITS TUNA CREAM PUFFS

8½-ounce package cream-puff mix
½ cup grated mild Cheddar cheese
1 tablespoon lemon juice
3 tablespoons water
1 teaspoon flour
½ teaspoon powdered mustard
½ teaspoon onion salt
⅛ teaspoon ground black pepper
⅛ teaspoon garlic salt
7-ounce can tuna fish, drained

Prepare cream-puff mix according to package directions, dividing batter into 30 tiny cream puffs. Bake as directed on package. Cool. Mix all remaining ingredients and heat only until cheese is melted. Use this mixture to fill cream puffs. Serve as hors d'oeuvre.

YIELD: 30 small puffs

BLEU CHEESE CARAWAY SEED SPREAD

⅓ cup finely crumbled Bleu cheese
3-ounce package cream cheese
⅓ cup mayonnaise
2 teaspoons caraway seed
¼ teaspoon ground white pepper

Combine all ingredients. Mix until thoroughly blended. Spread on toasted rounds of bread or crackers.

YIELD: About 1 cup

CARAWAY CHEESE POT

This is a delicious canapé spread, a mixture that can be replenished with additional cheese, caraway seed, brandy, and Kirsch as the supply runs low.

1 pound grated Cheddar cheese
3-ounce package cream cheese
¼ cup olive *or* salad oil
1 teaspoon powdered mustard
1 teaspoon caraway seed
2 tablespoons brandy
2 tablespoons Kirsch

Combine Cheddar and cream cheeses. Add oil and mix until smooth. Blend in mustard, caraway seed, brandy, and Kirsch. Turn into a jar. Cover and store in the refrigerator to use as needed.

The cheese spreads more easily if removed from the refrigerator 1 hour before serving.

HERBED CHEESE POT

Replace caraway seed, brandy, and Kirsch in the above recipe with ½ teaspoon each of marjoram and tarragon, and 4 tablespoons of sherry wine. Serve on toasted bread or crackers to accompany cocktails or salads.

YIELD: 1 pint

ONION-CHEESE-BACON SPREAD

8-ounce package cream cheese
4 teaspoons instant minced onion
2 tablespoons mayonnaise
¼ teaspoon salt
⅛ teaspoon ground black pepper
¼ teaspoon lemon juice
2 strips crisp bacon, crumbled

Soften cream cheese. Add onion to may-onnaise and add to cream cheese along with remaining ingredients. Spread on crackers or toast squares.

YIELD: 1 cup

ORIENTAL CREAM CHEESE SPREAD

3-ounce package cream cheese
1 tablespoon milk
¼ teaspoon salt
⅛ teaspoon garlic powder
¼ teaspoon ground turmeric

Mix all ingredients together until well blended. Spread thinly over crisp crackers.

YIELD: ¼ cup, enough to spread on 2 or 3 dozen crackers

SPICY BLEU CHEESE SPREAD

¾ cup finely crumbled Bleu cheese
½ cup (1 stick) butter or margarine
1 cup creamy cottage cheese
1½ teaspoons crumbled basil leaves
1½ teaspoons crumbled oregano leaves

½ teaspoon chili powder
⅛ teaspoon ground white pepper

Combine all ingredients. Mix until thoroughly blended.

YIELD: About 1⅔ cups

CURRIED CHICKEN LIVER TURNOVERS

½ cup sautéed chicken livers
2 hard-cooked eggs
1 teaspoon grated onion
¼ teaspoon salt
⅛ teaspoon ground black pepper
1 teaspoon curry powder
3 to 4 tablespoons heavy cream
Cream Cheese Pastry*

Chop liver and eggs very fine or press through a coarse sieve. Add remaining ingredients, using just enough cream to moisten. Roll Cream Cheese Pastry very thin. Cut into 2-inch circles. Place a teaspoon of curried liver filling on each round. Fold over and seal edges by crimping with a fork. Bake in a preheated hot oven (400° F.) 5 to 8 minutes or until browned. Serve hot.

YIELD: 2½ dozen

OYSTER TURNOVERS

25 frozen or fresh small oysters
¼ teaspoon ground black pepper
¼ teaspoon celery seed
¼ teaspoon salt
Butter Pastry*
Milk

Drain oysters and cut each in half. Add seasonings and mix well. Roll Butter Pastry ⅛ inch thick on a lightly floured board. Cut into 1½-inch circles with a cooky cutter. Place ½ oyster slightly off center of each circle. Fold pastry over.

Seal and crimp edges with a fork. Brush tops lightly with milk.

Place on cooky sheets. Bake in a preheated hot oven (425° F.) until browned, about 8 minutes.

YIELD: 50 turnovers

PICKLED SCALLOPS

25 to 30 (1 pound) bay scallops
3 to 4 tablespoons butter *or* margarine

1 cup cider vinegar
1½ tablespoons sweet pepper flakes
4 teaspoons instant minced onion
½ teaspoon whole allspice
2 teaspoons sugar
1½ teaspoons salt
⅛ teaspoon garlic powder

1 whole, hot red pepper, 1½ inches long
Toast rounds (optional)

Sauté scallops in butter or margarine. Put them in a flat casserole. Place the next 7 ingredients in a small saucepan. Bring to boiling point and boil 1 minute. Break pepper in half and add. Pour over sautéed scallops.

Marinate at least 24 hours before serving, turning scallops occasionally in marinade. Serve on toothpicks as an appetizer or on toast rounds.

YIELD: 6 servings

CELERY VICTOR

12 ribs of crisp-tender celery
2 sprigs parsley
¼ cup sliced fresh carrots
¼ cup sliced onion
1 teaspoon salt
1-inch depth of boiling chicken stock
  in saucepan

½ cup white wine vinegar
½ cup olive *or* salad oil
¼ teaspoon chervil leaves

1 teaspoon salt
⅛ teaspoon freshly ground
  black pepper

2-ounce can long anchovy fillets
Pimiento strips

Select tender inside ribs from 2 stalks of celery. Cut them 4 inches long, measuring from bottom of rib. Place in a saucepan with parsley, carrots, onion, 1 teaspoon salt, and hot chicken stock. Cover and cook slowly 10 minutes or until just tender. Remove celery to a shallow dish to cool.

Combine next 5 ingredients. Pour over the cooled celery. Refrigerate 3 to 4 hours or until serving time. Rinse anchovy fillets with water, cut each in half and arrange in 2 crosses over each rib. Garnish with pimiento strips.

YIELD: 6 servings

POTATO AND FISH ANTIPASTO

An Italian dish and most savory. Although "antipasto" means before the pasta, *the spaghetti or macaroni, it can be served as a main-dish salad.*

2 cups cold, cooked, diced potatoes
6¾-ounce can tuna fish
5-ounce can deveined, small shrimp *or*
   ¾ cup cold, deveined, cooked shrimp
2 tablespoons sliced ripe (black) olives
1 teaspoon salt
½ teaspoon oregano leaves
¼ teaspoon powdered mustard
⅛ teaspoon ground black pepper
3 tablespoons mayonnaise
1 tablespoon fresh lemon juice

2 tablespoons capers
3 fresh tomatoes, sliced
3 hard-cooked eggs, sliced

Combine the first 10 ingredients. Turn into the center of a serving platter. Sprinkle with capers. Arrange sliced tomatoes and eggs around the salad. Serve as an antipasto or as a main-dish salad.

YIELD: 6 to 8 servings

SPICED CAULIFLOWERETS

1 medium-head cauliflower

1 teaspoon salt
1 clove garlic, halved
1 teaspoon mixed pickling spices
1 tablespoon fresh lemon juice
1 cup boiling water

Tartar Sauce*

Cut off the outside leaves of cauliflower and break head into flowerets. Place in saucepan with next 5 ingredients. Cook, uncovered, 5 minutes. Cover and cook 10 minutes or until barely crisp-tender (DO NOT OVERCOOK). Serve with Tartar Sauce.

YIELD: About 1 dozen flowerets

TUNA-STUFFED MUSHROOMS

4 dozen 1-inch fresh mushrooms, whole

1 tablespoon butter *or* margarine
½ teaspoon salt
1 tablespoon oil, drained from tuna fish

2 teaspoons instant minced onion
1 tablespoon lemon juice
7-ounce can flaked tuna fish
¼ teaspoon salt (or to taste)
⅛ teaspoon ground black pepper
¹⁄₁₆ teaspoon garlic powder

¾ cup grated, sharp American cheese

Wash mushrooms. Remove and chop stems fine. Sauté whole caps in butter or margarine seasoned with the ½ teaspoon salt. Remove from skillet.

In the same skillet sauté stems in hot tuna-fish oil, cooking until all liquid is absorbed. Add the next 6 ingredients and ½ cup of the grated cheese. Mix well. Spoon the mixture into the mushroom caps. Sprinkle each cap with remaining grated cheese. Broil 1 to 2 minutes or until hot and cheese has melted. Garnish with parsley. Serve hot.

YIELD: 4 dozen

SPICED CRANBERRY JUICE

1 pound fresh cranberries
4 cups water
6 whole cloves
2 cinnamon sticks, each 2 inches long

1⅓ cups sugar
⅔ cup orange juice
½ cup lemon juice
⅛ teaspoon salt

Combine the first 4 ingredients in a saucepan. Cover and cook only until skins pop, about 8 to 10 minutes. Strain out spices. Add sugar and cook slowly 2 to 3 minutes to dissolve sugar. Cool. Stir in fruit juices and salt. Chill. Serve as an appetizer.

YIELD: 10 servings

HERBED APRICOT NECTAR

2 cups sliced fresh apricots

1 teaspoon tarragon leaves
2 tablespoons sugar
2 tablespoons fresh lemon juice

2 cups crushed ice

Place 1 cup of the apricots in the bowl of an electric blender. Add next 3 ingredients and blend 1 minute or until smooth. Repeat, using the remaining apricots and blend. Mix well with finely crushed ice. Serve as a beverage or as an appetizer.

YIELD: 6 servings

HOT TOMATO AND CLAM JUICE

1 (17½-ounce) can tomato juice
2 (7½-ounce) bottles clam juice
½ teaspoon salt
¼ teaspoon ground thyme
1/16 teaspoon ground black pepper
1/16 teaspoon garlic powder

Combine all ingredients in a saucepan. Cook only until hot. Serve hot in soup bowls or bouillon cups.

YIELD: 6 servings

BEVERAGES Hot and Cold

SPICES are used in many of our most popular beverages: ginger in ginger ale; anise in anisette and other liqueurs; caraway in kümmel cordial; and coriander in gin (it may surprise you, but most of the coriander grown in the United States ends up in the gin bottle).

The English spice the wassail bowl; the Swedish brew a spicy hot *gloeg;* and Mexicans are addicted to hot chocolate that includes an admixture of cinnamon. Punch is named after an Indian word meaning "five." At festivities, punches are most often a mixture of five ingredients: alcohol, water, lemon, sugar, and spice.

Just a bit of cardamom is delightful in coffee. Try 4 or 5 tiny black seeds with the ground coffee for a 6-cup coffee maker. For lemonade and other summer drinks, use a *spiced sugar syrup:* cook in the water, which will be used to make the syrup, a stick of cinnamon, three or four whole cloves, and the same number of whole allspice berries.

In concocting syrups of varying concentrations, use the following proportions:

Very thin syrup	1 part sugar to 4 parts water
Thin syrup	1 part sugar to 2 parts water
Medium syrup	3 parts sugar to 4 parts water
Heavy syrup	1 part sugar to 1 part water

CAFE BRULOT

This spectacular coffee is the perfect climax to a de luxe dinner. In New Orleans they serve it in special brûlot *cups, but demitasse cups will do very nicely.*

1 quart strong black coffee

1 cinnamon stick, 2 inches long
8 whole cloves
1 piece orange peel, 3 inches long
1 piece lemon peel, 2 inches long
6 lumps sugar
1 cup brandy
¼ cup Cointreau
1 teaspoon vanilla extract

Make black coffee, using 2½ tablespoons ground coffee to each cup of water. Keep coffee warm while mixing remaining ingredients. In a chafing dish, combine remaining ingredients. Heat and stir to dissolve sugar. Ignite and stir in hot coffee. Continue stirring until flame goes out. Serve hot.

YIELD: 8 servings

HOT SPICED ORANGE TEA

1 quart boiling water
¼ cup sugar
10 whole cloves
2 cinnamon sticks, each 2 inches long

4 tea bags
¼ cup fresh orange juice
2 tablespoons fresh lemon juice
Rind of ¼ medium-size orange
1 slice fresh lemon

Combine the first 4 ingredients in a saucepan. Mix well and bring to boiling point. Remove from heat and add tea bags. Steep 4 minutes. Strain. Stir in remaining ingredients. Place over low heat to keep warm (DO NOT BOIL). Remove and discard orange rind. Serve in cups, using cinnamon sticks as muddlers, if desired.

YIELD: 6 servings

MEXICAN CHOCOLATE
(CHOCOLATE DE MOLINILLO)

7 cups milk
4 cinnamon sticks, each 2 inches long
9 squares (9 ounces) semisweet chocolate

Heat milk and cinnamon in a 2½-quart saucepan (DO NOT BOIL). Add chocolate, and when melted remove from heat. Beat vigorously with a rotary beater or place a *molinillo* (Mexican hand mill) in the saucepan and twirl the handle backward and forward between palms of the hands until chocolate is rich with foam. Serve in individual cups.

YIELD: 10 servings

BRAZILIAN HOT CHOCOLATE

2 squares (2 ounces) unsweetened chocolate
¼ cup sugar

¼ teaspoon salt
¼ teaspoon ground cinnamon
3 teaspoons instant coffee
___
2 cups hot water
2 cups hot milk
1½ teaspoons vanilla extract

Melt chocolate over hot water in the top of a double boiler. Add next 4 ingredients. Stir in ¼ cup of the water and cook over direct medium-low heat ½ minute. Add remaining water and milk. Cook only until hot, stirring to prevent a skin from forming over the top. Add vanilla extract. Serve hot.

YIELD: 6 servings

MINTED HOT CHOCOLATE

½ teaspoon mint flakes
4¾ cups milk
___
¼ cup sugar
¼ cup cocoa
¼ teaspoon salt
¾ cup water
2 teaspoons vanilla extract

Heat mint flakes with milk, only until hot. Cover and steep while making the syrup. Mix the next 5 ingredients together in a 2-quart saucepan. Bring to boiling point and boil 2 minutes, stirring frequently. Pour hot milk through a sieve to strain out mint flakes. Add to the syrup. Heat only until hot, stirring to prevent a skin from forming over the top. Serve hot with whipped cream or a marshmallow, if desired.

YIELD: 8 servings

SPICED PARTY COCOA

6 tablespoons cocoa
⅛ teaspoon salt
½ cup sugar

¼ cup water
12 whole cloves
___
4 cups milk
⅔ cup light cream *or* top milk
6 cinnamon sticks, each 4 inches long

Mix the first 5 ingredients together in a saucepan. Stir and boil gently for 3 minutes. Add milk and cream. Cook until hot (DO NOT BOIL), stirring constantly to prevent skin from forming on surface. Serve in mugs with a stick of cinnamon in each as a muddler.

YIELD: 6 servings

CHOCOLATE MILK, SPANISH STYLE

3 squares (3 ounces) unsweetened chocolate
2 tablespoons butter *or* margarine
___
¾ cup sugar
½ teaspoon ground cinnamon
¼ teaspoon ground nutmeg
___
1 cup hot strong coffee
1 tablespoon vanilla extract
Milk
Heavy cream, whipped (optional)

Melt chocolate and butter together over hot water. Blend in sugar and spices. Gradually stir in coffee. Boil 3 minutes. Remove from heat. Cool. Add vanilla extract. For each serving, stir 2 tablespoons of the sauce into ¾ cup cold milk. Serve in tall glasses, topped with whipped cream, if desired.

YIELD: 12 servings

HOT BUTTERSCOTCH PUNCH

¾ cup light-brown sugar
⅓ cup hot water
1 tablespoon butter *or* margarine
5 cups milk
¹⁄₁₆ teaspoon salt
1¾ teaspoons vanilla extract
Heavy cream, whipped
Ground nutmeg

Melt sugar over medium-low heat in a 2-quart saucepan, stirring constantly. Add hot water and bring mixture to boiling point. Add butter or margarine and cook 1 to 2 minutes. Add milk and heat only until hot, stirring constantly. Blend in salt and vanilla extract. Serve hot in punch cups or mugs. Garnish with whipped cream and ground nutmeg.

YIELD: 6 servings

SOUTHERN EGGNOG

6 large eggs, separated
½ cup sugar (or to taste)
1 cup Bourbon *or* rye whisky, brandy (or other spirits to taste)
⅓ cup rum
2 cups milk
2 cups heavy cream, whipped
Ground nutmeg

Beat egg yolks until thick and lemon-colored. Gradually beat in sugar. Stir in desired spirits and rum. Cover and chill several hours or overnight. Just before serving, stir in milk. Fold in whipped cream and egg whites beaten until they stand in soft, stiff peaks. Serve in punch cups and garnish with ground nutmeg.

YIELD: About 24 servings

HOT SPICED FRUIT PUNCH

½ cup sugar
1 cup water
2 cinnamon sticks, each 2 inches long

1 teaspoon cracked ginger
½ teaspoon whole cloves
½ teaspoon whole allspice

½ cup fresh lemon juice
2½ cups pineapple juice
2 cups grapefruit juice
1½ cups apricot nectar
Fresh orange slices, cut in half
Whole cloves

Place first 3 ingredients in a saucepan. Put next 3 ingredients in a tea ball or tie them in a cheesecloth bag and add. Bring to boiling point and boil 5 minutes. Remove spices and add fruit juices. Heat, but DO NOT BOIL. Serve in mugs or punch cups. Stud orange slices with whole cloves and float a slice in each cup.

YIELD: 12 servings

point and cook 5 minutes. Remove from heat. Add remaining water and fruit juices. Serve over ice in punch cups or glasses. Garnish with fresh mint or a curl of lemon peel, if desired.

YIELD: 10 servings

SPICED CRANBERRY PUNCH

½ cup sugar
1 cup water
½ teaspoon whole cloves
3 cinnamon sticks, each 2 inches long
___
2 cups cranberry juice
½ cup lemon juice
1 cup orange juice
___
1 quart ginger ale
Whole cloves
Fresh lemon and orange slices

Mix first 4 ingredients in a saucepan. Bring to boiling point and boil 5 minutes. Strain out spices. Cool. Mix with fruit juices. Just before serving, pour into a punch bowl over ice. Add ginger ale. Stud lemon and orange slices with whole cloves and float over the top. Serve in punch cups.

YIELD: 12 servings

SPICED RUM CIDER

This drink is better if the cider is a little on the hard side.
1 cup apple cider
2 teaspoons light-brown sugar
1 tablespoon butter *or* margarine
___
4 tablespoons light rum
2 cinnamon sticks, each 4 inches long

Put first 3 ingredients in a saucepan. Heat, but DO NOT BOIL. Pour 2 tablespoons of rum in each of 2 teacups. Fill with the hot cider mixture. Stir with a stick of cinnamon, one stick for each cup.

YIELD: 2 servings

SPICED APPLE PUNCH

⅓ cup sugar
3 cups water
3 cinnamon sticks, each 2 inches long
2½ cups (20 ounces) apple juice
½ cup lemon juice
1 cup orange juice

Combine sugar, 1 cup of the water, and cinnamon in a saucepan. Bring to boiling

SPICED FRUIT PUNCH

¾ cup sugar
2½ cups water
3 cinnamon sticks, each 2 inches long
¾ teaspoon whole cloves
½ teaspoon whole allspice
½ teaspoon cracked ginger
___
¾ cup lemon juice
4 cups pineapple juice
3 cups grapefruit juice
2¼ cups apricot nectar *or*
    orange juice
___
Fresh orange and lemon slices
Whole cloves

Combine the first 6 ingredients in a saucepan. Bring to boiling point and boil 5 minutes. Strain out spices and cool. Add fruit juices. Pour into a punch bowl over ice just before serving. Stud orange and lemon slices with whole cloves and float on the top. Serve in punch cups.

YIELD: 18 servings

LADIES' DELIGHT

1½ cups sugar
6 cups water
½ teaspoon ground nutmeg
3 cups diced, fresh pineapple
3 cups fresh orange juice
1 cup fresh lime juice
4 bananas
Fresh lime slices

Boil sugar and 2 cups of the water together in a 1-quart saucepan for 3 minutes. Remove from heat, add nutmeg, and cool. Place 1 cup of the pineapple and ¼ cup of the orange juice in the bowl of an electric blender. Blend 1 minute or to a pulp. Repeat, using remaining pineapple. (If a blender is not available chop pineapple very fine.) Strain pulp through a coarse

sieve and mix with sugar syrup and fruit juices. Serve in tall glasses over ice cubes. Cut bananas in half crosswise and then cut each half into lengthwise halves. Stick one piece and a slice of lime in each glass.

YIELD: 12 servings in tall glasses

MINT FRUIT PUNCH

1 tablespoon mint flakes
1 cup water
½ cup sugar

½ cup fresh lemon juice
2½ cups (20-ounce can) pineapple juice
2½ cups (20-ounce can) grapefruit juice
1½ cups (12-ounce can) apricot nectar
1 cup water
Green maraschino cherries

Heat mint flakes and water to boiling point in a small saucepan. Boil 5 minutes. Strain out mint flakes, add sugar, and cool. Stir in next 5 ingredients. Pour into a punch bowl over ice. Garnish with green maraschino cherries. Serve in punch cups.

YIELD: 12 servings

LEMON BEER PUNCH

Credit for this popular Puerto Rican punch goes to Berta Cabanillas and Carmen Ginorio, authors of Puerto Rican Dishes. *Offhand, the idea of mixing lemon, grapefruit, and beer sounds rather horrible. However, it ends up tasting like a delicate champagne, or "like dandelion wine," said one taster old enough to have weathered Prohibition.*

1 cup sugar
1 cup water
1 cup lemon juice
All the lemon rinds

FRESH PINEAPPLE PUNCH

Save those peelings! With a minimum of effort you can make a delightful spiced fruit punch. This recipe comes from Jamaica, B.W.I.

Peelings from 1 medium-size fresh
   pineapple
Peelings from 1 fresh orange
8 whole cloves
1 cinnamon stick, 2 inches long
½ cup sugar
1 quart boiling water
½ cup fresh orange juice
½ cup fresh lemon juice
Fresh mint

Wash pineapple and orange peelings. Place in a large bowl with spices and sugar. Pour in boiling water and mix well. Cover and let stand overnight. Just before serving, strain and mix the liquid with fruit juices. Pour over ice. Serve in punch cups. Garnish with fresh mint leaves.

YIELD: 8 servings

½ cup grapefruit juice
12-ounce bottle light beer
Fresh lemon slices
Whole cloves

Mix sugar with water in a saucepan. Bring to boiling point, add lemon rinds. Cover and let stand 5 minutes. Remove lemon rinds. Cool syrup. Add fruit juices. Pour into a punch bowl over ice. Add beer just before serving. Float lemon slices studded with cloves on punch. Serve in punch cups.

YIELD: 6 servings

RECEPTION PUNCH

¾ cup sugar
1½ cups water
¾ teaspoon anise seed

1½ quarts grape juice
4½ cups light beer
Fresh lemon slices
Whole cloves

Combine the first 3 ingredients in a saucepan. Bring to boiling point and cook 5 minutes. Cool, then strain into grape juice. Just before serving, add beer and pour over ice. Stud lemons with cloves and float over the top. Serve in punch cups.

YIELD: 16 servings

ROSEMARY LEMONADE

1 cup sugar
4 cups water
⅔ cup lemon juice
½ teaspoon rosemary leaves
Dash salt
Fresh lemon slices

Combine sugar, 1 cup of the water, 1 tablespoon of the lemon juice, rosemary, and salt in a 1-quart saucepan. Mix well. Bring to boiling point and boil 5 minutes. Strain out rosemary leaves. Cool. Add remaining water and lemon juice. Serve cold with lemon slices in tall glasses.

YIELD: 5 servings

ROSEMARY FRUIT PUNCH

2 (20-ounce) cans pineapple juice
2½ teaspoons rosemary leaves
1/16 teaspoon salt
½ cup sugar
1½ cups lemon juice
2 cups water
Fresh lemon slices
Fresh mint

Place 1 cup pineapple juice and rosemary leaves in a 2-quart saucepan. Bring to boiling point. Remove from heat. Cover and steep 5 minutes. Strain out rosemary leaves and add salt and sugar. Cool. Stir in remaining pineapple juice, lemon juice, and water. Pour into a punch bowl over ice. Float lemon slices and mint leaves over the top. Serve in punch cups.

YIELD: 12 servings

ROSEMARY GIN PINEAPPLEADE

2 (20-ounce) cans pineapple juice
2½ teaspoons rosemary leaves
2 tablespoons sugar
Dash salt
1 cup lemon juice
3 cups gin
Fresh lemon slices
Whole cloves

Place ½ cup of the pineapple juice and rosemary leaves in a 2-quart saucepan. Bring to boiling point. Remove from heat. Cover and steep 5 minutes. Strain out rosemary leaves and mix the infusion with remaining juice and next 4 ingredients. Pour into a punch bowl over ice. Stud lemon slices with cloves and float them over the top. Serve in punch cups.

YIELD: 12 servings

RHUBARB PUNCH

2 pounds (2 quarts) fresh, diced rhubarb
4 cups water
2 cinnamon sticks, each 2 inches long
24 whole cloves
3½ cups sugar
2 cups orange juice
1 cup lemon juice
1 cup lime juice
6 cups cold water
1 teaspoon vanilla extract
Fresh mint

Cook first 4 ingredients together in a large covered saucepan 10 minutes, or until rhubarb is tender. Strain through a coarse sieve. Add sugar to the hot liquid and stir until it is dissolved. Stir in the next 5 ingredients. Pour into a punch bowl over ice. Garnish with sprigs of fresh mint.

YIELD: 1 gallon

BREADS

"All life moving to one measure—Daily bread."
W. W. GIBSON

AVANELLE'S BEST RYE BREAD

Here is a recipe for the best rye bread we've ever eaten. Rye flour isn't always easy to find, but health and specialty food stores generally stock it.

3 envelopes active dry yeast
1 cup warm water (110° to 115° F.)

3 teaspoons salt
2 tablespoons caraway seed
½ cup unsulphured molasses
½ cup hot water
2 tablespoons shortening

3½ cups sifted all-purpose flour
2¾ cups sifted rye flour
Corn meal

Soften yeast in warm water. Mix the next 5 ingredients and cool to lukewarm. Add yeast. Blend all-purpose flour with rye flour and gradually stir into yeast mixture. Turn dough onto a pastry board rubbed with a little flour to prevent sticking. Knead until dough is smooth and satiny.

Form dough into a ball and place in greased bowl, turning to bring greased side to the top. Cover with a towel and let rise in a warm place (80° to 85° F.) until double in size (1½ to 2 hours). Punch down dough. Form into a ball. Cover and let rest 10 minutes.

Shape into 2 loaves. Place in 2 greased 9 x 5 x 3-inch loaf pans, sprinkled with corn meal. Cover; let rise in a warm place until double in size (about 1 hour). Brush

111

lightly with cold water. Bake 10 minutes in a preheated very hot oven (450° F.); reduce heat to moderate (350° F.). Bake 25 to 30 minutes. Cover with foil or brown paper after baking 25 minutes to prevent burning the crust.

YIELD: 2 loaves

BLACK PEPPER CRACKLING BREAD

Black pepper bread is very popular in many parts of Italy. This bread, sprinkled with bits of crackling, is especially good served with salads and stews.

2 envelopes active dry yeast
½ cup warm water (110° to 115° F.)
1 teaspoon sugar
1 cup scalded milk
⅓ cup shortening

1 tablespoon sugar
2 teaspoons salt
1 large egg

About 6 cups sifted all-purpose flour
2 teaspoons ground black pepper
3 cups cracklings *(see below)*
Melted butter *or* margarine

Combine yeast, warm water, and 1 teaspoon sugar. Let stand 5 minutes to soften. Combine hot milk and shortening and cool to lukewarm. Add to yeast mixture. Stir in the next 3 ingredients and 2 cups of the flour. Beat batter until it falls in a sheet from the spoon. Gradually add remaining flour, kneading it in. Continue kneading on a lightly floured board until dough is smooth and satiny.

Place dough in a greased bowl, turning to bring greased side to the top. Cover with a towel and let rise in a warm place (80° to 85° F.) until double in size (about 1 hour). Punch down dough. Form into 2 balls of equal size. Cover and let rest 10 minutes.

Roll each ball of dough ½ inch thick in a 14 x 9-inch rectangle. Brush surface with melted butter or margarine. Sprinkle each with 1 teaspoon ground black pepper and 1½ cups cracklings. Roll up in jelly-roll fashion. Place in a greased 9 x 5 x 3-inch loaf pan. Brush top with melted butter or margarine. Cover and let rise in a warm place (80° to 85° F.) until double in size. Bake in a preheated moderate oven (375° F.) 40 minutes or until bread has browned.

TO MAKE CRACKLINGS

Cut 3 pounds salt pork (fat back) into thin slices. Place in a large baking pan and cook in a preheated very hot oven (450° F.) 5 minutes. Reduce heat to 350° F. and cook 25 minutes, or until pork is crisp and brown. Save fat for other cooking purposes.

YIELD: 2 loaves

BLACK PEPPER YEAST RING

2 envelopes active dry yeast
2 cups warm water (110° to 115° F.)
1 tablespoon salt
1 tablespoon coarsely ground
   black pepper
About 6½ cups sifted all-purpose flour
Melted shortening
Melted butter *or* margarine

Soften yeast in warm water. Add salt and black pepper. Gradually stir in about 4½ cups of the flour. Then work in remaining flour with hands. Knead dough until smooth and satiny. Place in an ungreased bowl, cover and let rise in a warm place (80° to 85° F.) until dough has doubled in size. Punch down dough, shape into a ball, cover and let rest 10 minutes.

Shape dough in 2 round twisted rings of equal size. Place on a lightly greased baking sheet. Brush tops lightly with melted butter or margarine. Cover and let rise in a warm place until double in size (30 to 40 minutes). Bake in a pre-heated very hot oven (450° F.) 25 minutes or until done.

YIELD: 2 rings

BLACK PEPPER LOAF BREAD

Divide dough in half and shape into 2 loaves. Place in 2 lightly greased 9 x 5 x 3-inch loaf pans. Cover. Let rise in a warm place until double in size (30 to 40 minutes). Bake in a preheated hot oven (400° F.) 35 minutes or until done.

YIELD: 2 loaves

DANISH CHRISTMAS BREAD

2 envelopes active dry yeast
½ cup warm water (110° to 115° F.)
1 cup sugar
2 teaspoons salt
1 teaspoon ground cardamom
1 cup (2 sticks) soft butter
 or margarine
2 large eggs
1 cup seedless raisins
½ cup diced citron
½ cup scalded milk
7 cups sifted all-purpose flour

Soften yeast in warm water with 1 tablespoon of the sugar. Gradually blend remaining sugar, salt, and cardamom into the soft butter or margarine. Add eggs, yeast, raisins, and citron. Cool milk to lukewarm and add. Stir in 2 cups of the flour. Beat batter until it falls in sheets from the spoon. Stir in 4 more cups of flour.

Turn dough onto a pastry board and knead in the remaining 1 cup of flour. Place dough in a greased bowl, turning to bring the greased side to the

top. Cover and let rise in a warm place (80° to 85° F.) 1 hour or until double in size. Punch down dough. Form into a ball. Cover and let rest 10 minutes.

Shape into 2 loaves and place each in a greased 9 x 5 x 3-inch loaf pan. Cover and let rise in a warm place 40 minutes or until loaves have doubled in size. Bake in a preheated moderate oven (350° F.) 50 to 60 minutes.

YIELD: 2 loaves

DILLY ONION BREAD

An unusual and delicious bread for ham, corned beef, or beef sandwiches.

2 envelopes active dry yeast
½ cup warm water (110° to 115° F.)
¼ cup sugar
1¼ cups scalded milk
½ cup shortening
———
2 large eggs, beaten
3½ teaspoons salt
3 tablespoons dill seed
¼ cup instant minced onion
———
6 to 7 cups sifted all-purpose flour
Melted butter *or* margarine

Soften yeast in warm water with 1 table-spoon of the sugar. Mix hot milk and shortening and cool to lukewarm. Add softened yeast, remaining sugar, and the next 4 ingredients. Mix well. Stir in 2 cups of the flour. Cover and let rise in a warm place (80° to 85° F.) 1 hour or until batter is bubbly. Stir in enough of the remaining flour to make a stiff dough.

Knead on a lightly floured board until dough is smooth and satiny. Punch down dough. Form into a ball. Cover and let rest 10 minutes. Shape into 2 loaves and place each in a 9 x 5 x 3-inch loaf pan. Brush tops with melted butter or margarine. Let rise in a warm place until loaves have doubled in size. Bake in a preheated moderate oven (375° F.) 50 minutes or until browned.

YIELD: 2 loaves

HERB BREAD

Some yeast doughs require kneading, others do not. But apparently the ancient Egyptians believed in thorough kneading. According to the historian Herodotus, "Dough they knead with their feet but clay with their hands."

This herb bread makes particularly good cold turkey and pork sandwiches.

1 envelope active dry yeast
¼ cup warm water (110° to 115° F.)
¼ cup sugar
1½ cups scalded milk
½ cup shortening, melted
2 large eggs, beaten
3 teaspoons salt
6 to 7 cups sifted all-purpose flour
1 teaspoon sage leaves
¾ teaspoon thyme leaves
¾ teaspoon marjoram leaves

Soften yeast in warm water along with 1 tablespoon of the sugar. Cool milk to lukewarm and mix with softened yeast, remaining sugar, shortening, eggs, salt, and 2 cups of the flour. Mix well. Cover and let rise in a warm place (80° to 85° F.) 1 hour or until bubbly. Combine herbs and add to the mixture. Stir in rest of flour to make a stiff dough. Knead on a floured board until satiny and elastic. Place in greased bowl, cover, and place in a warm place (80° to 85° F.) until double in bulk. Punch down dough and let rest for 10 minutes.

Shape into 2 loaves and place in greased 9 x 5 x 3-inch loaf pans. Brush tops with milk. Let rise until double in bulk. Bake in a preheated moderate oven (375° F.) 50 minutes or until done.

CARAWAY SEED ONION BREAD
In the above recipe omit herbs and add 3 tablespoons caraway seed and ¼ cup instant minced onion.

YIELD: 2 loaves

NORWEGIAN YULE BREAD (JULEKAKA)
½ medium-size, unpeeled navel orange
1 cup raisins

THE
SPICE MILLER

1 cup boiling water
1 envelope active dry yeast
¼ cup warm water (110° to 115° F.)
1 teaspoon sugar

⅔ cup sugar
½ cup (1 stick) butter *or* margarine
1¾ teaspoons salt
¾ teaspoon ground cardamom
1 cup scalded milk

About 5 to 6 cups sifted all-purpose flour
⅓ cup slivered citron
1 large egg white, lightly beaten
Chopped, blanched almonds

Wash orange, remove and discard any seeds, and put orange through a food chopper, using the medium blade. Set aside for later use. Combine raisins and boiling water, let stand 1 minute for raisins to soften, then drain well. Turn raisins onto paper towels to absorb excess water. Set aside.

Soften yeast in warm water with the 1 teaspoon of sugar added. Combine the next 5 ingredients. Stir until butter or margarine is melted and cool to lukewarm. Stir in yeast and 2½ cups of the flour. Beat until batter falls in sheets from spoon. Add orange, raisins, and citron and mix until well blended. Add enough of the remaining flour to make a soft dough. Turn onto a lightly floured board and knead until smooth and satiny. Place dough in a greased bowl, turning to bring greased side to the top. Cover and let rise in a warm place (80° to 85° F.) until dough has doubled in size (about 1½ hours. Punch down dough. Form into a ball, cover, and let rest 10 minutes.

Place in a buttered round 9-inch layer-cake pan. Flatten dough slightly to spread it over the bottom of the pan. Cover and let rise in a warm place until double in size (30 to 40 minutes). Bake in a preheated moderate oven (350° F.) 1 hour

or until done. Brush top with lightly beaten egg whites and sprinkle with chopped almonds. Return to oven to bake 10 minutes. Remove from pan to cool on a wire rack. Serve for Christmas breakfast or for holiday entertaining.

YIELD: One round 9-inch loaf

POPPY SEED EGG BRAID

2 envelopes active dry yeast
½ cup warm water (110° to 115° F.)
¼ cup sugar

1½ cups scalded milk
¼ cup (½ stick) soft butter
    or margarine
3 teaspoons salt

3 large eggs
7¼ to 7½ cups sifted all-purpose flour
1 large egg, beaten
2 tablespoons cold water
⅓ to ½ cup poppy seed

Soften yeast in warm water with 1 tablespoon of the sugar. Combine remaining sugar with next 3 ingredients. Stir to melt butter and cool to lukewarm. Add yeast, the 3 eggs and 3½ cups flour. Beat until the batter is smooth. Add remaining flour, a little at a time, until the dough leaves the sides of the bowl clean. Turn onto a lightly floured board and knead 5 minutes or until the dough is smooth and little bubbles can be seen beneath the surface. Shape into ball and place in greased bowl, turning to bring greased side to the top. Cover and let rise in a warm place (80° to 85° F.) 45 minutes or until dough has doubled in size. Punch down dough and let rise 20 minutes longer.

Divide dough in half and divide each half into thirds (sixths of original dough). Pat each portion into a 12 x 3-inch strip.

Sprinkle 1 teaspoon poppy seeds down the middle of each strip. Roll up

¾ cup corn meal
3 cups cold water

¼ cup unsulphured molasses
2 tablespoons caraway seed
3 tablespoons shortening
5 teaspoons salt
2 cups unseasoned, mashed potatoes

2 envelopes active dry yeast
1 teaspoon sugar
¼ cup warm water (110° to 115° F.)

1 cup sifted all-purpose flour
4½ cups unsifted, stone-ground
    rye flour
5½ cups unsifted stone-ground,
    whole-wheat flour

strip sidewise. Press outer edge into roll and pinch ends of roll to seal. Smooth strip by rolling back and forth over the board. Form into two 3-strip braids. First place 3 strips side by side on the board. Then, starting from the middle, braid toward each end. Pinch the ends to prevent separation. Place each braid in a greased 9 x 5 x 3-inch loaf pan. Brush tops with remaining egg mixed with cold water and sprinkle with poppy seeds. Let rise about 45 minutes or until dough comes to top of pan. Bake in a preheated hot oven (400° F.) 25 to 35 minutes or until well browned. Cool on wire racks.

YIELD: 2 loaves

PUMPERNICKEL BREAD

The first loaf of pumpernickel bread was made during the wheat famine of 1443. A Swiss baker, Pumper Nickel, developed it as a means of producing the maximum amount of bread from the least amount of available wheat.

Mix corn meal and cold water together in a saucepan. Bring to boiling point, stir, and cook 3 to 4 minutes or until mixture is the consistency of thick mush. Turn into a 4-quart mixing bowl or dish pan. While mixture is still warm, add the next 5 ingredients. Mix well and cool to lukewarm.

Combine the next 3 ingredients and let stand 10 minutes or until yeast has softened and the mixture is bubbly. Add to corn meal mixture. Mix the last 3 ingredients and set aside ¼ cup to use later. Stir 7 cups of the flour into corn meal mixture, 1 cup at a time. At this point the dough is very stiff and sticky and looks as though no more flour can be added. Nevertheless, turn the dough onto a pastry board and knead in, ½ cup at a time, all the remaining flour mixture, *except* the reserved ¼ cup. DO NOT UNDER-KNEAD. This dough is very stiff and should not be sticky at this stage.

Place dough in a greased bowl, turning to bring the greased side to the top. Cover and let rise in a warm place (80° to 85° F.) 1 hour or until dough has doubled in size. Punch down dough and knead in the reserved ¼ cup flour mixture. Cover and let dough rest 10 minutes.

Divide dough into 2 equal parts. Shape each into a round loaf or into a long loaf pointed at the ends and wide in the middle. Place on a greased cooky sheet that has been sprinkled with corn meal. Or if desired, shape dough into 2 loaves and place in two 9 x 5 x 3-inch loaf pans that have been greased and sprinkled with corn meal. Cover and let rise in a warm place 45 minutes. Brush tops with cold water. Bake in a preheated moderate oven (375° F.) 45 minutes or until bread is done. Remove from pans. Cool on wire racks.

YIELD: 2 loaves

SESAME SEED SALLY LUNN BREAD

This eighteenth-century English recipe came to our attention in Williamsburg, Virginia. The sesame seed is our contribution and adds crunchiness; the sugar-cinnamon variation is especially good for breakfast.

2 envelopes active dry yeast
½ cup warm water (110° to 115° F.)
¼ cup sugar
3 large eggs, at room temperature
1½ cups scalded milk
2 teaspoons salt
6½ cups sifted all-purpose flour
1 cup shortening, melted
Butter *or* margarine
Toasted Sesame Seed*

Soften yeast in warm water with 1 tablespoon of the sugar. Add remaining sugar. Beat in eggs. Cool milk to lukewarm and add. Gradually stir in 4 cups of the flour

*An asterisk after the name of a dish indicates that the recipe for this dish appears in the book. Consult the Index for the page number.

and beat until batter falls in sheets from spoon. Cool shortening to lukewarm and add. Stir in salt and remaining flour. Scrape down bowl. Grease top of dough to prevent crusting. Cover and let rise in a warm place (80° to 85° F.) until dough has doubled in size (about 1 hour). Punch down dough. Cover and let rest 10 minutes.

Divide dough in half. Butter two 8½-inch Sally Lunn or Turk's head molds or two 8-inch gelatine ring molds, and sprinkle with Toasted Sesame Seed. Place one half of the dough in each. Cover and let rise in a warm place 45 minutes or until dough has doubled in size. Bake in a preheated moderate oven (350° F.) 1 hour or until done. Serve hot with butter, if desired.

CINNAMON SALLY LUNN BREAD

Omit the sesame seed in the above recipe. Sprinkle the insides of the buttered molds with a mixture of ¼ cup sugar and 1 teaspoon ground cinnamon.

YIELD: 2 Sally Lunn rings

SPICED PUMPKIN RAISIN BREAD

2 envelopes active dry yeast
½ cup warm water (110° to 115° F.)
½ cup sugar
1½ teaspoons ground cardamom
2 teaspoons ground ginger
1 cup mashed, cooked pumpkin
2 large eggs
1 cup scalded milk
8½ cups sifted all-purpose flour
½ cup (1 stick) butter *or* margarine, melted
2 teaspoons salt
1½ cups seedless raisins

Soften yeast in warm water with 1 tablespoon of the sugar in a mixing bowl. Mix spices with remaining sugar and add to yeast together with pumpkin and eggs. Beat well. Cool milk to lukewarm and add. Gradually beat in 4 cups of the flour. Beat until the batter falls in sheets from the spoon. Cool melted butter or margarine to lukewarm and stir into the mixture along with the salt. Add remaining flour, stirring and kneading it in until all the flour is used. Knead dough on a lightly floured board until smooth and satiny. Form into a ball and place in a greased bowl, turning to bring the greased side to the top. Cover and let rise in a warm place (80° to 85°F.) 50 minutes or until double in size.

Turn out onto a lightly floured board and gradually knead in the raisins. (If dough sticks to board and hands, sprinkle lightly with additional flour.) Place 1¾ pounds of dough in each of 2 lightly greased 9 x 5 x 3-inch loaf pans. (There will be a small amount of dough left. Make it into rolls. These may be eaten the same day, while the loaves are better after they have aged overnight.) Brush tops with melted butter or margarine. Cover and let rise in a warm place 45 minutes or until double in size. Bake in a preheated moderate oven (375° F.) 45 minutes or until done. (The rolls should bake in about 20 minutes.)

YIELD: 2 loaves, plus about 16 rolls

STOLLEN

2 envelopes active dry yeast
½ cup warm water (110° to 115° F.)
2 teaspoons sugar

1 cup scalded milk
½ cup sugar
½ cup (1 stick) soft butter or
    margarine
2 large eggs
6 cups sifted all-purpose flour
1½ teaspoons salt
1½ teaspoons ground nutmeg

2 teaspoons grated lemon rind
1½ cups seedless raisins
1⅓ cups chopped almonds
¼ cup (½ stick) butter or margarine,
    melted
¼ cup sugar
½ teaspoon ground cinnamon
2 cups sifted confectioners' sugar
3 tablespoons water

Place the first 3 ingredients in a mixing bowl large enough for mixing the dough. Let stand until yeast softens. Cool milk to lukewarm and add to yeast along with the ½ cup sugar and butter or margarine. Mix well. Beat in eggs. Stir in 3 cups of the flour, together with the salt, nutmeg, and lemon rind. Beat until batter drops in sheets from the spoon. Stir in remaining flour, raisins, and 1 cup of the almonds. Turn onto a lightly floured board. Knead until dough is smooth and satiny. Put dough into a greased bowl, turning to bring the greased side to the top. Cover and let rise in a warm place (80° to 85° F.) 1 hour or until dough has doubled in size. Punch down dough. Cover and let rest 10 minutes.

Divide the dough in half. Roll each half into a rectangular sheet ½ inch thick and about 12 inches long. Brush each with melted butter or margarine. Mix the ¼ cup sugar with the cinnamon and sprinkle it, together with the remaining almonds, over the dough. Fold sides of each piece of dough to the middle and stretch to make long loaves, thick at the middle, narrow at the ends. Place each on a greased baking sheet. Brush tops with melted butter or margarine. Cover and let rise in a warm place (80° to 85° F.) 45 minutes or until double in size.

Bake in a preheated moderate oven (375° F.) 20 minutes or until browned. Combine confectioners' sugar and water and spread over top of the warm loaves when they are placed on wire racks to cool.

YIELD: 2 stollens

YEAST CINNAMON COFFEE CAKE

1 cup scalded milk
1 envelope active dry yeast

½ cup (1 stick) butter *or* margarine
¼ cup sugar
1 teaspoon salt

1 large egg
About 3½ cups sifted all-purpose flour
⅓ cup (⅔ stick) butter *or* margarine, melted
½ cup sugar
1½ teaspoons ground cinnamon

Cool the milk to lukewarm. Add yeast and let stand until softened. Mix together the next 3 ingredients. Beat in egg. Add yeast and milk. Stir in enough flour to make a soft dough. Knead on a lightly floured board until smooth and satiny. Place in a greased bowl, turning to bring the greased side to the top. Cover and let rise in a warm place (80° to 85° F.) 1 hour or until doubled in size. Punch down dough and knead lightly ½ minute.

Roll dough to ¼-inch thickness on a lightly floured board. Shape with a 2-inch biscuit cutter. Dip each disk in melted butter or margarine and then in remaining sugar mixed with cinnamon. Stand disks on edge in a well-buttered 8½-inch ring mold, filling the mold. Cover and let rise in a warm place 30 minutes or until double in size. Bake in a preheated moderate oven (350° F.) 35 to 40 minutes. There will be enough of the dough left to make 6 rolls.

YIELD: 1 coffee cake, plus 6 rolls

KING'S CAKE

This traditional New Orleans Mardi Gras cake makes for wonderful eating and lots of fun at parties. Baked into each cake is a tiny doll, bean, or pecan. The man who wins the slice with the little token wins the right to choose his queen.

2 envelopes active dry yeast
½ cup warm water (110° to 115° F.)
½ cup sugar
½ cup shortening
⅓ cup scalded milk

2 teaspoons salt
1 teaspoon ground nutmeg
1 teaspoon grated lemon rind

3 large eggs
4½ to 5 cups sifted all-purpose flour
⅔ cup (4 ounces) glacé orange peel
⅔ cup (4 ounces) citron
1 dried bean, pecan, *or* tiny doll
Lemon Glaze*
Glacé cherries, candied orange peel, *or* citron

Soften yeast in warm water with 1 tablespoon of the sugar. Add remaining sugar and shortening to hot milk. Stir until shortening is melted and milk has cooled to lukewarm. Add yeast and the next 3 ingredients. Beat in eggs. Stir in 2 cups of the flour and beat until batter falls in sheets from the spoon. Add orange peel and citron. Mix in 2 cups of the remaining flour.

Turn onto a pastry board and gradually knead in the rest of the flour. Continue kneading until dough is smooth and satiny. Place dough in a greased bowl, turning to bring the greased side to the top. Cover and let rise in a warm place (80° to 85° F.) 1¼ hours or until dough has doubled in size. Punch down dough and divide into 3 equal parts. Cover and let rest 10 minutes.

Wrap a bean, pecan, or tiny doll in foil and put it into one piece of the dough. Roll each piece of dough into a strip 30 inches long and form the 3 strips into 1 long braid. Shape into an oval on a greased cooky sheet. Cover and let rise in a warm place until double in size. Bake in a preheated moderate oven (375° F.) 25 minutes or until browned. Cool. Frost with Lemon Glaze. Decorate with glacé cherries, candied orange peel, or citron.

This recipe makes a large cake. If desired, divide the dough in half and make 2 smaller cakes.

YIELD: One 12-inch cake

POPPY SEED KRINGLE

1 envelope active dry yeast
¼ cup warm water (110° to 115° F.)
3 tablespoons sugar
¾ teaspoon salt
2¼ cups sifted all-purpose flour
⅓ cup shortening
¼ cup scalded milk
1 medium-size egg, beaten
Quick Poppy Seed Filling*
Confectioners' Sugar and Water Glaze*
Glacé fruit
Poppy seed

Soften yeast in warm water with 1 teaspoon of the sugar. Combine the remaining sugar, salt, and flour. Add shortening and cut it in, with 2 knives or a pastry blender, to coarse meal consistency. Cool milk to lukewarm and add. Stir in yeast and egg. Mix well. Place dough in a greased bowl, turning to bring greased side to the top. Cover and let rise in a warm place (80° to 85° F.) 2 hours or until almost double in size.

Punch down dough and roll on a lightly floured board into a 16 x 8-inch rectangle. Spread with Quick Poppy Seed Filling. Starting at the long side, roll up as for jelly roll. Place on a lightly greased cooky sheet. Bring ends together to form a ring. Let rise in a warm place 30 minutes or until double in size. Bake in a preheated moderate oven (350° F.) 25 minutes. Cool on wire racks. Frost with Confectioners' Sugar and Water Glaze. Decorate with glacé fruit and poppy seed.

YIELD: 1 kringle

SPICED SUGAR PLUM COFFEE RING

1 envelope active dry yeast
¼ cup warm water (110° to 115° F.)

1 cup scalded milk
⅓ cup sugar
⅓ cup shortening
1½ teaspoons salt

1 large egg, beaten
3½ cups sifted all-purpose flour
2 tablespoons melted butter or margarine
2 tablespoons light corn syrup
½ cup light-brown sugar
¼ cup pecan halves
¼ cup glacé cherries
½ cup (1 stick) butter or margarine, melted
¾ cup sugar

CINNAMON BRUNCH ROLLS

½ cup (1 stick) butter *or* margarine
3 cups sifted all-purpose flour
2 envelopes active dry yeast
½ cup warm water (110° to 115° F.)
1 tablespoon sugar
3 large eggs
1 teaspoon salt
1 teaspoon vanilla extract
½ cup chopped nuts
¼ cup sugar
½ teaspoon ground cinnamon

Blend butter or margarine with 1½ cups flour until the mixture resembles corn meal. Soften yeast in warm water. Add sugar and stir into the flour mixture. Cover and let stand 20 minutes. Beat in eggs, salt, and vanilla extract. Gradually add the remaining flour.

Pinch off pieces of dough the size of walnuts and roll in nuts mixed with the ¼ cup sugar and cinnamon. Roll each into a 6-inch long rope and tie the ends together to form a knot. Place on greased cooky sheets. Let rise about 10 minutes at room temperature. Bake in a preheated hot oven (425° F.) 12 to 15 minutes.

YIELD: 2 dozen rolls

TRADITIONAL DANISH CHRISTMAS BUNS

These buns, often called "St. Lucia's Christmas Buns," are served in Scandinavian homes at the St. Lucia's Day breakfast. Traditionally, the oldest daughter of the house, wearing a crown of greens and lighted candles, brings coffee and "St. Lucia's Buns" to the bedside of her parents.

2 envelopes active dry yeast
½ cup warm water (110° to 115° F.)

2 teaspoons ground cinnamon
1 teaspoon ground cloves

Soften yeast in warm water. Combine next 4 ingredients. Cool to lukewarm. Add yeast and egg. Gradually stir in flour. Beat vigorously. Cover and let rise in a warm place (80° to 85° F.) until double in size.

Mix 2 tablespoons melted butter or margarine with corn syrup and light-brown sugar. Turn into a buttered 10-inch ring mold and spread uniformly over the bottom. Top with pecan halves and glacé cherry halves.

Shape dough into 1-inch balls. Roll them in ½ cup melted butter or margarine and then into the ¾ cup sugar mixed with the cinnamon and cloves. Place 2 layers of balls over cherries and nuts. Cover and let rise in a warm place until double in bulk. Bake in a preheated moderate oven (375° F.) 25 minutes or until done. Let stand in pan 20 minutes. Turn out onto serving plate. Serve warm with butter or margarine. If this cake is made the day before it is to be used, heat before serving.

YIELD: 1 ring

⅓ cup sugar
2 teaspoons salt
1 teaspoon ground cardamom
½ cup (1 stick) butter *or* margarine
¾ cup scalded milk

1 large egg
4⅓ cups sifted all-purpose flour
Raisins
1 large egg white

Soften yeast in warm water with 1 table-spoon of the sugar. Place remaining sugar and next 4 ingredients in a large bowl. Cool milk to lukewarm, add, blend well. Stir in yeast, 1 egg, and 2 cups of the flour. Beat until the batter falls in sheets from a spoon. Add remaining flour and knead dough on a lightly floured board until it is creamy and satiny (about 5 minutes). Place dough in a greased bowl, turning to bring greased surface to the top. Cover and let rise in a warm place (80° to 85° F.) until dough is double in size. Punch down dough and shape into a ball. Cover and let rest 10 minutes.

Divide dough into 18 pieces of equal size and roll each piece into a rope 12 inches long and ½ inch thick. Curl ends and put 2 rolls together back to back. Stick a raisin in the center of each curl or, if desired, form each 12-inch rope into the shape of an *S,* coiling or curling each

end, and sticking a raisin in each coil. Place buns on a greased baking sheet. Brush with egg white beaten only until foamy. Cover and let rise in a warm place (80° to 85° F.) until double in size (about 40 minutes). Bake in a pre-heated hot oven (400° F.) 10 to 12 minutes.

YIELD: 1½ dozen rolls

HAMANTASCHEN WITH POPPY SEED FILLING

A 3-cornered pastry, filled with poppy seed and honey, is traditional for Purim, a jolly, light-hearted Jewish festival which celebrates the ancient story of Queen Esther and how she saved her people.

1 envelope active dry yeast
¼ cup warm water (110° to 115° F.)
½ cup sugar

¼ cup (½ stick) soft butter *or* margarine
1 teaspoon salt
1 cup scalded milk

2 large eggs, lightly beaten
5 cups sifted all-purpose flour
Poppy Seed Filling *(see below)*
1 large egg yolk
1 to 2 tablespoons water

Soften yeast in warm water in 1 table-spoon of the sugar. Combine remaining sugar with the next 3 ingredients. Stir to melt butter and cool to lukewarm. Stir in yeast, eggs, and about 2 cups of the floor. Beat batter until it is smooth and falls in sheets from the spoon. Blend in all but 2 tablespoons of the remaining flour. Knead on board, working in re-maining 2 tablespoons of flour. Place dough in a large greased bowl, turning to bring greased side to the top. Cover and let stand in warm place (80° to 85° F.)

for 2 hours or until double in bulk. Punch down dough, cover, and let rest 10 minutes.

Roll dough ⅛ inch thick on a lightly floured board. Cut into 4-inch circles. Place a scant tablespoon Poppy Seed Filling in the center of each. Moisten edges of dough with a little water. Bring edges on 2 sides of circle firmly together over filling, leaving about ⅓ of the circle open, forming a cornucopia. Then fold over the flap to meet the first 2 edges and pinch them firmly together, forming a triangle. Brush with egg yolk mixed with water. Bake in a preheated moderate oven (350° F.) 20 to 25 minutes or until brown.

HAMANTASCHEN POPPY SEED FILLING
1 cup poppy seed
½ cup water *or* milk
¼ cup honey
2 tablespoons sugar
⅛ teaspoon salt

1 teaspoon fresh lemon juice
1 large egg, lightly beaten

Combine first 5 ingredients in a saucepan. Stir and cook over moderate heat 10 minutes or until thick, stirring constantly. Add lemon juice. Add a little of the hot mixture to the beaten egg and then stir into the remaining poppy seed mixture. Cool thoroughly before using.

YIELD: 2½ dozen hamantaschen

HOT CROSS BUNS
2 envelopes active dry yeast
1 teaspoon sugar
½ cup warm water (110° to 115° F.)
¾ cup scalded milk

6 tablespoons butter *or* margarine
⅓ cup sugar

2 teaspoons salt
1 teaspoon ground ginger
1 teaspoon ground nutmeg

2 large eggs
5½ cups sifted all-purpose flour
⅓ cup finely chopped citron
¾ cup dried currants
Glaze *(see below)*

Soften yeast with the 1 teaspoon sugar in warm water. Combine hot milk with next 5 ingredients. Stir until butter or margarine is melted. Cool to lukewarm. Add yeast. Beat in eggs. Stir in 2 cups of the flour and beat until the batter falls in sheets from spoon. Add citron and currants. Add another 2½ cups flour, mixing it in well.

Turn mixture onto a pastry board and knead in remaining 1 cup flour. Continue kneading until dough is smooth and satiny. Place dough in a lightly greased bowl, turning to bring the greased side to the top. Cover and let rise in a warm place (80° to 85° F.) until double in size, about 1 hour. Punch down dough. Form into a ball. Cover and let rest 10 minutes.

Shape into 3 dozen rolls about the size of walnuts. Place in lightly greased pans, about 1 inch apart. Cover and let rise in a warm place 45 minutes or until double in size. Bake in a preheated moderate oven (375° F.) 15 to 20 minutes or until browned. In the meantime, make the glaze. Brush tops of buns lightly with glaze while they are still in the pans. Cool partially and with a spoon dribble glaze in the shape of a cross on top of each bun. Serve warm.

GLAZE
Add about 2 tablespoons milk and ¾ teaspoon vanilla extract to 1½ cups sifted confectioners' sugar. Mix well.

YIELD: 3 dozen buns

HUNGARIAN PRESSBURGER HORNS
(POZSONI PATKS)

1 envelope active dry yeast
1 tablespoon sugar
¼ cup warm water (110° to 115° F.)

5½ cups sifted all-purpose flour
1 teaspoon salt
1 cup (2 sticks) butter *or* margarine
2 large egg yolks
1 cup sour cream
¾ cup scalded milk
Poppy Seed Filling *(see below)*

Combine the first 3 ingredients and let stand while assembling remaining ingredients. Blend flour with salt. Add butter or margarine and cut it in with 2 knives or pastry blender to coarse crumb consistency. Mix egg yolk and sour cream and stir into the mixture. Stir in yeast. Cool milk to lukewarm. Add and mix to form a smooth dough, handling it as little as possible. Cover and allow to rise in a warm place (80° to 85° F.) until double in size (about 2 hours). Punch down dough and let rest 10 minutes.

Roll ½ the dough at a time ¼ inch thick on a lightly floured board. Cut into 3-inch squares. Place a teaspoon of Poppy Seed Filling on each. Fold dough over in cornucopia fashion. Seal edges to form neat horns. Place on lightly greased baking sheets, 1 inch apart. Brush tops with milk 2 to 3 times as they dry. Let stand 10 minutes. Bake in a preheated moderate oven (350° F.) 25 minutes or until golden brown.

POPPY SEED FILLING FOR PRESSBURGER HORNS

2 cups poppy seed
¾ cup sugar
2 tablespoons honey *or* light
  corn syrup

½ cup hot milk
1½ teaspoons grated lemon rind
2 teaspoons vanilla extract

Combine all ingredients and mix well.

YIELD: 6½ dozen rolls

POPPY SEED WHOLE-WHEAT ROLLS

2 envelopes active dry yeast
1 teaspoon sugar
½ cup warm water (110° to 115° F.)

1½ cups scalded milk
½ cup unsulphured molasses
2 large eggs

3¾ cups sifted all-purpose flour
3¾ cups unsifted whole-wheat flour
3 teaspoons salt

½ cup shortening, melted
1 large egg white
Poppy seed

Combine first 3 ingredients and let stand for yeast to soften. Cool milk to lukewarm and add to yeast. Stir in molasses and eggs. Combine the next 3 ingredients and add 4 cups of it to the yeast mixture. Beat batter until it falls in sheets from the spoon. Cool shortening to lukewarm, add, and mix well. Add remaining 3½ cups flour mixture, working it in thoroughly on a lightly floured board. Knead until dough is smooth and satiny. Shape into ball and place in a greased bowl, turning to bring greased side to the top. Cover and let rise in a warm place (80° to 85° F.) until dough has doubled in size (1 to 1½ hours). Punch down dough.

Form into 2 balls, cover, and let rest 10 minutes. Shape into rolls of desired size and place on a greased baking sheet 1 inch apart. Brush tops with egg white beaten only until frothy. Sprinkle tops with poppy seed. Cover and let rise in a warm place until double in size. Bake in a preheated hot oven (400° F.) 12 to 15 minutes.

YIELD: 5 to 6 dozen rolls

SESAME SEED CHEESE ROLLS

1 envelope active dry yeast
¼ cup warm water (110° to 115° F.)
1 teaspoon sugar

1 cup warm water (110° to 115° F.)
¼ cup sugar
2 tablespoons shortening
2 teaspoons salt

1 large egg, lightly beaten
½ pound (2 cups) shredded sharp Cheddar cheese
⅓ cup Toasted Sesame Seed*
4 to 5 cups sifted all-purpose flour
1 large egg white

Soften yeast in warm water containing the teaspoon of sugar. Combine the next 4 ingredients. Cool to lukewarm. Add yeast mixture, egg, cheese, and sesame seed. Gradually stir in 3½ cups of the flour. Turn onto lightly floured board. Gradually knead in the remaining flour. Knead gently 2 to 3 minutes. Place in a large greased bowl, turning to bring

greased side to the top. Cover and let rise in a warm place (80° to 85° F.) until double in size. Punch down dough. Form into a ball. Cover and let rest 10 minutes.

Shape into small rolls in attractive, assorted shapes. Place on lightly greased baking sheets. Brush tops with egg whites beaten only until frothy. Sprinkle with sesame seeds. Cover. Let rise in warm place until double in bulk. Bake in a preheated hot oven (400° F.) 15 minutes or until browned.

YIELD: 3 dozen rolls

SESAME SEED CHEESE BREAD
Shape the above dough into 2 loaves. Place in 2 greased 9 x 5 x 3-inch loaf pans. Cover and let rise until double in bulk. Bake in a preheated moderate oven (375° F.) 40 minutes or until browned.

YIELD: 2 loaves

CRANBERRY-ORANGE BREAD

1½ cups coarsely chopped raw cranberries
1½ tablespoons grated orange rind
3 tablespoons sugar

3 cups sifted all purpose flour
3 teaspoons double-acting baking powder
½ teaspoon soda
¾ teaspoon salt
1 teaspoon ground mace
1¼ cups sugar

2 large eggs, beaten
¾ cup orange juice
¾ cup water
½ cup shortening, melted
1 cup chopped pecans

Combine the first 3 ingredients and set aside. Sift together the next 6 ingredients. Mix eggs with orange juice and water. Add to flour mixture along with cranberry mixture, shortening, and pecans. Stir only until ingredients are blended.

Turn into a well-greased, lightly floured 9 x 5 x 3-inch loaf pan. Bake in a preheated moderate oven (350° F.) 1½ hours or until a cake tester inserted in the center comes out clean. Cool in pan 20 minutes. Turn out onto wire rack to finish cooling. Store airtight. This bread slices better if made a day before serving.

YIELD: 1 loaf

DATE AND NUT BREAD

7-ounce package pitted, dried dates
1 cup boiling water
1 teaspoon soda
1 cup sugar
½ cup shortening

¾ teaspoon ground ginger
¾ teaspoon ground nutmeg
¾ teaspoon ground cinnamon
½ teaspoon salt

1 large egg
1 cup chopped nuts
1¾ cups flour

Chop dates and soak in boiling water with soda for 15 minutes. Gradually blend sugar with shortening. Add next 4 ingredients. Mix well. Beat in egg. Combine nuts and flour and add to sugar and shortening alternately with date and water mixture. Turn into a well-greased, lightly floured 9 x 5 x 3-inch loaf pan. Bake in a preheated moderate oven (350° F.) 1½ hours or until cake tester inserted in center comes out clean.

YIELD: 1 loaf

POPPY SEED TEA BREAD

3 cups sifted all-purpose flour
1 teaspoon salt
3½ teaspoons double-acting
    baking powder

½ cup poppy seed
¾ cup sugar
¼ cup shortening
2 large eggs
1 teaspoon grated lemon rind
1⅓ cups milk

Sift the first 3 ingredients together and mix with poppy seed. Beat sugar, shortening, and eggs together. Blend in grated lemon rind and milk. Add, all at one time, to the flour mixture. Mix only until ingredients are blended (about 30 strokes), using the folding method of mixing. Stop at the end of the 15th stroke to scrape down bowl and spoon. Turn into a well-greased, lightly floured 9 x 5 x 3-inch loaf pan. Bake in a preheated moderate oven (350° F.) 1 hour. Cool. Serve with butter, cream cheese, or dried fruit and nut sandwich spreads.

YIELD: 1 loaf

SAFFRON-LEMON TEA BREAD

Saffron was grown and widely used in England for centuries. In the fourteenth-century cook book, Forme of Cury, *a collection of recipes used and compiled by the master cooks of Richard II, saffron was called for in more than half the recipes. Henry VIII was so fond of saffron that he wouldn't allow the ladies of the court to use it as a hair dye.*

Saffron, used delicately, is delightful. Used with too heavy a hand, however, it gives a medicinal flavor. This recipe was tested with ground saffron, but if whole saffron threads must be used, crumble them to a powder before measuring.

2 cups sifted all-purpose flour
2 teaspoons double-acting
    baking powder
1 teaspoon salt

½ cup shortening

¼ teaspoon soda
⅛ teaspoon powdered saffron
2 teaspoons grated lemon rind

¾ cup sugar
2 large eggs
¾ cup water
2 tablespoons fresh lemon juice

Sift together first 3 ingredients and set aside for later use. Mix shortening with next 3 ingredients. Gradually blend in sugar. Beat in eggs, 1 at a time. Combine water and lemon juice and add to the batter alternately with the sifted flour mixture, beginning and ending with flour. Beat batter ½ minute.

Turn into a well-greased, lightly floured 9 x 5 x 3-inch loaf pan. Bake 1 hour in a preheated moderate oven (350° F.). Cool in pan 10 minutes. Turn out onto a wire rack to finish cooling. Spread with softened cream cheese or butter or margarine for tea sandwiches.

YIELD: 1 loaf

SESAME SEED LOAF
⅓ cup (⅔ stick) butter or margarine

¾ cup sugar
1 large egg
1½ cups milk
3 cups sifted all-purpose flour
3½ teaspoons double-acting
      baking powder
1 teaspoon salt
6 tablespoons Toasted Sesame Seed*

Melt butter or margarine. Add sugar and egg and mix well. Beat in milk. Sift together flour, baking powder, and salt; add to mixture. Fold in all but 1 tablespoon sesame seed. Pour into a well-greased 9 x 5 x 3-inch loaf pan. Sprinkle remaining toasted sesame seed on top. Bake in a preheated moderate oven (325° F.) 1 hour or until done.

YIELD: 1 loaf

SPICED NUT BREAD
3 cups sifted all-purpose flour
1 teaspoon double-acting
   baking powder
1 teaspoon salt
1 teaspoon soda
¾ teaspoon ground nutmeg
¾ teaspoon ground ginger

2 large eggs, beaten
1½ cups light-brown sugar
½ cup (1 stick) butter or margarine,
   melted
1 cup chopped nuts
1½ cups sour milk or buttermilk

Sift together the first 6 ingredients. Set aside. Beat eggs in a large mixing bowl. Gradually blend in light-brown sugar. Stir in butter or margarine and chopped nuts. Add flour mixture alternately with milk, mixing only enough to blend ingredients. Turn into a well-greased, lightly floured 9 x 5 x 3-inch loaf pan. Bake in a preheated moderate oven (350° F.) 1¼ hours, or until done. Cool in pan

10 minutes. Turn out onto a wire rack to finish cooling. This bread cuts better if made the day before using. Store airtight.

YIELD: 1 loaf

BUTTER CINNAMON STICKS

2 cups sifted all-purpose flour
¼ teaspoon salt
1 cup (2 sticks) butter *or* margarine
⅔ cup quick-cooking rolled oats
½ to ⅔ cup water
Melted butter *or* margarine
1 teaspoon ground cinnamon
½ cup light-brown sugar

Mix flour and salt. Cut in butter or margarine to coarse crumb consistency. Blend in rolled oats. Gradually add enough water to make a dough. Chill until dough is stiff enough to handle, at least 2 hours.

Divide dough into 6 parts. Roll each into a 4 x 18-inch rectangle. Brush surface with melted butter or margarine. Mix cinnamon with brown sugar and sprinkle over the top. Roll up as for jelly roll, starting at the long side. Cut into 6 sticks, each 3 inches long. Place on an ungreased cooky sheet. Bake in a preheated hot oven (425° F.) 15 minutes or until lightly browned. Serve for breakfast or at tea time.

YIELD: 3 dozen cinnamon sticks

CHILI CORN MEAL CHEESE BISCUITS

1 cup sifted all-purpose flour
½ teaspoon salt
3 teaspoons double-acting baking powder
1 cup yellow corn meal
2 teaspoons chili powder
½ cup shredded sharp American cheese
¼ cup shortening
About ½ cup milk

Sift together in a mixing bowl the first 5 ingredients. Blend in cheese. Cut in shortening with 2 knives or pastry blender to coarse crumb consistency. Stir in enough milk to make a soft dough. Knead on a lightly floured board 30 seconds.

Roll out dough to ½-inch thickness. Cut with a 2-inch biscuit cutter dipped in flour. Bake on ungreased cooky sheets in a preheated very hot oven (450° F.) 12 minutes or until browned.

YIELD: 1 dozen biscuits

CHILI CHEESE PINWHEELS

2 cups sifted all-purpose flour
3 teaspoons double-acting baking powder
¾ teaspoon salt
¼ cup shortening
1 cup grated Cheddar cheese
⅔ cup milk
2 tablespoons melted butter *or* margarine
½ to ¾ teaspoon chili powder

Sift first 3 ingredients together. Cut in shortening and ½ cup of the cheese. Blend until the mixture resembles coarse meal. Gradually stir in only enough milk to form a soft dough, then roll it ¼ inch thick. Brush melted butter or margarine over surface of dough. Combine remaining cheese with chili powder and sprinkle over dough. Roll in jelly-roll fashion. Cut into slices ¾ inch thick. Bake 12 to 15 minutes on well-greased cooky sheets in a preheated very hot oven (450° F.).

YIELD: 16 biscuits

CINNAMON PINWHEEL BISCUITS

2 cups sifted all-purpose flour
3 teaspoons double-acting
   baking powder
1 teaspoon salt

¼ cup shortening
½ cup milk
⅓ cup (⅔ stick) butter *or* margarine
1½ teaspoons ground cinnamon
½ cup sugar
Melted butter *or* margarine

Sift the first 3 ingredients together. Cut in shortening. Add milk and stir to form a soft dough. Turn onto a lightly floured board. Knead lightly for about 20 seconds. Roll dough into a 16 x 6-inch rectangle.

Combine butter or margarine, cinnamon, and sugar, then spread over dough. Roll up in jelly-roll fashion and cut into 1-inch slices. Place in greased muffin tins. Brush tops with melted butter or margarine. Bake in a preheated hot oven (400° F.) 15 to 20 minutes.

YIELD: 16 biscuits

POPPY SEED SNAILS

2 cups sifted all-purpose flour
3 teaspoons double-acting
   baking powder
½ teaspoon salt
2 tablespoons sugar

¼ cup shortening
¾ cup milk
¼ cup (½ stick) butter *or* margarine,
   melted
Poppy Seed Filling *(see below)*
2 tablespoons honey

Sift together first 4 ingredients. Add shortening and cut it in with a pastry blender or 2 knives to crumb consistency. Stir in milk. Knead 20 seconds on a lightly floured board. Roll into a 12 x 8 x ¼-inch rectangle. Brush surface with 2 tablespoons of the melted butter or margarine. Spread with Poppy Seed Filling. Roll, starting at the 12-inch side, in jelly-roll fashion. Cut into slices 1 inch thick. Combine remaining 2 tablespoons butter or margarine and 2 tablespoons honey and put 1 teaspoon in each of twelve 2-inch muffin tins, into which then place a biscuit. Bake in a preheated hot oven (400° F.) 20 minutes or until browned. Serve hot.

POPPY SEED FILLING FOR "SNAILS"

¼ cup water
½ cup poppy seeds
3 tablespoons honey
½ teaspoon grated lemon rind

Combine water, poppy seeds, and honey in a small saucepan. Bring to boiling point and boil 5 minutes. Add lemon rind. Cool.

YIELD: 1 dozen snails

ALLSPICE DATE COFFEE CAKE

2 cups sifted all-purpose flour
3 teaspoons double-acting
   baking powder
½ teaspoon salt

⅓ cup shortening
½ cup light-brown sugar
1¼ teaspoons ground allspice
2 large eggs
1 cup diced, pitted dates
¾ cup milk

3 tablespoons sugar
2 teaspoons grated orange rind
1 teaspoon grated lemon rind
¼ cup finely chopped nuts

Sift together first 3 ingredients and set aside. Mix shortening with brown sugar and allspice until fluffy. Beat in eggs. Stir in dates. Add flour mixture alternately with milk. Turn into a greased, lightly floured 9-inch square pan. Mix last 4 ingredients together and sprinkle over the top. Bake in a preheated moderate oven (375° F.) 40 minutes or until done. Cool pans on wire rack for 10 minutes. Turn out of pan onto rack to finish cooling. Serve warm.

YIELD: One 9-inch square cake

CINNAMON STREUSSEL COFFEE CAKE

2 cups sifted all-purpose flour
3 teaspoons double-acting
  baking powder
1 teaspoon salt
½ cup sugar
1 teaspoon ground cinnamon

⅓ cup shortening
½ cup milk
1 large egg, well beaten
Melted butter or margarine

2 tablespoons all-purpose flour
2 tablespoons butter or margarine
5 tablespoons sugar
¾ teaspoon ground cinnamon

Sift the 2 cups of flour, baking powder, salt, the ½ cup sugar, and the 1 teaspoon

of cinnamon into a large mixing bowl. Cut in shortening until mixture resembles coarse corn meal. Add milk to egg and stir into dry ingredients until just mixed. Spread in a greased 8 x 8 x 2-inch pan. Brush with melted butter or margarine. Combine remaining ingredients and mix until they form coarse crumbs. Sprinkle over top of cake. Bake in a preheated hot oven (400° F.) for 25 to 30 minutes or until done.

YIELD: One 8-inch square cake

RICH CINNAMON COFFEE CAKE

1 cup sugar
1 teaspoon ground cinnamon
½ cup (1 stick) butter or margarine
2 large eggs

1¼ cups sifted all-purpose flour
2 teaspoons double-acting
  baking powder
¼ teaspoon salt

½ cup milk
2 tablespoons melted butter or
  margarine
1 tablespoon sugar
⅛ teaspoon ground cinnamon

Gradually blend sugar and 1 teaspoon of cinnamon with ½ cup of butter or margarine. Beat in eggs, 1 at a time. Sift the next 3 ingredients together and add alternately with milk to the sugar mixture. Beat batter 30 seconds. Pour into a well-greased, lightly floured 8 x 8 x 2-inch pan.

Bake in a preheated moderate oven (350° F.) 60 minutes or until a toothpick or cake tester inserted in center comes out clean. Remove cake from oven and brush surface with the melted butter or margarine. Combine the 1 tablespoon sugar and the ⅛ teaspoon cinnamon and sprinkle over the top. Serve hot with butter or margarine.

YIELD: One 8-inch square cake

FRESH PEAR KUCHEN

1 cup sifted all-purpose flour
2 teaspoons double-acting
   baking powder
½ teaspoon salt
1 tablespoon sugar

3 tablespoons shortening
½ cup milk
2 large, firm, ripe pears

½ teaspoon ground ginger
¼ teaspoon ground nutmeg
½ cup sugar
½ teaspoon grated lemon rind
2 tablespoons butter or margarine

Sift together the first 4 ingredients. Cut in shortening with a pastry blender until the mixture is the consistency of oatmeal. Stir in milk. Spread dough in the bottom of a buttered 9-inch pie plate, over which arrange pears, cut into ½-inch slices, pushing them into the dough slightly. Combine remaining ingredients and mix to form coarse crumbs. Sprinkle over pears.

Bake in a preheated moderate oven (375° F.) 35 minutes or until pears are tender and a cake tester inserted in cake comes out clean. Cut into wedges and serve warm, topped with whipped cream, if desired.

YIELD: 6 servings

FRESH PLUM KUCHEN

1 cup sifted all-purpose flour
2 teaspoons double-acting
   baking powder
½ teaspoon salt
1 tablespoon sugar

3 tablespoons shortening
⅓ cup milk
12 to 15 (¾ pound) fresh
   Italian plums

⅓ cup sugar (white or brown)
¼ teaspoon ground nutmeg
½ teaspoon ground cinnamon

1 tablespoon butter or margarine
2 tablespoons chopped walnuts

Sift the first 4 ingredients together. Add shortening and cut it in with a pastry blender or 2 knives to the consistency of oatmeal. Add milk all at once and stir just enough to mix into dry ingredients. Spread dough in bottom of a greased 8-inch pie pan. Cut plums in half, remove pits and arrange, skin-side down, over dough. Combine sugar and spices. Add butter and nuts. Mix until crumbly. Crumble over plums. Bake in hot oven (400° F.) 20 to 25 minutes. Serve warm or cold, topped with whipped cream, if desired.

YIELD: 6 servings

CINNAMON APPLESAUCE MUFFINS

2 cups sifted all-purpose flour
¼ cup sugar
3 teaspoons double-acting
   baking powder
½ teaspoon salt
½ teaspoon ground cinnamon

2 large eggs, beaten
1 cup milk
½ cup applesauce
¼ cup shortening, melted
½ cup chopped dates or raisins
1 tablespoon melted butter or
   margarine
2 tablespoons sugar
½ teaspoon ground cinnamon

Sift first 5 ingredients together into a mixing bowl. Combine eggs, milk, and applesauce and stir into the flour mixture, using 14 strokes. Then, stir in shortening and dates, using only 8 to 10 strokes. Fill well-greased muffin pans ¾ full. Bake in a preheated hot oven (400° F.) 27 minutes or until done. Remove from pan. Dip tops in melted butter or margarine and then in the 2 tablespoons of sugar mixed with ½ teaspoon of ground cinnamon. Serve hot with butter.

YIELD: 15 muffins

CINNAMON-BANANA MUFFINS

2 cups sifted all-purpose flour
1 teaspoon salt
2 teaspoons double-acting
   baking powder
1½ teaspoons ground cinnamon
⅓ cup sugar

1 large egg, well beaten
1 cup milk
¼ cup shortening, melted

1 cup (2 or 3) mashed, fully-ripe
   bananas
¼ teaspoon ground cinnamon
1 tablespoon sugar

Sift together into a mixing bowl first 5 ingredients. Combine egg, milk, and shortening. Add to dry mixture. Add mashed bananas and stir only until all ingredients are blended. Batter will be lumpy. Fill greased muffin tins ¾ full. Combine ¼ teaspoon of cinnamon and 1 tablespoon of sugar. Sprinkle over top of each muffin. Bake in a preheated hot oven (425° F.) for 20 to 25 minutes.

YIELD: 1 dozen muffins

APPLE PANCAKES

1 cup sifted all-purpose flour
½ teaspoon double-acting
   baking powder
½ teaspoon salt
⅛ teaspoon soda
¼ teaspoon ground nutmeg
¼ cup sugar

2 large eggs, well beaten
1 cup milk
1 tablespoon melted shortening
¾ cup shredded apple (about 1
   medium-size)
1 teaspoon fresh lemon juice
Cinnamon sugar (optional)

Sift together the first 6 ingredients. Combine eggs and milk and gradually stir into flour mixture. Add melted butter or margarine and beat slightly with a rotary beater. Mix shredded apple with lemon juice to prevent discoloration and blend with the batter.

For each pancake, drop 2 tablespoons of batter onto a lightly greased hot griddle. Bake until pancakes are brown on the bottom and bubbles form over the top. Turn to brown on the other side. Serve at once with syrup, honey, jelly, or sprinkle with cinnamon sugar.

YIELD: Approximately 16 pancakes

APPLESAUCE PANCAKES

1 cup sifted all-purpose flour
½ teaspoon salt
1½ teaspoons double-acting
    baking powder

1 cup applesauce
¼ teaspoon grated lemon rind
¼ teaspoon ground cinnamon
1 tablespoon sugar
¾ teaspoon vanilla extract

2 large eggs, separated
1½ tablespoons melted butter *or*
    margarine

Sift the first 3 ingredients together into a mixing bowl. Blend in the next 5 ingredients. Beat egg yolks slightly and add to the mixture along with butter or margarine. Beat egg whites until they stand in soft, stiff peaks and fold into the batter. For each pancake, pour ¼ cup batter onto a lightly greased hot griddle. Bake until brown on the bottom and bubbles form over the top. Turn and brown on the other side. Serve hot, with maple syrup or jelly.

YIELD: Approximately 10 pancakes

ONION CORN MEAL PANCAKES

¾ cup corn meal
½ cup sifted all-purpose flour
3 tablespoons instant minced onion
2 teaspoons double-acting
    baking powder
¾ teaspoon salt

2 tablespoons shortening
1¼ cups milk

Combine the first 5 ingredients in a mixing bowl and mix well. Add shortening and blend it in to fine crumb consistency. Stir in milk. For each pancake, pour 2 tablespoons of batter onto a lightly greased hot griddle. Cook over medium heat until brown on the bottom and bubbles form over the top. Turn to brown on other side (DO NOT COOK TOO FAST). Serve at once.

YIELD: 1 dozen pancakes

PANCAKES WITH CARAWAY CHEESE FILLING

4 large eggs
1 teaspoon salt
1 cup milk
1 cup sifted all-purpose flour

1 tablespoon butter *or* margarine
Caraway Cheese Filling *(see below)*
½ cup sour cream
Paprika

Combine the first 4 ingredients. Beat with a rotary beater until smooth. Let the batter stand 30 minutes. Melt butter or margarine in a 6-inch skillet and let it brown lightly. Pour in 2 to 3 tablespoons of batter. Rotate pan to spread batter uniformly. Brown lightly on the bottom, turn to brown the other side.

As pancakes are cooked, place them on a baking sheet and keep warm until all are fried. Place 2 to 3 tablespoons Caraway Cheese Filling in a strip across the center of each. Fold edges of pancakes from both sides to the center. Place in a 12 x 7½ x 2-inch baking dish. Top with sour cream. Bake in a preheated moderate oven (350° F.) 10 to 15 minutes or until hot. Garnish with paprika. Serve hot as a main dish for lunch or supper.

CARAWAY CHEESE FILLING

2½ cups creamy cottage cheese
⅓ cup sour cream
1½ teaspoons instant minced onion
1 teaspoon caraway seed
¼ teaspoon salt
$\frac{1}{16}$ teaspoon ground black pepper

Put cottage cheese through a sieve. Add remaining ingredients. Mix well.

YIELD: 6 servings, 2 pancakes each

CARDAMOM SOUR CREAM WAFFLES

This recipe was given to us by a friend who lived in Norway for a number of years. Sour cream and butter make these waffles rich and cardamom adds a delicate flavor. In Norway they are served with lingonberry jam or preserves.

1 cup sifted all-purpose flour
2 tablespoons sugar
1 teaspoon soda
1 teaspoon cardamom
½ teaspoon salt
———
2 large eggs, separated
¼ cup (½ stick) butter *or* margarine, melted
1 cup thick commercial sour cream
1 cup buttermilk *or* sour milk

Sift together first 5 ingredients. Set aside to use later. Beat egg yolks until thick and lemon-colored. Beat in melted butter or margarine. Add sour cream and buttermilk. Mix only until blended. Mix

with dry ingredients. Beat egg whites until they stand in soft, stiff peaks; fold into the mixture. Pour batter into waffle iron and bake 4 to 5 minutes or until steam subsides. Serve cold with butter or margarine and lingonberry preserves or jam, if desired.

YIELD: 12 waffles

GINGERBREAD WAFFLES

2 cups sifted all-purpose flour
1 teaspoon salt
1 teaspoon double-acting baking powder
½ teaspoon soda
2 teaspoons ground ginger
½ cup sugar
———
2 large eggs, beaten
½ cup unsulphured molasses
⅔ cup milk
½ cup shortening, melted

Sift together the first 6 ingredients into a mixing bowl. Combine eggs and molasses and add to the dry mixture. Mix well. Stir in milk and shortening. Spoon batter onto lightly oiled hot waffle iron. (The amount used for one waffle depends upon the size of waffle iron.) Bake 2 to 3 minutes on low heat. Serve topped with ice cream or with fruit and sweetened whipped cream. This batter may be made ahead of time, stored in a covered container in the refrigerator, and baked as needed. It will keep 5 days.

YIELD: 3 large, square waffles or 12 servings

CURRIED SPOON BREAD

½ cup yellow corn meal
2 tablespoons curry powder
½ teaspoon salt
½ teaspoon celery salt
½ teaspoon onion salt

¼ teaspoon ground white pepper
¹⁄₁₆ teaspoon garlic powder

½ cup cold water
1½ cups boiling water
1⅔ cups shredded sharp Cheddar
    cheese
2 large eggs, separated
1 teaspoon double-acting
    baking powder

Combine the first 7 ingredients in a 6-cup saucepan. Stir in cold water. Add boiling water. Mix well. Cook over low heat until very thick, stirring frequently. Blend in cheese. Combine egg yolks and baking powder and add gradually. Beat egg whites until they stand in soft peaks; fold into the mixture. Pour into a buttered 1-quart casserole. Place in a pan of hot water. Bake in a preheated slow oven (325° F.) 1½ hours or until done. Serve as the main dish for lunch or supper.

YIELD: 6 servings

HUSH PUPPIES

"Hush Puppies" are said to have originated at fish fries in South Carolina. The tantalizing aroma of the frying fish would set the dogs to yelping hungrily. The fish cook would fry bits of corn meal batter and toss them to the dogs saying: "Hush, puppies, hush, puppies."

1 cup white corn meal
⅓ cup sifted all-purpose flour
1 teaspoon double-acting
    baking powder
¼ teaspoon soda
1 teaspoon salt
3 tablespoons instant minced onion

¾ cup sour milk
2 tablespoons water
1 large egg, beaten

Combine first 6 ingredients. Mix thoroughly. Stir in remaining ingredients. Let stand 10 minutes for batter to thicken. Drop from a teaspoon into deep fat preheated to 370° F. or until an inch square of bread browns in the fat in 1 minute. Drain in absorbent paper. Keep warm in a slow oven (300° F.) while cooking remaining batter.

YIELD: About 1½ dozen

GRILLED ONION CORN BREAD SQUARES

8-inch squares cold corn bread
¼ cup (½ stick) butter *or* margarine,
    melted
½ teaspoon onion powder

Cut cold corn bread into 8 squares. Split each in half. Combine melted butter or margarine with onion powder and brush over the cut sides of corn bread squares. Place under the broiler to brown, watching closely to prevent burning. Serve hot.

CHILI CORN BREAD SQUARES

In the above recipe, replace onion powder with ½ teaspoon chili powder.

CURRIED CORN BREAD SQUARES

In the above recipe, replace onion powder with ¼ to ½ teaspoon curry powder.

GARLIC CORN BREAD SQUARES

In the above recipe, replace onion powder with ¼ teaspoon garlic powder.

YIELD: 8 squares

ONION CORN STICKS

1½ cups sifted corn meal
½ cup sifted all-purpose flour
¼ cup instant minced onion
1 teaspoon salt
1 teaspoon soda
1 teaspoon double-acting
  baking powder
2 teaspoons sugar
2 large eggs, beaten
2 cups sour milk *or* buttermilk
3 tablespoons melted shortening

Combine first 7 ingredients in a mixing bowl. Stir in remaining ingredients. Mix well. Spoon into hot, greased corn-stick pans. Bake in a preheated hot oven (425° F.) 15 to 20 minutes or until browned. Serve hot.

YIELD: 2 dozen corn sticks

BROWN-AND-SERVE CINNAMON ROLLS

12 (1 package) soft brown-and-serve
  rolls
¼ cup (½ stick) butter *or* margarine,
  melted
2 tablespoons sugar
½ teaspoon ground cinnamon

Bake rolls as directed on package. Quickly dip tops and sides in melted butter or margarine and then into sugar mixed with cinnamon. Serve piping hot.

YIELD: 1 dozen rolls

BROWN-AND-SERVE POPPY SEED ROLLS

12 (1 package) brown-and-serve rolls
1 tablespoon melted butter *or*
  margarine
1 tablespoon light corn syrup
Poppy seed

Place rolls on a baking sheet. Mix butter or margarine with corn syrup and brush over tops of rolls. Sprinkle with poppy seed. Bake in a preheated very hot oven (475° F.) 10 to 12 minutes or until brown. Serve hot.

YIELD: 1 dozen rolls

BROWN-AND-SERVE STICKY ROLLS

24 (2 packages) brown-and-serve rolls
2 tablespoons butter *or* margarine
2 tablespoons light corn syrup
½ cup light-brown sugar
½ teaspoon ground mace
¼ cup chopped pecans

Bake rolls according to directions on the package. Melt the butter or margarine. Add the next 3 ingredients. Stir until the brown sugar is dissolved. Add the pecans and pour over the tops of the rolls. Serve warm.

YIELD: 2 dozen rolls

CINNAMON BISCUIT COFFEE RING

20 (2 packages) ready-to-cook biscuits
⅓ cup (⅔ stick) butter *or* margarine,
  melted
⅓ cup sugar
1 teaspoon ground cinnamon

Dip each unbaked biscuit in melted butter or margarine and then into the sugar mixed with cinnamon. Stand up in a well-buttered 8-inch ring mold until mold is filled. Bake in a preheated hot oven (400° F.) 30 minutes or until brown.

YIELD: One 8-inch ring

CINNAMON CLOVER LEAF BISCUITS

Roll each unbaked biscuit into a ball. Dip in melted butter or margarine and then into cinnamon-sugar mixture. Place 3 balls in each buttered cupcake pan. Bake in a preheated hot oven (425° F.) 15 minutes or until browned.

YIELD: 20 biscuits

PARSLEY-CHEESE BISCUIT RING

¼ cup (½ stick) butter or margarine, melted
1 tablespoon parsley flakes
½ teaspoon instant minced onion
20 (2 packages) ready-to-cook biscuits
½ cup grated sharp American cheese

Melt butter or margarine. Stir in parsley flakes and instant minced onion. Dip one biscuit at a time into the mixture and then into cheese. Stand biscuits in 2 layers in a buttered 6¼-inch ring mold. Bake in a preheated hot oven (400° F.) 20 minutes or until well browned. Serve hot.

YIELD: 6 to 8 servings

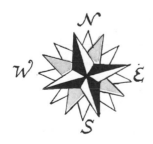

POPPY SEED BISCUITS

10 (1 package) ready-to-cook biscuits
2½ teaspoons melted butter or margarine
2½ teaspoons corn syrup
5 teaspoons poppy seed

Split each biscuit in half. Brush each with melted butter or margarine and corn syrup. Sprinkle ¼ teaspoon poppy seed on each. Place each split biscuit back together to make 10 biscuits. Bake on an ungreased cooky sheet in a preheated very hot oven (475° F.) for 10 to 12 minutes.

YIELD: 10 biscuits

CINNAMON YEAST ROLLS

1 package (14½ ounces) yeast-roll mix
2 tablespoons melted butter or margarine
¼ cup sugar
½ teaspoon ground cinnamon
½ teaspoon melted butter or margarine

Mix yeast dough as directed on package. Roll dough ½ inch thick in a 9 x 14-inch rectangle. Brush surface with 2 tablespoons melted butter or margarine. Combine sugar and cinnamon and sprinkle over the top. Roll up in jelly-roll fashion, starting at the long side (14-inch side). Place in a greased 9 x 5 x 3-inch loaf pan. Brush top with ½ teaspoon melted butter or margarine. Cover and let rise in a warm place (80° to 85° F.) until loaf has doubled in size. Bake in a preheated moderate oven (375° F.) 40 minutes or until browned.

YIELD: 1 loaf

QUICK CARDAMOM COFFEE RING

1 package (14½ ounces) yeast-roll mix
3 tablespoons melted butter *or* margarine
_____
⅓ cup sugar
¼ teaspoon ground cardamom
1 teaspoon grated lemon rind
_____
½ cup diced glacé fruit *or* raisins

Prepare yeast dough according to recipe on the package. Roll dough ¼ inch thick in an 8 x 18-inch rectangle. Brush surface with melted butter or margarine. Combine next 3 ingredients. Sprinkle over the surface of dough to within ½ inch of the edge. Sprinkle with glacé fruit or raisins.

Roll up in jelly-roll fashion, starting at the long side (18-inch side). Place on a greased baking sheet in a ring, pinching edges together. Let rise in a warm place (80° to 85° F.) until double in size. Bake in a preheated moderate oven (375° F.) 30 minutes or until done. If desired, brush top with additional melted butter or margarine and sprinkle with more glacé fruit.

YIELD: One 9-inch ring

QUICK POPPY SEED CRESCENT

1 package (14½ ounces) yeast-roll mix
Quick Poppy Seed Filling *(see below)*
1 tablespoon melted butter *or* margarine
Poppy seed
Glacé fruit (optional)

Make yeast dough according to directions on the package. Roll dough ¼ inch thick in an 8 x 16-inch rectangle. Spread surface within 1 inch of the edges with Poppy Seed Filling. Roll in jelly-roll fashion, starting at the long side (16-inch side).

Place on a lightly greased cooky sheet. Turn ends to form a crescent. Let rise in a warm place (80° to 85° F.) 10 minutes or until almost double in size. Bake in a preheated moderate oven (350° F.) 30 minutes or until browned. Remove from oven and brush top with melted butter or margarine. Sprinkle with poppy seed and garnish with glacé fruit, if desired.

QUICK POPPY SEED FILLING

½ cup sugar
½ cup water
1 cup poppy seed
½ teaspoon ground cinnamon
½ cup seedless raisins
2 tablespoons strained honey
1 teaspoon grated lemon rind

Mix sugar and water in a saucepan. Bring to boiling point and boil 5 minutes. Add poppy seed, cinnamon, raisins, and honey. Cook 3 more minutes. Remove from heat and stir in lemon rind. Cool. Use as filling for crescent.

YIELD: One 12-inch crescent

GARLIC FRENCH BREAD

1 loaf unsliced French bread, 10 to 12 inches long
¼ cup (½ stick) soft butter *or* margarine
½ teaspoon instant minced garlic

Slice bread in 10 pieces about 1 inch thick, cutting to within ¼ inch from the bottom. Mix butter or margarine with instant minced garlic and spread between slices. Wrap loaf in foil and heat in a preheated hot oven (425° F.) 20 to 25 minutes. Serve hot.

ONION FRENCH BREAD

In the above recipe, replace garlic with ¾ teaspoon instant minced onion.

ture between slices and over top. Sprinkle with Parmesan cheese. Wrap in foil and place in a preheated moderate oven (350° F.) 20 minutes or hot oven (400° F.) 15 minutes.

YIELD: 2 loaves

PARSLEY-CHEESE CROUSTADES

1 loaf unsliced white, whole-wheat, *or* rye bread

½ cup (1 stick) soft butter *or* margarine
1 tablespoon parsley flakes
⅛ teaspoon garlic powder

About 13 thin slices American cheese

Cut bread in slices ¾ inch thick to within ¼ inch from the bottom of loaf, leaving a solid crust to hold slices intact. Blend together the next 3 ingredients; spread on both sides of each slice of bread and insert a slice of cheese in between each 2 slices. Place bread on a baking sheet. Spread top and sides with remaining butter or margarine. Bake in a preheated moderate oven (350° F.) 15 minutes or until cheese has melted and bread is brown and crusty.

YIELD: 1 loaf

CURRIED FRENCH BREAD
In the above recipe, replace garlic with 1 teaspoon curry powder.

CHILI FRENCH BREAD
In the above recipe, replace garlic with 1 teaspoon chili powder.

CARAWAY SEED FRENCH BREAD
In the above recipe, replace garlic with 2 teaspoons caraway seed.

YIELD: 6 servings

HERBED ITALIAN BREAD

½ cup (1 stick) soft butter *or* margarine
1 tablespoon catsup
1 teaspoon ground oregano
¹⁄₁₆ teaspoon garlic powder

2 loaves Italian bread
½ cup grated Parmesan cheese

Combine the first 4 ingredients. Cut bread diagonally into slices from 1½ to 2 inches thick, cutting almost to the bottom, but leaving loaf intact. Spread the butter mix-

SPICED FAN-TAN LOAF

½ cup (1 stick) soft butter *or* margarine
½ teaspoon ground allspice
½ teaspoon ground nutmeg
¼ cup sugar

1 loaf sliced, day-old, close-textured bread

Combine first 4 ingredients; spread between slices of bread. Return loaf to its original shape and place in a 9 x 5 x 3-inch loaf pan. Cut the loaf, lengthwise, through the center. Heat in a preheated hot oven (425° F.) 20 minutes or until hot. If a softer loaf is desired, wrap loaf in foil and heat.

YIELD: 1 loaf

SESAME SEED FRANKFURTER ROLLS

8 (1 package) frankfurter rolls
1¼ cups (2½ sticks) butter *or* margarine, melted
⅓ cup Toasted Sesame Seed*

Split rolls in half lengthwise. Dip each half into melted butter or margarine. Roll in sesame seed. Place on cooky sheet. Bake in a preheated hot oven (400° F.) for 20 minutes. Serve hot.

YIELD: 16 halves

CINNAMON TAFFY TOAST

2 tablespoons soft butter *or* margarine
½ teaspoon ground cinnamon
⅓ cup unsulphured molasses
8 slices toasted bread

Blend together butter, cinnamon, and molasses. Spread on toasted bread. Place under broiler until topping is bubbly.

YIELD: 8 servings

POPPY SEED FRENCH TOAST

3 large eggs, beaten
1 cup milk
⅛ teaspoon salt
2 tablespoons poppy seed
1 tablespoon honey
_____
12 slices firm-textured bread
Butter *or* margarine

Combine first 5 ingredients. Beat until well mixed. Quickly dip bread, one slice at a time, into the mixture. Brown, on both sides, in butter or margarine. Serve at once with jelly, jam, syrup, or honey and with crisp bacon, sausage, or ham.

YIELD: 6 servings

POPPY SEED HONEY TOAST

8 slices white bread
¼ cup (½ stick) soft butter *or* margarine
2 tablespoons honey
1½ teaspoons poppy seed

Toast bread only on one side. Combine remaining ingredients. Spread over untoasted side of bread. Place under broiler just long enough to brown. Serve hot.

YIELD: 4 servings

LOST BREAD
(PAIN PERDU)
We call it French toast. But in the Cajun country of Louisiana, it is known as "Lost Bread," because the bread loses its iden-

tity when dipped into the egg and milk mixture and sautéed.

3 large eggs, well beaten
1 tablespoon sugar
½ teaspoon ground nutmeg
½ cup milk

6 slices day-old bread

Combine the first 4 ingredients. Dip bread slices, one at a time, into the mixture. Sauté in butter or margarine until browned, turning to brown both sides. Sprinkle with sugar or serve with jam, jelly, or syrup.

YIELD: 6 slices

RAISED CINNAMON DOUGHNUTS

2 envelopes active dry yeast
¾ cup warm water (110° to 115° F.)

1 cup shortening
½ cup sugar
1½ teaspoons ground nutmeg
1½ teaspoons ground cinnamon
1½ teaspoons salt
¾ cup hot water

2 large eggs
7½ cups sifted all-purpose flour

½ cup sugar
1½ teaspoons ground cinnamon

Soften yeast in warm water and set aside. Combine next 6 ingredients and cool to lukewarm. Stir in softened yeast, eggs, and 4 cups of the flour. Beat until batter falls in sheets from spoon. Stir in as much flour as you can, then turn dough onto a pastry board and knead in remaining flour. Knead until dough is smooth and satiny. Place dough in a greased bowl, turning to bring the greased side to the top. Cover bowl and let rise in a warm place (80° to 85° F.) about 1 hour or until dough has doubled in size. Punch down dough and shape it into a ball. Cover and let rest 10 minutes.

Divide dough in half. Store one-half in a covered bowl in the refrigerator until ready for use. Roll remaining half ¼ inch thick on a lightly floured board. Cover and let rise 30 minutes. Shape with a doughnut cutter dipped in flour. Fry 3 to 4 doughnuts at a time in deep fat preheated to 375° F. until golden, turning to brown both sides. Drain on paper towels. Roll doughnuts in a mixture of sugar and cinnamon. Repeat, using rest of dough. Store airtight.

YIELD: 4 dozen doughnuts

DUTCH DOUGHNUTS
(OLYKOEKS)

1 envelope active dry yeast
¼ cup warm water (110° to 115° F.)
1 tablespoon sugar
3 tablespoons shortening
1 cup scalded milk

¾ cup sugar
1 teaspoon ground nutmeg
3 teaspoons salt
2 large eggs, beaten

About 5 cups sifted all-purpose flour

Raisins
Diced citron
Diced raw apples
¼ cup sugar
¾ teaspoon ground cinnamon

Soften yeast in water with the 1 table-spoon sugar in a mixing bowl. Add shortening to hot milk, cool to lukewarm, and add to softened yeast. Stir in next 4 ingredients. Gradually add enough flour to make a soft dough. Mix well and knead on a lightly floured board 6 minutes or until dough is smooth and satiny.

Place dough in a greased bowl, turning to bring the greased side to the top. Cover bowl and let rise in a warm place (80° to 85° F.) about 50 minutes or until dough has doubled in size. Punch down dough, form into a ball, cover, and let rest 10 minutes.

Pinch off 1¼-inch balls of dough. Place 2 whole raisins, 2 pieces citron, and a dice of apple in the center of each. Shape into balls. Place on lightly greased cooky sheets. Cover and let rise in a warm place 40 minutes or until double in size. Carefully lift balls from cooky sheet with a spatula that has been dipped in flour.

Drop into hot, deep fat, preheated to 375° F. (or until a bread cube browns in 1 minute). Fry until golden. Drain on paper towels. Roll in remaining sugar mixed with cinnamon. Store airtight.

YIELD: 50 balls

SPICED POTATO DOUGHNUTS

4 cups sifted all-purpose flour
3 teaspoons double-acting baking powder
2 teaspoons salt
2½ teaspoons ground nutmeg
¼ teaspoon soda

2 large eggs, well beaten
1¼ cups sugar
¼ cup shortening, melted
1 cup freshly mashed, fluffy, unseasoned potatoes
1 tablespoon grated lemon rind
⅓ cup buttermilk
Confectioners' sugar (optional)
Cinnamon sugar (optional)

Sift together the first 5 ingredients and set aside. Beat eggs with sugar and shortening. Stir in mashed potatoes and lemon rind. Add flour mixture alternately with milk. Turn dough onto a lightly floured board. Roll to ¼-inch thickness. Shape with a doughnut cutter dipped in flour.

Drop 4 to 5 doughnuts at a time into deep fat preheated to 375° F. or until a bread cube browns in 60 seconds. Cook, turning to brown both sides, until doughnuts are brown and rise to the surface. Drain on paper towels. Roll in confectioners' sugar or in cinnamon sugar (1½ teaspoons ground cinnamon to ½ cup sugar). Store airtight.

YIELD: 3 dozen doughnuts

STEAMED BROWN BREAD

1 cup sifted all-purpose flour
2 teaspoons soda
1 teaspoon salt
1 teaspoon ground cinnamon
½ teaspoon ground allspice

1 cup quick-cooking oatmeal
2 cups corn meal
1 cup seedless raisins
1 cup unsulphured molasses
2 cups sour milk *or* buttermilk

Sift together the first 5 ingredients and mix with oatmeal and corn meal. Measure out ¼ cup and mix with raisins and set aside for later use. Stir molasses and milk into the remaining dry mixture. Add raisins and mix well.

Pour batter into 4 well-greased and lightly floured 20-ounce canned fruit or vegetable cans. Cover with 2 thicknesses of foil and tie in place with a strong cord. Place on a rack in a large kettle. Pour in enough hot water to come half way up the side of cans. Cover kettle and steam 2 hours, timing after water begins to boil. Add more water to the kettle, if necessary.

Remove from water. Remove foil from tops and cool at least 30 minutes before removing from cans. Store in a bread or cake box.

YIELD: 4 loaves

CAKES, Frostings, and Fillings

CAKE is a festive food. We serve it at weddings, birthdays, and during religious holidays. However, it may also be used to spruce up an otherwise ordinary meal. In the days of George and Martha Washington, it was known as a "Great Cake," to distinguish it from cookies and French pastries, and also because it was baked in a deep pan, layer cakes being unknown at that time.

The variety of cakes ranges from the fluffy angel food, which should be eaten while still fresh, to the heavy fruit cake, which will keep for months. Some, like pound cake, are plain, require no frosting, and make a pleasing dessert to serve with coffee. Others are created in layers, separated by filling, coated with frosting, and decorated for visual appeal.

Since the ingredients listed in recipes for most cakes are expensive, some cooks tend to purchase less costly ingredients. We consider this unwise. Cake is judged by flavor, and the flavor depends greatly on the quality of ingredients —so always buy the best.

144

The lighter cakes may be improved in flavor by the addition of some sweet spice, such as mace, which is known as "the pound-cake spice." In heavier cakes, such as fruit cake and the true spice cakes, the stronger flavored spices—such as allspice, ginger, and black pepper—may be used. Up to ⅛ teaspoonful of black pepper included in the latter cake appears to enhance the flavor of the *other* spices, rather than impose its own characteristic flavor.

A perfect cake can be made if the recipe and the following basic rules are followed:

First, use a good recipe, and read it carefully before you start.

Then, assemble all utensils and ingredients. Be sure that you have standard measuring cups and spoons, mixing bowls with rounded bottoms, a wooden spoon for mixing (unless you have an electric mixer), rubber bowl scraper, a rotary or electric beater, a flour sifter, wire cake racks, baking pans of specified size and material, and an oven thermometer (unless your oven is reliably thermostatically controlled.)

Use only fresh, top-quality ingredients, because your finished cake will only be as good as the products that are used to create it. (For example, any person with a sensitive taste can tell the difference between cakes made with natural and synthetic vanilla flavoring.)

Before you start your cake, prepare your pans. Make sure that they are the size specified in the recipe. Unless you are making angel-food or sponge cakes, which require ungreased pans, grease the inside bottoms of the pans generously with unsalted fat and sprinkle lightly with flour—or, if preferred, you may line the pans with wax or brown paper.

Next, measure all ingredients accurately, never packing or shaking the measuring cup, except when measuring brown sugar, which should be *firmly packed* in the cup). As we go to press, news has reached us that one of the sugar companies is introducing a new, free-pouring brown sugar which does not need packing. We have not tried it. All our recipes were developed using the old-fashioned variety.

To mix the cake, shortening should be soft so that sugar can easily be mixed with it until creamy and fluffy, almost to the consistency of whipped cream. If soda is used, add it at this time. Spices and flavorings, such as vanilla extract, also should be blended with the shortening and sugar.

Beat in the eggs, one at a time, unless otherwise specified. (All the cake recipes in this book were tested using *large* eggs.) Sift flour before measuring and sift again with baking powder, if the latter is used. Salt may be sifted with flour or it may be added along with the spices to the shortening. Add the flour and the milk or other liquid ingredients alternately, adding about ⅓ of each at a time, beginning with the flour. Beat the batter about 20 seconds after each addition. (If all the ingredients were to be mixed at one time, a longer total mixing time would be required to produce equally uniform mixing. This overbeating would result in a coarse-textured cake.)

Pour batter into pans, placing an equal quantity in each pan and spreading it evenly out to the edges of the pans.

Unless otherwise directed, place pans in an oven preheated to the baking temperature specified in the recipe. Put rack in the middle of the oven where the temperature is most even. If you need two racks, have one slightly above the middle and the other slightly below. Do not place the racks too close together or the pans too close to the oven walls. The heat must circulate freely on all sides of each pan. Time your cake to bake the number of minutes or hours given in the recipe. Do not even peek until the given minimum time has elapsed. To test the cake, open oven door and press a finger lightly against the center of the top of the cake. If the cake springs back, leaving no impression, it is done. Or test cake with a toothpick or wire cake tester. Stick it into the center. If it comes out clean, the cake is done.

Let cakes cool in pans: 10 minutes for layer cakes and 20 minutes for loaf cakes. Then turn them out onto wire racks to cool. Once cool, frosting, if desired, may then be applied.

ANGEL-FOOD CAKES

Tall and tender angel-food cakes are assured if the following rules are observed:

Have all ingredients at room temperature.

Separate eggs carefully, making sure that not even a trace of yolk is mixed with egg whites.

Beat whites until stiff enough to form peaks that bend the slightest bit when the beater is removed; but avoid overbeating to the point where the whites have a dull, dry appearance. (Overbeaten eggs make a tough, dry, coarse-textured cake.)

You can't win, either, if you underbeat the eggs: this makes a tough, leathery cake, as does baking at too high a temperature.

When folding together sugar and eggs, turn spatula gently and no longer than needed to combine ingredients.

Pour batter into ungreased pan that has been rinsed in cold water.

Place in cold oven and set oven control to "slow" (300° F.).

Do not attempt to remove cake from pan until it is completely cold. Many standard recipes suggest that the pan be inverted during the cooling period. Actually, this seems to have little effect, since a spatula must be used to loosen the cooled cake from the side of the pan.

Cut cake with a sharp knife which has been dipped in hot water and use a sawing motion.

THE ROAD TO
THE KITCHEN

BEEFSTEAK CAKE

How this fine-grained, old-fashioned cake from Williamsburg, Virginia, came to be called "Beefsteak Cake" will probably remain a mystery forever. We were unable to unearth the answer in our research, but the most likely reason for the name is that the cake was served after a beefsteak dinner.

3¼ cups sifted all-purpose flour
3 teaspoons double-acting
   baking powder
¾ teaspoon salt

2½ cups sugar
1 cup (2 sticks) soft butter *or*
   margarine
4 large eggs
1 cup milk
1 teaspoon vanilla extract

3 tablespoons unsulphured molasses
½ teaspoon ground allspice
½ teaspoon ground cinnamon
½ teaspoon ground cloves

Brown Sugar Frosting*

Sift together the first 3 ingredients and set aside. Gradually add sugar to butter or margarine. Beat in eggs, 1 at a time. Add flour mixture alternately with the milk. Add vanilla extract. Beat batter ½ minute. Pour ⅔ of the batter into 2 well-greased, lightly floured, 9-inch round layer-cake pans. Stir molasses and spices into the remaining batter and turn into a third pan.

    Bake each 35 minutes or until done in a preheated moderate oven (375° F.). Remove from oven. Cool in pans 10 minutes. Turn onto wire racks to finish cooling. Frost with Brown Sugar Frosting in

   *An asterisk after the name of a dish indicates that the recipe for this dish appears in the book. Consult the Index for the page number.

layer-cake fashion, with the dark layer in the middle.

YIELD: One 9-inch, 3-layer cake

BIRTHDAY CAKE

2 cups sifted cake flour
2 teaspoons double-acting
   baking powder
¼ teaspoon salt

½ teaspoon ground mace
½ cup shortening
1¼ cups sugar
1½ teaspoons vanilla extract
4 large egg whites, unbeaten
½ cup milk
Birthday Cake Filling and Frosting*

Sift together the first 3 ingredients and set aside. Mix mace with shortening. Gradually blend in sugar and vanilla extract. Beat until fluffy. Beat in 1 egg white at a time. Stir in flour mixture alternately with milk. Beat batter ½ minute. Turn into 2 well-greased, lightly floured, 8-inch round layer-cake pans.

    Bake in a preheated moderate oven (375° F.) 25 minutes or until cake tester inserted in center comes out clean. Cool in pans 10 minutes. Turn onto a wire rack to finish cooling. Spread Birthday Cake Filling between layers and ice the cake with remaining Frosting. Store airtight.

YIELD: One 8-inch, 2-layer cake

BLACK PEPPER SPICE CAKE

2½ cups sifted cake flour
1 teaspoon double-acting
   baking powder
1 teaspoon salt

¾ teaspoon soda
¾ teaspoon ground cloves
¾ teaspoon ground cinnamon
⅛ teaspoon ground black pepper
1½ teaspoons vanilla extract
¾ cup shortening

1 cup sugar
¾ cup light-brown sugar
3 large eggs
1 cup sour milk
Brown Sugar Seven-Minute Frosting*

Sift the first 3 ingredients together and set aside. Combine the next 6 ingredients and mix well. Gradually blend in sugars. Beat in eggs, 1 at a time. Stir in ⅓ of the flour mixture. Then add ½ cup sour milk. Repeat, using remaining ⅔ flour mixture and ½ cup milk. Turn batter into 3 well-greased, lightly floured 9-inch round cake pans. Bake in a preheated moderate oven (375° F.) 25 minutes or until a cake tester or toothpick inserted in the center comes out clean. Cool 10 minutes in pans. Turn out onto wire racks to finish cooling. Frost with Brown Sugar Seven-Minute Frosting.

YIELD: One 9-inch, 3-layer cake

SPICED CARROT CAKE

1 teaspoon ground cinnamon
1 teaspoon ground mace
½ teaspoon salt
1 cup (2 sticks) soft butter *or*
   margarine

2 cups sugar
4 large eggs
1½ cups finely grated carrots

⅔ cup chopped nuts
2½ cups sifted all-purpose flour
3 teaspoons double-acting
   baking powder
⅓ cup hot water
Date and Nut Filling*
Brown Sugar Seven-Minute Frosting*

Mix together first 4 ingredients. Gradually add sugar, mixing well after each addition. Beat in eggs, 1 at a time. Stir in carrots and nuts. Sift flour with baking powder and add alternately with water. Beat batter ½ minute.

Turn mixture into 2 well-greased, lightly floured, 9-inch round layer-cake pans. Bake in a preheated moderate oven (375° F.) 35 minutes or until cake tester inserted in center comes out clean. Cool in pan 10 minutes. Turn out onto wire racks to finish cooling.

Put layers together with Date and Nut Filling. Frost with Brown Sugar Seven-Minute Frosting. Decorate with walnut or pecan halves, if desired.

YIELD: One 9-inch, 2-layer cake

CINNAMON CHOCOLATE CAKE

2⅔ cups sifted all-purpose flour
¾ cup cocoa
1 teaspoon salt

2¼ cups light-brown sugar
¾ cup shortening
1½ teaspoons soda
¾ teaspoon ground cinnamon
¼ teaspoon ground cloves
2 teaspoons vanilla extract

2 large eggs
1½ cups sour milk *or* buttermilk
Mocha Frosting*

Sift the first 3 ingredients together and set aside. Gradually add 1 cup brown sugar to shortening, along with next 4 ingredients. Beat in 1 egg. Gradually add rest of brown sugar and remaining egg. Add flour mixture alternately with milk. Beat batter ½ minute. Turn into 3 well-greased, lightly floured, 9-inch round layer-cake pans. Bake in a preheated moderate oven (375° F.) 30 minutes or until a cake tester inserted in center comes out clean. Cool in pans 10 minutes. Remove from pans onto wire racks to finish cooling. Frost with Mocha Frosting.

YIELD: One 9-inch, 3-layer cake

OLD-FASHIONED DEVIL'S FOOD CAKE

When Professor Gussie Tabb of the home economics staff at Georgia Women's College taught us how to bake this cake, we had to grate a whole cupful of unsweetened chocolate. Since then, the recipe has been adapted to use melted chocolate, and your arms don't ache for a week after making it. This was a regular Sunday-best cake in our home.

4 squares (4 ounces) unsweetened
   chocolate
1 cup sugar
1 cup water
2½ cups sifted all-purpose flour

1 teaspoon double-acting
   baking powder
½ teaspoon salt
¾ teaspoon ground cinnamon
¼ teaspoon ground cloves
1 teaspoon soda
2 teaspoons vanilla extract
1 cup (2 sticks) soft butter *or* margarine
¾ cup sugar
3 large eggs
½ cup buttermilk *or* sour milk
Chocolate Cream Frosting*

Combine the first 3 ingredients in a saucepan and cook over low heat until chocolate is thoroughly melted and the mixture is of smooth custard consistency, stirring frequently to prevent scorching. Cool. Sift together next 3 ingredients and set aside. Cream together the next 5 ingredients. Gradually blend in sugar. Beat in eggs, 1 at a time. Stir in ½ cup of the flour mixture. Blend in cooled chocolate. Add remaining flour mixture alternately with milk. Beat batter ½ minute.

Turn into 2 well-greased, lightly floured, 9-inch round layer-cake pans. Bake in preheated moderate oven (375° F.) 30 minutes or until done. Cool in pans 10 minutes. Turn onto wire racks to finish cooling. Frost with Chocolate Cream Frosting.

YIELD: One 9-inch, 2-layer cake

POTATO FUDGE CAKE

It may seem a bit odd to put grated, raw potatoes in a chocolate cake; but the bland potato flavor is covered by the chocolate and spices and the potatoes do keep the cake moist.

2¼ cups sifted cake flour
2¼ teaspoons double-acting
   baking powder
¾ teaspoon salt

½ teaspoon ground allspice
½ teaspoon ground cloves
½ teaspoon ground cinnamon
1 cup shortening
2 cups sugar
2 squares (2 ounces) unsweetened
  chocolate, melted

1 cup grated raw potatoes
1½ teaspoons vanilla extract
½ cup chopped almonds

4 large eggs
½ cup milk
Potato Fudge Frosting*

Sift first 3 ingredients together and set aside. Mix spices with shortening. Gradually add sugar. Blend in chocolate. Add next 3 ingredients. Beat in eggs, 1 at a time. Add flour mixture alternately with milk. Beat batter ½ minute. Turn into 2 well-greased, lightly floured, 9 x 9 x 2-inch baking pans. Bake in a preheated moderate oven (375° F.) 35 minutes or until done. Cool in pans 10 minutes. Turn out onto wire rack to finish cooling. Frost with Potato Fudge Frosting.

YIELD: One 9-inch square, 2-layer cake

SOUR CREAM CHOCOLATE CAKE

½ cup shortening
1 teaspoon soda
¼ teaspoon salt
½ teaspoon ground cinnamon
2 teaspoons vanilla extract

1¾ cups sugar
4 squares (4 ounces) unsweetened
  chocolate, melted
2 large eggs
2 cups sifted cake flour
½ cup sour cream
¾ cup strong, cold coffee
Brown Sugar Frosting*

Mix together first 5 ingredients. Gradually blend in 1 cup of the sugar. Stir in chocolate. Gradually add remaining sugar, mixing well. Beat in eggs, 1 at a time. Stir in flour alternately with sour cream and coffee. Beat batter ½ minute. Turn into 2 well-greased, lightly floured, 8 x 8 x 2-inch pans.

Bake in a preheated moderate oven (375° F.) 35 to 40 minutes, or until done. Cool in pans 10 minutes. Turn out onto wire racks to finish cooling. Frost with Brown Sugar Frosting.

YIELD: One 8-inch square, 2-layer cake

CRANBERRY MERINGUE CAKE

2 cups sifted all-purpose flour
½ teaspoon salt
2 teaspoons double-acting
  baking powder

1 teaspoon ground mace
1 tablespoon grated orange rind
1 teaspoon grated lemon rind
⅔ cup shortening

1⅓ cups sugar
3 large eggs
⅔ cup milk
Jellied Whole Fresh Cranberries
  (see below)
Meringue* for 8-inch pie

Sift together the first 3 ingredients and set aside. Combine next 4 ingredients. Gradually blend in sugar. Beat in eggs, 1 at a time. Add flour mixture alternately with milk, beginning with flour. Turn batter into 2 well-greased, lightly floured, 8-inch round layer-cake pans.

Bake in a preheated moderate oven (375° F.) 30 minutes or until a cake tester inserted in the center comes out clean. Cool in pans 10 minutes. Turn out onto wire racks to finish cooling.

Spread Jellied Whole Fresh Cranberries between layers. Place cake on a cooky sheet or on an ovenproof cake plate. Spread top and sides with Meringue, building the meringue up around the rim to form a cradle for cranberries. Bake in a preheated moderate oven (375° F.) 10 to 15 minutes or until meringue has lightly browned. Cool. Spread cranberries over top of cake.

JELLIED WHOLE FRESH CRANBERRIES
4 cups fresh cranberries
2 cups sugar
¾ cup water
¼ teaspoon salt
1 tablespoon cornstarch
1 tablespoon water

Wash cranberries. Place in a saucepan with sugar, water, and salt. Cover. Bring to boiling point and cook 8 minutes or until skins pop. Blend cornstarch with the 1 tablespoon water. Add to cranberries. Cook 1 minute. Remove from heat, cool, and chill. Follow directions given above.

YIELD: One 8-inch, 2-layer cake

SPICED 1-2-3-4 CAKE
3 cups sifted all-purpose flour
4 teaspoons double-acting
  baking powder
¾ teaspoon salt

2 teaspoons pumpkin pie spice
1 cup (2 sticks) butter *or* margarine
2 cups sugar
4 large eggs
1 cup milk
1½ teaspoons vanilla extract
Brown Sugar Seven-Minute Frosting*

Sift together the first 3 ingredients and set aside. Blend pumpkin pie spice with soft-

ened butter or margarine. Gradually add sugar, mixing well after each addition. Beat in 1 egg. Then stir in ½ cup of the flour mixture. Beat in remaining eggs, 1 at a time. Add remaining flour mixture alternately with milk and vanilla extract. Beat batter ½ minute.

Turn into 3 well-greased, lightly floured, 9-inch round layer-cake pans. Bake in a preheated moderate oven (375° F.) 25 minutes or until a toothpick inserted in the center comes out clean. Cool cake in pans 10 minutes. Turn out onto wire rack to finish cooling. Frost with Brown Sugar Seven-Minute Frosting. Store in a tightly closed box.

YIELD: One 9-inch, 3-layer cake

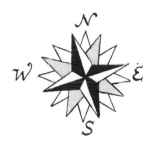

GUM DROP CAKE
3 cups sifted all-purpose flour
4½ teaspoons double-acting
  baking powder
¾ teaspoon salt

1 cup chopped gum drops
1 teaspoon ground mace
3 teaspoons vanilla extract
¾ cup shortening
1¾ cups sugar
3 large eggs
2 large egg yolks
1 cup milk
Marshmallow Seven-Minute Frosting*

Sift together first 3 ingredients. Blend in gum drops and set aside to use later. Mix mace and vanilla extract with shortening.

Add sugar gradually. Beat in whole eggs and egg yolks, 1 at a time. Add flour mixture alternately with milk.

Grease three, 9-inch round layer-cake pans. Line with brown or wax paper cut to fit bottoms of pans. Grease and flour paper lightly. Bake in a preheated moderate oven (375° F.) 25 minutes or until a toothpick inserted in the center comes out clean. Cool cakes in pans 10 minutes. Turn onto wire racks to finish cooling. Frost with Marshmallow Seven-Minute Frosting.

YIELD: One 9-inch, 3-layer cake

ORANGE-COCONUT CAKE

2 cups sifted all-purpose flour
2 teaspoons double-acting
   baking powder
½ teaspoon salt
¾ teaspoon ground mace
⅔ cup shortening
2 teaspoons grated orange rind
½ teaspoon grated lemon rind
1⅓ cups sugar
2 large eggs
1 large egg yolk
⅔ cup fresh orange juice
Fresh Coconut Seven-Minute Frosting*

Sift together first 3 ingredients and set aside. Mix together next 4 ingredients. Gradually blend in sugar. Beat in eggs and yolk, 1 at a time. Add flour mixture alternately with fresh orange juice, mixing well after each addition, beginning and ending with flour.

Pour batter into 2 well-greased, lightly floured, 8-inch round layer-cake pans. Bake in a preheated moderate oven (375° F.) 25 minutes or until a cake tester or toothpick inserted into center comes out clean. Cool in pans 10 minutes. Turn out on wire racks to finish cooling. Frost with Fresh Coconut Seven-Minute Frosting. Sprinkle with additional fresh coconut. If desired, garnish with sliced bananas, dipped first in fresh lemon or lime juice.

YIELD: One 8-inch, 2-layer cake

BOHEMIAN POPPY SEED CAKE

¾ cup poppy seed
¾ cup milk
2¼ cups sifted all-purpose flour
4 teaspoons double-acting
   baking powder
½ teaspoon salt
1½ cups sugar
½ cup shortening
2 teaspoons vanilla extract
½ cup milk
3 large egg whites
Chocolate Cream Frosting*

Soak poppy seed in milk overnight. Sift together the next 3 ingredients and set aside. Gradually blend sugar into shortening along with vanilla extract. Add soaked poppy seed alternately with flour mixture and milk. Beat egg whites until they stand in soft, stiff peaks and gently fold into the batter. Turn into 2 well-greased, lightly floured, 9-inch round layer-cake pans. Bake in a preheated moderate oven (350° F.) 30 minutes or until a toothpick inserted in the center comes out clean. Cool in pans 10 minutes. Turn onto wire racks to finish cooling. Frost with Chocolate Cream Frosting.

YIELD: One 9-inch, 2-layer cake

PUMPKIN SPICE CAKE

Here's a hearty fall-into-winter cake, fine-textured and beautifully spiced. The addition of the pumpkin helps keep the cake moist—but you'll hardly notice the flavor.

GRATED FRESH APPLE CAKE

This cake must be made with all-purpose flour and by the one-bowl method of mixing. Use fall apples such as Northern Spy, McIntosh, Winesap, or Jonathans, rather than Greenings or Delicious. This cake has fine flavor and excellent keeping qualities if stored in a cake safe.

2 cups sifted all-purpose flour
1¼ cups light-brown sugar
1 teaspoon salt
1 teaspoon soda
1 teaspoon double-acting
   baking powder
½ teaspoon ground nutmeg

½ cup shortening
1½ cups coarsely grated uncooked
   apples
2 tablespoons milk
2 large eggs
Butterscotch Sauce* *or* Lemon Sauce*

Sift the first 6 ingredients together in a mixing bowl. Add shortening, apples, and milk. Mix just enough to dampen ingredients. Beat 2 minutes by hand or with an electric beater at low speed. Add eggs and beat 2 more minutes at low speed.

Turn batter into a well-greased, lightly floured 9 x 9 x 2-inch pan. Bake in a preheated moderate oven (350° F.) 45 minutes or until a cake tester inserted in center comes out clean. Cool in pan 10 minutes. Turn out onto a wire rack to finish cooling. Serve, cut into squares, topped with Butterscotch Sauce or, if preferred, with Lemon Sauce.

YIELD: One 9-inch square cake

ABRAHAM LINCOLN MARBLE CAKE

2 cups sifted all-purpose flour
½ teaspoon salt

2 cups sifted cake flour
1½ cups light-brown sugar
¾ teaspoon salt
2 teaspoons double-acting
   baking powder
¼ teaspoon soda
½ teaspoon ground cloves
½ teaspoon ground cinnamon
½ teaspoon ground mace
1 teaspoon ground ginger

½ cup shortening
¾ cup dry, mashed, cooked pumpkin
2 large eggs
¼ cup milk
Lemon Frosting*

Sift the first 9 ingredients together into the bowl of an electric mixer. Add shortening and pumpkin. Mix by hand just enough to dampen the ingredients. Beat with an electric beater 2 minutes at low speed. Add eggs and milk and beat 2 minutes more.

Turn into 2 well-greased, lightly floured, 8-inch round layer-cake pans. Bake in a preheated moderate oven (375° F.) 35 minutes or until a toothpick inserted in the center comes out clean. Cool in pans 10 minutes. Turn onto wire racks to finish cooling. Frost with Lemon Frosting.

YIELD: One 8-inch, 2-layer cake

2 teaspoons double-acting
  baking powder

½ cup shortening
1 cup sugar
1½ teaspoons vanilla extract

2 large eggs
⅔ cup milk
¼ cup unsulphured molasses
1 teaspoon ground cinnamon
¼ teaspoon ground cloves

Sift together the first 3 ingredients and set aside. Cream together the next 3 ingredients. Beat in eggs, 1 at a time. Add milk alternately with flour mixture. Beat batter ½ minute. Place ⅓ of the batter in a small bowl. Stir in molasses and spices.

Spoon light and dark batters alternately into a well-greased, lightly floured, 9 x 9 x 2-inch pan or into a 9 x 3-inch tube pan. Bake the 9 x 9 x 2-inch 45 minutes in a preheated moderate oven (350° F.), the tube cake in a slow oven (325° F.) 1 hour or until a cake tester inserted in the center comes out clean. Cool in pan 10 minutes. Turn onto a wire rack to finish cooling. Serve without frosting, or frost as desired with coconut, chocolate, or Browned Butter Frosting.*

YIELD: One 9-inch square or 9-inch tube cake

BLUEBERRY CAKE WITH LEMON SAUCE

1 teaspoon ground mace
½ teaspoon soda
¼ teaspoon salt
1½ teaspoons vanilla extract
½ cup (1 stick) soft butter *or* margarine

1 cup sugar
3 large eggs
2 cups sifted all-purpose flour
¾ cup sour milk *or* buttermilk
1 cup fresh blueberries
1 tablespoon flour
Lemon Sauce*

Blend together the first 5 ingredients. Gradually add sugar. Beat in eggs, 1 at a time. Add flour alternately with milk.

Wash blueberries, drain well, and dredge in 1 tablespoon flour. Carefully stir into batter. Turn into a well-greased, lightly floured 9 x 9 x 2-inch pan. Bake in a preheated moderate oven (350° F.) 45 minutes or until a toothpick inserted in center comes out clean. Cut into squares. Serve hot with Lemon Sauce.

YIELD: One 9-inch square cake

SPICED BLUEBERRY MARY ANN CAKE

1½ cups sifted all-purpose flour
1½ teaspoons double-acting
  baking powder
½ teaspoon salt

¾ teaspoon ground cinnamon
¾ teaspoon ground nutmeg
⅓ cup shortening

½ cup sugar
2 large eggs
¾ cup milk

2 cups fresh blueberries
5 tablespoons sugar
½ cup heavy cream, whipped
Ground nutmeg

Sift together the first 3 ingredients and set aside. Blend spices with shortening. Gradually mix in the ½ cup sugar. Beat in eggs, 1 at a time. Add flour mixture alternately with milk. Beat batter ½ minute.

Pour batter into an 8½-inch well-greased, lightly floured Mary Ann cake pan, or if one is not available, bake in one 9-inch round layer-cake pan. Bake in a preheated moderate oven (375° F.) 35 to 40 minutes or until a toothpick inserted in center comes out clean. Cool in pan 10 minutes. Turn onto wire rack to finish cooling.

Top with blueberries sweetened with 4 tablespoons of the sugar. Garnish with a wreath of whipped cream sweetened with the remaining 1 tablespoon sugar. Sprinkle cream with nutmeg.

YIELD: One 8½ or 9-inch cake

SPICED BLUEBERRY TEA SQUARES

Don't be surprised to find that the blueberries have dropped to the bottom of the baked cake. It's right where they belong.

1¾ cups sifted all-purpose flour
2 teaspoons double-acting
   baking powder
½ teaspoon salt
½ teaspoon ground ginger
½ teaspoon ground nutmeg
⅓ cup shortening
1 cup sugar
2 large eggs
⅔ cup milk
1½ cups fresh blueberries

2 tablespoons flour
1 tablespoon sugar

Sift first 3 ingredients together and set aside. Mix spices with shortening. Blend in sugar. Beat in eggs, 1 at a time. Add flour mixture alternately with milk. Mix last 3 ingredients together and carefully stir into the batter.

Turn batter into a well-greased, lightly floured 9 x 9 x 2-inch pan. Bake in a preheated moderate oven (375° F.) 35 to 40 minutes or until done. Cut into squares.

YIELD: One 9-inch square cake

CINNAMON CRUMB CAKE

2 cups sifted all-purpose flour
2 teaspoons double-acting
   baking powder
½ teaspoon salt

½ cup shortening
2 teaspoons vanilla extract
1 cup sugar
2 large eggs
1 cup chopped dates *or* seedless raisins
1 cup milk
⅔ cup coarsely chopped pecans

¾ cup light-brown sugar
1 teaspoon ground cinnamon
2 tablespoons butter *or* margarine
3 tablespoons flour

¼ cup sifted confectioners' sugar
2 teaspoons cream
½ teaspoon vanilla extract

Sift together first 3 ingredients and set aside. Blend shortening with vanilla extract. Gradually mix in sugar. Beat in eggs, 1 at a time. Stir in dates or raisins. Add flour mixture alternately with milk.

Turn into a well-greased and lightly floured 9 x 9 x 2-inch pan and sprinkle pecans over the top. Mix next 4 ingredients and sprinkle over the nuts. Bake in a preheated moderate oven (350° F.) 1 hour and 10 minutes, or until a cake tester inserted in the center comes out clean. Mix remaining ingredients and spread over cake while it is still warm.

YIELD: One 9-inch square cake

COCONUT-PINEAPPLE CAKE

1 cup sifted all-purpose flour
1½ teaspoons double-acting
    baking powder
¼ teaspoon salt
1 teaspoon ground allspice
_____
2 large eggs
1 cup sugar
2 tablespoons shortening
½ cup hot milk
Coconut-Pineapple Topping *(see below)*

Sift together first 4 ingredients and set aside. Beat eggs until light and lemon-colored. Gradually beat in sugar. Add shortening to hot milk. Stir until melted. Add flour mixture and hot milk alternately to eggs and sugar.

   Turn into a well-greased, lightly-floured 8 x 8 x 2-inch pan. Bake in a preheated moderate oven (350° F.) 40 minutes or until a toothpick inserted in center comes out clean. Remove from oven and spread with Coconut-Pineapple Topping. Place under broiler until brown and bubbly, watching closely to prevent burning.

COCONUT-PINEAPPLE TOPPING

3 tablespoons melted butter *or*
    margarine
⅓ cup drained, crushed pineapple
½ cup flaked coconut
½ cup light-brown sugar
¼ teaspoon ground allspice

Combine all ingredients and mix well.

YIELD: One 8-inch square cake

LAZY DAISY CHOCOLATE CAKE

1½ cups sifted all-purpose flour
1 cup light-brown sugar
3 tablespoons cocoa
1 teaspoon soda
½ teaspoon salt
1 teaspoon ground cinnamon
1 teaspoon ground ginger
½ teaspoon ground cloves
_____
6 tablespoons cooking oil
1 tablespoon cider vinegar
1½ teaspoons vanilla extract
1 cup water
_____
2 tablespoons butter *or* margarine
6 tablespoons dark-brown sugar
2 tablespoons undiluted evaporated milk
⅓ cup chopped pecans

Sift the first 8 ingredients together into an 8 x 8 x 2-inch baking pan. Make 3 holes in the flour mixture: pour oil in one, vinegar in the second, and vanilla extract in the third. Pour water over all. Stir with a fork until all ingredients are blended (do not remove batter from pan).

Bake in a preheated moderate oven (350° F.) 45 minutes or until a cake tester inserted in the center comes out clean. Soften butter or margarine and blend with rest of ingredients. Spread over hot cake. Place under broiler to brown.

YIELD: One 8-inch square cake

ONE-EGG SPICE CAKE

Here's a fine picnic or busy-day cake. Serve it right from the pan to avoid disturbing the topping.

1½ cups sifted all-purpose flour
¾ teaspoon salt
2 teaspoons double-acting
    baking powder
⅓ cup shortening
½ teaspoon ground ginger
½ teaspoon ground cinnamon
½ teaspoon ground allspice
1 cup sugar
1 large egg
¾ cup milk
Broiled Coconut Topping*

Sift together the first 3 ingredients and set aside to use later. Mix shortening with spices. Gradually blend in sugar. Beat in egg. Add flour mixture alternately with milk. Beat batter ½ minute.

Turn batter into a well-greased, lightly floured 9 x 9 x 2-inch pan. Bake in a preheated moderate oven (350° F.) 35 minutes or until a toothpick inserted in center comes out clean. Spread cake, while hot, with Broiled Coconut Topping. Place under broiler until topping is bubbly and brown (about 5 minutes), watching closely to prevent burning.

YIELD: One 9-inch square cake

FRESH PEACH CAKE

4 medium (1 pound) fresh peaches
⅔ cup sugar
1 tablespoon flour
⅛ teaspoon salt
¼ teaspoon ground cinnamon
¼ cup (½ stick) butter *or* margarine
1 cup sifted all-purpose flour
½ cup sugar
1 teaspoon double-acting
    baking powder
¼ teaspoon salt
1 large egg, beaten
¼ cup milk
2 tablespoons melted shortening
Heavy cream, whipped (optional)

Wash, peel, and slice peaches. Combine next 4 ingredients. Add peaches. Mix well and turn into an 8 x 8 x 2-inch baking pan. Dot with butter or margarine.

Sift together the next 4 ingredients. Combine egg and milk and add to dry ingredients along with melted shortening. Mix only until ingredients are blended. (DO NOT OVERBEAT.) Spread over peaches, being sure to cover them uniformly.

Bake in a preheated hot oven (425° F.) 30 minutes or until cake has browned and cooked all the way through to the fruit. To serve, cut into squares and turn into serving dishes cake-side down. Top with whipped cream, if desired.

YIELD: One 8-inch square cake

SESAME SEED
BUTTER CAKE

2 cups sifted all-purpose flour
½ teaspoon salt
2 teaspoons double-acting

baking powder

¼ cup Sautéed Sesame Seed *(see below)*
1 cup sugar
1 teaspoon vanilla extract
½ cup (1 stick) soft butter *or* margarine
2 large eggs
1 cup milk
Sesame Seed Frosting *(see below)*
1 tablespoon Sautéed Sesame Seed
  (see below)

Sift the first 3 ingredients together, add the ¼ cup Sautéed Sesame Seed, and set aside. Gradually blend sugar and vanilla extract with butter or margarine. Beat in eggs, 1 at a time. Add flour mixture alternately with milk. Beat batter ½ minute. Turn mixture into a well-greased, lightly floured 9 x 9 x 2-inch pan. Bake in a preheated moderate oven (350° F.) 35 minutes or until a cake tester or toothpick inserted into the center comes out clean. Cool cake in pan 10 minutes. Turn out onto a wire rack to finish cooling. Spread top and sides with Sesame Seed Frosting and sprinkle with the 1 tablespoon Sautéed Sesame Seed.

SAUTEED SESAME SEED

Melt 1½ tablespoons butter or margarine in a skillet. Add ½ cup sesame seed. Stir and cook over moderate heat until seeds are golden.

SESAME SEED FROSTING

2 tablespoons butter *or* margarine
1⅓ cups sifted confectioners' sugar
About 2 teaspoons milk
½ teaspoon vanilla extract
3 tablespoons Sautéed Sesame Seed

Heat butter or margarine in a saucepan until golden. Remove from heat and stir in sugar and enough milk to make frost-ing of smooth, spreading consistency. Add vanilla extract and sesame seed. Mix well.

YIELD: One 9-inch square cake

SPICED VELVET CAKE

2 cups sifted all-purpose flour
1 teaspoon double-acting
  baking powder
½ teaspoon salt

1 teaspoon soda
¾ teaspoon ground cinnamon
½ teaspoon ground cloves
½ teaspoon ground nutmeg
½ cup shortening
1 cup sugar
3 tablespoons honey *or*
  unsulphured molasses
1 large egg
1 cup sour milk *or* buttermilk
Heavy cream, whipped (optional)

Sift together the first 3 ingredients and set aside. Add soda and spices to shortening and mix well. Gradually blend in sugar and honey or molasses. Beat in egg. Add flour mixture alternately with milk. Beat batter ½ minute.

Turn batter into a well-greased, lightly floured 9 x 9 x 2-inch pan. Bake in a preheated moderate oven (350° F.) 45 minutes or until a toothpick inserted in the center comes out clean. Cut into squares and serve with whipped cream if desired.

YIELD: One 9-inch square cake

SPICED APPLESAUCE-DATE CAKE

½ teaspoon soda
½ teaspoon salt
½ teaspoon ground cloves
½ teaspoon ground cinnamon
½ teaspoon ground nutmeg

1½ teaspoons grated lemon rind
½ cup (1 stick) soft butter *or* margarine
___
1 cup sugar
2 large eggs
1 tablespoon cold, strong coffee
1 cup applesauce
1 cup chopped dates
2 cups sifted all-purpose flour

Mix together first 7 ingredients. Gradually blend in sugar. Beat in eggs, 1 at a time. Stir in coffee and applesauce. Combine dates and flour and gradually add to the mixture. Beat batter ½ minute. Turn into a well-greased, lightly floured, 9 x 5 x 3-inch loaf pan. Bake in a preheated slow oven (325° F.) 1½ hours or until cake tester inserted in center comes out clean. Let cool in pan 10 minutes. Turn out onto wire rack to finish cooling.

YIELD: One 9-inch loaf cake

PRESIDENT HARRISON MOLASSES CAKE

Our great-grandmothers may not have had the vote, but judging from the titles of many old recipes, they certainly were conversant with current events.

¼ teaspoon salt
1 teaspoon soda
½ teaspoon ground cloves
½ cup (1 stick) soft butter *or* margarine
___
½ cup sugar
1 cup unsulphured molasses
2 large eggs
2½ cups sifted all-purpose flour
½ cup sour cream
Browned Butter Frosting*

Blend the first 4 ingredients together until fluffy. Gradually add sugar, mixing well.

Mix in molasses and ½ cup of the flour. Beat in eggs, 1 at a time. Add remaining flour alternately with sour cream. Beat batter ½ minute.

Turn into a well-greased, lightly floured 9 x 5 x 3-inch loaf pan. Bake in a preheated slow oven (325° F.) 1¼ hours. Cool in pan 20 minutes. Turn onto a wire rack to finish cooling. When cold, frost with Browned Butter Frosting. Store airtight.

YIELD: One 9-inch loaf cake

FOURTH-OF-JULY CAKE

Fourth-of-July Cake is a rich, but not-too-sweet, yeast coffee cake. In Colonial days it was decorated with a wreath of gilded boxwood sprays or blueberry clusters and leaves. An excellent choice for Sunday brunch, afternoon tea, or between-meals snack.

2 envelopes active dry yeast
1 cup warm water (110° to 115° F.)
1½ cups sugar

4½ cups sifted all-purpose flour
1 cup (2 sticks) butter *or* margarine
1 teaspoon salt
1½ teaspoons ground ginger
1½ teaspoons ground mace
3 large eggs

2 tablespoons brandy
2 tablespoons sweet sherry
1 cup seedless raisins
1 cup dried currants
½ cup thinly sliced citron

Butter Cream Frosting*

Soften yeast in warm water. Beat in 2 tablespoons of the sugar and 1 cup of the flour. Cover and let rise in a warm place (80° to 85° F.) until double in size.

Blend butter or margarine with salt, spices and remaining sugar. Beat in eggs, 1 at a time. Add next 5 ingredients. Mix well. Beat in remaining flour and continue beating until batter is smooth. Turn into a greased 10 x 4-inch tube pan. Cover and let rise in a warm place until double in size, about 2 hours.

Bake in a preheated moderate oven (350° F.) 1 hour or until browned. Turn onto a wire rack to cool. Spread top and sides with Butter Cream Frosting. If desired, place boxwood or blueberry leaves around the top edge of cake.

YIELD: One 10-inch tube cake

EASTER MARBLE CAKE

3 cups sifted all-purpose flour
4 teaspoons double-acting
　　baking powder
¾ teaspoon salt

1 teaspoon ground mace
2 teaspoons vanilla extract
1 cup (2 sticks) soft butter *or*
　　margarine
2 cups sugar
5 large eggs, separated

1 cup milk
3 drops yellow food coloring (optional)
Easy White Frosting*

Sift together the first 3 ingredients and set aside. Mix mace and vanilla extract with butter or margarine. Gradually blend in sugar. Beat in 1 egg yolk. Add flour mixture alternately with milk. Beat 4 of the egg whites until they stand in soft, stiff peaks. (Save remaining egg white for frosting.) Fold into the mixture.

Divide the batter into 2 equal parts and blend the 4 egg yolks (and yellow food coloring, if used) into 1 part. Drop white and yellow batters alternately into a well-greased, lightly floured 10 x 4-inch tube pan. Bake in a preheated slow oven (325° F.) 1 hour and 20 minutes or until a cake tester inserted in the center comes out clean. Remove from oven. Cool in pan 20 minutes. Turn out onto a wire rack to finish cooling. Frost top and sides with Easy White Frosting.

YIELD: One 10-inch tube cake

GRANDMOTHER DAY'S GOLDEN SPICE CAKE

One of Grandmother's favorite cakes.

3 cups sifted all-purpose flour
2 teaspoons double-acting
　　baking powder

½ teaspoon salt
1 teaspoon ground ginger
1 teaspoon ground mace
1 tablespoon vanilla extract

¾ cup (1½ sticks) soft butter *or*
　　margarine
2 cups sugar
9 large egg yolks
1 large egg
1 cup milk

Sift together flour and baking powder and set aside to use later. Add the next 4 ingredients to softened butter or margarine and mix until blended. Gradually mix in 1 cup of the sugar. Beat in 3 egg yolks. Add remaining sugar alternately with remaining egg yolks, beating and mixing well after each addition. Beat in whole egg. Add flour mixture alternately with milk and beat batter ½ minute. Turn into a well-greased, lightly floured 10 x 4-inch tube pan.

Bake in a preheated slow oven (325° F.) 1¼ hours or until a cake tester inserted in the center comes out clean and top is golden brown. Cool in pan 20 minutes. Turn onto a wire rack to finish cooling. Store airtight. This cake is best made 2 or 3 days before it is to be served.

YIELD: One 10-inch tube cake

SPICED LEMON LOAF CAKE

4 cups sifted all-purpose flour
4 teaspoons double-acting
  baking powder

1 teaspoon ground mace
½ teaspoon salt
1 cup (2 sticks) soft butter *or*
  margarine

2 cups sugar
6 large eggs
1 teaspoon grated lemon rind
1 cup milk

Sift together flour and baking powder and set aside. Mix together the next 3 ingredients. Gradually add sugar, mixing well after each addition. Beat in eggs, 1 at a time. Add lemon rind. Add flour mixture alternately with milk. Beat batter ½ minute. Turn batter into a well-greased, lightly floured 10 x 4-inch tube pan.

Bake in a preheated slow oven (325° F.) 1¼ hours or until a cake tester inserted in the center comes out clean. Cool in pan 20 minutes. Turn out onto a wire rack to finish cooling. Store airtight.

YIELD: One 10-inch tube cake

POPPY SEED CAKE

2 cups sifted cake flour
2 teaspoons double-acting
  baking powder
7 tablespoons (2¼-ounce box)
  poppy seed
½ cup (1 stick) soft butter *or*
  margarine
2 teaspoons vanilla extract
1½ cups sugar
1 cup milk
¼ teaspoon salt
4 large egg whites
Confectioners' sugar (optional)

Sift together flour and baking powder. Mix in poppy seed and set aside. Mix together butter or margarine and vanilla extract. Gradually add 1¼ cups of the sugar, mixing well after each addition. Add flour alternately with milk. Add salt to egg whites and beat until they stand in soft, stiff peaks, into which gradually beat in remaining ¼ cup sugar. Carefully fold into the batter. Turn into a well-greased, lightly floured 9 x 3½-inch tube pan.

Bake in a preheated moderate oven (350° F.) 55 minutes or until a cake tester inserted in the center comes out clean. Cool in pan 10 minutes. Turn onto a wire rack to finish cooling. Sift confectioners' sugar over top, if desired.

YIELD: One 9-inch tube cake

GEORGIA POUND CAKE

1½ cups (3 sticks) soft butter *or*
  margarine
1½ teaspoons ground nutmeg *or* mace

1 teaspoon vanilla extract

1 pound sifted confectioners' sugar
6 large eggs
3 cups sifted all-purpose flour
Confectioners' sugar

Place butter or margarine in a mixing bowl. Blend in next 2 ingredients. Gradually stir in sugar. Beat in eggs, 1 at a time. Gradually stir in flour. Grease and lightly flour the bottom of a 10 x 4-inch tube pan. (DO NOT GREASE THE SIDES.) Bake in a preheated slow oven (325° F.) 1 hour and 20 minutes or until a cake tester inserted in the center comes out clean. Sprinkle top with confectioners' sugar. Store airtight.

YIELD: One 10-inch tube cake

OLD-FASHIONED POUND CAKE

1 cup (2 sticks) soft butter or
   margarine

1½ teaspoons ground nutmeg or mace
2 teaspoons vanilla extract
½ teaspoon salt (optional)

1⅔ cups sugar
6 large eggs
2 cups sifted all-purpose flour

Have all ingredients at room temperature. Place butter or margarine in a mixing bowl of the electric mixer. (This cake may be mixed by hand, but the cake will be slightly smaller.) Add next 3 ingredients and mix well. Add sugar gradually, mixing well after each addition. Beat in 5 of the eggs, 1 at a time. Gradually stir in flour. Beat in remaining egg. Grease the bottom only of a 9 x 3½-inch tube pan and flour it lightly. Spoon in batter. Place in a cold oven. Turn oven control to 300° F. (slow). Bake 1½ hours or until cake tester inserted in center comes

out clean. Cool in pan at least 20 minutes. Turn onto a wire rack to finish cooling. Store airtight in a tightly closed tin cake box.

YIELD: One 9-inch tube cake

QUEEN'S SPICE CAKE

This recipe was taken from Grandmother Day's handwritten cook book and in her old-fashioned hand was the comment: "This is very nice indeed."

Since alcoholic beverages aren't always available, this recipe was tested with orange juice. No reason why you can't follow Grandmother Day's example and use brandy or wine, of course.

2½ cups sifted all-purpose flour
2 teaspoons double-acting
   baking powder
½ teaspoon salt

1 teaspoon ground cinnamon
¾ teaspoon ground nutmeg
¼ teaspoon ground cloves
1 cup (2 sticks) soft butter or
margarine

1½ cups sugar
3 large eggs
1 cup seedless raisins
½ cup milk
⅓ cup fresh orange juice *or* brandy
Orange Glaze *(see below)*

Sift together the first 3 ingredients and set aside. Add spices to butter or margarine and stir until fluffy. Gradually blend in sugar. Beat in eggs, 1 at a time. Stir raisins into flour mixture and add alternately with milk and orange juice or brandy. (If raisins are too dry, steam in a sieve over boiling water.) Turn batter into a well-greased, lightly floured 9 x 3½-inch tube pan. Bake in a preheated moderate oven (350° F.) 1¼ hours or until a cake tester inserted in center comes out clean. Cool in pan 10 minutes. Turn onto a wire rack to finish cooling. Cover top with Orange Glaze, letting the glaze drip down the sides. Store airtight.

ORANGE GLAZE
Mix 4 teaspoons orange juice and ¼ teaspoon vanilla extract with 1 cup sifted confectioners' sugar.

YIELD: One 9-inch tube cake

SOUR CREAM SPICE CAKE
3 tablespoons soft butter *or* margarine
3 tablespoons dark corn syrup
1 cup chopped pecans
3 cups sifted cake flour
3 teaspoons double-acting
    baking powder
¼ teaspoon soda
¾ teaspoon salt
1 teaspoon ground ginger
1 teaspoon ground cinnamon
¾ teaspoon ground cloves
¾ cup (1½ sticks) soft butter *or*
    margarine

1½ cups sugar
3 large eggs
1½ cups sour cream
Confectioners' sugar

Mix together butter or margarine and corn syrup. Spread in bottom of a 9 x 3½-inch tube pan. Sprinkle with chopped nuts. Sift together flour and baking powder and set aside. Mix together the next 6 ingredients. Gradually blend in sugar. Beat in eggs, 1 at a time. Add flour mixture alternately with sour cream. Turn batter into the prepared tube pan.

Bake in a preheated moderate oven (325° F.) 1 hour 20 minutes or until a cake tester inserted in the center comes out clean. Turn out onto a wire rack immediately. Cool. Sprinkle with sifted confectioners' sugar.

YIELD: One 9-inch tube cake

SPICED RUM CAKE
2½ cups sifted all-purpose flour
2 teaspoons double-acting
    baking powder
½ teaspoon salt
1 cup raisins
1 cup (2 sticks) soft butter *or*
    margarine
1 teaspoon grated lemon rind
1 teaspoon ground cinnamon
1 teaspoon ground ginger
½ teaspoon ground cloves
½ teaspoon soda
2 cups sugar
2 large eggs
1 cup sour milk
½ cup water
2 tablespoons rum *or* 1 tablespoon
    rum extract

Sift together the first 3 ingredients, mix with raisins, and set aside. Blend together the next 6 ingredients. Gradually mix in 1 cup of the sugar. Beat in eggs, 1 at a time. Add flour mixture alternately with milk. Beat batter ½ minute. Turn into a well-greased, lightly floured 9 x 3½-inch tube pan.

Bake in a preheated moderate oven (350° F.) 1 hour or until a cake tester inserted in the center comes out clean. Boil the remaining 1 cup sugar and water together 2 to 3 minutes. Remove from heat, add rum, and dribble over cake. If cake does not absorb all the sauce, spoon it on later. Let cake stand a day or two before serving. This cake is very moist, as it should be. Store airtight.

YIELD: One 9-inch tube cake

STEVENS' MOLASSES CAKE

½ teaspoon salt
1 teaspoon soda
1 teaspoon ground cinnamon
1 teaspoon ground nutmeg
¾ cup (1½ sticks) soft butter *or* margarine

2 cups unsulphured molasses
2 large eggs
3½ cups sifted all-purpose flour
1 cup milk
1 cup dried currants

Blend the first 5 ingredients together until fluffy. Gradually add molasses. Stir in 1 cup of the flour. Beat in eggs, 1 at a time. Add remaining flour alternately with milk. Stir in currants. Turn batter into a well-greased, lightly floured 10 x 4-inch tube pan.

Bake in a preheated slow oven (325° F.) 1½ hours or until a cake tester inserted in center comes out clean. Cool in pan 20 minutes. Turn onto a wire rack to finish cooling. Store airtight.

YIELD: One 10-inch tube cake

SWISS CARROT CHRISTMAS CAKE

In this delicately spiced cake the characteristic carrot flavor gets lost; but it is carrot that keeps the cake moist for months. Bread crumbs and ground almonds take the place of flour.

⅔ cup grated raw carrots, firmly packed
1⅔ cups finely ground, unblanched almonds
¾ cup fine, dry bread crumbs
½ teaspoon ground nutmeg
½ teaspoon ground cinnamon
1 teaspoon double-acting baking powder
6 large eggs, separated
1¼ cups sugar
1 teaspoon grated lemon rind
3 tablespoons fresh lemon juice
Confectioners' Sugar and Water Glaze*
Candied fruits (glacé cherries, angelica, and pineapple

Combine carrots and almonds in a mixing bowl. Mix bread crumbs with spices and baking powder and blend with the carrots and almonds. Beat egg yolks until thick and lemon-colored. Gradually beat in sugar, lemon rind, and juice. Continue beating until thick. Stir into carrot mixture. Beat egg whites until they stand in soft peaks and carefully fold into the batter. Line a greased 8-inch spring-form pan with wax paper. Grease and sprinkle bottom and sides with bread crumbs. Turn mixture into prepared pan.

Bake in a preheated moderate oven (350° F.) 1 hour or until cake tester inserted into center comes out dry and clean. Cool. Remove from pan. Spoon Confectioners' Sugar and Water Glaze over sides and top of cake. Decorate with candied fruits. Store in a tightly covered cake box. This cake improves with age.

YIELD: One 8-inch round loaf cake

WEDDING RING CAKE

2½ cups sifted all-purpose flour
½ teaspoon salt
3 teaspoons double-acting
  baking powder
_____
⅔ cup shortening
½ teaspoon ground mace
1½ cups sugar
6 large egg whites, unbeaten
1 cup milk
Spiced Comfort Frosting*

Sift together first 3 ingredients and set aside. Mix shortening with mace. Gradually add 1 cup of the sugar, creaming well after each addition. Beat in 2 egg whites. Blend in the remaining sugar. Beat in the remaining egg whites, 1 at a time. Stir in flour alternately with milk. Beat batter ½ minute. Turn into a well-greased, lightly floured 10½-inch gelatine ring mold.

Bake in a preheated moderate oven (350° F.) 50 minutes or until done. Turn out on wire rack to cool. Frost with Spiced Comfort Frosting and decorate as desired.

YIELD: One 10½-inch ring loaf cake

BLACK PEPPER FRUIT CAKE

We found this cake extra-special in flavor. The black pepper blends with all the other spices, enhancing them in a most provocative way.

4 cups golden seedless raisins
2½ cups thinly sliced citron
2 cups thinly sliced glacé cherries
1½ cups thinly sliced, dried figs
1 cup thinly sliced, dried dates
½ cup finely cut, candied lemon peel
1½ cups thick orange marmalade
½ cup apricot nectar
2 teaspoons ground mace
2 teaspoons ground nutmeg
1 teaspoon ground cardamom
½ teaspoon ground black pepper
_____
4½ cups sifted all-purpose flour
2 teaspoons double-acting
  baking powder
2 teaspoons salt
_____
2½ cups sugar
2 cups (4 sticks) soft butter *or*
  margarine
2 tablespoons dark rum
8 large eggs
3 cups coarsely chopped,
  blanched almonds

Combine the first 12 ingredients and let stand overnight. Sift flour with baking powder and salt and set aside to use later. Gradually add sugar to butter or margarine. Add rum. Beat in eggs, 1 at a time. Gradually blend in flour mixture. Stir in fruit mixture and almonds, a little at a time. Line 3 greased 9 x 5 x 3-inch loaf pans with brown paper and grease lightly. Divide the batter equally among the pans.

Bake in a preheated very slow oven (275° F.) 3 to 3¼ hours (keeping a large shallow pan of hot water in oven on rack underneath the cake) or until a cake tester or toothpick inserted in the center comes out clean. Cool in pan 30 minutes. Turn onto a wire rack to finish cooling. Wrap cake in a cloth soaked in brandy or wine. Store airtight.

YIELD: 3 loaves, 3 pounds each

GROOM'S CAKE

This is the cake that is never tasted at the wedding. Rather, it is wrapped prettily in small cubes and given to each guest as a sort of souvenir. Romantic young ladies tuck their bit of Groom's Cake under their pillows to induce dreams of handsome suitors.

But you don't have to wait for a wedding to bake this cake: It's a delicious Christmas cake as well. If you wish to bake it in a 10-inch tube pan, bake 3½ hours in a very slow oven (275° F.). Keep a large pan of hot water on the rack underneath the cake to prevent its drying out during the long baking period.

2 cups (½ pound) coarsely chopped
   pecans

2 cups (11 ounces) coarsely chopped,
   blanched almonds
8 cups (2½ pounds) coarsely chopped,
   seedless raisins
6 cups (3 pounds) mixed glacé fruit
1 cup unsulphured molasses
½ cup hot water
___
1 cup (2 sticks) soft butter *or* margarine
1 teaspoon ground cinnamon
1 teaspoon ground nutmeg
½ teaspoon ground allspice
¼ teaspoon ground cloves
½ teaspoon soda
1¼ cups sugar
6 large eggs
2¼ cups sifted all-purpose flour
½ cup milk
Wine *or* brandy

Combine the first 6 ingredients. Mix well and let stand while preparing remaining ingredients. (This softens the fruit.) Blend butter or margarine with spices and soda. Gradually mix in sugar. Beat in eggs, 1 at a time. Blend ¼ cup of the flour with fruit and nuts and stir into the mixture. Add remaining 2 cups flour and milk. Mix well. Line 2 greased 15 x 12 x 1-inch pans with brown paper. Grease paper lightly. Add the batter and spread uniformly over pans.

Bake in a preheated slow oven (300° F.) 1¾ hours, keeping a large shallow pan of water on rack underneath cake. Cool 20 minutes. Turn onto a wire rack. Remove brown paper. When cold, wrap cakes in a clean cloth or towel saturated in wine or brandy. Store tightly covered. Before the wedding day, cut cakes into pieces to fit the favor boxes. Wrap each in cellophane or foil and pack in individual boxes.

YIELD: 88 pieces, each 2½ x ¾ inch

HONEY FRUIT CAKE

4 cups sifted all-purpose flour
1 teaspoon salt
1 teaspoon double-acting baking
   powder

2 cups light-brown sugar
1½ cups (3 sticks) soft butter *or*
   margarine

½ cup strained honey
½ teaspoon soda
2 teaspoons ground ginger
1 teaspoon ground cinnamon
1 teaspoon ground nutmeg
½ teaspoon ground cloves

6 large eggs

1½ cups chopped walnuts, pecans, *or*
   almonds

2 cups light, seedless raisins
5 cups diced, mixed glacé fruit

⅓ cup milk *or* sherry wine

Sift together the first 3 ingredients and set aside for later use. Gradually add sugar to butter or margarine. Stir in the next 6 ingredients. Beat in eggs, 1 at a time. Combine next 3 ingredients and gradually stir into the mixture. Add flour mixture alternately with milk or wine. Mix well.

Bake in a preheated slow oven (300° F.) in paper-lined, greased cake pans, keeping a large shallow pan of hot water on a rack underneath the cakes. Types and sizes of pans, with approximate baking times for each, are given below:

Pan type	Pan size (inches)	Number of pans required	Approx. baking time (hours)
tube	10 x 4	1	3¼
loaf	9 x 5 x 3	2	2¼
loaf	7½ x 3½ x 2¼	4	1¾
loaf	4½ x 2½ x 2	12	1

Let cakes stand in pans 30 minutes after removing from oven. Then turn onto a wire rack to finish cooling. Store airtight.

YIELD: 6½ pounds of fruit cake

SPICED JAPANESE FRUIT CAKE

This recipe never saw Japan! It is from the South where it has come to be expected on a lavishly set Christmas table. No one seems to know where it got its name. The batter for the two light and one dark layer begins in the same mixing bowl, but spices are added to that part of the batch which will be baked as the dark layer.

3 cups sifted all-purpose flour
3 teaspoons double-acting baking
   powder
½ teaspoon salt

2 cups sugar
1 cup (2 sticks) soft butter *or* margarine
4 large eggs
2 teaspoons vanilla extract
1 cup milk

½ teaspoon ground cinnamon
½ teaspoon ground allspice
⅛ teaspoon ground cloves

¼ cup chopped raisins
¼ cup chopped nuts
¼ cup chopped citron

Spiced Japanese Fruit Cake Filling and
  Frosting (see below)

Sift first 3 ingredients together and set
aside. Gradually add sugar to butter or
margarine, mixing well after each addition. Beat in eggs and vanilla extract.
Add flour mixture alternately with milk.
Mix well.

Turn ⅔ of the batter into 2 well-
greased, lightly floured, 9-inch round
layer-cake pans. Add the next 6 ingredients to the remaining batter. Mix well.
Turn into 1 paper-lined and greased 9-
inch round layer-cake pan.

Bake in a preheated moderate oven
(375° F.) 25 to 30 minutes or until done.
Cool in pans 10 minutes. Turn out onto

wire racks to finish cooling. Frost with
Spiced Japanese Fruit Cake Filling and
Frosting.

SPICED JAPANESE FRUIT CAKE FILLING AND FROSTING

2 cups sugar
⅓ cup cornstarch
¼ teaspoon salt
2 cups water

2 tablespoons butter or margarine
¼ cup fresh lemon juice
1 cup flaked coconut
1 cup chopped raisins
1 teaspoon ground nutmeg
½ teaspoon ground cinnamon
1½ teaspoons grated lemon rind
2 teaspoons grated orange rind

½ cup flaked coconut

Mix sugar, cornstarch, and salt in a saucepan. Gradually blend in water. Cook
over medium heat until thick, stirring constantly. Remove from heat and add next
8 ingredients. Cool. Spread between
layers and over top and sides of Spiced
Japanese Fruit Cake. Sprinkle the remaining ½ cup of coconut over top and
sides. This cake is even more delicious
when eaten the day after it is baked.

YIELD: One 9-inch, 3-layer cake

KINGSTON BLACK FRUIT CAKE

*While recipe-hunting on the island of
Jamaica, we dipped into the bottomless
fruited rum crock! All year round, year
after year, the Jamaican homemaker keeps
dried fruits soaking in native rum, adding
more rum and more fruit as needed. This
fragrant mixture is used in a variety of
concoctions during the year, but most generously when preparing Christmas cakes.*

The fruit for this cake should be soaked in rum for at least one week and the baked cake should be aged one month. This same batter may also be steamed as a pudding (see below), if desired.

3¼ cups (1 pound) dried currants
2¼ cups (¾ pound) seedless raisins
2 cups (¾ pound) seeded chopped, raisins
1¼ cups (½ pound) sliced citron
1¼ cups (½ pound) sliced, dried figs
1 cup (½ pound) cooked prunes, drained
1½ cups (½ pound) blanched almonds, toasted and sliced
1 cup (6-ounce package) chopped, pitted, dried dates
1 cup (7 ounces) glazed whole cherries, sliced
½ cup (4-ounce can) diced, glazed orange peel
3 cups dark Jamaica rum
_____
1 cup (2 sticks) soft butter *or* margarine
1½ teaspoons ground cinnamon
1½ teaspoons ground allspice
1½ teaspoons ground nutmeg
2 cups dark-brown sugar
5 large eggs
2 cups sifted all-purpose flour
2 teaspoons double-acting baking powder
½ teaspoon salt

Prepare all the fruit and almonds. Mix well. Stir in rum and let soak one week. On the day the cake is to be made, place butter or margarine and spices in a mixing bowl or dish pan large enough for mixing cake. Mix well. Gradually blend in sugar. Beat in 2 of the eggs. Sift flour with baking powder and salt, add 1 cup to the butter-sugar mixture. Beat in remaining eggs. Stir in rum-soaked fruit. Add remaining flour. Mix well.

Line 2 greased 9 x 5 x 3-inch loaf pans with brown paper and grease lightly. Divide the batter equally between the 2 pans. Bake in a preheated slow oven (275° F.) 2½ hours or until a toothpick or cake tester inserted in the center comes out clean, keeping a large shallow pan of hot water on rack underneath cake during baking period to prevent cake from baking too dry. Cool in pan 1 hour. Turn cakes onto a wire rack and remove brown paper. When cool, wrap in foil and store in a tightly closed cake tin or box. Age at least one month before serving.

YIELD: 2 loaf cakes, 3 pounds each

STEAMED BLACK FRUIT PUDDING

If desired, after baking half the batter in a 9 x 5 x 3-inch pan, steam the remaining batter in a covered 1½-quart pudding mold 3 hours in boiling water, having the water come halfway up the side of the mold. Serve with Brandy Hard Sauce.*

YIELD: One 3-pound loaf cake and one plum pudding, serving 8 to 10

LIGHT FRUIT CAKE

1½ cups diced, candied pineapple
1½ cups light raisins
1 cup diced citron
¼ cup diced, candied orange peel
1 cup chopped, blanched almonds
_____

2 cups sifted all-purpose flour
2 teaspoons double-acting
   baking powder
¼ teaspoon salt

1½ teaspoons ground mace
1½ teaspoons ground ginger
½ cup (1 stick) soft butter *or*
   margarine
¾ cup sugar
3 large eggs
¼ cup milk

Combine first 5 ingredients and mix with ¼ cup of the flour and set aside. Sift together remaining flour, baking powder, and salt. Blend mace and ginger with butter or margarine. Gradually add sugar. Stir in fruit and almond mixture. Turn batter into a greased 9 x 5 x 3-inch pan, lined with brown paper and greased lightly.

Bake in a preheated slow oven (300° F.) 2 hours. Cool in pan 30 minutes. Turn out onto wire rack to finish cooling. Store airtight.

YIELD: 3½-pound cake

MARTHA WASHINGTON'S SOUR CREAM GREAT CAKE

Martha Washington had as light a hand with cakes as was possible in the days before modern baking powder. "Great cakes" were loaf cakes, since this was the only type of cake pan then available. This is a moist and delicious cake.

1 teaspoon soda
½ teaspoon salt
½ teaspoon ground mace
½ teaspoon ground nutmeg
1 teaspoon ground cinnamon
¾ cup (1½ sticks) soft butter *or*
   margarine

2 cups sugar
4 large eggs, separated

1 cup seedless raisins
1 cup currants
½ cup diced citron
1 tablespoon grated lemon rind

1 cup sour cream
2 tablespoons lemon juice
3½ cups sifted all-purpose flour

Mix together the first 6 ingredients until fluffy. Gradually blend in sugar. Beat in egg yolks, 1 at a time. Stir in next 4 ingredients. Add sour cream and lemon juice alternately with flour. Beat egg whites until they stand in soft, stiff peaks and fold into the batter. Turn into a well-greased, lightly floured 10-inch tube pan.

Bake in a preheated slow oven (275° F.) 2 hours and 20 minutes or until a cake tester inserted in the center comes out clean. Cool in pan 30 minutes. Turn out onto a wire rack to finish cooling. Store airtight.

YIELD: One 10-inch tube cake

RICH FRUIT CAKE

This pound-cake type fruit-cake recipe was given us by a research baker whose recipes are used by professional bakers all over the country. Tuck this cake away in an airtight tin container and it will keep for months at room temperature.

1½ cups (3 sticks) soft butter *or*
   margarine
1 teaspoon soda
1½ teaspoons salt
1½ teaspoons ground cinnamon
1 teaspoon ground ginger *or* allspice
½ teaspoon ground nutmeg *or* mace

1 cup sugar
¾ cup unsulphured molasses
4 cups sifted all-purpose flour
5 large eggs
6 cups (3 pounds) mixed, diced,
   glazed fruit
1½ cups coarsely chopped nuts

Mix together the first 6 ingredients. Blend in sugar and molasses. Stir in one cup of the flour. Beat in eggs, 1 at a time. Gradually stir in the remaining flour. Add fruit and nuts, mix well. Spoon batter into a well-greased, lightly floured 10-inch tube pan or into two 9 x 5 x 3-inch loaf pans. Bake the 10-inch cake 3 hours, the 9 x 5 x 3-inch cakes 2 hours in a preheated slow oven (300° F.), keeping a large shallow pan of hot water on rack underneath cakes while baking. Cool cakes in pan 30 minutes. Turn out on wire rack to finish cooling. Store airtight.

YIELD: 7 pounds

SPICED BANANA
FRUIT CAKE

Just in case November and most of December slipped by without your having done anything about the Christmas fruit cake, here's an excellent last-minute cake which can be baked and eaten at once. Unlike the traditional fruit cake, this one lacks keeping quality and should be eaten within two weeks.

3½ cups sifted all-purpose flour
4 teaspoons double-acting
   baking powder
1 teaspoon salt

½ teaspoon soda
2 teaspoons ground cinnamon
2 teaspoons ground ginger
1 teaspoon ground nutmeg
1⅓ cups shortening

1⅓ cups sugar
4 large eggs
2 cups (4 to 6) mashed, ripe
   bananas
1 cup raisins
1½ cups chopped nuts
4 cups glazed, diced fruit

Sift together the first 3 ingredients and set aside. Mix soda, spices, and shortening together. Gradually blend in sugar. Beat in eggs, 1 at a time. Add flour mixture alternately with mashed bananas. Mix raisins, nuts, and fruit and stir into batter. Turn into a greased, paper-lined 10 x 4-inch tube pan.

Bake in a preheated slow oven (300° F.) 3½ to 4 hours. Or, if desired, bake in two 9 x 5 x 3-inch loaf pans 2 hours at same temperature, keeping a pan of hot water on rack underneath cake throughout baking period. Store airtight.

YIELD: 5½-pound cake

CINNAMON-CHOCOLATE
SPONGE ROLL

The success secret of this recipe is to beat the eggs until very thick. Beating over hot—but not boiling—water makes the eggs fluff up more quickly and to a greater volume.

4 large eggs
¾ teaspoon double-acting
   baking powder
¼ teaspoon salt

¾ cup sugar
½ teaspoon ground cinnamon
1 teaspoon vanilla extract
¾ cup sifted cake flour
Confectioners' sugar
Cinnamon Chocolate Frosting*

Place first 3 ingredients in a mixing bowl and set *over* a pan of hot water (not in it).

Beat until foamy. Mix sugar with cinnamon and gradually beat into eggs. Continue beating until the mixture is very thick.

Remove bowl from hot water and beat in vanilla extract. Fold in flour. Line a greased 15½ x 10½ x 1-inch jelly-roll pan with waxed or brown paper cut to fit. Grease paper. Pour batter into pan.

Bake in a preheated hot oven (400° F.) 12 to 13 minutes, or until cake springs back when touched in center with finger. Turn upside-down onto a cloth dusted with confectioners' sugar. Quickly remove paper and trim off edges of cake. Roll up in cloth in jelly-roll fashion. Cool. Unroll and spread with Cinnamon-Chocolate Frosting. Roll again. Dust outside of cake with confectioners' sugar or frost with additional Cinnamon Chocolate Frosting.

YIELD: 12 servings

LIL'S BEST SPONGE CAKE

Sponge and angel-cake batters cling more easily to the sides of an ungreased baking pan if the pan has been rinsed with cold water and well-drained (though not dried, of course) just before adding the batter. If you follow these directions, you'll be rewarded with a tall and lovely cake with a tender, golden crumb.

6 large eggs, separated
1¼ cups sugar
¾ teaspoon ground mace
1 teaspoon grated lemon rind
1 tablespoon grated orange rind

1 tablespoon fresh lemon juice
½ teaspoon salt
1½ cups sifted cake flour
Confectioners' sugar (optional)

Beat egg yolks until very thick and lemon-colored. Gradually beat in next 4 ingredients, beating well after each addition. Beat in lemon juice. Add salt to egg whites, beat until stiff but NOT DRY. Pile on top of egg-yolk mixture. Sift flour over egg whites and carefully fold into the mixture. Turn into an ungreased 10 x 4-inch tube pan that has been rinsed in cold water and well drained.

Bake in a preheated slow oven (325° F.) 1 hour or until browned and cake pulls away from the sides of the pan. Invert on a wire rack to cool. Loosen cake from sides of pan and tube with a spatula. Invert cake on a wire rack and lift off pan. If desired, dust top with sifted confectioners' sugar.

YIELD: One 10-inch tube cake

LAYER SPONGE CAKE

Rinse two 9 x 9 x 2-inch layer-cake pans in cold water and drain well. Divide the above sponge cake batter evenly between the 2 pans. Bake in a preheated slow oven (325° F.) 30 to 35 minutes or until a toothpick inserted in the center comes out clean. Serve plain or frost, as desired.

YIELD: One 9-inch square, 2-layer cake

PASSOVER SPONGE CAKE

6 large eggs, separated
1 whole egg

1½ cups sugar
1½ tablespoons fresh lemon juice
1 teaspoon grated lemon rind

¾ cup sifted potato starch
¼ teaspoon salt
½ teaspoon ground ginger
Sifted confectioners' sugar

Beat together egg yolks and whole egg until frothy with a rotary or an electric beater. Gradually beat in next 3 ingredients. Sift together potato starch, salt, and ginger. Add gradually, blending thoroughly. Beat egg whites stiff, but NOT DRY. Carefully fold into the batter. Turn into an ungreased 10 x 4-inch tube pan.

Bake in a preheated moderate oven (350° F.) 50 to 60 minutes or until toothpick inserted in center comes out clean. Cool in pan 30 minutes. Turn onto a wire rack to finish cooling. Sift confectioners' sugar over the top. Store airtight.

YIELD: One 10-inch tube cake

SPICED ANGEL-FOOD CAKE

1½ cups sifted fine granulated sugar
1¼ cups sifted cake flour
¾ teaspoon ground mace
½ teaspoon salt
10 to 12 (1½ cups) large
   egg whites
1½ teaspoons cream of tartar
2½ teaspoons vanilla extract
Confectioners' sugar (optional)
Seven-Minute* or Spiced Comfort
   Frosting* (optional)

Sift sugar, flour, and mace together 6 times and set aside to use later. Add salt to egg whites and beat until whites are frothy. Add cream of tartar and beat until whites stand in soft, stiff peaks. Add vanilla extract and ¼ cup of the flour-sugar mixture and carefully fold into the egg whites, using a rubber scraper. Gently fold in remaining sugar-flour mixture, about ¼ at a time, using about 15 strokes for each addition and turning the bowl a little each time.

Rinse a 10 x 4-inch tube pan in cold water and drain it well. Pour batter into the pan. Run the rubber scraper through the batter 3 or 4 times to remove any large air bubbles that might be in the mixture. Place cake in a cold oven. Set oven control to slow (300° F.). Bake 1¼ hours or until cake tester inserted in the center comes out clean and top is golden brown. Remove cake from oven and invert over a cake rack or 3 inverted teacups. Let stand until cold (about 2 hours).

Carefully loosen cake from the sides of the pan with a spatula. Invert pan on a cake rack and lift off the cake. Serve plain, or sprinkle top generously with confectioners' sugar, or frost with Seven-Minute Frosting or Spiced Comfort Frosting. Store airtight.

YIELD: One 10-inch tube cake

SPICED HOT MILK SPONGE CAKE

1½ cups sifted cake flour
1½ teaspoons double acting
   baking powder
½ teaspoon salt
½ teaspoon ground mace
½ teaspoon ground ginger
¼ teaspoon ground cloves

5 large eggs
1½ cups sugar
½ cup hot milk
1 teaspoon grated lemon rind
1 teaspoon vanilla extract
Sifted confectioners' sugar

Grease and line the bottom *only* of a 10 x 4-inch tube pan and set aside. Sift together the first 6 ingredients and set aside. Beat eggs 7 to 10 minutes or until they are lemon-colored and very thick (about as thick as whipped cream). Gradually beat in sugar. Add all the flour mixture at one time, mixing *only* until blended, using as few strokes as possible. Quickly blend in hot milk, lemon rind, and vanilla extract. Turn into the prepared cake pan.

Bake in a preheated moderate oven (350° F.) 1 hour or until cake tester inserted in the center comes out clean. Cool cake in pan 30 minutes. Turn out onto a wire rack to finish cooling. Sprinkle confectioners' sugar over the top. Store airtight.

YIELD: One 10-inch tube cake

PEANUT BUTTER CUPCAKES

2 cups sifted all-purpose flour
3 teaspoons double-acting
   baking powder
½ teaspoon salt
___
½ cup shortening
½ cup peanut butter
½ teaspoon ground cloves
½ teaspoon ground cinnamon
___
1⅓ cups light-brown sugar
2 large eggs
1 cup milk
Peanut Butter Frosting*

Sift together the first 3 ingredients and set aside. Blend shortening with peanut butter, cloves, and cinnamon. Gradually add sugar, mixing well after each addition. Beat in eggs, 1 at a time. Add flour mixture alternately with milk, beginning and ending with flour. Line cupcake pans with #110 paper cupcake liners. Spoon in batter, filling them ¾ full. Bake in a preheated moderate oven (375° F.) 20 to 25 minutes or until a toothpick inserted in center comes out clean. Remove from oven and cool on wire racks. Frost with

Peanut Butter Frosting. Store in a tightly covered cake box.

YIELD: 2 dozen cupcakes

SESAME SEED CUPCAKES

1¾ cups sifted all-purpose flour
2 teaspoons double-acting
   baking powder
___
½ teaspoon ground cinnamon
½ teaspoon ground ginger
½ teaspoon ground nutmeg
¼ teaspoon ground cloves
½ teaspoon salt
½ cup shortening
___
1 cup sugar
1 large egg
¾ cup milk
Browned Butter Frosting*
Toasted Sesame Seed*

Sift together flour and baking powder and set aside. Add spices and salt to shortening and mix well. Gradually blend in sugar. Beat in egg. Add flour mixture alternately with milk. Beat batter ½ minute. Spoon batter into well-greased, lightly floured 2½-inch cupcake pans or into cupcake pans lined with #110 paper cupcake liners, filling them ¾ full.

Bake in a preheated moderate oven (375° F.) 20 minutes or until a toothpick inserted in the center comes out clean. Cool in pans 10 minutes. Turn out onto a wire rack to finish cooling. Frost tops with Browned Butter Frosting and sprinkle with Toasted Sesame Seed. Store airtight.

YIELD: About 2 dozen cupcakes

APPLE UPSIDE-DOWN GINGERBREAD

¼ cup (½ stick) butter *or* margarine
½ cup light-brown sugar
2 large baking apples
___
3 tablespoons sugar

FIVE-SPICE GINGERBREAD

Here is a light and fluffy gingerbread, subtly flavored with five sweet spices. It comes from the Cajun country of Louisiana.

½ teaspoon salt
1½ teaspoons soda
1 teaspoon ground ginger
¾ teaspoon ground cinnamon
½ teaspoon ground allspice
½ teaspoon ground nutmeg
½ teaspoon ground cloves
½ cup shortening
___

1 cup sugar
1 large egg
1 cup pure sugar-cane syrup
2½ cups sifted all-purpose flour
1 cup hot water
Lemon Sauce* (optional)

Combine the first 8 ingredients and mix well. Gradually blend in sugar. Beat in egg. Add syrup alternately with flour. Add hot water, a little at a time, beating after each addition. Turn into a well-greased, lightly floured 9 x 9 x 2-inch pan.

Bake in a preheated moderate oven (350° F.) 55 to 60 minutes or until a toothpick inserted in the center comes out clean. Serve warm or cold, topped with Lemon Sauce, or topped with fruit and whipped cream; or serve plain.

YIELD: One 9-inch square gingerbread

1 teaspoon soda
1 teaspoon salt
1¼ teaspoons ground ginger
½ teaspoon ground cinnamon
⅓ teaspoon ground nutmeg
½ cup shortening
___

1 large egg
1 cup unsulphured molasses
½ cup milk
2¼ cups sifted all-purpose flour
½ cup hot water
Heavy cream, whipped (optional)

Melt butter or margarine in a 10-inch heavy bottom skillet. Sprinkle brown sugar uniformly over bottom. Peel, core, and cut apples into ½-inch crosswise slices. Arrange them in bottom of skillet, overlapping edges.

Combine next 7 ingredients and mix well. Beat in egg. Stir in molasses. Add milk alternately with flour. Beat in hot water.

Spoon batter over apples and bake in a preheated slow oven (325° F.) 45 to 50 minutes or until a toothpick inserted in center comes out clean. Cool in pan 10 minutes. Invert onto a serving plate, but do not remove pan for 5 minutes. This permits sugar and butter topping to run down over cake. Serve with whipped cream, if desired.

YIELD: One 9-inch square gingerbread

MUSTER GINGERBREAD

This is a sheet-type gingerbread—a cross between a cooky and a cake—one which can easily be eaten out of hand.

1½ cups sifted all-purpose flour
½ teaspoon double-acting
    baking powder
½ teaspoon salt
___

¼ cup shortening
½ teaspoon soda
½ teaspoon ground cinnamon
½ teaspoon ground ginger
½ teaspoon ground nutmeg
¼ teaspoon ground cloves

¼ cup sugar
½ cup unsulphured molasses
1 large egg
½ cup hot water

Sift together the first 3 ingredients and set aside. Blend shortening with soda and spices. Gradually add sugar and molasses, mixing well. Stir in ½ cup of the flour mixture. Beat in egg. Add remaining flour alternately with hot water. Beat batter ½ minute. Turn batter into a well-greased, lightly floured 9 x 9 x 2-inch pan.

Bake in a preheated moderate oven (350° F.) 25 minutes or until a cake tester inserted in the center comes out clean. Cool and cut into 12 bars. Store airtight.

YIELD: 12 bars

MUSTARD GINGERBREAD

Mustard enhances other flavors, sometimes at the expense of its own character-istic flavor. In this gingerbread, for instance, you'll hardly notice it. The original recipe comes from a handwritten cook book in Mystic, Connecticut.

2¼ cups sifted all-purpose flour
1½ teaspoons double-acting
    baking powder
½ teaspoon salt

½ teaspoon soda
½ teaspoon ground cloves
1 teaspoon powdered mustard
1 teaspoon ground cinnamon
1 teaspoon ground ginger
½ cup shortening

½ cup sugar
1 cup unsulphured molasses
1 large egg
1 cup hot water
Heavy cream, whipped (optional)

Sift together the first 3 ingredients and set aside. Add soda and spices to shortening and mix well. Gradually blend in sugar and molasses. Beat in egg. Add flour mixture alternately with hot water. Beat batter ½ minute. Turn batter into a well-greased, lightly floured 9 x 9 x 2-inch pan.

Bake in a preheated moderate oven (350° F.) 45 to 50 minutes or until a toothpick inserted in center comes out clean. Cool in pan 10 minutes. Turn out onto a wire rack to finish cooling. If desired, serve warm with whipped cream.

YIELD: One 9-inch square gingerbread

QUICK GINGERBREAD

2 cups sifted all-purpose flour
⅓ cup sugar
1 teaspoon salt
½ teaspoon soda
1 teaspoon double-acting
    baking powder

1 teaspoon ground cinnamon
1½ teaspoons ground ginger
½ teaspoon ground cloves

1 cup unsulphured molasses
½ cup melted shortening
½ cup sour milk *or* buttermilk
1 large egg, lightly beaten
¼ cup hot water

Sift the first 8 ingredients together into a mixing bowl. Stir in molasses, shortening, milk, and egg. Beat in hot water. Turn into a well-greased, lightly floured 9 x 9 x 2-inch pan. Bake in a preheated moderate oven (350° F.) 45 minutes or until done.

YIELD: One 9-inch square gingerbread

SPICED BANANA
VALENTINE CAKES

1 package white cake mix
1½ cups mashed, ripe bananas
½ teaspoon ground mace *or* nutmeg
Lemon Frosting*

Mix cake according to directions on package, replacing liquid called for with mashed bananas. (If directions call for liquid *and* eggs, reduce liquid to ½ cup and add only 1 cup mashed, ripe bananas. Add eggs as specified.) Blend in mace or nutmeg. Bake in 16 well-greased, lightly floured individual heart-shaped molds in a preheated moderate oven (350° F.) 20 minutes or until a toothpick inserted in center comes out clean. Cool in pans 10 minutes. Turn onto wire rack to finish cooling. Frost with Lemon Frosting.

YIELD: 16 individual heart-shaped cakes

TOASTED SESAME
SEED CAKE

1 package white cake mix
½ teaspoon ground mace
Mocha Frosting*
Toasted Sesame Seed*

Mix cake according to package directions, adding ½ teaspoon ground mace to the batter. Turn into a well-greased, lightly floured 9-inch tube pan.

Bake in a preheated moderate oven (350° F.) 1 hour or until done. Cool 10 minutes in pan. Turn out onto wire rack to finish cooling. Frost top and sides with Mocha Frosting. Sprinkle with Toasted Sesame Seed.

YIELD: One 9-inch tube cake

SHEET CAKES

There may be times when dozens of guests are coming to visit and you need cake in quantity. These sheet cakes are easy to make, economical, and of fine flavor and texture. Baking Gold Coconut Cake is a good way to use up the yolks left over after baking an Angel Cake.

GOLD COCONUT
SHEET CAKE

3¾ cups sifted all-purpose flour
2 tablespoons double-acting
   baking powder

1 cup (2 sticks) soft butter *or*
   margarine
½ teaspoon salt
1 teaspoon ground mace
4 teaspoons vanilla extract

2⅓ cups sugar
10 large egg yolks
1½ cups milk
Marshmallow Seven-Minute Frosting*
1 can (3½ ounces) flaked coconut

Sift together flour and baking powder and set aside. Mix together the next 4 ingredients. Gradually blend in sugar. Beat in egg yolks, 2 at a time. Add flour mixture alternately with milk. Beat batter ½ minute. Turn into 2 well-greased, lightly floured 15½ x 10½ x 1-inch jelly-roll pans.

Bake in a preheated moderate oven (350° F.) 30 minutes or until a cake tester inserted in center comes out clean. Cool in pans 15 minutes. Turn onto wire racks to finish cooling. Frost with Marshmallow Seven-Minute Frosting and sprinkle with flaked coconut. Cut each cake into 24 servings.

YIELD: 2 cakes, each 15½ x 10½ x 1-inch

SPICE SHEET CAKE

7 cups sifted all-purpose flour
8 teaspoons double-acting
  baking powder
2 teaspoons salt
2 teaspoons ground ginger
1 teaspoon ground nutmeg
2 teaspoons ground cinnamon
½ teaspoon ground cloves
1½ cups (3 sticks) soft butter or
  margarine
4 cups sugar
4 large eggs
3 cups milk
Browned Butter Frosting*
1 can (3½ ounces) flaked coconut

Sift together first 3 ingredients and set aside to use later. Mix spices with butter or margarine. Gradually blend in sugar. Beat in eggs, 1 at a time. Add flour mixture alternately with milk. Beat batter ½ minute. Turn batter into 2 well-greased, lightly floured 15½ x 10½ x 1-inch jelly-roll pans.

Bake in a preheated moderate oven (375° F.) 30 minutes or until a cake tester inserted in the center comes out clean. Cool in pans 15 minutes. Turn onto wire racks to finish cooling. Spread tops with Browned Butter Frosting and sprinkle with coconut. Cut each cake into 18 or 24 squares.

YIELD: 2 cakes, each 15½ x 10½ x 1 inch

SPICED MARBLE SHEET CAKE

4 cups sifted cake flour
1 teaspoon salt
4 teaspoons double-acting
  baking powder
5 teaspoons vanilla extract
2 cups sugar
1 cup (2 sticks) soft butter or
  margarine
4 large eggs
1⅓ cups milk
⅓ cup maple-flavored syrup
1 tablespoon cocoa
2 teaspoons instant coffee
¼ teaspoon ground cinnamon
¼ teaspoon ground allspice
Maple Frosting*

Sift together first 3 ingredients and set aside. Gradually blend vanilla extract and sugar into butter or margarine. Beat in eggs, 1 at a time. Add sifted dry ingredients alternately with milk. Place ⅓ of the batter in a small bowl and stir remaining ingredients into it. Spoon light and dark batters alternately into a well-greased and floured 15½ x 10½ x 2-inch jelly-roll pan.

Bake in a moderate oven (375° F.) 30 to 35 minutes or until a cake tester inserted into the center comes out clean. Cool in pan 10 minutes. Turn onto a wire rack to finish cooling. Frost with Maple Frosting.

YIELD: 1 cake, 15½ x 10½ x 1 inch

SPICED CHOCOLATE SHEET CAKE

5⅓ cups sifted all-purpose flour
1½ cups sifted cocoa
2 teaspoons salt
1½ cups shortening
3 teaspoons soda

1750
SPICE SMUGGLERS
ON BANDA

2 teaspoons ground cinnamon
¾ teaspoon ground cloves
4 teaspoons vanilla extract

4½ cups dark-brown sugar
4 large eggs
2 cups buttermilk *or* sour milk

Chocolate Fudge Frosting*

Sift together the first 3 ingredients and set aside. Blend together the next 5 ingredients. Gradually add sugar. Beat in eggs, one at a time. Add flour mixture alternately with milk. Beat batter ½ minute. Divide batter between 2 well-greased, lightly floured 15½ x 10½ x 1-inch pans. Spread batter to cover bottoms of pans uniformly.

Bake in a preheated moderate oven (375° F.) 30 to 35 minutes or until a toothpick inserted into the center of cake comes out clean. Cool in pans 10 minutes. Turn onto wire racks to finish cooling. Spread tops with Chocolate Fudge Frosting. Cut cakes into serving-size pieces.

YIELD: 2 cakes, each 15½ x 10½ x 1 inch

POPPY SEED CHEESE CAKE

¼ cup graham cracker crumbs
½ teaspoon ground cinnamon
1¼ cups sugar
3 tablespoons flour
3 tablespoons poppy seed
6 packages (3 ounces each) soft cream cheese
6 large eggs, separated
1 cup sour cream
1½ teaspoons vanilla extract
⅛ teaspoon salt
½ teaspoon cream of tartar
Confectioners' sugar (optional)

Butter the inside of a 9-inch spring-form pan and sprinkle with graham cracker crumbs mixed with cinnamon. Set aside. Combine ¾ cup of the sugar with flour and poppy seed. Add cream cheese and beat until the mixture is fluffy and smooth. Beat egg yolks until light and lemon-colored. Blend with the cheese mixture. Stir in sour cream and vanilla extract. Add salt to egg whites and beat until they are foamy. Add cream of tartar and beat until they stand in soft, stiff peaks. Gradually beat in remaining ½ cup sugar and fold into the mixture. Turn into the prepared spring-form pan. Place on a rack in a larger pan. Pour in hot water, having it come to the top of the rack, yet not touching the cheese-cake pan.

Bake in a preheated slow oven (325° F.) 1¾ hours or until cake is firm in the center. Turn off heat and let pan cool in the oven 1 hour. Remove from oven. Loosen the cake from the sides of the pan with a spatula, but do not remove the pan side until ready to serve. Serve, with side removed, on a cake plate. Sift confectioners' sugar over the top, if desired.

YIELD: One 9-inch cheese cake

"FUDGY" CINNAMON SQUARES

½ teaspoon soda
½ teaspoon ground cinnamon
¼ teaspoon salt
1 teaspoon vanilla extract
⅓ cup shortening

¾ cup sugar
2 squares (2 ounces) unsweetened chocolate, melted
1 large egg
1¼ cups sifted all-purpose flour
¾ cup buttermilk *or* sour milk
Chocolate Fudge Frosting*

Combine the first 5 ingredients. Gradually blend in sugar and chocolate. Beat in egg. Add flour alternately with milk. Beat batter ½ minute.

Turn into a well-greased, lightly floured 8 x 8 x 2-inch pan. Bake in a preheated moderate oven (350° F.) 40 minutes or until a toothpick inserted in the center comes out clean. Cool in pan 10 minutes. Turn onto a wire rack to finish cooling. Spread top with Chocolate Fudge Frosting. Cut into squares.

YIELD: One 8-inch square cake (nine 2½-inch squares)

FROSTINGS and FILLINGS

George Washington concocted a cake recipe and he concluded it with the advice that if the cake turned out well, not to bother icing it. However, should it burn or otherwise misbehave, the icing must not be omitted.

In most of the uncooked frosting recipes included in this book, the suggested quantity of confectioners' sugar to be used is approximate. It is best to add what is needed to make the frosting of a consistency easiest to spread.

Cakes should always be allowed to cool thoroughly before frosting is applied.

Use a pastry brush to remove loose crumbs before the cake is frosted.

Frostings made with browned butter or melted chocolate become firm more readily than those made with softened butter.

When cake must stand unfrosted for a day or more, or when the frosting is to be very elaborate, it is a good idea first to spread a glaze over the whole surface. Such a glaze may be as simple as a mixture of Confectioners' Sugar and Water,* which lends itself to easy spreading.

While any cake may be frosted, certain classical cakes, such as pound cake, angel-food cake, sponge cake, and most Christmas fruit cakes, are usually served unfrosted. If desired, such cakes may be dusted lightly with confectioners' sugar. To achieve a fanciful effect, place a lace paper doily over the cake's top and dust, then remove doily carefully to leave an attractive design.

For more lavish effects, select a cooked frosting, such as Comfort Frosting,* or one of the Seven-Minute Frosting* variations.

*An asterisk after the name of a dish indicates that the recipe for this dish appears in the book. Consult the Index for the page number.

BIRTHDAY CAKE FILLING AND FROSTING

2 large egg whites
1½ cups sugar
¼ teaspoon cream of tartar
¼ cup water
⅛ teaspoon salt

1 teaspoon vanilla extract
½ cup raisins
6 dried figs
½ cup boiling water
⅓ cup chopped nuts
¼ teaspoon ground nutmeg

Combine the first 5 ingredients in the top part of a double boiler. Place over hot water and beat with an electric or rotary beater until mixture stands in peaks. Remove from heat and add vanilla extract. Continue beating until frosting stands in very stiff peaks. In the meantime, simmer raisins and figs in boiling water. Drain and chop fine. Add to ⅓ of the frosting along with nuts and nutmeg. Mix well and spread between layers. Frost top and sides with remaining frosting.

YIELD: Filling and frosting for an 8-inch, 2-layer cake

BROWN SUGAR FROSTING

⅓ cup (⅔ stick) butter or margarine
1 cup dark-brown sugar

¼ cup cold water
2½ cups sifted confectioners' sugar
2 teaspoons vanilla extract

Brown butter or margarine in a saucepan. Add brown sugar and water. Bring to a boil and boil 1 minute. Cool. Add confectioners' sugar and vanilla extract. Mix well.

YIELD: Frosting for tops and sides of two 8-inch round or square cake layers

BROWN SUGAR SEVEN-MINUTE FROSTING

¾ cup brown sugar (light or dark)
1 large egg white
2 tablespoons water
¼ teaspoon ground mace
⅛ teaspoon cream of tartar
Dash salt
1 teaspoon vanilla extract

Place all ingredients in the top of a double boiler. Set over the bottom of a double boiler filled to a depth of about 2 inches with boiling water. Beat with an electric beater until frosting stands in soft peaks, keeping the water boiling rapidly. Remove from heat and continue beating until frosting stands in very stiff peaks. Spread over cold cake.

YIELD: Frosting for tops and sides of two 8-inch cake layers or for tops only of two 9-inch layers

CREAM CAKE FILLING

2 teaspoons unflavored gelatine
3 tablespoons water

⅓ cup sugar
3 tablespoons cornstarch
⅛ teaspoon salt
¼ teaspoon ground mace

⅓ cup milk

1 cup scalded milk
1 large egg, beaten
1¼ teaspoons vanilla extract

Soften gelatine in water and set aside. Combine the next 4 ingredients in the top of a double boiler. Blend in cold milk. Add hot milk. Stir and cook over hot water until mixture has thickened, about 12 minutes. Add a little of the hot mixture to the egg and then gradually stir egg into remaining hot mixture.

Stir and cook 2 minutes. Add softened gelatine. Chill until filling is firm enough to spread. Add vanilla extract. Spread between layers of cold Boston cream pie or other cake layers.

YIELD: Filling for top of one 10-inch layer

CHOCOLATE FROSTING

1 tablespoon butter *or* margarine
1 square (1 ounce) unsweetened chocolate
1 cup sifted confectioners' sugar
About 1½ tablespoons water
¾ teaspoon vanilla extract

Melt butter or margarine and chocolate over hot water. Add sugar and enough

water to make frosting of thin-spreading consistency. Blend in vanilla extract. Spread over top of Boston cream pie or other cakes.

YIELD: Frosting for one 10-inch layer

CREAMY LIME FROSTING

½ cup sugar
2 tablespoons cornstarch
¹⁄₁₆ teaspoon salt

½ cup milk
½ cup (1 stick) butter *or* margarine
¼ teaspoon ground mace
About 3½ cups sifted confectioners' sugar
1 tablespoon milk
½ teaspoon grated lime rind
1 teaspoon vanilla extract

Combine the first 3 ingredients in a saucepan. Blend in milk. Stir and cook over low heat until very thick. Cool. Add butter or margarine and mace. Gradually add enough confectioners' sugar along with the 1 tablespoon milk to make frosting of smooth-spreading consistency. Mix in lime rind and vanilla extract.

YIELD: Frosting for tops and sides of two 8-inch cake layers or for tops only of two 9-inch layers

DATE AND NUT FILLING

½ cup sugar
½ cup undiluted evaporated milk
2 large egg yolks
¼ cup (½ stick) butter *or* margarine

1 teaspoon vanilla extract
½ cup shredded coconut
½ cup chopped nuts
⅓ cup chopped dates

Combine the first 4 ingredients in a saucepan. Mix well. Stir and cook over medium heat 12 minutes or until thickened. Remove from heat and stir in remaining ingredients. Beat until of spreading consistency. Spread between layers.

YIELD: Filling for top of one 8 or 9-inch layer

SPICED CHOCOLATE FROSTING

1 package (6 ounces) semisweet chocolate pieces
1 square (1 ounce) unsweetened chocolate
1 can (15 ounces) sweetened condensed milk
¼ teaspoon ground cinnamon
⅛ teaspoon ground cloves

Melt chocolate over hot water in top of a double boiler. Stir in remaining ingredients. Stir and cook over hot water or very low heat about 5 minutes or until well blended and of spreading consistency. Cool. Spread over top and sides of cake.

YIELD: Frosting for two 8- or 9-inch cake layers

EASY FUDGE FROSTING

4 cups sifted confectioners' sugar
4 tablespoons cocoa
½ cup heavy cream or undiluted evaporated milk
4 tablespoons butter or margarine
1½ teaspoons light or dark corn syrup
2½ teaspoons vanilla extract
½ teaspoon confectioners' sugar

Combine the first 5 ingredients in a saucepan. Mix thoroughly. Cook over medium-low heat *only* until mixture boils around the edges, 3 to 4 minutes, stirring a couple of times to prevent scorching. Remove from heat. Cool. (To hasten cooling, place in a pan of ice water.)

Add vanilla extract. Beat about ½ minute. Then, measure the ½ teaspoon

confectioners' sugar and mix with a little of the frosting against the side of the pan. Mix with remaining frosting. Beat until of spreading consistency. (This step helps frosting to firm quickly.) Spread on cake.

YIELD: Frosting and filling for a 9-inch, 2-layer cake

EASY CHOCOLATE FROSTING

⅓ cup (⅔ stick) butter or margarine
⅔ cup heavy cream or undiluted evaporated milk
1⅓ cups sugar
¼ teaspoon salt
2 squares (2 ounces) unsweetened chocolate
2 teaspoons vanilla extract
About 4½ cups sifted confectioners' sugar

Combine the first 4 ingredients in a heavy-bottom saucepan. Bring to a full rolling boil. Remove from heat. Add chocolate and vanilla. Mix well. Gradually stir in enough confectioners' sugar to make frosting of smooth-spreading consistency.

YIELD: Frosting and filling for an 8- or 9-inch, 3-layer cake

FLUFFY MINT FROSTING

2 teaspoons mint flakes
¼ cup boiling water
1 large egg white
¾ cup sugar
¼ teaspoon cream of tartar

Steep mint flakes in boiling water 7 minutes. Pour through a fine strainer into the top of a double boiler. Add remaining ingredients. Place over bottom of a double boiler, filled to a depth of about 2 inches with boiling water.

Beat with an electric beater until frosting stands in soft, stiff peaks, keeping water boiling rapidly. Remove from heat and continue beating until frosting stands in very stiff peaks. Spread over cold chocolate or molasses cake.

YIELD: Frosting for tops and sides of two 8-inch cake layers or for tops only of two 9-inch layers

GRAPEFRUIT SEVEN-MINUTE FROSTING

1 large egg white
¾ cup sugar
2 tablespoons fresh grapefruit juice
Dash salt
___
1 teaspoon grated grapefruit rind
⅛ teaspoon grated lemon rind
1 teaspoon vanilla extract

Place the first 4 ingredients in the top of a double boiler. Place over the bottom of a double boiler containing rapidly boiling water. (Keep water boiling while beating.) Beat with an electric beater until mixture stands in soft peaks. Remove from heat, add remaining ingredients, and beat until frosting stands in very stiff peaks. Spread over cold cake.

YIELD: Frosting for tops and sides of two 8-inch cake layers or for tops only of two 9-inch layers

LEMON SEVEN-MINUTE FROSTING

2 large egg whites
1½ cups sugar
2 tablespoons water
2 tablespoons fresh lemon juice
1/16 teaspoon salt
½ teaspoon vanilla extract
½ teaspoon grated lemon rind

Place all ingredients in the top of a double boiler. Set over the bottom of a double boiler, filled to a depth of about 2 inches with boiling water. Beat with an electric beater until frosting stands in soft, stiff peaks, keeping the water boiling rapidly. Remove from heat and continue beating until frosting stands in very stiff peaks. Spread over cold cake.

YIELD: Frosting for tops and sides of three 8-inch cake layers or for tops only of three 9-inch layers

PFEFFERNUESSE FROSTING

1 large egg white
2 teaspoons light corn syrup
¼ teaspoon ground cardamom
___
1½ cups sifted confectioners' sugar

Combine the first 3 ingredients in a 1-quart mixing bowl. Gradually beat in confectioners' sugar with an electric or rotary beater. Place 12 to 14 pfeffernuesse and 2 tablespoons frosting, at a time, in a mixing bowl. Stir with a fork until all pfeffernuesse are lightly covered. Repeat using all cookies and frosting.

Lift out with a fork onto a wire cooling rack. Have a pan, wax paper, or foil underneath to catch frosting that drips through the wires. Let stand until frosting has hardened.

YIELD: Frosting for 9 dozen pfeffernuesse

SEVEN-MINUTE FROSTING I

¼ cup water
1 large egg white
¾ cup sugar
¼ teaspoon cream of tartar
Dash salt
1 teaspoon vanilla extract

Place all ingredients in the top of a double boiler. Set over the bottom of a double boiler, filled to a depth of about 2 inches with boiling water. Beat with an electric beater until frosting stands in soft, stiff peaks, keeping water boiling rapidly. Remove from heat and continue beating until frosting stands in very stiff peaks. Spread over cold cake.

ANISE SEVEN-MINUTE FROSTING

In the above recipe, bring the ¼ cup water to boiling point, add ½ teaspoon anise seed, cover, and steep 10 minutes. Strain out and discard the seeds and combine liquid with the above remaining ingredients in the top of a double boiler. Proceed as in above directions.

FRESH COCONUT SEVEN-MINUTE FROSTING

In the above recipe, replace ¼ cup of water with ¼ cup water drained from the coconut. At end of beating period, beat in ½ cup grated fresh coconut.

YIELD: Frosting for tops and sides of two 8-inch cake layers or for tops only of two 9-inch layers

SEVEN-MINUTE FROSTING II

2 large egg whites
1½ cups sugar
⅛ teaspoon salt
1 tablespoon light corn syrup
¼ cup water
1½ teaspoons vanilla extract

Place all ingredients in the top of a double boiler. Place over the bottom of a double boiler, filled to a depth of about 2 inches with boiling water. Beat with an electric beater until frosting stands in soft, stiff peaks, keeping the water boiling rapidly. Remove from heat and continue beating until frosting stands in very stiff peaks. Spread over cold cake.

MARSHMALLOW SEVEN-MINUTE FROSTING

Cut 12 regular size marshmallows into small pieces and add to the above frosting as soon as it is removed from the heat. Beat as in above directions.

YIELD: Frosting for 9-inch, 2-layer cake

SPICED BUTTER FROSTING

¼ cup (½ stick) soft butter *or* margarine
¼ teaspoon ground ginger
½ teaspoon ground mace
1 teaspoon vanilla extract

1 large egg yolk
About 2½ cups sifted confectioners' sugar
2 tablespoons light cream *or* undiluted evaporated milk

Combine first 4 ingredients. Add egg yolk and enough sugar and cream or milk to make frosting of a smooth-spreading consistency.

YIELD: Frosting for a 9 x 5 x 3-inch loaf cake

SPICED COMFORT FROSTING

2 cups sugar
½ cup water
1 tablespoon light corn syrup
_____
¼ teaspoon salt
¼ teaspoon cream of tartar
2 large egg whites
¼ teaspoon ground mace
1 teaspoon vanilla extract

Combine the first 3 ingredients in a saucepan. Stir and cook over low heat until sugar is dissolved. Boil, covered, 3 minutes. Then boil uncovered, and without stirring, until a firm ball forms when dropped in cold water or until the syrup temperature reaches 250° F. on candy thermometer.

Remove syrup from heat. Quickly add salt and cream of tartar to egg whites and beat until they stand in stiff peaks. Gradually beat in hot syrup. Beat in mace and vanilla extract. Continue beating until mixture is of spreading consistency and stands in peaks.

YIELD: Frosting for 9-inch, 2-layer cake

BROWNED BUTTER FROSTING

½ cup (1 stick) butter or margarine
About 4½ cups sifted confectioners' sugar
About 5 tablespoons milk
1½ tablespoons light corn syrup
1½ teaspoons vanilla extract

Brown butter or margarine until golden in a saucepan large enough for mixing frosting. Add sugar alternately with milk, corn syrup, and vanilla extract. Mix well. Spread over cold cake.

YIELD: Frosting for 2 dozen cupcakes, for an 8-inch, 2-layer cake, or for one 9-inch loaf cake

MAPLE-FLAVORED BROWNED BUTTER FROSTING

⅔ cup (1⅓ sticks) butter or margarine
About 6 cups sifted confectioners' sugar
4 tablespoons light cream or undiluted evaporated milk
2 tablespoons maple-flavored syrup
2 teaspoons vanilla extract

Melt butter or margarine in a saucepan large enough for mixing frosting. Cook only until butter has lightly browned. Add enough confectioners' sugar alternately with cream or milk, syrup, and vanilla extract to make frosting of smooth-spreading consistency.

YIELD: Frosting for a 9-inch, 2-layer cake

BUTTER CREAM FROSTING

2 to 2½ cups sifted confectioners' sugar
2 to 3 tablespoons heavy cream or undiluted evaporated milk
¼ cup (½ stick) soft butter or margarine

Melt butter or margarine in a saucepan and heat until lightly browned. Remove from heat. Stir in cocoa. Add confectioners' sugar alternately with milk. Blend in vanilla extract. Spread over tops of cold sheet cakes or top and sides of layer cake.

YIELD: Frosting for 2 sheet cakes, each 15½ x 10½

CHOCOLATE GLAZE

Melt 2 tablespoons butter or margarine and 2 squares (2 ounces) unsweetened chocolate in a small saucepan over hot water. Remove from heat and stir in 2 tablespoons confectioners' sugar.

YIELD: Glaze for one 8 or 9-inch layer cake

CINNAMON-CHOCOLATE FROSTING

1 package (12 ounces) semisweet chocolate pieces
¼ cup (½ stick) butter *or* margarine
⅔ cup sifted confectioners' sugar
¾ teaspoon ground cinnamon
¼ cup milk
1 teaspoon vanilla extract
⅛ teaspoon salt

Melt chocolate and butter over hot water. Remove from heat and stir in remaining ingredients. Beat until of smooth-spreading consistency.

YIELD: Frosting for the inside of sponge-cake roll

¼ teaspoon ground mace
½ teaspoon vanilla extract

Add sugar and cream or milk alternately to butter or margarine, using just enough to make frosting of smooth-spreading consistency. Stir in mace and vanilla extract. Spread over cold cake.

YIELD. Frosting for top and sides of a 10 x 4-inch tube cake

CONFECTIONERS' SUGAR AND WATER GLAZE

Stir 4 teaspoons water into 1 cup sifted confectioners' sugar. Mix well.

YIELD: Glaze for a 9-inch square cake

CHOCOLATE FUDGE FROSTING

1 cup (2 sticks) butter *or* margarine
⅔ cup sifted cocoa
About 7 cups sifted confectioners' sugar
About ½ cup undiluted evaporated milk
2 teaspoons vanilla extract

CINNAMON-CHOCOLATE FUDGE FROSTING

½ teaspoon ground cinnamon
¼ cup (½ stick) butter *or* margarine
1 teaspoon vanilla extract
1 square (1 ounce) unsweetened chocolate, melted

2 cups sifted confectioners' sugar
¼ cup commercial sour cream

Mix together the first 4 ingredients. Add confectioners' sugar alternately with sour cream. Beat until of smooth-spreading consistency.

YIELD: Frosting for top of one 8-inch square cake

CHOCOLATE CREAM FROSTING

⅔ cup (1⅓ sticks) butter *or* margarine
2 squares (2 ounces) unsweetened chocolate
About 4 cups sifted confectioners' sugar
5 to 6 tablespoons heavy cream *or* undiluted evaporated milk
2 teaspoons vanilla extract

Melt butter or margarine in a saucepan large enough for mixing frosting. Heat to brown butter lightly. Add chocolate and stir until it has melted. Add sugar and enough cream to make frosting of smooth-spreading consistency. Stir in vanilla extract.

YIELD: Frosting for a 9-inch, 2-layer cake

POTATO FUDGE FROSTING

This frosting is deliciously smooth and creamy. Since it does not have the keeping qualities of richer frostings, it should be eaten within three days.

⅓ cup (⅔ stick) soft butter *or* margarine
2 squares (2 ounces) unsweetened chocolate
⅓ cup cold, smooth, mashed potatoes
⅛ teaspoon salt
1½ teaspoons vanilla extract

About 3 cups sifted confectioners' sugar
About 2 tablespoons milk

Melt butter or margarine in a saucepan. Cook until lightly browned. Add chocolate and stir until it is melted. Add next 3 ingredients and mix well. Add confectioners' sugar alternately with milk until frosting is of smooth-spreading consistency. Spread as desired over cake.

SPICED POTATO FUDGE FROSTING

Add ½ teaspoon ground cinnamon and ⅛ teaspoon ground cloves to the potato mixture in the above frosting recipe.

YIELD: Frosting for a 9-inch, 2-layer cake

LEMON FROSTING

3½ to 4 cups sifted confectioners' sugar
3 tablespoons milk *or* light cream
½ cup (1 stick) soft butter *or* margarine
1/16 teaspoon salt
¼ teaspoon ground mace
½ teaspoon grated lemon rind
1½ teaspoons vanilla extract

Add sugar and milk alternately to butter or margarine. Stir in remaining ingredients. Mix until fluffy.

YIELD: Frosting for an 8-inch, 2-layer cake

LEMON GLAZE

1½ cups sifted confectioners' sugar
2 teaspoons fresh lemon juice
5 teaspoons water
Yellow, green, and red food coloring

Combine sugar, lemon juice, and water. Mix well. Divide the frosting into 3 equal parts, coloring each as desired with yellow, green, or red food coloring.

YIELD: Frosting for top of a 12-inch King's Cake* or coffee cake.

MAPLE FROSTING

1 cup (2 sticks) soft butter *or* margarine
1 tablespoon vanilla extract
Dash ground cloves
¼ teaspoon salt

6 cups sifted confectioners' sugar
About ⅔ cup maple-flavored syrup

Combine first 4 ingredients. Beat until light and fluffy. Add sugar alternately with maple-flavored syrup, blending after each addition. Beat until thick enough to spread.

YIELD: Frosting for top of a 15½ x 10½-inch sheet cake

MOCHA FROSTING

½ cup (1 stick) soft butter *or* margarine
¼ cup cocoa
4 teaspoons instant coffee
½ teaspoon ground cinnamon

About 4 cups sifted confectioners' sugar
4½ tablespoons top milk *or* undiluted evaporated milk
1 teaspoon vanilla extract

Mix together the first 4 ingredients. Beat until fluffy. Add sugar alternately with milk. Stir in vanilla extract.

YIELD: Frosting for a 9-inch, 2-layer cake

NEVER-FAIL FROSTING

This frosting never fails if beaten stiff enough. It is ideal for a cake that is to be eaten the same day it is baked.

1 large egg white
1 cup sugar
¼ teaspoon cream of tartar
¼ teaspoon ground mace (optional)
1 teaspoon vanilla extract
½ cup boiling water

Place first 5 ingredients in the smaller bowl of the electric mixer. Add water. Beat at high speed until *very* stiff. Spread as desired over cake.

YIELD: Frosting for top and sides of an 8- or 9-inch, 2-layer cake

PEANUT BUTTER FROSTING

⅓ cup (⅔ stick) soft butter *or* margarine
⅓ cup peanut butter
Dash ground cloves
2½ cups sifted confectioners' sugar
1 teaspoon vanilla extract
3 tablespoons milk

Blend together butter or margarine, peanut butter, and cloves. Gradually add remaining ingredients. Mix well. Spread over cooled cake.

YIELD: Frosting for 2 dozen cupcakes or for an 8-inch, 2-layer cake

BROILED COCONUT TOPPING

3 tablespoons melted butter *or* margarine
⅓ cup light-brown sugar
2 tablespoons evaporated milk *or* light cream
¼ teaspoon ground nutmeg
½ cup shredded coconut

Combine all ingredients and spread over *hot* cake. Broil for about 5 minutes.

YIELD: Topping for one 9-inch square cake

BROILED COCONUT-ORANGE TOPPING

⅓ cup (⅔ stick) butter *or* margarine
¾ cup light-brown sugar
¼ cup orange juice
1 cup flaked coconut
¼ teaspoon grated orange rind
¼ teaspoon grated lemon rind
½ teaspoon ground nutmeg

Melt butter or margarine in a saucepan. Stir in remaining ingredients. Spread over top of a square cake or gingerbread. Brown lightly under broiler, watching closely to prevent burning.

YIELD: Topping for an 8- or 9-inch square cake

NUTMEG-LEMON TOPPING

2 large egg yolks

½ cup sifted confectioners' sugar
1 tablespoon fresh lemon juice
¼ teaspoon grated lemon rind
¼ teaspoon ground nutmeg
½ teaspoon vanilla extract

¾ cup heavy cream, whipped

Beat egg yolks. Gradually blend in next 5 ingredients. Fold in whipped cream. Serve over sponge cake.

YIELD: Topping for an 8-inch cake

EASY WHITE FROSTING

1 large egg white
¼ teaspoon cream of tartar
⅛ teaspoon salt
¼ teaspoon ground mace
¾ cup sugar
1 teaspoon vanilla extract
¼ cup boiling water

Place all ingredients in the small, deep bowl of the electric mixer. Beat with elec-

tric beater, at high speed, until very stiff. Spread over top and sides of cake.

YIELD: Frosting for a 10-inch tube cake or an 8- or 9-inch square cake

CHEESE DISHES

God of the country, bless today Thy cheese,
For which we give Thee thanks on bended knees . . .
From the hollow Holland, from the Vosges, from Brie,
From Roquefort, Gorgonzola, Italy!
Bless them, good Lord, Bless Stilton's royal fare,
Red Cheshire, and the tearful, cream Gruyère!
Bless Kantercaas, and bless the Mayence round,
Where aniseed and other grains are found;
Bless Edam, Pottekees, and Gouda then,
And those that we salute with "Sir" like men.

—M. Thomas Braun

HUNDREDS of cheeses have been created throughout the world—
France alone is said to have introduced about 400—but there are
actually fewer than 20 distinct types. Of these, fewer than 10 types are
properly used in cooking.

191

There are the very hard, ripened seasoning cheeses, Parmesan and Romano. These have such a sharp and distinct flavor, a small quantity has great pungency.

Firm ripened cheeses used for cooking include Cheddar—called "American" cheese in the United States—Gouda, Provolone, and Swiss. Flavors in this group vary from sharp to mild and sweet.

Unripened cheeses used in cooking are the familiar cottage cheese; mild Italian Mozzarella, which becomes stretchy as soon as heated; and Italian Ricotta, which is white, somewhat related to cottage cheese, but having a more pronounced flavor.

When cooking cheeses, there is one basic rule: Cook over low heat, as high heat or overcooking makes cheese tough, stringy, or leathery and may cause mixtures of cheese, egg, and milk to curdle. To accelerate melting and blending of cheese with other ingredients, grate, shred, or dice the cheese.

As to the art of spicing cheese, the list of spices and herbs that may be used is long: Herbs such as basil, marjoram, oregano, savory, and thyme add delightful aroma. Spice seeds such as caraway, celery, dill, and sesame contribute not only flavor but texture. And of the true spices, black, white, and red peppers are used; also mustard and ginger.

AMERICAN MAH-JONG

1 cup uncooked long-grain rice
4 cups canned tomatoes
1 cup chopped green pepper
1½ cups (6 ounces) grated, sharp
    American cheese
1 cup chopped pimiento-stuffed olives
¼ cup instant minced onion
½ teaspoon ground black pepper
2 teaspoons salt
1 teaspoon ground turmeric
1 bay leaf, crumbled
1 cup hot water

Combine all ingredients. Turn into a buttered 2-quart casserole. Cover and bake in a preheated slow oven (300° F.) 2 hours or until rice is tender. Serve hot as a main dish.

YIELD: 8 servings

CARAWAY SEED MACARONI RAREBIT

½ pound elbow macaroni
2 tablespoons butter *or* margarine

1 pound shredded Cheddar cheese
1 tablespoon caraway seed
¾ cup milk
½ teaspoon salt
¼ teaspoon ground black pepper

1 teaspoon powdered mustard
1 tablespoon water
Paprika

Cook macaroni as directed on the package. Drain and rinse in hot water. Melt butter or margarine in top of double boiler over hot water. Add the next 5 ingredients. Stir and cook until cheese has melted. Mix mustard with water and let stand 10 minutes. Add to the mixture.

Stir and cook until the sauce is the consistency of heavy cream, never letting the water in the double boiler boil. Add to macaroni. Mix lightly with a fork. Turn into a serving dish. Sprinkle with paprika.

YIELD: 6 servings

CHEESE AND CORN CASSEROLE

2 cups (1 pound) whole kernel corn
1 cup grated Cheddar cheese
1 tablespoon instant minced onion
2 tablespoons chopped green pepper
2 tablespoons chopped pimiento
1 cup soft bread crumbs
2 tablespoons butter *or* margarine, melted
1¼ teaspoons salt
¼ teaspoon ground ginger
⅛ teaspoon ground black pepper
¼ cup light cream

6 strips crisp bacon

Combine all ingredients except bacon. Turn into a buttered 1-quart casserole. Bake in a preheated moderate oven (350° F.) 50 minutes or until done. Serve with strips of crisp bacon.

YIELD: 6 servings

CHEESE AND EGG CROWN CASSEROLE

7 slices white bread
Soft butter *or* margarine
1 cup grated, sharp Cheddar cheese

3 large eggs, lightly beaten
2 cups milk
1 teaspoon salt
½ teaspoon powdered mustard
⅛ teaspoon ground white pepper
⅛ teaspoon garlic powder

Spread bread slices lightly with butter or margarine. Cut 2 slices twice on the bias, making 8 triangular pieces. Cut remaining bread into cubes (3½ cups) and place half the cubes over bottom of a buttered 1-quart casserole. Sprinkle with grated cheese and top with remaining bread cubes. Mix remaining ingredients and pour over bread cubes and cheese. Arrange triangles of bread upright around edge of dish to form a crown. Place in a pan of hot water.

Bake in a preheated slow oven (325° F.) 1 hour or until a knife inserted in center comes out clean. Serve at once.

YIELD: 6 servings

CHEESE AND RICE CROQUETTES

3 tablespoons butter *or* margarine
⅓ cup flour
1 cup milk

1 cup shredded American cheese
½ teaspoon salt
½ teaspoon ground ginger
1 teaspoon paprika
1/16 teaspoon cayenne
2 teaspoons parsley flakes
2 cups boiled rice

½ cup fine, dry bread crumbs
1 large egg, beaten
2 tablespoons milk
Fat for frying

Melt butter or margarine in a saucepan. Blend in flour. Stir in milk. Cook until very thick, stirring constantly. Add next 7 ingredients. Chill until mixture is firm enough to handle, about 1 hour. Shape into croquettes. Dip in fine, dry bread crumbs; then into egg mixed with the 2 tablespoons milk, and into bread crumbs

again. Fry in deep fat preheated to 340° F. until golden brown and heated through the center, about 40 seconds.

YIELD: 6 croquettes

CHEESE AND RICE PATTIES

Shape the above mixture into patties 1 inch thick and 2½ inches in diameter. Brown on both sides in hot bacon fat, butter, or margarine.

YIELD: 6 patties

CHEESE SOUFFLE SANDWICHES

12 slices white bread
Soft butter *or* margarine
6 slices American cheese
—
5 large eggs, lightly beaten
1½ cups milk
¾ teaspoon salt
¼ teaspoon ground black pepper
1 teaspoon paprika
⅛ teaspoon garlic powder
¾ teaspoon powdered mustard
½ teaspoon ground oregano

Remove crusts from bread and spread both sides with butter or margarine. Place 6 slices in a 10 x 6 x 1¾-inch baking pan. Place one slice of cheese over each of the bread slices. Cover with remaining bread slices. Combine the remaining ingredients and pour over sandwiches. Chill in refrigerator 3 hours. Bake in a preheated slow oven (300° F.) 30 minutes.

Increase heat to 325° F. and bake 15 minutes longer or until custard is set, puffy, and lightly browned. Serve at once.

YIELD: 6 servings

HAM AND CHEESE PUDDING

8 slices day-old bread
¼ cup (½ stick) butter *or* margarine
½ teaspoon powdered mustard
1½ teaspoons water
2 cups ground cooked ham
1 tablespoon mayonnaise
2 cups grated, sharp Cheddar cheese
—
3 large eggs, lightly beaten
1½ cups milk
1 cup cream of tomato soup
1 teaspoon salt
Dash cayenne

Remove crusts from bread and spread with softened butter or margarine. Place 4 slices in a buttered 8 x 8 x 2-inch pan. Soak mustard in water 10 minutes to develop flavor and mix with ham and mayonnaise. Spread over bread. Sprinkle with 1 cup of the grated cheese.

Cover with remaining bread slices. Combine next 5 ingredients and pour over bread. Sprinkle remaining cheese over the top. Chill 1 hour. Bake in a preheated slow oven (325° F.) 1 hour or until well puffed and browned. Serve at once.

YIELD: 6 servings

HERBED POTATO-CHEESE PUDDING

1 cup cottage cheese
1 cup sour cream
2 cups hot mashed potatoes
1½ teaspoons salt
½ teaspoon marjoram leaves
2 tablespoons instant minced onion
⅛ teaspoon garlic powder
—

2 large eggs, well beaten
2 tablespoons butter *or* margarine

Combine first 7 ingredients. Carefully blend in eggs. Turn into a buttered 1-quart casserole. Dot with butter or margarine. Bake in a preheated moderate oven (350° F.) 1 hour or until firm.

YIELD: 6 servings

MACARONI AND CHEESE MOUSSE

½ teaspoon powdered mustard
1½ teaspoons water
¼ cup (½ stick) butter *or* margarine
1½ cups milk
1 cup soft bread crumbs
2 tablespoons sweet pepper flakes
1 tablespoon instant minced onion

1 cup diced, sharp Cheddar cheese
1 teaspoon salt
⅛ teaspoon ground black pepper
1 cup cooked elbow macaroni

3 large eggs

Soak mustard in water 10 minutes to develop flavor. Heat together butter and milk and pour over bread crumbs, pepper flakes, and instant minced onion. Stir in mustard and next 4 ingredients. Beat eggs well and carefully blend with the mixture. Turn into a buttered 1-quart casserole and place in a pan of hot water.

Bake in a preheated moderate oven (350° F.) 1 hour or until a knife inserted

in the center comes out clean. Serve hot.

YIELD: 6 servings

CHEDDAR FONDUE

1 teaspoon powdered mustard
2 teaspoons water
3 tablespoons butter *or* margarine
3 tablespoons flour
½ to ¾ teaspoon ground black pepper
1 cup milk
2 cups grated, sharp Cheddar cheese
French bread, fresh *or* toasted

Mix mustard and water and let stand 10 minutes to develop flavor. Melt butter or margarine in top of double boiler. Add flour and black pepper and mix well. Gradually stir in milk.

Stir and cook over low heat until of medium thickness. Place over hot water and stir in grated cheese. Cook until cheese is melted. (DO NOT PERMIT WATER IN THE BOTTOM PART OF THE DOUBLE BOILER TO BOIL.) Add mustard and blend thoroughly.

Serve at once over toasted or untoasted French bread. Or, if desired, serve in a chafing dish and let each person spear cubes of bread with toothpicks and dunk into the fondue. If desired, serve as a hot hors d'oeuvre.

YIELD: 1⅔ cups

ONION-CHEESE FONDUE

6 slices bread
Soft butter *or* margarine
1½ cups (6 ounces) shredded, sharp
    Cheddar cheese
3 large eggs, well beaten
¾ teaspoon powdered mustard
¾ teaspoon salt
⅛ teaspoon ground black pepper
1 tablespoon instant minced onion
3 cups milk

Spread bread with butter or margarine and cut each slice in half. Arrange in a buttered 12 x 8 x 2-inch baking dish. Sprinkle with cheese. Combine remaining ingredients. Pour over bread. Let stand 1 hour.

Bake in a preheated slow oven (325° F.) 40 minutes or until puffy and brown. Serve at once as the main dish.

YIELD: 6 servings

PARMESAN CHEESE CUSHIONS

1 long loaf of French bread, approximately 14 inches long, 3 inches wide
Warm water

4 large eggs, beaten
½ cup grated Parmesan cheese
½ teaspoon salt
¼ teaspoon ground black pepper
1 teaspoon parsley flakes

1 cup olive *or* salad oil

2 cups (1-pound can) tomatoes
¼ teaspoon instant minced garlic
¼ teaspoon sugar
½ teaspoon salt
2 tablespoons olive *or* salad oil

½ teaspoon oregano leaves
½ teaspoon ground black pepper
Grated Parmesan cheese

Cut bread into small pieces. Place in warm water and let stand until thoroughly soaked. Squeeze out the water and mix bread with the next 5 ingredients. Mix well and shape into 16 cushions or balls of equal size. Fry in the 1 cup hot oil until golden on both sides. Combine the next 5 ingredients. Cook 15 minutes, stirring occasionally. Add oregano and black pepper. Cook 5 minutes. Serve over the fried bread cushions. Sprinkle with grated Parmesan cheese.

YIELD: 16 servings

PUERTO RICAN PIZZA

1 envelope active dry yeast
½ cup lukewarm water
1 teaspoon sugar

¾ cup hot water
6 tablespoons lard *or* shortening
¼ cup sugar
1 teaspoon salt

1 large egg
About 5 cups flour
Pizza Filling *(see below)*

Mix yeast with warm water and the 1 teaspoon of sugar. Let stand 10 minutes to soften. Combine in a mixing bowl the next 4 ingredients. Stir until lard and sugar are completely blended. Cool to lukewarm. Stir in yeast and egg. Gradually add enough flour to make a soft dough. Knead until smooth and satiny. Place in a greased bowl, turning dough in bowl to bring greased sides to the top. Cover and let rise in a warm place (80° to 85° F.) about 1 hour or until dough has doubled in size.

Divide dough in two equal parts. Cover and let rest 10 minutes. Roll each out very thin on a greased cooky sheet in a 15 x 12-inch rectangle. Chill until ready to spread the Pizza Filling.

PIZZA FILLING
½ cup finely chopped green peppers
2 tablespoons olive *or* salad oil

2 cups drained canned tomatoes
2 tablespoons instant minced onion
1 teaspoon salt
1 teaspoon oregano leaves
½ teaspoon sugar
½ teaspoon ground black pepper
⅛ teaspoon instant minced garlic

Spanish sausage (chorizos)
Stuffed green olives, sliced
Mozzarella cheese
Anchovy fillets
Grated Parmesan cheese

Sauté green pepper in hot oil. Add next 7 ingredients. Stir and cook slowly 10 minutes or until thickened. Cool. Spread over pizza dough. Top a portion of the pizza as desired with each of the following: Cooked, thinly sliced sausage; olives; sliced cheese; and anchovies.

Bake in a preheated hot oven (400° F.) 15 to 20 minutes or until crust has browned and edges are crisp. Sprinkle with Parmesan cheese. Cut into 2 x 1-inch pieces if to be served as a hot hors d'oeuvre, or into larger pieces if served as the main dish.

YIELD: 2 pizzas, 15 x 12 inches

QUICHE LORRAINE

It would seem that every cook in northern France has her own recipe for this savory cheese main-dish pie. You can use crisp bacon strips with the Swiss cheese or Gruyère arranged over the pie crust. You can add onion if you like. Or, you can omit the bacon and onion and use 4 to 6 coarsely chopped anchovies instead.

6 strips crisp bacon
9-inch, unbaked 1-crust pie shell
   (Never-Fail Pastry I*)
12 thin slices Swiss cheese

4 large eggs
1 tablespoon flour
½ teaspoon salt
½ teaspoon powdered mustard
Few grains cayenne

2 cups light cream
1½ teaspoons melted butter *or*
   margarine

Cut bacon strips in halves. Line unbaked 9-inch pie shell with bacon and Swiss cheese. Beat next 5 ingredients together. Add light cream and melted butter and strain mixture over bacon and cheese.

Bake in a preheated moderate oven (375° F.) for 40 minutes, or until custard has set.

YIELD: 6 servings

*An asterisk after the name of a dish indicates that the recipe for this dish appears in the book. Consult the Index for the page number.

CHILI DISHES

CHILI CON CARNE AND "TEX-MEX" COOKERY

CHILI CON CARNE, enchiladas, and tacos top the list of those Southwestern favorites so often called "Tex-Mex" dishes. Meat, beans, rice, corn meal, tomatoes, onions and green peppers are the basic ingredients made irresistible with the addition of rich spicing.

The Mexican cook usually blends her own spices: oregano, cumin, garlic, whole (and hot) chili peppers. Cooks north of the Rio Grande prefer the more convenient chili powder, which is a blend of chili peppers, red peppers, oregano, cumin, and garlic powder. Depending on the formula used by the manufacturer, chili powder may also contain other spices such as ground cloves, allspice, and onions. Most chili powder is not particularly pungent, but you can make it plenty hot by adding red pepper or cayenne.

Chili powder originated in our own Southwest during the nineteenth century. While the use of chili peppers and oregano in combination has been traced back to the Aztecs, the premixed blend, chili powder, is said to be the invention of early Texans. The first Anglo-American settlement in Texas was developed between 1821 and 1835. Story has it that these early settlers found themselves virtually cut off from civilization and the various supplies they were used to getting, so naturally they had to improvise. Inasmuch as curry powder was one of the most popular seasonings of the time, these settlers looked for something to take its place.

198

The aromatic ingredients that grew wild in this region—such as chili peppers, oregano, and garlic—were used in place of those which had to be imported.

Although chili powder is the primary seasoning in most Mexican-type dishes, its use as a general seasoning is increasing. Try it with eggs, omelets, cottage cheese, shellfish, and oyster cocktail sauces, gravy, and stew seasonings.

BARBECUED CHILI SPARERIBS

1 cup (8 ounces) Spanish-style tomato sauce
1 tablespoon sugar
2 tablespoons cider vingegar
1 tablespoon lemon juice
2 teaspoons chili powder
½ teaspoon salt
½ teaspoon powdered mustard
½ teaspoon celery salt
½ teaspoon garlic salt
1/16 to ⅛ teaspoon cayenne
1 tablespoon instant minced onion

3 pounds spareribs

Combine all ingredients except spareribs. Heat only until hot. Leave ribs in one piece and place on a rack in 15½ x 10½ x 1-inch baking pan.

Bake in a preheated very hot oven (500° F.) 15 minutes. Reduce heat to 350° F. and bake 1½ hours or until very tender, turning and brushing at 15 minute intervals until ribs are done. If you like them crisp, place ribs under broiler 3 to 5 minutes. With scissors, cut ribs into 2- to 3-rib servings. Spoon any remaining sauce over the ribs.

YIELD: 6 servings

BEEF AND CHILI BEAN CASSEROLE

This is an ideal party dish.

1 pound beef stew meat
1 cup chopped onion

½ cup diced green pepper
5 sausage links, sliced

3 cups (1 pound, 4 ounces) canned red kidney beans
1 cup catsup
2 teaspoons salt

5 to 6 teaspoons chili powder
½ teaspoon oregano leaves
½ teaspoon instant minced garlic
¼ teaspoon cayenne
2 cups (½ pound) grated, sharp Cheddar cheese

Onion rings

Trim and discard excess fat from meat. Cut meat into ½-inch pieces and place in a saucepan with the next 3 ingredients. Sauté until meat begins to brown. Add 2 cups of the undrained beans, catsup, and salt. Cover and simmer 30 minutes. Drain the remaining 1 cup of beans, mash, and add to meat along with the next 5 ingredients. Turn into a 2-quart casserole.

Bake, uncovered, in a preheated slow oven (325° F.) 1 hour. Garnish with a few onion rings. Serve hot.

YIELD: 8 servings

BUSY-DAY CHILI

1 pound ground lean beef
1 tablespoon shortening

1 can (10½ ounces) condensed cream of tomato soup
2 tablespoons instant minced onion
2 tablespoons water
2 teaspoons salt
4 teaspoons chili powder

½ teaspoon tarragon leaves
⅛ teaspoon ground black pepper
1/16 teaspoon cayenne
1/16 teaspoon garlic powder
2 cups (1 pound) canned
    red kidney beans, undrained

Brown beef in hot shortening. Add remaining ingredients. Stir and cook 10 minutes or until thickened. Serve hot.

YIELD: 6 servings

CHILI BEAN LOAF

2 pounds ground chuck
3 tablespoons instant minced onion
2 tablespoons sweet pepper flakes
2 teaspoons salt
2 teaspoons chili powder
¼ teaspoon ground black pepper
¼ teaspoon garlic powder
2 large eggs, lightly beaten
½ cup fine, dry bread crumbs
1 cup (8 ounces) canned tomatoes

2 cups (1 pound) canned kidney beans

Combine the first 10 ingredients in a mixing bowl. Drain beans, mash, and add to meat. Mix well. Pack into a greased 9 x 5 x 3-inch loaf pan. Bake in a preheated moderate oven (350° F.) 1 hour or until done.

YIELD: 8 to 10 servings

CHILI BOILED KIDNEY BEANS

2 cups dried red kidney beans
9 cups cold water
¼ pound salt pork

2 teaspoons salt
3 teaspoons chili powder
¼ teaspoon ground black pepper
2 tablespoons instant minced onion

Green pepper rings
Grated cheese

Wash beans well. Add cold water. Cover and bring to boiling point. Boil 5 minutes. Turn off heat and let stand 1 hour. Score salt pork and add to beans. Cover and cook until tender, about 2 hours.

Add the next 4 ingredients. Cover. Cook 30 minutes or until beans are tender. Garnish each serving with a green pepper ring and a sprinkling of grated cheese.

YIELD: 8 servings

CHILI CON CARNE

2 pounds ground chuck
1 tablespoon shortening
1 cup diced green pepper

3½ cups (1 pound, 13 ounces)
    canned tomatoes
½ cup onion flakes
2 teaspoons salt

4 cups (2 pounds) canned red
    kidney beans
2 tablespoons chili powder
2 teaspoons oregano
½ teaspoon garlic powder
½ teaspoon ground black pepper

Brown meat in shortening in a 3-quart saucepan or Dutch oven. Add green pepper and cook until limp. Stir in next 3 ingredients. Cook slowly 15 minutes. Add undrained kidney beans and next 4 ingredients. Cook 10 minutes. Serve over hot cooked rice.

YIELD: 12 servings

CHILI CON CARNE CHEESE BALLS

1½ pounds ground chuck
1½ teaspoons salt
¼ teaspoon ground black pepper
1½ teaspoons chili powder

12 cubes American cheese, ½ inch each
2 to 3 tablespoons shortening *or* olive oil

½ cup finely chopped onion
⅓ cup finely chopped green pepper
1½ cups hot water
¾ cup catsup
4½ teaspoons chili powder
1½ teaspoons salt (or to taste)

Combine the first 4 ingredients and divide into 12 equal portions. Wrap each portion around a cube of cheese. Brown on all sides in shortening or oil. Remove meat balls. Add remaining 6 ingredients, bring to boiling point. Add meat balls, cover, and simmer 10 minutes. Serve over hot cooked rice.

YIELD: 6 servings

CHILI MEAT CROQUETTES WITH TOMATO SAUCE

4 cups ground cooked beef
2 cups Thick White Sauce*
1 cup fine, dry bread crumbs
2 tablespoons instant minced onion
2½ teaspoons salt
4 teaspoons chili powder
¼ teaspoon ground black pepper
¼ teaspoon garlic powder

*An asterisk after the name of a dish indicates that the recipe for this dish appears in the book. Consult the Index for the page number.

Flour
1 large egg, lightly beaten
1 tablespoon milk *or* water
Fine, dry bread crumbs
Chili Tomato Sauce*

Combine first 8 ingredients. Shape into pyramids, cones, cylinders, or balls. Chill thoroughly. Roll in flour. Dip in egg mixed with milk or water. Roll in bread crumbs. Fry in deep fat preheated to 375° F. for 3 minutes or until browned. Serve with Chili Tomato Sauce.

YIELD: 6 croquettes

CHILI MACARONI AND CHEESE

1½ cups uncooked elbow macaroni
1½ cups cubed sharp American cheese
2 tablespoons instant minced onion
2 tablespoons chopped pimiento
½ teaspoon salt
1 teaspoon chili powder
⅛ teaspoon ground black pepper
2 large eggs, beaten
2 cups milk

Cook macaroni according to package directions. Drain. Rinse in hot water. Drain again. Mix lightly with remaining ingredients. Turn into a 10 x 6 x 2-inch baking dish. Bake in a preheated slow oven (325° F.) 50 minutes or until browned over the top. Serve hot.

YIELD: 6 servings

CHILI-SIZE

This is a double hamburger topped with a snappy chili bean sauce. Tremendously popular on the West Coast.

2 teaspoons shortening
1 pound ground chuck (for sauce)
¼ cup instant minced onion

½ teaspoon instant minced garlic
1¾ cups water

2 tablespoons chili powder
1 tablespoon flour
1¼ teaspoons salt
1 cup (8 ounces) canned kidney beans

12 cooked, thin hamburgers
6 toasted hamburger buns
¾ cup grated Cheddar cheese

Melt shortening in a deep 9-inch skillet.
Add chuck. Soften onion and garlic in ¼
cup of the water and add to meat. Cook
slowly 15 minutes or until meat is brown.
Stir in the remaining water and the next 4
ingredients.

Cook slowly 45 minutes or until sauce
is of medium thickness. Place a cooked
hamburger on each half of a toasted hamburger bun. Cover with a generous serving of the chili meat sauce. Sprinkle with
a rounded tablespoon grated Cheddar
cheese. A serving consists of one roll and
2 thin hamburgers with the meat sauce.

YIELD: 6 servings

GRILLED CHILI SHRIMP

½ cup (1 stick) butter or margarine,
    melted
2 teaspoons fresh lemon juice
1½ teaspoons chili powder
½ teaspoon salt
⅛ teaspoon ground black pepper

1 pound uncooked, peeled shrimp

Combine all ingredients except shrimp.
String shrimp on skewers, brush with the
sauce and cook over charcoal grill. (The
cooking time depends upon the heat of
the fire.)

GRILLED CHILI
SWORDFISH KEBABS
Replace shrimp in the above recipe with

1-inch cubes of uncooked swordfish.

YIELD: 4 servings

CHILI SHRIMP ON RICE

¼ cup onion flakes
3 tablespoons water
1 tablespoon olive or salad oil

½ teaspoon garlic salt
2 teaspoons chili powder (or to taste)
1 teaspoon oregano leaves
¼ teaspoon ground cumin seed
1½ cups (12 ounces) canned tomatoes
2 cups (1 pound) canned
    red kidney beans, drained
1 pound peeled, deveined, raw shrimp

Soften onion in water and sauté 1 minute
in oil. Add all remaining ingredients.
Stir and cook over medium-low heat 15
minutes or until shrimp are tender. (DO
NOT BOIL, as high heat toughens shrimp.)
Serve over hot cooked rice.

YIELD: 6 servings

MEAT BALLS IN
ALMOND SAUCE

(ALBONDIGAS EN SALSA
DE ALMENDRA)

2 tablespoons minced onion
3 tablespoons olive oil
⅓ cup tomato purée
1¼ cups water
1½ teaspoons salt
⅔ cup blanched almonds
⅛ teaspoon instant minced garlic
3 slices bread, cubed
¼ cup hot milk
½ pound ground lean beef
½ pound ground lean pork
1 large egg, beaten
2 to 3 teaspoons chili powder
    (or to taste)
⅛ teaspoon ground black pepper

2 large hard-cooked eggs
3 cups cooked, diced potatoes
Sliced blanched almonds, toasted

Sauté onion 1 minute in 1 tablespoon of the oil. Add tomato purée, water, and ½ teaspoon of the salt. In the meantime, fry almonds, garlic, and ⅓ of the bread cubes in the remaining oil. Cool and put through a food chopper, using medium blade. Add to the tomato mixture. Cook slowly 10 minutes.

Soak the remaining bread cubes in hot milk. Drain and add to the meats along with the remaining salt and the next 3 ingredients. Cut hard-cooked eggs in lengthwise quarters. Then, cut quarters in crosswise halves and wrap enough meat around each piece to make a 2-inch ball.

Brown on all sides and add to the sauce. Simmer 15 minutes. Turn into a serving dish with meat balls in center. Place cooked potatoes on sauce around the meat balls. Garnish with almonds.

YIELD: 5 servings

MEXICAN CHICKEN
3-pound, ready-to-cook chicken
3 tablespoons butter *or* margarine
3 medium tomatoes, peeled and
    quartered
2 tablespoons instant minced onion
2½ teaspoons salt
½ cup water

1½ teaspoons chili powder
¼ teaspoon garlic powder
⅛ teaspoon ground black pepper
¼ cup chopped pimiento

1 tablespoon flour
1 tablespoon water

Cut chicken into serving-size pieces and brown in butter or margarine. Add tomatoes, onion, salt, and water. Cover and

simmer 20 to 30 minutes or until chicken is tender.

Add the next 4 ingredients 10 minutes before cooking time is up. Remove chicken to serving dish. Mix flour with water to a smooth paste and stir into the gravy. Cook ½ to 1 minute or until thickened. Pour into dish around chicken. Serve hot over rice.

YIELD: 6 servings

TOSTADAS WITH MEAT SAUCE
(GANACHA)
1 pound ground chuck
1 tablespoon olive *or* salad oil

1 cup (8 ounces) tomato sauce
2 tablespoons instant minced onion
1 teaspoon salt
2 teaspoons chili powder
1 teaspoon oregano leaves
¼ teaspoon garlic powder
¼ teaspoon ground black pepper

6 tortillas
2 to 3 tablespoons olive *or* salad oil
Shredded Monterey *or* Cheddar cheese
Finely shredded lettuce

Brown meat in the 1 tablespoon hot oil. Add the next 7 ingredients and simmer 5 minutes, stirring frequently. Fry tortillas until crisp in hot oil, adding more as needed. Place a tortilla on each serving plate. Top with meat sauce. Sprinkle with cheese and lettuce. If tortillas are not available, serve sauce on toast or corn-meal pancakes.

YIELD: 6 servings

CHILI CON CARNE PIE WITH CORN BREAD TOPPING

¼ cup instant minced onion
¼ cup water
1 tablespoon shortening
½ cup chopped green pepper
1 pound ground chuck

2 cups (1 pound) canned tomatoes
1½ teaspoons salt
¼ teaspoon ground black pepper
¼ teaspoon poultry seasoning
3 to 4 teaspoons chili powder
2½ cups (1 pound, 4 ounces) canned red kidney beans, undrained

1 package corn bread mix

Soften onion in water. Turn into a 10-inch skillet along with shortening, green pepper, and meat. Stir and cook 10 minutes or until meat is brown.

Add the next 6 ingredients. Cook 10 to 15 minutes or until mixture has thickened. Turn into a greased 1½-quart casserole. Make corn bread as directed on the package. Drop batter from a tablespoon over the top. Spread with a spatula to cover top uniformly.

Bake in a preheated hot oven (425° F.) 30 minutes or until corn bread has browned.

YIELD: 6 servings

MEAL-IN-ONE CORN PIE

1 pound ground chuck
1 tablespoon butter *or* margarine

2 tablespoons instant minced onion
¼ teaspoon instant minced garlic
3 tablespoons flour

2 cups fresh corn, cut from the cob
2 cups diced tomatoes
½ teaspoon sugar
2 teaspoons salt (or to taste)
1¾ teaspoons chili powder
¼ teaspoon ground black pepper

6 slices buttered, close-textured bread

Brown meat in butter or margarine. Add the next 3 ingredients. Stir and cook ½ minute. Add the next 6 ingredients. Cook 5 minutes. Turn into a buttered 10 x 6 x 2-inch baking dish. Top with buttered bread.

Bake in a preheated moderate oven (350° F.) 30 minutes or until bread is golden. Serve hot as the main dish.

YIELD: 6 servings

TAMALE PIE

1 pound ground chuck
¾ cup diced green pepper

¾ cup diced onion
½ teaspoon oregano leaves
¼ teaspoon ground cumin seed
2 teaspoons salt
3 teaspoons chili powder

¼ teaspoon instant minced garlic
¼ teaspoon ground black pepper
2 cups (1 pound) canned tomatoes

1½ cups yellow corn meal
1¼ cups water
3¾ cups boiling water
1¾ teaspoons salt

3 slices fresh tomato

Cook together, in a heavy 9-inch skillet, the first 7 ingredients. When meat begins to brown, add the next 3 ingredients. Simmer, uncovered, 15 minutes or until excess liquid has evaporated.

Mix corn meal with cold water, and gradually stir into boiling water. Add salt. Stir and cook until the mixture has thickened.

Spread a thin layer over the bottom of a 10 x 6 x 2-inch baking dish. Add meat and tomato mixture, smoothing with a spatula to cover uniformly. Spread a ¼-inch layer corn-meal mixture over the top. Put remaining cooked corn meal in a pastry bag, pushing it through the tube to make a frill around the edge.

Bake in a preheated moderate oven (375° F.) 30 minutes or until done. For a garnish, arrange sliced tomatoes over the top as desired 15 minutes before cooking time is up. Serve hot.

YIELD: 6 servings

CHILI BEAN SLOPPY JOES
1 pound ground chuck
1 tablespoon shortening

½ cup diced green pepper
¼ cup instant minced onion
1½ teaspoons salt
1 cup canned tomatoes

1 cup (8 ounces) drained
  kidney beans
⅛ teaspoon ground black pepper
1 to 2 teaspoons chili powder

Hamburger buns

Brown meat in shortening, stirring frequently. Add the next 4 ingredients. Stir and cook until mixture has thickened, about 10 minutes. Add next 3 ingredients. Cook until hot, 5 to 6 minutes. Serve between split hot hamburger buns.

YIELD: 8 servings

MEXICAN SANDWICHES
(TORTAS COMPUESTAS)
4 crusty French rolls

2 cups (1 pound) canned red kidney
  beans, drained
3 tablespoons kidney-bean liquid
1¼ teaspoons salt
¾ teaspoon chili powder
¼ teaspoon ground black pepper
⅛ teaspoon garlic powder

½ cup finely shredded lettuce

¼ pound sliced, cooked pork, tongue,
  turkey, *or* ham
1 avocado, cut in thin slices
1 large green pepper, cut in rings
  ⅛ inch thick

¼ to ⅓ cup French dressing

Cut rolls in half lengthwise, tear out soft centers, and set aside. Combine next 6 ingredients. Heat and then put through a sieve to form a paste. Cool. Spread over the bottom halves of rolls. Cover with shredded lettuce. Then top with the next 3 ingredients. Pour enough French dressing over each to moisten. Cover with remaining halves of rolls.

YIELD: 4 servings

TACOS

12 tortillas
Cooking oil

1 pound ground chuck
1 tablespoon cooking oil *or* fat
2 tablespoons instant minced onion
¼ teaspoon instant minced garlic
2½ to 3 teaspoons chili powder
1¼ teaspoons salt
½ teaspoon oregano leaves
¼ teaspoon ground cumin seed
2 teaspoons sweet pepper flakes

1 cup canned tomatoes
Shredded lettuce

Fry tortillas crisp in ½ inch hot oil, turning with tongs and shaping each into a *U*. Set aside in a warm place until ready to use.

Place the next 9 ingredients in a saucepan. Stir and cook 5 minutes or until mixture begins to brown. Add tomatoes. Stir and cook 10 minutes or until mixture thickens. Spoon in fried tacos (fried tortillas). Top with shredded lettuce.

YIELD: 6 servings

COOKIES and SMALL CAKES

HISTORY does not tell us when, where, or by whom the first cooky was made. However, we credit the Dutch—famous for their honey and nut cookies—with having introduced the name to America, since cooky derives from the Dutch *Koekje,* meaning "little cakes." The early Dutch settlers brought their family recipes along with them, thereby endowing America with a wide variety of these delicacies.

The Germans brought over their Christmas cookies, many of which, like the famous Pfeffernuesse,* were highly spiced. The English brought their tea biscuits, the Scotch their shortbreads and oatmeal cookies, and the Chinese their almond cakes.

Although cocoa is native to America, chocolate cookies came to the American Colonies by way of Europe long after Columbus and Sir Francis Drake had taken the cacao from the New World to Spain and France.

The use of sugar in cookies is relatively new. Early Europeans depended largely on honey for sweetening and, in Colonial times, molasses often pro-

*An asterisk after the name of a dish indicates that the recipe for this dish appears in the book. Consult the Index for the page number.

vided the sweetening. It was not until the introduction of modern sugar-refining equipment that we were able to cook with the sugar now familiar to us.

In making cookies, follow recipe directions faithfully. Overmeasurement of flour can cause the cookies to be tough and dry. On the other hand, dough having too little flour cannot be rolled. Rich, short cookies usually require ungreased baking sheets. The pans should be thin and small enough so that the hot air of the oven will circulate around them freely. Make each cooky the same size and thickness so that they all will bake at the same rate. Because cookies bake so quickly, and even continue baking a few minutes after they are removed from the oven, take care not to overbake. Test them a minute or two before you believe they may be done. Take them out as soon as they have a delicate brown crust and are "set" in the center.

As soon as rolled or dropped cookies have been pulled from the oven, remove them from the sheet with a spatula and place them on a wire rack. Most bar cookies, however, should be cooled in the pan. They are cut most easily when barely warm or even completely cold, rather than when hot.

All cookies should be stored in closed containers to safeguard the moist, soft varieties from drying out, and the crisp ones against absorbing moisture from the air. Store soft and crisp cookies in separate containers. The crisp cookies should be cold before they are placed in the containers.

CHRISTMAS CUT-OUT COOKIES

½ cup shortening
½ cup unsulphured molasses

2 cups sifted all-purpose flour
½ cup sugar
½ teaspoon soda
¼ teaspoon salt
1 teaspoon allspice

¼ cup milk
1 large egg white
Colored granulated sugar *or* Confectioners' Sugar and Water Glaze*

Melt shortening in a saucepan large enough for mixing cookies. Stir in molasses. Sift together the next 5 ingredients and add to molasses and shortening along with milk. Mix well. Chill dough 3 to 4 hours or until it is stiff enough to handle.

Roll dough to ⅛-inch thickness on a lightly floured board. Shape as desired with assorted cooky cutters, dipped in flour.

Bake on ungreased cooky sheets in a preheated moderate oven (350° F.) 10 minutes or until lightly browned around the edges. Cool on wire racks. Beat egg white *only* until frothy. Brush lightly over the tops of cookies and sprinkle with red and green granulated sugar. Or, if desired, frost with Confectioners' Sugar and Water Glaze after cookies are baked and cooled. Store airtight.

YIELD: 4 to 5 dozen cookies

EMPIRE BISCUIT

This is an old Richmond, Virginia, recipe that has been modernized in the testing. It dates back to early Colonial days and must have been the favorite recipe of some old Tory, since it is called an "empire" cooky.

¼ teaspoon ground mace
¼ teaspoon ground cinnamon
½ cup (1 stick) soft butter *or* margarine
¼ cup sugar
1¼ cups sifted all-purpose flour
Currant jelly
Confectioners' Sugar and Water Glaze*
Glacé red cherries
Angelica

Mix together the first 3 ingredients. Blend in sugar. Gradually stir in flour. Chill dough 1 hour or until it is stiff enough to handle. Roll to ¹⁄₁₆-inch thickness on a lightly floured board. Shape with a 1½-inch round cooky cutter. Place on ungreased cooky sheets. Bake 4 to 6 minutes, in a preheated hot oven (400° F.), or until lightly browned around the edges. Cool on wire rack. Put two cookies together with a thin layer of currant jelly. Frost tops with Confectioners' Sugar and Water Glaze. Garnish with bits of glacé red cherries and angelica.

YIELD: 2 dozen cookies

GINGERBREAD MEN
¾ cup unsulphured molasses
¾ cup (1½ sticks) butter *or* margarine
3⅔ cups sifted all-purpose flour
1 teaspoon double-acting baking powder
1 teaspoon salt
½ teaspoon soda
2 teaspoons ground ginger
2 teaspoons ground cinnamon
¾ cup dark-brown sugar
1 large egg

Heat molasses in a saucepan large enough for mixing cookies. Remove from heat and stir in butter or margarine. Cool.

Sift together the next 6 ingredients, add brown sugar, and mix well. Stir into the molasses and butter mixture. Add egg and mix well. Chill 1 to 2 hours or until dough is stiff enough to roll.

Divide dough in half. Roll each half ⅛ to ¼ inch thick on a lightly floured board, chilling the second half while the first half is being rolled and cut.

Use a gingerbread-man cooky cutter dipped in flour. Place on lightly greased cooky sheets. Decorate in gingerbread-man fashion with raisins or currants or, if desired, wait until cookies are baked and cooled and then decorate with Confectioners' Sugar and Water Glaze.*

Bake in a preheated moderate oven (350° F.) 12 to 15 minutes or until lightly browned around the edges. Cool on wire racks. Store airtight.

YIELD: About 16 gingerbread men

NUREMBERGERS
Nurembergers are spiced honey cookies from the German city famous for its toys. In the thirteenth and fourteenth centuries, Nuremberg was a great trading center for the spices of the Orient.

2½ cups sifted all-purpose flour
½ teaspoon soda
½ teaspoon ground cloves
¾ teaspoon ground cinnamon
1 teaspoon ground allspice
1 cup strained honey
¾ cup light-brown sugar
1 large egg, lightly beaten
1 tablespoon fresh lemon juice
1 teaspoon grated lemon rind
½ cup chopped nuts
¾ cup chopped citron

Blanched almonds
Candied lemon peel

Sift together the first 5 ingredients and set aside. Mix honey with brown sugar in a saucepan large enough for mixing cookies. Heat to boiling point. Cool. Stir in next 3 ingredients. Gradually add flour mixture. Blend in chopped nuts and citron, saving a little of the citron for use as garnish.

Chill dough overnight or until it is stiff enough to roll. Roll to ¼-inch thickness on a lightly floured board. (This dough is supposed to be sticky. Do not add more flour.) Shape with 2-inch cooky cutter. Place on greased cooky sheets. Decorate to resemble a daisy by using a dice of citron as the center and strips of almond and candied lemon peel for the petals.

Bake in a preheated moderate oven (350° F.) 10 minutes. Cool and store airtight 3 or 4 days before eating. These cookies improve with age.

YIELD: 5½ dozen cookies

ORANGE CUT-OUT CHRISTMAS COOKIES

2 cups sifted all-purpose flour

1 teaspoon double-acting
  baking powder
½ teaspoon salt

½ teaspoon ground mace
2 teaspoons grated orange rind
½ cup shortening

1 cup sugar
1 large egg
2 tablespoons orange juice
Confectioners' Sugar and Water Glaze*

Sift together the first 3 ingredients and set aside. Blend mace and orange rind with shortening. Gradually mix in sugar. Beat in egg and orange juice. Stir in flour, a little at a time. Chill dough overnight, 3 to 4 hours, or until it is stiff enough to handle. Roll to ⅛-inch thickness on a lightly floured board.

Bake on ungreased cooky sheets in a preheated hot oven (400° F.) 8 minutes or until cookies are light brown around the edges. Cool and frost with Confectioners' Sugar and Water Glaze. Or, if desired, serve plain. Store airtight.

YIELD: 7 dozen cookies

ANISE COOKIES

Anise is a favorite sweet spice in Europe, especially in the Scandinavian countries and in Germany. Our modern wedding cake is said to date back to the anise-flavored cakes eaten by the Romans after elaborate meals.

To crush anise seeds, use a mortar and pestle, if available, or place seeds in a custard cup and crush with the back of a spoon.

1 cup light-brown sugar
½ to ¾ teaspoon crushed anise seed
¾ cup (1½ sticks) soft butter *or*
  margarine

PEPPER

CINNAMON

CINNAMON

CINNAMON

CLOVE

CLOVES

NUTMEG

NUTMEG

NUTM

THE
SPICE MERCHANT

2 cups sifted all-purpose flour
1 teaspoon double acting
   baking powder
⅛ teaspoon salt

1 large egg, beaten
2 tablespoons milk

Gradually blend brown sugar and crushed anise seed into butter or margarine. Sift together the next 3 ingredients and add to the mixture alternately with combined egg and milk. Mix well. Fill a cooky press with the dough. Form cookies in desired shapes on ungreased cooky sheets.

Bake in a preheated hot oven (400° F.) 8 to 10 minutes. Cool on wire racks. Store airtight.

YIELD: 8 dozen cookies

BRANDY SNAPS

1 cup sifted cake flour
⅔ cup sugar
2 teaspoons ground ginger
1 teaspoon ground cinnamon

½ cup unsulphured molasses
½ cup (1 stick) butter or margarine

Sift together the first 4 ingredients and set aside. Heat molasses *just* to boiling point in a saucepan large enough for mixing cookies. Stir in butter or margarine. Add flour mixture. Mix well. Drop ½-teaspoon portions of dough onto greased cooky sheets, 2 inches apart to allow room for spreading.

Bake in a preheated slow oven (300° F.) 15 to 18 minutes. Remove cookies from oven and cool 2 minutes. Carefully slip a spatula underneath the wafers and remove them from the pan onto a cooling rack. Quickly roll each around the index finger or the handle of a wooden spoon. If wafers become brittle before they are shaped, place in oven a minute to reheat. Then remove from pan and roll. Store airtight.

HONEY ROLLED WAFERS

In the above recipe, reduce sugar to ½ cup, omit ginger, and replace molasses with ½ cup honey. Bake and shape as directed for Brandy Snaps.

YIELD: 30 snaps

BROWN SUGAR SAND TARTS

2 cups sifted all-purpose flour
¼ teaspoon ground nutmeg
1 cup light-brown sugar

⅔ cup (1⅓ sticks) soft butter or
   margarine
1 large egg, lightly beaten
1 tablespoon milk

¼ cup granulated sugar
1 teaspoon ground cinnamon

Sift together the first 3 ingredients. Add butter or margarine and cut it in until the mixture resembles coarse meal. Add egg and milk and mix well to form a dough. Shape into 1-inch balls. Place on lightly greased cooky sheets 2 inches apart. Flatten to ¹⁄₁₆-inch thickness with the bottom of a glass covered with a wet cloth. Combine granulated sugar and cinnamon. Sprinkle each cooky lightly with this mixture. Bake in a preheated hot oven (400° F.) 8 to 10 minutes or until the edges have lightly browned (DO NOT OVERBAKE).

ROLLED COOKIES

Chill the above dough 1 to 2 hours or until stiff enough to handle. Roll to ⅛-inch thickness on a lightly floured board. Cut into assorted shapes with cooky cutters dipped in flour. Bake 8 to 10 minutes in preheated hot oven (400° F.) on lightly greased cooky sheets.

YIELD: 6 to 7 dozen thin cookies

BUTTER WAFERS

2 cups sifted all-purpose flour
1 cup sugar
½ teaspoon ground cinnamon
½ teaspoon ground allspice

¾ cup (1½ sticks) soft butter *or* margarine

1 large egg, lightly beaten
1½ teaspoons vanilla extract
1 tablespoon milk

Colored granulated sugar (optional)

Sift together the first 4 ingredients into a mixing bowl. Add butter or margarine and work it in with the tips of fingers or pastry blender. Combine next 3 ingredients. Stir into the mixture. Mix well to form a dough. Shape into ½-inch balls.

Place 2 inches apart on an ungreased cooky sheet. Flatten to ¹⁄₁₆-inch thickness with the bottom of a glass covered with a damp cloth. If desired, sprinkle colored sugar in the center of each cooky. Bake in a preheated hot oven (400° F.) 6 to 8 minutes or until lightly brown around the edges. DO NOT BAKE TOO BROWN. Cool on a wire rack. Store airtight.

YIELD: 5 dozen wafers

CINNAMON-CHOCOLATE SNAPS

¼ teaspoon salt
¼ teaspoon ground cloves
2 teaspoons soda
1 teaspoon ground cinnamon
2 teaspoons vanilla extract
¾ cup shortening

1 cup light-brown sugar
¼ cup unsulphured molasses
⅓ cup cocoa
1 large egg
2 cups sifted all-purpose flour

Blend together in a mixing bowl the first 6 ingredients. Gradually mix in brown sugar and molasses. Stir in cocoa. Beat in egg. Add flour and mix well.

Chill dough 1 hour or until it is stiff enough to handle. Shape into 1-inch balls. Dip tops in granulated sugar. Place on lightly buttered cooky sheets 2 inches apart. Sprinkle each cooky with 2 or 3 drops of water. This produces a crinkled top.

Bake in a preheated moderate oven (325° F.) 12 to 15 minutes. DO NOT OVERBAKE. Cool on wire racks. Store airtight.

YIELD: 4½ dozen snaps

CRACKLE TOP SPICE COOKIES

¾ cup (1½ sticks) soft butter *or* margarine
2 teaspoons soda
¼ teaspoon salt
1 teaspoon ground cinnamon
1 teaspoon ground nutmeg
1 teaspoon ground allspice
1 teaspoon ground ginger

¾ cup sugar
½ cup unsulphured molasses
1 large egg
2½ cups sifted all-purpose flour
Granulated sugar

Blend together first 7 ingredients. Gradually add sugar, mixing well after each addition. Stir in molasses. Beat in egg.

Gradually stir in flour. Chill dough until stiff enough to handle.

Shape into ¾-inch balls. Dip tops in granulated sugar. Place on greased cooky sheets 2 inches apart to allow room for spreading. Sprinkle each cooky with 2 or 3 drops water to produce a crackled surface. Bake in a preheated moderate oven (375° F.) 10 to 12 minutes or until just done, not hard. Cool on wire rack. Store airtight.

YIELD: 7 dozen cookies

FENNEL SEED COOKIES

½ cup (1 stick) soft butter *or* margarine
1 teaspoon ground fennel seed
¼ teaspoon salt

1 cup sugar
1 large egg
1¾ cups sifted all-purpose flour
1½ teaspoons double-acting baking powder

Combine the first 3 ingredients. Blend in sugar. Beat in egg. Sift flour with baking powder and gradually stir into the mixture. Refrigerate 2 hours. Shape into 1-inch balls and place on lightly greased cooky sheets. Press flat with the bottom of a glass covered with a damp cloth, bake in a preheated moderate oven (375° F.) 10 minutes. Cool on wire racks. Store airtight.

YIELD: 4 dozen cookies

GRANDMOTHER DAY'S GINGER WAFERS

On Grandmother Day's handwritten, original recipe she penned: "I make 100 dozen of these every Christmas, using 9 pounds of flour." Since her recipe called for 3 pounds of flour, she obviously made 3 huge batches.

If desired, keep this dough in the re-frigerator 2 to 3 weeks in a covered container. Bake cookies as needed.

¾ cup unsulphured molasses
½ cup (1 stick) butter *or* margarine
⅓ cup sugar
1 large egg yolk

2 cups sifted all-purpose flour
¼ teaspoon soda
¼ teaspoon salt
1 teaspoon ground ginger
1 teaspoon ground cinnamon

Heat molasses (DO NOT BOIL) in a saucepan large enough for mixing cookies. Add butter or margarine and stir until melted. Blend in sugar and cool. Beat in egg yolk. Sift together remaining ingredients. Gradually stir into the molasses mixture.

Chill 2 or more hours or until dough is stiff enough to handle. Form into ½-inch balls. Place 2 inches apart on greased cooky sheets. Flatten to ¹⁄₁₆-inch thickness. Bake in a preheated hot oven (400° F.) 4 to 5 minutes.

YIELD: 5 to 6 dozen cookies

HONEY COOKIES

4 cups sifted all-purpose flour
1½ teaspoons salt
1 teaspoon soda
1 teaspoon double-acting baking powder
2 teaspoons ground cinnamon
2 teaspoons ground ginger
½ teaspoon ground cloves

1 cup shortening
1¼ cups strained honey
¼ cup sugar
1 large egg

Sift together the first 7 ingredients and set aside for later use. Melt shortening in a saucepan large enough for mixing cookies. Add honey and sugar. Cool. Beat in egg. Gradually stir in the flour mixture. Beat 20 strokes. Cool dough enough to handle easily.

Shape into 1½-inch balls. Place on lightly greased cooky sheets 2 inches apart to allow room for spreading. Bake 15 minutes or until lightly browned in a preheated moderate oven (350° F.). Store airtight.

YIELD: 4 dozen cookies

LURKA LOGS

The recipe for these delicate cardamom-scented cookies was given to us by the wife of one of the Indian U.N. representatives. We learned from our friend that lurka *means "boy," while* log *means "people." Boy people will find a cooky jar full of Lurka Logs an irresistible temptation.*

2¼ cups sifted all-purpose flour
1½ teaspoons double-acting
    baking powder
½ teaspoon ground cardamom
½ teaspoon salt
1 cup (2 sticks) soft butter *or*
    margarine
1¼ cups sugar
2 large eggs

Granulated sugar
Flaked coconut

Sift together flour and baking powder and set aside. Mix together the next 3 ingredients. Gradually blend in sugar. Beat in eggs. Gradually stir in flour mixture. Drop rounded ½ teaspoon portions of dough 2 inches apart on ungreased cooky sheets. Flatten to ⅛-inch thickness with the bottom of a glass covered with a damp cloth. Sprinkle tops with granulated sugar and coconut.

Bake in a preheated moderate oven (375° F.) 8 to 10 minutes or until cookies are lightly browned around the edges. Cool on pans ½ minute. Transfer to wire racks to finish cooling. Store airtight.

YIELD: About 8 dozen cookies

MEXICAN SESAME-ANISE COOKIES

A favorite recipe of a staff member of the Mexican Consulate General in New York, these cookies are crisp and rich and delicately anise-flavored.

1 tablespoon anise seed
2 tablespoons boiling water
⅔ cup sugar
¾ cup (1½ sticks) soft butter *or*
    margarine
⅛ teaspoon soda
1 large egg
2 cups sifted all-purpose flour
1 large egg, lightly beaten
Toasted Sesame Seed*

Combine anise seed and boiling water and steep while mixing dough. Gradually blend sugar with butter or margarine and soda. Beat in egg. Strain anise-seed liquid into the mixture. Discard seed. Stir in flour, a little at a time. Mix well.

Chill dough overnight or until stiff

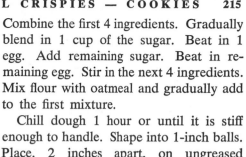

Combine the first 4 ingredients. Gradually blend in 1 cup of the sugar. Beat in 1 egg. Add remaining sugar. Beat in remaining egg. Stir in the next 4 ingredients. Mix flour with oatmeal and gradually add to the first mixture.

Chill dough 1 hour or until it is stiff enough to handle. Shape into 1-inch balls. Place, 2 inches apart, on ungreased cooky sheets.

Bake in a preheated moderate oven (350° F.) 12 to 15 minutes. Cool on wire racks. Store airtight.

YIELD: 6½ dozen crispies

OATMEAL COOKIES

1 cup (2 sticks) soft butter *or* margarine
⅔ cup shortening
2 teaspoons soda
1 teaspoon ground cinnamon
½ teaspoon ground allspice
¼ teaspoon ground cloves
½ teaspoon salt
2 teaspoons vanilla extract

⅔ cup sugar
2⅓ cups light-brown sugar
4 large eggs

2 cups quick-cooking oatmeal
1 cup chopped nuts
1½ cups seedless raisins

4 cups sifted all-purpose flour

Blend together the first 8 ingredients. Gradually mix in white and brown sugars. Beat in eggs, 1 at a time. Stir in next 3 ingredients. Gradually stir in flour. Drop tablespoon portions of dough, 2 inches apart, onto lightly greased cooky sheets.

Bake in a preheated moderate oven (375° F.) 10 minutes or until lightly browned around the edges. Cool 1 minute on cooky sheets. Then place on wire racks to finish cooling. Store airtight.

enough to handle. Shape dough into ½-inch balls. Place on ungreased cooky sheets, 3 inches apart. Place a piece of waxed paper over cookies and flatten to ¹⁄₁₆-inch thickness with the bottom of a glass. Remove waxed paper. Brush tops with lightly beaten egg. Sprinkle each with Toasted Sesame Seeds. Bake in a preheated hot oven (400° F.) 7 to 8 minutes or until lightly browned.

YIELD: 6 dozen cookies

OATMEAL CRISPIES

1 teaspoon soda
1 teaspoon salt
1 teaspoon ground nutmeg
1 cup shortening

2 cups sugar
2 large eggs

1 cup seedless raisins
¾ cup chopped nuts
1 teaspoon grated lemon rind
1 tablespoon lemon juice

1½ cups sifted all-purpose flour
3 cups quick-cooking oatmeal

Since this cooky dough keeps well in the refrigerator in a covered bowl, bake off as many cookies as desired at a time. Return remaining dough to the refrigerator and bake fresh batches as needed.

YIELD: 8 dozen 3-inch cookies

OLD-FASHIONED CORIANDER COOKIES

Coriander seed was used in cooky doughs in Colonial days. Judging by the number of times it is mentioned in antique cooky recipes, it must have been one of the favorite spices.

½ cup shortening
½ teaspoon salt
¼ teaspoon soda
5 teaspoons ground coriander seed
___
1 cup sugar
1 large egg
2 cups sifted all-purpose flour
½ cup buttermilk *or* sour milk

Cream together first 4 ingredients. Gradually blend in sugar. Beat in egg. Add flour alternately with milk, blending well. Drop dough from a teaspoon onto lightly greased cooky sheets about 2 inches apart, keeping them round. Bake in a preheated moderate oven (375° F.) 15 minutes or until lightly browned around the edges. Cool on wire racks. Store airtight.

YIELD: 3 dozen cookies

ORANGE-COCONUT COOKIES

¾ cup shortening
½ teaspoon soda
½ teaspoon salt
¾ teaspoon ground mace
1 teaspoon grated lemon rind
1½ teaspoons grated orange rind
___
1 cup sugar
1 large egg
1 tablespoon orange juice
2 cups sifted all-purpose flour
¾ cup sour cream
1 cup flaked cocount

Blend together the first 6 ingredients. Gradually add sugar, mixing well after each addition. Beat in egg. Add orange juice. Stir in flour alternately with sour cream. Add coconut.

Drop rounded teaspoonsful of dough, 2 inches apart, on lightly greased cooky sheets. Bake in a preheated moderate oven (375° F.) 12 to 14 minutes. Cool. Store airtight.

YIELD: 3½ dozen cookies

ROLLED SESAME SEED WAFERS

½ cup sugar
1 teaspoon vanilla extract
½ cup (1 stick) soft butter *or* margarine
2 large eggs
1¼ cups sifted all-purpose flour
¼ cup Toasted Sesame Seed*

Gradually blend sugar and vanilla extract into butter or margarine. Beat in eggs, 1 at a time. Stir in flour and 3 tablespoons of the sesame seed. Drop 1 rounded ½ teaspoon of dough at a time onto ungreased cooky sheets, 2 inches apart. Flatten to ¹⁄₁₆-inch thickness with the bottom of a glass covered with waxed paper or a wet towel. Sprinkle each with Toasted Sesame Seed.

Bake in a preheated slow oven (325° F.) 5 minutes or until wafers have browned lightly around the edges. As cookies are removed from the pan, roll wafers around the index finger or the handle of a wooden spoon, sesame seeds to the outside. If cookies cool before rolling is finished, return to oven to heat about ½ minute. Store airtight.

YIELD: 5 dozen wafers

SESAME SEED-PEANUT BUTTER COOKIES

1 cup sifted all-purpose flour
1 teaspoon double-acting
  baking powder
3 tablespoons Toasted Sesame Seed*

¼ teaspoon soda
¼ teaspoon salt
½ teaspoon ground nutmeg
½ cup shortening

½ cup creamy peanut butter
1 cup light-brown sugar
1 large egg

3½ tablespoons Toasted Sesame Seed*

Sift together flour and baking powder and mix with the 3 tablespoons Toasted Sesame Seed. Set aside. Combine the next 4 ingredients. Add peanut butter and mix well. Gradually add sugar. Beat in egg. Stir in flour mixture.

Drop ½-teaspoon portions of dough, 2 inches apart, onto ungreased cooky sheets. Sprinkle each with ¼ teaspoon Toasted Sesame Seed. Bake in a preheated moderate oven (375° F.) 10 minutes or until edges have lightly browned. Cool on wire racks. Store airtight.

YIELD: 3½ dozen cookies

SESAME SEED WAFERS

4 cups sifted all-purpose flour
2 teaspoons double-acting
  baking powder
½ teaspoon salt

1¾ cups sugar
1 cup (2 sticks) soft butter or
  margarine
2 large eggs
2 teaspoons vanilla extract
3 tablespoons Toasted Sesame Seed*
¼ cup water

Sift together first 3 ingredients and set aside. Gradually add sugar to butter or margarine. Beat in eggs. Stir in vanilla extract and sesame seed. Add flour mixture alternately with water. Chill dough 3 to 4 hours.

Drop teaspoon-size portions, 2 inches apart, onto ungreased cooky sheets. Flatten to ¹⁄₁₆-inch thickness with the bottom of a glass covered with a damp cloth. Bake in a preheated moderate oven (375° F.) 10 minutes or until lightly browned around the edges. Cool and store airtight.

YIELD: 7 dozen cookies

SPANISH COOKIES
(MANTECADITOS)

1 cup shortening
2 tablespoons butter or margarine
½ teaspoon salt
1 teaspoon crushed anise seed
1½ teaspoons grated lemon rind
1 teaspoon vanilla extract

in egg. Gradually stir in nuts and flour mixture.

Shape into 2 rolls, 2 inches in diameter. Wrap in foil. Chill overnight or until ready to use. Slice ⅛ inch thick. Bake on lightly greased cooky sheets in a preheated hot oven (400° F.) 5 or 6 minutes. Store airtight.

YIELD: 3½ dozen cookies

1¼ cups sugar
2 small eggs
2 cups sifted all-purpose flour

Blend together the first 6 ingredients. Gradually add sugar. Beat in eggs. Gradually stir in flour. If dough is too soft to shape into balls, chill until it is firm enough to handle.

Shape into 1-inch balls. Place on lightly greased cooky sheets, 1½ inches apart. Bake in a preheated moderate oven (350° F.) 8 to 10 minutes or until browned around the edges. Cool and store airtight.

YIELD: 6 dozen cookies

SPICED ICE-BOX COOKIES

2¼ cups sifted all-purpose flour
1 teaspoon double-acting
    baking powder
¼ teaspoon salt
½ teaspoon ground nutmeg
¾ teaspoon ground ginger
_____
¾ cup (1½ sticks) soft butter *or*
    margarine
¾ cup sugar
1½ teaspoons vanilla extract
1 large egg
½ cup chopped nuts

Sift first 5 ingredients together and set aside for later use. Cream butter or margarine with sugar and vanilla extract. Beat

SPICED PEPPERMINT CRISPS

2 cups sifted all-purpose flour
1½ teaspoons double-acting
    baking powder
_____
½ cup shortening
½ teaspoon salt
½ teaspoon ground nutmeg
_____
1 cup sugar
2 large eggs
2 tablespoons milk
⅓ cup crushed peppermint-stick candy

Sift together flour and baking powder and set aside. Mix together the next 3 ingredients. Gradually blend in sugar. Beat in eggs. Stir in milk. Gradually add flour mixture, mixing well after each addition. Drop from a teaspoon onto an ungreased baking sheet 2½ inches apart. Swirl dough with spoon to flatten. Sprinkle each with crushed peppermint-stick candy.

Bake in a preheated moderate oven (350° F.) 10 to 12 minutes. Cool slightly before removing from baking sheet. Cool on wire rack. Store airtight.

YIELD: 5 to 6 dozen crisps

SPICED TEA WAFERS

2¼ cups sifted all-purpose flour
1 teaspoon ground ginger
1 teaspoon ground nutmeg
_____
1¼ cups soft light-brown sugar

⅔ cup (1⅓ sticks) butter *or*
 margarine
1 large egg, beaten
1½ teaspoons vanilla extract

Sift together the first 3 ingredients. Add sugar and mix well, being sure the sugar is free from lumps. Add butter or margarine and cut it in with a pastry blender or fingers to crumb consistency. Stir in egg and vanilla extract. Chill dough 1 hour or until it is stiff enough to handle.

Shape into ½-inch balls and place on lightly greased cooky sheets 1½ inches apart to allow room for spreading. Flatten cookies to ¹⁄₁₆ inch thick with a glass covered with a wet cloth. Decorate tops as desired with blanched almonds, other nuts, glacé fruit, colored sugar, or cinnamon sugar, if desired.

Bake in a preheated hot oven (400° F.) 4 to 5 minutes or until edges have browned lightly. Cool and store airtight.

YIELD: 7 dozen cookies

SPICED BROWN-SUGAR FRUIT DROPS

These delicious cookies are dainty enough for a tea party and yet hearty enough for afternoon snacks. They have a rich, delicately spiced brown-sugar flavor and are filled with pecans, dates, and raisins. If the cookies are not overbaked, they have a better flavor and remain soft for a longer period of time.

3½ cups sifted all-purpose flour
1 teaspoon double-acting
 baking powder
¼ teaspoon salt

1 cup (2 sticks) soft butter *or*
 margarine
¼ teaspoon soda
2 teaspoons apple pie spice
2 teaspoons vanilla extract

2¼ cups dark-brown sugar
2 large eggs
⅓ cup milk
½ cup chopped pecans
¾ cup chopped dates
¾ cup seedless raisins
Glacé cherries, halved

Sift together the first 3 ingredients and set aside. Mix together the next 4 ingredients. Gradually blend in sugar. Beat in eggs. Add flour mixture alternately with milk. Stir in nuts and fruit. Drop from a teaspoon, 1 inch apart, onto greased cooky sheets. Push half of a glacé cherry in the top of each cooky.

Bake in a preheated moderate oven (350° F.) 10 to 12 minutes or until browned around the edges. DO NOT BAKE TOO BROWN. Cool and store airtight.

YIELD: 6 dozen cookies

BLIND DATE COOKIES

3 dozen pitted, dried dates
3 dozen pecans

½ teaspoon ground nutmeg
1 teaspoon vanilla extract
¼ teaspoon lemon extract
½ cup shortening
¾ cup light-brown sugar

1 large egg

1¾ cups sifted all-purpose flour
1½ teaspoons double-acting
    baking powder
½ teaspoon salt
½ cup milk

Stuff dates with pecans and set aside. Mix together the next 5 ingredients until well blended. Beat in egg. Sift flour with baking powder and salt and add to the creamed mixture alternately with milk. Drop dough, in rounded ½ teaspoonsful, 2 inches apart, onto lightly greased cooky sheets. Press a stuffed date into the center of each. Cover date completely with a little more dough. Bake in a preheated moderate oven (375° F.) 15 minutes or until lightly browned around the edges. Cool on wire rack. Store airtight.

YIELD: 3 dozen cookies

CARDAMOM FORK COOKIES

1 cup (2 sticks) soft butter *or*
    margarine
2 teaspoons soda
1 teaspoon ground cardamom
½ teaspoon salt
———
2 cups light-brown sugar
2 large eggs
———
4½ cups sifted all-purpose flour
2 teaspoons cream of tartar

Combine the first 4 ingredients. Gradually blend in sugar. Beat in eggs. Sift flour with cream of tartar and gradually stir into the mixture.

Chill dough 3 to 4 hours or until it is stiff enough to handle. Shape into ½-inch balls. Place on ungreased cooky sheets. Dip a fork in flour and press into each cooky in crisscross style. Bake in a preheated moderate oven (350° F.) 10 minutes. Cool. Store airtight.

YIELD: 8 dozen cookies

CHOCOLATE HERMITS

1 teaspoon salt
¾ teaspoon soda
½ teaspoon ground cinnamon
½ teaspoon ground cloves
½ cup shortening
———
1½ cups dark-brown sugar
2 squares (2 ounces) unsweetened
    chocolate, melted
1 large egg
⅓ to ½ cup sour milk *or* buttermilk
2½ cups sifted all-purpose flour
———
2 teaspoons vanilla extract
½ cup chopped pecans
¾ cup seedless raisins

Mix together the first 5 ingredients. Gradually add brown sugar. Stir in chocolate. Beat in egg. Gradually stir in milk and flour. Add remaining ingredients. Mix well. Drop dough from a teaspoon onto lightly greased cooky sheets, 2 inches apart.

Bake in a preheated moderate oven (375° F.) 15 minutes or until done. Cool on wire racks. Store airtight.

YIELD: 4 dozen hermits

SPICED CHOCOLATE NUT COOKIES

This delicious recipe requires lots of nutmeats and almost no flour. It works beautifully, however, and we consider it one of our best cooky recipes of this type. It is rich with nutmeats and unusual in both flavor and texture, a crunchy cooky with a slightly crinkly top.

3 squares (3 ounces) unsweetened
    chocolate
2 cups shelled pecans
1 cup sugar
⅛ teaspoon salt
2 large eggs, lightly beaten
¼ cup fine, dry bread crumbs

2 tablespoons flour
¾ teaspoon ground cinnamon
½ teaspoon ground cloves
Confectioners' sugar

Grate chocolate and set aside for later use. Chop pecans very fine, using a nut chopper, electric blender, or a sharp knife. Gradually blend sugar and salt with beaten eggs. Stir in chocolate and pecans. Combine bread crumbs, flour and spices, and mix well.

Shape dough into 1-inch balls. Roll in confectioners' sugar. Place on buttered cooky sheets. Bake in a preheated slow oven (325° F.) 15 minutes or until cookies have crackled over the top. Cool on wire racks. Store airtight.

YIELD: 4 dozen cookies

ENGLISH TEA COOKIES

2¼ cups sifted all-purpose flour
1½ teaspoons double-acting
    baking powder
¼ teaspoon salt
1¼ teaspoons ground nutmeg
1¼ cups sugar

⅔ cup (1⅓ sticks) butter or
    margarine
2 large eggs
½ cup milk
1 tablespoon confectioners' sugar
¼ cup seeded raisins

Sift first 5 ingredients together into a mixing bowl. Add butter or margarine; cut it in until mixture resembles coarse meal. Combine eggs and milk, stir into the flour mixture. Drop dough from teaspoon onto lightly greased cooky sheets. Dust confectioners' sugar over the tops. Place a seeded raisin in the center of each.

Bake in a preheated moderate oven

(375° F.) 9 minutes or until edges have lightly browned. Cool on wire racks. Store airtight.

YIELD: 4 dozen cookies

FRUIT AND NUT COOKIES

3½ cups sifted all-purpose flour
1½ teaspoons double-acting
    baking powder
½ teaspoon salt

1 teaspoon ground mace
1 teaspoon ground cinnamon
1 cup (2 sticks) soft butter or
    margarine

2¼ cups sugar
2 large eggs

4 ounces (½ package) pitted, dried
    dates, chopped
1 cup seedless raisins
½ cup chopped nuts

⅓ cup milk
Seeded raisins (optional)

Sift together the first 3 ingredients and set aside. Combine the next 3 ingredients. Gradually blend in 1 cup of the sugar. Beat in eggs. Add remaining sugar and mix well. Stir in next 3 ingredients. Add flour mixture alternately with milk.

Drop from a teaspoon, 1½ inches apart, onto lightly greased cooky sheets. Top each with a seeded raisin, if desired.

Bake in a preheated moderate oven (375° F.) 12 minutes or until cookies have lightly browned around their edges. Cool on wire rack. Store airtight.

YIELD: 7½ dozen cookies

GUNNING GINGERBREAD COOKIES

Gunning Gingerbread goes back many, many years. Our ancestors packed it with them on hunting trips and sailors liked it because of its long-keeping quality. The original recipe was baked in sheets; but we prefer them baked as drop cookies.

1 teaspoon salt
1 teaspoon soda
1½ teaspoons ground ginger
½ cup shortening

⅔ cup sugar
1 cup unsulphured molasses
1 tablespoon cider vinegar
3 tablespoons water
3 cups sifted all-purpose flour

Mix together the first 4 ingredients. Gradually add sugar and molasses. Combine vinegar and water and add to the mixture alternately with flour. Drop dough from a tablespoon, 2 inches apart, onto lightly greased cooky sheets.

Bake in a preheated hot oven (400° F.) 12 minutes or until browned lightly around the edges. Cool on wire racks. Store airtight.

YIELD: 3 dozen cookies

OLD-TIME CINNAMON SUGAR COOKIES

½ teaspoon soda
½ teaspoon salt
2 teaspoons ground cinnamon
1 cup (2 sticks) soft butter *or*
   margarine

1½ cups light-brown sugar
1 large egg
½ cup thick, commercial sour cream
4 cups sifted all-purpose flour

Blend first 4 ingredients. Gradually add brown sugar. Beat in egg. Stir in sour cream and flour. Mix well. Drop rounded-teaspoon portions of dough, 2 inches apart, onto lightly greased cooky sheets. Bake in a preheated hot oven (400° F.) 10 to 12 minutes or until lightly browned around the edges. Store airtight.

YIELD: 4 dozen large cookies

OLD-TIME NUTMEG HERMITS

4 cups sifted all-purpose flour
1 teaspoon soda
1½ teaspoons ground nutmeg
½ teaspoon salt

2 cups light-brown sugar
1 cup (2 sticks) soft butter *or*
   margarine
4 large eggs
¼ cup milk
2 cups seedless raisins
1 cup chopped nuts
Seeded raisins (optional)

Sift together first 4 ingredients and set

aside. Gradually blend brown sugar with butter or margarine. Beat in eggs. Add flour mixture alternately with milk. Stir in seedless raisins and nuts. Drop from a teaspoon, 1½ inches apart, onto lightly greased cooky sheets. Top each cooky with a big seeded raisin, if desired.

Bake in a preheated moderate oven (375° F.) 12 to 15 minutes. Cool on wire racks. Store airtight.

YIELD: 5 dozen cookies

SESAME SEED FORK COOKIES

3 cups sifted all-purpose flour
½ teaspoon salt
2¼ teaspoons double-acting
　　baking powder

1½ teaspoons vanilla extract
¾ cup (1½ sticks) soft butter or
　　margarine
1¼ cups sugar
1 large egg
2 tablespoons milk
⅓ to ½ cup Toasted Sesame Seed*

Sift together the first 3 ingredients and set aside. Mix vanilla extract with butter or margarine. Gradually blend in sugar. Beat in egg. Add milk. Gradually stir in flour mixture. Mix well. This dough is stiff, but do not add more milk.

Shape into 1-inch balls. Dip each into Toasted Sesame Seed. Place on ungreased cooky sheets 2 inches apart. Flatten in crisscross fashion with the tines of a fork. Bake in a preheated hot oven (400° F.) 10 minutes or until lightly browned. Cool on wire rack. Store airtight.

YIELD: 4½ dozen cookies

SOFT MOLASSES COOKIES

It took seven years of testing, off and on, to recapture just that certain flavor and texture of Soft Molasses Cookies we re-member so well from childhood. Once the recipe was perfected to our satisfac-tion, we baked 29,000 of them for visitors at the 1950 Eastern States Exposition.

1 cup (2 sticks) soft butter or
　　margarine
½ teaspoon salt
3 teaspoons soda
2 teaspoons ground ginger
2 teaspoons ground cinnamon
1 teaspoon powdered mustard
1 teaspoon instant coffee
1 teaspoon ground cloves

1 cup sugar
1 cup unsulphured molasses
1 large egg
4¾ cups sifted all-purpose flour
¾ cup water or milk
Walnut halves or seeded raisins

Combine the first 8 ingredients. Gradu-ally blend in sugar and molasses. Beat in egg. Add the flour alternately with the water or milk. Beat the batter ½ minute. Drop teaspoonsful of dough, 2 inches apart, onto greased cooky sheets, being careful to keep the cookies round. Press a walnut half or a raisin in the center of each. Bake 15 minutes or until done in a preheated moderate oven (375° F.). Cool. Store airtight.

YIELD: 5 dozen large cookies

SOFT RAISIN COOKIES

½ cup (1 stick) soft butter or
　　margarine
¾ teaspoon soda
½ teaspoon salt
½ teaspoon ground ginger
½ teaspoon ground nutmeg
1 teaspoon ground cinnamon

1½ cups dark-brown sugar
1 large egg
⅓ cup sour milk or buttermilk

2½ cups sifted all-purpose flour
¾ cup seedless raisins
3 dozen seeded raisins (optional)

Mix together the first 6 ingredients. Blend in 1 cup of the brown sugar. Beat in egg. Blend in remaining sugar. Stir in milk. Gradually add flour and seedless raisins. Drop heaping-teaspoon portions, 1 inch apart, onto lightly greased cooky sheets. Place a big seeded raisin in the center of each, if desired.

Bake in a preheated moderate oven (375° F.) 15 minutes or until lightly browned. Cool on wire racks. Store airtight.

YIELD: 3 dozen cookies

SPICED NUGGETS

¾ cup (1½ sticks) soft butter *or* margarine
½ teaspoon salt
⅛ teaspoon ground white pepper
½ teaspoon ground mace
1 teaspoon ground ginger
_____
¾ cup sugar
1 large egg
¾ cup seedless raisins
1 cup flaked coconut
½ cup chopped nuts
2 cups sifted all-purpose flour

Combine the first 5 ingredients. Gradually blend in sugar. Beat in egg. Rinse raisins, drain well, and pat dry between paper towels. Stir into the mixture. Add coconut and nuts. Stir in flour. Drop from a teaspoon onto greased cooky sheets.

Bake in a preheated moderate oven (350° F.) 15 to 18 minutes or until lightly browned around the edges. Remove cookies to wire racks to cool. Store airtight.

YIELD: 5 dozen cookies

COCONUT-ALMOND BARS

1½ cups brown sugar
1¼ cups sifted all-purpose flour
½ cup (1 stick) soft butter *or* margarine
_____
½ teaspoon salt
½ teaspoon ground mace
2 large eggs, beaten
1 teaspoon vanilla extract
1 cup flaked coconut
1 cup chopped blanched almonds

Gradually add ½ cup of the sugar and 1 cup of the flour to butter or margarine. Pat the mixture uniformly over the bottom of a 13 x 9 x 2-inch pan.

Bake in a preheated moderate oven (375° F.) 12 minutes. Remove from oven. Combine remaining sugar and flour with mace and salt. Beat in eggs and vanilla extract. Stir in coconut and almonds. Spread uniformly over the pre-baked crust. Bake in preheated moderate oven (375° F.) 20 minutes or until golden brown. Cool in pan. Cut into 24 bars. Store airtight.

YIELD: 2 dozen bars

SPICED COCONUT HONEY CHEWS

2 cups sifted cake flour
¼ teaspoon salt
¼ teaspoon soda
1¼ cups sugar
_____
½ cup (1 stick) butter *or* margarine, melted
½ cup honey
1 teaspoon ground nutmeg
4 large egg whites
2 tablespoons milk
_____
1⅓ cups moist, shredded coconut

Sift together first 4 ingredients. Add the next 5 ingredients. Mix well, but do not

together the next 5 ingredients. Blend in brown sugar and lemon rind. Add butter or margarine and mix well. Stir in milk and mix until smooth. Add oats. Put half the dough into a buttered 8 x 8 x 2-inch baking dish. Cover with fruit mixture. Roll remaining dough between 2 sheets of wax paper to fit top of pan. Remove paper and place dough over filling.

Bake in a prchcatcd moderate oven (350° F.) 25 to 30 minutes. Cool and cut into bars.

YIELD: 16 bars

LEBKUCHEN

Literally translated lebkuchen *means "lively cake." The many spices give this traditional German Christmas cooky its lively flavor; the honey gives it the characteristic texture and keeping qualities. Since lebkuchens improve with age, make them 3 to 4 days before serving.*

¾ cup honey
¾ cup sugar
1 large egg
1 teaspoon grated lemon rind
1 tablespoon milk

2¾ cups sifted all-purpose flour
½ teaspoon salt
½ teaspoon ground cloves
1 teaspoon ground cinnamon
1 teaspoon ground allspice

⅓ cup chopped citron
½ cup chopped blanched almonds
Confectioners' Sugar and Water Glaze*

Heat honey to boiling point (DO NOT BOIL) in a saucepan large enough for mixing dough. Stir in sugar. Beat in egg. Blend in lemon rind and milk.

Sift together the next 5 ingredients and gradually stir into the honey-sugar mixture. Add citron and almonds. Chill dough overnight.

overbeat. Stir in coconut. Pour into 2 well-greased, wax-paper lined 8 x 8 x 2-inch pans. Bake in a preheated moderate oven (350° F.) 35 minutes or until top is firm when pressed lightly with the fingers. Turn out onto wire racks. Remove paper at once. Cool. Cut each into 24 squares. Store airtight. The flavor of these chews improves with age.

YIELD: 48 squares

DATE-FILLED SPICE BARS

1 cup chopped, pitted dates
½ cup sugar
¼ cup fresh orange juice
½ cup water

1 cup sifted all-purpose flour
¼ teaspoon salt
¼ teaspoon soda
½ teaspoon ground nutmeg
½ teaspoon ground cinnamon

½ cup light-brown sugar
1 teaspoon grated lemon rind
½ cup (1 stick) butter *or* margarine
¼ cup milk
1½ cups quick-cooking rolled oats

Combine first 4 ingredients in a saucepan. Cook until thick. Cool and set aside. Sift

Spread in 2 lightly greased and lightly floured 9 x 9 x 2-inch pans. Bake in a preheated hot oven (400° F.) 15 minutes or until done. While cookies are hot, quickly brush tops with Confectioners' Sugar and Water Glaze. Cool in pans. Cut each square into 32 bars. Store airtight.

YIELD: 64 bars

POPPY SEED COCONUT BARS

2 cups sifted cake flour
¼ teaspoon salt
¼ teaspoon soda
1¼ cups sugar

½ cup (1 stick) butter or margarine, melted
⅓ cup honey
½ teaspoon almond extract
1½ teaspoons vanilla extract
4 large egg whites
2 tablespoons milk

1 cup shredded, moist coconut
⅓ cup poppy seed

Sift the first 4 ingredients together into a mixing bowl. Add the next 6 ingredients. Mix well. Stir in coconut and poppy seeds. Pour into 2 well-greased, wax-paper lined 9 x 9 x 2-inch baking pans.

Bake in a preheated moderate oven (350° F.) 30 minutes or until top is firm when pressed lightly with fingers. Turn out onto wire racks. Remove paper at once from bottom of cakes. When cool, cut each cake into 16 bars. Store airtight.

YIELD: 32 bars

RICH JELLY BARS

2 cups sifted all-purpose flour
⅔ cup sugar
½ teaspoon double-acting baking powder

¾ cup (1½ sticks) soft butter or margarine
1 large egg
2 teaspoons vanilla extract
1 teaspoon ground mace

Apricot, pineapple, or peach jam or jelly

Sift together the first 3 ingredients. Add the next 4 ingredients all at once and mix until a dough is formed.

Divide the dough into 4 equal parts. Shape into rolls 13 inches long and ¾ inch wide. Place on 2 ungreased cooky sheets 4 inches apart and 2 inches from edge of sheets. Make a depression ⅓ inch deep, with a knife handle, lengthwise down the center of each strip. Fill the depression with jelly or jam.

Bake in a preheated moderate oven (350° F.) 15 to 20 minutes or until lightly browned around the edges. While warm, cut into diagonal bars. Cool on wire racks. Store airtight.

YIELD: 3½ dozen bars

ROYAL CAKE
(FYRSTEKAKE)

2¼ cups sifted all-purpose flour
2 teaspoons double-acting baking powder
¾ cup sugar

¾ cup (1½ sticks) butter *or*
   margarine
1 large egg yolk
2 tablespoons milk
Cardamom-Almond Filling *(see below)*

Sift together into a mixing bowl the first 3 ingredients. Add butter or margarine and cut it in to crumb consistency. Beat egg yolk with milk and add. Mix well.

Press ⅔ of the dough ¼ inch thick into the bottom of a 13 x 9 x 2-inch baking pan. Spread surface with Cardamom-Almond Filling. Roll remaining dough ⅛ inch thick into a rectangle. Cut in strips ½ inch wide with a pastry cutter. Place them over the top of filling in crisscross fashion.

Bake in a preheated slow oven (300° F.) about 45 minutes. Cool in pan. Cut into bars when cold.

CARDAMOM-ALMOND FILLING

1¼ cups unblanched almonds

1¼ cups sifted confectioners' sugar
¾ teaspoon ground cardamom
½ teaspoon ground cinnamon

1 large egg white
6 tablespoons water

Put almonds through a food chopper, using the fine blade, or use blender. Add next 3 ingredients. Stir in egg white and water.

YIELD: Fifty-four 1 x 2-inch bars

SPICED COOKY BARS

1½ cups seedless raisins

¼ teaspoon salt
½ teaspoon ground mace
1 teaspoon ground ginger
1½ teaspoons grated lemon rind
½ cup shortening

1 cup sugar

3 tablespoons unsulphured molasses
2⅔ cups sifted all-purpose flour
1 teaspoon double-acting
   baking powder
½ cup milk

Rinse raisins in hot water, pat dry with paper towels, and set aside. Combine the next 5 ingredients. Gradually blend in sugar and molasses. Sift flour with baking powder and mix with raisins. Add alternately with milk to first mixture. Mix well, cover, and let dough stand 1 hour.

Divide dough in half and place each half on a lightly greased 15½ x 12-inch cooky sheet. Roll dough with a lightly floured rolling pin to completely cover the cooky sheet, being careful to keep the edges straight and being sure the dough does not extend over the edge of pan.

Bake in a preheated hot oven (400° F.) 7 to 8 minutes. While hot, mark off in 3 x 2-inch bars with a sharp-pointed knife or tracing wheel. Cool on wire racks. Store airtight.

YIELD: 5 dozen bars

RICH CLOVE COOKIES

1 cup (2 sticks) soft butter *or*
   margarine
½ teaspoon ground mace
¼ teaspoon ground cloves
2 teaspoons vanilla extract

½ cup sugar
1 large egg yolk
2½ cups sifted all-purpose flour
Whole cloves
Sifted confectioners' sugar

Combine the first 4 ingredients. Gradually blend in sugar. Beat in egg yolk. Gradually stir in flour. Chill dough 1 hour or until it is stiff enough to handle. Shape into 1-inch balls. Place, 1 inch apart, on ungreased cooky sheets. Insert a whole clove in the center of each.

Bake in a preheated slow oven (325° F.) 20 minutes or until lightly browned. DO NOT BAKE TOO BROWN. Roll in confectioners' sugar. Store airtight.

YIELD: 4 dozen cookies

SPICED PECANETTES

¾ cup (1½ sticks) soft butter *or* margarine
¼ teaspoon ground cloves
½ teaspoon ground nutmeg
½ teaspoon ground ginger

½ cup sugar
1 cup chopped pecans
2 cups sifted all-purpose flour

Sifted confectioners' sugar *or* Chocolate Glaze*

Combine the first 4 ingredients. Gradually add sugar. Stir in nuts. Add flour, a little at a time. Chill dough, if necessary, 1 hour or until it is stiff enough to handle. Shape into 1-inch balls. Place, 1 inch apart, on ungreased cooky sheets.

Bake in a preheated slow oven (325° F.) 20 to 25 minutes or until lightly browned around the edges. DO NOT OVERBAKE. Remove from cooky sheets and roll in confectioners' sugar while warm. Cool and roll in confectioners' sugar again. Or, if desired, omit the confectioners' sugar and top each with ¼ teaspoon Chocolate Glaze.

YIELD: 4 dozen pecanettes

SPICED SHORTBREAD GEMS

¾ teaspoon ground mace
½ teaspoon ground ginger
1½ teaspoons vanilla extract
1 cup (2 sticks) soft butter *or* margarine

⅓ cup sugar
2¼ cups sifted all-purpose flour
1 cup chopped pecans *or* walnuts
Confectioners' sugar

Mix together the first 4 ingredients. Gradually blend in the ⅓ cup of sugar. Stir in flour, a little at a time, along with nuts.

Shape into 1-inch balls or in small crescents. Place on ungreased cooky sheets 1 inch apart. Bake in a preheated moderate oven (350° F.) 20 minutes or until golden brown. Remove from cooky sheets and, while warm, roll in confectioners' sugar. Store airtight.

YIELD: 3 dozen cookies

SPICED SPRITZ

1 cup (2 sticks) soft butter *or* margarine
¼ teaspoon salt
½ teaspoon ground cloves
¾ teaspoon ground nutmeg

½ cup light-brown sugar
1 large egg
2¼ cups sifted all-purpose flour

Blend together the first 4 ingredients. Sift brown sugar, press out any lumps, and gradually blend with butter mixture. Stir in egg. Gradually add flour. Press dough through a cooky press, using any desired disk, onto ungreased cooky sheets.

Bake in a preheated moderate oven (375° F.) 7 to 10 minutes or until lightly browned around edges. Remove from cooky sheets and cool on wire racks. Decorate as desired with nuts or candy decorettes.

YIELD: 7 dozen cookies

ITALIAN TWISTS
(CENCI)

6 large eggs
¼ cup sugar
1 teaspoon salt
1 teaspoon vanilla extract
1 teaspoon almond extract
4 cups sifted all-purpose flour
3 teaspoons double-acting
    baking powder
1 tablespoon soft butter *or* margarine
Cinnamon sugar

Beat together the first 3 ingredients until eggs are frothy. Add vanilla and almond extracts. Sift flour with baking powder and gradually add to egg mixture along with butter or margarine. Mix well.

Turn onto a lightly floured board and knead about 10 minutes. Divide dough into 3 parts. Roll each to noodle thinness. Cut into strips ¾ inch wide with a fluted pastry wheel.

Fry in deep fat preheated to 350° F. 1 minute or until twists are golden brown. Drain on paper towels. Sprinkle with cinnamon sugar (mix ½ teaspoon ground cinnamon with ⅓ cup sifted confectioners' sugar). Store airtight.

YIELD: 7½ dozen twists

PFEFFERNUESSE

"Pepper Nuts" or "Spice Nuts" are English for this traditional German Christmas cooky.

¾ cup strained honey
¾ cup unsulphured molasses
¼ cup shortening
1 large egg
4 cups sifted all-purpose flour
1 teaspoon salt
1 teaspoon soda
1 teaspoon double-acting
    baking powder
1 teaspoon ground nutmeg
1 teaspoon ground allspice
¾ teaspoon ground cardamom seed
½ teaspoon ground black pepper
¼ teaspoon ground anise seed
Pfeffernuesse Frosting*

Heat honey and molasses (DO NOT BOIL) in a saucepan large enough for mixing the dough. Add shortening. Cool. Beat in egg.

Sift remaining ingredients together and gradually stir in honey mixture. Let dough stand 30 minutes to stiffen enough to handle.

Moisten hands and shape dough into ¾-inch balls. Bake on lightly greased cooky sheets in a preheated moderate oven (350° F.) 13 to 15 minutes. Frost with Pfeffernuesse Frosting. If a soft cooky is desired, store airtight.

YIELD: 11 dozen pfeffernuesse

RUM BALLS

1 cup fine, dry cooky *or* cake crumbs
1 cup sifted confectioners' sugar
2 tablespoons cocoa
½ teaspoon ground cinnamon
½ teaspoon ground ginger
1 cup chopped pecans
2 tablespoons light *or* dark corn syrup
¼ cup dark rum
Confectioners' sugar

Combine the first 6 ingredients. Mix well. Stir in corn syrup and rum. Shape into 1-inch balls with hands dusted with confectioners' sugar. Roll balls in sifted confectioners' sugar. Store in a covered jar in the refrigerator until ready to serve.

BRANDY BALLS

Replace the rum in the above recipe with ¼ cup brandy.

YIELD: 30 balls

SPICED COCONUT PUFFS

3 large egg whites
¹⁄₁₆ teaspoon salt
1 tablespoon cornstarch
1 cup sugar
½ teaspoon ground mace
2 cups shredded coconut
1 teaspoon vanilla extract
½ teaspoon almond extract
Glacé cherries *or* pecans, halved (optional)

Add salt to egg whites and beat until stiff, but not dry. Combine cornstarch, sugar, and mace. Gradually beat into egg whites. Cook over hot water in double boiler, stirring constantly, until mixture begins to thicken. Remove from heat. Add coconut and vanilla and almond extracts. Drop by rounded teaspoonsful onto greased cooky sheets, 2 inches apart. Top each with half of a glacé cherry or a pecan half, if desired.

Bake in a preheated slow oven (300° F.) for 15 to 18 minutes or until just slightly browned. Cool on wire racks. Store airtight.

YIELD: Approximately 4 dozen puffs

SPICED MADELEINES

Madeleines are said to have originated in Commercy, France, in the early eighteenth century. For many decades, the recipe was a closely guarded secret of one man. It was finally sold to the pastry makers of Commercy for a considerable sum.

Madeleines are little cakes—very light —baked in special Madeleine shell pans. The original recipe does not contain spice, but a pinch of mace and cardamom improves the flavor.

1¼ cups sifted cake flour
½ teaspoon double-acting
    baking powder
¼ teaspoon salt
½ teaspoon ground mace
⅛ teaspoon ground cardamom
3 large eggs
⅔ cup sugar
2 teaspoons grated lemon *or*
    orange rind
¾ cup (1½ sticks) butter *or*
    margarine, melted

Sift together the first 5 ingredients and set aside. Beat eggs in a 2-quart bowl until they are light and lemon-colored. Gradually beat in sugar. Continue beating until the volume has increased 4 times. Gradually fold in flour mixture and lemon or orange rind. Stir in butter.

Brush madeleine pans (12 shells to a pan) with additional melted butter, using about 2 tablespoons. Spoon 1 tablespoon of batter into each shell, filling it ⅔ full.

Bake in a preheated moderate oven (350° F.) 12 minutes or until a toothpick inserted in center comes out clean. Remove cakes from pan onto a wire rack to cool. Repeat until all batter is used, washing and buttering pans after each use. Sift confectioners' sugar over the top.

YIELD: 36 cakes

SWEDISH SPICE COOKIES

1 teaspoon ground mace
½ teaspoon ground ginger
1 cup (2 sticks) soft butter *or* margarine
½ cup sugar
1 large egg yolk
2 teaspoons vanilla extract

2½ cups sifted all-purpose flour
Sifted confectioners' sugar

Blend together the first 6 ingredients until fluffy. Gradually stir in flour. Put dough through a cooky press, using the broad plate, onto an ungreased cooky sheet.

Bake in a preheated moderate oven (350° F.) 10 minutes or until cookies have browned lightly around the edges. Cool on wire racks. Roll in confectioners' sugar.

YIELD: 3½ dozen cookies

BLACK PEPPER CHRISTMAS COOKIES

3 cups sifted all-purpose flour
2 teaspoons double-acting baking powder

3 teaspoons ground ginger
2 teaspoons ground cinnamon

½ teaspoon ground cloves
½ teaspoon ground black pepper
1 cup (2 sticks) soft butter *or* margarine

1½ cups sugar
1 large egg

Sift flour with baking powder and set aside. Mix together the next 5 ingredients. Gradually blend in sugar. Beat in egg. Gradually stir in flour mixture. Chill dough several hours, overnight or until it is stiff enough to handle. Roll dough on a lightly floured board to ⅛-inch thickness. Shape as desired with assorted cooky cutters dipped in flour. Decorate before or after baking, with nuts, glacé fruits, or colored granulated sugar. Or if desired, decorate with Confectioners' Sugar and Water Glaze* or other cooky decorations after baking. Bake in a preheated moderate oven (375° F.) 8 to 10 minutes or until lightly browned around the edges. Cool on wire racks. Store airtight.

YIELD: 5 dozen cookies

SESAME SEED COOKIES

1 package (11 ounces) vanilla cooky mix
3 tablespoons Toasted Sesame Seed*

Mix cooky mix as directed on package. Add 2 tablespoons Toasted Sesame Seed and mix well. Drop dough from the end of a teaspoon onto lightly greased cooky sheets. Flatten slightly with the bottom of a glass covered with a damp cloth. Garnish with additional Toasted Sesame Seed. Bake as directed on package. Cool on wire racks. Store airtight.

YIELD: 3 dozen cookies

DESSERTS

THE dessert should complement the meal. If the main course has been as hearty as roast pork and pan-browned potatoes, it is appropriate to serve an Anise Fruit Compote* or Baked Pears with Ginger Sauce.* Seafood demands citrus desserts, such as an Orange Trifle* or Lemon Meringue.* A soup-and-salad supper leaves space and appetite for a more filling dessert, a Pineapple Cottage Pudding* or an Apple Pudding.*

Select the dessert that is harmonious to the occasion, whenever possible. For the family—especially if there are small children—a custard or milk-rich pudding will provide nutrients that are both healthful and pleasing. When you invite friends in for coffee and dessert, you might like to offer something imaginative—Bay-Roc Coconut Pudding* or Chocolate Charlotte.* A summer dinner on the patio will end most happily if you serve something cool and sweet, while the Christmas holidays call for the traditional Steamed English Christmas Pudding.*

*An asterisk after the name of a dish indicates that the recipe for this dish appears in the book. Consult the Index for the page number.

GRATED FRESH APPLE SNOW

2 cups grated, good-flavored raw apples
¼ cup fresh lemon juice
⅛ teaspoon ground nutmeg
⅛ teaspoon salt
2 tablespoons sugar

2 large egg whites
¼ cup sugar
Grated, unsweetened chocolate

Combine the first 5 ingredients and chill. Beat egg whites until they stand in soft peaks. Gradually beat in the ¼ cup of sugar. Continue beating until stiff. Fold into the grated apple mixture. Serve in sherbet glasses. Garnish with grated, unsweetened chocolate.

YIELD: 6 servings

SHREDDED APPLE WHIP

2 tablespoons sugar
⅛ teaspoon sugar
1 teaspoon cornstarch

2 large eggs
1 cup milk
2 tablespoons sugar

1 cup shredded, good-flavored
  raw apple
Ground nutmeg

Combine first 3 ingredients in the top of a double boiler. Blend in 1 whole egg and 1 egg yolk, saving 1 egg white for later use. Add milk. Stir and cook over hot water (NOT BOILING) until custard coats a metal spoon. Remove from heat, cool, and chill.

Beat egg white until it stands in soft, stiff peaks. Beat in remaining 2 tablespoons of sugar. Fold in shredded apple. Spoon 2 tablespoons of custard into each sherbet glass and fill with apple whip. Garnish with ground nutmeg.

YIELD: 6 servings

SPICED FRESH BLUEBERRY CUP

¼ cup sugar
½ cup water
½ teaspoon fresh lemon juice
1 cinnamon stick, 2 inches long
3 whole cloves
Dash salt

2 cups fresh blueberries
Fresh mint (optional)

Place first 6 ingredients in a saucepan and bring to boiling point. Boil 1 minute. Pour syrup through a sieve over washed blueberries to strain out spices. Chill. Serve in sherbet glasses for dessert. Garnish with a sprig of fresh mint, if desired.

YIELD: 4 servings

SPICED ORANGES IN RED WINE

½ cup sugar
½ cup water
2 slices lemon

1 cinnamon stick, 2 inches long
4 whole cloves

½ cup Burgundy
6 to 10 navel oranges (depending on
  size)

Mix the first 5 ingredients together in a
saucepan and boil 4 minutes. Chill and
add Burgundy. Peel oranges in spiral
fashion, being sure to remove all the white
portion of rind. Cut oranges into sections
and add to the spiced wine syrup.

YIELD: 6 servings

BAKED APPLE SURPRISE

Wrote the poet, Byron,
  All human history attests
  That happiness for man,—the hungry
    sinner!—
  Since Eve ate apples, much depends on
    dinner.
Just a reminder that men invariably love
any kind of apple dessert.

6 large baking apples, such as
  Rome Beauty

½ teaspoon lemon rind
½ cup seedless raisins
½ cup sugar
⅛ teaspoon salt
½ teaspoon ground nutmeg
¾ teaspoon ground cinnamon

6 teaspoons butter *or* margarine
Boiling water

Wash apples. Cut a slice ¼ to ½ inch
thick off the top of each, remove, and set
aside. Scoop out all the pulp you can,
leaving shell intact. Chop apple pulp fine
and mix with next 6 ingredients. Fill cavities of apples with the mixture. Top each
with 1 teaspoon of butter or margarine
and the reserved apple slice. Place in a
baking pan. Pour in ½-inch boiling water.
Cover pan with foil. Bake in a preheated
moderate oven (350° F.) 30 minutes.
Remove foil and bake 30 minutes longer.

YIELD: 6 servings

BAKED BANANAS

6 firm, ripe (not too soft) bananas
2 tablespoons fresh lemon juice

¼ teaspoon salt
½ teaspoon ground nutmeg
¼ teaspoon ground cinnamon
¼ teaspoon ground ginger
4 tablespoons strained honey
⅓ cup maple syrup

1 tablespoon butter *or* margarine
6 thin slices lemon
Heavy cream, whipped (optional)

Peel and split bananas in half lengthwise.
Brush with lemon juice. Place in a buttered baking dish. Mix the next 6 ingredients and pour over all. Dot with butter or margarine. Top each banana with
a slice of lemon. Bake in a preheated
moderate oven (350° F.) 20 to 25 minutes. Baste with spiced syrup while baking. Serve with or without whipped
cream.

YIELD: 6 servings

BANANA-STUFFED BAKED APPLES

6 large baking apples, such as
  Rome Beauty
2 small bananas
1 teaspoon fresh lemon juice

5 tablespoons sugar
$\frac{1}{16}$ teaspoon salt
$\frac{1}{2}$ teaspoon ground nutmeg

Heavy cream, whipped (optional)
1 cup fresh orange juice

Wash, pare, and core apples. Place in a baking dish. Peel bananas, dice, and mix with lemon juice. Spoon into cavities of apples. Combine next 3 ingredients and sprinkle over apples. Pour orange juice over all.

Cover and bake in a preheated moderate oven (375° F.) 55 minutes or until apples are tender when pierced with a toothpick, basting with orange juice 4 times while baking. Serve warm or cold with a little of the syrup poured over each. Top with whipped cream, if desired.

YIELD: 6 servings

BAKED PEARS WITH GINGER SAUCE

6 large, firm Bartlett pears
$\frac{1}{2}$ cup sugar
$\frac{1}{4}$ cup ($\frac{1}{2}$ stick) butter or margarine
Hot water
Ginger Sauce*

Wash pears. Cut out most of the core of each, starting from the stem end, but not cutting through the blossom end. Gradually blend sugar with butter or margarine and spoon into the cavities in the pears, filling them. Stand stuffed pears in a baking dish, spaced so that they do not touch. Pour in $\frac{1}{2}$ inch of hot water. Cover and bake in a preheated moderate oven (375° F.) 1 hour or until tender, basting several times with water in pan. Uncover 15 minutes before baking time is up. Serve with Ginger Sauce.

YIELD: 6 servings

SPICED PEARS IN ORANGE JUICE

4 firm, ripe Bartlett pears
$\frac{1}{3}$ cup sugar
1 cup fresh orange juice
1 tablespoon fresh lemon juice
1 cinnamon stick, 2 inches long
4 whole cloves
$\frac{1}{8}$ teaspoon ground nutmeg
Dash salt

Peel, quarter, and core pears. Place in a baking dish. Mix together in a saucepan the remaining ingredients. Bring to boiling point and pour over pears. Cover and bake 30 minutes in a preheated moderate oven (350° F.). Remove cover and cook 10 minutes or until pears are tender. Cooking time depends upon ripeness of pears. Cool in pan. Serve at room temperature.

YIELD: 6 servings

ANISE FRUIT COMPOTE

A few anise seeds cooked with the sugar syrup for fruits gives delicious flavor to raw and stewed fruits.

1 cup sugar
$\frac{1}{4}$ teaspoon anise seeds
$1\frac{1}{2}$ cups water
Dash salt

$\frac{1}{2}$ cup fresh navel-orange sections
$\frac{1}{2}$ cup fresh grapefruit sections
$\frac{1}{2}$ cup seeded grape halves
$\frac{1}{2}$ cup diced ripe pears
$\frac{1}{2}$ cup diced unpeeled apples
$\frac{1}{2}$ cup diced fresh pineapple

Combine the first 4 ingredients in a saucepan. Mix well and bring to boiling point. Cook 3 to 4 minutes. Cool. Strain over mixed fruit. Chill and serve.

YIELD: 6 servings

FIGS IN ANISE-RUM SAUCE

1-pound ring of dried figs
2 cups water
½ teaspoon anise seed
½ cup sugar
¼ cup light rum
Heavy cream (optional)

Snip tough stems off and wash dried figs. Add water and let soak 3 or 4 hours. Add anise seed and cook 45 minutes or until tender. Add sugar and cook a minute longer. Cool and add rum. Delicious with or without heavy cream.

YIELD: 6 servings

APPLE AND PLUM COMPOTE

½ cup sugar
1 cup water
2 cinnamon sticks, each 2 inches long
2 teaspoons lemon juice
4 large cooking apples
9 Italian plums

Boil the first 4 ingredients together in a covered saucepan 5 minutes. Peel, core, and quarter apples. Add to boiling syrup.

Cover and cook 8 minutes or until apples are almost tender. Cut plums in half, remove pits, and add. Cook 2 minutes. Serve warm or chilled.

YIELD: 6 servings

APPLESAUCE CREAM

¾ teaspoon ground cinnamon
¾ teaspoon grated lemon rind
3 tablespoons sugar (or to taste)
1½ cups (15-ounce jar) sweetened applesauce
1 cup heavy cream, whipped
Shaved semisweet chocolate

Blend the first 4 ingredients. Fold in whipped cream. Chill. Spoon into sherbet glasses. Garnish with shaved semisweet chocolate.

YIELD: 6 servings

HUNGARIAN APPLESAUCE

8 medium-large cooking apples
1 cup water
2 tablespoons flour
1½ cups sugar
1 teaspoon ground nutmeg
¼ teaspoon salt
½ cup sour cream

Wash and peel apples. Cut in quarters and remove cores. Place in saucepan with water. Cover and cook until apples are tender, but not falling to pieces. Mix flour with ¼ cup of the sugar, add to apples, and cook until thickened. Stir in remaining sugar, nutmeg, salt, and sour cream. Serve warm or cold.

YIELD: 6 to 8 servings

BLUEBERRY AND PINEAPPLE COMPOTE

⅓ cup sugar
½ cup water

1 tablespoon lemon juice
1 cinnamon stick, 2 inches long
½ teaspoon whole cloves

¾ teaspoon vanilla extract
2 cups fresh blueberries
2 cups fresh pineapple wedges
Fresh mint leaves

Combine the first 5 ingredients in a saucepan. Mix well. Cover, bring to boiling point, and boil 2 minutes. Strain off spices, add vanilla extract and fruit. Chill. Serve in sherbet glasses. Garnish with fresh mint leaves.

YIELD: 6 servings

CHERRY AND PINEAPPLE COMPOTE

½ cup sugar
1 cup water
2 cinnamon sticks, each 2 inches long
½ teaspoon fresh lemon juice

2 cups fresh pineapple wedges
2 cups pitted, fresh, sweet cherries
1½ cups fresh cantaloupe balls

Boil the first 4 ingredients together 5 minutes in a covered saucepan. Add pineapple wedges and cherries. Heat thoroughly, but DO NOT BOIL. Cool. Chill. Just before serving, add cantaloupe balls.

YIELD: 6 servings

FRESH FRUIT COMPOTE

1 cup sugar
¾ cup water
1⁄16 teaspoon salt
2 cinnamon sticks, each 2 inches long

¼ teaspoon whole cloves
¼ teaspoon whole allspice
3 large apples
3 large pears
3 large navel oranges
1 pound seedless grapes

Fresh strawberries *or* fresh mint leaves

Combine the first 4 ingredients in a saucepan. Mix well. Tie cloves and allspice in a cheesecloth bag and add. Bring mixture to boiling point. Wash and dice unpeeled apples and add. Peel and dice pears and add. Cover and cook slowly 10 minutes or until fruit is tender. Remove and discard spice bag and cinnamon. Chill.

Shortly before serving, peel and section oranges, then add to the syrup along with grapes. Serve in sherbet glasses garnished with a whole uncapped fresh strawberry or a sprig of fresh mint.

YIELD: 12 servings

RHUBARB AND PINEAPPLE COMPOTE

4 cups diced fresh rhubarb
1 cup sugar
½ teaspoon ground ginger
2 cups fresh pineapple wedges

Place rhubarb and sugar in the top of a double boiler. Mix well. Cover and cook over boiling water 35 minutes or until rhubarb is tender. Remove from heat and stir in ginger. Cool. Add pineapple. Chill and serve.

YIELD: 6 servings

PEACH AND BLUEBERRY COMPOTE

⅓ cup water
¾ cup sugar
Dash salt
2 cinnamon sticks, each 2 inches long
1 teaspoon fresh lemon juice

3 cups (about 8 medium) sliced fresh ripe peaches
1 cup fresh blueberries
Fresh mint (optional)

Mix together the first 5 ingredients and bring to boiling point. Add peaches, cover, and cook 10 minutes or until peaches are tender. Remove from heat and cool. Carefully blend in blueberries. Chill. Remove cinnamon sticks. Serve in sherbet glasses. Garnish with fresh mint leaves, if desired.

YIELD: 6 to 8 servings

CODDLED PEARS IN SPICED RUM SAUCE

(WITH LEMON ICE)

This is an elegant dessert, and can be served most charmingly with a tiny bow of yellow or green baby ribbon tied to the stem of the pear. Spice the pears at least 24 hours before serving, or make them days in advance and let them "live" in the rum syrup until needed.

2 cups sugar
1½ cups water
⅛ teaspoon salt
4 cinnamon sticks, each 2 inches long
½ teaspoon whole cloves
½ teaspoon whole allspice
4 whole ginger roots, each 1 inch long
12 medium-size, whole, fresh, firm, ripe Bartlett pears
¾ cup light rum
12 scoops lemon ice *or* lemon sherbet

Combine the first 4 ingredients in a saucepan. Mix well. Tie remaining spices in a cheesecloth bag and add. Bring to boiling point. Peel pears, leave whole with stems attached. Add a few at a time to the syrup, cover, and cook slowly until pears are tender, 10 to 20 minutes, turning to cook uniformly. Repeat until all pears are cooked. Remove spice bag. Add rum. Let pears stand in syrup at least 24 hours. Just before serving, place a scoop of lemon ice or sherbet in bottom of serving dish. Stand a whole pear, stem end up, on each. Spoon a little of the spiced rum sauce over the top.

YIELD: 12 servings

PEAR COMPOTE AU GELEE

6 firm, ripe pears
2 tablespoons fresh lemon juice
¾ cup sugar
2 cups water
1 cinnamon stick, 2 inches long
1 slice lemon
½ cup currant jelly, melted

Wash and peel pears. Cut in half, if large, and remove cores. If small, core only and leave whole. Rub with some of the lemon juice to prevent discoloration. Combine remaining lemon juice with next 3 ingredients. Bring to boiling point. Add pears, cover, and simmer 20 minutes or until pears are tender but still firm.

Carefully transfer pears to a bowl. Cover and cool. Add the lemon slice to the syrup. Cook until the mixture begins to thicken, about 5 minutes. Strain, cool, and chill. Glaze pears by spooning a little of the melted jelly over each. Place in serving dishes and serve with chilled syrup.

YIELD: 6 servings

ENGLISH APPLE TRIFLE

8 cups (2 pounds) sliced cooking apples
2 tablespoons water
¾ cup sugar
¼ teaspoon salt
½ teaspoon ground nutmeg
1 teaspoon grated lemon peel
12 lady fingers
1 cup Soft Custard *(see below)*
½ cup heavy cream, whipped
1 tablespoon sugar

ORANGE TRIFLE

12 lady fingers
About ¼ cup orange marmalade
2 tablespoons sweet sherry wine
Soft Vanilla Custard *(see below)*
½ cup heavy cream, whipped
Ground nutmeg

Cut lady fingers in lengthwise halves and spread each half with orange marmalade. Then put two halves together in sandwich fashion. Arrange lady fingers in a 1-quart glass bowl, sprinkling each layer with sherry, over which spoon Soft Vanilla Custard. Pour all remaining custard over the top. Cover and chill overnight or until ready to serve. Just before serving, spread with whipped cream sweetened with 1 tablespoon of sugar. Garnish with ground nutmeg. Serve at the table from the serving dish.

SOFT VANILLA CUSTARD

¼ cup sugar
¼ teaspoon nutmeg
¼ teaspoon salt
2 large eggs
_____
1½ cups milk
1 teaspoon vanilla extract

Combine first 4 ingredients in the top part of a double boiler or 1-quart saucepan. Mix well. Stir in 1½ cups milk. Cook over hot water (NOT BOILING) or very low heat until custard coats a metal spoon, stirring frequently. Remove from heat and cool. Add 1 teaspoon of vanilla extract.

YIELD: 6 servings

STUFFED PEACHES WITH CUSTARD SAUCE

6 large, firm, ripe, fresh peaches
Orange juice
½ cup finely chopped seedless raisins

Place apples and water in a saucepan. Cover and cook over low heat until apples are tender. Remove from heat and put through a sieve. Add next 4 ingredients. Mix well. Cool. Arrange lady fingers, applesauce, and custard in alternating layers in an 8-inch bowl, having lady fingers on the bottom and custard over the top. Chill until ready to serve. Just before serving, cover with whipped cream sweetened with 1 tablespoon of sugar.

SOFT CUSTARD

2 tablespoons sugar
¼ teaspoon ground nutmeg
¹⁄₁₆ teaspoon salt
_____
1 large egg
1 cup milk

Combine first 3 ingredients in a 3-cup saucepan or in the top of a double boiler. Add egg and mix until blended. Add milk. Stir and cook over low heat or hot water (NOT BOILING) only until custard coats a metal spoon. Remove from heat. Cool and chill.

YIELD: 6 to 8 servings

½ cup finely chopped pecans,
   almonds, *or* walnuts
¼ cup diced fresh oranges
¼ teaspoon ground cinnamon
⅛ teaspoon ground cloves

Soft Custard Sauce*

Peel peaches. Cut in half, remove seeds, and dip in orange juice to prevent discoloration. Combine next 5 ingredients. Spoon an equal amount into 6 of the peach halves. Top with remaining peach halves. Place a stuffed peach in each of 6 dessert dishes. Serve with Soft Custard Sauce spooned over the top.

YIELD: 6 servings

PEARS ZABAGLIONE

½ cup sugar
2 cups water
1 tablespoon grated, fresh lemon peel
1 tablespoon grated, fresh orange peel
⅛ teaspoon salt
2 cinnamon sticks, each 2 inches long

6 peeled, medium-size pears
Fresh lemon juice
Zabaglione Sauce *(see below)*

Combine the first 6 ingredients in a 1½-quart saucepan. Bring to boiling point. Cut pears in half, remove cores, dip in lemon juice, and add half the pears to the boiling syrup. Cover and cook 25 minutes or until pears are tender. Transfer cooked pears to a bowl. Repeat, using the remaining pears. Cool in syrup. Chill. Serve in a sauce dish with Zabaglione Sauce.

ZABAGLIONE SAUCE

4 large egg yolks
½ cup sifted confectioners' sugar
1/16 teaspoon salt
½ cup sweet sherry wine
½ teaspoon grated lemon rind

Beat egg yolks in top of a 1-quart double boiler until light and lemon-colored. Gradually beat in sugar. Add salt. Cook over hot water until mixture is foamy. DO NOT ALLOW WATER TO BOIL. Add wine and lemon rind. Beat until well blended. Remove from hot water and cool.

YIELD: 6 servings

BAY-ROC COCONUT PUDDING

This recipe, rich with fresh coconut and topped with Lime Meringue, is so delectable it seems like lily-gilding to serve it with a Cream and Brandy Sauce. With it, however, it becomes the best pudding imaginable. The recipe comes from the Bay-Roc Hotel, Montego Bay, Jamaica, B.W.I.

¾ cup (1½ sticks) soft butter *or*
   margarine
½ teaspoon ground mace
¾ cup sugar
1 large egg, beaten
3 large egg yolks
3 cups finely grated fresh coconut
1¼ cups evaporated milk *or*
   light cream
1 teaspoon vanilla extract

Lime Meringue*
Cream and Brandy Sauce*

Cream butter or margarine, mace, and sugar together until fluffy. Add next 5 ingredients. Butter individual baking dishes, 2½ inches deep, and fill ¾ full. Bake in a pan of hot water in a preheated moderate oven (350° F.) 45 minutes or until firm. Remove from oven and cool. Top with Lime Meringue and return to 325° F. oven for 15 to 20 minutes. Serve with Cream and Brandy Sauce.

YIELD: 8 servings

OLD-FASHIONED BUTTERMILK PUDDING

½ cup (1 stick) soft butter *or* margarine
½ teaspoon ground mace
⅔ cup sugar
3 large eggs
___
3 tablespoons flour
½ teaspoon salt
½ teaspoon grated lemon rind
___
2 cups fresh buttermilk
2 teaspoons vanilla extract
Ground nutmeg

Cream butter or margarine, mace, and sugar together until fluffy. Beat in eggs, one at a time. Add the next 3 ingredients. Mix well. Stir in buttermilk and vanilla extract. Turn into a 1-quart casserole. Sprinkle with nutmeg. Place in pan of hot water. Bake in a preheated slow oven (325° F.) 1 hour and 10 minutes or until a knife inserted in center comes out clean.

YIELD: 6 servings

PUMPKIN FLAN

We were jubilant when we discovered Pumpkin Flan. This rich and delicately spiced Puerto Rican custard is a specialty of a small Bronx restaurant, El Radiante, owned and managed by Mr. and Mrs. Gabriel Guardarramos.

¾ cup sugar
½ teaspoon salt
1 teaspoon ground cinnamon
1 cup mashed, cooked pumpkin
5 large eggs, lightly beaten
___
1½ cups undiluted evaporated milk
⅓ cup water
1½ teaspoons vanilla extract
Caramel (*see below*)
___
½ cup heavy cream, whipped
1 tablespoon sugar
¼ teaspoon ground ginger

Combine sugar, salt, and cinnamon. Add pumpkin and eggs. Mix well. Stir in next 3 ingredients. Mix well and turn into caramel-coated 8 x 8 x 2-inch pan. Place in a pan of hot water. Bake in a preheated moderate oven (350° F.) 1 hour and 20 minutes, or until a knife inserted in the center comes out clean. Remove from oven. Cool and chill. To serve, run a spatula around the sides of pan, turn out onto a serving plate, and cut into squares. Top with whipped cream mixed with the 1 tablespoon sugar and ¼ teaspoon ground ginger.

CARAMEL

Melt ½ cup sugar over medium low heat until it forms a golden syrup, stirring constantly to prevent burning. Pour immediately into an 8 x 8 x 2-inch pan, turning and rolling the pan from side to side to coat with caramel. Set aside to use later.

YIELD: 9 servings

SPICED SQUASH PUDDING

¾ cup sugar
1 tablespoon flour
¾ teaspoon salt
1 teaspoon ground ginger
½ teaspoon ground nutmeg

3 large eggs

1½ cups mashed, cooked butternut *or* hubbard squash

1½ cups milk

2 tablespoons light, mild molasses

2 tablespoons melted butter *or* margarine

Heavy cream, whipped

Combine the first 5 ingredients. Beat in eggs. Stir in next 4 ingredients. Mix well. Pour into a buttered 1½-quart casserole. Bake in a preheated moderate oven (350° F.) 1¼ hours or until firm in the center. Serve with whipped cream.

SPICED PUMPKIN PUDDING

Replace squash in the above recipe with mashed, cooked pumpkin.

YIELD: 8 servings

BAKED TRIFLE

⅓ cup sugar

1 tablespoon cornstarch

¼ teaspoon salt

3 large egg yolks

3 cups milk

½ teaspoon ground nutmeg

1½ teaspoons vanilla extract

Two 8-inch sponge-cake layers

Meringue* for 9-inch pie

Combine first 3 ingredients in a saucepan. Blend egg yolks with 2 tablespoons of the milk; add and mix well. Heat remaining milk and stir into the mixture. Stir and cook over hot water or low heat until custard coats a metal spoon. Cool. Add nutmeg and vanilla extract. Split each sponge-cake layer. Place one split layer in the bottom of a 2-quart casserole. Cover with custard. Repeat, using remaining cake and custard, having custard as top layer. Let stand 1 hour for custard to soak into cake. Top with Meringue. Bake in a preheated slow oven (325° F.) 30 minutes or until Meringue is brown.

YIELD: 8 servings

CHOCOLATE MOUSSE

1 package (6 ounces) semisweet chocolate pieces

¼ teaspoon salt

½ teaspoon ground cinnamon

2 tablespoons water

4 large eggs, separated

2 teaspoons vanilla extract

½ cup heavy cream, whipped

Place the first 4 ingredients in the top of a double boiler and cook over hot water until chocolate has melted. Beat egg yolks until thick and lemon-colored. Gradually beat in melted chocolate and vanilla extract. Fold in whipped cream. Spoon into sherbet glasses. Chill until firm and ready to serve. Top with additional whipped cream, sweetened to taste, if desired.

YIELD: 8 servings

THE KITCHEN

MOCHA CREAM

1 package chocolate-chiffon pie filling
1 cup boiling milk

¼ cup sugar
2 tablespoons instant coffee
½ teaspoon ground allspice

1½ teaspoons vanilla extract
½ cup heavy cream, whipped

Beat chocolate-chiffon pie filling into milk, continue beating until it stands in peaks. Combine next 3 ingredients and beat into the mixture. Fold in vanilla extract. Cool and then fold in cream. Serve in sherbet glasses plain or topped with additional whipped cream.

YIELD: 6 servings

LIME CREAM

1 cup sugar
2 tablespoons cornstarch
½ teaspoon ground mace
⅛ teaspoon salt

1 cup water
¼ cup fresh lime juice
1 large egg, lightly beaten
1 teaspoon grated lime rind
1 teaspoon vanilla extract
1 cup heavy cream, whipped
Grated lime rind (optional)

Combine the first 4 ingredients in a saucepan or the top of a double boiler. Gradually stir in water. Cook over boiling water until mixture has thickened, stirring constantly. Add lime juice and cook until thickened. Add a little of the hot mixture to the egg and then stir into the remaining hot mixture. Stir and cook 1 to 2 minutes over low heat or hot water. Remove from heat and add lime rind and vanilla extract. Cool. Fold in whipped cream. Serve in sherbet glasses garnished with additional whipped cream, if desired, and grated lime rind.

LEMON CREAM

Replace lime juice and lime rind with lemon juice and lemon rind in the above recipe.

YIELD: 6 servings

SPICED VANILLA CREAM

½ pound marshmallows
1 cup milk
½ teaspoon ground nutmeg

2 teaspoons vanilla extract
1 cup heavy cream, whipped
10-ounce package frozen strawberries
   (optional)

Place first 3 ingredients in a saucepan. Stir and cook over low heat *only* until marshmallows have melted. Remove from heat, stir in vanilla extract. Chill in a bowl of ice water until the mixture begins to thicken. Fold in whipped cream. Spoon into sherbet glasses. Chill until firm and ready to serve. Top with thawed frozen strawberries just before serving, if desired.

YIELD: 5 to 6 servings

CRANBERRY TAPIOCA PARFAIT

1 large egg, separated
2 cups milk
5 tablespoons sugar

3 tablespoons quick-cooking tapioca
½ teaspoon salt
¼ teaspoon ground mace
½ teaspoon vanilla extract

2 teaspoons lemon juice
1 teaspoon grated lemon rind
1 cup heavy cream, whipped
Tart Cranberry-Orange Sauce*

Beat egg yolk and ¼ cup of the milk in a saucepan. Add remaining milk, 3 tablespoons of the sugar, and next 4 ingredients. Stir and cook over medium heat 6 to 7 minutes or until mixture has thickened. Beat egg white until it stands in soft, stiff peaks. Gradually beat in remaining sugar, one tablespoon at a time. Fold in tapioca along with lemon juice and rind. Cool. Fold in whipped cream.

Fill parfait glasses with alternating layer of pudding and Tart Cranberry-Orange Sauce. Top with additional whipped cream, if desired.

YIELD: 8 to 10 servings

GEORGIA PEACH PUDDING

9 cups (4 pounds) sliced fresh peaches
1¼ cups sugar
½ teaspoon ground cinnamon
⅛ teaspoon salt
2½ tablespoons tapioca
1 cup sifted all-purpose flour
⅓ cup (⅔ stick) butter *or* margarine
Sliced fresh peaches

Combine peaches with ¾ cup of the sugar and next 3 ingredients. Turn into a 10 x 6 x 2-inch baking dish. Mix remaining sugar with flour. Add butter or margarine and cut into crumb consistency.

Sprinkle crumbs over peaches. Bake in a preheated moderate oven (375° F.) 1¼ hours or until peaches are tender and crumbs are brown. Garnish with slices of fresh peaches.

YIELD: 8 servings

APPLE CHARLOTTE

4 cups finely diced apples
¾ cup sugar
¼ teaspoon salt
½ teaspoon ground cloves
¼ teaspoon grated lemon rind
½ cup orange juice
3 tablespoons cooking sherry
¼ cup (½ stick) butter *or* margarine
3 cups soft bread crumbs
Heavy cream (optional)

Mix together first 7 ingredients. Melt butter or margarine and add to bread crumbs. Mix well. Fill a buttered 1-quart casserole with alternating layers of bread crumbs and apples, beginning and ending with bread crumbs. Cover and bake in a preheated moderate oven (350° F.) 30 minutes. Remove cover and bake 15 minutes or until crumbs are brown and apples are tender. Serve warm with cream, if desired.

YIELD: 6 servings

SWEDISH APPLE CAKE WITH VANILLA CREAM SAUCE

½ cup (1 stick) butter *or* margarine, melted
3 cups stale cake, dry bread crumbs *or* graham cracker crumbs
3¾ cups (two 18-ounce cans) applesauce
2 teaspoons ground cinnamon
Vanilla Cream Sauce (*see below*)

Combine melted butter and crumbs in a skillet or saucepan. Cook 5 minutes over medium heat, stirring frequently to prevent scorching. Mix applesauce with cinnamon. Fill a buttered 8 x 8 x 2-inch baking pan with alternate layers of buttered crumbs and applesauce, having crumbs as bottom and top layers. Bake until brown and the cake is set, about 45 minutes, in a preheated moderate oven (350° F.). Serve warm or cold with Vanilla Cream Sauce.

VANILLA CREAM SAUCE
2 large eggs, well beaten
⅓ cup sugar
¹⁄₁₆ teaspoon salt
1 cup top milk or light cream
1 teaspoon vanilla extract

Combine beaten eggs, sugar, and salt. Stir in top milk or light cream. Cook over very low heat until slightly thickened. Remove from heat. Cool. Stir in vanilla extract. Serve over Swedish Apple Cake.

YIELD: 9 servings

CHOCOLATE BREAD PUDDING
⅛ teaspoon salt
¼ teaspoon ground cloves
½ teaspoon ground cinnamon
½ cup sugar
1 cup soft bread crumbs
2¾ cups hot milk
2 teaspoons vanilla extract
2 tablespoons butter or margarine
2 squares (2 ounces) unsweetened chocolate
¼ cup cold milk
2 large egg yolks
Meringue* for 8-inch pie

Combine first 5 ingredients. Add hot milk, vanilla extract, and butter or mar-

garine. Melt chocolate over hot water and add. Combine cold milk with egg yolks and add. Turn into a buttered 1-quart casserole. Bake in a preheated slow oven (325° F.) 45 minutes or until knife inserted in the center comes out clean. Top with Meringue. Bake 15 minutes or until golden.

YIELD: 6 servings

COCONUT BREAD PUDDING
1 cup soft bread crumbs
4 cups hot milk
2 tablespoons butter or margarine
¼ teaspoon salt
2½ teaspoons vanilla extract
1 large egg
2 large egg yolks
½ cup sugar
½ teaspoon ground mace
1 cup flaked coconut
½ teaspoon grated lemon rind

Soften crumbs in 1 cup of the hot milk. Mash well. Add remaining hot milk, butter or margarine, salt, and vanilla extract. Beat whole egg and egg yolks together slightly. Blend in sugar and mace. Add to bread crumb mixture along with coconut and lemon rind. Turn into a buttered 1½-quart casserole. Set in a pan of hot water and bake in a preheated slow oven (325° F.) 1½ hours. Serve warm.

YIELD: 6 servings

OLD-FASHIONED BREAD PUDDING
6 slices stale bread
3 tablespoons butter or margarine
½ cup seedless raisins
½ cup sugar
¾ teaspoon ground ginger
½ teaspoon ground cinnamon

½ teaspoon salt
3 cups milk
3 large eggs
Heavy cream, whipped (optional)

Trim crust from bread. Spread each slice with butter or margarine. Place 2 slices in the bottom of a 9 x 5 x 3-inch loaf pan. Add a layer of raisins. Repeat, using remaining buttered bread and raisins.

Combine next 5 ingredients. Beat eggs lightly and add to the mixture. Pour over bread. Push the bread down into the liquid with the back of a tablespoon. Let stand 2 hours. Place in a pan of hot water. Bake in a preheated slow oven (325° F.) 1¼ hours or until a knife inserted in the center comes out clean. Serve plain or with whipped cream.

YIELD: 8 servings

ORANGE BREAD PUDDING

1 cup diced, fresh orange sections
1½ cups day-old bread, cubed

⅔ cup sugar
1 tablespoon cornstarch
¼ teaspoon salt
½ teaspoon ground nutmeg

2 large egg yolks
1½ cups milk

2 tablespoons butter or margarine
1 teaspoon grated orange rind
1 teaspoon vanilla extract

Meringue* for 8-inch pie

Place oranges and bread cubes in a 1-quart casserole and set aside. Combine the next 4 ingredients in a saucepan. Blend in egg yolks and ¼ cup of the milk. Mix in remaining milk. Stir and cook over very low heat until custard coats a metal spoon and has slightly thickened, about 10 minutes. Add the next 3 ingredients. Pour into the casserole over the oranges and bread cubes. Place in a pan of hot water.

Bake in a preheated slow oven (325° F.) 1½ hours or until pudding is firm in center. Cover with Meringue. Reduce heat to slow (300° F.). Return pudding to oven, leaving it in the pan of hot water. Bake 20 minutes or until the Meringue has browned. Serve warm.

YIELD: 6 servings

ORANGE SOUFFLE BREAD PUDDING

⅔ cup sugar
¾ teaspoon ground mace
1 teaspoon grated lemon rind
1 tablespoon grated orange rind
2 tablespoons fresh lemon juice
½ cup fresh orange juice
1 teaspoon vanilla extract
2 cups soft bread cubes, crust removed
½ cup (1 stick) butter or margarine, melted

4 large eggs, separated
¼ cup milk
¼ teaspoon salt

Combine the first 9 ingredients in a mixing bowl. Beat egg yolks until thick and lemon-colored, add milk, and pour over bread cube mixture. Add salt to egg whites and beat them until they stand in soft, stiff peaks. Fold into custard. Turn into a 1-quart casserole, having only the bottom buttered. Place in a pan of hot water. Bake in a preheated slow oven (325° F.) 55 minutes or until soufflé is done. Serve warm.

YIELD: 6 servings

BAKED PEARS IN CASSEROLE, A LA PARISIENNE

12 slices bread
Butter *or* margarine
2 tablespoons sugar
¾ teaspoon ground cinnamon
6 ripe fresh pears
_____
6 tablespoons fresh orange juice
2 teaspoons fresh lemon juice
¼ teaspoon grated lemon rind
_____
½ cup sugar
2 tablespoons butter *or* margarine
Sweet *or* sour cream (optional)

Cut bread into 2¾-inch rounds. Put each 2 slices together in sandwich fashion to make 6 servings. Butter tops and bottoms of each serving. Place in a buttered 8½ x 1¾-inch casserole. Sprinkle with the 2 tablespoons of sugar mixed with cinnamon. Peel pears, leaving them whole with stems attached. Place 1 each on a round of bread. Mix together the next 3 ingredients and spoon over pears. Sprinkle with remaining ½ cup of sugar. Dot with butter or margarine.

Cover and bake in a preheated moderate oven (350° F.) 1 hour. Remove cover and baste with juice formed in the bottom of the pan. Bake, uncovered, 30 minutes or until pears are tender, basting 2 times. Serve with sweet or sour cream, if desired. The bread becomes cake-like.

YIELD: 6 servings

BANANA PUDDING

½ teaspoon ground nutmeg
¼ cup sugar
2 tablespoons flour
¼ teaspoon salt
_____
1 large egg
2 large egg yolks
1½ cups milk
_____
1½ teaspoons vanilla extract
½ teaspoon ground nutmeg
½ teaspoon grated lemon rind
_____
4-ounce package vanilla wafers, ginger or lemon snaps

3 or 4 medium bananas, sliced
Meringue* for 8-inch pie

Combine first 4 ingredients. Add whole egg, egg yolks, and ¼ cup of the milk. Heat remaining milk and gradually stir into the egg and sugar mixture. Stir and cook over low heat or hot water until mixture coats a metal spoon. Add next 3 ingredients. Arrange vanilla wafers, lemon or ginger snaps, and sliced bananas in alternate layers in a buttered, 1-quart casserole, having wafers as bottom layer and bananas as top layer. Pour custard over all. Top with Meringue. Bake in a preheated moderate oven (325° F.) 15 minutes or until brown. This pudding is best served warm.

YIELD: 6 servings

PEACH MACAROON PUDDING

1½ cups mashed, ripe, fresh peaches
¾ cup almond macaroon crumbs
2 tablespoons fresh orange juice,
    Kirsch, *or* brandy
_____
½ cup sugar
½ teaspoon ground mace
1 teaspoon vanilla extract
½ cup (1 stick) soft butter *or*
    margarine
4 large eggs, separated
⅛ teaspoon salt

Combine the first 3 ingredients. Gradually blend ¼ cup of the sugar, mace, and vanilla extract into the butter or margarine. Mix until light and fluffy. Beat one egg yolk at a time into the fruit mixture. Add salt to egg whites and beat until they stand in soft, stiff peaks. Gradually beat in the remaining ¼ cup of sugar and fold into the mixture. Turn into a 1½-quart casserole which has been but-

tered on the bottom only. Place in a pan of hot water (NOT BOILING) and bake in a preheated slow oven (325° F.) for 50 minutes. Reduce temperature to 300° F. (slow) and bake 10 minutes more or until well-puffed and firm.

YIELD: 6 servings

OLD-TIME FRESH PEACH CRUMB PUDDING

16 medium-size (4 pounds) fresh
    peaches
1 cup sugar
½ teaspoon ground cinnamon
1½ cups sifted all-purpose flour
½ cup (1 stick) butter *or* margarine

Peel peaches and cut into quarters. Combine ½ cup of the sugar, cinnamon, and 3 tablespoons of the flour and mix with peaches. Turn into a buttered 10 x 6 x 2-inch baking dish. Combine the remaining sugar and flour. Mix in butter or margarine until the mixture is of crumb consistency. Sprinkle over peaches, covering them uniformly. Bake in a preheated moderate oven (375° F.) 1 hour or until peaches are tender and crumbs are browned.

YIELD: 6 to 8 servings

BAKED INDIAN PUDDING

¼ cup corn meal
2 cups hot milk
_____
¼ cup sugar
⅛ teaspoon soda
½ teaspoon salt
½ teaspoon ground ginger
½ teaspoon ground cinnamon
_____
¼ cup unsulphured molasses
1 cup cold milk
Heavy cream, whipped, *or* ice cream
    (optional)
Ground nutmeg

Gradually stir corn meal into hot milk. Cook over low heat or hot water 15 minutes or until thick, stirring constantly. Remove from heat. Blend together the next 5 ingredients and add. Stir in molasses and cold milk. Pour into a buttered 1-quart casserole. Bake in a preheated very slow oven (275° F.) 2 hours. Serve warm with whipped cream or ice cream, if desired. Garnish with nutmeg.

YIELD: 6 to 8 servings

TIPSY CARAMEL PUDDING

1 cup milk
½ cup sugar
1 teaspoon ground nutmeg
1½ teaspoons vanilla extract
2 tablespoons butter *or* margarine
7 tablespoons cream of wheat
¼ teaspoon salt
3 large eggs, separated
⅓ cup mixed glacé fruit
¼ cup Kirsch *or* rum
4 tablespoons Caramel *(see below)*
Heavy cream, whipped (optional)

Combine the first 5 ingredients in a saucepan. Heat to boiling point. Stir in cream of wheat and salt. Stir and cook until mixture has thickened, 6 to 8 minutes. Cool slightly. Beat egg yolks lightly, into which gradually beat a little of the hot mixture. Then add to remaining hot mixture. In the meantime, soak glacé fruit in Kirsch or rum and add. Beat egg whites until they stand in soft, stiff peaks. Fold into the mixture. Turn into a 1-quart mold, coated with Caramel. Place in a pan of hot water. Bake in a preheated moderate oven (350° F.) 1 hour. Serve warm, with whipped cream if desired.

CARAMEL
Melt ¼ cup of sugar in a small heavy skillet or saucepan over low heat. Stir in 2 tablespoons of boiling water. Sugar will lump. Boil until lumps are dissolved. Add ¼ teaspoon vanilla extract.

YIELD: 6 servings

RICE CUSTARD PUDDING

¼ cup long-grain rice
2 cups hot milk
½ teaspoon salt
½ cup sugar
1 teaspoon grated lemon rind
1 teaspoon vanilla extract
½ teaspoon grated nutmeg
1 tablespoon butter *or* margarine
1 large egg, beaten
2 large egg yolks, beaten
Lemon Meringue*

Cook rice, milk, and salt in top of a double boiler over hot water 20 minutes, or until rice is almost tender. Combine the next 7 ingredients and gradually add to rice. Mix well. Turn into a buttered 1-quart casserole. Bake in a pan of hot water in a preheated moderate oven (350° F.) 1 hour or until pudding is soft-firm, and lightly browned. Top with Lemon Meringue and bake in a slow oven (325° F.) 15 minutes longer.

YIELD: 6 servings

SPICY APPLE SQUARES

1 cup sifted all-purpose flour
½ teaspoon soda
½ teaspoon salt
1 teaspoon ground allspice
½ cup light-brown sugar
1 cup quick-cooking oatmeal
½ cup (1 stick) soft butter *or* margarine
2½ cups sliced apples
¼ cup dried currants

¼ cup sugar
3 tablespoons butter *or* margarine
Date and Nut Sauce*

Sift together first 5 ingredients. Add oatmeal and mix well. Blend in ½ cup butter or margarine until the mixture resembles coarse crumbs. Pat ½ of the mixture into the bottom of a buttered 9-inch square baking pan. Combine apples, currants, and the ¼ cup of sugar and spread over crumbs. Dot with butter or margarine. Cover with remaining crumbs. Bake in a preheated moderate oven (350° F.) 45 minutes or until apples are tender and top is brown. Cut into squares and serve warm with Date and Nut Sauce.

YIELD: 8 servings

PEAR AND APPLE BETTY

3 firm, ripe, fresh pears
3 tart fresh apples

1 cup lightly crumbled corn flakes
½ cup sugar
½ teaspoon ground nutmeg
½ teaspoon grated lemon rind
¼ teaspoon salt

2 tablespoons butter *or* margarine
Heavy cream, whipped, sour cream, *or* Hard Sauce* (optional)

Wash, pare, and slice fruit. Turn ¼ of the amount into a buttered 1-quart baking dish. Combine the next 5 ingredients and sprinkle ¼ of the mixture over fruit. Dot with ½ tablespoon butter or margarine. Repeat with 3 more layers, using remaining ingredients.

Bake in a preheated moderate oven (350° F.) 1 to 1½ hours or until fruit is tender. (Baking time depends upon the ripeness of fruit.) Serve with whipped or sour cream or Hard Sauce, if desired.

YIELD: 6 servings

NEW ENGLAND APPLE SHORTCAKE

4 medium-size apples, such as Rome Beauty, which holds shape when cooked

1 cup sugar
2 cups water
½ teaspoon salt
2 cinnamon sticks, each 2 inches long
2 slices lemon

Warm Shortcake Biscuit *(see below)*
Butter *or* margarine
¼ teaspoon vanilla extract
1 tablespoon sugar
½ cup heavy cream, whipped

Wash, peel, quarter, and core apples. Cut quarters in half lengthwise. Set aside. Combine the next 5 ingredients in a 1½-quart saucepan. Mix well and bring to boiling point. Add apples. Cover and cook 10 minutes or until apples are tender, stirring once or twice and being careful not to break apples. (The apple slices should hold their shape.) Turn off heat and allow apples to stand, covered, 5 minutes.

Carefully remove apples from syrup. Boil syrup until thick. Return apples to syrup and spoon on the bottoms of buttered, warm Shortcake Biscuit, spooning some of the syrup over apples. Top with remaining biscuit halves and apples. Add vanilla extract and the 1 tablespoon sugar to cream. Beat with a rotary or an electric beater until it stands in soft, stiff peaks. Spoon over shortcake.

SHORTCAKE BISCUIT
2 cups sifted all-purpose flour
1 teaspoon salt
2 teaspoons double-acting baking
   powder
2 tablespoons sugar
___
⅓ cup shortening
About ⅔ cup milk

Sift together the first 4 ingredients. Add shortening and cut it in to crumb consistency. Stir in enough milk to make a soft dough. Knead about 20 seconds on a lightly floured pastry board. Roll dough to ½-inch thickness. Shape with a 3-inch biscuit cutter. Bake in a preheated very hot oven (450° F.) 12 minutes.

YIELD: 8 servings

FRESH PEACHES ON GINGERBREAD WAFFLES
3 cups sliced fresh peaches
4 tablespoons sugar
Gingerbread Waffles*
½ teaspoon vanilla extract
¾ cup heavy cream, whipped

Mix peaches with 3 tablespoons of the sugar and let stand 10 to 15 minutes. Just before serving, spoon peaches over Gingerbread Waffles. Top with whipped cream, sweetened with the remaining 1 tablespoon sugar and flavored with vanilla extract. Serve as a luncheon or supper dessert.

YIELD: 6 servings

APPLE ROLLS
2 cups sifted all-purpose flour
3 teaspoons double-acting
   baking powder
½ teaspoon salt
2 tablespoons sugar
___
¼ cup shortening
About ½ cup milk
3 medium-size cooking apples
1½ cups sugar
2 cups water
¼ cup sugar
½ teaspoon ground nutmeg
½ teaspoon grated lemon rind
¼ cup (½ stick) butter or margarine
Heavy cream, whipped (optional)

Sift the first 4 ingredients together into a mixing bowl. Cut in shortening until the mixture is the consistency of coarse crumbs. Stir in only enough milk to make a soft dough. Roll out on a lightly floured board into a 17 x 12 x ⅛-inch rectangle. Peel and dice apples and sprinkle over dough. Roll up as for jelly roll. Cut into 10 slices. Combine the 1½ cups sugar and 2 cups water and boil 3 or 4 minutes.

Pour mixture into a 12 x 8 x 2-inch baking pan into which place the rolls, cut-side down. Combine remaining ¼ cup sugar, nutmeg, and lemon rind. Sprinkle over rolls. Dot with butter or margarine.

Bake in a hot oven (400° F.) 45 minutes or until done. Serve warm, with some of the sauce poured over each serving. Top with whipped cream, if desired.

YIELD: 10 servings

BLUEBERRY CURLS WITH BLUEBERRY SAUCE
2 cups sifted all-purpose flour
2 tablespoons sugar
3 teaspoons double-acting
   baking powder
¾ teaspoon salt

⅓ cup shortening
⅔ cup milk
1 cup fresh blueberries
3 tablespoons sugar
¼ teaspoon ground cinnamon
Blueberry Sauce*
¼ cup heavy cream, whipped

Sift together the first 4 ingredients. Cut in shortening until the mixture resembles corn meal. Gradually stir in milk. Turn onto a lightly floured board. Knead about 20 strokes. Roll into a 10 x 8 x ¼-inch rectangle. Mix blueberries, sugar, and cinnamon and sprinkle over dough. Roll dough, beginning at the 10-inch side, in jelly-roll fashion. Cut into 1-inch slices. Place each in a greased cupcake pan. Bake in a preheated moderate oven (375° F.) 30 to 35 minutes. Serve topped with Blueberry Sauce and whipped cream.

YIELD: 10 servings

POPPY SEED AND APPLE STRUDEL

The pastry for this strudel must be rolled, pulled, and coaxed to tissue-paper thinness. Clear the dining-room table, spread it with a clean sheet, and go to it.

STRUDEL DOUGH
2 cups sifted all-purpose flour
¼ teaspoon salt
1 large egg, beaten
½ cup warm water
1 cup (2 sticks) butter *or* margarine, melted

POPPY SEED AND APPLE FILLING
2 cups poppy seeds
3 quarts finely chopped, good-flavored apples (about 4½ pounds)
1½ cups sugar

1½ teaspoons grated lemon rind
1 teaspoon ground cinnamon
½ teaspoon salt
1 cup fine, dry bread crumbs

Sift flour and salt into a mixing bowl. Add beaten egg. Gradually add water, mixing well with a fork. After all the water has been added, stir in 2 tablespoons of the melted butter or margarine. Knead on a lightly floured board for at least 30 minutes or until dough is smooth, bubbly, elastic, and no longer sticks to the board. Or, to save all that effort, put dough through a food chopper 8 times, using medium blade.

Place dough in the center of a large table covered with a floured cloth. Cover with a warm bowl and let stand for 30 minutes. Meanwhile, prepare the filling by combining all the ingredients except the bread crumbs. Divide dough into two parts. Roll one part as thinly as possible into a rectangle. Brush with melted butter. Placing hands under the dough, pull and stretch with the fingers very gently until the dough is paper thin. Brush again with melted butter.

Cover the surface with ½ cup dry bread crumbs and then ½ of the filling. Roll up as for jelly roll, holding the cloth high and allowing the strudel to roll itself over and over. Cut the roll in half. Pinch edges together so that juice does not run out. Place rolls on ungreased cooky sheet and brush tops with melted butter.

Repeat above procedure with second ball of dough, using remaining bread crumbs, filling, and additional melted butter if necessary. Bake in a preheated hot oven (400° F.) 30 minutes. Reduce temperature to 350° F. and continue baking 30 more minutes, basting the dough from time to time with melted butter. The crust should be brown and very crisp. To serve, cut in crosswise slices as desired. Freeze any leftover strudel for future use.

YIELD: 4 rolls, each 14 inches long

APPLE PANDOWDY

6 cups sliced, tart cooking apples

¾ to 1 cup sugar
¼ teaspoon salt
¼ teaspoon ground nutmeg
¼ teaspoon ground cinnamon

2 tablespoons butter *or* margarine
Shortcake Topping *(see below)*
Hard Sauce*

NOTE: If apples are *not* tart, add 1 tablespoon lemon juice and ½ teaspoon grated lemon rind.

Turn apples into a 9 x 9 x 2-inch baking pan. Combine next 4 ingredients. (The amount of sugar depends upon the tartness of the apples.) Sprinkle over the top. Cover baking pan with a piece of foil and bake in a preheated hot oven (400° F). about 20 minutes or until apples are *almost* tender.

Remove pan from oven and increase oven temperature to 425° F. Cover with Shortcake Topping, rolled to ¼-inch thickness, cut to fit top of pan. Prick dough with a fork at 4 or 5 places. Brush top with milk. Bake 30 minutes or until crust has browned. To serve, cut into squares and serve apple-side up, topped with Hard Sauce or whipped cream, if desired.

SHORTCAKE TOPPING

2 cups sifted all-purpose flour
3 teaspoons double-acting
  baking powder
½ teaspoon salt

½ cup (1 stick) butter *or* margarine
About ⅔ cup milk

Sift together first 3 ingredients in a mixing bowl. Add butter or margarine and cut it in to crumb consistency. Stir in enough milk to make a soft dough. Knead about 20 seconds on a lightly floured board. Roll dough ½ inch thick to fit pan. Proceed as in above directions.

YIELD: 8 servings

APPLE COBBLER

6 cups sliced, tart, cooking apples
1 cup sugar
¼ teaspoon salt
½ teaspoon ground cinnamon
¼ teaspoon ground nutmeg

2 tablespoons butter *or* margarine
9-inch, unbaked 1-crust pie shell
  (Never-Fail Pastry I*)

NOTE: If apples are very juicy, mix 3 tablespoons flour with the 1 cup sugar to thicken the juice.

Combine first 5 ingredients and turn into a 9 x 9 x 2-inch baking dish. Dot with butter or margarine. Cover with unbaked pastry rolled ⅛-inch thick, 2 inches larger than the baking dish. Trim, turn under, and flute edge. Cut a vent in the pastry to allow for the escape of steam.

Bake in a preheated very hot oven (450° F.) 10 minutes. Reduce heat to 350° F. (moderate) and continue baking 30 minutes, or until apples are tender and pastry is brown. Serve warm or cold.

YIELD: 9 servings

PEACH COBBLER

7 cups sliced, fresh peaches (4 pounds)
1 tablespoon fresh lemon juice

1¼ cups sugar
¼ teaspoon salt
¼ teaspoon ground cinnamon
3½ tablespoons quick-cooking tapioca

2 to 3 tablespoons butter *or* margarine
Unbaked 1-crust pie shell (Never-Fail
  Pastry I*)

Mix peaches with lemon juice in a 1½-quart casserole. Combine next 4 ingredients and sprinkle over peaches. Dot with butter or margarine. Cover with unbaked pastry, rolled ⅛-inch thick and 2 inches larger than diameter of casserole. Trim, turn under and flute edge. Cut 2 to 3 vents in top to allow for escape of steam. Bake in a preheated hot oven (425° F.) 45 minutes or until crust is brown. Serve warm or cold.

YIELD: 6 servings

APPLE PUDDING

¼ teaspoon soda
¼ teaspoon ground cloves
¼ teaspoon ground cinnamon
¼ teaspoon ground nutmeg
⅛ teaspoon salt
¼ cup (½ stick) soft butter *or*
  margarine
½ cup sugar
1 large egg, well beaten
½ cup sifted all-purpose flour
1½ cups chopped, good-flavored apples
  (about 3 small apples)
Lemon Sauce*

Combine the first 6 ingredients. Add sugar gradually. Beat in egg. Stir in flour.

Fold in apples. Turn into a buttered 8 x 8 x 2-inch pan.

Bake in a preheated moderate oven (350° F.) 35 to 40 minutes or until firm when pressed in center with finger. Cut into squares and serve hot or warm with Lemon Sauce.

YIELD: 6 servings

BAKED BLUEBERRY PUDDING

2 cups sifted all-purpose flour
1½ cups sugar
2 teaspoons double-acting
  baking powder
½ teaspoon salt
½ teaspoon ground nutmeg
¾ teaspoon ground cinnamon
⅔ cup (1⅓ sticks) butter *or*
  margarine
2 large eggs
¾ cup milk
2 cups fresh blueberries
Lemon Sauce*

Sift together into the large bowl of the electric mixer the first 6 ingredients. Add butter or margarine and blend it in until the particles are the size of a small pea. Add eggs and milk. Beat mixture 3 minutes at low speed or until all ingredients are thoroughly blended.

Turn batter into a well-greased, lightly floured 9 x 9 x 2-inch pan. Wash blueberries and drain them well. Spread over the batter. Bake in a preheated moderate oven (350° F.) 1 hour or until done. Serve warm or cold with Lemon Sauce.

YIELD: 8 servings

PEACH PUDDING

1 cup sifted all-purpose flour
1 cup sugar
½ teaspoon salt
½ teaspoon ground cinnamon

1½ teaspoons double-acting
    baking powder
4 tablespoons butter *or* margarine
½ cup milk
6 cups (3 pounds) thinly sliced,
    fresh peaches
Heavy cream, whipped (optional)

Sift flour with ½ cup of the sugar, salt, cinnamon, and baking powder. Cut in 2 tablespoons of the butter or margarine until mixture is crumbly. Stir in milk. Spread batter in a buttered 8 x 8 x 2-inch pan. Cover with sliced peaches. Blend the remaining ½ cup sugar with remaining butter or margarine and sprinkle over peaches.

    Cover with foil and bake in a preheated moderate oven (375° F.) 20 minutes. Remove cover and bake 40 minutes or until done. Cut pudding into squares and top with whipped cream, if desired.

YIELD: 6 servings

PEAR PUDDING

5 cups (2¼ pounds) sliced,
    fresh pears
⅔ cup sugar
1½ tablespoons quick-cooking tapioca
3 tablespoons fresh lemon juice
¼ teaspoon salt
¾ teaspoon grated lemon rind

2 tablespoons butter *or* margarine

1 cup sifted all-purpose flour
⅓ cup sugar
½ teaspoon salt
½ teaspoon ground mace
1½ teaspoons double-acting
    baking powder

¼ cup shortening
1 large egg, beaten
½ cup milk
Lemon Sauce* (optional)

Combine the first 6 ingredients. Turn into a buttered 9 x 9 x 2-inch baking dish. Dot with butter or margarine. Sift together the next 5 ingredients. Add shortening and mix until crumbly. Stir in egg and milk. Beat until ingredients are blended. Spoon batter over pears, spread with a spatula to cover them uniformly. Bake in a preheated moderate oven (350° F.) 1 hour or until browned and pears are tender. Cut into squares and serve warm or cold. Top with Lemon Sauce, if desired.

YIELD: 6 to 9 servings

PINEAPPLE COTTAGE PUDDING

2½ cups (1 pound, 14 ounce can)
    crushed pineapple

¼ cup light-brown sugar
⅟₁₆ teaspoon salt
½ teaspoon grated lemon rind

1¾ cups sifted all-purpose flour
2½ teaspoons double-acting
    baking powder
½ teaspoon salt
½ teaspoon ground mace
1 teaspoon vanilla extract
⅓ cup shortening
¾ cup sugar

1 large egg
⅔ cup milk
Heavy cream, whipped, *or*
    Vanilla Sauce*

Drain pineapple and turn into buttered 8 x 8 x 2-inch baking pan. Combine the next 3 ingredients and sprinkle over pineapple. Sift together flour, baking powder, and salt. Set aside. Mix together the next 4 ingredients. Beat in egg. Add flour mixture alternately with milk. Spread batter uniformly over pineapple.

    Bake in a preheated moderate oven (350° F.) 50 minutes or until a toothpick inserted in the center comes out clean. Serve warm or cold, cut in squares topped with whipped cream or Vanilla Sauce.

YIELD: 6 servings

RHUBARB GINGER PUDDING

4 cups diced, fresh rhubarb
1 cup sugar
⅛ teaspoon salt
3 tablespoons quick-cooking tapioca
1 teaspoon grated lemon rind

2 tablespoons butter *or* margarine
Cottage Pudding Batter *(see below)*

Combine first 5 ingredients. Turn into a 1½-quart casserole. Dot with butter or margarine. Top with Cottage Pudding Batter. Bake in a preheated moderate oven (350° F.) 1¼ hours. Serve warm.

COTTAGE PUDDING BATTER

¼ cup shortening
½ cup sugar
1 large egg

1½ cups sifted all-purpose flour
1½ teaspoons double-acting
    baking powder
½ teaspoon salt
½ teaspoon ground ginger
¼ teaspoon ground nutmeg

½ cup milk

Cream shortening with sugar. Beat in egg. Sift together next 5 ingredients. Add alternately with milk. Beat batter ½ minute. Spread uniformly over rhubarb.

YIELD: 6 servings

BAVARIAN CREAM CAKE

1 package yellow cake mix
½ teaspoon ground mace

2 envelopes unflavored gelatine
½ cup cold water
2 cups hot, canned fruit-cocktail juice

6 tablespoons fresh lemon juice
½ teaspoon grated lemon rind
¼ teaspoon salt
1½ teaspoons ground mace
½ cup sugar

2 cups drained, canned fruit cocktail
4 large egg whites
½ cup sugar
2½ cups heavy cream, whipped

Make up yellow-cake mix as directed on package, blending ½ teaspoon ground mace into batter. Bake as directed in a 9 x 9 x 2-inch square pan that has been well greased and lightly floured. Soften gelatine in cold water. Add hot fruit-cocktail juice. Stir in next 5 ingredients. Mix well. Chill until mixture begins to thicken. Stir in fruit cocktail. Beat egg whites until they stand in soft peaks. Gradually beat in remaining ½ cup sugar, beating until stiff. Fold into gelatine mixture along with 1 cup of the cream, whipped. (Save remaining 1½ cups cream for later use.)

Turn into a 9-inch square pan that has been rinsed in cold water. Chill until firm and ready to use. Place cold cake on serving plate. Unmold gelatine layer over cake layer. If necessary, trim gelatine to fit cake. Whip remaining cream and frost top and sides of cake. Sprinkle top with ground mace, if desired.

YIELD: 16 servings

BAVARIAN PEACH CAKE

½ package yellow cake mix
1 envelope unflavored gelatine
¼ cup water
1 cup hot peach juice

ITALIAN PEACH TORTE

4 medium-large fresh peaches
Juice of 1 lemon
¼ cup (½ stick) butter *or* margarine
⅓ cup sugar
¼ cup chopped, unblanched almonds

Dip peaches in boiling water for only a few seconds. Then dip in cold water. Remove skins and cut into halves. Dip in fresh lemon juice to prevent discoloration. Melt butter or margarine in an 8 x 8 x 2-inch baking pan. Add sugar and almonds. Mix well and spread uniformly over bottom. Arrange peaches, cut-side down, over the mixture. Set aside.

TORTE

½ cup shortening
½ cup sugar
½ teaspoon vanilla extract
½ teaspoon ground cinnamon

2 large eggs

2 teaspoons double-acting
  baking powder
¼ teaspoon salt
½ cup sifted all-purpose flour

1 cup fine vanilla wafer crumbs
½ cup milk

Mix together the first 4 ingredients. Beat in eggs. Sift together the next 3 ingredients and mix with vanilla wafer crumbs. Add to the first mixture alternately with milk. Beat batter ½ minute. Pour over peaches in the prepared pan.

Bake in a preheated moderate oven (350° F.) 1¼ hours or until a cake tester inserted in center comes out clean. Let cake cool in pan 20 minutes. Turn out on wire rack to finish cooling. Serve warm or cold, cut into squares.

YIELD: One 8-inch square torte

---

3 tablespoons lemon juice
½ teaspoon ground mace
½ teaspoon grated lemon rind
⅛ teaspoon salt
¼ cup sugar

1 cup drained, diced, canned peaches
¼ cup sugar
2 large egg whites, beaten
1½ cups heavy cream, whipped
2 tablespoons sugar

Prepare yellow-cake mix as directed on package. Bake as directed in an 8-inch layer-cake pan. Soften gelatine in water. Add peach juice. Blend in next 5 ingredients. Chill until the mixture begins to thicken. Stir in peaches. Gradually beat remaining ¼ cup sugar into beaten egg whites and fold into gelatine along with ½ cup of the cream, whipped.

Turn into a lightly oiled round, 8-inch layer-cake pan. Chill until firm and ready to use. Place cake layer on plate, over which unmold the gelatine layer. If necessary, trim gelatine to fit cake. Whip remaining cream and sweeten with 1 tablespoon sugar. Spread over top and sides of cake.

YIELD: 8 servings

PEACH AND RASPBERRY TORTE

½ teaspoon ground mace
1 teaspoon vanilla extract
½ cup shortening

1 cup sugar

1 cup sifted all-purpose flour
½ cup cornstarch
½ teaspoon salt
1½ teaspoons double-acting
    baking powder

¼ cup milk
2 large eggs, beaten
Fresh Peach and Raspberry
    Cream Topping (see below)
1 cup sliced fresh peaches
½ cup fresh raspberries

Combine the first 3 ingredients. Gradually blend in sugar. Sift together the next 4 ingredients. Add to shortening and sugar mixture alternately with milk and eggs. Grease and line the bottom of a 9-inch layer-cake pan with wax paper. Add the batter and spread over the bottom to cover uniformly.

Bake in a preheated moderate oven (350° F.) ¾ hour or until a toothpick inserted in the center comes out clean. Cool in pan 20 minutes. Turn onto wire rack and remove wax paper at once. Turn torte right side up.

Top with Peach and Raspberry Cream Topping. Garnish with sliced peaches and raspberries.

FRESH PEACH AND RASPBERRY CREAM TOPPING

Whip 1 cup heavy cream until it stands in soft, stiff peaks. Add 2 tablespoons sugar and 1 teaspoon vanilla extract. Mix lightly. Fold in ½ cup each, coarsely diced, fresh peaches and fresh raspberries.

YIELD: 6 to 8 servings

POINCIANA STEAMED APPLE PUDDING

The recipe for this tempting pudding is a hand-me-down in the Day family— from great-grandmother to grandmother to mother to niece. This is a good holiday and cold-weather pudding, since it requires steaming and is best if served warm.

½ cup sifted all-purpose flour
½ teaspoon soda
1 teaspoon double-acting
    baking powder
1 teaspoon ground cinnamon
½ teaspoon salt
½ cup sugar

1½ cups fine, dry bread crumbs

½ cup unsulphured molasses
2 large eggs, beaten
2 tablespoons melted shortening

1½ cups chopped, tart cooking apples
1½ cups chopped seedless raisins
Hard Sauce* or heavy cream, whipped
Dried prunes or apricots (optional)

Sift together first 6 ingredients and mix with bread crumbs. Add next 3 ingredients. Mix well. Stir in apples and raisins. Turn batter into a well-greased, 1-quart mold, filling it ⅔ full. Cover tightly with lid that fits the mold or with foil tied in place with a strong cord. Place mold on a wire rack in deep kettle. Pour in hot water to come halfway up sides of the mold. Cover kettle and bring water to boiling point. Turn down heat just enough to keep water boiling, and start counting the time from this point.

Steam 2½ hours or until done. Replenish with more boiling water as necessary to keep it at its original level. Pudding is done when cake tester inserted in the center comes out clean. Remove pudding from the steamer and place it in a preheated moderate oven (350° F.) 5 to 10 minutes or until top is no longer sticky. Serve hot with Hard Sauce or whipped cream. To decorate, arrange soaked dried prunes or apricots in bottom of mold before pouring in.

YIELD: 8 servings

STEAMED BLUEBERRY PUDDING

¼ cup (½ stick) soft butter *or* margarine
⅓ cup sugar
½ teaspoon ground nutmeg
1 teaspoon vanilla extract

1 large egg
¾ cup sifted all-purpose flour
½ teaspoon double-acting baking powder
¼ cup milk
½ cup fresh blueberries
1 tablespoon flour
Lemon Sauce*

Combine the first 4 ingredients. Beat in egg. Sift flour with baking powder and add alternately with milk. Beat batter ½ minute. Carefully mix blueberries with the 1 tablespoon flour and fold into the batter.

Turn into 6 well-greased, lightly floured 6-ounce custard cups. Cover each with foil. Hold in place with a rubber band. Place cups on a rack or jar lids in a deep 10-inch skillet or saucepan. Pour in boiling water to come halfway up the sides of cups. Cover and steam 1 hour, adding additional water if needed. Serve warm with Lemon Sauce.

YIELD: 6 servings

STEAMED CARROT PUDDING

¾ cup sugar
⅔ cup sifted all-purpose flour
1 teaspoon salt
1 teaspoon double-acting baking powder
1 teaspoon ground nutmeg
½ teaspoon ground ginger
¼ teaspoon ground cloves

2 teaspoons grated lemon rind
1⅓ cups fine, dry bread crumbs
1½ cups (1¼ pounds) grated raw carrots

1 large egg, beaten
⅓ cup shortening
Hard Sauce*

Sift together the first 7 ingredients. Blend in next 3 ingredients. Stir in egg and shortening. Mix well. Turn into a well-greased, lightly floured 1-quart mold, filling it ⅔ full. Cover tightly. Place in a deep kettle. Pour in hot water to come halfway up the side of the mold. Cover and steam 2½ hours, adding more water to kettle as necessary. Unmold and serve warm with Hard Sauce or whipped cream.

YIELD: 8 servings

STEAMED ENGLISH CHRISTMAS PUDDING

This traditional Christmastime recipe originally called for three whole nutmegs, painstakingly grated. You might prefer to use ground nutmeg, as we have done. The results are excellent.

2 cups (½ pound) ground beef suet
15-ounce package seedless raisins
11-ounce package currants
1⅓ cups (½ pound) chopped citron
3 cups fine, dry bread crumbs
3 large eggs, beaten

1 tablespoon grated lemon rind
2 tablespoons fresh lemon juice
2¼ cups (1 pound) dark-brown sugar
1½ teaspoons salt
3 teaspoons ground nutmeg
½ cup cider *or* pineapple juice

Foamy Sauce*

Put suet and raisins through a food chopper, using the medium blade. Stir in next 10 ingredients. Turn into a well-greased, lightly floured 2-quart mold. Cover tightly. Place on a rack in a deep kettle. Pour in boiling water to come halfway up the side of mold. Cover and steam 3 hours, counting time after water begins to boil. Add more water as needed to keep it at its original level. Serve with Foamy Sauce.

YIELD: 12 servings

STEAMED HOLIDAY PUDDING

Here is the traditional English "plum pudding." About 150 years ago an Englishman who'd spent Christmas in France wrote, "No prejudice can be stronger than that of the French against the plum pudding. A Frenchman will dress like an Englishman, swear like an Englishman and get drunk like an Englishman, but if you want to offend him forever, compel him to eat plum pudding."

If you're of French extraction, you may want to skip this one.

¼ cup shortening
½ cup dark-brown sugar
2 large eggs

1½ cups soft bread crumbs
½ teaspoon salt
1 teaspoon double-acting
   baking powder
1 teaspoon ground allspice
1 teaspoon ground cinnamon
¾ teaspoon ground nutmeg
¼ teaspoon ground cloves
2 teaspoons instant coffee

1 cup chopped nuts
1 cup chopped dates
1 cup moist mincemeat
Hard Sauce* *or* heavy cream, whipped

Mix shortening with brown sugar. Beat in eggs. Combine the next 8 ingredients and add to the mixture. Mix well. Stir in nuts, dates, and mincemeat. Turn into a greased, lightly-floured 1-quart mold, filling it ¾ full. Cover tightly with lid that fits mold or with foil held in place with an elastic band or tied with a strong cord. Place in a deep kettle on a rack. Pour in hot water to come halfway up side of mold. Cover kettle and bring water to boiling point. Steam 2½ hours or until a cake tester inserted in center comes out clean. Serve hot with Hard Sauce or whipped cream.

YIELD: 8 servings

OLD-FASHIONED APPLE DUMPLINGS

King George III, English monarch at the time of the American Revolution, was

*considered dim-witted by some of his sub-
jects. Witness this little poem about the
king staring in perplexity at an apple
dumpling:*

*"How?" cried the staring monarch,
with a grin—*
*"How the devil got the apple in?"
It's very simple, of course—you wrap
squares of dough around it.*

Never-Fail Pastry IV*
or 1½ boxes pastry mix
6 medium-size baking apples, such as
Rome Beauty
___
¾ cup light-brown sugar
1 teaspoon ground cinnamon
½ teaspoon ground nutmeg
⅛ teaspoon salt
___
6 teaspoons butter *or* margarine
Hard Sauce* *or* heavy cream, whipped

Make pastry according to directions.
Wash and peel apples. Remove cores,
being careful not to cut through the blossom end. Combine next 4 ingredients.
Roll half the dough at a time to ⅛-inch
thickness in a 21 x 7-inch rectangle. Cut
into three 7-inch squares. Place an apple
in the center of each. Fill cavity with
sugar and spice mixture. Top with a teaspoon of butter or margarine. Bring opposite corners of pastry together over the
top, pressing sides together firmly. Repeat, using all pastry, apples, sugar mixture, and butter. Brush with milk and
sprinkle surface lightly with sugar, if desired.

Bake on a cooky sheet in a preheated
hot oven (425° F.) 35 minutes or until
apples are tender and pastry is brown.
Baking time depends upon the variety
and ripeness of apples. Serve with
whipped cream or Hard Sauce, if desired.

YIELD: 6 servings

CRANBERRY DUMPLINGS

2 cups fresh cranberries
1 cup sugar
1 cup water
¼ teaspoon salt
___
1 cup sifted all-purpose flour
2 tablespoons sugar
½ teaspoon salt
1 teaspoon double-acting
baking powder
¼ teaspoon ground mace
___
1 large egg, beaten
½ cup milk
Heavy cream, whipped (optional)

Wash cranberries and place in a saucepan. Add the 1 cup sugar, water, and
¼ teaspoon salt. Cover, bring to boiling
point and cook 10 minutes or only until
skins pop. Sift together the next 5 ingredients. Combine egg and milk and add to
the dry ingredients. Stir only to blend
ingredients.

Drop from a tablespoon on top of hot
cranberries. Cover and simmer 20 minutes without lifting the cover. Serve at
once, with whipped cream if desired.

YIELD: 6 servings

PEAR AND APPLE DUMPLINGS

Never-Fail Pastry III* *or* 1 box
pastry mix
2 large, firm, ripe pears
2 large, tart apples
___
¾ cup sugar
½ teaspoon ground nutmeg
½ teaspoon ground cinnamon
¼ teaspoon salt
___
6 teaspoons butter *or* margarine
Light cream *or* Hard Sauce*

Make pastry according to directions. Peel,
core, and slice pears and apples and mix
with next 4 ingredients.

Divide unbaked pastry into thirds and roll each ⅛-inch thick in a 12 x 6-inch rectangle and cut into two 6-inch squares. Place ½ cup fruit mixture in center of each and dot with 1 teaspoon butter or margarine. Moisten edges of pastry and bring point over apples and press them together. Place in a buttered 13 x 9 x 2-inch baking pan. Brush with milk. Bake in a preheated hot oven (425° F.) 45 minutes or until fruit is tender and pastry is brown. Serve warm with light cream or Hard Sauce, or serve plain.

YIELD: 6 servings

APPLE TURNOVERS WITH GOLDEN LEMON SAUCE

Never-Fail Pastry IV* or 1½ boxes
  pastry mix
6 medium-size (2¼ pounds) raw, tart
  baking apples
½ cup boiling water
¾ cup sugar
¼ teaspoon salt
½ teaspoon ground cinnamon
½ teaspoon ground nutmeg
4 teaspoons butter or margarine
Golden Lemon Sauce*

Make pastry according to directions. Set aside. Wash, peel, core, and cut apples into eighths. Place in a saucepan with boiling water. Cover and cook gently 10 minutes or until apples are tender. Cool. Stir in next 4 ingredients. Divide unbaked pastry dough into 8 equal parts. Roll into 7-inch circles ⅛ inch thick. Invert a 6¾-inch bread-and-butter plate on each and cut around it with a pointed knife or pastry wheel. Place ¼ cup apple mixture on one side of each. Dot each with ½ teaspoon butter or margarine. Dampen edges with a little water. Fold dough over in half-moon fashion. Press edges together tightly and crimp with a fork.

Bake on ungreased cooky sheets in a preheated hot oven (425° F.) 30 minutes or until lightly browned. Serve with Golden Lemon Sauce.

YIELD: 8 servings

CHARLOTTE RUSSE

There are several types of "charlottes" and considerable speculation as to how this type of pudding got its name. One account has it that this is the modern spelling of charlyt, *which once meant custard. Another, that it was created for the French princess, Charlotte. This has always been a great ladies' luncheon dessert.*

1 pound jelly roll
1 envelope unflavored gelatine
¼ cup water
½ cup scalded milk
½ cup sugar
½ teaspoon ground nutmeg
2 teaspoons vanilla extract
1½ cups heavy cream, whipped
Uncapped fresh strawberries or
  sliced bananas

Cut jelly roll in slices ½ inch thick. Place 1 slice in the bottom and stand remaining

slices around the sides of an 8-inch spring-form pan and set aside. Soften gelatine in water. Add to hot milk, along with sugar mixed with nutmeg. Stir in vanilla extract. Chill in a pan of ice water until mixture begins to thicken, stirring frequently. Beat the mixture with a rotary or electric beater until fluffy.

Whip 1 cup of the cream and beat in ⅓ of it. Fold in the ⅔ cup whipped cream. Pour into the jelly roll-lined, spring-form pan. Chill until firm and ready to serve. Just before serving, remove sides of pan and place on a serving plate. Whip remaining ½ cup cream and garnish the top and around the base of the mold. Top with uncapped fresh strawberries or sliced bananas.

YIELD: 12 servings

CHOCOLATE CHARLOTTE

3 envelopes unflavored gelatine
¾ cup water
1 cup scalded milk
6 squares (6 ounces) unsweetened chocolate
2 cups sugar
9 tablespoons hot water
½ teaspoon ground cinnamon
¼ teaspoon ground cloves
¼ teaspoon salt
2 tablespoons vanilla extract
3½ cups heavy cream, whipped
13 lady fingers

Soften gelatine in water. Add milk and stir until gelatine is dissolved. Melt chocolate over hot water, blend with 1 cup of the sugar and all the hot water. Add to hot-milk mixture. Stir in remaining sugar mixed with spices and salt. Add vanilla extract. Chill until the mixture begins to thicken.

Beat with a rotary or an electric beater until fluffy. Fold in 3 cups of whipped cream. Rinse a 7-inch spring-form mold with cold water. Fill with chocolate mixture. Refrigerate until firm and ready to serve. Unmold onto a serving plate. Arrange lady fingers around the sides of mold. Garnish with remaining whipped cream put through a pastry tube or bag.

YIELD: 8 servings

MOLDED CHOCOLATE PUDDING

2 teaspoons unflavored gelatine
3 tablespoons water
1 large egg

½ cup sugar
¼ cup unflavored cocoa
⅛ teaspoon salt
¼ teaspoon ground cloves
¼ teaspoon ground cinnamon

¾ cup light cream *or* undiluted evaporated milk
1 teaspoon vanilla extract
1 cup heavy cream, whipped

Soften gelatine in water and set aside. Beat egg lightly in top of a double boiler. Add the next 5 ingredients. Blend in cream or evaporated milk. Stir and cook over hot water (NOT BOILING) until thickened, about 10 minutes. Stir in softened gelatine. Cool until the mixture begins to set.

Quickly fold in vanilla extract and whipped cream. Turn into an oiled 1-quart mold. Chill until firm and ready to serve. Unmold onto a serving plate and garnish with additional whipped cream, if desired.

YIELD: 6 servings

CHRISTMAS PLUM PUDDING MOLD

2 envelopes unflavored gelatine
¼ cup water

1½ cups hot pineapple juice
¼ cup fresh lemon juice
½ cup sugar
½ teaspoon ground nutmeg
½ teaspoon ground ginger

1 cup dried light raisins
1 cup chopped, dried dates
2 cups glacé mixed fruit
1 cup chopped, blanched almonds

2 cups heavy cream, whipped
Grated nutmeg (optional)

Soften gelatine in water. Stir in next 5 ingredients and mix well. Chill until mixture is about as thick as fresh egg whites. Place in a pan of ice water and beat with a rotary beater until fluffy. Stir in fruits and almonds. Fold in whipped cream. Turn into an oiled 2-quart mold. Chill until firm and ready to serve. Unmold onto a serving plate. Serve with additional whipped cream, garnished with grated nutmeg and red and green glacé fruits, if desired.

YIELD: About 12 servings

CINNAMON CREAM
2 cinnamon sticks, each 2 inches long
1⅓ cups light cream
1 cup sugar

1 envelope unflavored gelatine
⅓ cup milk
1 cup sour cream
1 teaspoon vanilla extract
Fresh, frozen, *or* canned fruit

Heat together for 10 minutes the first 3 ingredients. Soften gelatine in milk and stir into hot cream. Cool and chill until mixture begins to thicken. Remove cinnamon. Beat sour cream until of smooth, fluffy consistency. Fold into the mixture along with vanilla extract. Turn into 6 oiled individual molds or into an oiled 1-quart mold. Chill until firm and ready to serve. Unmold and serve with fruit.

YIELD: 6 servings

FRUITY GINGER CREAM
1 envelope unflavored gelatine
¼ cup water

6 tablespoons sugar
1/16 teaspoon salt
1 teaspoon ground ginger

2 large eggs, separated
1 cup milk
¾ cup glacé fruit
¾ cup heavy cream
¾ teaspoon grated lemon rind
1 tablespoon sugar
6 glacé cherries

Soften gelatine in water. Combine the next 3 ingredients with egg yolks and milk in the top of a double boiler. Mix well. Stir and cook over hot water (NOT BOIL-ING) until custard coats a metal spoon. Blend in gelatine. Chill until mixture begins to thicken.

Stir in fruit. Beat ½ cup of the cream with rotary egg beater until stiff and fold it in along with lemon rind. Beat egg whites until they stand in soft, stiff peaks, into which beat remaining 1 tablespoon sugar. Carefully fold into the gelatine mixture. Turn into an oiled 1-quart mold or into 6 individual gelatine molds. Chill until firm and ready to serve.

Unmold onto serving plate. Decorate as desired with glacé cherries and remaining ¼ cup cream whipped and sweetened to taste with sugar.

YIELD: 6 servings

MOLDED COCONUT PUDDING

2 envelopes unflavored gelatine
½ cup milk
1 cup sugar
¾ teaspoon ground nutmeg
¼ teaspoon salt
2 cups milk
1 teaspoon vanilla extract
1 cup heavy cream, whipped
1 cup flaked coconut
Caramel Sauce*

Soften gelatine in ½ cup milk and set aside. Combine sugar, nutmeg, and salt in a saucepan. Stir in milk and heat *only* to boiling point. Add gelatine and vanilla extract. Chill in a pan of ice water until the mixture begins to thicken. Fold in whipped cream and coconut. Turn into a lightly oiled 5-cup mold. Chill until firm and ready to serve. Unmold onto a serving plate just before serving. Serve with Caramel Sauce.

YIELD: 6 to 8 servings

FRESH FRUIT ANGEL MOLD

1 pint heavy cream
¼ cup confectioners' sugar
½ teaspoon ground nutmeg

2½ cups sliced, peeled oranges
2½ cups sliced bananas
8- *or* 9-inch baked angel-food cake

Whip cream stiff. Fold in sugar and nutmeg. Mix oranges with bananas. Tear cake into chunks. In an 8-inch springform pan, place alternate layers of cake, whipped cream, and fruit, having whipped cream between each layer of cake and fruit and over the top.

Chill overnight or several hours. Just before serving, remove rim from springform pan and place cake on a serving plate. Cut into wedges and serve.

YIELD: 8 to 10 servings

PINEAPPLE REFRIGERATOR CAKE

24 lady fingers
2 cans (1 pound, 4½ ounces each) crushed pineapple, drained
½ teaspoon ground nutmeg
½ teaspoon ground ginger
2 cups heavy cream
¼ cup confectioners' sugar
1 teaspoon vanilla extract
Ground nutmeg

Line bottom and sides of an 8-inch spring-form pan with lady fingers, reserving the rest for later use. Combine pineapple and spices. Whip cream until stiff and add confectioners' sugar and vanilla extract.

Spread ½ of the crushed pineapple mixture over the bottom of lady finger-lined pan. Top with half the whipped cream. Add another layer of each: lady fingers, pineapple mixture, and whipped cream. Refrigerate overnight or several hours. Just before serving, remove sides from the spring form, place on a serving plate, and garnish with a sprinkling of ground nutmeg.

YIELD: 10 servings

REFRIGERATOR PLUM BREAD PUDDING

3 cups (1½ pounds) sliced fresh
   Italian plums
1 cup sugar
¼ teaspoon ground cinnamon
1 tablespoon fresh lemon juice

2 teaspoons cornstarch
1 tablespoon cold water
¼ teaspoon vanilla extract
6 slices bread
Butter *or* margarine
Ground cinnamon
Heavy cream, whipped (optional)

Place first 4 ingredients in a saucepan. Cover and cook 10 minutes. Mix cornstarch with water and add. Cook 1 minute or until thickened. Remove from heat and cool slightly. Stir in vanilla extract. Butter bread and sprinkle with cinnamon. Arrange bread and plums in alternate layers in a 9 x 5 x 3-inch loaf pan. Chill several hours or overnight. Spoon into individual serving dishes. Top with whipped cream, if desired.

YIELD: 6 to 8 servings

BANANA CREAM

¼ cup sugar
2 cups (about 8 medium)
   mashed bananas
⅓ cup orange juice
2 tablespoons lemon juice
⅛ teaspoon salt
1 teaspoon ground ginger
2 tablespoons dark rum

1 cup heavy cream, whipped

Mix together all ingredients except cream. Fold in cream. Pour into an ice-cube tray and freeze until mushy. Turn into a mixing bowl and beat with the electric beater until fluffy. Return to ice-cube tray and freeze until firm and ready to serve. If the cream seems to be a bit hard, let stand at room temperature 15 to 20 minutes to soften enough to serve.

YIELD: 6 to 8 servings

CHARLOTTE PLOMBIERE

¾ cup sugar
⅛ teaspoon salt
4 large egg yolks, beaten

1½ cups scalded top milk
1½ teaspoons ground ginger

1½ cups heavy cream
1½ teaspoons vanilla extract
1½ teaspoons lemon extract

Lady fingers
Heavy cream, whipped (optional)

Combine first 3 ingredients. Gradually stir in milk. Cook over hot water until of custard consistency, stirring constantly. Cool. Stir in ginger. Turn into freezing tray and freeze until partially frozen (about 45 minutes). Place in chilled bowl, beat quickly with rotary beater until smooth. Fold in next 3 ingredients.

Return to freezing tray and freeze until

stiff enough to spread, stirring 2 or 3 times. Spoon into 8-inch spring-form pan lined on the bottom and sides with lady fingers. If desired, garnish top with whipped cream put through pastry tube. Place in freezer and freeze firm. When ready to serve, remove from spring-form pan and place on a serving plate. To serve, cut in wedges.

YIELD: 8 servings

GINGER ICE CREAM
2¼ teaspoons ground ginger
¼ teaspoon salt
1¼ cups sugar

2 cups milk
2 cups heavy cream
3 teaspoons vanilla extract

Combine the first 3 ingredients. Add milk and stir until sugar is dissolved. Stir in cream and vanilla extract. Turn into 2 ice-cube trays or into an 8 x 8 x 2-inch baking dish.

Freeze until almost firm. Remove from freezer and turn into the large bowl of the electric mixer. Beat until the mixture is fluffy, starting at low speed and increasing the speed to highest as the mixture softens. (Do not beat enough to melt mixture.) Return to ice-cube trays or baking dish and freeze until firm and ready to serve, stirring once before the mixture completely freezes.

YIELD: 10 to 12 servings

MEXICAN PARFAIT
1 square (1 ounce) unsweetened
    chocolate
½ teaspoon ground cinnamon
⅔ cup sugar
¾ cup water
3 large egg whites, beaten
1½ teaspoons vanilla extract
2 cups heavy cream, whipped

Grate chocolate, blend with cinnamon, and set aside. Heat sugar and water to boiling point and cook without stirring 5 minutes. Gradually beat syrup into beaten egg whites and continue beating until mixture cools. Fold in chocolate and cinnamon mixture, vanilla extract, and whipped cream. Turn into 2 ice-cube trays. Freeze until firm and ready to serve.

YIELD: 8 servings

FROZEN CHRISTMAS PUDDING

This elegant dessert can be made days ahead of time and stored in the freezer. Serve this after a comparatively light main course.

1 quart vanilla ice cream
¼ teaspoon ground ginger
¼ teaspoon ground mace
¼ teaspoon ground cardamom seed
1 cup heavy cream
1 cup glacé mixed fruit
1 tablespoon sugar
½ cup heavy cream
Green *or* red food coloring (optional)

Let ice cream stand at room temperature only long enough to soften. Add spices to the 1 cup cream and beat until stiff. Fold into the ice cream along with glacé fruit. Turn into a 1½-quart plum-pudding or gelatine mold or into individual gelatine molds.

Freeze firm. The morning or day before serving, dip mold quickly (flash dip) into boiling water. Turn out onto serving plate. Return to freezer for surface to harden. Add sugar to remaining cream, whip until stiff, and add a few drops food coloring if desired. Spread over top and sides.

Return to freezer until ready to serve. Garnish with holly leaves and red or green birthday candles. Bring to table with candles lighted.

YIELD: 10 servings

FROZEN PLUM PUDDING

1 quart vanilla ice cream

2 cups heavy cream, whipped
¾ teaspoon ground cardamom seed
½ cup chopped glacé cherries
½ cup chopped citron
¼ cup sweet sherry
¼ cup chopped, blanched almonds
¼ cup macaroon crumbs

¼ cup heavy cream, whipped
1 tablespoon sugar
1 drop red *or* green food coloring
Glacé cherries, citron, *or* candied orange peel (optional)

Soften ice cream until it can be easily stirred. Fold in the next 7 ingredients. Turn into a 2-quart mold. Cover. Freeze overnight or at least 12 hours. The same day pudding is to be served, unmold it onto the serving plate. (To unmold, flash dip mold in hot water. Invert onto a chilled serving plate and lift off mold.)
Return to freezer for surface to harden.

Then, sweeten cream with sugar and color as desired with food coloring. Spread over top and sides of mold. Return to freezer until ready to serve. Decorate with glacé cherries, citron, or candied orange peel, if desired.

YIELD: 12 to 15 servings

SPICED LEMON CREAM
(WITH CHOCOLATE SAUCE)
1 package lemon gelatine
2 cups hot water

⅔ cup sugar
¼ cup lemon juice
½ teaspoon grated lemon rind
⅛ teaspoon salt
¼ teaspoon ground mace

½ cup heavy cream, whipped

¼ cup graham cracker crumbs
¼ teaspoon ground cinnamon
⅛ teaspoon ground cloves

Spiced Chocolate Sauce*

Dissolve gelatine in hot water. Add next 5 ingredients. Chill until the mixture begins to thicken. Beat until fluffy with a rotary beater. Fold in whipped cream. Combine the next 3 ingredients and sprinkle half over bottom and sides of 8 lightly buttered 5-ounce gelatine molds. Fill with the mixture. Cover with remaining crumbs. Place in freezer. Just before serving, unmold onto serving plates and top with Spiced Chocolate Sauce.

YIELD: 8 servings

MINT PARFAIT
¼ cup mint flakes
¾ cup boiling water
1 cup sugar
¼ teaspoon salt
3 large egg whites, stiffly beaten

¼ teaspoon green food coloring
2 cups heavy cream, whipped
½ teaspoon vanilla extract
Spiced Chocolate Sauce* (optional)

Combine mint flakes and ¼ cup of the boiling water, cover, and steep while cooking sugar syrup. Blend sugar with the remaining ½ cup boiling water in a small saucepan. Add salt. Bring to boiling point and boil rapidly 5 minutes or until a soft ball forms when a little of the syrup is dropped in very cold water.

Strain mint water through a fine sieve and add to the cooked syrup. Bring to boiling point and pour in a fine stream over the beaten egg whites. Beat until mixture is thick and cool. Fold in coloring, whipped cream, and vanilla extract. Turn into 2 ice-cube trays or a 9 x 9 x 2-inch pan. Freeze, without stirring, until firm and ready to serve. Serve plain or top with Spiced Chocolate Sauce.

YIELD: 9 or 10 servings

VANILLA CREAM PUFFS

1 cup water
½ cup (1 stick) butter *or* margarine
⅛ teaspoon salt
1 cup sifted all-purpose flour
4 large eggs
Rich Vanilla Cream Puff Filling
  (see below)

Heat first 3 ingredients to boiling point. Stir in flour, all at once. Cook over low heat until mixture leaves the pan and forms a ball (1 to 2 minutes), stirring constantly. Remove from heat and cool slightly (about 5 minutes). Beat in eggs, one at a time. Beat until dough is smooth and velvety and holds its shape when spoon is raised. (If the mixture spreads when a spoonful is dropped on a pan, cook it over hot water, *just long enough*

to stiffen the mixture).

Drop from a tablespoon onto ungreased cooky sheets. Bake in a preheated hot oven (400° F.) 20 to 25 minutes or until brown and dry. Allow to cool slowly. Cut off tops with a sharp knife. Scoop out any filament of soft dough. Fill with Rich Vanilla Cream Puff Filling. Replace tops. Dust with confectioners' sugar or serve with your favorite dessert sauce.

YIELD: 12 puffs

SPICED CHOCOLATE ECLAIRS

Spread dough on lightly greased cooky sheets in 5 x 1½-inch strips 1 inch high and 2 inches apart to allow room for spreading. Bake in a preheated hot oven (400° F.) 30 minutes. Cool on wire racks. Cut off tops and fill with Rich Vanilla Cream Puff Filling *(see below)*. Replace tops of eclairs. Ice with Spiced Chocolate Frosting.*

YIELD: 8 eclairs

RICH VANILLA CREAM PUFF FILLING

½ cup sugar
⅛ teaspoon salt
½ teaspoon ground nutmeg
⅓ cup flour
2 cups milk
2 large eggs, beaten
1 teaspoon vanilla extract

Combine first 4 ingredients in a saucepan. Gradually stir in milk. Cook over low heat, stirring constantly until thickened. Remove from heat. Stir a little of this mixture into 2 beaten eggs. Then, blend into the hot mixture in the saucepan. Cook over low heat until very thick (1 to 2 minutes), stirring constantly. Cool. Blend in vanilla extract.

MERINGUES

A meringue is a baked foam made from egg white, sugar, and air, plus salt and flavoring. There are two types: soft and hard. Soft meringue, usually made with 2 tablespoons sugar per egg white, is used as a topping for pies and puddings. Hard meringue (glacé), containing about 4 to 5 tablespoons sugar per egg white, is used as a shell for holding ice cream, fruit, custard, or other sweet filling.

The essential points in making a good meringue are as follows:

1. Use finely granulated sugar. (Confectioners' sugar is unsatisfactory because it contains starch.)

2. The egg whites should be at room temperature. Remove from refrigerator at least an hour before using.

3. Add salt (and cream of tartar, if used) to egg whites and beat until stiff but not dry. The foam should stand in well-defined peaks with their tip ends rounding only slightly when the beater is slowly withdrawn. The beating incorporates air and coagulates the protein of the egg white, making it strong enough to retain the air bubbles during and after baking. If underbeaten, the meringue will "weep" (uncoagulated egg white will run out). If overbeaten, the protein will become so brittle that it will break, releasing the air and sugar, producing a flat meringue with "beads" of separated sugar solution. Beating with a fine wire whip produces a meringue with the greatest volume. However, a hand or electric rotary beater may be used. The latter is very useful for making a hard meringue, which may require a total beating time of about 30 to 40 minutes—but can easily overbeat a soft meringue if not closely watched.

4. When the egg whites have been beaten, add the sugar ½ to 1 tablespoon at a time, beating after each addition until the sugar is well blended. Merely folding in the sugar is not sufficient. The sweetened foam should stand in rather stiff peaks (very stiff peaks for hard meringue). Some authorities like to add all the sugar to the egg whites before any beating is done. Meringue produced by this method has a finer texture and holds up longer, but has a smaller volume and requires a longer beating time.

5. Liquid ingredients, such as vanilla extract, lemon juice, and vinegar, if used, are added after the sugar and beaten in well. If spices are used, they should be mixed with the sugar. Ginger, nutmeg, and mace are suitable for use over cream-type fruit or custard pie fillings.

6. When making hard meringues, it is recommended that an acid stabilizer, such as cream of tartar, lemon juice, or vinegar, be added to

strengthen the egg-white foam so that it will stand up during the long baking. A stabilizer also is useful when making soft meringue from whites of grades B or C eggs, which produce a weaker foam than do fresh ones, but the stabilizer is unnecessary when making a soft meringue from fresh eggs.

7. To prevent a soft meringue from shrinking away from the edge of the pie crust or pudding dish, it first is spooned in a ring against the inner edge of crust or dish. Then the remainder is placed in the middle and spread evenly. Finally, the surface may be decorated by pulling up points with the back of a spoon or by adding the last portion from a pastry tube.

8. Bake the meringue in a preheated oven. Hard meringues must be baked in a very slow oven (225° to 275° F.) for at least an hour. The process resembles drying more than it does baking. Excellent results have been obtained by preheating a well-insulated oven, inserting the meringue, turning off the heat, and allowing to stand overnight.

9. Soft meringues should be baked at a somewhat higher temperature for a shorter time, the higher the temperature the shorter the time. The authors have obtained best results by placing the meringue over a cold filling and baking at 325° F. for 15 minutes. A meringue baked over a cold filling tends to weep, but the weeping is kept to a minimum by baking at a low temperature (325° F.). One baked over a warm filling tends to bead. The beading is held to a minimum by baking at a higher temperature (400° F. for 8 to 10 minutes). However, some authorities recommend that all soft meringues be baked at 400° to 425° F.

10. Hard meringues should be covered and stored in a dry place, since their high content of sugar gives them a tendency to absorb moisture. The stabilizer converts some of the sugar to invert sugar, which is even more absorbent than ordinary sugar.

SOFT MERINGUE

Ingredient	8-inch pie	9-inch pie
Salt	⅛ teaspoon	¼ teaspoon
Large egg whites	2	3
Sugar	4 tablespoons	6 tablespoons
Vanilla extract	¼ teaspoon	½ teaspoon

Add salt to egg whites. Beat until soft peaks form when the beater is raised. Beat in sugar, 1 tablespoon at a time. Continue beating until stiff peaks form when the beater is raised. Beat in vanilla extract. Spoon meringue over cold filling, sealing the inside edge of crust.

Bake in a preheated slow oven (325° F.) 15 minutes. If meringue is spread over a warm filling, bake in a preheated hot oven (400° F.) 10 minutes. Cool on wire rack away from draft.

LEMON MERINGUE

For an 8-inch pie, add 1 tablespoon fresh lemon juice along with vanilla extract in the above meringue recipe. For a 9-inch pie, increase the lemon juice to 1½ tablespoons. Spread over filling and bake as in above directions.

LIME MERINGUE

Replace lemon juice with fresh lime juice in the above recipe.

SPICED MERINGUE

In the above recipe for a 9-inch pie, blend ¼ teaspoon ground ginger, mace, or nutmeg with the sugar. Spread over pies with cream-fruit fillings (as banana cream pie) or custard fillings. Bake according to above directions.

HARD MERINGUE DESSERT SHELLS (GLACE)

Ingredient	6 shells	12 shells
Salt	⅛ teaspoon	¼ teaspoon
Cream of tartar	⅛ teaspoon	¼ teaspoon
Large egg whites	2	4
Sugar	½ cup	1 cup
Vanilla extract	¼ teaspoon	½ teaspoon

Add salt and cream of tartar to egg whites. Beat with an electric beater at high speed, until whites are stiff enough to hold their shape. Beat in sugar, 2 tablespoons at a time, at low speed. Egg whites should stand in very stiff peaks and should be shiny and moist. This is important for successful meringue. Beat in vanilla extract.

Mark 3-inch circles on brown paper. Butter the paper lightly and dust with cornstarch. Spread each with a layer of meringue mixture ¼ inch thick. Build a border with more meringue to a height of 1½ inches, leaving the center unfilled. Place paper on a cooky sheet. Bake in a preheated very slow oven (250° F.) 1¼ hours. Turn off heat and cool in oven ½ hour. Remove from oven. When cold, transfer to a tin box. Cover tightly.

9-INCH MERINGUE SHELL

Make the meringue recipe for 6 meringue shells. Using a round 9-inch layer-cake pan as a guide, mark a 9-inch circle on brown paper. Butter lightly and dust with cornstarch. Spread the circle with a layer of meringue mixture ¼ inch thick. Build a border with remaining meringue to a height of 1½ inches. Place paper on a cooky sheet. Bake in a very slow oven (250° F.) 2 hours. Cool in oven ½ hour. Remove from paper. Fill with cream filling or fruit.

SPICED LEMON CREAM MERINGUES

4 large egg yolks
½ cup sugar
½ teaspoon ground mace
⅟₁₆ teaspoon salt

¼ cup fresh lemon juice
½ teaspoon grated lemon rind
½ cup heavy cream, whipped
½ teaspoon vanilla extract

6 Hard Meringue Dessert Shells*
Combine the first 4 ingredients in the top of a double boiler. Mix well. Stir in lemon juice. Cook over hot (NOT BOILING) water, 10 minutes or until thick and smooth, stirring frequently. Remove from heat and cool. Fold in remaining ingredients. Pile the mixture in baked Meringue Dessert Shells.

YIELD: 6 servings

EGG DISHES

RALPH WALDO EMERSON wrote: "There is always a best way of doing everything, if it be to boil an egg. . . ." So far as we know, he never got around to writing an essay on egg cookery. Had he done so, he might have pointed out some of the following rules.

As one of the most delicate protein foods, eggs should be cooked at low to moderately-low temperatures; high heat toughens eggs. Keep the heat low, too, when making soft custards and sauces in which egg is used as a thickener.

When combining hot mixtures and eggs in custards, cream fillings, soufflés, etc., pour the hot mixture slowly into the beaten egg, stirring or beating constantly. Adding a bit of egg mixture to a mass of hot food cooks the egg before it can be stirred smoothly through the hot mixture.

Eggs can be separated most easily into yolks and whites when they are cold. The whites whip lighter and to larger bulk if allowed to come to room temperature before they are beaten. It is safer to separate one egg at a time, using a custard cup for the white. Even a small speck of yolk in the white prevents whipping. When beating eggs, such as in making sponge cake, where both whites and yolks must be beaten, beat the whites first, then the yolks. This saves washing the beater.

Egg sizes are graded from jumbo, extra large, large, medium, and small to peewee. Recipes in this book were tested with large eggs weighing about 2 ounces each, or 8 eggs to the pound.

Whenever cupfuls of whole eggs, yolks, or whites are specified, allow 4 to 5 whole eggs per cup; 14 to 17 yolks, and 7 to 8 whites, respectively.

THE
SPICE
WAREHOUSES

SOFT-COOKED EGG

Place egg (or eggs) in a saucepan with sufficient cold water to cover the egg to a depth of about 1 inch. Cover and bring water just to boiling point. Remove from heat and let stand 2 to 4 minutes, depending on the degree of doneness desired. Cool under running cold water to prevent further cooking.

HARD-COOKED EGG

Follow directions for cooking soft-cooked egg except let the egg stand in the hot water 20 minutes. Cool immediately in cold water to reduce the formation of a dark ring around the yolk where the white meets the yolk.

SPANISH FRIED EGGS WITH BREAD CUBES

¼ cup olive *or* salad oil
⅛ teaspoon garlic powder
6 slices stale bread, cut into ¼-inch cubes
6 large eggs
Salt (to taste)
Ground black pepper (to taste)
Paprika

Heat oil with garlic powder in a 9-inch skillet. Sauté bread cubes in hot oil until golden brown. Break eggs over this. Lower heat, cover, and cook slowly until eggs have set, but are not hard-cooked. Sprinkle with salt and pepper. Garnish with paprika. Remove eggs carefully from pan, having a layer of bread cubes attached under each serving.

YIELD: 6 servings

CHEESE-BAKED EGGS

¼ pound sharp Cheddar cheese
4 large eggs

6 tablespoons light cream
1 teaspoon powdered mustard
Dash cayenne
½ teaspoon salt

2 tablespoons butter *or* margarine

Shred cheese on a coarse shredder and sprinkle over the bottom of a buttered glass, 9-inch pie plate. Break 4 eggs over cheese, being careful not to break the yolks. Combine next 4 ingredients and pour over the eggs. Dot with butter or margarine. Bake in a preheated moderate oven (350° F.) 15 to 20 minutes or until eggs are set and cheese has melted.

YIELD: 4 servings

SWISS EGGS

1½ cups coarsely shredded Cheddar cheese
6 large eggs

½ cup light cream
1½ teaspoons powdered mustard
¾ teaspoon salt
Dash cayenne

3 tablespoons butter *or* margarine
Bacon *or* ham

2 pounds fresh Asparagus, Cooked*
2 cups (3 ounces) chow mein noodles
12 strips crisp bacon

Melt butter or margarine in a saucepan. Blend in flour. Remove from heat and stir in milk or milk and chicken stock. Stir and cook until of medium thickness. Add next 5 ingredients. Mix lightly. Place asparagus on chow mein noodles. Spoon creamed eggs over asparagus and noodles. Top each serving with 2 strips crisp bacon. Serve as a luncheon or supper dish.

YIELD: 6 servings

EGGS, SPRING STYLE

6 large hard-cooked eggs
2 tablespoons butter *or* margarine
1½ tablespoons flour
⅔ cup milk

¾ teaspoon salt
½ teaspoon ground black pepper
¼ teaspoon ground nutmeg

½ pound fresh spinach
2 tablespoons grated Romano cheese
1 cup flour
2 large eggs, lightly beaten
1 cup fine, dry bread crumbs
Olive oil

Sprinkle cheese over the bottom of a well-buttered 11¼ x 7½ x 1½-inch baking pan. Break eggs over cheese, being careful not to break yolks. Combine next 4 ingredients and pour over eggs. Dot with butter or margarine.

Bake in a preheated moderate oven (350° F.) 15 minutes or until eggs are set and cheese has melted. Serve hot with bacon or ham for breakfast or lunch.

YIELD: 6 servings

CREAMED EGGS WITH ASPARAGUS ON CHOW MEIN NOODLES

¼ cup (½ stick) butter *or* margarine
¼ cup flour
2 cups milk *or* 1 cup milk and
   1 cup chicken stock

6 large hard-cooked eggs
1 tablespoon instant minced onion
1 teaspoon salt
½ teaspoon ground marjoram
⅛ teaspoon ground black pepper

*An asterisk after the name of a dish indicates that the recipe for this dish appears in the book. Consult the Index for the page number.

Peel eggs, cut in half lengthwise, remove and mince yolks. Set aside. Melt butter or margarine in a saucepan. Blend in flour. Add milk. Stir and cook until thickened. Add next 3 ingredients and egg yolks. Wash spinach and cook only in water that clings to the leaves. Drain well and chop fine. Add to sauce along with the cheese. Cool. Spoon into egg whites. Roll in flour, then in beaten egg, then in crumbs and pan-fry in hot oil until golden. Serve hot.

YIELD: 6 servings

SCRAMBLED EGGS ON ANCHOVY TOAST

6 large eggs, lightly beaten
1 teaspoon salt
¼ teaspoon ground black pepper
1½ teaspoons chili powder

4 teaspoons butter or margarine

¼ cup (½ stick) butter or margarine
6 anchovies, minced
Dash garlic powder

6 slices toast
⅔ cup grated, sharp Cheddar cheese

Combine first 4 ingredients in a bowl. Melt the 4 teaspoons butter or margarine in a frying pan. Add eggs. Stir and cook over low heat until done, stirring constantly. Combine the next 3 ingredients and spread over the toast. Top with scrambled eggs. Sprinkle with grated cheese. Serve hot.

YIELD: 6 servings

HERBED SCRAMBLED EGGS AND TUNA FISH

1 can (7 ounces) tuna fish, flaked
4 large eggs
1 tablespoon fresh lemon juice

¾ teaspoon salt
⅛ teaspoon ground black pepper
½ teaspoon poultry seasoning
½ teaspoon parsley flakes

Drain oil from tuna fish into 8-inch skillet. Remove tuna fish from can, flake, and set aside to use later. Heat the oil in the pan. Add unbeaten eggs and tuna fish. Stir and when they begin to set, stir in remaining ingredients. Cook until eggs are set. Serve hot with grits, home-fried potatoes, and a vegetable for lunch or supper, or with a vegetable salad and toast.

YIELD: 2 or 3 servings

INDIAN EGG CURRY
(UNDAH KA SALUN)

¼ cup onion flakes
¼ teaspoon instant minced garlic
3 tablespoons water

2 tablespoons vegetable oil or butter or margarine
2 teaspoons ground coriander
½ teaspoon ground cumin
½ teaspoon ground ginger
1 teaspoon ground turmeric
¼ teaspoon ground red pepper

1 cup chicken stock, milk, or coconut milk
6 large hard-cooked eggs
1 teaspoon salt
1 cup cooked green peas
1 teaspoon lemon juice
3 cups cooked rice

Combine first 3 ingredients and let stand 5 minutes or until all water has been absorbed. Fry in vegetable oil or butter or margarine until onions begin to brown. Add spices. Stir and cook 2 minutes. Blend in stock, coconut milk, or milk.

Cook slowly 10 minutes, stirring occasionally. Peel eggs, cut them in half lengthwise and add to the sauce along with peas. Cook only until eggs and peas are hot. Stir in lemon juice just before serving. Serve on rice.

YIELD: 6 servings

CURRIED EGGS, JAMAICAN STYLE

½ cup sliced scallions
1 tablespoon curry powder
2 tablespoons coconut oil, butter, *or* margarine
¼ cup flour
1 cup chicken stock
1 cup coconut milk *or* chicken stock
½ teaspoon salt
¼ teaspoon ground black pepper
¼ teaspoon ground ginger
⅛ teaspoon garlic powder
3 cups cooked rice
12 large hard-cooked eggs

Sauté scallions and curry powder in coconut oil, butter, or margarine. Blend in flour. Stir in 1 cup stock. Cook until mixture begins to thicken, stirring all the time. Add coconut milk or chicken stock and cook until of medium thickness. Add seasonings. Turn rice onto a serving platter. Peel eggs, leave whole and ar-

range over rice. Pour curry sauce over all.

YIELD: 6 servings

MADRAS EGG CURRY

1 tablespoon instant minced onion
½ teaspoon instant minced garlic
1 tablespoon water
1 tablespoon shortening *or* cooking oil
2 teaspoons curry powder
1 tablespoon tomato paste
¾ cup water
1 teaspoon salt
1 teaspoon fresh lemon juice
6 large hard-cooked eggs

Soften instant minced onion and garlic in the 1 tablespoon water. Sauté in shortening or oil along with curry powder 3 to 4 minutes. Add tomato paste and water. Cook 3 or 4 minutes. Add salt and lemon juice. Stir and cook until the gravy is of medium thickness, about 1 minute. Peel hard-cooked eggs; cut in half lengthwise and add. Heat. Serve with rice.

YIELD: 6 servings

NARGISI EGG KEBABS

6 large hard-cooked eggs
2 cups ground cooked beef *or* lamb
1¼ teaspoons salt
¼ teaspoon ground ginger
¼ teaspoon ground cumin
¼ teaspoon ground cinnamon
¼ teaspoon ground turmeric
½ teaspoon ground coriander
1/16 teaspoon ground cloves
1/16 teaspoon ground red pepper
2 large eggs, uncooked
1 tablespoon milk
Fine, dry bread crumbs
Vegetable shortening *or* cooking oil
Fresh lime *or* lemon juice

Peel hard-cooked eggs and set aside. Put meat through the food chopper, using the finest blade, grinding it almost to paste consistency. Combine with salt, spices, and one of the uncooked eggs. Using fingers, coat meat mixture around each hard-cooked egg. Beat the remaining uncooked egg and mix with milk, into which dip the egg-meat balls and then dip in bread crumbs.

Fry in shallow hot shortening or oil until browned on all sides. Sprinkle with lime or lemon juice. Serve hot or cold whole, or cut in half lengthwise.

YIELD: 6 servings

EGGS IN SPICED ASPIC

2 cans (10½ ounces each)
  beef consommé

¼ teaspoon instant minced onion
¼ teaspoon rosemary leaves
⅛ teaspoon salt
⅛ teaspoon garlic powder
Dash cayenne
¾ teaspoon whole black peppers
1 teaspoon parsley flakes

4 large eggs, cooked 2 minutes
Watercress
Pimiento

Combine consommé with next 7 ingredients. Simmer slowly 15 minutes. Strain to remove whole spices. Cool and chill until consommé begins to jell. Spoon 2 tablespoons of consommé into each of four 6-ounce custard cups. Cook 4 eggs 2 minutes, below boiling point, in a covered saucepan. (Do not cook eggs longer since they are very soft-cooked.) Peel and put one in each cup. Finish filling cup with consommé and chill until firm. Just before serving, unmold onto a serving plate. Garnish with watercress and pimiento strips.

YIELD: 4 servings

HOT EGG SALAD

2 tablespoons butter *or* margarine

2 tablespoons flour
1 tablespoon salt
⅛ teaspoon ground black pepper
1¼ teaspoons marjoram leaves
1 cup milk
1 tablespoon instant minced onion

5 cups diced, cooked potatoes

9 large hard-cooked eggs, 8 diced,
  1 sliced
1¼ cups diced celery
¼ cup diced green pepper
¼ cup chopped green olives
¼ cup mayonnaise

Salad greens

Melt butter or margarine. Blend in next 6 ingredients. Stir and cook until the mixture is of medium thickness. Add pota-

toes and cook only until hot. Add next 5 ingredients. Mix lightly. Serve on salad greens. Garnish each with a slice of hard-cooked egg.

YIELD: 8 servings

CAJUN-STUFFED EGGS

12 hard-cooked pullet eggs
1 can (3 ounces) broiled mushrooms
2 tablespoons mayonnaise
1 teaspoon powdered mustard
1½ teaspoons chili powder
½ teaspoon celery salt
½ teaspoon garlic salt
¼ teaspoon ground black pepper
½ teaspoon salt
Dash cayenne
Paprika
Parsley

Peel eggs, cut into lengthwise halves. Remove egg yolks and place in a bowl. Reserve egg whites for future use. Chop mushrooms finely with chopping knife. Add to egg yolks. Mash and mix well. Blend in mayonnaise and all seasonings except paprika and parsley. Stuff the mixture into cavities of hard-cooked egg whites. Garnish with paprika and parsley sprigs.

YIELD: 24 stuffed egg halves

DEVILED EGGS

6 large hard-cooked eggs
¼ teaspoon salt
⅛ teaspoon ground black pepper
1 teaspoon Dijon-type prepared mustard
½ teaspoon instant minced onion
⅛ teaspoon garlic powder
Dash cayenne
1 teaspoon cider vinegar
¼ cup minced celery
3 tablespoons mayonnaise
½ teaspoon fresh lemon juice
_____
Paprika

Peel eggs, cut in half, and remove yolks. Mash yolks. Add all remaining ingredients except paprika. Mix well. Pile into the cavities of egg whites. Garnish with paprika.

YIELD: 6 servings

FISH and SHELLFISH

YOU can almost surely count on finding a bargain at your fish market, where prices fluctuate according to season, local supply, and the preference of buyers. Do not hesitate to ask your fish dealer which is the best fish or seafood buy for the day.

Fresh 'fish may be whole, drawn, dressed, or in fillets or steaks. *Whole fish* are sold as caught. *Drawn fish* have only the viscera removed. *Dressed fish* have the viscera, head, tail, and usually the fins removed. *Fillets* are boneless slices of fish cut lengthwise away from the backbones. Steaks are crosswise slices, usually ¾ to 1 inch thick, still including bones.

Fish fillets cost more per pound than whole fish, but since there is little waste in either fillets or fish steaks, you will get more servings per pound. A whole fish weighing 1 pound makes only 2 servings after cleaning and dressing; but 1 pound of boneless fillets will make 3 or 4 servings.

How to cook fish depends largely on fat content. Choose a "fat" fish (such as salmon, shad, mackerel, lake trout, or whitefish) for baking and broiling. "Lean" fish (such as haddock, flounder, cod, sea bass, striped bass, rosefish, pike, perch, and carp) are preferred for cooking in water, since they are firmer after cooking. They may be baked or broiled, of course, if liberally basted with fat. Select fat or lean fish for frying.

TIMETABLE FOR COOKING FISH AND SHELLFISH

Fish or shellfish (market form)	Cooking method	Weight or thickness (approximate)	Temperature	Cooking Time (Approx. total) (in minutes)
Fish (fillets)	Baked		350° F.	25 to 35
	Broiled			10 to 15
	Simmered			10
	Deep-fat fried		375° F.	1 to 4
Fish (steaks)	Baked	½ to 1 inch	350° F.	25 to 35
	Broiled	"		10 to 15
	Simmered	"		10
	Deep-fat fried	"	375° F.	2 to 4
Fish (Pan-dressed)	Baked	½ to 1 pound	350° F.	25 to 30
	Broiled	"		10 to 15
	Simmered	"		10
	Deep-fat fried	"	375° F.	2 to 4
Fish (Whole)	Baked	3 to 4 pounds	350° F.	40 to 60
Clams (Live)	Baked		450° F.	15
	Broiled			5 to 8
(Shucked)	Deep-fat fried		375° F.	2 to 3
Crabs (Live)	Simmered			15
(Soft-shell)	Deep-fat fried	4-ounce	375° F.	3 to 4
Lobster (Live)	Baked	¾ to 1 pound	400° F.	15 to 20
		1 to 1½ "	400° F.	20 to 25
	Broiled	¾ to 1 "		10 to 12
		1 to 1½ "		12 to 15
	Simmered	¾ to 1 "		10 to 15
		1 to 1½ "		15 to 20
	Deep-fat fried	¾ to 1 "		3 to 4
		1 to 1½ "		4 to 5

TIMETABLE FOR COOKING FISH AND SHELLFISH (continued)

Fish or shellfish (market form)	Cooking method	Weight or thickness (approximate)	Temperature	Cooking Time (Approx. total) (in minutes)
Oysters (Live)	Baked		450° F.	15
	Broiled			5
(Shucked)	Baked		400° F.	10
	Broiled			5
	Deep-fat fried		375° F.	2
Scallops (Shucked)	Baked		350° F.	25 to 30
	Broiled			8 to 10
	Simmered			4 to 5
	Deep-fat fried		350° F.	3 to 4
Shrimp	Baked		350° F.	20 to 25
	Broiled			8 to 10
	Simmered			5
	Deep-fat fried		350° F.	2 to 3
Lobster (Tails)	Baked	4 to 8 ounces	450° F.	20 to 25
	Broiled	"		8 to 10
	Simmered	"		10
	Deep-fat fried	"	350° F.	3 to 4

There are five different species of canned salmon on the market. Chinook or King salmon is salmon-red or lighter in color and has a firm flesh. Red or Sockeye is firm-fleshed and deep orange in color. Silver salmon and pink salmon are lighter in color, while Chum salmon is a pale pink or white. The food value of these varieties is the same.

Shellfish, such as crabs, lobsters, clams, and oysters, should be alive if purchased in the shell, except hard-shell crabs and lobsters, which may be purchased already cooked in the shell.

Shucked shellfish are those which have been parted from their shells. Oysters, clams, and scallops are marketed in this way.

The edible portion of shellfish is often sold cooked, ready to eat. Shrimp, crab, and lobster meat are also marketed in this way.

Whatever variety of fish or seafood you cook, DO NOT OVERCOOK. Consult the timetable.

Many spices enhance fish dishes: all the culinary herbs, for instance, onion and garlic products; allspice; cloves; black, white, or red peppers; ginger; mace; mustard; saffron; sesame seeds; turmeric. There are spice blends, too, some of them especially created for seafood: seafood seasoning; shrimp spice or crab boil; mixed pickling spice; Italian seasoning; curry powder; chili powder; and barbecue spice.

The following recipe combines some spices into a tasty seasoning.

SAVORY FISH SEASONER

¼ cup (½ stick) butter *or* margarine
¼ teaspoon crumbled basil leaves
¼ teaspoon crumbled marjoram leaves
¼ teaspoon crumbled savory leaves
¼ teaspoon ground black pepper
2 tablespoons fresh lemon juice

Melt butter or margarine in a small saucepan. Add herbs and black pepper. Heat ½ minute. Stir in lemon juice. Brush over fish while broiling or baking.

YIELD: ¼ cup

BROILED FISH

2½ pounds fish steaks (halibut, sword, *or* salmon)

¼ cup (½ stick) butter *or* margarine, melted
½ teaspoon basil, marjoram, thyme, *or* poultry seasoning
¼ teaspoon ground black pepper
2¼ teaspoons salt
2 tablespoons lemon juice

Parsley
Lemon slices

If fish is frozen, let it thaw completely before broiling. Wash in cold water and pat dry with paper towels. Combine next 5 ingredients in a small saucepan, heat ½ minute and brush over both sides of fish.

Place fish on lightly oiled broiler racks. Place in a preheated broiler 4 inches from the source of heat. Broil 5 minutes. Baste both sides of fish and turn. Broil another 5 minutes or until fish is brown and flaky when tested with a fork. Serve garnished with parsley and lemon slices.

BROILED FISH, ITALIAN STYLE

Prepare fish steaks and broil as in above directions, but baste with the following sauce: ¼ cup olive oil, 1 teaspoon lemon juice, ½ teaspoon each, basil leaves and mint flakes, 1½ teaspoons salt, and ¼ teaspoon ground black pepper, heated together ½ minute in a small saucepan.

YIELD: 6 servings

MEDITERRANEAN BROILED FISH

2 pounds fillet of haddock, ½ inch
   thick

⅓ cup fresh lemon juice
1 teaspoon mint flakes
2 teaspoons oregano leaves
1¼ teaspoons salt
¼ teaspoon ground black pepper

2 tablespoons butter, margarine, *or*
   olive oil
Parsley *or* lemon slices

Wipe fish with a damp cloth. Place serving-size pieces on a broiler rack. Combine next 5 ingredients and brush over fish. Then brush with melted butter, margarine, or olive oil.

Place under preheated broiler, having oven control set to broil, 4 inches from the source of heat. Broil 5 minutes. Turn fish with 2 pancake turners or spatulas. Brush with seasoned lemon juice and butter, margarine, or oil. Broil 5 minutes or until brown. Brush again with seasoned lemon juice. Serve hot. Garnish with parsley or thin lemon slices.

YIELD: 6 servings

BAKED HADDOCK FILLETS
(WITH FRESH GRAPEFRUIT SECTIONS)
1½ pounds fillet of haddock
1 teaspoon salt
⅛ teaspoon ground black pepper
¾ cup soft bread crumbs
3 tablespoons butter *or* margarine,
   melted
¼ teaspoon thyme leaves
12 fresh grapefruit sections

Wipe fish with a damp cloth and sprinkle both sides with salt and ground black pepper. Place in a shallow, buttered baking dish. Mix bread crumbs with 2 table-

spoons of the melted butter or margarine and thyme. Sprinkle over fish. Top with grapefruit sections. Brush with remaining butter or margarine.

Bake in a preheated moderate oven (350° F.) 25 minutes or until fish is flaky. Place under broiler to brown, 3 to 4 minutes.

YIELD: 5 to 6 servings

SAVORY BAKED HADDOCK

1½ pounds fillet of haddock
Salt (to taste)
½ teaspoon powdered mustard
2 teaspoons water
½ cup mayonnaise

1 teaspoon instant minced onion
1 teaspoon fresh lemon juice
½ teaspoon thyme leaves
1⁄16 teaspoon ground black pepper

Paprika

Wipe fish with a damp cloth and arrange in a buttered baking dish. Sprinkle with salt. Soak mustard in water 10 minutes and add to mayonnaise along with next 4 ingredients. Spread on fish. Bake in a preheated moderate oven (350°, F.) 25 minutes or until top is brown and fish is flaky. Garnish with paprika.

YIELD: 6 servings

BAKED FILLET OF HADDOCK WITH SESAME SEED CRUMBS

"In the hands of an able cook fish can become an inexhaustible source of perpetual delight," wrote Brillat-Savarin. This is one of our favorite fish recipes.

1½ pounds fillet of haddock
Dash salt
6 pats butter *or* margarine

3 cups soft bread crumbs
1 teaspoon salt
¼ teaspoon ground black pepper
2 tablespoons Toasted Sesame Seed*
⅓ cup (⅔ stick) butter *or* margarine, melted

Cut fish into 6 pieces of equal size. Place in a buttered, shallow 9-inch square baking pan. Rub a dash of salt lightly over each serving and top with a pat of butter or margarine.

Combine remaining ingredients and sprinkle over fish, covering it completely. Bake in a preheated moderate oven (350° F.) 25 to 30 minutes or until crumbs are brown. Serve hot.

BAKED FILLET OF HADDOCK WITH HERBED BREAD CRUMBS
In the above recipe omit sesame seed and add ½ teaspoon ground thyme to the crumbs.

YIELD: 6 servings

BAKED FISH STEAKS WITH SOY SAUCE
2 pounds fish steaks (any kind)

1½ tablespoons soy sauce
⅛ teaspoon ground cinnamon
¼ teaspoon salt
½ teaspoon ground ginger
½ teaspoon grated lemon rind

2 tablespoons salad oil
Parsley

Wipe fish with a damp cloth and place in a buttered, shallow baking pan. Combine the next 5 ingredients and pour over fish. Heat oil and pour over fish. Bake in a preheated slow oven (325° F.) 25 minutes or until fish is flaky.

Turn oven control to broil. Place fish under broiler 5 minutes or until browned.

Serve with a little of the sauce spooned over each serving. Garnish with parsley.

YIELD: 6 servings

CURRIED STUFFED FISH
1 fish, 3 to 4 pounds (bass, blue, red snapper, *or* other fish suitable for stuffing)
1 teaspoon salt
⅛ teaspoon ground black pepper

2½ cups soft bread crumbs
1 tablespoon instant minced onion
1 teaspoon salt
1 teaspoon curry powder
¼ teaspoon garlic powder
⅛ teaspoon ground black pepper
2 tablespoons butter *or* margarine, melted
1 tablespoon hot water

Salad oil

Have fish scaled, cleaned, and ready to stuff. Mix the salt and pepper and rub into body cavity of fish. Combine next 8 ingredients and spoon into the cavity. Close opening with skewers or toothpicks. Make a gash 3 inches long and ¼ inch deep across the top of the fish to prevent top from cracking.

Brush fish with salad oil. Place in a buttered baking pan. Bake in a preheated slow oven (325° F.) 50 minutes or until fish is flaky when tested with a fork.

YIELD: 6 servings

HALIBUT STEAK WITH TOMATO-BREAD STUFFING

2 pounds halibut fish steaks, ¾ pound each
1 teaspoon salt
1¼ teaspoons ground black pepper

2 cups soft bread crumbs
1 tablespoon onion flakes
1 tablespoon parsley flakes
3 tablespoons butter *or* margarine, melted
½ cup canned tomatoes *or* ⅔ cup chopped fresh tomatoes
1 teaspoon poultry seasoning

1½ tablespoons butter *or* margarine
⅓ cup boiling water
Lemon-Mayonnaise Sauce*

Purchase fish steaks of equal weight and shape, which can be placed one on top of

the other. Place one steak in an oiled baking dish. Mix ½ teaspoon of the salt and ¼ teaspoon of the black pepper and sprinkle over fish slices. Combine the remaining salt and black pepper with the next 6 ingredients and spread over fish in sandwich fashion. Cover with the second steak.

Dot top with the 1½ tablespoons butter or margarine. Pour boiling water in pan around fish. Bake in a preheated moderate oven (350° F.) 35 minutes or until fish is flaky when tested with a fork. Garnish with lemon slices and paprika. Serve with Lemon-Mayonnaise Sauce.

YIELD: 6 servings

BAKED STUFFED MARINATED FISH

1 whole fish, 3 to 4 pounds (bass, red snapper, weak, *or* blue)

½ teaspoon salt
½ teaspoon whole thyme leaves
1 tablespoon whole, mixed pickling spices
1½ tablespoons lemon juice
1 tablespoon slivered lemon rind
1 can (10½ ounces) beef bouillon
¼ cup salad oil
¼ cup onion flakes

2 cups soft bread crumbs
1 tablespoon onion flakes
¼ teaspoon salt
⅛ teaspoon ground black pepper
¼ teaspoon thyme leaves
3 tablespoons butter *or* margarine, melted

2 medium carrots, peeled and thinly sliced
1 tablespoon instant minced onion

Have fish cleaned, scaled, and ready to stuff. Leave head, tail, and backbone attached, if desired. Combine next 8 ingredients, heat but DO NOT BOIL, and then cool. Place fish in a close-fitting dish. Cover with marinade. Cover tightly with aluminum foil and place in refrigerator to marinate a full 24 hours, turning several times.

Remove fish from marinade. With a paper towel, wipe off excess spices. Strain marinade and save liquid. Combine next 6 ingredients and spoon into cavity of fish. Close opening with skewer or toothpicks.

Place fish in a buttered, shallow baking pan. Add carrots and instant minced onion. Add marinade liquid. Bake, covered, in a preheated moderate oven (350° F.) about 1 hour or until fish is done, basting several times. Season to taste with additional salt and pepper.

YIELD: 4 to 6 servings

FISH PATTIES

1 pound frozen perch fillets
2 tablespoons butter *or* margarine

3 cups unseasoned mashed potatoes
1 large egg
1 tablespoon instant minced onion
1½ teaspoons poultry seasoning
¾ teaspoon salt (or to taste)
1/16 teaspoon ground black pepper
1/16 teaspoon garlic powder

Flour
Shortening

Defrost fish and sauté in butter or margarine until fillets are flaky, about 10 minutes. Flake fish and mix with next 7 ingredients. Cool. Shape into 12 patties, ½ inch thick. Roll in flour and fry in hot, shallow shortening until browned on both sides. Serve hot.

YIELD: 6 servings, two patties each

SALMON CHEESEBURGERS
(WITH TOMATO GRAVY)

1 can (1 pound) pink *or* red salmon
Milk

¾ cup fine, dry bread crumbs
1 large egg, beaten
1 teaspoon salt
¼ teaspoon ground black pepper
1 small bay leaf, finely crumbled
1 tablespoon instant minced onion

6 slices processed American cheese
Shortening
Tomato Gravy*

Drain the liquid from salmon into a measuring cup and add enough milk to make 1 cup. Flake salmon and mix with liquid and the next 6 ingredients. Mix well. Shape into 12 thin patties 3½ inches in diameter.

Cut cheese slices into 3-inch rounds and place 1 round between each 2 patties, sandwich fashion, being sure to press edges together. Brown on both sides in hot shortening in a heavy skillet. Serve with Tomato Gravy, or between toasted hamburger buns, omitting Tomato Gravy.

YIELD: 6 servings

TUNA FISH AND RICE BALLS

2 cups cooked rice
7-ounce can tuna fish, drained
2 large eggs, lightly beaten
¾ teaspoon salt
¼ teaspoon ground black pepper
¾ teaspoon ground thyme
2 teaspoons instant minced onion
2 tablespoons fine, dry bread crumbs
_____

1 large egg, beaten
1 tablespoon milk
Fine, dry bread crumbs
Shortening

Combine the first 8 ingredients. Mix well. Shape into 12 balls. Mix remaining beaten egg and milk, into which roll fish balls. Then roll in bread crumbs. Fry in deep fat preheated to 375° F. Drain on paper towels. Serve hot.

YIELD: 6 servings

TUNA LOAF
(WITH EGG SAUCE)

3 cans (7 ounces each) tuna fish
_____

1½ cups soft bread crumbs
2 large eggs
2 tablespoons instant minced onion
¼ teaspoon instant minced garlic
1 tablespoon parsley flakes
2 teaspoons salt
1 teaspoon ground thyme
¼ teaspoon ground black pepper
1 tablespoon fresh lemon juice
⅔ cup milk
_____

Egg Sauce*

Flake tuna fish. Add next 10 ingredients and mix well. Pack mixture firmly in a greased 1½-quart casserole or loaf pan. Bake in a preheated moderate oven (350° F.) 1 hour or until loaf has browned over the top. Turn out onto a serving platter. Serve with Egg Sauce.

YIELD: 8 servings

TUNA AND BROCCOLI AU GRATIN

½ teaspoon powdered mustard
1 teaspoon water
1 bunch (1½ pounds) Broccoli, Cooked*
2 tablespoons butter *or* margarine
1½ tablespoons flour
1 cup milk
½ teaspoon salt
⅛ teaspoon ground black pepper
2 teaspoons lemon juice
6½-ounce can tuna fish
½ cup grated sharp Cheddar cheese
1 cup soft bread crumbs
3 tablespoons butter *or* margarine, melted

Mix mustard with water and let stand 10 minutes. Cook broccoli. Melt butter or margarine in a saucepan. Blend in flour. Stir in milk and cook until of medium thickness. Add mustard, salt, black pepper, and lemon juice.

Arrange drained, cooked broccoli in a 10 x 5 x 2-inch baking dish. Flake tuna fish and strew over the top along with cheese. Cover with sauce. Sprinkle with bread crumbs blended with melted butter or margarine. Bake in a preheated moderate oven (350° F.) 30 minutes or until crumbs are appetizingly brown. Serve hot as the main dish.

HAM AND BROCCOLI AU GRATIN
Replace tuna fish in the above recipe with 2 cups diced, cooked ham.

YIELD: 6 servings

CODFISH, PORTUGUESE STYLE

6 slices eggplant, ¾ inch thick
⅔ cup olive oil
2 cups sliced onions

3 tablespoons capers
1 teaspoon cumin seed
1 cup cooked rice

2½ teaspoons salt
¼ teaspoon coarsely ground black pepper
1 teaspoon paprika
⅛ teaspoon ground red pepper

1½ pounds codfish fillets
2 cups diced fresh tomatoes
3 whole cloves
3 tablespoons fresh lemon juice
½ cup hot water
2 tablespoons butter *or* margarine

Peel eggplant slices and sauté in hot olive oil until light yellow. Place in a 10 x 6 x 2-inch baking dish. Separate onions into rings, sauté in same oil, and scatter over eggplant. Combine next 3 ingredients and spread over onion.

Mix the next 4 ingredients, rub on both sides of fish, and arrange on rice. Top with tomatoes. Add cloves and lemon juice to water and pour over all. Dot with butter or margarine. Cover and bake in a preheated moderate oven (350° F.) 30 minutes. Remove cover and bake 10 to 15 minutes longer. Serve hot.

YIELD: 6 servings

SCALLOPED SALMON

1 can (7¾ ounces) salmon
1 tablespoon fresh lemon juice

⅓ cup (⅔ stick) butter *or* margarine, melted
1¼ cups cracker crumbs

¼ teaspoon ground black pepper
½ teaspoon powdered mustard
¼ teaspoon thyme leaves
1 teaspoon salt
1 tablespoon onion flakes

Milk

Drain and flake salmon, saving the liquid to use later. Add lemon juice to salmon and set aside. Combine the next 7 ingredients and put half the mixture in a buttered 9-inch pie plate. Spread to cover pie plate uniformly. Add salmon and smooth the surface with a spatula.

Pour salmon liquid in a measuring cup and add enough milk to make 1 cup liquid. Pour over salmon. Top with remaining cracker-crumb mixture. Bake in a preheated hot oven (400° F.) 25 minutes or until crumbs are brown. A good supper or luncheon dish.

YIELD: 6 servings

POACHED SALMON WITH SWEDISH LEMON SAUCE (LAX MED CITRONSAS)

3 tablespoons instant minced onion
2 teaspoons salt
1 teaspoon whole black pepper
1 large bay leaf
2 tablespoons dill seed
1 quart boiling water
2 tablespoons white vinegar

6 slices fresh salmon
Swedish Lemon Sauce*
Salt to taste
Paprika

Combine the first 7 ingredients in a deep 10-inch skillet or saucepan. Bring to boiling point. Place fish on a plate or in a pie pan and tie in a cheesecloth. (This prevents fish from breaking.)

Immerse in the boiling mixture. Reduce heat. Cover and cook 10 minutes or until fish is flaky. Remove from water, unwrap, and transfer to a serving dish. Sprinkle fish with salt to taste. Serve with Swedish Lemon Sauce. Garnish with paprika.

YIELD: 6 servings

FISH CURRY

¼ cup onion flakes
¼ teaspoon instant minced garlic
3 tablespoons water
2 tablespoons salad oil *or* shortening
1 teaspoon ground turmeric
1 cup canned tomatoes
2 teaspoons salt
1½ pounds fillets (halibut, perch, *or* cod)
1 tablespoon ground coriander
1 teaspoon ground cumin seed
½ teaspoon ground ginger
½ teaspoon ground red pepper
¼ teaspoon ground fennel seed
2 teaspoons lemon juice

Soften onion flakes and garlic in water. Stir and cook in hot oil or shortening until they begin to change color. Add turmeric, stir, and cook 3 to 4 minutes. Add tomatoes and salt and cook 5 minutes or until sauce has thickened.

Cut fish into serving-size pieces and rub both sides with remaining spices blended. Add any remaining spice to the sauce. Place fish in the sauce. Cover and cook slowly 10 to 15 minutes or until fish is flaky. Add lemon juice. Do not stir. Shake pan gently back and forth to prevent fish from sticking to pan. Serve hot with rice.

YIELD: 6 servings

FISH AND EGGPLANT STEW

½ cup diced onion
2 cups diced fresh tomatoes
3 cups diced eggplant
1 cup diced green pepper
2 large radishes, sliced
3 cups boiling water
___
3 teaspoons salt
1 pound white-meat fish (perch fillets, codfish, *or* fillet of haddock)
½ teaspoon ground black pepper
¼ teaspoon instant minced garlic
Dash cayenne
1 tablespoon fresh lemon juice
Soy sauce (optional)

Combine the first 6 ingredients with 2 teaspoons of the salt in a 3-quart saucepan. Cover and cook 15 minutes or until vegetables are tender. Mix remaining salt with black pepper, garlic, and cayenne and rub on both sides of fish. Add to stew along with lemon juice. Cover and cook 10 minutes or until fish is flaky. Serve with soy sauce, if desired. Serve as main dish.

YIELD: 8 servings

MARINER'S STEW

2 cups canned tomatoes
1 tablespoon flour
___
1½ cups sliced onions
2 teaspoons salt
½ teaspoon ground black pepper
1 tablespoon parsley flakes
¾ teaspoon crumbled oregano leaves
¼ teaspoon powdered mustard
___
¼ teaspoon whole allspice
1 small ginger root
2 pounds haddock *or* perch fillets, diced
2 tablespoons butter *or* margarine
2 large eggs, beaten
2 tablespoons fresh lime *or* lemon juice

Place tomatoes in a 2-quart saucepan and break up with a fork. Add flour and mix until smooth. Add next 6 ingredients. Tie allspice and ginger in a bag, add, and cook, covered, for 15 minutes. Add fish and cook 10 minutes or until fish is flaky. Remove from heat and discard spice bag. Stir in beaten eggs. Add lime or lemon juice. Cook until slightly thickened, 2 to 3 minutes. Serve hot.

YIELD: 8 servings

FISH RAGOUT

4 medium potatoes
_____
1½ cups water
1 small bay leaf
2½ teaspoons salt (or to taste)
_____
12-ounce package frozen perch fillets, thawed
⅓ cup onion flakes
1 tablespoon paprika
¹⁄₁₆ teaspoon ground red pepper
1 tablespoon butter _or_ margarine
½ cup sour cream

Wash, peel, and slice potatoes. Place in a saucepan with next 3 ingredients. Cover and cook 15 minutes or until potatoes are tender. Add fish and onion flakes. Cover and cook 10 minutes or until fish is flaky. Stir in paprika, red pepper, and butter or margarine. Cook 2 to 3 minutes. Stir in sour cream. Heat only until cream is hot. Serve hot as the main dish.

YIELD: 6 servings

ESCOVITCHED FISH

Escovitched fish is "soused" or pickled fish and is served throughout the Caribbean. This particular recipe is of Jamaica, B.W.I., origin. Though Jamaicans living along the shore have access to more than a thousand varieties of fish, those living inland traditionally have had to eat salted or pickled fish.

1 pound fillet of haddock _or_ swordfish
3 tablespoons butter _or_ margarine
_____
1 cup cider vinegar
3 tablespoons finely chopped green pepper
4 teaspoons instant minced onion
1½ teaspoons salt
½ teaspoon whole allspice
½ teaspoon whole black pepper
⅛ teaspoon garlic powder
_____
1 hot red pepper, 1½ inches long

Rinse fish and cut into 1-inch squares. Sauté in butter or margarine. Place in a 10 x 6 x 2-inch baking dish. Place the next 7 ingredients in a saucepan. Break red pepper in half and add. Heat to boiling point and pour over fish. Cover and marinate a full 24 hours, turning the fish occasionally in marinade. Serve as an entrée or as an hors d'oeuvre on toasted squares of bread.

YIELD: 4 servings or about 4½ dozen hors d'oeuvres

IMPERIAL CRABMEAT, BALTIMORE

½ cup chopped green pepper
1 tablespoon butter *or* margarine

½ teaspoon salt
¼ teaspoon ground black pepper
¼ teaspoon powdered mustard
1 teaspoon worcestershire sauce
¼ cup mayonnaise

1 pound cooked, fresh crabmeat *or* 2
   cans (6½ ounces each) crabmeat
⅓ cup chopped pimiento
⅔ cup soft bread crumbs
2 tablespoons butter *or* margarine,
   melted
½ teaspoon paprika

Sauté green pepper in butter or margarine 1 minute. Mix with the next 5 ingredients. Flake crabmeat and add. Turn into a buttered 1-quart casserole. Combine pimiento, bread crumbs, butter, and paprika and sprinkle over the top. Bake in a preheated moderate oven (350° F.) 30 minutes or until crumbs are brown. Serve hot as the main dish.

YIELD: 6 servings

CRABMEAT FONDUE

2 cups milk

2 tablespoons butter *or* margarine
1¾ cups soft bread crumbs
½ teaspoon salt
¼ teaspoon ground black pepper
¼ teaspoon instant minced garlic
½ teaspoon instant minced onion
¼ teaspoon ground ginger
6½-ounce can crabmeat, flaked

5 large eggs, separated
1 cup shredded Cheddar cheese
Tomato Gravy*

Heat milk. Add the next 8 ingredients. Beat egg yolks and stir into the mixture.

Stir and cook over low heat 5 minutes or until thickened. Add cheese and mix well. Beat egg whites until they stand in soft, stiff peaks and fold into the mixture.

Turn into a 1½-quart casserole, having *only* the bottom buttered. Place in a pan of hot water. Bake in a preheated slow oven (325° F.) 1½ hours or until center is firm. Serve at once with Tomato Gravy.

YIELD: 6 servings

CRABMEAT HASH

2 tablespoons butter *or* margarine
1 can (7¾ ounces) crabmeat, flaked
1 cup diced, cooked potatoes
2 large eggs, lightly beaten
2 tablespoons chopped green pepper
1 tablespoon instant minced onion
1 teaspoon salt
½ teaspoon basil leaves
⅛ teaspoon ground black pepper

Melt butter or margarine in an 8- or 9-inch skillet. Add remaining ingredients and cook 10 minutes or until green pepper is tender. Cook, without stirring, 5 minutes or until hash has browned over the bottom. Fold over in omelet fashion. Serve as the main dish for lunch or supper.

YIELD: 4 servings

CRABMEAT NEWBURG

3 cups (1 pound) crabmeat
¼ cup (½ stick) butter *or* margarine,
   melted
1½ teaspoons salt
½ teaspoon ground mace
¼ teaspoon ground red pepper

1½ cups light cream
¼ teaspoon garlic powder
4 large eggs, beaten

1 teaspoon fresh lemon juice *or*
   2 tablespoons dry sherry

Toast *or* patty cases
Paprika

Flake crabmeat and add to melted butter or margarine. Cook over low heat until hot, about 5 minutes, stirring constantly. Add salt, mace, and red pepper. Mix well. Combine the next 3 ingredients and add to crabmeat. Cook until mixture begins to thicken (10 to 15 minutes). Add lemon juice or sherry. Serve over toast or in patty cases. Garnish with paprika.

YIELD: 4 servings

CRABMEAT ON PILOT CRACKERS

1 cup light cream *or* undiluted
  evaporated milk
1 cup cooked rice
1½ teaspoons salt
½ teaspoon ground basil
1½ teaspoons instant minced onion

1 cup (6½-ounce can) flaked crabmeat
2 tablespoons butter *or* margarine
1 teaspoon paprika
¼ cup catsup
Pilot crackers
Parsley flakes

Combine the first 5 ingredients and heat over hot water or very low heat 10 minutes. Stir in crabmeat, butter or margarine, and paprika. Heat thoroughly for 10 minutes. Stir in catsup. Serve over pilot crackers. Garnish with parsley flakes.

YIELD: 5 servings

CRABMEAT SUPREME

2 tablespoons butter *or* margarine
1 tablespoon cracker meal
¾ cup milk

1 teaspoon double-acting baking powder
1 large egg, beaten
1 tablespoon lemon juice
1 teaspoon salt
¼ teaspoon ground black pepper
½ teaspoon poultry seasoning
½ teaspoon powdered mustard

2 cans (6½ ounces each) crabmeat

Melt butter or margarine. Blend in cracker meal. Stir in milk and cook until thickened, stirring constantly. Remove from heat. Stir in next 7 ingredients. Flake crabmeat, remove any bones, and place in a buttered 1-quart casserole. Pour sauce over crabmeat. Bake in a preheated moderate oven (350° F.) 25 minutes. Pop under broiler about 5 minutes or until browned.

YIELD: 4 servings

STEAMED LOBSTER
(WITH CURRY BUTTER)

1 inch boiling water
1 (1- to 2-pound) live lobster
Curry Butter *(see below)*

NOTE: If live lobsters are not available in your locality, use the frozen lobster tails. Prepare them for steaming as directed on the package and steam as for live lobster in following directions. Serve with Curry Butter.

Place live lobster on a rack in a large kettle and pour in 1 inch boiling water. Cover and steam from 15 to 20 minutes or until lobster turns pink. (Count cooking time after steam has formed.)

Remove lobster from kettle and place on its back on a cutting board. Split lengthwise with a heavy, sharp knive, running it from the mouth through the body and tail. Remove the dark vein. Undeveloped spawn, red in color, is frequently found and may be removed or eaten, as desired. Crack the large claws. Serve in the shells with melted Curry Butter.

CURRY BUTTER

For each serving of lobster, melt 2 tablespoons butter or margarine and blend in 1 teaspoon curry powder. Serve in individual small paper, glass, or china cups, into which dip chunks of steamed lobster.

YIELD: 1 serving

STUFFED LOBSTER, RHODE ISLAND STYLE

1 inch boiling water
1 (1 to 2 pounds) live lobster
1 cup soft, fine bread crumbs
1½ teaspoons paprika
¼ teaspoon chili powder
⅛ teaspoon cayenne
1/16 teaspoon ground black pepper
1/16 teaspoon salt
2 tablespoons butter or margarine
½ teaspoon paprika
Lemon slice

Place rack in bottom of saucepan large enough to steam lobster. Put live lobster on the rack. Pour in boiling water, having

it come 1 inch up side of pan. Cover, bring to boiling point, reduce heat, and steam 15 minutes or until lobster turns red. DO NOT OVERCOOK. Remove lobster from saucepan and cool.

Slit shell by inserting a knife or scissors at tail end and cutting the entire length of lobster. Remove tail meat in one piece. Remove and discard the black vein from the tail meat, and the stomach and lungs from the front end of the lobster. Cut meat in ½-inch cubes and mix with all remaining ingredients except the last 2 ingredients. Pile mixture in lobster shell. Bake in a preheated hot oven (400° F.) 15 minutes. Sprinkle with the ½ teaspoon paprika. Serve on a large serving platter. Garnish with lemon slice. Crack the claws with a lobster cracker and pick out meat with a lobster pick.

YIELD: 1 serving

CURRIED LOBSTER

⅓ cup (⅔ stick) butter or margarine
⅓ cup flour
2 teaspoons chopped fresh onion
1½ teaspoons curry powder

2 cups milk *or* 1 cup milk and 1 cup
  lobster stock
1 teaspoon salt
⅛ teaspoon ground black pepper
2 cans (5 ounces each) lobster *or*
  1½ cups cooked lobster chunks
Patty cases *or* chow mein noodles

Melt butter or margarine in a saucepan. Remove from heat. Blend in next 3 ingredients. Stir and cook 1 minute. Gradually add milk or milk and lobster stock. Cook until of medium thickness. Add salt, black pepper, and lobster. Heat only until hot. Serve in patty cases or over chow mein noodles.

YIELD: 6 servings

DEVILED LOBSTER, JAMAICAN STYLE

⅓ cup minced green pepper
3 tablespoons butter *or* margarine
3 tablespoons flour

2 cups strained, canned tomatoes
2 tablespoons instant minced onion
¼ cup minced green olives
3 teaspoons salt
¼ teaspoon ground black pepper
¾ teaspoon marjoram leaves
⅛ teaspoon cayenne
½ teaspoon sugar

2 teaspoons lime juice
2 cups cooked lobster meat

Fresh lime slices

Sauté green pepper in butter or margarine 4 minutes or until limp. Blend in flour and cook until bubbly. Add the next 8 ingredients and cook until medium thickness. Stir in lime juice and lobster. Cook only until hot over medium-low heat. Serve over hot cooked rice. Garnish each serving with a slice of fresh lime.

YIELD: 4 servings

LOBSTER A LA KING

3 tablespoons butter *or* margarine
3 tablespoons flour
2 cups milk

2 cans (5 ounces each) lobster *or* 1½
  cups cooked fresh lobster
¼ cup diced pimiento
1 tablespoon instant minced onion
2 large hard-cooked eggs, diced
1 teaspoon salt
2 teaspoons paprika
¾ teaspoon basil leaves
¼ teaspoon ground black pepper
¼ teaspoon garlic powder

½ cup sliced mushrooms
1 tablespoon butter *or* margarine
2 teaspoons fresh lemon juice

Melt butter or margarine in a 1½-quart saucepan. Remove from heat and blend in flour. Stir and cook until bubbly. Remove from heat and stir in milk. Cook over medium-low heat until of medium thickness, stirring constantly. Add next 9 ingredients. Sauté mushrooms in butter or margarine until tender and limp. Add and cook ½ minute. Stir in lemon juice just before serving. Serve in patty cases.

SHRIMP A LA KING
Replace lobster in the above recipe with fresh or canned shrimp.

YIELD: 6 servings

LOBSTER NEWBURG

6 frozen lobster tails
⅓ cup (⅔ stick) butter *or* margarine
¼ cup flour
1½ cups lobster stock *(see below)*
1½ cups light cream
2 teaspoons salt
1½ teaspoons powdered mustard
¼ teaspoon ground white pepper
⅛ teaspoon cayenne

⅛ teaspoon garlic powder
4 large egg yolks
2 tablespoons dry sherry *or* brandy
Toast *or* patty cases

Steam lobster tails as directed on package. Cool, remove meat from shells, and dice. Set aside. (Reserve shells for making lobster stock.) Melt butter or margarine in a saucepan. Remove from heat and blend in flour. Stir and cook until bubbly. Remove from heat and add lobster stock and cream. Stir and cook until sauce is smooth and of medium thickness. Add seasonings. Beat egg yolks until foamy, into which beat a little of the hot sauce. Gradually stir into remaining hot sauce. Cook only until hot. DO NOT BOIL. Add sherry or brandy and lobster. Heat 1 minute. Serve on toast or patty cases.

LOBSTER STOCK
Combine in a 3-quart saucepan cracked lobster shells, 3 cups water, 1 teaspoon salt, 1 bay leaf, and ½ teaspoon each of whole allspice and whole black peppers. Bring to boiling point, cover, and simmer 15 minutes. Strain. Use 1½ cups of the liquid in Lobster Newburg.

YIELD: 6 servings

LOBSTER SHORTCAKE

2 cups cooked fresh, frozen, or
   canned lobster
¼ cup (½ stick) butter *or* margarine
¼ cup flour
2 cups milk
1 tablespoon parsley flakes
¾ teaspoon instant minced onion
1¼ teaspoons salt
¼ teaspoon ground black pepper
2 teaspoons fresh lemon juice
Corn Bread Squares *(see below)*
Paprika

Break lobster into chunks and set aside. Melt butter or margarine in a saucepan. Remove from heat and blend in flour. Stir and cook until bubbly. Remove from heat and add milk. Cook until of medium thickness, stirring constantly. Add the next 5 ingredients and mix well.

Blend in lobster, being careful not to break chunks too much. Heat only until hot. DO NOT BOIL. Serve in shortcake fashion between layers and over top of split corn bread squares. Garnish with paprika.

CORN BREAD SQUARES
Mix and bake a 10-ounce package of unsweetened corn-bread mix according to package directions, or bake your own, using your favorite recipe. Cut into 6 squares and split each, forming 2 layers.

YIELD: 6 servings

LOBSTER THERMIDOR

6 frozen lobster tails, about 5 ounces
   each, *or* 3½ cups chunks from cooked
   fresh lobster
3 tablespoons butter *or* margarine
2 tablespoons flour
1 cup milk *or* light cream
½ teaspoon thyme leaves
¼ teaspoon powdered mustard
⅛ teaspoon ground black pepper
¾ teaspoon paprika
1 teaspoon salt
1 teaspoon instant minced onion
2 tablespoons sherry
⅓ cup grated Parmesan cheese
Paprika

If frozen lobster tails are used, cook as directed on the package. If fresh lobster is used, cook in accordance with recipe for Steamed Lobster.* Remove meat and cut into large chunks. Melt butter or margarine in a saucepan. Remove from heat and blend in flour. Stir and cook until bubbly. Remove from heat, stir in milk or cream, and cook, stirring constantly, until of medium thickness. Add next 7 ingredients together with lobster meat, saving a few chunks of the meat for top of casserole.

Refill lobster shells or turn into 6 individual buttered baking dishes or a 1-quart casserole. Place reserved lobster meat over top. Sprinkle with Parmesan cheese. Place under broiler until brown (about 3 minutes). Garnish with paprika.

YIELD: 6 servings

QUICK LOBSTER THERMIDOR

1 can (10½ ounces) cream of
   mushroom soup
¼ cup hot water
½ teaspoon powdered mustard
⅛ teaspoon salt
⅛ teaspoon ground black pepper
1 can (6½ ounces) lobster, diced

1½ tablespoons fresh lemon juice
5 tablespoons grated Parmesan cheese
Paprika

Combine the first 6 ingredients in a saucepan. Stir and cook over low heat *only* until hot. Add lemon juice and mix lightly until blended. Turn into a buttered 1-quart casserole or into 5 individual casseroles. Sprinkle with grated Parmesan cheese. Bake in a preheated moderate oven (350° F.) 15 to 20 minutes. Garnish with paprika.

YIELD: 5 servings

BAKED SCALLOPS, UNITED NATIONS STYLE

This recipe was given to us by one of the chefs of the United Nations Restaurant. Bay scallops are the little fellows. If not available, cut larger sea scallops in quarters and prepare the same way.

2 dozen (1 pound) bay scallops
Salt
Ground black pepper

½ teaspoon parsley flakes
¼ teaspoon instant minced onion
¹⁄₁₆ teaspoon garlic powder
1 teaspoon fresh lemon juice
⅓ cup (⅔ stick) butter *or* margarine

6 lemon wedges

Place 4 scallops in each of 6 sea shells. Sprinkle with salt and ground black pepper to taste. Mix the next 5 ingredients. Top each portion with a heaping teaspoon of the mixture. Bake in a very hot oven (450° F.) 5 minutes or until butter has melted and scallops are hot. Serve as first course with lemon wedges.

YIELD: 6 servings

PICKLED FISH, PUERTO RICAN STYLE
(PESCADO EN ESCABECHE)

This dish originated in Spain and was brought to the United States via Puerto Rico. We learned of it from Berta Cabanillas and Carmen Ginorio, authors of Puerto Rican Dishes.

2 pounds swordfish, cod, *or* halibut
3 teaspoons salt
½ teaspoon ground black pepper
⅓ cup flour
1 cup olive oil

¾ cup cider vinegar
¼ cup water
2 tablespoons onion flakes
3 tablespoons chopped green pepper
8 bay leaves
½ teaspoon whole allspice
1½ teaspoons whole black pepper
½ teaspoon salt
½ teaspoon instant minced garlic
½ cup pitted, small, whole green olives
2 dried, hot red peppers, 1½ inches long, broken in half

Cut fish into serving-size pieces, ½ inch thick. Mix the 3 teaspoons salt with the ½ teaspoon ground black pepper and rub half of it into both sides of the fish. Mix remaining salt and black pepper with flour and roll fish in mixture.

Heat 3 tablespoons of the oil in a skillet, add fish, and sauté both sides, adding more oil if necessary. Place remaining ingredients in a saucepan, heat to boiling point, and boil 1 minute. Pour over fish. Add remaining olive oil. Marinate at least 24 hours before serving, turning fish from time to time. Serve cold as an entrée or as an hors d'oeuvre.

YIELD: 6 servings (main dish)

SCALLOPS A LA AVANELLE

3 tablespoons butter *or* margarine

1 teaspoon chopped chives
½ teaspoon parsley flakes
⅛ teaspoon tarragon leaves
1/16 teaspoon garlic salt
1/16 teaspoon ground black pepper
¾ teaspoon fresh lemon juice

¼ teaspoon salt
4 dozen (2 pounds) bay scallops
½ cup soft bread crumbs
3 tablespoons butter *or* margarine, melted

Soften 3 tablespoons butter or margarine. Add next 6 ingredients. Sprinkle salt over scallops. Arrange 6 scallops in each of 8 sea shells or small individual casseroles. Top each with 1 teaspoon of the herbed mixture and sprinkle with soft bread crumbs mixed with 3 tablespoons of melted butter or margarine. Bake in a preheated very hot oven (500° F.) 5 minutes.

YIELD: 8 servings

BOMBAY SHRIMP BALLS
(JHINGA KOFTA)

3 cups cooked, deveined shrimp (3 cans, 5½ ounces each)
1 tablespoon instant minced onion
¼ teaspoon instant minced garlic
1 tablespoon water

2 large eggs
3 tablespoons flour
1 teaspoon ground coriander seed
½ teaspoon ground turmeric
1 teaspoon salt
⅛ teaspoon garlic powder

½ teaspoon ground black pepper
½ teaspoon powdered mustard
½ teaspoon ground cumin seed
⅓ cup water
Curry Sauce *(see below)*
¼ cup evaporated milk *or*
    coconut milk
1 teaspoon lemon juice

Grind shrimp twice in food chopper, using finest blade. Soften instant minced onion and garlic in 1 tablespoon water and add. Blend in the next 9 ingredients and mix until of pastelike consistency. Add water and cook 5 minutes or until the mixture almost sticks to the pan. Shape mixture into 1½-inch balls and brown in hot shortening or oil. Drain. Add Curry Sauce and cook 5 minutes. Add milk and heat 1 to 2 minutes without stirring. Add lemon juice. Serve hot on rice.

CURRY SAUCE
¼ cup onion flakes
3 tablespoons water
2 tablespoons shortening *or* oil
⅛ teaspoon garlic powder
¾ teaspoon salt
1¾ teaspoons curry powder
1¼ cups water

Mix onion flakes with the 3 tablespoons water and let stand for 3 minutes. Fry in shortening or oil until onions are almost brown. Add next 3 ingredients, stirring and cooking 1 or 2 minutes. Add water. Cook, uncovered, over low heat 10 minutes, to form a medium-thick sauce.

YIELD: 6 servings

SCAMPI
1 pound medium-large fresh shrimp
1 cup (2 sticks) butter *or* margarine
¼ cup olive oil

1 tablespoon parsley flakes
¾ teaspoon basil leaves
½ teaspoon oregano leaves
¾ teaspoon garlic powder
¾ teaspoon salt
1 teaspoon fresh lemon juice

Peel and devein shrimp, leaving tails attached. Split down the inside, lengthwise, being careful not to cut through the shrimp. Spread open to simulate a butterfly. Place in a shallow baking dish.

Melt butter or margarine, add remaining ingredients, and pour over shrimp. Bake in a preheated very hot oven (450° F.) 5 minutes. Place under the broiler 5 minutes or until shrimp are flecked with brown.

YIELD: 5 to 6 servings

SHRIMP AND LOBSTER STEW
⅓ cup onion flakes
½ teaspoon instant minced garlic
2½ cups water
2 tablespoons butter *or* margarine
2½ cups canned tomatoes
2 jars (8 ounces each) clam juice
2 cups sliced carrots
2 cups sliced celery
1 bay leaf
1 teaspoon salt (or to taste)
1 package (12 ounces) frozen shrimp
1 package (10 ounces) frozen
    lobster tails
1 teaspoon rosemary
½ teaspoon crumbled saffron strands
3 tablespoons flour

Soften onion flakes and instant minced garlic in ¼ cup of the water. Sauté them in butter or margarine 2 minutes in a kettle large enough for making stew. Add 2 cups of the water and the next 6 ingredients. Cover and simmer 30 minutes.

Peel and devein shrimp, remove meat from lobster tails as directed on package, and add both to the kettle. Stir in spices. Cover and simmer 10 minutes or *only* until lobster and shrimp turn pink. Blend flour with the remaining ¼ cup water and add. Cook 1 minute. Serve hot in bowls.

YIELD: 8 servings

SHRIMP ETOUFFEE

2 packages (12 ounces each) frozen
  shrimp
⅓ cup onion flakes
¼ cup sweet pepper flakes
¼ teaspoon instant minced garlic
½ cup water
2 tablespoons butter *or* margarine
½ cup chopped celery
1½ cups water

¼ cup tomato paste
2 tablespoons instant minced green
  onion
1 tablespoon parsley flakes
3 teaspoons salt
¼ teaspoon ground red pepper
¼ teaspoon ground black pepper
1 tablespoon fresh lemon juice

Defrost shrimp. Soften onion and sweet pepper flakes and instant minced garlic in the ½ cup water. Sauté in butter or margarine along with celery until celery is tender, about 4 minutes. Add shrimp and the 1½ cups water.

Cover and cook slowly 10 minutes. Stir in the next 7 ingredients. Cover and cook slowly 5 minutes. Serve hot with rice.

YIELD: 6 servings

SHRIMP JAMBALAYA

¼ cup salad *or* olive oil
¼ cup diced celery
½ cup diced green pepper
1 cup raw, long-grained rice

1 cup canned tomatoes
3½ cups beef *or* chicken stock
¼ cup instant minced onion
1 teaspoon salt
⅛ teaspoon ground black pepper
1/16 teaspoon cayenne
½ teaspoon ground thyme leaves
1 teaspoon parsley flakes

1 cup diced, cooked ham
2 cups peeled, deveined, cooked shrimp

Heat oil in a heavy saucepan or Dutch oven. Add celery, green pepper, and rice. Stir and cook until rice begins to stick to bottom of pan and has browned lightly. Add the next 8 ingredients. Cover and cook 25 minutes, or until rice is tender.

Add ham and shrimp 6 minutes before cooking time is up. Serve hot.

YIELD: 6 servings

SHRIMP POLENTA

Polenta is the Italian version of corn-meal mush, to which chopped meat, cheese, seafood, etc., may be added. When cooled and firm, slice and brown in butter. Polenta was a favorite dish of Napoleon Bonaparte.

1 cup yellow corn meal
1 teaspoon salt
1 cup cold water

3 cups boiling water
⅔ cup chopped onion
2 tablespoons olive *or* cooking oil
6 medium-sized mushrooms, sliced

1 teaspoon salt
1½ teaspoons oregano leaves
½ teaspoon basil leaves
2 packages (5 ounces each) frozen shrimp, thawed
2 tablespoons parsley flakes
1 can (6 ounces) tomato paste

¼ cup grated Cheddar *or* Parmesan cheese

Combine the first 3 ingredients in a mixing bowl. Stir into the boiling water. Stir and cook until the mixture has thickened, about 15 minutes, adding more water if necessary. In the meantime, sauté onion in oil. Add mushrooms. Cover and cook slowly 10 minutes. Add next 6 ingredients. Heat and cook 5 minutes or until shrimp turns pink. Turn polenta onto a platter. Top with shrimp mixture. Sprinkle with grated cheese. Serve as the main dish.

YIELD: 4 servings

SHRIMP AND RICE ACADIAN

⅓ cup onion flakes
¼ teaspoon instant minced garlic
3 tablespoons water
1 tablespoon shortening
1 tablespoon flour

2 cups (1 pound) canned tomatoes
3 cups water
¼ cup sweet pepper flakes
1 tablespoon parsley flakes
3 teaspoons salt
½ teaspoon sugar
¾ teaspoon ground thyme
⅛ teaspoon cayenne

1 cup uncooked, long-grained rice
1 pound deveined, fresh or frozen shrimp *or* 2 cans (6½ ounces each) shrimp
½ cup grated American cheese

Soften onion and garlic in the 3 tablespoons water and set aside. Melt shortening, blend in flour, stir, and cook until mixture has browned. Add onion and garlic. Stir and cook 2 minutes. Add the next 8 ingredients. Mix well and stir in rice. Cover and cook 50 minutes.

If fresh shrimp is used, add to rice 10 minutes before cooking time is up. Add cheese and mix lightly, being careful not to break up rice grains. If canned shrimp is used, drain and add along with cheese. Serve hot.

YIELD: 6 servings

SHRIMP-STUFFED EGGPLANT

1 large (1½ pounds) eggplant
¼ cup chopped onion
3 tablespoons butter *or* margarine
1 pound cooked shrimp

¼ cup fine, dry bread crumbs
1 large egg yolk

1 teaspoon salt
2 teaspoons chili powder
¼ teaspoon ground black pepper
⅛ teaspoon garlic powder

¾ cup soft bread crumbs

Wash eggplant, cut in half lengthwise, and parboil 15 minutes. Scoop out pulp to within ½ inch of the skin and chop fine. Sauté onion in 1 tablespoon of the butter or margarine and mix with eggplant. Break shrimp into pieces and add along with the next 6 ingredients.

Fill eggplant shells with the mixture. Melt remaining butter or margarine and mix with the soft bread crumbs. Sprinkle over eggplant. Bake in a preheated moderate oven (350° F.) 35 to 40 minutes, or until crumbs are brown.

YIELD: 6 servings

SHRIMP-STUFFED GREEN PEPPERS

6 large green peppers
Boiling water
½ teaspoon salt

1½ cups diced, cooked ham
6½-ounce can (1 scant cup) diced shrimp
½ cup finely chopped celery
1 tablespoon instant minced onion
1 cup soft bread crumbs
1 cup diced, fresh tomato
1 teaspoon powdered mustard
¾ teaspoon salt
⅛ teaspoon ground black pepper

2 tablespoons butter or margarine
½ cup soft bread crumbs

Cut tops from green peppers and scoop out seeds, leaving the shells intact. Par-boil in boiling water with the ½ teaspoon salt, about 5 minutes in a covered saucepan. Remove from water and drain. Place in a 9 x 9 x 2-inch baking pan. Set aside.

Combine next 9 ingredients and spoon into peppers. Melt butter or margarine and mix with remaining ½ cup bread crumbs. Sprinkle over tops of peppers. Pour in ½ cup boiling water. Bake in a preheated moderate oven (350° F.) 40 to 50 minutes or until done. Serve hot.

YIELD: 6 servings

SHRIMP AND VEGETABLES, ORIENTAL STYLE

3 tablespoons butter or margarine
1 cup sliced fresh green beans

1½ cups sliced celery
1½ cups sliced fresh mushrooms
1 cup thinly sliced white onions

2 cups shredded lettuce
1 pound cooked shrimp
¼ cup soy sauce
1 teaspoon cornstarch
¼ teaspoon ground ginger
⅛ teaspoon ground black pepper

Melt butter or margarine in a 10-inch skillet. Add green beans. Cover and cook 5 minutes. Add next 3 ingredients. Cover and cook slowly 8 to 10 minutes or until vegetables are crisp-tender. Add lettuce and shrimp and heat 2 minutes.

Blend soy sauce with cornstarch, ginger, and black pepper. Add to the mixture. Cook ½ minute or until sauce has thickened. Serve hot.

YIELD: 6 servings

JAMS and JELLIES

ANYONE can make delicious jams and jellies. Even city dwellers. It's easy and it's fun. And when the winter solstice casts its gloomy shadow over your home, what could be a more refreshing reminder of the coming spring than a newly opened jar of Spiced Grape Jelly*—made by you?

Jams, jellies, conserves, and other spreads are usually made at the height of the summer fruit season. And today, when science has revealed the secrets of the chemistry of fruits and sugar, and the nature of the cooking process itself, you can count on perfect results every time you set out to make one of these delicious spreads.

Jellies are made from fruit juice cooked with sugar. *Jams* are made from crushed fruit and sugar cooked until the mixture is thick and homogeneous. *Marmalades* are jamlike preserves, containing the juice, pulp, and rind of the fruit itself. *Conserves* are jamlike preserves, containing *two* or more fruits plus raisins and nuts. *Fruit butters* are made of fruit pulp cooked with a comparatively small amount of sugar until thick and butterlike.

HOW TO MAKE JELLY

Good jelly has the characteristic color and flavor of the fruit from which it is made. It is clear or translucent. It is firm enough to hold its shape when unmolded and will break with a sharp line; yet it is flexible enough so that it cuts easily. To make a jelly of this high quality, consult the following chart and follow the directions carefully.

*An asterisk after the name of a dish indicates that the recipe for this dish appears in the book. Consult the Index for the page number.

304

JELLY MAKING CHART (WITHOUT COMMERCIAL PECTIN)

Fruit	Water (AMOUNT FOR EACH QUART PREPARED FRUIT)	Boiling Time (TO EXTRACT JUICE FROM FRUIT)	Sugar (AMOUNT FOR EACH CUP JUICE)	Spice†
	Cups	Minutes	Cups	
Apples, tart	1	20 to 25	¾	A, B, C, D
Crab apples	1	20 to 25	1	A, B, C, D
Currants, red	¼	5 to 10	1	A, B, C
Gooseberries	¼	5 to 10	¾	B, C, D
Grapes, Concord	¼	5 to 10	¾ to 1	A, B, C, D, E
Mayhaws	2	20	¾ to 1	A, B, C, D
Plums, sour	½	15 to 20	¾	A, C
Quince	2	20 to 25	¾	A, B, C, D
Scuppernong	¼	5 to 10	¾	C, D

†Suggested spicing for one 4- to 6-cup batch of jelly (choose one):

A. Four 2-inch cinnamon sticks
B. Four 2-inch cinnamon sticks and 24 whole cloves
C. 1 tablespoon mixed pickling spice
D. 1½ teaspoons whole allspice and ½ teaspoon whole cloves
E. 1 teaspoon ground cardamom

A good rule to remember when adding spices to jelly is that spices should enhance and not overshadow the delicate flavor of the fruit. Light-colored spices, such as cardamom, may be used either in the ground or whole form. In the ground form, they should be added to the jelly at the end of the cooking period. However, most spices would darken the jelly; an exception is grape juice, or other dark juices, if spices are added in the ground form. Therefore, spices should be used whole and should be tied in a bag, cooked with juice and the sugar, and removed at the end of the cooking period.

DIRECTIONS FOR MAKING JELLY

1. Select fruit that contains the right amounts of pectin and acid, for it is these two substances, combined with the proper amount of sugar, that give jelly its body. As fruit ripens, its pectin and acid contents decrease. Hence, for best results, use a mixture of 3 parts of *just*-ripe fruit for color and flavor plus 1 part of slightly *under*-ripe fruit for pectin and acid.

2. Wash fruit and discard any that is spoiled or over-ripe. Do not peel or core firm fruits such as apples or quinces, since they contain a concentra-

tion of pectin in the core and in the pulp just under the skin. Cut fruit in uniform pieces. If fruit is soft, such as grapes or berries, crush the fruit to start the flow of juice.

3. Place fruit in a large saucepan with the correct amount of water. Cover, bring to boiling point, and boil as indicated in the above chart. Overcooking fruit tends to destroy the pectin, flavor, and color.

4. Drip boiled fruit juice through a jelly bag made of 2 thicknesses of cheesecloth. The bag may be squeezed gently to expell most of the juice from the pulp. Then restrain through a cotton flannel bag or through 4 thicknesses of cheesecloth to obtain a clear juice.

5. Wash jelly glasses or jars. Place upside down in a pan of water. (If jelly glasses are used, put lids in with them.) Bring water to boiling point. Keep glasses in the boiling water until you are ready to fill them. (If dome cap jars are used, place lids in the boiling water.) No further boiling is necessary.

6. Measure juice in a large saucepan. Do not cook more than 4 to 6 cups at a time for best results.

7. Measure the sugar. The amount varies with the fruit, but averages about ¾ cup to 1 cup per cup of juice.

8. Add sugar to cold juice. Stir and cook until sugar is dissolved. Boil rapidly, uncovered, and without stirring, until jelly is done. To test, pour jelly from the side of a metal spoon. If two distinct drops, formed on the side of the spoon, run together into one drop or into a "sheet," the jelly has cooked sufficiently.

9. Remove jelly from heat and let stand while draining glasses or jars. Place hot jars on a tray, handling them with tongs.

10. Skim off and discard scum that has formed over the top of jelly. Fill jelly glasses to within ¼ inch from the top of glasses. Fill dome cap jars to within ½ inch from the top of jars and seal at once. Cover jelly in glasses with a clean towel and let stand until cold. Pour ¼ inch of melted paraffin over the top. Let stand until firm. Repeat with another layer of paraffin. Cover with clean, dry lids.

11. Label with the name of jelly and the date it was made.

12. Store in a clean, cool, dry place.

MARMALADES

Marmalades are prepared from pulpy fruits, preferably those rich in pectin and acid. Citrus fruits are favorite marmalade fruits. Apples, cranberries, grapes, and quinces may also be used, since they provide pectin and acid. Berries, carrots, pears, pineapple, and tomatoes may be used with any of the above fruits, but cannot be used alone to make marmalade because they are deficient in jelly-forming materials.

SPICE·BATTLE
1605
THE DUTCH AND THE
PORTUGUESE FIGHT
FOR THE POSSESSION
OF THE SPICE ISLANDS

Since the preparation and cooking of marmalade varies with the fruit used, directions with each recipe should be followed carefully.

JAMS

Jams are usually made from crushed fruits such as apricots, berries, cherries, peaches, plums, and grapes. The fruit is cooked with sugar to a soft jellylike consistency and contains no free juice or liquid.

The standard proportion of sugar varies from ¾ to 1 part by weight of sugar to 1 part by weight of the prepared fruit, or ¾ cup sugar to 1 cup of fruit.

Heat the fruit and sugar slowly, stirring constantly, until all the sugar has dissolved. Bring the mixture to the boiling point and stir and boil rapidly until it is thick. The cooking time varies with the fruit. Each recipe in this book specifies the approximate cooking time. Pour into sterilized jars and seal as for jelly.

CONSERVES

Conserves may be made with any two or more fruits cooked together with sugar to a jamlike consistency. A true conserve also contains raisins and chopped or sliced nuts.

1. Wash fruit. Peel and core apples or pears; pit stone fruits; peel peaches and apricots; quarter, dice, or crush fruit according to the type of fruit used. For better texture, fruits with tough skins such as blueberries, cranberries, grapes, and plums, unless peeled, should be cooked a short time before adding sugar. The amount of sugar varies with the fruit used.

2. Blanch almonds to remove skins and slice thinly or chop coarsely. Blanch walnuts to prevent darkening the conserves. Pecans do not need to be blanched. Chop nuts to the size of corn kernels.

3. Tie whole spices—such as allspice, cinnamon, cloves, ginger, or whole mixed pickling spice—in a bag and cook with the fruit and sugar. Add ground allspice shortly before cooking time is up. Use only enough spice to enhance the natural flavor of the conserve.

FRUIT BUTTERS

Prepare fruit butters from tart apples, apricots, grapes, pears, plums, and quinces. Apple butter cooked with apple cider has an especially delightful flavor.

Wash fruit and discard any that is spoiled and prepare it as follows:

Apples: Peel and core (or not) as desired. Measure fruit and add an equal amount of cider or use half cider and half water.

Apricots and peaches: Blanch fruit. Remove pits. Crush fruit and cook in own juice.

Grapes: Remove from stems, crush, and cook in own juice.

Pears: Remove stems and cut into quarters. Do not peel or core. Add half as much water as fruit.

Plums: Remove pits. Crush and cook in own juice.

Quinces: Remove blossom end but do not peel or core. Cut into small pieces. Add half as much water as fruit.

Cook fruit until soft, stirring frequently. Rub fruit through a fine sieve or colander to remove fibers and to give smooth consistency. Add sugar. Usually the best proportion is ½ cup sugar to 1 cup pulp. However, this proportion varies with the sweetness of fruit and the taste of the user. Some authorities recommend ⅔ to ¾ cup sugar per cup fruit pulp. Bring mixture to boiling point and cook until thick and no rim of liquid separates around the edge of butter when a small quantity is dropped on a cold plate. Stir butter constantly while cooking to prevent burning.

Ladle into hot sterilized jars while butter is boiling hot. Seal airtight.

HOW TO SPICE FRUIT BUTTERS

Use only fresh spices. Tie whole spices in a cheesecloth bag, using only enough to give delicate flavor, usually 1½ to 2 teaspoons whole sweet spices (allspice, cloves, cracked ginger, mace, or nutmeg and two to three 2-inch cinnamon sticks) to a 6-cup batch of fruit butter. Cook with the fruit and sugar mixture. If ground spices are used, add them at the end of the cooking period, using 1 teaspoon of a favorite ground sweet spice or a blend of sweet spices totaling 1 teaspoon.

JELLIES AND JAMS MADE WITH COMMERCIAL PECTIN

Today, one can make good jelly and jam with commercial pectin, which is available in two forms: liquid pectin such as Certo and powdered pectin such as Sure-Jell. The use of either of the pectins enables one to use fruit that is low in pectin, shortens the preparation time, and insures success if the detailed instructions that come in every package are followed.

APPLE BUTTER

6 pounds tart cooking apples
2 cups apple cider
___
3½ cups sugar
¼ teaspoon salt
4 cinnamon sticks, each 2 inches long
___
1 teaspoon whole allspice
½ teaspoon whole cloves
½ teaspoon ground nutmeg

Wash apples, do not peel or core, and slice into a 4-quart saucepan. Add cider. Cover and cook until apples are mushy, 20 to 25 minutes. Push apples through a sieve or food mill. Mix the pulp with the next 3 ingredients. Tie allspice and cloves in a cheesecloth bag and add. Cook, uncovered, rapidly, until the mixture begins to thicken, stirring frequently to prevent scorching. Reduce heat to prevent spattering and stir and cook until the mixture falls in sheets from the spoon. Total cooking time is about 1 hour. Add nutmeg 5 minutes before cooking time is up. Remove and discard cinnamon sticks and spice bag. Ladle into hot sterilized jars. Seal airtight immediately.

YIELD: 6 jars, ½ pint each

APPLE, PLUM, AND PEAR CONSERVE

4 cups (about 4 medium) peeled, diced apples
4 cups (about 9 large) sliced plums
4 cups (about 3 large) sliced, peeled pears

6 cups sugar
½ teaspoon salt
3 cinnamon sticks, each 2 inches long
1½ teaspoons ground allspice
1 cup coarsely chopped pecans

Combine fruit and sugar in a 4-quart saucepan. Let stand overnight or 6 hours. Add salt and cinnamon, stir, and cook, uncovered, over medium heat until mixture has thickened, about 1½ hours. Add allspice and pecans. Cook 5 more minutes. Remove and discard cinnamon. Ladle into hot, sterilized jars, leaving ½-inch space at top. Seal at once. Serve as a spread on bread or as a meat or poultry accompaniment.

YIELD: 10 jars, ½ pint each

RHUBARB AND LEMON CONSERVE

2½ quarts (2½ to 3 pounds) diced, fresh rhubarb
5½ cups sugar
⅓ cup fresh lemon juice
4 cinnamon sticks, each 2 inches long
___
1 cup seedless raisins
1 cup chopped pecans
2 tablespoons grated lemon rind

Place the first 4 ingredients in a 4-quart saucepan. Mix well. Cook, uncovered, over medium heat 1 hour or until the mixture has thickened, stirring frequently to prevent scorching. Skim off scum.

Stir in remaining ingredients and heat thoroughly. Remove and discard cinnamon. Ladle marmalade into hot, sterilized jars. Seal airtight immediately. Serve as marmalade or as a relish, since this is not as sweet as most marmalades.

YIELD: 6 jars, ½ pint each

SPICED PEACH AND PINEAPPLE MARMALADE

9 cups (about 5 pounds) thinly sliced peaches
½ cup fresh orange juice
Rind of 1 medium-size orange, thinly sliced
1 cup crushed pineapple

7 cups sugar
¼ teaspoon salt
1 teaspoon whole cloves

Place first 4 ingredients in saucepan. Bring to boiling point. Stir in sugar and salt. Tie cloves in a cloth bag and add. Stir and cook, uncovered, until mixture has thickened (40 to 50 minutes). Remove and discard spice bag. Ladle into hot, sterilized jars. Seal at once.

YIELD: 8 jars, ½ pint each

PEAR AND PINEAPPLE JAM

2 cups fully ripened, crushed pears
2 cups crushed, canned pineapple
⅛ teaspoon salt

3 cinnamon sticks, each 2 inches long
1 box (1¾ ounces) powdered pectin

5 cups sugar
½ teaspoon grated lemon rind
3 to 4 drops yellow food coloring

Combine the first 5 ingredients in a 4-quart saucepan. Cook over high heat, stirring constantly, until mixture comes to a full rolling boil. (A full rolling boil cannot be stirred down.) Boil 1 minute. Stir in sugar.

Bring fruit to a full rolling boil and boil hard 1 minute, stirring constantly. Blend in lemon rind. Remove jam from heat and skim off foam. Remove and discard cinnamon. Cool and stir 7 minutes to prevent pineapple from floating.

Add enough yellow coloring (3 to 4 drops) to give jam an attractive yellow color. Quickly ladle into hot, sterilized jars, leaving ½-inch space at the top. Seal airtight immediately.

YIELD: 7 jars, ½ pint each

SPICED PINEAPPLE JAM

1 can (20 ounces) crushed pineapple
Water
1 box (1¾ ounces) powdered pectin
2 tablespoons mixed pickling spice
3 cups sugar

Measure pineapple and add water to make 3¼ cups. Place in a 6-quart saucepan with pectin. Mix well. Tie spices in a cheesecloth bag and add to pineapple. Stir and cook over high heat until mixture comes to a hard boil.

Add sugar all at one time. Mix well. Bring to a full rolling boil and boil hard 1 minute. (A full rolling boil cannot be stirred down.) Remove and discard spice bag and ladle into hot, sterilized jars. Seal airtight immediately.

YIELD: 4 jars, ½ pint each

RHUBARB AND ORANGE JAM

6 cups (1½ pounds) diced, fresh
  rhubarb
2 cups diced, peeled oranges
4½ cups sugar
⅛ teaspoon salt

1 teaspoon ground cinnamon
¼ teaspoon ground cloves

Place all ingredients except spices in 4-quart saucepan. Stir and cook over low heat 40 minutes or until mixture has thickened. Add spices and cook 2 more minutes. Ladle into hot, sterilized jars. Seal with paraffin and cover with lids.

YIELD: 7 glasses, 6 ounces each

SPICED TOMATO JAM

2½ pounds (about 8 medium)
  fresh tomatoes
1 teaspoon grated lemon rind
¼ cup fresh lemon juice
¼ teaspoon salt
1 tablespoon mixed pickling spice
1 box (1¾ ounces) powdered pectin
5 cups sugar

Place 2 to 3 tomatoes at a time in a sieve and dip in boiling water and then in cold water. Slip off the skins with a knife. Crush and place in a 6-quart saucepan. Simmer 10 minutes, uncovered, and measure. (There should be 3 cups.) Return to saucepan, add lemon rind, lemon juice, and salt. Tie spices in a cheesecloth bag and add. Stir in pectin and bring to a hard boil over high heat. Stir in all the sugar at once. Bring to a full rolling boil and boil hard 1 minute, stirring constantly. (A full rolling boil cannot be stirred down.) Let stand 5 minutes. Remove and discard spice bag and ladle jam into hot, sterilized jars. Seal airtight.

YIELD: 6 jars, ½ pint each

CHERVIL JELLY

3 tablespoons chervil leaves
2½ cups boiling water
¼ cup cider vinegar
1 box (1¾ ounces) powdered pectin
4½ cups sugar
3 to 4 drops green food coloring

Place chervil and boiling water in a bowl. Cover and let stand 15 minutes. Strain into a 2½-quart saucepan. Add vinegar and pectin. Bring to a rapid boil over high heat. Stir in all sugar at one time.

Bring to a full rolling boil and boil hard 1 minute, stirring constantly. (A full rolling boil cannot be stirred down.) Remove jelly from heat and stir in food coloring. Skim off foam with a metal spoon and pour jelly into hot, sterilized jars. Seal airtight immediately.

TARRAGON JELLY

In the above recipe, replace chervil with the same amount of tarragon leaves.

YIELD: 3 jars, ½ pint each

CINNAMON-RHUBARB JELLY

3 pounds (3 quarts) diced, fresh rhubarb
1½ cups water
1 box (1¾ ounces) powdered pectin
6 cinnamon sticks, each 2 inches long
2 drops red food coloring
4½ cups sugar

Cook rhubarb with water in a covered saucepan 15 to 20 minutes or until mushy. Remove from heat and strain as directed in Step 4 in "Directions for Making Jelly" *(see above)*. Measure 3 cups juice. If there is insufficient juice, add water to make 3 cups. Pour into a 5-quart saucepan. Stir in pectin and cinnamon. Cook over high heat until mixture comes to a full rolling boil, stirring constantly. Add the food coloring and all the sugar at one time. Mix well. Bring to a full rolling boil. Boil hard 1 minute, stirring constantly. Remove from heat and skim off foam with a metal spoon. Pour into hot, sterilized jars, leaving a ½-inch space at the top of each jar. Seal airtight immediately.

YIELD: 4 jars, ½ pint each

SPICED GRAPE JELLY

3½ pounds (3½ quarts) Concord grapes
1½ cups water
1 box (1¾ ounces) powdered pectin
7 cups (3 pounds) sugar
1 teaspoon ground allspice
½ teaspoon ground cloves

Cook grapes with water in a covered saucepan. Strain as directed in Step 4 in "Directions for Making Jelly" *(see above)*. Measure 5 cups juice and pour into a 5-quart kettle. Add pectin. Cook over high heat, stirring constantly, until mixture comes to a full rolling boil. Boil rapidly 1 minute, stirring constantly. Add sugar and spices. Boil again rapidly 1 minute, stirring constantly. Remove jelly from heat, skim off foam, and pour into hot, sterilized jars, leaving a ½-inch space at the top of each. Seal airtight.

CARDAMOM JELLY

Replace allspice and cloves in the above recipe with 1 teaspoon ground cardamom or cardamom to taste.

YIELD: 10 jars, ½ pint each

SPICED GRAPE JELLY
(USING BOTTLED GRAPE JUICE)

3½ cups sugar
2 cups (1 pint) bottled grape juice
1 cup water
1½ teaspoons whole allspice
½ teaspoon whole cloves
2 cinnamon sticks, each 2 inches long
1 box (1¾ ounces) powdered pectin

Measure sugar and set aside. Pour grape juice and water into a 5-quart kettle. Tie cloves and allspice in a cheesecloth bag and add. Stir in cinnamon and pectin. Stir and cook over high heat until the mixture comes to a full rolling boil. (A full rolling boil cannot be stirred down). Add sugar all at one time. Mix well. Bring to a full rolling boil. Stir and boil 1 minute. Remove jelly from heat and skim off foam with a metal spoon. Remove and discard spice bag and cinnamon sticks. Ladle jelly into hot, sterilized jars, leaving a ½-inch space at the top of each. Seal airtight immediately.

YIELD: 3 jars, ½ pint each

FRESH TOMATO AND ORANGE MARMALADE RELISH

5½ pounds (about 23 small) firm, ripe
    tomatoes
About 5 pounds sugar
3 medium-size navel oranges
2 medium-size lemons
2 cinnamon sticks, each 2 inches long
1 tablespoon whole cloves
3 ounces diced, crystallized ginger

Dip tomatoes in hot water and then into cold water. Remove and discard skins. Place a colander in a bowl and slice the tomatoes into it so that any juice will be caught in the bowl. Weigh the tomatoes plus ½ cup of the juice. This weight should be about 5 pounds. Put into a 10-quart kettle. Add sugar to equal the weight of tomatoes and juice.

Slice oranges and lemon about ¹⁄₁₆ inch thick, then cut the slices into quarters. Measure. (There should be 3¾ cups oranges and 1¼ cups lemons.) Add to tomatoes and sugar. Tie cloves in a cheesecloth bag and add together with the cinnamon. Mix well. Bring to boiling over high heat. Reduce to moderate and cook until fruit is clear and juice has been reduced by one-half, about 60 to 70 minutes, stirring occasionally.

Add ginger 10 minutes before cooking time is up. Remove and discard spice bag and cinnamon and ladle into hot, sterilized jars. Seal at once. Serve as a relish with meats or as a spread on bread.

YIELD: Approximately 11 jars, ½ pint
    each

MEATS

"MANKIND," says a Chinese manuscript, "for the first seventy-thousand ages ate their meat raw, clawing or biting it from the living animal just as they do in Abyssinia to this day."

—CHARLES LAMB, "Dissertation on Roast Pig"

From those early challenging days when raw meat was devoured to today's Steak au Poivre,* Veal Scallopine,* and Rosemary Shish Kebabs,* almost everyone has relished the taste of meat. Correctly cooked and imaginatively seasoned, it has great appeal.

With few exceptions (broiling beef steak, for instance), meat should be cooked slowly, using low to moderate temperatures during the cooking period. Like all other protein foods, meat is toughened by prolonged heating at high temperatures. There is everything to be gained from low-temperature meat cookery: not only is the meat more tender, but it is juicier, more flavorful, and will shrink less, thus providing more edible meat per pound purchased. As a bonus, you will lessen the time spent watching, basting and fussing, as well as being spared the chore of scrubbing a fat-spattered oven or burned skillet.

The meat recipes included in the following sections have all been carefully tested, and ingredient lists specify the animal and cut that should be used. Cooking temperatures and approximate cooking time are given in each recipe but, for your convenience, timetables for cooking meats are listed below. Methods of braising, broiling and roasting follow.

For information on spicing meats, see below. See also Marinating Techniques.*

*An asterisk after the name of a dish indicates that the recipe for this dish appears in the book. Consult the Index for the page number.

314

SIMPLIFIED CHART FOR SPICING MEATS

Any and every meat is complemented by one or more spices and herbs. It is important to know what the possible combinations are, however. Certain spices can be added to all meats; others go only with those meats (given in parentheses) following spice. A dagger (†) marking a spice or herb indicates a particularly pungent seasoning, to be used lightly for the most pleasing effect.

' Allspice	†Mint (lamb)
†Bay leaf	Mixed pickling spice
Caraway	Mustard
Celery seed	†Nutmeg (veal)
Chili powder	Onion
†Cinnamon (beef)	†Oregano
Cloves (pork)	Paprika
Coriander (beef, pork)	Pepper, black or white
Cumin	†Pepper, red
Curry powder	Poultry seasoning
Dill (veal, lamb)	†Rosemary (veal, lamb)
†Fennel (veal, pork, lamb)	†Saffron (veal)
†Garlic	†Sage
†Ginger	Tarragon (lamb)
†Mace (veal)	Thyme
Marjoram	

BROILING

Broiling may be done on top of the range, in the oven broiler, or over a charcoal grill. Slash edges of fat in several places to prevent curling. To cook "rare," use a high temperature for a short time. To cook "well-done," start at a high temperature to sear the meat to retain the juices, but then reduce the heat and cook more slowly for a longer time to permit the interior to cook. Do not add salt during the early stages of cooking, since this would tend to draw out the juices.

PAN BROILING

Pan broiling is suitable for slices of meat thinner than 1 inch. Preheat a heavy skillet over high heat. Rub in bottom of skillet just enough fat to keep meat from sticking. Lay the meat in the hot skillet until one side has been seared. Turn and sear the other side. Then reduce heat and continue cooking, turning occasionally, at the temperature and for the time required for the degree of "doneness" desired.

OVEN BROILING

Since oven broilers vary from range to range, consult the directions given with your particular stove. Some broilers have provisions for adjusting the temperature of the heat source, while others require that the rack be raised or lowered to adjust the speed of cooking. Both the broiler oven and the broiler pan should be preheated. The rack should be greased with some of the fat of the meat to prevent sticking. Usually, the top of the meat is placed between 2 and 4 inches below the flame or electric heating element. Broil one side until brown. Season. Turn with tongs to prevent piercing the meat. Broil the other side. Season. Serve at once on a heated platter. (Directions for grilling are same as those given for oven broiling.)

TIMETABLE FOR BROILING MEAT
(In a preheated oven broiler)

Cut	Thickness (inches)	Approximate minutes per side
Beef steaks: (club, rib, T-bone, porterhouse, small sirloin, strip steak, filet mignon)	1	5 (rare)
		6 (medium)
		7 to 8 (well-done)
	1½	8 to 9 (rare)
		10 (medium)
		12 to 13 (well-done)
	2	16 (rare)
		18 (medium)
		20 to 21 (well-done)
Large sirloin	1	10 (rare)
		12 (medium)
		14 (well-done)
	1½	12 (rare)
		14 (medium)
		16 (well-done)
Lamb chops, rib and loin	1	5 (medium)
		6 (well-done)
Ham and picnic slices (cook before eating)	½	4 (well-done)
	1	9 (well-done)
	1½	10 to 15 (well-done)
Ham and picnic slices (fully cooked)	½	3 to 5 (*do not turn*)
	¾	3
	1	5

ROASTING

Place roast on a rack in a shallow pan, fat-side up so that it will be self-basting. Do not add water, oil, or fat. If a meat thermometer is available, insert its bulb into the center of the thickest part of the meat, being sure that it does not touch either the bone or fat. Cook, uncovered, at a low temperature (325° F.) to conserve nutriments and to minimize loss of weight. If a meat thermometer is used, the meat will be done when the thermometer reads the temperature shown in the table below. Approximate cooking times for roasting various cuts of beef, lamb, pork, and veal are given below.

TIMETABLE FOR ROASTING BEEF AT 325° F.
(Starting from refrigerator temperature)

Cut	Ready-to-cook weight (pounds)	Approximate roasting time (hours)	Meat thermometer reading (°F.)
Rib roast, standing (bone-in)	4	1¾	140 (rare)
		2¼	160 (medium)
		3	170 (well-done)
	6	3¼	140 (rare)
		3¾	160 (medium)
		4¼	170 (well-done)
	8	3½	140 (rare)
		4½	160 (medium)
		5	170 (well-done)
Rolled rib roast	4 (4½ to 5 inches wide)	2¾	140 (rare)
		3¼	160 (medium)
		3½	170 (well-done)
	6 (5½ to 6½ inches wide)	3½	140 (rare)
		4¼	160 (medium)
		4¾	170 (well-done)
Rump roast (bone-in) (Also see "Braising")	4	2½	140 (rare)
		3	160 (medium)
		3¼	170 (well-done)
Rump roast, rolled (Also see "Braising")	4	2¼ to 3	140 (rare)
		3 to 3½	160 (medium)
		3¼ to 3¾	170 (well-done)
Sirloin tip	4	2¼	140 (rare)
		2¾	160 (medium)
		3¼	170 (well-done)

NOTE: A thin roast will require less roasting time than will a thick one of the same weight.

TIMETABLE FOR BRAISING BEEF
(Starting from refrigerator temperature)

Cut	Ready-to-cook weight (pounds)	Approximate cooking time, after browning (hours)
Pot roast (eye of round, heel of round, rump, or sirloin tip)	3	3
	5	3½
Pot roast or steak (round or chuck)	2 to 4 (1 to 2 inches thick)	2½
	2 to 4 (½ inch thick)	1 to 1½
Flank steak (rolled with stuffing)	1½ to 2	2
Short ribs	2 x 2 x 4 inches	2

HINTS ON BAKING HAM

Each of the following recipes calls for the use of a specific weight and type of ham. If another weight or type is used, the baking time, and the meat thermometer temperature, should be changed to that shown in the timetable.

We recommend that all commercial hams be baked with dry heat (uncovered) in a slow oven (325° F.). The dry heat gives the ham a baked, rather than a boiled, flavor, while the low temperature prevents loss of weight and nutrients and permits the interior to be cooked before the outside is overdone.

The use of a meat thermometer is the most accurate method of determining when a ham is done. The thermometer should be inserted into the middle of the thickest part of the ham, but must not touch the bone.

In order that the ham may be self-basting, it should be placed on the rack with its fat-side up. Therefore, a half ham should be set on its cut end.

Whether or not ham is scored after baking with the glaze or before the glaze is applied, depends upon your objective. Since fat melts and oozes out of the scores during baking, it is inclined to break or spot the glaze. Hams scored and studded with cloves after the baking period is completed are likely to be more attractive and taste almost as good since, even with pre-scoring, the flavor of the glaze and cloves does not penetrate much over ½ inch. (This is a trick taught the authors by one of New York's finest caterers.)

When brown sugar is used for the glaze, all lumps should be crushed before measuring. Then it should be packed into the measuring cup tightly enough to maintain its shape after removal from the cup.

TIMETABLE FOR BAKING HAM AT 325° F.
(Starting from refrigerator temperature)

Type	Ready-to-cook weight (pounds)	Approximate baking time (hours)	Meat thermometer reading (° F.)
Fully Cooked Ham			
Bone-in, whole	8 to 10	2¼ to 2½	130
"	10 to 12	2½ to 3	130
Bone-in, half	5 to 8	1½ to 2¼	130
Boneless, whole	10 to 12	2½ to 2¾	130
Boneless, half	5 to 8	1½ to 2¼	130
Cook-Before-Eating Ham			
Bone-in, whole	8 to 10	3¼ to 3½	160
"	10 to 12	3½ to 4	160
"	12 to 15	4 to 4½	160
Bone-in, half	6 to 8	2½ to 3½	160
Bone-in, smoked picnic	4 to 6	2½ to 3	170
Smoked boneless			
Shoulder butt	2	2	170
"	3	3	170

TIMETABLE FOR ROASTING LAMB AT 325° F.
(Starting from refrigerator temperature)

Cut	Ready-to-cook weight (pounds)	Approximate roasting time (hours)	Meat thermometer reading (° F.)
Leg	6	3	175 (medium)
		3½	180 (well-done)
	8	4	175 (medium
		4½	180 (well-done)
Crown roast	5	3¾	180 (well-done)
Shoulder	3	2¾	180 (well-done)
(bone-in)	5	3¼	180 (well-done)
Shoulder (boned	3	2¼	180 (well-done)
and rolled)	5	3	180 (well-done)

TIMETABLE FOR ROASTING PORK AT 325° F.
(Starting from refrigerator temperature)

Cut	Ready-to-cook weight (pounds)	Approximate cooking time (hours)
Loin	3	2¾
	5	3
	8	3½
	12	4
Fresh ham (leg)	8	4½
	10	5½
	14	6½
Shoulder (bone-in)	5	4
	8	5
Shoulder (boneless)	4	3 to 3½
	6	4¾

TIMETABLE FOR ROASTING VEAL AT 325° F.
(Starting from refrigerator temperature)

Cut	Ready-to-cook weight (pounds)	Approximate roasting time (hours)	Meat thermometer reading (° F.)
Leg (bone-in)	5	3½	180
	8	4½	"
Loin or rib roast	5	2¾	"
	8	3½	"
Shoulder (bone-in)	5	3½	"
	8	4	"
Shoulder (boned and rolled)	4	3½	"
	8	4½	"

NOTE: Cover veal roast with thin strips of salt pork or fat bacon if it lacks a fat covering.

AMOUNTS OF MEAT TO BUY
Boneless meat— ¼ pound per serving (boneless roast, ham, and ground meat)
Bone-in meat—½ pound per serving (leg of lamb, chops, rib roast, and steaks)
Bony meat—¾ to 1 pound per serving (spareribs, short ribs)

BEEF

CAJUN ROAST BEEF

The Cajun people of Louisiana and Eastern Texas prefer this method of preparing both the choice and cheaper cuts of beef. The gravy is so good that we would almost be satisfied to have it by itself over rice.

¼ cup instant minced onion
¼ teaspoon instant minced garlic
1 tablespoon salt
1½ teaspoons ground black pepper
¾ teaspoon ground red pepper
3 tablespoons water
¼ cup cider vinegar

5-pound boneless beef roast (eye of
    round, rump, *or* rolled rib)
1 teaspoon cornstarch
1 teaspoon water

Combine the first 7 ingredients and let stand 5 minutes to soften onion and garlic. With a paring knife, cut 1-inch slits about 1½ inches apart in all sides of the meat, sticking the knife to the middle of the roast. Pry open slits and fill each with about ½ teaspoon of the mixture, using the point of a teaspoon. Cover and marinate overnight in the refrigerator.

Place roast on a rack in a baking or roasting pan. Cover with foil or roaster cover. Bake in a preheated slow oven (325° F.) 3½ hours, or until meat is tender, removing cover 40 minutes before cooking time is up to permit meat to brown.

Remove roast to a platter. Skim excess fat from pan drippings with a large spoon. Blend cornstarch with the 1 teaspoon water. Add to drippings. Stir and cook until gravy is slightly thick. Serve meat with rice or potatoes and gravy.

YIELD: 12 to 14 servings

CARAWAY SAUERKRAUT WITH POT ROAST

Serve this with Potato Dumplings* or buttered noodles.

3- to 5-pound pot roast (rump, shoulder,
    or round beef roast)
2 tablespoons beef suet *or* shortening

1 cup water
2 bay leaves
¼ cup instant minced onion
2 teaspoons salt
¼ teaspoon ground black pepper

1½ tablespoons flour
2 tablespoons water

3 cups canned sauerkraut
1½ cups diced apples
½ cup water
½ cup sauerkraut juice
¾ teaspoon caraway seed

Brown meat in beef suet or shortening in a Dutch oven or heavy saucepan. Add the next 5 ingredients. Cover, bring to boiling point, reduce heat and simmer 3 to 3½ hours, or until meat is tender.

Mix flour with water to a smooth paste and blend with gravy. Stir and cook ½ minute. In the meanwhile, combine remaining ingredients in a 1½-quart saucepan. Cover and cook slowly 15 minutes. Serve with sliced pot roast.

YIELD: 6 to 10 servings

MARINATED SHORT RIBS OF BEEF

3 pounds short ribs of beef
1 tablespoon powdered mustard
2 tablespoons water

1 tablespoon instant minced onion
1 tablespoon fresh lemon juice

2 tablespoons wine vinegar
¼ cup salad *or* olive oil
1 tablespoon salt
1 teaspoon ground black pepper
1½ teaspoons chili powder
½ teaspoon instant minced onion
¼ teaspoon cayenne

Trim excess fat from beef and cut into serving-size pieces, 2 x 2 x 4 inches. Set aside. Mix mustard with water and let stand 10 minutes for flavor to develop. Add remaining ingredients. Pour over meat.

Cover and marinate in the refrigerator overnight or about 12 hours. Turn meat in marinade occasionally. Place meat in a roasting pan or casserole, saving marinade. Cook, uncovered, in a preheated hot oven (450° F.) 20 minutes.

Pour in marinade. Cover and cook in a slow oven (325° F.) 1½ to 2 hours, or until meat is tender. Baste with marinade occasionally. Thicken gravy with 2 tablespoons flour mixed until smooth with 3 tablespoons water. Stir and cook 1 to 2 minutes or until gravy has thickened.

YIELD: 4 servings

SAUERBRATEN

No spice cookbook would be complete without a good recipe for German-style sauerbraten. Remember that this dish starts with a one, two, or better still, three-day marinating period. Potato Dumplings are the classic accompaniment.*

4- to 5-pound eye of round roast
1 tablespoon powdered mustard
3 tablespoons water

1 bay leaf
1 teaspoon whole black pepper
1½ teaspoons salt
1½ teaspoons poultry seasoning
½ teaspoon tarragon leaves

½ teaspoon instant minced garlic
2 tablespoons onion flakes
2 tablespoons light-brown sugar
1 cup water
1 beef bouillon cube
½ cup red wine vinegar

2 tablespoons shortening
Flour
½ cup sour cream (optional)

Place beef in a bowl just large enough to hold it and the marinade. Mix mustard with the 3 tablespoons water and let stand 10 minutes. Mix with the next 11 ingredients in a saucepan, bring to boiling point and pour over meat. Cool. Cover and refrigerate 24 to 48 hours, turning meat occasionally to marinate uniformly.

Remove beef from marinade and wipe dry with paper towel, saving marinade. Brown in shortening in a Dutch oven or heavy saucepan. Pour in marinade, cover, and cook in a preheated slow oven (325° F.) 3 to 3½ hours, or until meat is tender; or, if desired, cook over low heat the same length of time.

Remove meat to a platter. Strain gravy and thicken. For each cup of gravy, blend 1½ tablespoons flour with 2 tablespoons water. Add to gravy and cook 1 minute or until thickened. If desired, stir in sour cream. Serve gravy with meat.

YIELD: 8 to 10 servings

VEGETABLE POT ROAST

3- to 4-pound pot roast (rump, heel of round, *or* sirloin tip)
1 tablespoon shortening *or* beef suet
2 teaspoons salt
½ teaspoon ground black pepper
About ½ cup water
1 small bay leaf
____
¼ teaspoon instant minced garlic
½ cup chopped green pepper
½ cup diced celery
1 cup diced potatoes
1 cup chopped onion
1 cup sliced carrots
2 cups diced, fresh tomatoes

Brown roast on all sides in shortening or suet in a Dutch oven or heavy saucepan. Sprinkle meat with salt and black pepper. Add water and bay leaf. Cover and simmer 2 to 2¼ hours, or until meat is almost tender, adding additional water if necessary. Add remaining ingredients. Cook, covered, 1 hour or until meat is tender and vegetables are soft. Slice meat and serve with vegetables and juice spooned over each serving.

YIELD: 6 to 8 servings

GLAZED CORNED BEEF

5 pounds corned beef (brisket)
Water (to cover)
Whole cloves
4 teaspoons powdered mustard
2 tablespoons water
____
2 teaspoons cider vinegar
¼ cup dark corn syrup
¼ teaspoon ground allspice

Place corned beef along with enough water to cover it in a 4-quart saucepan. Bring to boiling point, reduce heat, and simmer, covered, 4 hours or until meat is tender. Remove meat from water and drain. Place on a rack in a shallow baking pan, fat-side up. Score fat in 1-inch squares. Stud each square with a whole clove. Set aside.

Mix mustard with water and let stand 10 minutes for flavor to develop. Add remaining ingredients and mix well. Spoon half of the glaze over the clove-studded corned beef. Bake in a preheated moderate oven (350° F.) 20 minutes. Remove meat from the oven and spoon remaining glaze over the top. Bake 20 additional minutes, or until corned beef is glazed and browned.

YIELD: 8 servings

CORNED BEEF PATTIES

1 teaspoon powdered mustard
1 tablespoon water
12-ounce can corned beef
____
¼ cup minced green pepper
¼ teaspoon salt
¼ teaspoon ground black pepper
¼ cup fine, dry bread crumbs
⅓ cup mayonnaise
1 large egg, beaten

Flour
1 to 2 tablespoons shortening

Mix mustard with water and let stand 10 minutes. Chop corned beef fine and mix with mustard and next 6 ingredients. Shape into eight 3 x ½-inch patties. Dip in flour. Brown on both sides in enough shortening to prevent sticking to pan. Serve in warm, split hamburger buns or on a plate with tomato sauce.

YIELD: 8 servings

CORNED BEEF AND VEGETABLE CASSEROLE

2 cups cooked, diced potatoes
2 cups cooked, sliced carrots
1 cup cooked, sliced celery
⅓ cup onion flakes
1½ teaspoons salt
1 teaspoon thyme leaves
¼ teaspoon ground black pepper
¼ teaspoon instant minced garlic
___
1 can (12 ounces) corned beef
¼ cup vegetable cooking water
¾ cup soft bread crumbs
2 tablespoons butter or margarine, melted

Combine the first 8 ingredients and turn half into a 1½-quart casserole. Break corned beef into small pieces over the vegetables. Cover with remaining vegetables. Add vegetable water. Combine bread crumbs and butter or margarine and sprinkle over the top. Bake in a preheated moderate oven (350° F.) 45 minutes or until browned. Serve hot with a salad.

YIELD: 6 servings

BEEF BOURGUIGNONNE

A delicious French stew. We like to add just ¼ cup of wine minutes before the

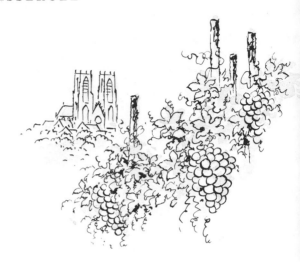

stew is removed from the heat. To our taste, it perks up the flavor agreeably.

2 pounds chuck or top round of beef
¼ cup flour
¼ cup (½ stick) butter or margarine
___
1½ teaspoons salt (or to taste)
1 small bay leaf
½ teaspoon instant minced garlic
¼ cup chopped parsley
½ cup thinly sliced carrots
2 cups water or consommé
1 cup Burgundy or other dry red wine
___
12 small, fresh white onions
¾ teaspoon thyme leaves
½ teaspoon ground black pepper
1 cup sliced fresh or canned mushrooms
1 tablespoon butter or margarine
¼ cup Burgundy or other dry red wine (optional)

Trim off and discard excess fat from meat. Cut meat into 1-inch cubes. Roll in flour. Melt butter or margarine in a heavy 2-quart saucepan. Add meat, stir, and cook until browned. Stir in all remaining flour and cook 1 minute. Add the next

7 ingredients. Cover and simmer 1¾ hours or until meat is almost tender.

In the meantime, peel onions. Add, cover, and cook 30 minutes. Add thyme and black pepper. Sauté mushrooms in the 1 tablespoon butter or margarine and add. Cover and cook 5 minutes. If you wish to give the dish a fresher flavor, add the remaining ¼ cup wine 2 minutes before removing from heat. Serve hot over mashed potatoes, rice, or noodles.

YIELD: 6 servings

STEAK AU POIVRE

3½- to 4-pound sirloin steak, cut 1½
   inches thick
3 tablespoons cracked black pepper
1 teaspoon salt
¼ cup (½ stick) butter or margarine
¼ cup olive or salad oil
¼ cup chicken or veal stock
2 tablespoons white wine or brandy

Slash the fat around edges of steak at 2-inch intervals so edges will not curl in broiling. Rub each side with 1½ table-spoons black pepper, pushing it in with the ball of hand. Sprinkle both sides lightly with salt. Heat butter or margarine and oil in a 12-inch skillet.

Add steak and sear on each side, then cook 5 to 7 minutes on each side. (Cooking time depends upon the degree of rareness desired.) Transfer steak to a serving platter. Drain off all liquid but 2 tablespoons. Add stock and wine or brandy. Heat and pour over steak. Serve at once.

YIELD: 5 servings

BLACK PEPPER STEAK

To each pound tender steak, cut ¾ to 1 inch thick, rub ¼ teaspoon coarsely ground black pepper into one side of the meat. Place in a preheated broiler 4 inches from the source of heat, with oven control set to broil. Broil 5 to 7 minutes or as desired. Turn steak and sprinkle with additional coarsely ground black pepper, ¼ teaspoon to each pound of meat. Broil as desired. Sprinkle with salt and serve at once.

YIELD: For each serving, allow about ⅓-
   to ½-pound boneless steak or ½-
   to ¾-pound bone-in steak.

BROILED STEAK WITH HERBED BUTTER

One 3- to 4-pound, 1 inch thick, sirloin, porterhouse or T-bone steak, or four
   ¾- to 1-pound club or rib steaks
___
Beef suet
¼ teaspoon thyme leaves
¼ teaspoon savory leaves
⅛ teaspoon powdered mustard
¼ cup (½ stick) soft butter or
   margarine

Slash the fat edge of steak at 2-inch intervals to prevent curling while broiling. Preheat broiler and broiling rack. Rub broiler rack with suet to prevent meat from sticking. Place steak on broiler and broil 5 to 8 minutes on each side. (Cooking time depends on thickness of steak, amount of bone, and degree of rareness desired.) While meat is cooking, blend 4 remaining ingredients. Place meat on a heated serving platter and spread with herbed butter. Serve at once.

YIELD: 4 servings

MEXICAN STEAK

3½- to 4½-pound sirloin steak, cut 2
   inches thick
½ teaspoon oregano leaves

4 medium-size onions, sliced
3 medium-size green peppers, sliced
4 strips bacon
Salt
Coarsely ground black pepper

Rub ¼ teaspoon oregano into each side of steak. Place on a broiler rack. Cover with 2 onions and 1½ green peppers. Top with 2 strips of bacon. Place under the broiler with oven control set to 400° F. (hot). Cook 10 minutes or until bacon is crisp. Remove from oven and spoon the cooked bacon, onions, and green peppers into a casserole. Place in oven to keep warm.

Turn meat and cover with remaining onions and green peppers. Top with remaining bacon. Broil 10 minutes or until bacon is crisp. Remove from oven and spoon onions and green peppers into the casserole. Return to oven to keep warm.

Increase broiler heat to broil and broil steak on both sides until brown. Place on cutting board or serving platter. Sprinkle both sides with salt and coarsely ground black pepper. Serve with the onions and green peppers and French fried potatoes.

YIELD: 5 to 6 servings

COUNTRY-STYLE STEAK WITH CURRY GRAVY

2 pounds boneless chuck *or* round
  steak
¼ cup flour
2 teaspoons salt
¼ teaspoon ground black pepper
2 tablespoons shortening
2 cups sliced onion

1 cup boiling water
½ cup sliced carrots
½ cup sliced celery

1 tablespoon flour
¾ teaspoon curry powder
½ teaspoon salt
Dash garlic powder

Trim excess fat from meat and discard it. Cut steak into serving-size pieces. Score meat or beat with a mallet on a board to break up fibers. Dredge in flour mixed with the 2 teaspoons salt and black pepper. Brown on both sides in shortening in a 10-inch skillet. Add onions, cover, and cook 10 minutes or until onions are limp. Add next 3 ingredients.

Cover and simmer 20 minutes or until meat is tender. Place steak and vegetables on a warm platter. Combine remaining ingredients and add to pan drippings. Stir and cook until gravy is thick. Serve over mashed potatoes or rice.

YIELD: 6 servings

HOME-STYLE STEAK

2 pounds round steak, cut ½ inch
  thick
1 teaspoon salt
Flour

⅓ cup onion flakes
¼ cup water
2 tablespoons shortening

½ cup water
½ cup canned tomatoes
1 beef bouillon cube
2 teaspoons paprika
Dash cayenne
¼ teaspoon ground black pepper

Cut steak into 6 serving-size pieces. Rub both sides with salt and sprinkle lightly with flour. Soften onion in the ¼ cup water and then sauté in shortening. Add meat and brown on both sides. Add remaining ingredients. Cover and cook until meat is tender, 35 to 40 minutes. Serve hot with mashed potatoes or rice.

YIELD: 6 servings

CHINESE-STYLE STEAK

Don't overcook the cucumbers if you'd capture the Chinese flavor and texture of this dish.

1½ pounds round *or* rump steak

¼ cup salad oil
2½ teaspoons salt
¼ teaspoon ground ginger
½ teaspoon ground black pepper

1 tablespoon instant minced onion
1 tablespoon water
1 tablespoon shortening
3 cups sliced unpeeled cucumbers
⅓ cup beef stock
2¼ teaspoons cornstarch

Cut steak across the grain into strips ¼ inch wide. Combine the next 4 ingredients and pour over meat. Soften onion in water and add. Let stand 1 hour. Melt shortening in a 10-inch skillet. Add beef and marinade. Cook, uncovered, until browned. Add cucumbers and stock

mixed with cornstarch. Cover and cook 5 minutes. Serve at once with hot cooked rice.

YIELD: 6 servings

STEAK IN SOUR CREAM SAUCE

2 pounds round steak
2 teaspoons salt
½ teaspoon ground black pepper
3 tablespoons butter *or* margarine
2 tablespoons flour

2 cups beef stock *or* 2 bouillon cubes
  and 2 cups boiling water
1 tablespoon instant minced onion
2 teaspoons paprika
⅛ teaspoon powdered mustard

½ cup sour cream

Cut beef into narrow strips ½ inch wide and 2 inches long. Rub with salt and black pepper. Brown in butter or margarine. Cover and cook slowly 10 minutes. Blend in flour. Add the next 4 ingredients. Stir and cook until mixture begins to thicken, about 2 minutes. Cover and simmer 10 minutes. Add sour cream. Mix well and heat (DO NOT BOIL). Serve over mashed potatoes or cooked rice.

YIELD: 6 servings

STEAK WITH GREEN PEPPER SAUCE

1 teaspoon powdered mustard
1 tablespoon water

1 teaspoon ground black pepper
2 tablespoons bacon drippings
2 tablespoons red wine vinegar
¾ cup chopped onion
¾ cup chopped green pepper

2 pounds round steak
1 can (6 ounces) tomato paste

Blend mustard with water and let stand 10 minutes to develop flavor. Add the next 5 ingredients and set aside. Score steak crisscross on both sides with a knife, being careful not to cut through the meat. Place meat in a pan, over which pour sauce. Let stand 3 hours. Remove meat and place in a shallow baking dish. Add tomato paste to the mixture and pour over meat. Bake, uncovered, in a preheated moderate oven (350° F.) 1 hour or until meat is tender.

YIELD: 6 servings

SWISS STEAK

1½ pounds round *or* flank steak
3 tablespoons flour

1 teaspoon salt
¼ teaspoon coarsely ground
    black pepper
⅟₁₆ teaspoon garlic powder

2 tablespoons shortening
1 cup hot water
3 tablespoons onion flakes
2 tablespoons flour
1 cup milk *or* water

Cut steak into 5 serving-size pieces. Pound with a mallet until meat is very thin. Dredge in the 3 tablespoons flour mixed with the next 3 ingredients. Brown

on both sides in hot shortening in a heavy 10-inch skillet. Add hot water and onion flakes. Cover and simmer 25 to 30 minutes or until meat is tender and most of the water has evaporated.

Remove meat to a warm serving platter. Blend the 2 tablespoons of flour in pan drippings. Add milk or water. Stir and cook 1 minute, or until of medium thickness. Serve hot with mashed potatoes or rice.

YIELD: 5 servings

BEEFSTEAK-CHEESE ROLLS
(IN TOMATO SAUCE)

1 can (6 ounces) tomato paste
1 cup water
1 tablespoon light-brown sugar
2 tablespoons cider vinegar
¼ cup chopped onion
¼ cup chopped green pepper
1¼ teaspoons salt
¼ teaspoon ground black pepper
1 teaspoon oregano leaves

6 strips of sharp Cheddar cheese,
    each 3 x ½ x ½ inches
6 cubed steaks, ¼ inch thick
Shortening

Combine the first 9 ingredients in a saucepan. Cook slowly until thickened, about 10 minutes. Place a cheese strip across the center of each steak. Roll up and fasten ends with toothpicks. Brown on all sides in a little hot shortening. Add tomato sauce. Simmer 10 minutes. Serve on rice, noodles, or spaghetti.

YIELD: 6 servings

ROLLED CUBED STEAKS, WESTERN STYLE

½ cup chopped green pepper
2 tablespoons shortening

3 tablespoons instant minced onion
1 medium-size pimiento, chopped
1 can (6 ounces) tomato paste
½ cup chopped ripe (black) olives
¼ cup grated, sharp American cheese
¼ cup fine, dry bread crumbs
1½ teaspoons salt
2 teaspoons chili powder
¼ teaspoon ground black pepper

4 cubed minute steaks
Salt
Ground black pepper
½ cup water

Sauté green pepper in shortening. Remove from heat and add next 9 ingredients. Mix well. Sprinkle meat with salt and black pepper. Divide the stuffing in half and place an equal amount of one of the halves on each of the steaks. Roll up. Fasten ends with toothpicks.

Place rolls, folded-side down, in a 10 x 6 x 2-inch baking pan. Combine the remaining half of stuffing with the ½ cup water. Pour over meat. Bake, uncovered, in a preheated moderate oven (350° F.) 1 hour or until meat is tender. Serve hot with rice or potatoes.

YIELD: 4 servings

ROLLED FLANK STEAK WITH CELERY STUFFING

2 pounds flank steak
1 teaspoon salt
¼ teaspoon ground black pepper

2 tablespoons instant minced onion
½ cup finely chopped celery
¼ cup (½ stick) butter *or* margarine
2 cups soft bread crumbs
1½ teaspoons salt
½ teaspoon ground thyme
¼ teaspoon ground black pepper

1 tablespoon shortening
¾ cup boiling water
1 tablespoon cornstarch
1 tablespoon water
1/10 teaspoon ground ginger
1/16 teaspoon garlic powder

Score steak. Mix salt with the ¼ teaspoon black pepper and rub into both sides of meat. Combine the next 7 ingredients and spread uniformly over meat. Roll in jelly-roll fashion, starting from the long side. Tie in place with string or fasten end with skewers. Sprinkle lightly with flour and brown on all sides in shortening.

Place on a rack in a Dutch oven or baking dish. Add water. Cover and cook slowly 1½ hours or bake in a preheated slow oven (325° F.) 2 hours. Mix remaining ingredients, add to pan juices, and cook 1 minute or until thickened. To serve, place meat on platter, cut strings, and slice crosswise. Serve with gravy.

YIELD: 6 servings

STUFFED BEEF ROLLS

6 cubed minute steaks, cut ¼ inch thick
⅓ cup flour
1½ teaspoons salt
¼ teaspoon ground black pepper

3 cups croutons (toasted bread cubes)
3 tablespoons onion flakes
1½ tablespoons parsley flakes
1 teaspoon celery seed
¾ teaspoon salt
___
1½ cups beef stock
1½ tablespoons flour
3 tablespoons water
Salt

Dredge steak in the ⅓ cup flour mixed with the 1½ teaspoons salt and black pepper and pound it into the steak with a mallet or wooden potato masher. Combine the next 5 ingredients with ⅓ cup of the meat stock. Divide the mixture into 6 equal parts and spread one on each steak. Roll up and fasten ends with toothpicks. Brown in 2 tablespoons shortening. Add remaining stock.

Bake 1 hour or until tender in a preheated moderate oven (350° F.), basting 4 times. Remove beef rolls to serving platter and keep warm. Blend the 1½ tablespoons flour with water until smooth and add to pan drippings. Stir and cook 1 minute or until of desired thickness. Add salt to taste. Serve over beef rolls.

YIELD: 6 servings

STUFFED STEAK ROLLS

4 minute steaks, ¼ inch thick
1 teaspoon salt
¼ teaspoon ground black pepper
___
2 tablespoons instant minced onion
⅛ teaspoon instant minced garlic
1 teaspoon chili powder
½ cup finely chopped celery
½ cup finely chopped dill pickle
___
1 cup (8 ounces) Spanish-type tomato sauce
2 tablespoons shortening
½ cup water

Sprinkle steaks with a mixture of salt and black pepper. Combine the next 5 ingredients and place a rounded tablespoon of the mixture on each steak. (Save stuffing that is left to use later.) Roll up tightly as for jelly roll. Fasten edges in place with toothpicks. Brown on all sides in shortening. Transfer to a casserole.

Combine remaining stuffing and tomato sauce with water. Pour over steak rolls. Cover. Bake in a preheated moderate oven (350° F.) 50 minutes or until meat is tender. Serve hot.

YIELD: 4 servings

HAMBURGERS IN VARIETY

It would be possible to write a whole cookbook on the various ways of preparing hamburgers. The following are a few of our favorite recipes.

Preground hamburger is almost certain to have a comparatively high fat content. Ground round is lowest in fat, highest in cost, and inclined to be a bit dry. Ground chuck is juiciest, most flavorful, and generally cheaper than ground round.

In mixing and shaping hamburger patties, handle as lightly and as little as possible. Too much handling makes them tough and dry.

And if in the past you have used only pepper and salt to season them, do branch out and try curry powder, chili powder, ground cumin, a pinch of ginger, herbs, and the dehydrated onion and garlic seasonings.

BLEU CHEESE HAMBURGERS

1½ pounds ground chuck
1½ teaspoons salt
¼ teaspoon ground black pepper
¼ teaspoon instant minced garlic
1 tablespoon instant minced onion

3 tablespoons finely crumbled
   Bleu cheese

Combine first 5 ingredients. Shape into 12 thin patties of equal size. Place 1½ teaspoons Bleu cheese in the center of each of 6 patties. Top with remaining patties. Pinch edges together to hold in cheese. Brown on both sides in a hot buttered skillet or over a slow-burning charcoal fire. Serve in hot hamburger buns.

YIELD: 6 servings

COMPANY HAMBURGERS

½ pound ground chuck
¼ pound ground lean pork
¼ pound ground veal
1 tablespoon instant minced onion
1 teaspoon salt
¼ teaspoon ground ginger
¼ teaspoon ground black pepper
¹⁄₁₆ teaspoon garlic powder

3 slices day-old bread, cubed
½ cup water

Place the first 8 ingredients in a bowl. Soak bread cubes in water 3 minutes, squeeze dry, and add to meat. Mix well, but lightly. Shape into 5 patties of equal size. Cook over medium heat in a heavy skillet 30 minutes to be sure pork is well cooked, turning to brown both sides. Serve between hamburger buns.

YIELD: 5 servings

CURRIED CHEESEBURGERS

1½ pounds ground chuck
2 tablespoons instant minced onion
1½ teaspoons salt
1 teaspoon curry powder
⅛ teaspoon garlic powder
¼ teaspoon ground black pepper

6 slices American cheese

Combine first 6 ingredients. Shape into 12 thin patties of equal size. Cut cheese slices about ¼ inch smaller than the diameter of meat patties and place one on each of 6 patties. Cover with remaining patties. Press edges together well to prevent cheese from oozing out. Brown on both sides in a hot greased skillet or cook over slow-burning charcoal fire. Serve between split, hot hamburger buns.

YIELD: 6 servings

DILL PICKLE HAMBURGERS

1½ pounds ground chuck

1 teaspoon salt
½ teaspoon garlic salt
¼ teaspoon ground black pepper
1 tablespoon instant minced onion

6 slices dill pickle, ⅛ inch thick

Shape meat into 12 thin patties of equal size and shape. Mix next 4 ingredients and sprinkle an equal amount over each patty, using all the mixture. Place a slice of dill pickle on center of each of 6 patties. Top with remaining patties, being sure to press edges together.

Pan broil 15 minutes, turning to brown both sides. Or, if desired, broil over slow-burning charcoal fire. Serve between split, warm hamburger buns.

YIELD: 6 servings

HAMBURGER CHEESEWICHES

1 pound ground, lean beef
Garlic salt
Onion salt
Ground black pepper
4 slices American cheese

Shape meat into 8 patties, ¼ inch thick and 4 inches in diameter. Sprinkle on both sides with garlic and onion salts and black pepper. Place a thin slice of cheese on each of 4 patties, over which place another patty, sandwich-style. Grill on both sides over hot embers about 10 minutes or until brown, turning once. (The time depends upon the heat of the fire.) Serve on toasted hamburger buns.

YIELD: 4 servings

HAMBURGER PUFFS

2 tablespoons instant minced onion
¾ teaspoon salt
1 teaspoon powdered mustard
½ teaspoon double-acting
    baking powder
¼ teaspoon ground black pepper
¼ teaspoon garlic powder
⅛ teaspoon ground ginger
_____
4 large eggs, separated
1 pound ground chuck
Tomato and Bacon Sauce*

Combine the first 7 ingredients. Add egg yolks and beat lightly. Blend in meat. Beat egg whites until they stand in soft, stiff peaks. Fold into the mixture. Drop from a tablespoon onto a greased heavy skillet. Cook over medium-low heat until well puffed over the top and browned underneath. Turn to brown other side. Serve with Tomato and Bacon Sauce.

YIELD: 8 servings

MUSHROOM BURGERS WITH HERB AND TOMATO SAUCE

3 tablespoons butter *or* margarine
¾ cup finely chopped, fresh
    mushrooms
_____
1½ pounds ground chuck
2 teaspoons salt
2 teaspoons instant minced onion
1 teaspoon Dijon-type prepared
    mustard
¼ teaspoon ground black pepper
⅛ teaspoon garlic powder
⅛ teaspoon ground ginger
_____
Herb and Tomato Sauce *(see below)*

Melt butter or margarine in a 10-inch skillet. Add mushrooms and sauté quickly, about 5 minutes. Remove mushrooms from skillet with a slotted spoon. Mix with the next 7 ingredients. Shape into 6 patties. Fry in pan drippings, turning to brown both sides. Remove from pan and keep warm while making sauce. Save pan drippings for sauce.

HERB AND TOMATO SAUCE

1 tablespoon butter *or* margarine
_____
1 tablespoon chopped green pepper
1 tablespoon chopped celery
½ cup diced, fresh mushrooms
_____

1 cup canned tomatoes
1 tablespoon instant minced onion
1 teaspoon salt
½ teaspoon oregano leaves
⅛ teaspoon garlic powder

1 teaspoon cornstarch
¼ cup water

Add butter or margarine to pan drippings. Heat and then add next 3 ingredients. Sauté until vegetables are tender. Stir in next 5 ingredients. Cover and cook 5 minutes. Blend cornstarch with water and add. Cook 5 minutes, stirring frequently. Serve hot over Mushroom Burgers.

YIELD: 6 servings

ORIENTAL-STYLE HAMBURGERS

1½ pounds ground chuck
2 tablespoons instant minced onion
½ teaspoon salt

½ cup soy sauce

½ teaspoon ground ginger
½ teaspoon ground black pepper
¼ teaspoon instant minced garlic

Mix beef with onion and salt. Shape into 6 patties of equal size. Place in a 10 x 6 x 2-inch baking pan. Combine remaining ingredients. Pour over meat and let stand at room temperature 2 hours.

Remove from sauce and broil 7 minutes on one side and 4 minutes on the other, or until browned on both sides. Serve between warm hamburger buns.

YIELD: 6 servings

POLISH HAMBURGERS

½ pound ground lean beef
½ pound ground veal
1 teaspoon salt
1 teaspoon instant minced onion
¼ teaspoon celery salt
¼ teaspoon ground black pepper
1/16 teaspoon ground nutmeg
¾ teaspoon fresh lemon juice
1 large egg, beaten

1 tablespoon soft butter or margarine
⅛ teaspoon ground black pepper

Combine the first 9 ingredients. Mix well. Shape into 4 patties. Mix butter or margarine with remaining black pepper. Spread an equal amount over each patty. Oven broil or pan fry until meat is done, turning to brown both sides. Serve in warmed hamburger buns, or as the meat course with potatoes and other vegetables.

YIELD: 4 patties

GRILLED SALISBURY STEAK

2 pounds ground chuck
2 teaspoons salt
½ teaspoon thyme leaves

¼ teaspoon ground black pepper
¼ teaspoon garlic powder
1 tablespoon instant minced onion
2 tablespoons minced green pepper
———
Flour
Melted butter, margarine, *or* salad oil
Herbed Tomato Sauce*

Mix first 7 ingredients together and shape into 6 steaks, ¾ inch thick. Sprinkle lightly with flour and broil in melted butter, margarine, or salad oil 15 to 18 minutes, turning to brown both sides. Serve with Herbed Tomato Sauce.

YIELD: 6 servings

HERBED MEAT BALLS

1 pound ground chuck
1½ teaspoons salt
———
½ teaspoon thyme leaves
⅛ teaspoon garlic powder
1/16 teaspoon cayenne
1 tablespoon parsley flakes
⅓ cup fine, dry bread crumbs
———
1 tablespoon shortening
———
1 beef bouillon cube
½ cup tomato juice
1 tablespoon instant minced onion
———
1 tablespoon paprika
1 cup sour cream

Combine beef, 1 teaspoon of the salt, and the next 5 ingredients. Shape into 1-inch balls. Brown on all sides in shortening. Add the next 3 ingredients and remaining ½ teaspoon salt. Cook 5 minutes. Stir in paprika and sour cream. Heat only until cream is hot. Serve over hot cooked noodles.

YIELD: 6 servings

MARINATED MEAT BALLS

1½ pounds ground chuck
¼ cup fine, dry bread crumbs
1 large egg, beaten
1 teaspoon salt
¼ teaspoon ground black pepper
———
½ teaspoon celery salt
¼ teaspoon salt
½ teaspoon crumbled rosemary leaves
¼ teaspoon garlic powder
⅛ teaspoon ground black pepper
1 tablespoon instant minced onion
½ cup salad oil

Combine first 5 ingredients. Shape into 1½-inch balls. Mix remaining ingredients and pour over meat. Let stand in the refrigerator 5 to 6 hours or overnight. Broil, until browned, over slow-burning charcoal fire or about 15 minutes in oven broiler, basting with marinade as often as meat looks dry. Serve between hot, split frankfurter buns.

YIELD: 18 meat balls

MEAT BALLS AND VEGETABLES HAWAIIAN

1 pound ground chuck
¼ cup fine, dry bread crumbs
1 teaspoon salt
¼ teaspoon ground black pepper
———
2 tablespoons salad oil
⅓ cup onion rings
1 cup thin, diagonal-sliced carrots
1 cup thin, diagonal-sliced celery
1 can (1 pound) bean sprouts, drained
1 cup beef bouillon *or* 1 beef bouillon cube and 1 cup hot water
1 teaspoon ground ginger
1 tablespoon cornstarch
3 tablespoons soy sauce

2 cups beef bouillon
1 tablespoon flour
2 tablespoons water

Combine the first 6 ingredients and shape into 1½-inch balls. Roll in the 3 tablespoons flour. Brown in shortening, adding it as needed. Stir in green peppers and onions and brown lightly. Add bouillon.

Cover and cook slowly 15 minutes or until meat is tender. Mix remaining flour with water to a smooth paste. Add and cook until gravy is medium thick. Serve hot with potatoes or rice.

YIELD: 6 servings

Combine the first 4 ingredients. Shape into 1-inch balls and brown in hot oil. Add vegetables and ¾ cup of the bouillon or bouillon cube and ¾ cup of the water. Cover and cook 10 minutes or only until vegetables are crisp-tender.

Blend ginger and cornstarch with remaining bouillon or water and soy sauce. Add to vegetables and mix well. Stir in meat balls. Cook until sauce has thickened and meat balls are hot. Serve over hot rice.

YIELD: 6 servings

MEAT BALLS IN GREEN PEPPER GRAVY

1½ pounds ground lean meat
1½ teaspoons salt
¾ teaspoon celery salt
1 teaspoon oregano leaves
½ teaspoon ground black pepper
⅛ teaspoon garlic powder

3 tablespoons flour
2 to 3 tablespoons shortening
4 cups sliced green peppers
1½ cups onion rings

MEAT BALLS IN MUSHROOM SAUCE

1 pound ground chuck
¼ pound ground, lean sausage
1¼ teaspoons salt
¾ teaspoon poultry seasoning
3 tablespoons catsup
1 large egg, lightly beaten
¼ cup fine, dry bread crumbs

2 tablespoons shortening

1 can (10½ ounces) cream of
    mushroom soup
½ can water
1 teaspoon paprika
¼ teaspoon ground thyme
1/16 teaspoon garlic powder

Combine the first 7 ingredients. Shape into 1½-inch balls. Brown on all sides in hot shortening. Reduce heat and cook 10 minutes or until meat is well done. Stir in the next 5 ingredients. Heat thoroughly. Serve hot over cooked noodles.

YIELD: 6 servings, 3 balls each

SAVORY MEAT BALLS

1 pound ground chuck
⅓ cup fine, dry bread crumbs
1 teaspoon salt
1 teaspoon ground coriander
½ teaspoon ground cumin seed
1/16 teaspoon cayenne
___
1 tablespoon shortening
2 cups sliced onion
___
½ pound (2 cups) diced,
    fresh mushrooms
1 teaspoon lemon juice
1 beef bouillon cube
___
1 teaspoon salt
¼ teaspoon ground black pepper
¼ teaspoon instant minced garlic
1 tablespoon paprika
___
1 cup sour cream

Combine first 6 ingredients. Shape into 1-inch balls. Brown on all sides in shortening. Add onion and sauté until they are limp and transparent. Add next 3 ingredients and cook until mushrooms are tender. Stir in next 4 ingredients and cook 2 to 3 minutes. Add sour cream and stir and cook only until cream is hot. Serve over cooked rice or noodles. Garnish with chopped parsley.

YIELD: 6 servings

TIKIA KEBABS

This recipe is from Pakistan and quite snappily seasoned.

1½ pounds ground chuck
3 tablespoons instant minced onion
1½ tablespoons salad *or* olive oil
1½ teaspoons salt
¾ teaspoon ground cumin seed
¾ teaspoon ground coriander
¼ teaspoon ground cinnamon
    (optional)
¼ teaspoon cayenne

Combine all ingredients. Shape into 1½-inch balls. Thread on skewers. Broil over slow-burning charcoal or under oven broiler, turning frequently to brown all sides. Serve hot.

YIELD: 6 servings

CARROT MEAT LOAF

2 tablespoons bacon fat *or* shortening
1½ cups chopped onion
___
1½ cups (4 medium) finely shredded,
    raw carrots
1½ cups (6 small) finely shredded,
    raw potatoes
1½ pounds ground lean beef
¼ pound beef liver, seared and
    ground
½ cup fine, dry bread crumbs
1 tablespoon salt
½ teaspoon ground black pepper
1½ teaspoons poultry seasoning
2 large eggs, beaten
___
2 strips bacon

Heat bacon fat or shortening in a saucepan. Add onions and sauté until limp. Mix with next 9 ingredients. Turn into a greased 9 x 5 x 3-inch loaf pan. Arrange bacon strips over the top. Bake in a preheated moderate oven (350° F.) 1 hour or until done.

YIELD: 8 servings

COMPANY MEAT LOAF

1 teaspoon powdered mustard
1 tablespoon water
2 pounds ground chuck
___
1 cup fine, dry bread crumbs
3 tablespoons instant minced onion
⅔ cup minced green pepper
1½ cups finely chopped tomatoes
2 teaspoons salt (or to taste)
½ teaspoon ground black pepper
2 large eggs, lightly beaten
___
8 whole carrots, cooked

Mix mustard with water and let stand 10 minutes. Combine meat with mustard and next 7 ingredients. Pat ½ of the mixture in a 9 x 5 x 3-inch loaf pan, having bottom of pan lined with brown or wax paper. Place whole, peeled, cooked carrots lengthwise over the meat. Pat the remaining meat over the carrots. Bake in a preheated moderate oven (350° F.) 1 hour or until meat is done. Cool in pan about 10 minutes. Turn out onto serving dish. Garnish with boiled whole new potatoes, sprinkled with paprika.

YIELD: 8 servings

ITALIAN MEAT LOAF

The Ricotta cheese that is spread over this meat loaf partially melts, and mingles with the meat juices to form a rich sauce.

1 pound ground lean beef
1 cup soft bread crumbs
½ cup grated Romano cheese
2 tablespoons instant minced onion
¼ cup chopped parsley
¼ teaspoon instant minced garlic

2¼ teaspoons salt
1¼ teaspoons basil leaves
½ teaspoon ground black pepper
3 large eggs, beaten
2 teaspoons olive *or* salad oil
2 tablespoons fine, dry bread crumbs
½ pound Ricotta cheese (Italian cottage cheese)

Combine the first 6 ingredients. Add 2 teaspoons of the salt, 1 teaspoon of the basil leaves, ¼ teaspoon of the black pepper, and 2 of the eggs. Mix well. Brush bottom and sides of a 9 x 5 x 3-inch loaf pan with oil and sprinkle with fine, dry bread crumbs. Turn ½ of the meat mixture into the pan and spread uniformly over the bottom.

Mix remaining salt, basil, black pepper, and egg with Ricotta cheese. Spread over meat. Top with remaining meat mixture, being sure to spread it to the sides of pan to completely cover cheese. Bake 1 hour or until done in a preheated moderate oven (350° F.). The Ricotta cheese makes its own sauce to be spooned over meat slices.

YIELD: 8 servings

SKILLET MEAT LOAF

1½ pounds ground chuck
½ pound ground lean pork
¾ cup fine cracker crumbs
¼ cup instant minced onion
¼ teaspoon instant minced garlic
2 teaspoons salt
1 teaspoon poultry seasoning
¼ teaspoon ground black pepper
⅛ teaspoon cayenne
1 large egg, lightly beaten

1½ cups chopped canned tomatoes
1 tablespoon shortening
1 teaspoon cornstarch
1 tablespoon water

Combine first 10 ingredients with ½ cup of the tomatoes. Mix well and shape into a round loaf 6 inches in diameter. Heat shortening in a deep 9-inch skillet. Place the meat in the hot shortening. Pour remaining tomatoes over meat. Cover tightly and cook over high heat 5 minutes or until steam escapes. Reduce heat and simmer 50 minutes or until meat is done. Remove meat from pan. Thicken pan drippings with cornstarch blended with water. Stir and cook 1 minute or until sauce has thickened. Serve over meat loaf.

YIELD: 8 servings

BEEF AND MACARONI STEW

A common enough dish—but uncommonly good!

1 pound ground chuck
1 tablespoon butter *or* margarine

¼ cup diced green pepper
¼ cup instant minced onion
2½ teaspoons salt
¼ teaspoon ground black pepper
¼ teaspoon instant minced garlic
3½ cups (1 pound, 12 ounces)
    canned tomatoes
1 cup uncooked elbow macaroni

½ cup diced Cheddar cheese

Brown meat in butter or margarine in a 2½-quart saucepan. Add next 7 ingredients, mix well and cook, covered, 20 minutes or until macaroni is tender, stirring occasionally. Stir in cheese. Serve hot as the main dish.

YIELD: 4 servings

BEEF AND VEGETABLE STEW

As all good dumpling makers know, the stew should be boiling hot when dumpling batter is dropped on the surface, and the pot must be covered immediately. Cook for precisely 15 minutes without lifting the lid and peeking. This prevents soggy dumplings.

2½ pounds lean beef stew meat
½ cup flour
1 tablespoon salt
2 tablespoons shortening
3 cups hot water
4 medium-size potatoes, quartered
6 medium-size carrots, quartered
12 small white onions
¾ teaspoon oregano leaves
½ teaspoon salt
¼ teaspoon instant minced garlic
1 teaspoon chili powder
⅓ cup flour
½ cup water
Chili-Tomato Dumplings *(see below)*

Trim and discard excess fat from meat. Cut meat into ¾-inch pieces. Roll in flour blended with salt. Brown on all sides in hot shortening in a Dutch oven or heavy 4-quart saucepan. Add water. Cover and simmer 1½ hours. Add vegetables, cover, and cook 30 to 40 minutes or until vegetables are tender. Add seasonings. Mix remaining flour and water together until smooth and blend with the stew. Drop Chili-Tomato Dumpling batter from a tablespoon over hot stew. Cook as directed below.

CHILI-TOMATO DUMPLINGS

1½ cups sifted all-purpose flour
¾ teaspoon salt
2¼ teaspoons double-acting
    baking powder
1½ teaspoons chili powder

¾ cup tomato juice

VARIETY IS THE
SPICE OF LIFE

Sift together first 4 ingredients. Stir in tomato juice. Drop batter from a tablespoon over hot stew, cover, and cook 15 minutes *without lifting cover.*

YIELD: 8 servings

BEEF STEW FROM GREECE

2 pounds lean beef stew meat
3 tablespoons olive *or* salad oil

2 cups water
1 can (6 ounces) tomato paste
3 tablespoons wine vinegar
2½ teaspoons salt
½ teaspoon sugar
½ teaspoon ground black pepper
½ teaspoon instant minced garlic

2 cinnamon sticks, each 2 inches long
8 whole cloves
2 pounds small white onions

Trim off and discard excess fat from meat. Cut meat into 1-inch pieces. Brown on all sides in hot oil in a heavy saucepan. Mix next 7 ingredients, heat to boiling point, and pour over meat. Add cinnamon. Stick cloves in one of the

onions and add. Cover and simmer until meat is almost tender, about 1½ hours. Peel remaining onions and add. Continue cooking 30 to 40 minutes. Remove cinnamon and onion with cloves before serving.

YIELD: 6 servings

BEEF AND VEGETABLE STEW WITH WINE

2 pounds boneless chuck *or* rump of beef
⅓ cup flour
3½ teaspoons salt
2 tablespoons shortening

2 cups boiling water
1 cup dry red wine
1 teaspoon fresh lemon juice
1 bay leaf
6 whole black peppers
4 whole cloves

20 small white onions, peeled
6 medium-size carrots, peeled and quartered
¼ pound fresh snap beans, cut into 1-inch pieces
½ teaspoon instant minced garlic

3 tablespoons flour
¼ cup Sauterne
¼ cup Burgundy
3 cups fluffy, mashed potatoes

Trim off and discard excess fat from meat. Cut beef into 1-inch cubes. Mix the ⅓ cup flour and 2 teaspoons of the salt with meat. Brown in shortening on all sides in a Dutch oven or heavy saucepan. Add the next 6 ingredients. Cover and cook slowly 2 hours or until meat is almost tender. Add remaining salt, vegetables, and garlic.

Cover and cook 30 minutes or until vegetables are tender. Blend the 3 tablespoons flour with Sauterne until smooth; add to mixture along with Burgundy. Mix well and cook 1 to 2 minutes. Serve with mashed potatoes or, if desired, turn stew into a 2-quart casserole. Make a border around the edge of casserole with mashed potatoes. Brush top with a little milk. Place in a very hot oven (500° F.) to brown, about 10 minutes.

YIELD: 8 servings

BEEF STEW WITH SOUR CREAM

1½ pounds round steak
3 tablespoons flour
2 teaspoons salt
½ teaspoon ground black pepper
1 cup sliced onions
___
1 cup water
1 bay leaf
1 cup sliced celery
1 cup sliced carrots
½ cup diced potatoes
___
1 cup sliced mushrooms
¾ cup sour cream
2 teaspoons paprika

Trim excess fat from meat and save it for later use. Pound meat with a mallet and cut it into 2 x ½-inch strips. Roll in flour mixed with salt and black pepper. Melt some of the suet (fat) trimmed from meat in a Dutch oven or heavy saucepan. Add meat and brown on both sides. Add onions and sauté until they are limp. Stir in next 5 ingredients.

Cover and cook 25 minutes or until meat and vegetables are tender. Add mushrooms, cover, and cook 10 minutes. Blend in sour cream and paprika just before serving. Heat, but DO NOT BOIL.

YIELD: 6 servings

BEEF VINDALOO
(INDIAN DISH)

1 tablespoon ground coriander seed
½ teaspoon ground cumin seed
1 teaspoon ground turmeric
½ teaspoon powdered mustard
½ teaspoon ground red pepper
1 teaspoon ground black pepper
½ teaspoon ground ginger
2 tablespoons cider vinegar
___
3 tablespoons onion flakes
¼ teaspoon instant minced garlic
3 tablespoons cold water
2 tablespoons butter, margarine, *or* cooking oil
2 pounds lean shoulder of beef
2½ cups hot water
1½ teaspoons salt
2 tablespoons fresh lemon juice

Combine first 8 ingredients and mix to a paste. Rehydrate onion and garlic in cold water, and sauté in butter, margarine, or cooking oil. Add the above paste and cook 1 to 2 minutes. Trim and discard fat from beef. Cut meat into ½-inch pieces and add. Cook in its own juice 10 minutes. Add hot water and cook until tender (about 40 to 50 minutes). Add salt and lemon juice. Serve over rice.

YIELD: 6 servings

COLOMBIAN BEEF AND VEGETABLE STEW

2 pounds boneless beef stew meat

1 bay leaf
½ teaspoon cumin seed
6 whole black peppers
¼ teaspoon instant minced garlic
2 teaspoons salt
1 teaspoon cider vinegar
3 cups water

2 medium-size potatoes
2 large carrots
4 long ribs celery
4 ears corn, cut into 2-inch lengths
½ cup sliced onion
½ cup diced, fresh tomatoes

¼ teaspoon crumbled saffron
½ teaspoon oregano leaves
½ cup shelled fresh peas

Trim off and discard excess fat from meat. Cut meat into 1-inch pieces. Place in a 3-quart saucepan with next 7 ingredients. Cover and cook slowly 1 hour or until meat is almost tender. Peel potatoes and carrots and cut into lengthwise strips ½ inch wide and add. Cut celery into slices ½ inch wide and add along with remaining vegetables.

Cover and cook 15 to 20 minutes or until vegetables are almost tender. Mix saffron in 1 teaspoon water and add along with oregano and peas. Mix well, being careful not to break vegetables. Cook 5 minutes, covered. Serve in soup plates with 2 to 3 pieces of corn, having a plastic toothpick or corn holder inserted in one end of each piece.

YIELD: 6 to 8 servings

CREOLE BEEF STEW

2 pounds beef stew meat
⅓ cup flour

3½ teaspoons salt
½ teaspoon ground black pepper
2 tablespoons shortening
1 cup water

1 cup sliced onions
1 cup sliced fresh okra
1 cup fresh corn, cut from the cob
1 cup diced potatoes
2 cups (1 pound) canned tomatoes
¼ teaspoon instant minced garlic
½ teaspoon chili powder (or to taste)

Trim off and discard excess fat from meat. Cut beef into 1-inch cubes. Mix flour with salt and black pepper and sprinkle over meat. Mix well. Brown on all sides in shortening. Add water. Cover and simmer 1½ to 2 hours or until meat is tender. Add remaining ingredients 30 minutes before cooking time is up. Serve hot.

YIELD: 6 servings

DILLY BEEF WITH SOUR CREAM

This delicious party dish is of Scandinavian origin. If made in advance, do everything but add the cream, which should be stirred in just before serving. Under no circumstances let the cream boil.

2 pounds beef stew meat
⅓ cup flour
2¾ teaspoons salt
1 teaspoon ground black pepper
2 tablespoons shortening

1⅔ cups hot water
1 bay leaf
¾ teaspoon dill seed

4 teaspoons paprika
¾ cup sour cream

Trim off and discard excess fat from beef.

Cut meat into 1-inch pieces. Roll in flour mixed with salt and black pepper. Brown in hot shortening. Add the next 3 ingredients. Cover and cook slowly 1½ hours or until meat is tender. Add paprika and cook 5 minutes. Stir in sour cream. Cook only until hot. DO NOT BOIL. Serve over hot cooked rice, noodles, or mashed potatoes.

YIELD: 6 servings

HUNGARIAN GOULASH

Lots of onions go into a Hungarian Goulash and never, never use flour to thicken the sauce. Long, slow cooking gives the stew body.

2 pounds boneless rump, round steak,
   or stew meat
2 tablespoons shortening
3 cups thinly sliced onions
_____
2½ teaspoons salt (or to taste)
½ teaspoon ground black pepper
2 teaspoons paprika
⅛ teaspoon cayenne
1 cup water
_____
3 medium-size potatoes, cut into
   eighths
½ cup chopped green pepper
1 teaspoon paprika

Trim off and discard excess fat from meat. Cut meat into 1-inch cubes. Brown on all sides in a Dutch oven or large heavy saucepan. Add onions and sauté until they are golden brown. Add next 5 ingredients. Cover and cook slowly 1½ hours or until meat is almost tender. Add potatoes and green pepper. Cover and cook 30 minutes or until potatoes are tender. Add remaining paprika. Serve with cooked rice.

YIELD: 6 servings

KIDNEY RAGOUT

3 teaspoons salt
2 pounds veal *or* lamb kidneys
3 tablespoons bacon fat, butter, *or*
   margarine
_____
2 cups (1 pound) canned tomatoes
⅓ cup diced celery
¼ cup diced green pepper
3 tablespoons onion flakes
1 teaspoon sugar
_____
½ teaspoon basil leaves
½ teaspoon oregano leaves
¼ teaspoon ground black pepper
1 can (4 ounces) whole mushrooms,
   drained

Rub 1 teaspoon of the salt over kidneys and let them stand 2 hours to remove some of the strong flavor. Rinse in cold water. Remove membrane and white tubes and cut into slices ¼ inch thick. Sauté 5 minutes in bacon fat, butter, or margarine. Add next 5 ingredients, cover, and simmer 30 minutes. Add remaining ingredients. Cover and cook 10 minutes. Serve over hot rice or mashed potatoes.

YIELD: 6 servings

OVEN COMPANY STEW

2 pounds beef stew meat
¼ cup flour
3 teaspoons salt
_____
½ teaspoon ground black pepper
2 cups (1 pound) canned tomatoes
1 cup sliced celery
½ cup diced green pepper
3 tablespoons onion flakes
1 teaspoon basil leaves
1 teaspoon tarragon leaves
¼ teaspoon instant minced garlic
8 medium-size peeled potatoes,
   quartered
8 medium-size peeled carrots, quartered

1 can (6 ounces) mushroom caps, drained
3 tablespoons flour
¼ cup cold water

Trim off and reserve excess fat from meat. Cut meat into 1-inch cubes. Dredge in flour mixed with 1 teaspoon of the salt. Brown in some of the fat trimmed from meat. Turn into a 3½-quart casserole. Combine remaining salt with the next 10 ingredients and pour over meat. Cover and cook 2 hours in a preheated slow oven (325° F.).

Remove cover and add mushrooms and remaining 3 tablespoons flour blended until smooth with cold water. Return to oven and cook 30 minutes. Serve hot with a green salad and corn bread squares or garlic bread.

YIELD: 8 to 10 servings

OVEN VEGETABLE AND BEEF FRICASSEE

4 minute cube steaks (about 1½ pounds)
½ cup flour
2 tablespoons shortening

2 cups diced potatoes
2 cups sliced carrots
1 cup sliced onions
1 cup sliced celery
1 cup hot water or consommé
2 tablespoons lemon juice
1 bay leaf
1½ teaspoons salt
¼ teaspoon thyme leaves
¼ teaspoon ground black pepper

Cut steaks into strips ½ inch wide. Roll in flour and brown in shortening. Add remaining ingredients. Turn into a 2½-quart casserole. Cover and bake in a preheated moderate oven (350° F.) 1

hour, stirring twice to mix well. Serve hot.

YIELD: 6 to 8 servings

RAGOUT DE BOEUF

This stew should be marinated at least 6 hours; overnight is even better. Shredded carrots give body to the sauce. If yours is a small family, don't be afraid to freeze the leftovers.

2½ cups beef stock or consommé
⅓ cup chopped onion
1 tablespoon parsley flakes
1 tablespoon red wine vinegar
2 tablespoons olive or salad oil
¼ teaspoon ground thyme
½ teaspoon ground black pepper
½ teaspoon salt
1 crumbled bay leaf
¼ teaspoon instant minced garlic

2 medium-size carrots

3 pounds boneless chuck or top round

¼ pound diced salt pork
¼ cup (½ stick) butter or margarine
½ cup flour

8 small white onions

½ pound fresh mushrooms

Place the first 10 ingredients in a large bowl. Peel and shred carrots medium-fine and add. Trim off and discard excess fat from meat. Cut meat into 1½-inch cubes and add to marinade. Cover and marinate in the refrigerator 6 hours or overnight. Remove meat and drain, reserving marinade.

Fry salt pork to render fat. Add butter or margarine. Dredge meat in flour, add to hot fat, and brown on all sides. Bring marinade to boiling point and pour over meat. Cover and cook slowly 1½ to 2 hours or until meat is almost tender.

Peel onions and add. Cover and cook 25 minutes. Wash mushrooms, leave caps whole, slice stems, and add. Cover and cook 10 minutes. Serve hot.

YIELD: 8 servings

CAJUN MEAT PIE

This recipe is typical of the Bayou country of Louisiana and comes from Mrs. Grady Estilette of New Iberia. The crust is rich and the filling flavorful. In many restaurants in the Cajun country, this meat filling is served in small tarts as an accompaniment to the main dish.

3 cups sifted all-purpose flour
1½ teaspoons salt
1¼ cups shortening
2 large egg yolks, beaten
½ cup cold water

Sift flour and salt together into a mixing bowl. Cut in shortening with a pastry blender or 2 knives. Mix egg yolks with water and add. Toss mixture lightly to form a dough. Shape into a ball. Wrap in foil or wax paper and chill overnight or several hours.

MEAT FILLING
½ cup sifted all-purpose flour
½ cup cooking oil

3 tablespoons instant minced onion
3 tablespoons water
2 tablespoons finely diced celery
2 tablespoons finely diced green pepper
1 cup water
1½ pounds ground chuck
2½ teaspoons salt
¼ teaspoon ground black pepper
2 teaspoons chili powder
½ teaspoon powdered mustard
½ teaspoon garlic powder
1/16 teaspoon ground ginger
1 teaspoon fresh lemon juice

Blend flour with oil. Stir and cook 20 minutes or until the mixture is brown (roux). Soften onion in the 3 tablespoons of water and add to roux, along with celery and green pepper. Stir and cook over low heat 5 minutes. Remove from heat and stir in ½ cup of the water. Mix until well blended. Add meat and remaining ½ cup water. Stir and cook 15 minutes. Stir in remaining ingredients. Roll ½ of the pastry ⅛ inch thick and line a 10-inch pie plate. Add meat filling.

Roll ½ of the pastry ⅛ inch thick; cut into strips ½ inch wide and arrange over pie in lattice-crust fashion. Trim excess pastry from around edge of pie plate. Crimp edges with tines of a fork dipped in flour. Bake in a preheated very hot oven (450° F.) 10 minutes. Reduce heat to 350° F. (moderate) and bake 30 minutes.

YIELD: 8 to 10 servings

PANAMANIAN BEEF AND VEGETABLE STEW (SANCOCHO)

You may raise your eyebrows at the mention of green bananas in a stew, but these add exotic flavor to this delicious concoction of Panamanian origin.

2 pounds boneless lean pork
1 pound boneless beef stew meat
½ cup diced ham
___
1 tablespoon salt
½ teaspoon instant minced garlic
1 bay leaf
4 cups water
___
¼ cup onion flakes
3 tablespoons fresh lime juice
2½ cups diced potatoes
2 cups cubed yellow squash *or*
    pumpkin
⅓ cup finely chopped parsley
___
1 pound Spanish-style sausage
    (Chorizo)
1 teaspoon ground black pepper
1 teaspoon ground coriander
⅛ teaspoon ground red pepper
2 green bananas

Trim off and discard excess fat from pork, beef, and ham. Cut meat into 1-inch cubes. Place in a saucepan with next 4 ingredients. Cover and cook slowly 1½ hours or until meat is almost tender. Add next 5 ingredients.

Cut sausage into slices ¼ inch thick and add along with black pepper, coriander, and red pepper. Cover and cook 20 minutes. Cut bananas into slices ½ inch thick and add. Cover and cook 10 minutes. Serve in deep soup plates.

YIELD: 8 to 10 servings

CURRIED BEEF POT PIE

No pastry to roll here—just pour pancake batter over hot mixture and bake until browned.

2 pounds beef stew meat
1 tablespoon shortening
___
¼ cup instant minced onion
¼ teaspoon ground black pepper

⅛ teaspoon garlic powder
2¼ teaspoons salt
1½ teaspoons curry powder
2 tablespoons flour
___
1 cup beef stock *or* water
1 cup diced celery
Pancake Batter Topping *(see below)*

Trim off and discard excess fat from meat. Cut meat into ½-inch pieces. Brown in shortening. Add the next 6 ingredients and mix well. Stir in beef stock or water and celery. Bring to boiling point and cook, covered, 10 minutes. Turn into a 1½-quart casserole. Cover with Pancake Batter. Bake in a preheated moderate oven (350° F.) 45 minutes or until browned. Serve hot.

PANCAKE BATTER TOPPING
1½ cups sifted all-purpose flour
2¼ teaspoons double-acting
    baking powder
¾ teaspoon salt
___
¼ cup shortening
1 large egg, beaten
¾ cup milk

Sift together into a mixing bowl first 3 ingredients. Add shortening and cut it in until the mixture resembles crumbs. Combine egg and milk. Stir into the mixture. Mix only until ingredients are blended. Spoon over meat.

YIELD: 6 servings

HAMBURGER AND VEGETABLE PIE

A good, inexpensive family casserole.

⅓ cup diced green peppers
½ cup diced onion
2 tablespoons butter *or* margarine
1½ pounds ground chuck

1 cup (8 ounces) Spanish-type
    tomato sauce
1 teaspoon salt
¾ teaspoon oregano leaves
¼ teaspoon celery salt
¼ teaspoon ground black pepper
¼ teaspoon instant minced garlic

1 cup cooked sliced carrots
1 cup frozen peas
Unbaked pastry for 2-crust 9-inch pie
    (Never-Fail Pastry III*)

Sauté green pepper and onion in butter
or margarine until onions are limp. Add
meat and cook until it loses its red color.
Add next 6 ingredients. Mix well. Line
a 9-inch pie plate with half the pastry,
rolled ⅛ inch thick. Spread carrots over
the bottom. Top with meat mixture and
then with peas. Cover with remaining
dough rolled ⅛ inch thick.

Trim, turn under, and flute edges of
pastry. Cut a gash in the crust to allow
for the escape of steam. Bake in a preheated very hot oven (450° F.) 10 minutes. Reduce heat to moderate (350° F.)
and bake 40 minutes or until crust is
brown. Serve hot.

YIELD: 6 servings

HASTY MEAT PIE

2 cans (1½ pounds each) beef stew

2 tablespoons flour
¼ teaspoon salt
½ teaspoon poultry seasoning
⅛ teaspoon ground black pepper
¹⁄₁₆ teaspoon garlic powder
¼ cup water
12 unbaked oven-ready biscuits

Open cans of beef stew and turn into a
mixing bowl. Combine the next 6 ingredients and mix with the stew. Spoon
into a 1½-quart casserole. Top with unbaked biscuits. Bake in a preheated hot

oven (425° F.) 12 minutes. Cover with
foil and bake 15 minutes to thoroughly
cook biscuits through the center. Serve
hot.

YIELD: 6 servings

HERBED HAMBURGER PIE

1½ pounds ground lean beef
1 tablespoon butter *or* margarine
¼ cup flour

1 cup diced potatoes
1 cup sliced carrots
1 cup onion rings
½ cup diced celery
1 beef bouillon cube
1 cup hot water
2 teaspoons salt (or to taste)

½ teaspoon thyme leaves
½ teaspoon ground black pepper
¼ teaspoon garlic powder

12-ounce package unsweetened
    corn muffin mix

Brown meat in butter or margarine. Blend
in flour. Add the next 7 ingredients.
Cover, bring to boiling point, and simmer
5 minutes. Remove from heat and add
the next 3 ingredients. Turn into a 9 x 9
x 2-inch baking dish. Prepare corn muffin batter as directed on package. Spread
uniformly over meat. Bake in a preheated
moderate oven (375° F.) 40 minutes or
until top has browned. Serve hot.

YIELD: 6 servings

ITALIAN SALAMI PIE

*Around the Bay of Naples, this Salami
Pie is served each Easter along with
pastas, salads, and all kinds of favorite
Neapolitan dishes.*

1 envelope active dry yeast
1 cup warm water

½ teaspoon salt
½ teaspoon ground black pepper
2 tablespoons shortening
About 3¼ cups sifted all-purpose flour

Mix yeast with water and let stand 5 minutes to soften. Stir in salt, black pepper, and shortening. Gradually add enough flour to make a soft dough. Knead on a lightly floured board until dough is smooth and elastic.

Cover and let stand in a warm place (80° to 85° F.) until dough has doubled in volume. Cut off ¼ of the dough and reserve for later use. Roll remaining dough to fit the bottom and sides of a 2-quart casserole, about 2 inches deep, leaving a 1-inch rim of dough all around edge of casserole. Roll remaining dough to fit the top of the casserole and set aside while making filling.

FILLING

1 pound Italian sweet salami
   (Suprasado)
1 pound Mozzarella cheese

½ cup grated Parmesan cheese
1 teaspoon whole black pepper
¼ teaspoon onion powder
⅛ teaspoon sugar
⅛ teaspoon ground ginger
6 large eggs, beaten

Dice salami and Mozzarella cheese and mix with remaining ingredients. Turn into the yeast-dough lined casserole. Top with the dough rolled to fit the top of casserole. Press edges together, turn under, and flute as for other pie crusts.

Bake in a preheated slow oven (325° F.) 2 to 2¼ hours or until knife inserted in the center comes out clean. Slice in wedges and serve hot.

YIELD: 6 to 8 servings

MEAT AND VEGETABLE PIE

2 tablespoons butter *or* margarine
3 tablespoons flour
2 beef bouillon cubes
1½ cups hot water

1½ teaspoons salt
¼ teaspoon ground black pepper
2 cups diced cooked beef, lamb, *or* pork
1 cup onion rings
1 cup diced carrots
½ cup diced celery
¼ cup diced potatoes

½ teaspoon marjoram leaves
Unbaked 9-inch pie crust
   (Never-Fail Pastry I*)

Melt butter or margarine in a 2-quart saucepan. Blend in flour and cook until bubbly. Remove from heat and stir in bouillon cubes and water. Stir and cook until of medium thickness. Add next 7 ingredients. Cover and simmer 5 minutes. Add marjoram. Turn into a 1½-quart casserole.

Top with pastry rolled to ⅛ inch thickness. Trim, turn under, and flute edge. Cut a gash in top to allow for escape of steam. Bake in a preheated very hot oven (450° F.) 10 minutes. Reduce heat to 350° F. (moderate) and bake 30 minutes or until crust has browned and vegetables are tender. Serve hot.

YIELD: 6 servings

MEAT BALL DEEP-DISH PIE

1½ pounds ground chuck
1½ teaspoons salt
½ teaspoon ground black pepper
¼ teaspoon ground marjoram
2 tablespoons instant minced onion

2 tablespoons ham *or* bacon drippings

¾ cup diced green pepper
½ cup chopped celery
1 tablespoon instant minced onion

½ teaspoon sugar
½ teaspoon salt
¼ teaspoon ground black pepper
¼ teaspoon instant minced garlic
2 cups (1 pound) canned tomatoes

Unbaked 1-crust pie shell
  (Never-Fail Pastry I*)

Combine the first 5 ingredients. Shape into 1-inch balls. Brown on all sides in hot ham or bacon drippings. Remove meat from fat and add next 3 ingredients. Stir and cook until vegetables are limp. Add meat balls and next 5 ingredients. Cook, uncovered, 5 minutes.

Turn into a 1½-quart casserole. Cover with pastry, rolled ⅛ inch thick. Trim, turn under, and flute edge. Cut a gash in top of crust to allow for escape of steam. Bake in a preheated hot oven (425° F.) 30 minutes or until pastry has browned. Serve hot.

YIELD: 6 servings

SPICED MEAT PIE

Similar to the Cajun Meat Pie,* but the pastry isn't as rich and it is much easier to handle. Also, the filling is more lightly spiced.

½ teaspoon powdered mustard
1 tablespoon water
¼ cup (½ stick) butter *or* margarine
¼ cup flour

¾ pound ground chuck
2 tablespoons finely chopped celery
2 tablespoons finely chopped green
  pepper

1¼ cups hot water
1½ teaspoons salt
¼ teaspoon ground black pepper
1½ teaspoons chili powder

¼ teaspoon garlic powder
⅛ teaspoon ground ginger
2 tablespoons instant minced onion
1 teaspoon fresh lemon juice

Unbaked pastry for 2-crust 9-inch pie
  (Never-Fail Pastry III*)

Blend mustard with the 1 tablespoon water. Melt butter or margarine in a 2-quart saucepan. Blend in flour. Stir and cook over low heat 15 minutes or until mixture has browned. This makes a brown roux. Stir in next 3 ingredients and cook until the meat turns gray. Add mustard and all remaining ingredients except pastry. Cool.

Turn mixture into a 9-inch pie plate lined with unbaked pastry rolled to ⅛ inch thickness. Cover with remaining pastry rolled to ⅛ inch thickness. Trim, turn under, and flute edge. Cut a gash in top crust to allow for the escape of steam.

Bake in a preheated very hot oven (450° F.) 10 minutes. Reduce heat to 350° F. (moderate) and bake 30 minutes or until crust has browned. Cut into wedges and serve hot, as the main dish.

YIELD: 6 servings

INDIAN BARBECUED KEBABS
(BOTI KEBABS)

2 pounds lean sirloin steak
Boiling water

½ cup yogurt
¼ cup instant minced onion
1 tablespoon water
2 teaspoons salt
2 teaspoons poppy seed
1 teaspoon ground ginger
4 teaspoons ground coriander
2 teaspoons ground turmeric
½ teaspoon ground cumin seed
¼ teaspoon ground red pepper

16 green pepper squares
16 onion slices
16 mushroom caps
¼ cup salad oil

Cut meat into 1½ inch pieces and soak 5 minutes in boiling water, enough to cover. Drain. Add next 10 ingredients. Mix well to coat all sides of the meat with the seasonings. Let stand in the refrigerator 4 to 5 hours or overnight. String on skewers, alternating with next 3 ingredients.

Broil over a slow-burning charcoal fire until meat has browned and is tender, basting with the oil as often as the meat looks dry. (Cooking time depends upon heat of fire and the degree of cooking desired. An oven broiler may be substituted for the charcoal fire.) Serve in split hot frankfurter rolls or in French bread, split and cut to fit the kebabs.

YIELD: 8 servings

HERBED BEEF KEBABS

¼ cup salad oil
2 tablespoons cider vinegar
1 teaspoon onion salt
1 teaspoon celery salt
¾ teaspoon garlic salt
½ teaspoon salt
1 teaspoon oregano leaves
½ teaspoon ground black pepper
1 tablespoon prepared mustard
1 small bay leaf
2 pounds boneless sirloin of beef
16 (1½ inches each) green pepper squares
16 mushroom caps
16 tomato wedges

Combine first 10 ingredients in a saucepan. Heat to boiling point and cool. Cut meat into 1½-inch cubes and add to the

mixture along with 1½-inch green pepper squares. Mix well. Cover and let stand in the refrigerator 6 hours or overnight.

String meat, green pepper squares, and mushrooms on skewers. Cook over slow-burning charcoal fire 20 to 25 minutes or until meat and vegetables are tender, basting with marinade as often as kebabs look dry.

String tomato wedges on a separate skewer, brush with marinade, and cook 8 to 10 minutes, turning frequently. Serve with meat, green peppers, and mushrooms between long French rolls, cut to fit kebabs, or between frankfurter buns.

YIELD: 8 servings

SPICED BEEF KEBABS

1½ teaspoons salt
½ teaspoon garlic salt
¾ teaspoon chili powder
¼ teaspoon ground ginger
¼ teaspoon oregano leaves
½ teaspoon thyme leaves
¼ teaspoon ground black pepper
1 small bay leaf, crumbled
1½ tablespoons instant minced onion
¼ cup lemon juice
1 tablespoon cider vinegar
⅓ cup salad oil
1½ pounds boneless sirloin of beef

Combine first 12 ingredients in a mixing bowl. Cut beef into 1½-inch cubes. Add to marinade. Let stand in the refrigerator 6 hours or overnight. String meat on skewers. Broil over slow-burning charcoal fire or in oven broiler 15 to 20 minutes, turning skewers frequently to brown on all sides. Baste with marinade as often as meat looks dry. Serve between split, warmed frankfurter buns.

YIELD: 15 kebabs

BEEFSTEAK AND KIDNEY EN CASSEROLE

1 pound lean beef stew meat
¾ pound veal *or* lamb kidneys
¼ cup flour
2 tablespoons shortening *or* bacon fat

1½ teaspoons salt (or to taste)
½ teaspoon poultry seasoning
¼ teaspoon ground black pepper
2 tablespoons instant minced onion
1 tablespoon parsley flakes
½ cup diced celery
¾ cup hot water *or* beef stock

Fluffy mashed potatoes

Trim and discard excess fat from meat and kidneys and cut into 1-inch pieces. Dredge meat with flour and brown in shortening. Add the next 7 ingredients and turn into a 1-quart casserole. Cover and bake in a preheated moderate oven (350° F.) 1 hour or until meat is tender.

Remove from oven and spoon a 2-inch border of hot, fluffy mashed potatoes around the edge of casserole. Bake 15 minutes or until potatoes are brown. Serve hot with a vegetable and salad.

YIELD: 6 servings

STUFFED GREEN PEPPERS

6 squatty green peppers
1 cup boiling water
½ teaspoon salt

1 cup ground lean beef
1 cup cooked rice
1½ cups diced fresh tomato
2 tablespoons minced green pepper *(see directions below)*
1½ teaspoons salt
¼ teaspoon ground black pepper
½ teaspoon oregano leaves
3 tablespoons onions flakes

¾ cup soft bread crumbs
2 tablespoons butter *or* margarine, melted

½ cup Spanish-type tomato sauce
¾ cup boiling water

Wash green peppers. Cut a thin slice from the stem end. Remove seeds from peppers and use the slices for making the "minced green pepper." Parboil peppers 4 minutes in the salted water in a covered saucepan. Remove from water and drain.

Cook meat in a lightly greased skillet until it is no longer red. Mix in next 7 ingredients. Spoon into well-drained green peppers. Place in a 10 x 6 x 2-inch baking dish. Mix bread crumbs with butter or margarine and sprinkle over tops.

Combine tomato sauce and water and pour around peppers. Bake, uncovered, in a moderate oven (350° F.) 45 minutes, or until done. Serve with the sauce spooned over the tops.

YIELD: 6 servings

FAVORITE LIVER LOAF

1 pound beef liver, sliced
1 can (12 ounces) luncheon meat
2 slices firm-textured bread

1 large egg, lightly beaten
3 tablespoons onion flakes
¾ teaspoon powdered mustard
1 teaspoon ground marjoram
1 teaspoon salt
½ teaspoon ground black pepper
¼ teaspoon instant minced garlic
Dash cayenne
¾ cup milk

Cook liver in simmering water to cover, in covered saucepan 5 minutes. Remove from water and drain well. Put liver, luncheon meat, and bread through the food chopper, using the fine blade.

Add remaining ingredients and mix well. Turn into a 9 x 5 x 3-inch loaf pan. Bake in a preheated moderate oven (350° F.) 1 hour or until browned.

YIELD: 8 to 10 servings

GINGERED LIVER, CHINESE STYLE

2 pounds baby beef, lamb, or
calf liver

3 tablespoons salad oil
¼ teaspoon ground black pepper
¼ cup soy sauce
½ teaspoon ground ginger
1 tablespoon water

Slice liver in strips ¼ inch wide. Sauté

in hot oil 5 minutes, turning pieces of liver often. Add remaining ingredients. Cover and simmer 5 minutes. Serve with hot cooked rice.

YIELD: 6 servings

HERBED LIVER HASH

⅓ cup onion flakes
¼ cup water
2 tablespoons butter or margarine
2 tablespoons flour
1 cup beef stock or 1 beef bouillon cube
and 1 cup boiling water
½ cup milk

¼ teaspoon crushed red pepper
1 teaspoon salt
¼ teaspoon ground thyme
1½ cups diced, cooked beef or
pork liver

Soften onion flakes in the ¼ cup water. Sauté 1 minute in butter or margarine. Blend in flour. Add stock or water and bouillon cube and milk. Mix well. Stir in remaining ingredients. Cook until of medium thickness, stirring frequently. Serve over hot rice, toast, or corn bread squares.

YIELD: 4 servings

LIVER AND VEGETABLE MEAT LOAF

2 tablespoons bacon fat *or* shortening
1½ cups chopped onion

1½ cups finely shredded raw carrots
1½ cups finely shredded raw potatoes
1½ pounds ground lean beef
¼ pound beef liver, seared and ground
½ cup fine, dry bread crumbs
1 tablespoon salt
½ teaspoon ground black pepper
1½ teaspoons poultry seasoning
2 large eggs, beaten

2 strips bacon

Heat bacon fat or shortening in a saucepan. Add onions and sauté until limp. Mix with next 9 ingredients. Turn into a greased 9 x 5 x 3-inch loaf pan. Arrange bacon strips over the top. Bake in a preheated moderate oven (350° F.) 1 hour, or until done.

YIELD: 8 servings

LIVER TERRINE

1 pound beef *or* lamb liver
1 can (2 ounces) anchovies
3 large eggs, lightly beaten
1½ teaspoons salt
½ teaspoon powdered mustard
1 tablespoon water

½ teaspoon poultry seasoning
¼ teaspoon ground black pepper
2 tablespoons instant minced onion
¼ teaspoon instant minced garlic
1 cup Medium White Sauce*
2 strips crisp bacon, crumbled

Cook liver in boiling water only until it loses its red color. Put liver and anchovies through a food chopper, using the fine blade. Add eggs and salt. Soak mustard in water 10 minutes to develop flavor. Add to liver along with remaining ingredients. Mix well.

Turn into a 3-cup baking dish. Place in a pan of hot water and bake in a preheated slow oven (325° F.) 1½ hours or until a knife inserted in the center comes out clean. Cool. Cover and chill 24 hours. Serve cold in slices.

YIELD: 8 to 10 slices

ORIENTAL VEGETABLES AND BEEF

If you want to stretch a piece of roast beef, here's a way to make a virtue of necessity. Cook the vegetables quickly, until just crisp-tender. The texture suggests well-prepared sukiyaki.

2 tablespoons butter *or* margarine

¼ cup thinly sliced green pepper
1 cup sliced fresh mushrooms
1 cup sliced Chinese cabbage
1 cup thinly sliced fresh asparagus
1 cup sliced celery
1 cup sliced green onions (tops and bottoms)

2½ cups ⅛-inch strips cooked, cold roast beef
¼ cup soy sauce

1 teaspoon cornstarch
¼ teaspoon ground ginger
⅛ teaspoon ground black pepper
Salt (to taste)

Melt butter or margarine in a 10-inch skillet. Add vegetables, cover, and cook slowly 6 to 7 minutes or only until they are crisp-tender. Add beef. Blend soy sauce with next 4 ingredients. Add and cook 1 minute or just until sauce has thickened. Serve hot as the main dish.

YIELD: 6 servings

LAMB

GRILLED MARINATED LAMB CHOPS

¼ cup salad *or* olive oil
2 tablespoons wine vinegar
2 teaspoons prepared mustard
1 teaspoon crumbled rosemary leaves
1½ teaspoons salt
¾ teaspoon onion salt
¼ teaspoon ground black pepper
¼ teaspoon instant minced garlic
¼ teaspoon ground ginger

6 boneless loin lamb chops, trimmed
  well and cut 1-inch thick

Combine the first 9 ingredients in a mixing bowl. Wrap the narrow ends of boneless lamb chops around the wide part in pinwheel fashion. Fasten ends securely with toothpicks.

Marinate overnight or 5 to 6 hours in the marinade in a covered bowl in refrigerator. Cook slowly over slow-burning charcoal fire until well done and browned. Or if desired, broil in oven broiler 15 to 20 minutes. Baste with marinade as often as meat looks dry.

YIELD: 6 servings

LAMB CHOPS IN PIQUANT SAUCE

6 shoulder lamb chops, cut ½ inch
  thick

2 tablespoons olive *or* salad oil
2 tablespoons fresh lemon juice
1½ teaspoons salt
1 teaspoon ground black pepper
1 teaspoon oregano leaves
¼ teaspoon instant minced garlic

½ teaspoon powdered mustard
2 teaspoons water
6 anchovy fillets, chopped
⅛ teaspoon ground black pepper
¼ teaspoon instant minced garlic
½ teaspoon oregano leaves
1 teaspoon instant minced onion
1 tablespoon cider vinegar

Trim and discard excess fat from lamb chops and set aside. Mix the next 6 ingredients and rub on all sides of chops. Let stand, in refrigerator, overnight or 5 to 6 hours.

Mix mustard with water, let stand 10 minutes, and combine with remaining ingredients. Brush lamb chops on both sides with the mixture. Place meat in a 13 x 9 x 2-inch baking dish. Bake, uncovered, in a preheated moderate oven (350° F.) 1 hour or until chops are tender, turning once. Serve hot with rice or mashed potatoes.

YIELD: 6 servings

LAMB CURRY, AMERICAN STYLE

½ cup onion flakes
½ teaspoon instant minced garlic
⅓ cup water
2 pounds lean boneless leg *or*
  shoulder of lamb
4½ teaspoons curry powder
2 tablespoons shortening

1½ cups water *or* stock
1 bay leaf
2 teaspoons salt (or to taste)

¼ cup undiluted evaporated milk
1 teaspoon lemon juice

Soften onion and garlic in the ⅓ cup water. Set aside. Trim and discard excess fat from lamb. Cut meat into ½-inch pieces and mix with curry powder. Cook in hot shortening 20 minutes or until meat has browned. Add next 3 ingredients. Cover and cook slowly 30 to 40 minutes or until meat is tender. Add milk. Heat, but DO NOT BOIL. Stir in lemon juice just before serving. Serve with hot rice.

YIELD: 6 servings

CURRY OF LAMB

East meets West in the preparation of this lamb curry in that the curry powder is reinforced with a few additional spices. Nonetheless, it has an entirely authentic Indian taste, though perfectionists can rightfully claim that short cuts were taken here and there. If you like your curries hot, add ground red pepper to taste.

2½ pounds boneless lamb stew meat
2 tablespoons shortening
⅓ cup onion flakes
¼ cup water
1 tablespoon curry powder
1¾ cups stock *or* water
2 teaspoons salt (or to taste)
___
½ teaspoon powdered mustard
¼ teaspoon ground black pepper
¼ teaspoon ground cumin seed
⅛ teaspoon ground allspice
¼ teaspoon instant minced garlic
___
¼ cup undiluted evaporated milk
1 tablespoon fresh lemon juice

Trim and discard excess fat from lamb. Cut lamb into 1-inch pieces. Cook in hot shortening until meat is gray. Soften onion in ¼ cup water, add with curry powder to lamb; cook 3 minutes. Add stock and salt.

Cover and cook 50 minutes over low heat until much of the liquid has evaporated. Add next 5 ingredients 10 minutes before cooking time is up. Stir in milk and lemon juice just before serving. Heat, but do not boil. Serve with hot rice.

YIELD: 6 servings

CURRIED LAMB, INDIAN STYLE

Indian cookery acquires much of its characteristic flavor from some spices that are not too well known in America: from cardamom, coriander, cumin, turmeric, and saffron. One bit of spice cookery all Indian cooks insist on: spices must be cooked. Note that in this, and in certain other authentic Indian dishes, spices are heated in fat (not water) before other ingredients are added.

⅓ cup onion flakes
¼ cup water
3 tablespoons vegetable cooking oil *or* shortening
2 tablespoons ground coriander
1½ teaspoons ground cumin seed
1 teaspoon ground cardamom seed
1 teaspoon ground ginger
1 teaspoon ground turmeric
½ teaspoon garlic powder

¼ teaspoon ground black pepper
⅛ teaspoon cayenne
2 pounds boneless leg of lamb *or* lamb stew meat
2 cups water
1½ teaspoons salt (or to taste)
¼ cup yogurt *or* undiluted evaporated milk
1 teaspoon fresh lemon juice

Soak onion flakes in the ¼ cup water until they are soft. Cook in hot oil until golden. Add spices and stir and cook over low heat 1 minute. Trim excess fat from lamb and discard it. Cut meat into 1 inch cubes and add. Cook 10 to 15 minutes or until browned, stirring frequently. Add water and salt.

Cover and cook 30 minutes or until meat is tender. Remove cover and cook until liquid has been reduced to a slightly thickened sauce, about 10 minutes. Add yogurt or evaporated milk just before serving. Stir in lemon juice. Serve with rice and chutney.

YIELD: 6 servings

CURRIED LAMB WITH GRAPES

2 pounds boneless shoulder of lamb
¾ cup finely chopped onion
1 tablespoon curry powder
¼ cup salad oil *or* shortening

1 cup hot water *or* beef *or* lamb stock
1 bay leaf
¼ teaspoon ground cardamom
¼ teaspoon ground ginger
¼ teaspoon powdered mustard
2 teaspoons salt (or to taste)

¼ cup undiluted evaporated milk
1½ cups green seedless grapes

Trim and discard excess fat from lamb. Cut meat into 1-inch pieces. Set aside. Sauté onions and curry powder in oil or shortening until onions are golden, stir-

ring frequently. Add lamb and cook until browned on all sides, about 10 minutes. Add the next 6 ingredients. Cover and cook 50 minutes, or until lamb is tender. Stir in milk and grapes. Heat thoroughly, but DO NOT BOIL. Serve hot over cooked rice.

YIELD: 6 servings

KOFTAH CURRY

1 tablespoon onion flakes
¼ teaspoon instant minced garlic
1 tablespoon water

1½ pounds ground lamb *or* chuck
1½ teaspoons salt
¼ teaspoon ground cinnamon
⅛ teaspoon ground cloves
1 large egg, beaten

½ cup onion flakes
⅓ cup water
¼ cup shortening *or* vegetable oil
1 teaspoon turmeric
1 cup water
2 tablespoons tomato paste
1 teaspoon salt
2 teaspoons ground coriander
½ teaspoon ground cumin
¼ teaspoon ground black pepper
⅛ teaspoon cayenne

Soften onion and garlic in the 1 tablespoon water. Mix with the next 5 ingredients. Shape into 18 balls and set aside for later use. Soften onion flakes in the ⅓ cup water. Brown in 2 tablespoons of the hot shortening or oil. Add turmeric and cook with onions 2 to 3 minutes. Remove onion from pan with a perforated spoon. Add remaining shortening and heat. Add meat balls and brown on all sides. Add browned onions and remaining ingredients. Cover and cook over moderate heat 20 minutes. Serve with rice.

YIELD: 6 servings

LAMB KORMA
(GHOSHT KA KORMA)

2 pounds boneless, lean leg of lamb

½ cup yogurt
1 teaspoon ground cumin seeds
1 teaspoon ground turmeric
½ teaspoon ground cardamom

¼ cup cooking oil *or* shortening
⅔ cup instant onion flakes
½ teaspoon instant minced garlic
½ cup water

1 teaspoon ground ginger
1 teaspoon powdered mustard
½ teaspoon ground black pepper
½ teaspoon ground red pepper
½ teaspoon ground cinnamon
⅛ teaspoon ground cloves

2½ teaspoons salt
1 cup water
1 teaspoon lemon juice
2 tablespoons fresh *or* flaked coconut

Trim and discard excess fat from lamb and cut into 1-inch pieces. Blend with next 4 ingredients. Marinate 2 or more hours. Brown in 1 tablespoon of the shortening. Pour off excess fat. Soften onion and garlic in the ½ cup water.

In another pan, sauté onion until golden in remaining shortening or oil. Add next 6 ingredients, stir, and cook 2 minutes. Add lamb and salt, cover pan tightly, and cook slowly 20 minutes. Pour in the 1 cup water, stir to form a rich gravy.

Cover and cook 25 minutes, or until lamb is tender, adding more water if needed. Blend in lemon juice and coconut just before serving. Serve over rice.

YIELD: 6 servings

MALAI KORMA

If this recipe were made in southern India it would call for coconut milk instead of heavy cream. If you would like to try this variation buy a whole coconut and grate it. To one cup of freshly grated coconut, add 1 cup boiling water and let stand for 1 hour. Strain through a cheesecloth, squeezing out the last bit of moisture.

Incidentally, the best way to get at the coconut meat in the first place is to crack the shell by tapping it here and there with a hammer; or heat the uncracked coconut in a slow oven for a half hour to facilitate removal of the shell.

2 pounds lean leg of lamb
2 cups chopped onion
½ teaspoon ground ginger
1 teaspoon ground turmeric
1 cup yogurt
3 tablespoons butter *or* margarine
2 bay leaves
½ cup water
⅓ cup blanched almonds
½ cup heavy cream *or* undiluted evaporated milk
¼ teaspoon cayenne
1 teaspoon salt

Trim and discard excess fat from lamb and cut meat into 1-inch pieces. Add 1 cup of the onion, half of both the ginger and turmeric, and ¼ cup of the yogurt. Mix well, cover, and let stand overnight in the refrigerator. When ready to cook, sauté remaining chopped onion in 1 tablespoon of the butter or margarine until golden. Add marinated lamb and stir and cook 10 minutes, or until lamb is dry. Add rest of yogurt and bay leaves. Cook, uncovered, 10 minutes, or until lamb is dry. Add water and cook until meat is dry. Put almonds through a food chopper, using the medium blade, and add to lamb. Stir in remaining ginger, turmeric, and the rest of the ingredients. Cook, slowly, 10 to 12 minutes. DO NOT BOIL. Serve over hot cooked rice.

YIELD: 6 servings

LAMB VINDALOO, AMERICAN STYLE

3 pounds boneless lamb stew meat

2½ teaspoons salt
2 tablespoons curry powder
3 tablespoons cider vinegar
3 tablespoons water

1½ cups chopped onion
¾ teaspoon instant minced garlic
2 tablespoons butter or margarine
¾ cup beef or lamb stock or water
1/16 teaspoon ground red pepper

Trim and discard excess fat from meat. Cut meat into 1-inch pieces. Add next 4 ingredients and let stand overnight in the refrigerator. Sauté onion and instant minced garlic in butter or margarine. Add meat, cover, and cook slowly in its own juice 1½ hours. Add stock or water and red pepper. Heat thoroughly. Serve with rice.

YIELD: 6 servings

INDIAN CURRY PUFFS

In India curry puffs are filled with spiced vegetable mixtures for the vegetarians, various meat fillings for nonvegetarians, and flavorful sweets.

2 tablespoons instant minced onion
2 tablespoons water
2 tablespoons butter or margarine

2 teaspoons ground coriander
¼ teaspoon cayenne
¼ teaspoon ground ginger
¼ teaspoon ground cinnamon
¼ teaspoon garlic powder

¼ cup chopped fresh tomatoes
1½ cups finely ground lamb or beef
1¼ teaspoons salt

¼ cup water
2 teaspoons fresh lemon juice
Curry Puff Pastry *(see below)*
Large egg white, lightly beaten

Mix onion with water and let stand 3 to 5 minutes to soak. Sauté in butter or margarine. Add next 5 ingredients; stir and cook 1 minute. Stir in next 3 ingredients. Stir and cook 2 or 3 minutes. Add the ¼ cup water and lemon juice. Stir and cook until all water has disappeared. Turn onto a plate to cool.

Roll Curry Puff Pastry very thin on a lightly floured board. Cut into circles using a saucer as a guide for the large puffs; with a 2½-inch cooky cutter for appetizer size. Brush edges lightly with lightly beaten egg white. Place meat mixture on each—1 rounded tablespoon on larger puff or rounded ½ teaspoon on the smaller size. Fold over the dough and crimp edges with a fork, being sure they are well sealed.

Fry in deep fat preheated to 375° F. until golden brown. Drain on absorbent paper. Serve as main dish or hot appetizer. If desired, replace Curry Puff Pastry with plain pastry and bake 12 to 15 minutes in a preheated hot oven (400° F.).

CURRY PUFF PASTRY

2 cups sifted all-purpose flour
1 teaspoon salt
¼ cup (½ stick) butter or margarine
7 tablespoons yogurt

Sift flour with salt. Melt butter or margarine and add to flour. Mix well. Stir in yogurt gradually, working it in with the hands about 5 minutes. Knead until dough is satiny and smooth.

YIELD: About 6 main-dish puffs or 5 dozen appetizer puffs

BOILED LAMB WITH DILL SAUCE

2½ pounds lamb stew meat or
    shoulder of lamb

1 bay leaf
8 whole black peppers
½ teaspoon dill seed
2 teaspoons salt
2 cups water

2 tablespoons butter or margarine
2 tablespoons flour
2 cups lamb stock

¼ teaspoon dill seed
1 tablespoon cider vinegar
1 teaspoon sugar
½ teaspoon salt

Trim and discard excess fat from lamb. Cut meat into 1-inch pieces. Place in a saucepan with next 5 ingredients. Cover. Bring to boiling point and cook slowly 1½ hours, or until meat is tender. Melt butter or margarine in a 2-quart saucepan. Blend in flour. Stir and cook until mixture is bubbly.

Remove from heat. Drain 2 cups of stock from meat and add to flour and butter. Add remaining ingredients. Stir and cook until sauce has thickened. Add meat and heat. Serve with boiled potatoes or cooked rice.

YIELD: 6 servings

CURRIED LAMB KEBABS

2 pounds boneless leg of lamb

2 teaspoons salt
1 teaspoon ground black pepper
2 teaspoons curry powder
¼ teaspoon ground ginger
¼ teaspoon instant minced garlic
1½ tablespoons instant minced onion
1 tablespoon lemon juice
3 tablespoons olive or salad oil

Trim excess fat from lamb and cut meat into 1½-inch cubes. Place in a mixing bowl. Add remaining ingredients and rub well into the lamb. Cover and marinate in the refrigerator overnight or 5 to 6 hours.

String meat on skewers and cook over a slow-burning charcoal fire until meat is well done and browned. If desired, cook in oven broiler 15 to 20 minutes. Baste with marinade as often as the meat looks dry. Serve between thick diagonal slices of French bread or frankfurter buns.

YIELD: 6 servings

LAMB KEBABS, HAWAIIAN STYLE

2 pounds boneless leg of lamb

1 teaspoon sugar
½ teaspoon salt
½ teaspoon ground black pepper
¼ teaspoon ground ginger

6 tablespoons yogurt
2 teaspoons salt
1 teaspoon ground ginger
2 teaspoons poppy seed
4 teaspoons ground coriander
2 teaspoons ground turmeric
¼ teaspoon cayenne

¼ cup shortening, melted

Trim off and discard excess fat from lamb. Cut meat into 1-inch pieces. Place in a bowl, add boiling water to cover, and soak 5 minutes. Drain. Soften onion in the ¼ cup of water and mix with next 7 ingredients. Add to meat. Mix well to coat meat with the seasonings. Cover. Let stand in the refrigerator 4 to 5 hours or overnight. Broil in an oiled, shallow baking pan 8 minutes, turning and basting with melted shortening 2 times. String on toothpicks, using 2 kebabs per serving. Serve as a hot hors d'oeuvre.

YIELD: 16 to 18 servings

MOORISH KEBABS

This is a typical Moroccan dish, beautifully seasoned. When cut into ¾-inch cubes, these make particularly tempting hot hors d'oeuvres.

2 pounds boneless leg of lamb
¼ pound lamb suet

¼ cup finely chopped onion
2 tablespoons finely chopped parsley
4 tablespoons olive *or* salad oil
1 crumbled bay leaf
1½ teaspoons salt
2 teaspoons ground coriander seed
1 teaspoon ground cumin seed
3 teaspoons paprika
½ teaspoon ground black pepper
¼ teaspoon ground ginger
¼ teaspoon garlic powder

¼ teaspoon instant minced garlic
1 tablespoon soy sauce
⅓ cup lemon juice
⅓ cup wine vinegar

Trim excess fat from lamb and cut meat into 1½-inch cubes. Combine remaining ingredients; heat, cool, and pour over lamb. Mix well. Cover bowl and refrigerate overnight or 5 to 6 hours, stirring occasionally. String lamb on skewers.

Cook over a slow-burning charcoal fire until meat is well done and browned. (Cooking time depends upon the heat of the fire.) If desired, cook in oven broiler 15 to 20 minutes. Baste with marinade as often as meat looks dry. Serve between warm frankfurter buns or long French rolls.

YIELD: 6 servings

LAMB KEBABS, INDIAN STYLE

2 pounds boneless leg of lamb
Boiling water
¼ cup instant minced onion
¼ cup water

Trim excess fat from lamb and cut the lean portion into 1½-inch cubes. Chop suet very fine and add to lamb. Thoroughly mix the remaining ingredients and add to the meat. Mix well.

Cover and marinate in the refrigerator overnight or 5 to 6 hours. String meat on skewers and broil over a slow-burning charcoal fire until meat is thoroughly cooked and browned. If desired, broil in oven broiler 10 to 12 minutes, or until done. Serve kebabs in split, warm frankfurter buns or long French rolls.

YIELD: 6 servings

RUSSIAN LAMB KEBABS

An American adaptation of the Russian shashlik.

2 pounds boneless leg of lamb
½ pound fresh, button mushroom
    caps
¼ teaspoon instant minced garlic
½ teaspoon ground black pepper
½ teaspoon powdered mustard
2 teaspoons salt
1 tablespoon instant minced onion
1 tablespoon cider vinegar
1 tablespoon fresh lemon juice
⅓ cup olive *or* salad oil
4 slices bacon

Trim excess fat from lamb and cut lamb into 1½-inch cubes. Place in a bowl along with mushrooms and set aside. Combine the next 8 ingredients and pour over lamb and mushrooms. Cover and refrigerate 5 to 6 hours or overnight, turning in marinade 4 or 5 times. Cut bacon into 1-inch pieces.

Alternate lamb, bacon, and mushrooms on skewers, allowing space between each piece to permit thorough cooking. Broil over a slow-burning charcoal fire until well done and browned. (Cooking time depends upon heat of fire.) If desired, broil 15 to 20 minutes in oven broiler. Baste with marinade as often as meat looks dry.

YIELD: 8 servings

ROSEMARY SHISH KEBABS

2 pounds lean leg of lamb
1 teaspoon salt
1 teaspoon garlic salt
1 teaspoon crumbled rosemary leaves
¾ teaspoon onion salt
½ teaspoon ground black pepper
2 tablespoons prepared mustard
2 tablespoons cider vinegar
4 tablespoons olive *or* salad oil
16 small onion slices
16 green pepper squares
16 small, whole fresh mushrooms

Trim and discard excess fat from lamb and cut the lean portion into 1½-inch cubes. Combine the next 8 ingredients, add to lamb, and mix well. Marinate in the refrigerator overnight or 5 to 6 hours, turning meat in marinade 4 or 5 times.

String lamb on skewers, alternating with onion slices, green pepper squares, and mushrooms. Cook over a slow-burning charcoal fire until browned and thoroughly cooked, basting with marinade sauce left in bowl. (The cooking time depends upon the heat of the fire.) Serve in warm, split frankfurter buns.

YIELD: 8 servings

SPICED SHISH KEBABS

1 can (10½ ounces) beef bouillon
¼ cup salad *or* olive oil
2 tablespoons cider vinegar
2 tablespoons fresh lemon juice
1 teaspoon salt
1 teaspoon poultry seasoning
½ teaspoon ground black pepper
½ teaspoon onion powder
¼ teaspoon garlic powder

1 tablespoon mixed pickling spice
2 pounds boneless leg of lamb
8 green pepper squares, 1½ inches each
8 slices medium-small onion, ¼ inch thick
8 medium-size mushroom caps
8 wedges fresh, firm tomatoes

Place the first 9 ingredients in a saucepan. Tie pickling spice in a bag and add. Bring mixture to boiling point and boil 2 minutes. Trim and discard excess fat from lamb and cut into 1½-inch cubes and add to marinade. Cool. Cover and refrigerate overnight or 10 to 12 hours.

String lamb on skewers, alternating with green pepper squares, onion slices, and mushroom caps. Cook over slow-burning charcoal fire 20 to 25 minutes, basting with marinade as often as meat looks dry.

String tomato wedges on a skewer and cook over hot coals when meat is about half done. (This method prevents over-cooking tomatoes.) If desired, cook in oven broiler. Serve all in frankfurter rolls or wedges of French bread cut to fit kebabs.

YIELD: 8 servings

CURRIED LAMBURGERS

1½ pounds ground lean lamb
Onion salt
Garlic salt
¼ cup (½ stick) soft butter *or* margarine
¾ to 1 teaspoon curry powder
6 hamburger buns

Shape unseasoned ground lamb into 6 patties ½ inch thick. Sprinkle both sides with onion and garlic salts. Place in a folding wire broiler. Cook over slow-burning charcoal fire or in oven broiler 15 to 20 minutes, turning to brown both sides. In the meantime, blend butter or margarine with curry powder and spread generously on both sides of patties. Serve hot between warm hamburger buns.

YIELD: 6 patties

SAUSAGE-LIVER LOAF

2 pounds lamb's liver

½ pound lean pork sausage
1 cup fine, dry bread crumbs
2 large eggs, lightly beaten
2 tablespoons instant minced onion
1 tablespoon poultry seasoning
2 teaspoons salt
1 teaspoon celery salt
1 teaspoon powdered mustard
½ teaspoon ground black pepper
⅛ teaspoon cayenne
⅛ teaspoon garlic powder
¾ cup liver stock

2 slices lean bacon

Cook liver in simmering water to cover in covered saucepan 5 minutes. Remove from water and drain well, saving the stock to use later. Put liver through a food chopper, using the medium blade. Add next 12 ingredients. Mix well. Turn mixture into a greased 9 x 5 x 3-inch loaf pan, patting it uniformly against all sides of pan. Cut bacon strips in half and place over top. Bake in a preheated moderate oven (350° F.) 1 hour.

YIELD: 8 to 10 servings

LAMB'S LIVER AND BACON LOAF

2 pounds lamb's liver
3 tablespoons bacon fat

5 slices crisp bacon, crumbled
2 cups soft bread crumbs
¼ cup instant minced onion
3 teaspoons salt
3 teaspoons powdered mustard
2 teaspoons poultry seasoning
½ teaspoon ground black pepper

1 beef bouillon cube
¾ cup boiling water
2 large eggs, lightly beaten

Sauté liver in hot bacon fat only until the pink disappears. Put it through a food chopper, using the medium blade. Add the next 7 ingredients. Dissolve bouillon cube in boiling water and add. Mix well.

Stir in eggs. Turn into a greased 9 x 5 x 3-inch loaf pan. Bake in a preheated moderate oven (350° F.) 1 hour. (Left-over Lamb's Liver and Bacon Loaf makes delicious sandwiches.)

YIELD: 8 to 10 servings

LAMB LOAF WITH ROSEMARY SAUCE

2 pounds ground lean lamb
2 cups soft bread crumbs
3 tablespoons instant minced onion
1 tablespoon parsley flakes
1¾ teaspoons salt
¼ teaspoon ground black pepper
2 large eggs, lightly beaten
½ cup beef stock or water
⅛ teaspoon garlic powder

2 tablespoons butter or margarine
2 tablespoons flour

1 cup milk or light cream
¼ teaspoon salt
¼ teaspoon crumbled rosemary leaves
¹⁄₁₆ teaspoon ground white pepper

Combine the first 9 ingredients. Mix lightly, but well. Turn into a greased 9 x 5 x 3-inch loaf pan. Bake in a preheated moderate oven (350° F.) 1 hour or until meat is done.

In the meantime, melt butter or margarine in a saucepan. Blend in flour. Add remaining ingredients. Stir and cook until sauce is of medium thickness. Serve over slices of hot lamb loaf.

YIELD: 8 servings

CROWN ROAST OF LAMB

1 crown (16-rib) lamb roast
1 teaspoon salt
¼ teaspoon ground black pepper

¼ cup instant minced onion
¼ cup water

¾ cup chopped celery
4 cups hot mashed potatoes
1 cup fine, dry bread crumbs
2 tablespoons bacon fat

1 teaspoon salt
½ teaspoon crumbled rosemary leaves
¼ teaspoon ground black pepper
⅛ teaspoon garlic powder
___
16 small fresh mushrooms
½ inch boiling water
1 teaspoon fresh lemon juice
Melted butter *or* margarine
Lamb Gravy *(see below)*

Ask the butcher to grind the trimmings from the roast and use it for lamb loaf or patties. Mix 1 teaspoon salt with ¼ teaspoon ground black pepper and rub over both sides of meat. Stand roast on a rack in a shallow baking pan. Soften instant minced onion in water and mix with next 8 ingredients. Spoon into center of crown. Wrap ends of ribs with foil to prevent charring. Cover top of stuffing with foil. Bake in a preheated slow oven (325° F.) 2¾ hours. Remove foil from ends of ribs and stuffing. Continue baking 1 more hour. Wash and boil mushroom caps 1 minute in the boiling water and lemon juice. Dip each in melted butter or margarine and place on the end of each rib. Cook 5 minutes. Or, if desired, top rib ends with paper frills. Garnish with parsley. Serve with Lamb Gravy.

LAMB GRAVY

Drain drippings from roasting pan and blend with 1 tablespoon flour. Stir in 1 cup water, ¼ teaspoon salt (or to taste), ⅛ teaspoon crumbled rosemary leaves, and 1/16 teaspoon each, ground black pepper and garlic powder. Stir and cook 1 to 2 minutes or until slightly thickened.

YIELD: 8 servings

HERBED ROAST LEG OF LAMB, GREEK STYLE

A liberal use of olive oil, oregano, and lemon juice is characteristic of good Greek meat cookery.

6-pound leg of lamb
Garlic powder
1½ teaspoons salt
½ teaspoon ground black pepper
3 teaspoons oregano leaves
½ cup olive oil
2 tablespoons fresh lemon juice

Wipe lamb with a damp cloth. Make 5 slits ½ inch wide and 2 inches deep at intervals over the top of roast. Fill each slit with 1/16 teaspoon garlic powder.

Mix 1 teaspoon of the oregano, 1/16 teaspoon garlic powder, 1 teaspoon of the salt, and ¼ teaspoon of the black pepper and rub over the surface of the lamb. Combine remaining salt, black pepper, oregano, oil, and lemon juice. Heat and rub into lamb.

Put meat on a rack and place in a large, shallow baking pan. Cook, uncovered, in a preheated slow oven (325° F.) 3 to 3½ hours, basting several times with hot herbed oil and lemon juice. Remove lamb from roasting pan and place on a serving platter. Make gravy from pan drippings.

YIELD: 10 servings

ROAST LAMB, ITALIAN STYLE

Italian cooks use rosemary lavishly on many of their meat dishes, especially lamb. A pinch of sage and garlic goes beautifully with the rosemary.

6-pound leg of lamb
___
1¾ teaspoons salt
¾ teaspoon ground black pepper
1 teaspoon crumbled rosemary leaves
¼ teaspoon sage leaves
¼ teaspoon instant minced garlic
2½ tablespoons flour
___
½ cup wine vinegar
½ cup hot water
___

5 anchovy fillets, minced
2 teaspoons flour
2 tablespoons water
1 teaspoon Kitchen Bouquet
¼ teaspoon salt (or to taste)

Trim and discard excess fat from lamb. Place meat, skin-side up, in a shallow baking pan and cook 10 minutes in a preheated very hot oven (500° F.). Remove from oven. Mix the next 6 ingredients and rub over the entire surface of roast with the back of a wooden spoon.

Reduce oven heat to slow (325°F.) Add vinegar and water to roasting pan, cover pan with foil, return to oven, and cook 3½ hours, or until meat is tender. Remove meat to serving platter.

Strain spices from pan drippings. Combine remaining ingredients and blend with pan drippings. Stir and cook 1 minute or until thickened. Serve over hot sliced lamb.

YIELD: 10 servings

MARINATED LAMB ROAST

6-pound leg of lamb roast

2 tablespoons mixed pickling spice
1½ teaspoons poultry seasoning
1 teaspoon salt
2 tablespoons grated lemon rind
3 tablespoons fresh lemon juice
2 cans (10½ ounces each) beef
   bouillon

2 tablespoons shortening
2 medium-size carrots
1 medium-size onion

Trim and discard excess fat from lamb and place in a close-fitting pan. Combine the next 6 ingredients. Heat, but do not boil. Pour over lamb. Cool. Marinate in refrigerator full 24 hours, turning several times in marinade.

Before cooking, remove meat from marinade and wipe dry with paper towels. Brown on all sides in hot shortening. Add marinade and vegetables. Bake, covered, in a preheated slow oven (325° F.) 3½ hours or until meat is tender, basting with marinade 4 times.

Remove meat to a serving platter and keep warm. Strain pan drippings and thicken with flour, using 1½ tablespoons to each cup strained gravy. Stir and cook until thickened. Serve over sliced lamb.

YIELD: 10 servings

ARMENIAN ONION AND LAMB STEW

3 pounds boneless lamb stew meat
4 tablespoons flour
3 tablespoons salad oil *or* shortening
2½ cups water
3 teaspoons salt
1 teaspoon cumin seed
24 small white onions
1 cup diced tomatoes
2 teaspoons paprika
½ teaspoon ground black pepper

Trim and discard excess fat from meat. Cut lamb into 1-inch pieces. Mix flour with meat and brown in hot oil or shortening. Add water, salt, and cumin seed.

Cover and cook 1 hour, adding more water if necessary. Peel onions and add along with tomatoes. Cook, covered, 45 minutes. Stir in paprika and black pepper. Cook 5 minutes. Serve hot.

YIELD: 6 servings

CURRIED LAMB STEW

2 pounds boneless, lean lamb stew
   meat

1½ tablespoons curry powder
   (or to taste)
1 tablespoon salt
½ teaspoon ground black pepper
¼ cup flour

2 tablespoons shortening
2 cups water
1 bay leaf

1½ cups cubed potatoes
1½ cups sliced carrots
1 cup sliced celery
1 cup sliced onions
¼ teaspoon instant minced garlic

1 cup frozen peas, thawed

Trim and discard excess fat from meat. Cut lamb into 1-inch pieces. Combine next 4 ingredients, add to meat, and mix well. Brown on all sides in hot shortening in a Dutch oven or heavy saucepan. Add water and bay leaf.

Cover and cook 1½ hours or until meat is almost tender. Add the next 5 ingredients. Cover and cook 20 minutes. Add peas and cook covered, 10 minutes, or until peas are tender. Serve hot.

YIELD: 6 servings

ROSEMARY LAMB CASSEROLE

2 pounds boneless lamb stew meat

1 cup boiling water
3 teaspoons salt
½ teaspoon ground black pepper
¼ teaspoon instant minced garlic
1 bay leaf

4 medium-size potatoes
2 medium-size carrots
12 small white onions

½ teaspoon crumbled rosemary leaves
¼ cup flour
⅓ cup water

Trim fat from lamb, saving some to use for browning meat. Cut the lean meat into 1½-inch cubes. Melt 2 tablespoons chopped lamb fat in a skillet. Add meat and brown on all sides. Turn into

a 2-quart casserole. Add the next 5 ingredients.

Cover and cook in a preheated slow oven (325° F.) 45 minutes or until lamb is almost tender. Peel and quarter potatoes and carrots and add to casserole. Peel onions and add. Cover and cook 30 minutes. Blend the remaining ingredients until smooth and mix with the meat and vegetables. Cover and cook 25 minutes or until vegetables are tender.

YIELD: 6 servings

SPANISH LAMB STEW

2 pounds breast of lamb
⅓ cup flour
2 tablespoons shortening *or* olive oil

3 cups hot water
1 bay leaf
3½ teaspoons salt
½ teaspoon whole black pepper

¼ cup onion flakes
½ cup finely chopped green pepper
½ cup uncooked rice
2 cups (1 pound, 3 ounces) canned tomatoes
1 cup frozen peas, thawed
½ teaspoon thyme leaves

1 large egg, beaten
1 teaspoon olive oil
½ teaspoon cider vinegar

Cut lamb into 1½-inch pieces. Dredge in flour and brown in hot shortening or oil. Add the next 4 ingredients. Cover and cook slowly 1½ hours or until meat is almost tender. Add onion, green pepper, and rice. Cover and simmer 30 minutes.

Add tomatoes, peas, and thyme 10 minutes before cooking time is up. Combine the last 3 ingredients. Add to stew. Stir and cook 1 to 2 minutes or until thickened. Serve hot.

YIELD: 6 servings

CURRIED STUFFED EGGPLANT

1 large (1½ pounds) eggplant

1 cup chopped onion
1 cup chopped fresh mushrooms
1¼ teaspoons curry powder

2 tablespoons butter *or* margarine
1 cup ground cooked lamb
½ cup fine, dry bread crumbs
¼ teaspoon ground black pepper
1 teaspoon salt
Toasted Sesame Seed*
Fresh parsley

Wash eggplant. Wrap in foil and bake in a preheated moderate oven (350° F.) 50 minutes or until it is partially done. Cut in half and remove pulp to within ½ inch of the skin, being careful not to cut skin. Chop pulp and place it in a mixing bowl.

Sauté next 3 ingredients in butter or margarine 2 to 3 minutes. Add to eggplant pulp along with lamb, bread crumbs, and seasonings. Mix well. Spoon mixture into eggplant shells. Place halves in a close-fitting baking dish so they will hold their shape.

Bake in a preheated moderate oven (350° F.) 35 minutes or until browned. Garnish with Toasted Sesame Seed and parsley.

YIELD: 6 servings

STUFFED GRAPE LEAVES

Better not strip the leaves from your grape arbor. Special brining is required, so it's best to buy them in the can from a specialty store. Stuffed grape leaves, known as dolmas, *are great favorites in the Middle East.*

*An asterisk after the name of a dish indicates that the recipe for this dish appears in the book. Consult the Index for the page number.

⅓ cup finely chopped onions
½ pound ground lean shoulder of lamb
1 tablespoon olive *or* salad oil

1 tablespoon honey
1 tablespoon fresh lemon juice
½ cup chopped pine (pinola) nuts *or* almonds
2 tablespoons beef gravy
¼ cup chopped fresh mint
¼ teaspoon ground cinnamon
¼ teaspoon cracked black pepper
½ of a 7-ounce package wheat pilaf, cooked as directed on package

2 large eggs, beaten
½ teaspoon salt (or to taste)
24 grape leaves in brine
¼ cup olive oil
2 tablespoons fresh lemon juice

Sauté onion and lamb in the 1 tablespoon olive or salad oil until onions are transparent. Add the next 8 ingredients and mix well. Stir and cook 5 minutes. Remove from heat and blend in eggs and salt. Cool.

Lay grape leaves flat on a board and top each with a heaping tablespoon of the mixture. Roll or fold leaves to cover meat completely. Hold ends of leaves in place with toothpicks. Place in a large shallow dish. Pour remaining oil and lemon juice over the top. Marinate 2 to 3 hours or overnight. Serve cold.

YIELD: 6 to 8 servings

LAMB-STUFFED GREEN PEPPERS

6 medium-size green peppers
Boiling water
½ teaspoon salt
¼ teaspoon instant minced garlic
2 tablespoons instant minced onion
2 tablespoons water
2 tablespoons salad oil
1 cup soft bread crumbs
2 cups diced, leftover cooked lamb
1 teaspoon salt
½ teaspoon oregano leaves
¼ teaspoon ground cumin seed
¼ teaspoon ground black pepper

Wash green peppers, cut off tops, and remove seeds. Parboil 5 minutes in boiling water to cover and ½ teaspoon salt. Remove from water and drain. Soften instant minced garlic and onion in water and sauté in hot oil until limp and transparent. Blend in remaining ingredients. Spoon lamb into parboiled peppers. Place in a baking dish. Bake in a preheated moderate oven (350° F.) 30 minutes or until done.

YIELD: 6 servings

PORK

ROAST SUCKLING PIG
(WITH APPLE CIDER STUFFING)

If you've never tried this unbelievably delicious and entirely unusual feast—then gather up your nerve, call your butcher, and ask him to order a suckling pig for you.

12-pound, ready-to-cook suckling pig
1½ teaspoons salt
½ teaspoon ground black pepper
1/16 teaspoon garlic powder
Raisin, Nut, and Apple Cider Stuffing*
3 tablespoons butter *or* margarine, melted
2 cups boiling water
Small red apple
2 maraschino cherries
Cranberry necklace
Roast Suckling Pig Gravy *(see below)*

Wash pig in cold water and wipe dry. Rub the inside of pig with a mixture of the salt, black pepper, and garlic powder. Stuff pig loosely with the Apple Cider Stuffing. Close opening with skewers and lace tightly with a string. Wipe the outside of skin and rub with melted butter or margarine. Place a small block of wood in the pig's mouth to brace it for the apple that will be inserted later. Place pig, in kneeling position, on a rack in a large shallow pan. Pour 2 cups boiling water in the pan and cover pig loosely with foil. Roast pig in a preheated slow oven (325° F.) 5 hours or until meat is tender, basting every ¾ hour with hot water that is in the pan. Add more water if necessary. Remove pig to a large serving platter. Replace wooden block with the apple. Insert a cherry in each eye socket. Place cranberry necklace around the pig's neck. Garnish platter with parsley and spiced fruit, if desired.

ROAST SUCKLING PIG GRAVY

Measure fat in the suckling pig roasting pan. There should be ⅓ cup. Pour it back into the pan and heat. Add 2½ cups hot water or meat stock and stir with a wooden spoon to loosen the brown portion that is sticking to the bottom of the pan. Blend ⅓ cup flour with ½ cup water until smooth. Add to the pan liquid. Stir and cook until gravy has reached the desired thickness. Season with 1 teaspoon salt, ⅟₁₆ teaspoon ground black pepper, and ⅟₁₆ teaspoon garlic powder. Serve hot over meat and stuffing.

YIELD: Approximately 12 servings

MARINATED PORK ROAST

1½ teaspoons salt
1½ teaspoons whole allspice
1 teaspoon whole cloves
½ teaspoon whole black pepper
½ teaspoon ground marjoram
½ teaspoon ground sage
1 crumbled bay leaf
1 tablespoon slivered lemon rind
2 tablespoons fresh lemon juice

2 cans (10½ ounces each)
  beef bouillon

4- to 5-pound loin of pork roast
1 tablespoon fat
½ cup sliced onion
½ cup sliced carrots

Heat together the first 10 ingredients to boiling point. Pour over pork. Cool. Marinate 24 hours in refrigerator, turning several times. Remove meat from marinade and wipe off spices. Save marinade. Brown on all sides in shortening in a Dutch oven or heavy saucepan. Add marinade, onions, and carrots.

Cover. Bring to boiling point, reduce heat, and simmer 2 hours or until meat is tender. If desired, bake in a covered roasting pan in a preheated slow oven (325° F.) 3 hours. Remove meat from pan. Strain gravy and thicken, using 1½ tablespoons flour for each cup gravy. Add salt to taste.

YIELD: 6 to 8 servings

CURRIED FRESH PORK ROAST

2 tablespoons instant minced onion
2 tablespoons water
3 teaspoons curry powder
2 tablespoons salad *or* vegetable oil
½ teaspoon ground ginger
¼ teaspoon powdered mustard
¼ teaspoon ground cardamom
⅛ teaspoon cayenne
1¾ teaspoons salt
1½ cups hot water
4- to 5-pound loin of pork roast
1 tablespoon shortening

Soften instant minced onion in the 2 tablespoons water. Sauté softened onion and curry powder in salad oil 3 minutes or until lightly browned, stirring frequently. Stir in spices and salt. Gradually add the 1½ cups water. Heat just to boiling point. Pour over roast. Cool. Marinate in refrigerator 24 hours, turning several times.

Remove from the marinade, saving liquid. Brown roast on all sides in shortening. Place in a covered roasting pan. Add marinade and cover. Bake in a preheated slow oven (325° F.) 2½ hours. Remove cover and bake 30 minutes longer. Baste once. Remove meat from roasting pan. Thicken pan drippings with flour, using 1½ tablespoons for each cup gravy.

YIELD: About 6 servings

BARBECUED PORK CHOPS

2 teaspoons powdered mustard
⅓ cup water

⅓ cup cider vinegar
½ cup catsup
1½ teaspoons salt
1 teaspoon sugar
¼ to ½ teaspoon cayenne
2 tablespoons salad oil

6 lean, loin pork chops, cut 1 inch thick

Mix mustard with water and let stand 10 minutes for flavor to develop. Add the next 6 ingredients. Heat to boiling point. Arrange pork chops over a slow-burning charcoal fire.

Cook until browned on both sides and thoroughly cooked through the center, about 50 minutes, turning and brushing with warm barbecue sauce every 5 minutes or as often as chops look dry. Serve at once.

YIELD: 6 servings

PORK CHOPS WITH ORANGE SLICES

6 loin pork chops

1 teaspoon ground ginger

½ teaspoon powdered mustard
1 teaspoon salt
1 tablespoon light-brown sugar
2 tablespoons soy sauce

3 medium-size oranges, unpeeled
Confectioners' sugar

Trim excess fat from pork and place it in a 10-inch skillet to melt slowly. Combine next 5 ingredients. Rub well into the chops. Brown on both sides in hot fat. Reduce heat, cover, and cook slowly 30 minutes. Remove chops to serving dish.

Wash oranges and cut into crosswise slices ¼ inch thick. Dust them heavily with confectioners' sugar. Brown on both sides in the pork chop pan. Arrange slices on platter around the chops.

YIELD: 6 servings

PORK CHOPS, WESTERN STYLE

6 center cut pork chops, 1 inch thick
1 medium-size green pepper, sliced
4 potatoes, peeled and sliced
4 raw carrots, peeled and sliced

1 teaspoon salt
¼ teaspoon ground black pepper
1½ teaspoons chili powder
1 tablespoon instant minced onion
⅛ teaspoon garlic powder

1 cup tomato juice

Brown pork chops on both sides in their own fat. Cover with sliced vegetables. Mix the next 5 ingredients and sprinkle over vegetables. Add tomato juice. Cover and bake 1 hour in a preheated moderate oven (350° F.).

YIELD: 6 servings

PORK SATE

An Indonesian dish—cured, broiled meat.

2 tablespoons instant minced onion
2 tablespoons ground coriander seed
1 tablespoon light-brown sugar
1 teaspoon salt
¼ teaspoon ground black pepper
¼ teaspoon garlic powder
⅛ teaspoon ground red pepper
3 tablespoons fresh lemon juice
¼ cup soy sauce

1½ pounds boneless lean pork

Combine the first 9 ingredients. Trim off excess fat from pork and cut meat into 1½-inch cubes. Add to marinade. Mix well. Cover and refrigerate 10 to 12 hours or overnight.

When ready to cook, string meat on skewers and broil over a slow-burning charcoal fire, turning to brown on all sides. Baste often while cooking with salad oil or melted butter or margarine. Cooking time depends upon heat of fire. Pork should be cooked well-done. Serve hot in frankfurter rolls or French bread cut to fit the kebabs.

YIELD: 6 servings

PORK CHOP AND LIMA BEAN CASSEROLE

1½ cups dried lima beans
4 cups water
4 teaspoons salt
6 center cut pork chops

2 tablespoons flour

⅓ cup catsup
2 tablespoons light-brown sugar
3 tablespoons instant minced onion
¾ teaspoon powdered mustard
½ teaspoon ground black pepper
¼ teaspoon instant minced garlic
1 small bay leaf

Wash lima beans and soak overnight in water. Add 3 teaspoons of the salt. Bring to boiling point and simmer 1 hour or until beans are almost soft. Drain off water and save it. Turn beans into a 2½-quart casserole.

Trim fat from pork chops and save. Rub remaining salt on both sides of pork chops. Sprinkle with flour and brown on both sides in some of the fat trimmed from chops. Arrange over beans. Combine the reserved 1½ cups bean water with remaining ingredients. Pour over chops and beans.

Cover and bake in a preheated slow oven (325° F.) 1 hour or until chops and beans are tender. Remove cover and bake 30 minutes. Serve hot.

YIELD: 6 servings

BARBECUED SPARERIBS, HAWAIIAN STYLE

1½ tablespoons sugar
3 tablespoons soy sauce
1½ tablespoons wine vinegar
2½ teaspoons salt
¾ teaspoon ground black pepper
½ teaspoon ground ginger
¼ teaspoon cayenne
¼ teaspoon instant minced garlic

1½ teaspoons powdered mustard
2 tablespoons water
4 pounds lean spareribs

Combine the first 8 ingredients. Mix mustard with water and let stand 10 minutes

1522
THE PORTUGUESE
BUILD 'FORT TERNATE'
TO PROTECT THE
SPICE TRADE

to develop flavor. Add to sauce. Arrange spareribs in a large flat dish or platter.

Add sauce, being sure that all sides of ribs are well coated. Marinate in refrigerator 12 hours or overnight, turning occasionally to marinate uniformly.

To cook, place spareribs in a large, shallow pan such as a jelly-roll pan. Pour in all the marinade. Bake in a preheated moderate oven (350° F.) 1½ hours, turning once. Serve hot.

YIELD: 6 servings

CHINESE SPARERIBS

¼ cup soy sauce
¼ cup sherry wine
3 tablespoons honey
1 teaspoon salt
1 teaspoon ground black pepper
¼ teaspoon ground ginger
⅛ teaspoon instant minced garlic

4 pounds pork spareribs

Combine the first 7 ingredients. Pour over spareribs. Cover and marinate in refrigerator overnight or 12 hours, turning meat in sauce 4 times.

Remove spareribs from marinade and

place in a baking pan. Cook in a preheated moderate oven (350° F.) 1½ hours or until ribs are tender and browned, basting with marinade 5 times. Serve hot.

YIELD: 6 servings

PORK SAUSAGE AND RICE A LA MILANESA

1 pound small pork sausages
¾ cup diced onion
1½ cups uncooked rice
1 tablespoon salt

½ teaspoon ground black pepper
2 tablespoons paprika
3 cups chicken stock or 3 chicken bouillon cubes and 3 cups hot water

1 cup grated Parmesan cheese

Sauté sausage with onion until sausage is brown, draining off excess fat as it accumulates. Add rice and salt. Stir and cook until rice has browned lightly. Blend in next 3 ingredients.

Cook until rice is tender, about 15 minutes. Add cheese and mix lightly. Cook in a preheated moderate oven (350° F.) 25 minutes or until hot. Serve at once.

YIELD: 6 servings

PORK AND ASPARAGUS CASSEROLE

1 package (8 ounces) elbow macaroni

3 cups diced, cooked lean pork
1 can (10½ ounces) cream of mushroom soup
½ cup milk or chicken stock
2 tablespoons instant minced onion
2 teaspoons salt
1 teaspoon poultry seasoning
1 teaspoon basil leaves
½ teaspoon garlic powder
¼ teaspoon ground black pepper

1 package (10 ounces) frozen
asparagus
3 tablespoons fine, dry bread crumbs
2 tablespoons butter *or* margarine

Cook macaroni according to package directions. Drain well. Combine with the next 9 ingredients. Place half the mixture in the bottom of a buttered 12 x 7½ x 2-inch baking dish. Cut each asparagus stalk into 3 pieces, saving 8 of the nicest tips for a garnish.

Place asparagus over the macaroni and pork layer. Top with remaining macaroni mixture. Blend bread crumbs with melted butter or margarine. Sprinkle over the top.

Bake in a preheated moderate oven (350° F.) 1 hour or until browned. Arrange asparagus tips, saved for that purpose, over the top 10 minutes before baking time is up. Serve hot.

YIELD: 8 to 10 servings

SCALLOPED PORK AND SWEET POTATOES

Pour a spiced sauce over diced, leftover pork and cooked sweet potatoes, and bake until thoroughly hot. This makes a delicious—and economical—casserole.

3 cups diced, leftover pork roast
4 cups diced, cooked sweet potatoes
1 teaspoon salt
3 tablespoons butter *or* margarine
3 tablespoons flour
2 beef bouillon cubes
2 cups boiling water
¾ teaspoon salt
¼ teaspoon ground ginger
¼ teaspoon ground thyme
⅛ teaspoon garlic powder
3 slices bacon

Fill a buttered 1½-quart casserole with alternate layers of cooked pork and sweet potatoes, having pork as the bottom layer and sweet potatoes as the top. Sprinkle each layer with salt, dividing the 1 teaspoon salt between all layers.

Melt butter or margarine in a saucepan. Blend in flour. Dissolve bouillon cubes in hot water and gradually mix with the butter and flour. Cook until slightly thickened. Add seasonings. Pour over pork and sweet potatoes.

Bake in a preheated moderate oven (350° F.) 30 minutes. Fry bacon until about half done and place over the top. Bake 15 minutes, or until bacon is crisp.

YIELD: 6 servings

SPICED-GLAZED HAM

8- to 10-pound fully-cooked, bone-in, whole ham
1 tablespoon powdered mustard
2 tablespoons water
—
2 tablespoons paprika
1 teaspoon ground allspice
1 cup light-brown sugar
—
About 3 tablespoons pineapple juice
Whole cloves

Place ham, fat-side up, in a shallow baking pan. Insert a meat thermometer, if available, in the center, being sure that the point does not touch the bone. Bake in a preheated slow oven (325° F.) 1¾ to 2 hours.

Mix mustard with water and let stand 10 minutes. Add next 3 ingredients. Stir in enough pineapple juice to form a paste. Remove roast from oven. Spread ham thickly with the glaze and replace in oven, working quickly so that the ham cannot cool.

Bake an additional 30 minutes or until the thermometer registers 130° F. and the surface of the ham is golden brown and glazed. Cool 20 to 30 minutes. Score fat and stud with cloves.

YIELD: 16 to 20 servings

MUSTARD-GLAZED HAM

2 teaspoons powdered mustard
1 tablespoon water
½ teaspoon ground allspice
½ teaspoon ground cinnamon
½ teaspoon ground cloves
5- to 8-pound, fully-cooked, bone-in, half ham
___
½ cup dark corn syrup
¼ cup water
1 teaspoon cider vinegar
___
Whole cloves

Soak mustard in the 1 tablespoon water 10 minutes and blend with next 3 spices. Spread on all sides of ham. Let stand 2 hours. Place ham, cut-end down, on a rack set in a large baking pan. If available, insert a meat thermometer into the center of the ham, making sure that the tip does not touch the bone.

Combine next 3 ingredients and brush over ham. Bake in a preheated slow oven (325° F.) 1½ to 2¼ hours or until the thermometer registers 130° F., basting every 20 minutes with the corn syrup mixture. Remove from oven. Cool 20 to 30 minutes. Score fat and stud with cloves. Garnish as desired.

YIELD: 10 to 16 servings

JELLY-GLAZED HAM

5- to 8-pound, fully-cooked, bone-in, half ham
___
1 cup jelly (apple, currant, cranberry *or* guava)
2 tablespoons light corn syrup
1 tablespoon white vinegar

1 teaspoon powdered mustard
___
Whole cloves

Place ham, cut-side down, on a rack in a large, shallow baking pan. If available, insert a meat thermometer in the center, being sure that the point does not touch the bone. Bake, uncovered, in a preheated slow oven (325° F.) 1½ to 2¼ hours.

While ham is baking, combine next 4 ingredients in a saucepan. Place over low heat until jelly melts. Mix well. Remove ham from oven and score it diagonally in 1¼-inch diamonds. Stud each with a whole clove. Brush or spoon glaze generously over ham. Return to oven and bake 15 minutes.

Again spoon or brush ham with glaze, using all the remaining glaze. Bake 15 to 20 minutes longer or until the surface is beautifully browned and the meat thermometer indicates 130° F. Let stand 30 minutes before slicing.

YIELD: 14 to 16 servings

PARTY-BAKED HAM

10- to 12-pound, fully-cooked, bone-in, whole ham
___
2 cups apple juice *or* cider
1 teaspoon whole allspice
1 teaspoon whole cloves
½ teaspoon cracked ginger
3 cinnamon sticks, each 2 inches long
___
1 cup light honey
___
Whole cloves
Paprika

Place ham, fatty-side up, on a rack in a large baking pan. If available, insert a meat thermometer into the center of the ham, making sure that its tip does not touch the bone. Bring the next 5 ingredients to boiling point in a covered saucepan and boil 5 minutes. Using a pastry brush or small paint brush, brush a little of the mixture over the ham.

Bake in a preheated slow oven (325° F.) 1½ to 2 hours, basting with the spiced apple juice or cider at 15 minute intervals. Drizzle half the honey over ham. Bake 30 minutes. Drizzle ham with remaining honey and continue baking 30 minutes or until surface is golden and glazed and the meat thermometer indicates 130° F.

Remove ham from oven and cool 20 to 30 minutes. Score fat, stud with whole cloves, and sprinkle generously with paprika. Garnish as desired with spiced fruit.

YIELD: 20 to 24 servings

BAKED HAM STEAK WITH BANANAS AND SESAME SEED

2 center cut ham steaks, each ½ inch thick
⅓ cup orange juice
¼ cup dark corn syrup
2 large bananas
2 tablespoons Toasted Sesame Seed*

Slash fat around the edge of the steaks to prevent curling and place on a rack in a large, shallow baking pan (jelly-roll pan). Mix orange juice and corn syrup and brush over the surface of ham. Bake in a preheated moderate oven (350° F.) 30

minutes, basting twice with the orange and corn syrup.

Peel bananas, cut each in half crosswise, then split each half lengthwise. Place over the ham. Brush bananas with the orange juice and corn syrup mixture. Sprinkle with Toasted Sesame Seed. Continue baking 30 minutes, or until bananas have browned.

YIELD: 6 servings

HAM STEAK WITH APPLE STUFFING

2 tablespoons chopped celery
2 tablespoons butter *or* margarine
2 cups toasted bread cubes (croutons)
1 tablespoon instant minced onion
¼ teaspoon salt
⅛ teaspoon poultry seasoning
⅛ teaspoon ground black pepper
2 tablespoons water
1 cup finely diced apples
2 ham steaks, ½ inch thick
Whole cloves
2 tablespoons orange juice
1 tablespoon melted butter *or* margarine
Apple rings (optional)

Sauté celery in the butter or margarine. Add the next 7 ingredients. Mix well. Slash the fat around ham to prevent it from curling and place one of the steaks in a greased baking dish. Spread with apple stuffing. Top with remaining ham steak. Stud the fat around the edge with whole cloves, spacing them 1 inch apart.

Bake in a preheated moderate oven (350° F.) 1¼ hours or until done, basting 2 to 3 times with orange juice mixed with the butter or margarine. Garnish with apple rings if desired.

YIELD: 6 servings

HAM STEAK WITH STUFFED MUSHROOMS

12 large fresh mushrooms

1 cup fine, soft bread crumbs
½ cup finely chopped fresh tomato
¼ teaspoon ground thyme
¼ cup grated sharp American cheese
1 tablespoon parsley flakes
1 tablespoon fresh lemon juice
1½ teaspoons salt
⅛ teaspoon ground black pepper

¼ cup (½ stick) butter *or* margarine, melted
1 teaspoon fresh lemon juice
¼ cup buttered, soft bread crumbs
2- to 2½-pound ham steak, grilled
Parsley

Wash mushrooms, remove stems, and chop them very fine. Set mushroom caps aside. Combine stems with next 8 ingredients and 2 tablespoons of the butter or margarine. Sauté mushroom caps in remaining butter or margarine and remaining lemon juice. Fill with the crumb mixture.

Sprinkle buttered crumbs over the tops. Place on a baking sheet and broil 5 to 8 minutes, having the oven regulator set to broil. Serve with grilled ham steak. Garnish with parsley.

YIELD: 6 servings

BANANA-HAM ROLLS WITH MUSTARD-CHEESE SAUCE

6 firm-ripe bananas
Fresh lemon juice
6 slices boiled *or* baked ham
2 tablespoons melted butter *or* margarine
Mustard-Cheese Sauce*

Peel bananas, brush with lemon juice, and wrap each in a slice of ham. Place in a buttered baking pan. Pour melted butter or margarine over bananas. Bake in a preheated moderate oven (350° F.) only until bananas are hot, about 15 minutes. Serve with Mustard-Cheese Sauce as the main dish for lunch or supper.

YIELD: 6 servings

HAM AND VEAL LOAF

3 cups ground, leftover cooked ham
1 pound uncooked ground veal
1 cup crushed corn flakes
2 large eggs, lightly beaten
1 tablespoon instant minced onion
¾ teaspoon thyme leaves
1 teaspoon salt
1 teaspoon powdered mustard
¼ teaspoon ground black pepper
⅛ teaspoon garlic powder
1 cup milk

Combine all ingredients. Mix well. Turn into a greased 9 x 5 x 3-inch loaf pan. Bake in a preheated moderate oven (350° F.) 1¼ hours or until meat is done.

YIELD: 8 to 10 servings

HAM AND SHRIMP CREOLE

3 tablespoons butter *or* margarine
3 tablespoons flour

2 cups (1 pound, 3 ounces) canned tomatoes
¼ cup tomato paste
1½ cups hot water *or* stock
½ cup diced green pepper
2 tablespoons onion flakes
2 tablespoons chopped parsley
3 teaspoons salt
2 teaspoons chili powder
½ teaspoon sugar
¼ teaspoon garlic powder
⅛ teaspoon ground thyme

1 cup diced, cooked ham
1 cup cooked green peas

Wash and scrape potatoes. Place in a saucepan with boiling water and salt. Cover, bring to boiling point, and cook 25 minutes, or until potatoes are tender. Drain, if necessary, saving the water to use in cream sauce.

Melt butter or margarine. Remove from heat. Blend in flour. Cook about ½ minute or until bubbly. Remove from heat. Pour potato cooking water (stock) into a measuring cup and finish filling with milk. Add to the butter or margarine and flour mixture. Mix well. Stir and cook until of medium thickness. Add remaining ingredients. Heat 1 to 2 minutes.

YIELD: 6 servings

2 cups diced, cooked ham
½ pound peeled, deveined, raw shrimp

Melt butter or margarine in a 2½-quart heavy saucepan. Remove from heat. Blend in flour and cook until the mixture is bubbly. Remove from heat and add the next 11 ingredients.

Simmer 20 minutes, covered. Add ham and shrimp and cook, uncovered, 10 minutes, or until shrimp turns pink. Serve over hot rice.

YIELD: 6 servings

HAM AND CREAMED NEW POTATOES

12 small, new potatoes
1 inch boiling water
1 teaspoon salt
¼ cup (½ stick) butter or margarine
4 tablespoons flour
2 cups potato stock and milk
½ teaspoon salt
½ teaspoon basil leaves
⅛ teaspoon ground black pepper

HAM AND POPPY SEED NOODLE CASSEROLE

1 package (8 ounces) medium-fine noodles
2 tablespoons poppy seed
4 tablespoons butter or margarine
3 cups diced, cooked ham
2 tablespoons flour
2 cups milk
1 teaspoon salt
⅛ teaspoon ground black pepper
⅛ teaspoon garlic powder
½ cup buttered, soft bread crumbs

Cook noodles as directed on package. Drain. Cook poppy seed in 2 tablespoons of the butter or margarine until butter is golden. Mix with noodles.

Fill a 1½-quart casserole with alternating layers of noodles and ham, beginning with noodles and ending with ham. Melt remaining 2 tablespoons butter or margarine in a saucepan. Blend in flour. Cook until mixture is bubbly.

Remove from heat and stir in next 4 ingredients. Cook until sauce has slightly thickened. Pour over noodles. Sprinkle with buttered crumbs. Bake in a preheated moderate oven (350° F.) 35 minutes or until crumbs are brown.

YIELD: 6 servings

DEVILED HAM AND KALE

2 pounds fresh kale
1 cup boiling water

1¼ teaspoons salt
⅛ teaspoon ground black pepper
2 tablespoons bacon fat, butter, *or* margarine

2 cups diced, cooked, leftover ham
1 cup Medium White Sauce*
¾ teaspoon powdered mustard
⅔ cup soft bread crumbs
2 tablespoons butter *or* margarine, melted
Pimiento strips

Wash kale, trim off and discard coarse stems. Place kale in saucepan with boiling water. Cover and cook 25 minutes or until almost tender. Remove from heat and add next 3 ingredients. Turn into a 9 x 6 x 2-inch casserole.

Mix ham with Medium White Sauce and mustard. Spoon over kale. Mix bread crumbs with melted butter or margarine. Sprinkle over the top. Place in a preheated hot oven (400° F.) 10 minutes or until brown. Garnish with pimiento strips.

YIELD: 6 servings

HAM AND EGGPLANT SANDWICH

1 medium-size (1¼ pounds) eggplant
⅓ cup milk
⅔ cup flour
1½ teaspoons salt
½ teaspoon oregano leaves
⅛ teaspoon ground black pepper
⅔ cup shortening *or* salad oil
6 slices cooked ham, heated

Wash eggplant (do not peel) and cut into 12 crosswise slices ¼ inch thick. Dip slices in milk and then in flour mixed with salt, oregano, and black pepper. Brown on both sides in hot shortening or oil, adding shortening as needed. To serve, place 1 slice of ham between 2 slices eggplant in sandwich fashion.

YIELD: 6 servings

FRIED EGGPLANT HAM AND CHEESE SANDWICHES

1 medium-size (1¼ pounds) eggplant

1 cup fine, dry bread crumbs
1½ teaspoons salt
¼ teaspoon ground black pepper
¾ teaspoon onion powder
1 teaspoon finely crumbled oregano leaves
½ teaspoon celery salt

2 large eggs
2 tablespoons shortening
2 tablespoons milk
6 slices ham
6 slices American *or* Provolone cheese

Peel and slice eggplant crosswise, ¼ inch thick. There should be 12 slices. Combine the next 6 ingredients. Mix well. Set aside. Beat eggs with milk. Dip eggplant slices in egg and milk and then into seasoned crumbs. Brown on both sides in shortening, adding it as needed. To serve, arrange 1 slice each, ham and cheese, between 2 slices eggplant in sandwich fashion. Serve hot.

YIELD: 6 servings

CAJUN JAMBALAYA

1 cup rice
Water to cover
2 tablespoons butter *or* margarine

1 cup chopped green pepper
¾ cup chopped celery
1 cup diced, cooked ham
1 cup diced, cooked chicken
1 cup diced, cooked pork sausage

2 cups chicken stock
1½ cups canned tomatoes
¼ cup onion flakes
2 tablespoons chopped parsley
2 teaspoons salt (or to taste)
¾ teaspoon thyme leaves
½ teaspoon chili powder
¼ teaspoon instant minced garlic
¼ teaspoon ground black pepper

Soak rice in water to cover 30 minutes. Drain. Sauté in butter or margarine until rice begins to stick to bottom of pan. Add next 5 ingredients, stir and cook 5 minutes. Add stock, tomatoes, and seasonings. Cover and cook 15 minutes or until rice is almost tender. Turn off heat and let the mixture stand covered until ready to serve. Serve hot.

YIELD: 6 servings

HAM PATTIES

2 teaspoons powdered mustard
2 tablespoons water

3 cups ground, cooked ham
¾ cup fine, dry bread crumbs
½ teaspoon marjoram leaves
¼ teaspoon ground black pepper
¼ teaspoon garlic powder
¼ cup milk
2 large eggs, lightly beaten

2 tablespoons shortening

Mix mustard with water and let stand 10 minutes. Blend with the next 7 ingredients. Shape into 8 patties. Brown on both sides in hot shortening in a heavy skillet. Serve hot with mashed potatoes.

YIELD: 8 patties

HAM TIMBALES

Ham Timbales are an ideal main dish for a ladies' luncheon. Serve with a vegetable such as tiny peas, buttered snap beans amandine, or grilled tomato. Pass piping hot biscuits or corn sticks.

1 teaspoon powdered mustard
1 tablespoon water
3 tablespoons butter *or* margarine
3 tablespoons flour

1 cup milk
¾ teaspoon salt
⅛ teaspoon garlic powder
¼ teaspoon ground black pepper

3 cups ground, cooked ham
3 large eggs, beaten
Cheddar Cheese Sauce*

Mix mustard with water and set aside for 10 minutes. Melt butter or margarine in a saucepan. Remove from heat. Blend in flour. Cook until bubbly. Remove from heat and stir in next 4 ingredients. Cook until thickened. Add mustard, ham, and eggs. Mix only until ingredients are blended.

Turn into 6 buttered 6-ounce custard cups. Place in a pan of hot water. Bake in a preheated moderate oven (350° F.) 45 minutes or until a pointed knife inserted in the center comes out clean. Unmold onto serving plate. Serve with Cheddar Cheese Sauce.

YIELD: 6 servings

HAM PIE WITH SWEET POTATO CRUST

½ teaspoon powdered mustard
2 teaspoons water
¼ cup (½ stick) butter *or* margarine
¼ cup flour
1 cup milk
1 cup ham stock
1 cup diced celery

2 cups diced, cooked ham
1 tablespoon instant minced onion
¼ teaspoon ground black pepper
¼ teaspoon garlic powder
½ cup cooked peas

Sweet Potato Pastry *(see below)*

NOTE: To make ham stock, add 1¼ cups cold water to ham bone. Cover and cook slowly 1 hour.

Mix mustard with water and set aside 10 minutes for flavor to develop. Melt butter or margarine in a saucepan. Blend in flour. Stir and cook until mixture is bubbly. Remove from heat and add milk, stock, and celery. Cook 3 to 4 minutes or until sauce has thickened, stirring frequently. Stir in mustard and the next 5 ingredients.

Turn into a 10 x 6 x 2-inch baking dish. Cover with pastry, rolled ¼ inch thick. Trim and anchor edge to casserole. Make 2 slits in crust to allow for escape of steam. Bake in a preheated hot oven (400° F.) 25 minutes or until pastry has browned.

YIELD: 6 servings

SWEET POTATO PASTRY

1 cup sifted all-purpose flour
1 teaspoon double-acting
   baking powder
½ teaspoon salt

¾ cup cold, mashed sweet potatoes
⅓ cup shortening, melted
1 large egg, well beaten

Sift the first 3 ingredients together into a mixing bowl. Add remaining ingredients. Stir until well blended. Chill 1 hour or until dough is stiff enough to handle. Roll or pat to ¼ inch thickness to fit the top of 10 x 6-inch casserole or 9-inch pie plate.

YIELD: Sufficient pastry to cover a 10 x 6-inch casserole or a 9-inch pie plate

VEAL

MARINATED VEAL ROAST

1 can (10½ ounces) beef bouillon
1½ tablespoons fresh lemon juice
1 tablespoon grated lemon rind
1 tablespoon mixed pickling spice
1 teaspoon salt
¾ teaspoon poultry seasoning

3- to 4-pound boneless, rolled veal roast
2 tablespoons shortening
1 cup sliced carrots
3 tablespoons instant minced onion

Combine the first 6 ingredients in a sauce-pan. Bring to boiling point. Place veal in a close-fitting pan. Pour in marinade. Cool. Cover dish and marinate in the refrigerator a full 24 hours, turning meat in the marinade several times.

Remove meat from marinade and wipe dry with paper towels. Save marinade. Heat shortening in a Dutch oven or heavy skillet, add meat, and brown on all sides. Add marinade and vegetables. Cover and bake in a preheated slow oven (325° F.) 2½ to 3 hours or until meat is tender.

Remove meat to a platter. Keep warm while making gravy. Strain gravy and measure it. Thicken with flour, using 1½ tablespoons flour to each cup gravy. Heat to boiling point, stirring constantly. Serve over sliced veal.

YIELD: 6 to 8 servings

VEAL POT ROAST

When there's a "special" on shoulder of veal, pot roast it this way with dill seed and sour cream.

3-pound boneless, rolled shoulder of
  veal roast
1½ tablespoons shortening

½ cup hot water
6 medium-size potatoes
6 medium-size carrots
6 medium-size white onions
1 tablespoon salt
1 teaspoon dill seed
½ teaspoon ground black pepper
3 tablespoons flour
¼ cup water
½ cup sour cream
Paprika

Brown veal on all sides in shortening. Place on rack in a Dutch oven or heavy saucepan. Add water. Cover and cook slowly 1½ hours. Peel vegetables and add to veal along with salt and dill seed. Cover and cook 1 hour or until meat is tender.

Remove meat and vegetables to a platter and keep warm. Blend black pepper and flour with water and add to pan drippings. Stir and cook 1 minute or until gravy has thickened. Add sour cream. Heat but DO NOT BOIL. Serve gravy in a separate dish. Garnish potatoes and onions with paprika.

YIELD: About 6 servings

PAPRIKA VEAL STEAK

1½ pounds veal steak

½ cup flour
2 teaspoons salt
¼ teaspoon ground black pepper
1 tablespoon paprika
Dash cayenne

¼ cup shortening
1 cup water *or* beef bouillon
½ cup cold water
½ cup sour cream

Cut veal into 4 serving-size pieces. Mix together the next 5 ingredients and save out 1½ tablespoons to use later. Dredge meat in remaining flour mixture. Brown in hot shortening on both sides. Add water or bouillon. Cover and cook 30 minutes or until veal is tender. Remove meat from pan.

Blend the reserved 1½ tablespoons flour mixture with the ½ cup cold water and stir into pan drippings. Stir and cook 1 minute or until thickened. Blend in sour cream. Add meat and heat, but DO NOT BOIL.

YIELD: 4 servings

VEAL PAPRIKA
2 pounds veal stew meat
2 tablespoons shortening
2 tablespoons flour
1½ teaspoons salt
⅛ teaspoon garlic powder
3 tablespoons instant minced onion
1 cup sour cream
1 tablespoon paprika
Potato Dumplings (see below)

Cut veal into 1½-inch cubes. Brown in hot shortening. Mix flour with salt and garlic powder and sprinkle over meat. Mix well to coat veal uniformly. Add water and onion. Cover and cook slowly, 1 hour, or until veal is tender. Stir in sour cream and paprika. Heat but DO NOT BOIL. Serve with Potato Dumplings.

YIELD: 8 servings

POTATO DUMPLINGS
6 medium (2 pounds) potatoes
Boiling water to cover
1½ slices close-textured white bread
2 tablespoons butter or margarine
1 large egg, well beaten
2 teaspoons salt
¾ teaspoon ground nutmeg

⅔ cup sifted all-purpose flour
¼ cup cornstarch

Cook unpeeled potatoes in boiling water to cover until potatoes are tender. Drain off water. Cool and remove skins. Mash or put potatoes through a ricer. Refrigerate, uncovered, overnight or 5 to 6 hours. Cut bread slices into ½-inch squares. Sauté in butter or margarine until golden. Set aside. Stir egg, salt, and nutmeg into potatoes. Add flour and cornstarch. Shape into 2-inch balls. Poke 2 fried bread cubes into the center of each ball.

Place about 2 quarts of water and 2 teaspoons salt in a large saucepan. Bring to boiling and drop in only as many dumplings at one time as will lie uncrowded in one layer. Cook, uncovered, 5 minutes. Remove dumplings with a perforated spoon. Drain well. Serve also with pot roast and Sauerbraten.*

YIELD: 12 dumplings

VEAL CUTLETS PARMESAN

2 pounds veal cutlets, ½ inch thick
1½ teaspoons salt
¼ teaspoon ground black pepper
1½ teaspoons crumbled basil leaves
⅓ cup grated Parmesan cheese
1⅓ cups fine, dry bread crumbs
3 large eggs, beaten
⅓ cup olive or salad oil
Fresh lemon slices

Cut veal into 6 serving-size pieces and flatten to ¼ inch thickness with a mallet or ask the butcher to do this. Mix salt, black pepper, and basil and rub into both sides of meat. Blend cheese and bread crumbs.

Roll meat in crumbs, dip in eggs, and roll in crumbs again. Let stand ½ hour to make crumbs adhere. Heat oil in a 10-inch skillet, add meat, and brown slowly on both sides, allowing about 15 minutes for each side. Serve hot, each topped with a fresh lemon slice.

YIELD: 6 servings

VEAL IN SOUR CREAM SAUCE

(WITH POPPY SEED NOODLES)

2 pounds boneless shoulder of veal
⅓ cup flour
1½ teaspoons salt
¼ teaspoon ground black pepper
2 tablespoons shortening
1⅓ cups boiling water
2 tablespoons instant minced onion
¼ teaspoon instant minced garlic
½ cup sour cream
Poppy Seed Noodles*

Cut veal into ½-inch cubes. Roll in flour, mixed with salt and black pepper. Brown

*An asterisk after the name of a dish indicates that the recipe for this dish appears in the book. Consult the Index for the page number.

in hot shortening. Add water, onion, and garlic. Cover and cook 40 minutes or until veal is tender. Stir in cream and heat *only* until hot. Serve over hot Poppy Seed Noodles.

YIELD: 6 servings

PEPPERPOT VEAL STEW

2 pounds veal stew meat
2 tablespoons shortening

2¼ teaspoons salt
½ teaspoon ground black pepper
1 tablespoon paprika
¼ cup onion flakes
⅔ cup beef bouillon or hot water

2 medium-size green peppers, sliced
3 medium-size ripe tomatoes, quartered
½ teaspoon cornstarch

Cut meat into 1-inch cubes. Brown on all sides in hot shortening. Add the next 5 ingredients. Cover and simmer 1½ to 2 hours, or until meat is tender. Add green peppers and tomatoes 10 minutes before cooking time is up. Mix cornstarch with 2 teaspoons water and stir into the gravy. Cook 1 minute or until thickened. Serve hot over rice.

YIELD: 6 servings

VEAL, NEAPOLITAN STYLE

2 pounds boneless shoulder of veal or veal stew meat
1 cup diced onion
1 cup diced green pepper
3 tablespoons olive or salad oil
2 cups tomato sauce
2 teaspoons salt
1 teaspoon parsley flakes
½ teaspoon instant minced garlic
2 teaspoons crumbled oregano leaves
¼ teaspoon ground black pepper

Cut veal into 1-inch cubes and set aside. Sauté onion and green pepper in hot oil until onion is transparent. Add meat and brown on all sides. Stir in tomato sauce and spices. Cover and simmer 50 to 60 minutes or until veal is tender. Serve hot over rice.

YIELD: 6 servings

VEAL PAPRIKASH

¼ cup onion flakes
3 tablespoons water
2 pounds boneless veal stew meat
2 tablespoons shortening

1 tablespoon paprika
1¼ teaspoons salt
¹⁄₁₆ teaspoon ground red pepper
1 cup canned tomatoes
½ cup beef stock *or* water

½ cup sour cream

Soften onion flakes in the 3 tablespoons water. Set aside to use later. Cut veal into 1-inch pieces and brown in shortening. Add softened onion. Stir and cook 2 to 3 minutes.

Add the next 5 ingredients. Cover and cook 1 hour or until veal is tender. Stir in sour cream just before serving. Heat but DO NOT BOIL. Serve over hot rice.

YIELD: 6 servings

VEAL STEAK PAPRIKASH

Whether you spell it paprikash *or* paprikas, *someone's bound to come along and say it's wrong. Hungarian spelling would be* paprikas, *but to a non-Hungarian reader it would look like a typographical error. At any rate, this is a superb veal dish.*

2 pounds veal steak, ½ inch thick
2 tablespoons shortening
¾ cup diced green pepper
¾ cup diced raw tomato

1 cup sliced onion
½ cup water
1¼ teaspoons salt
⅛ teaspoon cayenne
1 tablespoon paprika

Cut veal into 6 serving-size pieces. Brown on both sides in hot shortening. Add vegetables and additional fat, if necessary. Cook until onions are limp. Stir in remaining ingredients. Cover and cook 45 minutes, or until meat is tender.

YIELD: 6 servings

HERBED BROILED LIVER

1½ pounds sliced calf *or* lamb liver
2 tablespoons melted butter *or* margarine
1 tablespoon fresh lemon juice
½ teaspoon crumbled thyme leaves
¼ teaspoon crumbled marjoram leaves
¾ teaspoon salt (or to taste)
⅛ teaspoon ground black pepper

Place liver on a buttered cold broiler grid. Combine remaining ingredients. Brush over top of liver. Place under broiler heat and broil 8 minutes or until browned. Turn liver, brush with seasoned butter, and broil 5 minutes, or until liver is done. Serve immediately.

YIELD: 6 servings

BREAST OF VEAL WITH POTATO STUFFING

5 pounds breast of veal
2 tablespoons soft chicken fat
3 teaspoons salt
½ teaspoon paprika
6 medium potatoes, peeled

¼ teaspoon ground black pepper
½ cup finely chopped onion
2 tablespoons parsley flakes

2 large eggs, beaten
⅔ cup matzo meal
2 tablespoons hot chicken fat

Ask the butcher to cut a deep pocket in the veal. Combine soft chicken fat, 1 teaspoon of the salt, and paprika and use a portion of it to rub the inside of the veal pocket.

Grate potatoes and mix with remaining salt and the next 6 ingredients. Stuff into the veal pocket. Fasten the pocket opening with skewers or toothpicks. Rub the remaining chicken fat and paprika mixture over the outside of the meat. Place on a rack in a baking pan.

Roast in a preheated slow oven (325° F.) 2½ hours, or cook 30 minutes per pound. Make gravy, if desired, from pan drippings, using 1½ tablespoons flour to each cup liquid. Add salt and ground black pepper to taste.

YIELD: 6 to 8 servings

ROSEMARY VEAL AND HAM CASSEROLE

2 pounds boneless shoulder of veal
2 tablespoons butter *or* margarine
3 cups water
¼ teaspoon instant minced garlic
¼ cup instant minced onion
1 teaspoon salt
¼ cup flour
½ cup milk
½ teaspoon crumbled rosemary leaves
1 pound diced, cooked ham
2¼-ounce can shoe-string potatoes

Cut veal into 1-inch cubes and sauté in butter or margarine until brown. Add water, garlic, onion, and salt. Cover, bring to boiling point, reduce heat, and cook 30 minutes or until meat is tender. Blend flour with milk to a smooth paste, thin with a little of the veal stock and add

to the meat. Stir in rosemary and ham. Cook 5 minutes. Cool.

Turn into a 2-quart casserole, cover, and refrigerate. Half an hour before serving, sprinkle shoe-string potatoes over the meat around the edge to form a border. Cook, uncovered, in a preheated moderate oven (350° F.) 30 minutes or until hot.

YIELD: 8 servings

LIL'S VEAL SCALLOPINE

1½ pounds veal steak, cut ½ inch
    thick and into 6 pieces
⅓ cup flour
1¼ teaspoons salt
¼ teaspoon ground black pepper
2 tablespoons butter *or* margarine
3 tablespoons olive oil
¼ teaspoon instant minced garlic
1¼ cups chicken stock *or* water
¾ cup dry sherry

1½ teaspoons parsley flakes
½ teaspoon thyme leaves
¼ teaspoon marjoram leaves

Pound steaks to ¼-inch thickness with a mallet. Dredge in flour mixed with salt and black pepper. Heat butter or margarine, oil, and garlic in a 10-inch skillet. Add as many pieces of veal at a time as the skillet will accommodate. Brown on all sides.

Push the browned meat to one side and repeat, using remaining veal. Pour in chicken stock and ½ cup of the sherry. Cover and cook 30 minutes or until meat is tender. Add herbs 10 minutes before cooking time is up. Just before serving, blend in the remaining ¼ cup sherry. Cook ½ minute or only until wine is hot. Serve with cooked rice.

YIELD: 6 servings

PASTAS

UNLESS you have had the adventure of exploring shops that specialize in Italian foods, you cannot possibly realize how many kinds—and colors—of pastas there are. There are over 300 shapes available, and many of them have names that sound like opera divas.

As to where the macaroni family originated, there are diverse reports. The story most often told is that Marco Polo returned to Venice from the courts of Kublai Khan, carrying spaghetti among his other treasures. Then there is the entirely apocryphal story that macaroni acquired its name when a nobleman from Palermo tasted his first pasta, dressed with grated Parmesan. As he ate, he kept exclaiming in ecstasy, *"Ma, caroni! Ma, caroni!"* In literal translation, this meant, "But the dears! The precious things!" More prosaically, perhaps, the word may also have been derived from the Italian *maccare,* to pound, as when making a paste. (Spaghetti, by the way, is the diminutive of the Italian word for string.)

To introduce still another anecdote, you may recall that Yankee Doodle Dandy stuck a feather in his cap and called it macaroni. There is a story behind that, too. In eighteenth-century England, there was a Macaroni Club. Its members were young men of wealth, who were considered dandies, and *avant-garde* as well. They made a great display of despising English food and voicing their preference for the exotic macaroni. When British army surgeon Shuckburg wrote "Yankee Doodle Dandy" in 1755, as a satire on the ragged uniforms of the Americans, he substituted "dandies" for the American soldiers, the feathers in their caps symbolizing macaroni.

But to return to more practical matters: cooking directions of the various macaroni products may vary according to their specific manufacturer. It is always best, of course, to follow the cooking directions on the package. General instructions are simple: to cook half a pound of macaroni, spaghetti, or noodles, lower the pasta into 3 quarts of rapidly boiling water, to which a tablespoonful of salt has been added. Do this so slowly that the water does not stop boiling. Cook, uncovered, stirring occasionally to prevent sticking. Seven to 10 minutes of cooking should be sufficient—it depends upon how much resistance you like when biting into the cooked product. Italians prefer it *al dente,* that is, well done yet firm enough to need a bit of chewing. Transfer cooked macaroni to a colander to drain. If it is to be eaten immediately, there is no need to rinse with cold water. However, if it is to be refrigerated for later use, rinse it both before and after storage.

Since all macaroni products are bland, the creation of a suitable sauce offers a challenge. As you will note in the following recipes, most spices and all herbs can be used to give these dishes zest.

MACARONI AND CHEESE, SOUTHWESTERN

1 package (8 ounces) elbow macaroni

2 cans (8 ounces each) Spanish-style tomato sauce
½ cup water
1 teaspoon salt
1 teaspoon chili powder
½ teaspoon ground black pepper
¼ teaspoon garlic powder
2 tablespoons instant minced onion

2 cups grated Cheddar cheese
2 tablespoons butter *or* margarine, melted
¾ cup soft bread crumbs

Cook and drain macaroni as directed on package. Combine the next 7 ingredients. Heat and add 1½ cups cheese. Mix well. Fill a buttered 10 x 6 x 2-inch baking dish with alternating layers of cooked macaroni and tomato-cheese sauce, having macaroni on bottom and sauce over the top.

Sprinkle with remaining cheese. Mix butter or margarine with bread crumbs and sprinkle over the top. Bake in a preheated moderate oven (350° F.) 45 minutes or until browned. Serve hot.

YIELD: 6 servings

HERBED TOMATO- MACARONI CASSEROLE

1 package (8 ounces) elbow macaroni
½ pound ground chuck
1 cup diced green pepper
2¼ teaspoons salt

2 cups (1 pound) canned tomatoes
2 teaspoons basil leaves
¼ teaspoon ground black pepper
½ teaspoon instant minced garlic
¼ cup onion flakes

½ cup soft, fine bread crumbs
1 tablespoon butter *or* margarine, melted
1 cup finely shredded Cheddar cheese

Cook macaroni as directed on package. Drain and set aside. Cook meat, green pepper, and ½ teaspoon of the salt together until meat begins to brown. Add macaroni and next 5 ingredients. Mix well.

Turn into a 2-quart casserole. Mix last 3 ingredients and sprinkle over the top. Bake in a preheated moderate oven (350° F.) 30 minutes or until browned. Serve hot as the main dish for lunch or supper.

YIELD: 6 servings

MEAT AND MACARONI, RANCH STYLE

1 pound ground chuck
1 tablespoon butter *or* margarine
¾ cup chopped green pepper

2 cans (8 ounces each) Spanish-style tomato sauce
¾ cup water
3 tablespoons instant minced onion
1½ teaspoons salt

1½ teaspoons chili powder
½ teaspoon ground black pepper
½ teaspoon garlic powder

1 cup grated sharp Cheddar cheese
1 package (8 ounces) elbow macaroni

Brown meat in butter or margarine. Add green pepper and cook 3 minutes, stirring frequently. Add the next 7 ingredients. Mix well and cook 10 minutes or until mixture has thickened. Stir in cheese. Cook macaroni as directed on package. Drain and add to the sauce. Mix well with a fork. Serve hot.

YIELD: 6 servings

RIGATONI AND SAUCE
(SALSA PER RIGATONI)

1½ pounds ground chuck
1 tablespoon olive *or* salad oil

3 cups hot water
3 cans (6 ounces each) tomato paste
1 bay leaf
2 teaspoons fennel seed
2½ teaspoons salt

¼ teaspoon ground red pepper
¼ teaspoon instant minced garlic
3 tablespoons instant minced onion
2 teaspoons sugar
2 teaspoons oregano leaves

1 package (8 ounces) rigatoni (large-ribbed, tubular macaroni)
½ cup grated Parmesan cheese

Brown meat in hot oil in a deep 10-inch skillet. Add next 5 ingredients. Bring to boiling point, reduce heat, and simmer 30 minutes. Add next 5 ingredients and cook 10 minutes. Cook macaroni as directed on package. Drain well and turn into a serving dish. Cover with sauce. Sprinkle with grated Parmesan cheese.

YIELD: 6 servings

SIMPLE SPAGHETTI SAUCE

4 large mushrooms, sliced
1 tablespoon olive oil

1 can (8 ounces) Spanish-style
    tomato sauce
¾ teaspoon oregano leaves
2 teaspoons instant minced onion
⅛ teaspoon garlic powder
1 bay leaf
¼ teaspoon salt (or to taste)
⅛ teaspoon ground black pepper

¾ of an 8-ounce package of spaghetti

Sauté mushrooms in olive oil. Add next
7 ingredients. Cook 5 minutes. Serve
over hot cooked spaghetti.

YIELD: 4 servings

SPAGHETTI WITH TOMATO-CLAM SAUCE

¼ cup olive *or* salad oil

1 can (6 ounces) tomato paste
1 can (8 ounces) Spanish-style
    tomato sauce
2 tablespoons minced green pepper
1 tablespoon instant minced onion
½ teaspoon salt
½ teaspoon oregano leaves
½ teaspoon poultry seasoning
¼ teaspoon ground black pepper
¼ teaspoon garlic powder

2 cans (7½ ounces each) minced
    clams
1 package (8 ounces) thin spaghetti

Heat oil in a 2-quart saucepan. Add the
next 9 ingredients. Bring to boiling point,
reduce heat, and cook, uncovered, 5 minutes. Drain clams and add. Heat but DO
NOT BOIL; overcooking toughens clams.
Cook spaghetti as directed on package.
Drain and serve with clam sauce.

YIELD: 6 servings

SPAGHETTI WITH SWEET AND HOT SAUSAGE SAUCE

½ pound ground chuck
2 tablespoons olive *or* salad oil
½ cup chopped green pepper
3 tablespoons instant minced onion

½ pound sweet Italian sausage
¼ pound hot Italian sausage
2½ cups (1 pound, 3 ounces)
    canned tomatoes
2 cans (6 ounces each) tomato paste
3½ teaspoons salt
1½ teaspoons sugar

½ teaspoon basil leaves
½ teaspoon oregano leaves
¼ teaspoon crushed red pepper
¼ teaspoon garlic powder

1 package (1 pound) spaghetti
Grated Romano *or* Parmesan cheese

Cook chuck in hot oil until it is no longer
pink. Add green pepper and onion. Stir
and cook 5 minutes. Blend in the next

THE SPAGHETTI

6 ingredients. Cover and simmer 1 hour.

Add all remaining ingredients except spaghetti and cheese. Cook 10 minutes. Serve hot over spaghetti, cooked as directed on the package. Sprinkle with grated Romano or Parmesan cheese.

YIELD: 10 to 12 servings

SPAGHETTI VILANOVA

1½ cups chopped onion
1 cup diced green pepper
⅓ cup olive oil
1¼ pounds ground chuck
½ pound hot Italian sausage

3 cans (8 ounces each) Spanish-type
   tomato sauce
2 teaspoons salt (or to taste)
2 teaspoons sugar
¾ teaspoon instant minced garlic

3 teaspoons Italian seasoning
½ cup finely shredded Romano or
   Parmesan cheese
1½ dozen ripe (black) olives,
   chopped
3 packages (8 ounces each) spaghetti
Mozzarella cheese

Sauté onion and green pepper in olive oil 10 minutes or until onion is limp and pepper is tender. Add chuck and sausage. Stir and cook until meat begins to brown, about 10 minutes. Add next 4 ingredients. Cook slowly 15 to 20 minutes, stirring occasionally. Add Italian seasoning, shredded cheese, and olives. Cook 5 minutes.

Cook spaghetti as directed on package, drain and turn into a 13 x 9 x 2-inch baking dish. Pour in sauce, covering the spaghetti. Slice Mozzarella cheese ⅛ inch thick and arrange over the top. Broil until cheese is brown and bubbly. Serve hot.

YIELD: 12 to 14 servings

CARAWAY SEED NOODLES

1 package (8 ounces) noodles
2 tablespoons caraway seed
3 tablespoons butter or margarine
1 teaspoon salt
¼ teaspoon ground black pepper

Cook noodles according to package directions. Drain thoroughly. Heat caraway seed in butter or margarine until butter begins to brown. Add salt and black pepper. Toss lightly with noodles. Serve hot with roast beef, corned beef, ham, pork, or sauerbraten.

POPPY SEED NOODLES

In the above recipe for Caraway Seed Noodles, replace caraway seed with 2 tablespoons poppy seed.

YIELD: 6 servings

CARAWAY SEED NOODLE RING
(WITH CREAMED TUNA FISH)

1 package (8 ounces) medium-width
   noodles
1 tablespoon butter or margarine
3 tablespoons caraway seed
3 tablespoons butter or margarine
3 tablespoons flour
1½ cups milk
2 cans (6 ounces each) tuna fish
¾ teaspoon salt
¼ teaspoon thyme leaves
⅛ teaspoon ground black pepper
Pimiento (optional)

Cook noodles as directed on the package. Drain and rinse with hot water. Melt the 1 tablespoon butter or margarine, add caraway seed, and cook until butter or margarine begins to brown. Add to noodles. Toss lightly. Turn into a buttered 1½-quart ring mold. Place in a pan of hot water to keep warm.

Melt the 3 tablespoons butter or margarine in a 1½-quart saucepan. Remove from heat. Blend in flour. Cook until bubbly. Remove from heat, stir in milk, and cook until of medium thickness, stirring frequently. Drain and flake tuna fish and blend with sauce. Add seasonings.

Heat, stirring as little as possible to avoid mashing tuna fish. Turn noodle ring onto a serving plate. Fill center with tuna mixture. Garnish with strips of pimiento, if desired.

YIELD: 6 servings

EGG BOWS LEONARDO

2 pounds Italian sweet sausage

1 teaspoon salt
1 can (6 ounces) tomato paste
3½ cups (1 pound, 13 ounces)
    canned plum tomatoes
¼ teaspoon instant minced garlic
1 tablespoon instant minced onion

1 teaspoon oregano leaves
½ teaspoon basil leaves
⅛ teaspoon ground black pepper

1 package (8 ounces) egg noodle
    bows (farfallette)

Cut sausage into slices ¼ inch thick and brown. Drain off fat. Add the next 5 ingredients, bring to boiling point and simmer, uncovered, 45 minutes. Stir in next 3 ingredients. Cook 10 minutes. Cook noodles according to package directions. Drain and turn onto a serving dish. Pour sauce over the top. Serve hot.

YIELD: 6 servings

BAKED LASAGNE

1 clove garlic, minced
¼ cup chopped onion
2 tablespoons olive oil
1 pound ground chuck

3 cups (1 pound, 8 ounces) canned
    Italian tomatoes
1 can (8 ounces) tomato sauce
1 teaspoon salt (or to taste)

1 teaspoon basil leaves
1 teaspoon oregano leaves
2 tablespoons parsley flakes

1 package (1 pound) lasagne noodles
1 pound Ricotta cheese
½ pound Mozzarella cheese
¼ pound grated Parmesan cheese

Sauté garlic and onion in hot oil until onion is limp. Add meat and cook until it begins to brown, stirring frequently. Add next 3 ingredients and simmer 40 minutes. Add next 3 ingredients. Cook 5 minutes. Cook lasagne noodles as directed on the package. Drain and rinse with hot water.

In a buttered 12 x 8 x 2-inch baking dish, layer half the ingredients, in this order: lasagne noodles, Ricotta, Mozzarella, meat sauce, and Parmesan cheese. Repeat, using the remaining ingredients. Bake in a preheated moderate oven (350° F.) 30 to 35 minutes or until lasagne is hot and cheese is melted.

YIELD: 8 servings

STUFFED NOODLES
(LASAGNE IMBOTTITE)

2 tablespoons olive oil
¼ cup diced celery
¼ cup tomato paste
2½ cups (1 pound, 3 ounces)
    canned Italian plum tomatoes
¼ teaspoon instant minced garlic
2 tablespoons instant minced onion

1½ teaspoons oregano leaves
1 teaspoon ground black pepper
½ teaspoon sugar
½ teaspoon basil leaves
¼ teaspoon salt (or to taste)

1½ packages (12 ounces) broad
   noodles, cooked
¾ cup grated Parmesan cheese
1 cup diced Mozzarella cheese
¾ pound Ricotta *or* pot cheese
¾ pound Italian sausage

Place the first 6 ingredients in a saucepan, cover, and simmer 1 hour. Add the
next 5 ingredients. Pour ½ cup of the
sauce in a 12 x 8 x 2-inch baking dish,
into which place a layer of: noodles,
Parmesan cheese, Mozzarella cheese, Ricotta or pot cheese, and sauce, beginning
with noodles and ending with sauce.

Slice sausage ⅛-inch thick and cook
only until browned. Place in a layer over
the sauce. Cover in layers with remaining noodles, cheese, and sauce, having
sauce on top. Bake 45 minutes in a preheated moderate oven (350° F.). Serve
hot. Sprinkle with additional grated
Parmesan cheese, if desired.

YIELD: 8 to 10 servings

POPPY SEED AND
ALMOND NOODLES

1 package (8 ounces) noodles
2 tablespoons poppy seed
½ cup slivered, blanched almonds
3 tablespoons chicken fat, butter, *or*
   margarine
¾ teaspoon salt
⅛ teaspoon ground white pepper

Cook noodles according to package directions. Drain thoroughly. Toast poppy
seed and almonds in chicken fat, butter,
or margarine. Add to noodles along with
salt and pepper. Toss lightly. Serve at
once.

YIELD: 6 servings

POPPY AND SESAME
SEED NOODLES

1 package (8 ounces) noodles

3 tablespoons poppy seed
3 tablespoons sesame seed
3 tablespoons butter *or* margarine

1 teaspoon salt
⅛ teaspoon ground black pepper
1 teaspoon grated orange rind
½ teaspoon grated lemon rind

Tuna Fish and Mushroom Sauce*
   (optional)

Cook noodles as directed on package.
Drain thoroughly. Cook poppy and
sesame seeds in butter or margarine until
butter begins to brown. Add next 4
ingredients. Toss lightly. Serve with Tuna
Fish and Mushroom Sauce, roast beef,
lamb, or pork.

YIELD: 6 servings

*An asterisk after the name of a dish indi-
cates that the recipe for this dish appears in the
book. Consult the Index for the page number.

SPAGHETTI WITH
ANCHOVY SAUCE

1 can (2 ounces) anchovy fillets
½ cup olive *or* salad oil

⅛ teaspoon ground black pepper

1/16 teaspoon garlic powder
1/2 teaspoon paprika
1 tablespoon parsley flakes
1/2 teaspoon instant minced onion

1 package (8 ounces) spaghetti
Pimiento

Dice anchovies and heat in oil 5 minutes or just long enough for oil to absorb the flavor of anchovies. Add next 5 ingredients and heat 1/2 minute. Cook spaghetti as directed on package. Serve with anchovy sauce. Garnish with pimiento cut into strips.

YIELD: 6 servings

SPAGHETTI WITH QUICK CLAM SAUCE

Here's a fine Friday dish which takes only minutes. When cooking spaghetti, follow the manufacturer's directions precisely.

2 tablespoons olive *or* salad oil

1/2 teaspoon garlic powder
1/4 teaspoon crumbled oregano leaves
1 tablespoon dried parsley flakes

1 can (7½ ounces) minced clams
1/8 teaspoon ground black pepper
1/2 teaspoon salt

1 package (8 ounces) spaghetti
Parmesan cheese

Heat oil in saucepan. Add next 3 ingredients and heat 1/2 minute. Add next 3 ingredients. Cook over low heat only until clams are hot. DO NOT BOIL. Serve hot over spaghetti, cooked as directed on package. Sprinkle with Parmesan cheese.

YIELD: 6 servings

SPAGHETTI MARINARA

1/2 cup olive *or* salad oil

8 cups peeled, diced, fresh tomatoes
1 tablespoon salt
1/2 teaspoon instant minced garlic
2 tablespoons onion flakes

1 teaspoon basil leaves
1 teaspoon sugar
1/2 teaspoon oregano leaves
1/2 teaspoon ground black pepper
1/3 cup tomato paste

1 package (8 ounces) spaghetti
Grated Parmesan cheese

Heat oil in a 9-inch skillet. Add next 4 ingredients. Cook slowly, uncovered, 30 minutes. Stir in next 5 ingredients. Cook, uncovered, 15 minutes or until sauce has thickened. Cook spaghetti as directed on package. Drain and serve with marinara sauce. Sprinkle with grated Parmesan cheese.

YIELD: 6 servings

ITALIAN SPAGHETTI WITH MEAT BALLS

3/4 cup chopped onion
1/4 cup olive oil

7 cups (2 cans; 1 pound, 13 ounces each) tomatoes
2 tablespoons salt
1 teaspoon sugar
½ teaspoon garlic powder
1 bay leaf
———
1 can (6 ounces) tomato paste
Meat Balls *(see below)*
¾ teaspoon basil leaves
½ teaspoon ground black pepper
———
1 package (8 ounces) spaghetti
Grated Parmesan *or* Romano cheese

Sauté onions in hot oil 4 minutes. Add the next 5 ingredients. Cover. Simmer over very low heat 2 hours. Add tomato paste, Meat Balls, basil, and black pepper 20 minutes before cooking time is up. Serve over spaghetti, cooked as directed on the package. Sprinkle with grated cheese.

MEAT BALLS

1 pound ground lean beef
1 cup soft bread crumbs
1 tablespoon parsley flakes
1 tablespoon grated Parmesan cheese
1 teaspoon salt
¼ teaspoon ground black pepper
⅛ teaspoon garlic powder
1 large egg, well beaten

Combine all ingredients. Shape into 12 balls and set aside. Do not brown.

YIELD: 6 servings

SPAGHETTI WITH MUSHROOM AND TOMATO SAUCE

1 pound fresh mushrooms
3 tablespoons olive oil
3½ cups (1 pound, 13 ounces) canned plum tomatoes
———

¼ teaspoon crushed red pepper
1 teaspoon garlic powder
1½ teaspoons basil leaves
3¼ teaspoons salt
2 teaspoons sugar
1 teaspoon parsley flakes
3 tablespoons instant minced onion
———
1 package (8 ounces) spaghetti
Grated Parmesan *or* Pecorino cheese

Wash and slice mushrooms (stems and caps). Sauté in hot oil 10 minutes or until mushrooms are tender. Break up tomatoes and add. Mix well. Cover and simmer 1 hour, stirring occasionally.

Add seasonings 10 minutes before cooking time is up. Serve over hot spaghetti, cooked as directed on the package. Sprinkle with grated Parmesan or Pecorino cheese.

YIELD: 6 servings

SPAGHETTI PEPERONI

½ pound peperoni sausage
½ pound ground lean beef
3½ cups (1 pound, 12 ounces) canned plum tomatoes
1 can (6 ounces) tomato paste
1 cup water
2 tablespoons instant minced onion
2 teaspoons salt
———
1 teaspoon crumbled oregano leaves
1 teaspoon chili powder
½ teaspoon sugar
½ teaspoon garlic powder
2 tablespoons parsley flakes
1 can (8 ounces) sliced mushrooms
———
1 package (1 pound) spaghetti
Grated Parmesan cheese

Chop sausage fine and cook 5 minutes in a 9-inch skillet. Add meat and cook until it begins to brown. Add the next 5 ingredients. Simmer, uncovered, 20 minutes. Stir in all remaining ingredients except spaghetti and cheese. Cook 10 minutes. Serve over spaghetti, cooked as directed on package. Sprinkle on Parmesan cheese.

YIELD: 8 to 10 generous servings

NEAPOLITAN SPAGHETTI

⅓ cup olive *or* salad oil

1 cup sliced onion
1 cup chopped green pepper
¾ teaspoon instant minced garlic

1½ pounds ground chuck

5 cups canned tomatoes
1 can (6 ounces) tomato paste
3 teaspoons salt
2 teaspoons sugar

½ teaspoon ground black pepper
2½ teaspoons Italian seasoning
3 packages (8 ounces each) spaghetti
Grated Parmesan *or* Romano cheese

Heat oil in a 4-quart saucepan. Add next 3 ingredients and cook until vegetables are limp. Add meat and cook until it is no longer red. Stir in next 4 ingredients. Simmer 2 hours, uncovered, stirring occasionally.

Add black pepper and Italian seasoning and cook 10 minutes. Cook spaghetti as directed on package. Drain and serve with spaghetti sauce. Top with grated Parmesan or Romano cheese.

YIELD: 12 to 14 servings

TUNA FISH SPAGHETTI

¼ teaspoon garlic powder
1 tablespoon chopped capers
2 tablespoons tuna oil and olive *or* salad oil
2 cups (1 pound) canned tomatoes
⅓ cup water

2 teaspoons salt
1 teaspoon instant minced onion
¾ teaspoon crumbled basil leaves
¼ teaspoon ground black pepper
½ teaspoon anchovy paste
1 tablespoon parsley flakes
1 can (6 ounces) tuna fish, drained

1 package (8 ounces) spaghetti
Parmesan cheese (optional)

Cook garlic powder and capers in oil 1 minute, using oil drained from tuna fish as part of the oil. Put tomatoes through a sieve and add along with water. Cook, uncovered, over low heat until sauce is of desired thickness.

Stir in next 7 ingredients. Heat and serve over spaghetti, cooked as directed on package. If desired, sprinkle with grated Parmesan cheese.

YIELD: 6 servings

SPAGHETTI WITH VEAL
(SPAGHETTI CON VITELLO)

1¾ pounds veal steak, cut 1 inch thick

¼ cup flour
2½ teaspoons salt
1½ teaspoons oregano leaves
¼ teaspoon ground black pepper
⅛ teaspoon garlic powder

3 tablespoons olive oil *or* shortening
⅓ cup onion flakes
½ cup hot water
1 package (8 ounces) spaghetti
¾ cup grated Parmesan *or* Romano cheese

Cut veal into 6 serving-size pieces. Dip in flour mixed with the next 4 ingredients. Brown on both sides in hot oil or shortening. Place in a 10 x 6 x 2-inch baking dish. Sprinkle with onion flakes. Rinse skillet with ½ cup hot water and pour liquid into baking dish.

Cover and bake in a preheated moderate oven (350° F.) 45 minutes or until veal is tender. Remove cover the last 15 minutes of cooking period.

Cook spaghetti as directed on package. Drain well. Arrange meat on a serving platter and surround with spaghetti. Add ½ cup of the cheese to liquid left in baking dish. Heat and pour over veal. Sprinkle with remaining grated cheese. Serve hot.

YIELD: 6 servings

MANICOTTI
2½ cups sifted all-purpose flour
¾ teaspoon salt
1 tablespoon melted butter or
  margarine
3 large eggs
About 3 tablespoons lukewarm water
Ricotta Cheese Filling (see below)
Tomato Sauce (see below)

Sift together flour and salt. Add butter or margarine and eggs. Mix well. Gradually stir in enough water to form a soft dough. Knead until smooth. Roll half the dough at a time very thin on a lightly floured board. Cut into 6 x 4-inch rectangles. Place ¼ cup Ricotta Cheese Filling in center of each.

Shape into rolls, having the dough completely covering the filling, and overlapping a fraction of an inch. Place in a single layer, lap-side down, in a 13 x 9 x 2-inch baking pan. Cover with cooked Tomato Sauce. Bake in a preheated hot oven (400° F.) 30 minutes. Serve 2 manicotti per person with sauce spooned over the top. Sprinkle with additional grated Parmesan cheese.

RICOTTA CHEESE FILLING
2 pounds Ricotta cheese
1 teaspoon salt
1 teaspoon ground black pepper

1 tablespoon parsley flakes
½ cup grated Parmesan cheese

Combine all ingredients and proceed as directed above.

TOMATO SAUCE
¼ cup olive or salad oil
2 cans (8 ounces each) tomato purée
4 cups (2 cans; 1 pound each Italian
  tomatoes
½ teaspoon instant minced garlic
1 large bay leaf
_____
2 teaspoons parsley flakes
½ cup chopped celery
1 teaspoon basil leaves
1 teaspoon oregano leaves
1½ teaspoons salt
½ teaspoon ground black pepper

Place the first 5 ingredients in a saucepan. Cook, uncovered, 30 minutes. Add remaining ingredients. Cook 10 minutes longer. Pour over manicotti and cook as directed above.

YIELD: 9 servings, 2 manicotti each

PICKLES, RELISHES, and MEAT ACCOMPANIMENTS

THESE accompaniments to meat have been selected because they contrast so pleasingly with the main dish—in flavor, temperature, color, and texture. About half of these recipes are for "fixings," which are to be served immediately or within several days. The balance of the recipes are for pickles and relishes, prepared in quantities so they may be canned and stored away for future use.

POACHED APPLE WEDGES

2 cups sugar
1½ cups water
¼ teaspoon salt
2 cinnamon sticks, each 4 inches long
  or 4 cinnamon sticks, each 2 inches long
¾ teaspoon whole cloves
4 medium-size baking apples, cored
  and cut into eighths

Combine sugar, water, and salt in a 10-inch skillet. Tie cinnamon and cloves in a cheesecloth bag and add. Bring to boiling point and boil 2 minutes. Add apples to boiling syrup. Cook, uncovered, until apples are barely tender, turning to cook uniformly. Cool apples in syrup. Use as an accompaniment to meat or poultry dishes.

YIELD: 1 quart

CURRIED APPLES

1 can (20 ounces) sliced apples
2 tablespoons butter *or* margarine
½ teaspoon curry powder
1 teaspoon sugar

Turn apples into a pie pan. Melt butter or margarine, add curry powder and sugar, and pour over apples. Bake in a preheated moderate oven (350° F.) 15 minutes or until hot. Serve with meat or poultry.

YIELD: 8 servings

GINGERED APPLE CHUTNEY RINGS

3 medium-size baking apples (Rome Beauty, or other good firm baking apples)
½ cup sugar
1 cup water
⅛ teaspoon salt
¼ teaspoon ground ginger
6 tablespoons fruit chutney (any kind)

Wash apples, remove cores, and cut in half crosswise. Place sugar, water, salt, and ginger in saucepan, mix well, and bring to boiling point. Add apples and cook slowly, uncovered, 25 minutes or until tender.

Remove from syrup and drain, being careful to keep apples intact. Cool. Fill centers with your favorite chutney just before serving. Serve with curries or other spiced meat dishes.

YIELD: 6 servings

SAUTEED BANANAS

4 small bananas
1 large egg, beaten
1 teaspoon fresh lemon juice
¼ cup fine, dry bread crumbs
½ teaspoon ground cinnamon
½ teaspoon ground ginger
1/16 teaspoon salt
3 tablespoons butter or margarine

Peel bananas, cut in half lengthwise, and then in half crosswise. Combine egg and lemon juice. Dip bananas in egg mixture. Roll in bread crumbs mixed with spices and salt. Sauté in butter or margarine, turning carefully to cook both sides. Serve with meats or poultry.

YIELD: 8 servings

SPICED MIXED FRUIT

1 can (1 pound, 4 ounces) sliced pineapple
1 can (1 pound, 4 ounces) whole apricots
1 can (1 pound, 4 ounces) figs
1 can (1 pound, 13 ounces) peach halves

⅔ cup light-brown sugar
1 cup cider vinegar
½ teaspoon salt
4 cinnamon sticks, each 2 inches long

2 teaspoons whole allspice
1½ teaspoons whole cloves
½ cup red maraschino cherries

Drain juices from fruits into a saucepan. Add the next 4 ingredients. Tie allspice and cloves in a bag and add to fruit juices. Heat to boiling point and boil 5 minutes. Add fruits, including cherries. Simmer 10 minutes. DO NOT BOIL. Cool. Remove spice bag.

Cover and chill at least 24 hours before serving. Serve as an accompaniment to meat or poultry. Store all leftover fruit in a covered jar in the refrigerator. It will keep several weeks.

BRANDIED SPICED MIXED FRUIT
After cooling above fruit mixture to room temperature, add ⅓ to ½ cup brandy.

YIELD: 2 quarts

SPICED CRANBERRY SAUCE

1 pound fresh cranberries
2 cups sugar
½ cup water
⅛ teaspoon salt
⅛ teaspoon ground cloves
⅛ teaspoon ground ginger
½ teaspoon ground allspice
½ teaspoon ground cinnamon

Wash cranberries and place in a saucepan with sugar, water, and salt. Cover, bring to boiling point, and cook 8 to 10 minutes or only until skins burst. Remove from heat. Stir in spices. Cool. Serve with meats and poultry.

YIELD: 3½ cups

CRANBERRY STUFFED PEARS
Fill cooked fresh or canned pear halves with Spiced Cranberry Sauce. Serve as a relish with meats or poultry.

TART CRANBERRY-ORANGE SAUCE

2 cups fresh cranberries
½ cup sugar
½ cup water
1 tablespoon grated orange rind

Wash cranberries and place in a saucepan with sugar and water. Cover, bring to boiling point, and cook only until

skins pop, 8 to 10 minutes. Add orange rind. Cool.

YIELD: 1½ cups

GRAPE OLIVES

2 cups Ribier grapes
1 cup sugar
1 cup water
½ cup cider vinegar
1 cinnamon stick, 2 inches long
¼ teaspoon whole cloves
¼ teaspoon whole allspice

Wash grapes, drain, and dry. Place in a 1-quart jar. Combine remaining ingredients. Bring to boiling point and boil 3 minutes. Pour over grapes, covering them completely with the pickling syrup. Cool, cover, and let stand in refrigerator 48 hours before using. Serve as you would olives with meat or poultry.

YIELD: 2 cups

CRANBERRY AND APPLE RELISH

1 pound fresh cranberries
2 medium-size unpeeled apples
2 teaspoons grated orange rind
2 tablespoons lemon juice
1½ cups sugar
½ teaspoon ground ginger
½ teaspoon ground cinnamon
¼ teaspoon ground cloves

Wash cranberries. Wash apples, cut into quarters, and remove cores. Put through a food chopper along with cranberries, using the medium blade. Stir in remaining ingredients. Chill in a covered jar overnight or several hours for flavors to blend.

YIELD: 3½ cups

PICKLED CAULIFLOWER

Boiling water
1 tablespoon fresh lemon juice
3 cups fresh cauliflowerets
1 cup fresh onion rings
½ green pepper, cut in strips
¼ red pepper, cut in strips
1 cup white vinegar
1¼ cups water
½ cup sugar
½ teaspoon salt
8 whole black peppers
½ teaspoon mustard seed
½ teaspoon celery seed
½ teaspoon tarragon leaves

Pour boiling water and lemon juice over cauliflowerets, onion rings, and pepper strips. Cover and let stand while preparing the vinegar mixture.

Combine vinegar, water, sugar, salt, and spices in a saucepan. Bring to boiling point. Boil 5 minutes. Drain water off cauliflower and onion and discard it. Add hot vinegar mixture. Cool, cover, and marinate overnight in refrigerator or until ready to serve.

YIELD: 5 cups

DATE CHUTNEY

1½ cups cider vinegar
1 cup sugar
½ teaspoon instant minced garlic

4 cups (2 pounds) coarsely chopped, pitted dates
¼ teaspoon cayenne
1 teaspoon ground ginger
¼ teaspoon salt

Combine the first 3 ingredients in a saucepan and cook 7 to 10 minutes or until a thin syrup is formed. Add remaining ingredients. Stir and cook 15 minutes or until thickened. Pack in hot, sterilized jars and seal airtight at once or, if desired, store in a covered jar in the refrigerator and serve as needed with curries, pork, poultry, or ham.

YIELD: 4 jars, 1 cup each

PEAR CHUTNEY

10 cups (5 pounds) sliced, firm, ripe pears
½ cup finely chopped green pepper
1½ cups seedless raisins

4 cups sugar
1 cup chopped crystallized ginger
3 cups cider vinegar
½ teaspoon salt

½ teaspoon whole allspice
½ teaspoon whole cloves
3 cinnamon sticks, each 2 inches long

Place pears and the next 6 ingredients in a saucepan. Tie allspice and cloves in a cloth bag and add along with cinnamon. Cook slowly until pears are tender and mixture is thick, about 1 hour. Remove spices. Ladle into hot, sterilized jars. Seal airtight.

YIELD: 8 jars, ½ pint each

GINGER PEARS

⅓ cup (2 ounces) cracked ginger
¼ cup fresh lemon juice
4 pounds fresh pears
5 cups sugar
2 teaspoons grated lemon rind
¼ cup cider vinegar

Soak ginger in lemon juice 6 to 8 hours or overnight. Wash, peel, quarter, and core pears. (If pears are extra large, cut them into eighths.) Add sugar to pears and mix well to coat each piece. Cover and let stand overnight or 6 to 8 hours. Stir in lemon-soaked ginger.

Cook, uncovered, over medium-low heat until pears are tender and clear (about 1 hour), stirring frequently. (Cooking time depends upon ripeness of pears.) Add grated lemon rind and vinegar 5 minutes before cooking time is up. Pack in hot, sterilized jars, filling them to within ½ inch from top. Seal airtight at once. Serve as a relish with meat or poultry or, if desired, serve on hot biscuits or toast.

YIELD: 7 jars, ½ pint each

PENNSYLVANIA GINGER PEARS

5 pounds firm, ripe pears
¼ cup slivered lemon rind
½ cup water
1 tablespoon cracked ginger
½ teaspoon salt
3 pounds light-brown sugar
⅓ cup fresh lemon juice

Peel, core, and quarter pears and place in a 5-quart saucepan. (If pears are very large, cut them into eighths.) Boil lemon rind in the water 10 minutes. Drain and discard water. Add rind to pears.

Tie ginger in a cloth bag and add to pears along with remaining ingredients. Simmer 1 hour or until pears are clear, stirring frequently. (Cooking time depends upon ripeness of pears.) Ladle into hot, sterilized jars. Seal airtight. Serve as a meat or poultry accompaniment.

YIELD: 5 jars, ½ pint each

SPICED PICKLED FIGS

10 pounds firm, ripe figs
Whole cloves
7 pounds sugar
1 quart cider vinegar
1 teaspoon whole allspice
4 cinnamon sticks, each 2 inches long

Wash figs, leave whole and unpeeled. Stick 2 cloves into each fig. Set aside to use later. Combine sugar, vinegar, allspice (tied in a bag) and cinnamon in a large preserving kettle, enamel or stainless steel. Mix well and bring to boiling point. Add figs and cook 5 minutes, uncovered. Remove from heat and cool. Cover and let stand overnight.

Remove figs from syrup the next day. Bring syrup to boiling point, pour over figs, and let them stand 48 hours. Remove figs from syrup again. Bring syrup to boiling point, add figs, and boil about ½ minute or only until figs are hot. Ladle into hot, sterilized 1-pint jars. Seal at once. Let stand at least 4 weeks before using.

YIELD: 8 to 10 pints

SPICED FRESH PEAR PICKLES

12 to 15 (5 pounds) fresh pears
    (Bartlett or Kieffer)
Whole cloves
-----
4 cups sugar
½ cup water
2 cups cider vinegar
4 cinnamon sticks, each 3 inches long
-----
1 teaspoon whole allspice
4 whole ginger roots, each 1½ inches
    long

Wash pears. Remove blossom ends but leave stems attached. If pears are very large, cut into halves or quarters; if small, leave whole. If Kieffer pears are used, cover with hot water and simmer 10 to 15 minutes or until almost tender. If Bartlett pears are used, cook only about 5 minutes. (Cooking time depends upon the ripeness and variety of the fruit.) Stud each pear with 3 whole cloves.

Mix next 4 ingredients in a 6-quart saucepan. Tie allspice and ginger in a cheesecloth bag, add, and boil 5 minutes. Drop in enough pears at one time to fill a jar. Cook until tender to toothpick test. Transfer pears to hot, sterilized jars. Repeat this procedure until all pears have been cooked.

Remove and discard spice bag. Bring syrup to boiling point, boil hard 1 minute and then pour in jars over fruit, filling them to within ½ inch of the tops. Pack a stick of cinnamon in each. Slide a knife down the side of each jar to release air bubbles. Wipe off tops. Seal at once. Let stand at least 6 weeks before using.

YIELD: 3 jars, 1½ pints each

SPICED FRESH PEACHES

25 firm, ripe peaches
Whole cloves
-----
2 cups sugar
½ cup peach cooking water
2 cups cider vinegar
3 cinnamon sticks, each 2 inches long
-----
1 teaspoon whole allspice
2½ cups light-brown sugar

Wash and peel peaches. Leave whole. Stud each with 2 to 3 whole cloves. Cover with boiling water and cook 5 minutes or until almost tender. Drain, saving ½ cup of the water for making syrup.

Combine next 4 ingredients in a 4-quart saucepan. Tie allspice in a cheesecloth bag and add. Mix well and boil 5 minutes. Add 1 layer of peaches at a time and simmer until thoroughly hot, 2 to 3 minutes. Remove peaches to a bowl. Repeat until all peaches have been cooked. Pour boiling syrup over peaches and let stand overnight.

The next morning, combine brown sugar and syrup, bring to boiling point; add peaches, bring to a full rolling boil; pack in hot, sterilized jars. Seal at once. This method of making spiced peaches prevents peaches from shriveling and floating.

YIELD: 3 quarts

SPICED GOOSEBERRIES

4 cans (1 pound each) gooseberries
2 cups light-brown sugar
½ cup cider vinegar
¼ teaspoon salt
___
¼ teaspoon ground allspice
¼ teaspoon ground cinnamon
¼ teaspoon ground cloves

Combine the first 4 ingredients in a 3-quart saucepan. Mix well. Cook over medium heat 30 to 40 minutes or until mixture has thickened, stirring frequently. Add spices 10 minutes before cooking time is up. Pack in hot, sterilized jars. Seal at once. If desired, store in a covered jar in the refrigerator and serve as needed.

YIELD: 4 jars, ½ pint each

TRESSA'S WATERMELON RIND PICKLE

Tressa Zimmer of Union, N. J., is famous for her watermelon rind pickles and justly so. These are crisp, translucent, deliciously spiced. They do require five days preparation time—no short cuts allowed. This permits gradual penetration of sugar and spices.

Crisp watermelon rind
Water to cover
1 tablespoon salt
8 teaspoons alum
___
9 cups sugar
1 quart cider vinegar
2 cinnamon sticks, each 2 inches long
___
1 tablespoon whole cloves
1 slice candied ginger *or* 2 roots ginger *or* ½ teaspoon cracked ginger

Cut off and discard the green and red portions of the rind. Cut rind into 1-inch squares. Measure or weigh. There should be 3½ quarts or 5 pounds prepared rind. Place rind in a large enamel or stainless steel preserving kettle. Add water to cover and salt. Bring to boiling point and cook gently only until rind can be easily pierced with a fork. Add alum. Cool. Cover and let stand overnight.

Turn rind into a colander or large sieve and hold under running water to rinse rind well. Drain. Return rind to the kettle. Add the next 3 ingredients. Tie cloves and ginger in a bag and add. Mix well. Bring to boiling point only, stirring until sugar has dissolved. DO NOT BOIL. Remove kettle from heat and allow to cool. Cover and let stand overnight.

The next morning, drain off syrup to another saucepan. Bring to boiling point and pour over rind. Let stand overnight. Repeat this procedure for 4 more days.

The last day heat the rind in the syrup,

THE HERB-
GARDEN

but DO NOT BOIL. Remove and discard spice bag. Pack the hot rind in hot, sterilized jars and fill with boiling syrup. Seal jars airtight. Let pickles stand at least 4 weeks before using.

YIELD: 5 jars, 1 pint each

SPICED CRANBERRY CATSUP

1 pound fresh cranberries
¼ cup cider vinegar
¾ cup water
1¾ cups light-brown sugar

½ teaspoon ground allspice
¾ teaspoon ground cinnamon
¾ teaspoon ground cloves
1 teaspoon paprika
⅛ teaspoon salt

Wash cranberries and place in a saucepan with vinegar, water, and sugar. Cover, bring to boiling point, and boil 8 to 10 minutes, or only until cranberries are soft. Put through a coarse sieve, pushing as much of the cranberries through as possible. Add remaining ingredients and stir and cook 10 to 12 minutes or until mixture has thickened. Cool. Cover and store in the refrigerator until ready to use. Or, if desired, double this recipe, turn into sterilized ½ pint jars and seal airtight. Serve when fresh cranberries are not available.

YIELD: 2 cups

PICKLED DILL BEANS

2½ pounds firm, young, tender, fresh
    snap beans
3 cups boiling water
2½ teaspoons salt
1¼ cups light-brown sugar
3 cups cider vinegar
1¼ cups water
2 tablespoons dill seed
½ teaspoon ground turmeric

½ teaspoon crushed red pepper
⅔ cup sliced, small white onions

Wash beans and keep them full length. Cut off ends and place in a 5-quart saucepan with boiling water and 1 teaspoon of the salt. Bring to boiling point and cook, uncovered, 5 minutes. Cover and cook 4 to 5 minutes or until beans are barely crisp-tender. Cooking time depends upon tenderness of beans.

Pack beans in hot, sterilized jars. Mix remaining ingredients, bring to boiling point, and boil 3 minutes. Pour hot pickling syrup into jars over beans. Seal airtight at once. Let stand about 6 weeks before using. Serve as a pickle.

YIELD: 7 jars, ½ pint each

MY BEST MUSTARD PICKLE

2 cups (2 medium-size) ground
    cucumbers
1 cup (2 medium-size) ground onions
¾ cup (1½ medium-size) ground red
    or green sweet peppers
3¾ cups (½ medium-size head)
    cauliflowerets
2 cups tiny, whole pickling onions,
    peeled
2 cups tiny cucumbers (gherkins)
6 tablespoons coarse salt
2 cups sugar
2 cups vinegar
2 tablespoons powdered mustard
¼ cup water
6 tablespoons all-purpose flour
2 teaspoons ground turmeric
1½ teaspoons celery salt

(If gherkins and tiny white onions are not available, use cucumber chunks and sliced, small white onions.)

Grind cucumbers, onions, and peppers separately, using the medium blade. Put each in a separate bowl. Separate cauliflower into bite-size flowerets. Place in a separate bowl. Place tiny onions and gherkins each in a separate bowl. Sprinkle each vegetable with 1 tablespoon salt. Add enough cold water to cover each vegetable. Let stand overnight.

Drain well. Turn into a large preserving kettle along with sugar and 1½ cups of the vinegar. Bring to boiling point. Mix mustard with the ¼ cup water and let stand 10 minutes to develop flavor, and add. Combine the remaining ½ cup vinegar with flour, turmeric, and celery salt and blend with the mixture.

Stir and cook until sauce has slightly thickened. Ladle into hot, sterilized jars. Seal at once. Let stand at least 6 weeks before serving.

YIELD: 5 pints

SLICED CUCUMBER AND ONION PICKLE

3 pounds small firm cucumbers
2 pounds small white onions
⅓ cup salt

4½ cups cider vinegar
¾ cup water
¾ cup sugar
2½ teaspoons celery seed
1½ tablespoons mustard seed
2¼ teaspoons ground turmeric

4 very large red peppers, coarsely diced

Wash cucumbers and cut into slices ¼ inch thick. Peel onions and cut into slices ¼ inch thick. Mix the 2 vegetables with salt and let stand overnight. The next morning, turn vegetables into a colander and place under running water to wash out salt. Press out the excess water.

Put the next 6 ingredients in a 5-quart kettle. Bring to boiling point. Add cucumbers and onions along with diced red peppers. Bring to boiling point and boil, uncovered, 10 to 15 minutes or only until cucumbers are transparent. (Pickles will be soft if overcooked.) Pack in hot, sterilized jars. Seal at once. Store in a cool place about 4 weeks before using.

YIELD: 7 jars, ½ pint each

PICKLED WHITE ONIONS

3 pounds 1-inch white onions
Cold water to cover
2 tablespoons coarse salt
Cold water to cover

3 cups white vinegar
1 cup water
½ cup sugar

½ teaspoon whole cloves
6 pods (1½ inches each) dried red pepper
6 small bay leaves

Soak unpeeled onions 2 hours in water to cover with 1 tablespoon of the salt added. Remove onions from water and peel them. Soak peeled onions 48 hours in water to cover with the remaining salt. Before cooking, drain onions and rinse them in cold water.

Place the next 3 ingredients in a 4-quart saucepan. Tie cloves in a cloth bag and add. Bring mixture to boiling point. Add onions and boil 3 to 5 minutes or until they are thoroughly hot. Remove spice bag.

Pack in hot, sterilized jars, having onions covered with boiling vinegar. Add 1 pod red pepper and 1 bay leaf to each jar. Seal airtight at once. Let onions stand 5 to 6 weeks before using.

YIELD: 3 quarts

PIES and PASTRIES

E UREKA! At last we have found a never-fail method for making light, flaky, and tender pastry! It has proven so dependable that we named it "Never Fail," and accordingly have specified it in many of the recipes that follow. You may of course substitute your own favorite pastry for our Never Fail if you so choose.

Very few cooks make good pie crust. This is unfortunate, because a fine pie is one of the most delicious desserts, while a pie with a tough or soggy crust is one of the worst. The technique for making a perfect crust is comparatively simple, once you have acquired the knack.

Detailed directions are given in the following recipes. If you follow them carefully, you should achieve good results every time. The most important factor is the handling of the mixture after it has been moistened.

NEVER-FAIL PASTRY

	I	II	III	IV
	One-crust pie		Two-crust pie	
Ingredient	9-inch	10-inch	9-inch	10-inch
Flour, cups	1	1½	2	3
Salt, teaspoons	½	¾	1	1½
Shortening, cups	⅓	½	⅔	1
Cold water, tablespoons	3	4½	5	7 to 8

The mixing of the dry ingredients (flour, salt, and spices when used) is simple. Just sift them together.

The cutting-in of the shortening follows. This is done in a bowl, using two knives or a pastry blender. The shortening should be cut into pieces about the size of peas. If they are too small, the crust will be crumbly instead of flaky. Each of the cut pieces must be coated with the dry flour mixture so that the pieces will not recombine. The bowl and knives should be dry to prevent lumping of the flour.

Now add the minimum amount of cold water required to just moisten, not wet, the flour. From this point on, great care must be used. The water must be distributed throughout the mass, and air incorporated without developing the gluten of the flour by pulling or working. First, partially distribute the water throughout the flour mixture in the bowl by gently tossing with two forks. Just lift up and gently turn over. (Do not use a stirring motion, which would cause one layer to rub against and pull another.)

As soon as the mixture has attained crumb consistency (pellets of shortening coated with moist flour mixture), turn out of the bowl onto a pastry board. (There is no need to dust the board with flour at this time because there already is sufficient free flour in the mixture.) Very gently shape it into a mound with the hands. Cut the mound in half with a spatula. Pick up one half, set it upon the other, and gently form it into a new mound. (Too heavy a hand makes a tough crust.) Cut the new mound in half and stack again. Repeat this until the dough holds together, about 10 times. This operation completes the mixing and incorporates air. (Since pastry dough contains no other leavening agent, this air is required to lighten the pastry.)

Finally, roll the dough to the required diameter and thickness, using very light pressure and working from the center towards the edges. (Do not pull the dough.) Sometimes it may be necessary to flour the board and rolling pin very lightly with flour during this last stage.

The pastry circles for both the bottom and top crusts should be about ⅛ inch thick and 2 inches larger in diameter than the outer edge of the pie plate.

For a 1-crust pie, fold pastry circle in half and place over pie plate, making sure that the fold is over the middle of the plate. Unfold and gently press the pastry against the inside walls of the pie plate to expel air bubbles, pushing the edges toward the center rather than pulling from the center out. The pastry should extend about ½ inch beyond the rim of the pie plate. Any additional should be trimmed off. Turn the edge under and press against the under side of the rim. Flute the top edge.

For a 2-crust pie, place the bottom crust as described above, except do not fold under or flute edge. Lay the upper crust over the filling in the same manner, press the edges of the 2 crusts together, and turn under and flute the double thickness. The gashes (steam vents) may be cut in the upper crust while it is folded in half or later, as desired.

Fill and bake as described under the individual pie or pie shell recipe.

FOR BAKED PIE SHELL

If shell is to be baked and then filled, as with Lemon Meringue Pie,* prick the entire surface with a fork to release air bubbles. Chill ½ hour. Remove from refrigerator and prick well again. Bake in a hot oven (425° F.) 12 to 15 minutes or until golden brown. If bubbles appear during baking, prick with a fork. Cool completely before adding the filling.

FOR UNBAKED PIE SHELL

If pie filling is to be baked in an unbaked pie shell, as in Old-Fashioned Pumpkin Pie,* chill the shell ½ hour. Fill and bake as directed.

NUTMEG PASTRY

Add ¾ teaspoon ground nutmeg to the flour in the above recipe for pastry for a 9-inch, 2-crust pie.

*An asterisk after the name of a dish indicates that the recipe for this dish appears in the book. Consult the Index for the page number.

BUTTER PASTRY

2 cups sifted all-purpose flour
½ teaspoon ground nutmeg
1 cup (2 sticks) butter *or* margarine
About 2 tablespoons water

Sift flour with nutmeg. Add butter or margarine and cut it in until pieces are the size of peas. Sprinkle enough water over flour to form a dough. Mix lightly with a fork. Shape into a ball. Chill until dough is stiff enough to handle, about 1 hour. Use as pastry for cocktail turnovers.

YIELD: Pastry for 50 turnovers, cocktail size

CREAM CHEESE PASTRY

1 cup sifted all-purpose flour
½ cup (1 stick) butter *or* margarine
1 package (3 ounces) cream cheese

Place flour in a bowl and work in butter or margarine and cream cheese with a pastry blender or fingers. Form into a roll when well blended. Wrap in wax paper and chill several hours or overnight or until stiff enough to roll. Use as the pastry for turnovers or for deep-dish 1-crust meat pies.

YIELD: Sufficient pastry for 2½ dozen 2-inch turnovers or a top for a 9-inch pie

VANILLA WAFER CRUMB CRUST

1¼ cups fine vanilla wafer crumbs
¼ cup light-brown sugar
½ teaspoon ground cinnamon
⅛ teaspoon ground mace

⅓ cup (⅔ stick) butter *or* margarine, melted

Combine first 4 ingredients thoroughly. Blend in melted butter or margarine. Pat uniformly on bottom and sides of a 9-inch pie plate. Bake in a preheated hot oven (400° F.) 6 minutes. Cool.

YIELD: One 9-inch pie crust

GRAHAM CRACKER POPPY SEED PIE CRUST

2 cups graham cracker crumbs
½ cup (1 stick) soft butter *or* margarine
¼ cup sugar
3 tablespoons poppy seed

Gradually blend graham cracker crumbs with softened butter or margarine. Add sugar and poppy seed and mix well. Pat the mixture firmly and uniformly over the bottom and sides of a 9-inch pie plate.

Bake in a preheated slow oven (325° F.) 8 to 10 minutes. Cool before adding the filling.

YIELD: One 9-inch pie crust

CINNAMON DEEP-DISH APPLE PIE

5 cups (5 medium-size) sliced cooking apples
2 cinnamon sticks, each 2 inches long

¾ cup sugar
½ teaspoon salt
1½ tablespoons quick-cooking tapioca

2 tablespoons butter *or* margarine
8-inch, unbaked 1-crust pie shell (Never-Fail Pastry I*)

Place apples in an 8 x 8 x 2-inch pan. Add cinnamon. Mix next 3 ingredients. Sprinkle over apples. Dot with butter or margarine. Cover with unbaked pastry rolled ⅛ inch thick (2 inches larger than diameter of pan). Trim, turn under, and flute edge. Cut a vent in pastry to allow for escape of steam. Bake in a preheated very hot oven (450° F.) 10 minutes. Reduce heat to moderate (350° F.) and bake 40 minutes or until apples are tender.

YIELD: One 8-inch pie

DEEP-DISH APPLE AND PEAR PIE

3 medium-size firm, ripe, fresh pears
3 medium-size tart apples

¾ cup sugar
2 tablespoons quick-cooking tapioca
¼ teaspoon salt
½ teaspoon ground allspice
½ teaspoon ground cinnamon

1 tablespoon fresh lemon juice
¼ teaspoon vanilla extract
3 tablespoons butter *or* margarine

9-inch, unbaked 1-crust pie crust (Never-Fail Pastry I*)

Wash and peel apples and pears. Cut into eighths or sixths. Remove cores. Combine next 5 ingredients. Mix with pears and apples along with lemon juice and vanilla extract. Turn into a 9 x 9 x 2-inch baking pan. Dot with butter or margarine.

Roll unbaked pastry to ⅛-inch thickness and 2 inches larger in diameter than the pan's and place over the top. Trim, turn under, and flute edge. Cut a vent in pastry to allow for escape of steam. Bake in a preheated very hot oven (450° F.) 10 minutes. Reduce heat to 350° F. (moderate) and bake 50 minutes. Serve warm or cold.

YIELD: One square 9-inch pie or 8 servings

DEEP-DISH BLUEBERRY PIE

4 cups fresh blueberries

1 cup sugar
3 tablespoons quick-cooking tapioca
½ teaspoon salt
1 tablespoon fresh lemon juice

2 cinnamon sticks, each 2 inches long
2 tablespoons butter *or* margarine

Unbaked pastry using 1 cup flour
    (Never-Fail Pastry I*)

Wash blueberries, drain, and mix with next 4 ingredients. Turn into a 10 x 6 x 2-inch baking dish. Add cinnamon sticks. Dot with butter or margarine. Top with unbaked pastry rolled to ⅛-inch thickness and 2 inches larger than the dimension of the baking dish.

Trim, turn under, and flute edge. Cut a vent in pastry to allow for escape of steam. Bake in a preheated hot oven (425° F.) 40 minutes or until done. Serve warm or cold.

YIELD: 6 to 8 servings

CAPE COD DEEP-DISH CRANBERRY PIE

"Mother and Grandmother also used to make a cranberry pie," wrote the late Joseph C. Lincoln in Cape Cod Yesterdays, *"that came to the table fat and puffy and inviting. It was baked in a deep dish and when cut it streamed juice, just as does a properly constructed blueberry pie. The triangular sections on our plates were islands set in red seas. We could—and often did—eat the pie with a spoon." He wrote, too, that the exact recipe had disappeared. From the general description we created this truly delectable pie. The tapioca is our idea since we wanted to make the "red sea" of juice more manageable.*

Unbaked pastry using 2 cups flour
    (Never-Fail Pastry III*)
6 cups fresh cranberries

2½ cups sugar
⅓ cup quick-cooking tapioca
½ teaspoon salt

3 cinnamon sticks, each 2 inches long
¼ cup unsulphured molasses
3 tablespoons butter *or* margarine

Roll ⅔ of the pastry into a 15 x 12-inch rectangular sheet ⅛ inch thick. Use this sheet to line the bottom and sides of a 10 x 6 x 2-inch baking dish. Wash cranberries and mix with next 3 ingredients. Turn into pastry-lined pie dish.

Tuck in cinnamon sticks. Dribble molasses over the top. Dot with butter or margarine. Roll remaining pastry ⅛ inch thick. Cut into strips ½ inch wide. Place over top in lattice fashion. Bake in a preheated hot oven (400° F.) 60 minutes or until done.

YIELD: 8 servings

DEEP-DISH PLUM PIE

5 to 6 cups (2¼ pounds) sliced, pitted, fresh Italian plums

1¼ cups sugar
3 tablespoons quick-cooking tapioca
¼ teaspoon salt
¾ teaspoon ground allspice

2 tablespoons butter *or* margarine
Unbaked 1-crust pie shell (Never-Fail Pastry I*)

Place plums in a 10 x 6 x 2-inch baking dish. Combine next 4 ingredients. Sprinkle over plums. Shake dish to distribute mixture uniformly. Dot top with butter or margarine. Cover with unbaked pastry rolled to ⅛-inch thickness and 2 inches larger than the diameter of the dish. Or, if desired, cover in lattice fashion with strips of pastry cut ½ inch wide.

Trim, turn under, and flute edge. If solid crust is used, cut a vent in pastry to allow for the escape of steam. Bake in a preheated very hot oven (450° F.) 10 minutes. Reduce heat to moderate (350° F.) and continue baking 30 to 40 minutes or until crust is brown. It is advisable to put a square of foil in the bottom of the oven to catch any of the juice that might boil out. Serve warm or cold.

YIELD: 6 to 8 servings

APPLE PIE

The English of 600 years ago put all sorts of things in pies: sparrows, eels, oysters, blackbirds, rooks, rump steak, pippins, dates, "raisins of ye sun," plover's eggs, and "lemman" rind—as many strange and unrelated things as the oddments to be found in a magpie's nest. Eventually, legend has it, "magpie's nest" was shortened to "pie."

9-inch, unbaked 2-crust pie shell (Never-Fail Pastry III*)
5 cups (4 to 5 large) sliced cooking apples
½ cup boiling water

1 cup sugar
½ teaspoon salt
½ teaspoon ground nutmeg
½ teaspoon ground cinnamon
3 tablespoons quick-cooking tapioca *(see below)*

2 tablespoons butter *or* margarine

(NOTE: Some varieties of apples do not need a thickening agent. If apples are not juicy, omit tapioca.) Line a 9-inch pie plate with half the unbaked pastry, rolled to ⅛-inch thickness. Set aside. Cook apples with water in a covered saucepan 5 to 6 minutes, or until apples are about half done, enough to shrink them and eliminate the space between the apples and the crust which so frequently occurs. Cool.

Turn into the pastry-lined pie plate. Combine next 5 ingredients and sprinkle over apples. Dot with butter or margarine. Cover with remaining pastry rolled to ⅛-inch thickness. Trim, turn under, and flute edge. Cut vents in top crust to allow for escape of steam.

Bake in a preheated very hot oven (450° F.) 10 minutes. Reduce heat to 350° F. (moderate) and cook 30 to 40 minutes or until crust has browned. Cool before serving.

YIELD: One 9-inch pie

APPLE CREAM PIE

½ cup sugar
½ cup dark-brown sugar
¼ cup all-purpose flour
¾ teaspoon ground ginger
½ teaspoon ground nutmeg
⅛ teaspoon ground cloves
¼ teaspoon salt

6 cups sliced, tart apples
½ cup heavy cream
9-inch, unbaked 1-crust pie shell
  (Never-Fail Pastry I*)
1 tablespoon dark-brown sugar

Combine the first 7 ingredients and mix with apples. Turn into an unbaked pie shell, over which pour cream. Sprinkle with the remaining 1 tablespoon brown sugar. Bake in a preheated hot oven (400° F.) 50 to 60 minutes, or until crust is brown and apples are tender. Cool before serving.

YIELD: One 9-inch pie

APPLE CUSTARD PIE

2 cups fresh, unsweetened applesauce

1 tablespoon butter or margarine
¾ cup sugar
¼ teaspoon salt
½ teaspoon ground cinnamon
½ teaspoon ground nutmeg
¼ teaspoon grated lemon rind

3 large eggs, beaten
1 cup milk
9-inch, unbaked 1-crust pie shell
  (Never-Fail Pastry I*)

Heat applesauce. Add next 6 ingredients. Cool. Stir in eggs and milk. Mix well and turn into an unbaked 9-inch pie shell. Bake in a preheated hot oven (450° F.) 10 minutes.

Reduce heat to moderate (350° F.) and bake 1½ hours, or until filling is firm in the center. To test, insert the point of a knife in center of pie. If it comes out clean, pie is done.

YIELD: One 9-inch pie

ENGLISH APPLE PIE

Everyone should love this crustless pie, especially those who ordinarily avoid eating pastry—or making it. And if pastry-making has been a problem, try our Never-Fail Pastry. Make sure wedge of pie can be cut without breaking by slicing apples paper-thin and allowing pie to cool completely before serving.*

3 pounds tart cooking apples

½ cup sugar
½ teaspoon ground nutmeg
¼ teaspoon salt
2 tablespoons fresh lemon juice
¾ cup light-brown sugar
1 cup sifted all-purpose flour

½ cup (1 stick) butter or margarine

¼ teaspoon ground nutmeg
¼ teaspoon salt

¼ cup (½ stick) butter *or* margarine

Peel and core apples, leaving 7 of them whole. Arrange the 7 whole apples in a 9-inch pie plate lined with unbaked pastry, rolled to ⅛ inch thickness. Dice the remaining apples and use to fill in the spaces around the whole apples. Combine the next 6 ingredients. Spoon into the cavities of apples, filling them full.

Sprinkle any remaining sugar mixture over the entire top, pressing it down to cover well. Divide the butter into 7 pieces and place one piece on the center top of each apple. Bake in a preheated moderate oven (350° F.) 1½ hours or until apples are tender. Cool completely before cutting.

YIELD: One 9-inch pie

Peel apples and cut into paper-thin slices. Mix with next 4 ingredients. Pack as firmly as possible in a 10-inch pie pan. Combine brown sugar and flour. Add butter or margarine and cut it in until mixture resembles coarse crumbs.

Sprinkle crumb mixture over apples and press it down firmly, especially at the edges to retain juice. Bake in a preheated moderate oven (350° F.) 1¼ hours or until apples are tender. Cover bottom of oven with foil to catch any juice that boils from pie. Serve cold.

YIELD: One 10-inch pie

JERSEY APPLE PIE

9 medium-size tart apples
9-inch, unbaked 1-crust pie shell
 (Never-Fail Pastry I*)

1 cup light-brown sugar
⅓ cup sifted all-purpose flour
½ teaspoon ground cinnamon
¼ teaspoon ground cardamom

LAYERED APPLESAUCE PIE

⅓ cup light-brown sugar
⅓ cup sugar
¼ teaspoon salt
1 teaspoon ground cinnamon
¼ teaspoon ground cloves
3 large eggs

1½ cups canned applesauce
½ cup undiluted evaporated milk *or*
 light cream
½ teaspoon vanilla extract
9-inch, unbaked 1-crust pie shell
 (Never-Fail Pastry I*)

Combine first 6 ingredients. Beat until mixture is light and fluffy. Blend in applesauce, milk or light cream, and vanilla extract.

Turn into an unbaked 9-inch pie shell. Bake in a preheated very hot oven (450° F.) 10 minutes. Reduce heat to moderate (350° F.) and bake 1 hour or until a knife inserted in center comes out clean.

YIELD: One 9-inch pie

APPLESAUCE MERINGUE PIE

2 cups thick, unsweetened applesauce
1 cup sugar
½ teaspoon ground allspice
½ teaspoon ground cinnamon
½ teaspoon ground cloves
½ teaspoon ground ginger
¼ teaspoon ground nutmeg
½ teaspoon grated lemon rind
½ cup (1 stick) butter or margarine, melted
3 large egg yolks, beaten

9-inch, unbaked pastry for 2-crust pie (Never-Fail Pastry III*)
Ginger Meringue (see below)

Combine the first 10 ingredients. Pour into a 9-inch pie plate lined with half the unbaked pastry rolled ⅛ inch thick. Cover with remaining pastry rolled to ⅛-inch thickness. Trim, turn under, and flute edge. Cut a vent in top crust to allow for the escape of steam.

Bake in a preheated moderate oven (350° F.) 1 hour or until crust is brown. Remove pie from oven and let stand until completely cold. Spread Ginger Meringue over top of crust. Bake in a preheated slow oven (300° F.) 15 to 20 minutes or until meringue has browned. Cool away from draft.

GINGER MERINGUE

Add ¹⁄₁₆ teaspoon salt to 3 large egg whites and beat until they are foamy. Add ¼ teaspoon cream of tartar and beat until egg whites stand in soft, stiff peaks. Beat in 6 tablespoons sugar, ½ tablespoon at a time. Beat in ¼ teaspoon ground ginger.

YIELD: One 9-inch pie

SPICED MARLBOROUGH PIE

3½ cups fresh applesauce
1 tablespoon butter or margarine

2 large eggs, beaten
½ teaspoon ground cinnamon
½ teaspoon ground cloves
¼ teaspoon ground nutmeg
2 teaspoons fresh lemon juice
¾ teaspoon grated lemon rind
1 cup sugar

9-inch, unbaked 1-crust pie shell (Never-Fail Pastry I*)
Heavy cream, whipped (optional)

Heat applesauce. Add butter or margarine and cool. Stir in next 7 ingredients. Turn into a 9-inch pie pan lined with unbaked pastry. Bake in a preheated moderate oven (375° F.) 1 hour or until crust has browned and the pie is firm in the center. Cool. Garnish with whipped cream just before serving if desired.

YIELD: One 9-inch pie

TWO-CRUST BLUEBERRY PIE

1 cup sugar
3½ tablespoons quick-cooking tapioca
¼ teaspoon salt
½ teaspoon ground cinnamon
¼ teaspoon ground cloves
½ teaspoon grated lemon rind

1 tablespoon fresh lemon juice
4 cups fresh blueberries
9-inch, unbaked pastry for 2-crust pie
  (Never-Fail Pastry III*)
2 tablespoons butter *or* margarine

Combine the first 6 ingredients. Mix with lemon juice and blueberries. Turn into a 9-inch pie plate lined with unbaked pastry. Dot with butter or margarine.

Top with pastry rolled to ⅛-inch thickness. Trim, turn under, and flute edge. Cut a vent in top crust to allow for escape of steam. Bake in a preheated hot oven (425° F.) 40 minutes or until crust has browned. Cool before serving.

YIELD: One 9-inch pie

LATTICE-CRUST CHERRY PIE

1 cup sugar
¼ teaspoon salt
½ teaspoon ground nutmeg
3 tablespoons cornstarch

½ cup cherry juice
1 tablespoon fresh lemon juice
3 cups drained, pitted, sour cherries
2 tablespoons butter *or* margarine
9-inch, unbaked pastry for 2-crust pie
  (Never-Fail Pastry III*)

Combine the first 4 ingredients in a 1½-quart saucepan. Stir in cherry juice. Cook until mixture is clear and has thickened. Cool. Add lemon juice and cherries.

Turn into a 9-inch pie plate lined with unbaked pastry, rolled to ⅛-inch thickness. Dot with butter or margarine. Roll remaining pastry to ⅛-inch thickness. Cut into strips ½ inch wide. Place over top in crisscross fashion. Trim, turn under, and flute edge.

Bake in a preheated very hot oven (450° F.) 10 minutes. Reduce heat to moderate (350° F.) and bake 30 minutes. Serve cold.

YIELD: One 9-inch pie

BROWN BETTY CRANBERRY AND APPLE PIE

5 cups (3 large) tart apples
2 cups fresh cranberries

9-inch, unbaked 1-crust pie shell
  (Never-Fail Pastry I*)

1 cup sugar
2 tablespoons cornstarch
½ teaspoon salt
½ teaspoon ground cinnamon
½ teaspoon ground nutmeg
1 cup soft bread crumbs

¼ cup (½ stick) butter *or* margarine

Peel and slice apples. Wash cranberries and mix with apples. Turn into an unbaked pie shell.

Combine the next 6 ingredients. Mix well. Add butter or margarine and mix with fingers until well blended. Sprinkle over the fruit. Bake in preheated very hot oven (450° F.) 10 minutes. Reduce heat to moderate (350° F.) and bake 45 to 50 minutes or until fruit is tender. Cool before serving.

YIELD: One 9-inch pie

LATTICE-TOP PEAR PIE

5 large *or* 6 medium-size fresh, ripe pears

¾ cup sugar
3 tablespoons quick-cooking tapioca
¼ teaspoon salt
1 teaspoon ground allspice
_____
2 tablespoons fresh lemon juice
½ teaspoon grated lemon rind
9-inch, unbaked pastry for 2-crust pie
   (Never-Fail Pastry III*)
2 tablespoons butter *or* margarine

Peel pears and cut into sixths or eighths, depending upon size of pears. Remove cores. Combine next 4 ingredients. Mix with pears, along with lemon juice and rind. Turn into a 9-inch pie plate, lined with unbaked pastry rolled to ⅛-inch thickness. Dot top with butter or margarine.

Cover, in lattice fashion, with pastry strips ½ inch wide, rolled ⅛ inch thick. Trim, turn under, and flute edge. Bake in a preheated very hot oven (450° F.) 10 minutes. Reduce heat to 350° F. (moderate) and bake 50 minutes, or until pears are tender and crust is brown.

YIELD: One 9-inch pie

RAISIN PIE

2½ cups (15 ounce box) seedless
   raisins
2¾ cups water
½ cup unsulphured molasses
½ teaspoon salt
¼ teaspoon ground cloves
1 teaspoon ground cinnamon
_____
3 tablespoons cornstarch
3 tablespoons water
1 teaspoon grated lemon rind
1 tablespoon fresh lemon juice
9-inch, unbaked pastry for 2-crust pie
   (Never-Fail Pastry III*)

Combine the first 6 ingredients in a saucepan. Blend cornstarch with water and add to raisin mixture. Stir and cook until thickened. Add lemon juice and rind. Cool.

Turn into a 9-inch pie plate, lined with unbaked pastry rolled to ⅛-inch thickness. Cover with remaining pastry rolled to ⅛-inch thickness. Trim, turn under, seal, and flute edge. Cut a vent in top crust to allow for the escape of steam. Bake in a preheated hot oven (425° F.) 40 minutes or until crust has browned. Cool before serving.

YIELD: One 9-inch pie

TWO-CRUST RHUBARB PIE

9-inch, unbaked pastry for 2-crust pie
   (Never-Fail Pastry III*)
5 cups diced, fresh rhubarb
1¼ cups sugar
¼ teaspoon salt
½ teaspoon ground cinnamon
¼ teaspoon ground nutmeg
3 tablespoons quick-cooking tapioca
2 tablespoons butter *or* margarine
1 teaspoon grated lemon rind

Line a 9-inch pie plate with half the unbaked pastry, rolled to ⅛-inch thickness. Combine remaining ingredients and turn into the pastry-lined pie plate. Roll remaining pastry to ⅛-inch thickness. Cut into strips ½ inch wide. Arrange over the top in crisscross fashion. Trim, turn under, and flute edge.

Bake in a preheated very hot oven (450° F.) 15 minutes. Reduce heat to moderate (350° F.) and bake 30 minutes or until done. Cool before serving.

YIELD: One 9-inch pie

CHOCOLATE CREAM PIE

1 cup sugar

¼ teaspoon salt
½ teaspoon ground cinnamon
4 tablespoons cornstarch
⅓ cup cocoa

2¼ cups milk
3 tablespoons butter *or* margarine
3 large egg yolks
1 teaspoon vanilla extract
9-inch, baked 1-crust pie shell
   (Never-Fail Pastry I*)
Meringue* for 9-inch pie

Mix ½ cup of the sugar with next 4 ingredients in top part of a double boiler. Blend in ¼ cup of the milk. Heat remaining milk and add. Stir and cook 6 minutes, or until very thick. Cover and continue cooking 12 minutes, stirring frequently. Add butter or margarine.

Beat egg yolks lightly and blend with remaining sugar, to which add a little of the hot mixture. Then stir into rest of the hot filling. Cook, uncovered, over hot water (NOT BOILING) until very thick, about 10 minutes. Add vanilla extract. Cool. Turn into a *cold* baked, 9-inch pie shell. Top with Meringue. Bake in a preheated slow oven (325° F.) 15 minutes or until browned. Serve cold.

YIELD: One 9-inch pie

GINGER CREAM PIE

¾ cup sugar

3 tablespoons cornstarch
3 tablespoons all-purpose flour
2 teaspoons ground ginger
½ teaspoon salt

2 cups scalded milk
4 large eggs, separated
1½ teaspoons vanilla extract
½ cup sugar
9-inch, baked 1-crust pie shell
   (Never-Fail Pastry I*)

Combine ½ cup of sugar and next 4 ingredients in the top of a double boiler or saucepan. Gradually stir in hot milk. Stirring occasionally, cook over hot water or very low heat until thickened, about 20 to 35 minutes. Cover and cook, without stirring, 5 minutes.

Beat egg yolks lightly with remaining ¼ cup sugar, add a little of the hot mixture, and then blend with remaining hot mixture. Stir and cook until very thick, about 10 minutes. Remove from hot water and cool. Add vanilla extract. Turn into a baked 9-inch pie shell.

Beat egg whites until they stand in soft, stiff peaks. Gradually beat in remaining ½ cup sugar. Spread over pie. Bake in a preheated slow oven (325° F.) 15 minutes or until browned. Sprinkle with 2 tablespoons of gingersnap crumbs, if desired. Cool thoroughly before serving.

YIELD: One 9-inch pie

FROZEN CREAMY LEMON PIE

2 large eggs, separated
⅓ cup lemon juice
1 teaspoon grated lemon rind
¾ cup sugar
¾ teaspoon ground mace
1½ cups heavy cream

9-inch, baked Vanilla Wafer Crumb
  Crust*
1 tablespoon sugar
¼ teaspoon vanilla extract
Ground mace

Mix in the top of a double boiler egg yolks, lemon juice and rind, and ½ cup of the sugar. Stir and cook over hot water (NOT BOILING) 6 to 8 minutes or until mixture thickens. Cool.

Beat egg whites until they stand in soft, stiff peaks and gradually beat in remaining ¼ cup sugar. Fold into the mixture. Whip 1 cup of the cream and fold into the filling. Turn into a pie plate lined with a baked Vanilla Wafer Crumb Crust. Freeze until ready to serve.

Combine remaining ½ cup cream, sugar, and vanilla extract and whip to form soft peaks. Spread over the top as desired. Sprinkle lightly with ground mace. Return to freezer for 20 minutes. Serve cut into wedges.

YIELD: One 9-inch pie

NEVER-FAIL LEMON MERINGUE PIE

Three rules must be observed to guarantee good results: Add the sugar in two parts, half with the cornstarch, half with the egg yolks. Use a double boiler—not of glass—with a top and bottom part that fit tightly enough to allow only the excess steam to escape. Be sure to cover the saucepan whenever specified in the directions.

1 cup sugar
⅓ cup cornstarch
½ teaspoon salt
¼ cup cold water
1¼ cups hot water
2 tablespoons butter *or* margarine

3 large egg yolks
⅓ cup lemon juice
1 teaspoon grated lemon rind
½ teaspoon ground nutmeg
1 teaspoon vanilla extract
9-inch, baked 1-crust pie shell
  (Never-Fail Pastry I*)
Meringue* for 9-inch pie

Combine ½ cup of the sugar with next 3 ingredients in the top of a double boiler. Stir in hot water. Stir and cook over rapidly boiling water 5 minutes or until thick. Cover and continue cooking over boiling water 8 minutes or until mixture is very thick, stirring occasionally. Add butter or margarine. Blend egg yolks with remaining ½ cup sugar and a little of the hot mixture. Then stir into the remaining hot mixture.

Cook, uncovered, over hot water (NOT BOILING) 10 minutes or until very thick, stirring frequently. Gradually stir in lemon juice and rind. Cool. Add nutmeg and vanilla extract. Turn into a baked 9-inch pie shell. Top as desired with Meringue. Bake in a preheated slow oven (325° F.) 15 minutes or until lightly browned. Serve cold.

YIELD: One 9-inch pie

MACAROON CREAM PIE

⅔ cup sugar
¼ cup cornstarch
¼ teaspoon salt
½ teaspoon ground mace
2 cups milk
3 large egg yolks, lightly beaten
1 teaspoon vanilla extract
½ cup Almond Macaroon Crumbs
  (see below)
9-inch, baked 1-crust pie shell
  (Never-Fail Pastry I*)
Meringue* for 9-inch pie

Mix the first 4 ingredients in the top part of the double boiler. Blend in 2 tablespoons of the milk. Heat remaining milk and add. Stir and cook over rapidly boiling water 15 minutes or until very thick.

Cover and cook 10 or more minutes, stirring occasionally. Add a little of the hot mixture to egg yolks and stir into hot mixture. Stir and cook over low heat 1 minute. Add vanilla extract and macaroon crumbs. Cool.

Turn into a *cold* baked pie shell. Top with meringue. Bake in a preheated slow oven (325° F.) 15 to 20 minutes or until browned.

ALMOND MACAROON CRUMBS

Heat macaroons 10 minutes in a preheated slow oven (325° F.). Cool and roll between sheets of wax paper with a rolling pin.

YIELD: One 9-inch pie

OPAL'S RUM CREAM PIE

The guests of Opal Lenigan of Morristown, New Jersey, always feel especially privileged when she serves her famous Rum Cream Pie. It may also be served as a frozen pie. If you like to cook in advance for an important party, make this pie a day or two ahead and store it in the freezer until ready to serve.

CHOCOLATE CRUMB CRUST

6 tablespoons melted butter *or* margarine
1½ cups fine, crisp chocolate cooky crumbs

Mix melted butter or margarine with the cooky crumbs. Turn into a buttered 9-inch pie plate. Pat crumbs over bottom and sides of plate to cover uniformly. Chill 1 hour.

RUM CREAM FILLING

1 envelope unflavored gelatine
¼ cup water
3 large eggs, separated
½ cup sugar
1 cup milk
¼ teaspoon ground nutmeg
¼ cup light *or* dark rum
⅛ teaspoon salt
½ cup heavy cream, whipped
Semisweet chocolate, grated

Soften gelatine in water and set aside. Beat egg yolks lightly in the top of a double boiler. Add sugar and milk. Stir and cook over hot water (NOT BOILING) 10 minutes or until custard coats a metal spoon. Remove from heat and stir in gelatine, nutmeg, and rum.

Chill over ice water until mixture begins to thicken. In the meantime, add salt to egg whites and beat them until they stand in soft, stiff peaks. Fold into the custard along with whipped cream. Turn into the prepared chocolate crumb crust. Chill until ready to serve. Sprinkle top with grated semisweet chocolate just before serving.

YIELD: One 9-inch pie

BUTTERMILK PIE

½ teaspoon salt
½ teaspoon ground nutmeg
½ teaspoon grated lemon rind
2 teaspoons vanilla extract
½ cup (1 stick) soft butter *or* margarine
_____
⅔ cup sugar
3 large eggs
3 tablespoons all-purpose flour
2 cups fresh buttermilk
9-inch, unbaked 1-crust pie shell
   (Never-Fail Pastry I*)

Combine the first 5 ingredients and mix until fluffy. Gradually blend in sugar. Beat in eggs, 1 at a time. Blend in flour. Stir in buttermilk. (This mixture appears curdled, but this is as it should be.)
   Turn into a 9-inch pie plate lined with unbaked pastry. Bake in a preheated very hot oven (450° F.) 10 minutes. Reduce heat to 325° F. (slow) and bake 35 minutes or until a knife inserted in the center comes out clean. Remove from oven and cool.

YIELD: One 9-inch pie

JAMAICAN FRESH COCONUT PIE

½ cup sugar
½ cup (1 stick) soft butter *or* margarine
_____

½ teaspoon ground nutmeg
1 large egg, beaten
2 large egg yolks, beaten
2 cups grated fresh coconut
1 teaspoon vanilla extract
¾ cup milk
_____
9-inch, unbaked 1-crust pie shell
   (Never-Fail Pastry I*)
Meringue* for 9-inch pie

Blend sugar with butter or margarine. Add the next 6 ingredients. Mix well. Turn into a 9-inch pie plate lined with unbaked pastry. Bake in a preheated hot oven (425° F.) 10 minutes. Reduce heat to moderate (350° F.) and bake 35 to 40 minutes or until filling is firm in the center. Remove from oven. Cool. Top with meringue. Bake in a preheated slow oven (325° F.) 15 minutes or until browned. Cool before serving.

YIELD: One 9-inch pie

MAPLE CUSTARD PIE

2 cups milk
_____
1 tablespoon cornstarch
¼ teaspoon salt
½ teaspoon ground nutmeg
_____
3 large eggs, lightly beaten
⅓ cup maple syrup
1½ teaspoons vanilla extract
9-inch, unbaked 1-crust pie shell
   (Never-Fail Pastry I*)
½ cup flaked coconut

Mix ¼ cup of the milk with next 3 ingredients. Stir in eggs. Heat together remaining milk, maple syrup, and vanilla extract and add to first mixture. Turn into a 9-inch pie plate, lined with unbaked pastry.
   Bake in a very hot oven (450° F.) 10 minutes. Reduce heat to slow (325° F.) and bake 40 to 45 minutes or until a

knife inserted in the center comes out clean. Sprinkle coconut over top of pie 5 minutes before baking time is up. Cool before serving.

YIELD: One 9-inch pie

SPICED PECAN PIE, GEORGIA STYLE

3 large eggs, lightly beaten
1 cup light corn syrup
½ cup sugar
¼ teaspoon salt

¼ teaspoon ground nutmeg
½ teaspoon ground cinnamon
1 teaspoon vanilla extract
2 tablespoons butter or margarine, melted

1 cup coarsely chopped pecans
1 tablespoon flour
9-inch, unbaked 1-crust pie shell (Never-Fail Pastry I*)

Combine the first 4 ingredients. Mix next 4 ingredients and add. Blend pecans with flour and stir into the mixture. Turn into a 9-inch pie plate lined with unbaked pastry. Bake in a preheated hot oven (400° F.) for 15 minutes. Reduce heat to moderate (350° F.) and bake 40 minutes longer or until a knife inserted in center comes out clean.

YIELD: One 9-inch pie

LOUISIANA PECAN PIE

3 large eggs
½ cup dark-brown sugar
½ teaspoon ground cinnamon
¼ teaspoon ground nutmeg
1 cup light corn syrup
3 tablespoons butter or margarine, melted
⅛ teaspoon salt
1½ teaspoons vanilla extract

1 cup chopped pecans
1 tablespoon all-purpose flour
9-inch, unbaked 1-crust pie shell (Never-Fail Pastry I*)
Heavy cream, whipped
Pecan halves

Combine the first 8 ingredients and mix well. Blend chopped pecans with flour and stir into the mixture. Turn into a 9-inch unbaked pie shell. Bake in a preheated moderate oven (375° F.) 40 minutes or until firm in center. Cool. Garnish with whipped cream and pecan halves just before serving.

YIELD: One 9-inch pie

PECAN RAISIN PIE

This is one of those easy recipes that can be modified to suit your taste so long as you don't tamper with the basic egg-and-syrup mixture. Use all pecans or, if you like, all raisins. Omit the bit of grated orange rind if you prefer the old-fashioned pecan-pie flavor.

1 cup corn syrup
3 large eggs
½ cup sugar
2 tablespoons butter *or* margarine,
    melted
¼ teaspoon salt
½ teaspoon grated orange rind
    (optional)
¾ teaspoon ground allspice

½ cup steamed seedless raisins
½ cup coarsely cut pecans
9-inch, unbaked 1-crust pie shell
    (Never-Fail Pastry I*)

Blend together the first 7 ingredients. If raisins are from newly opened package, quite moist, use as they are. If slightly dry, heat, covered in a sieve over hot water. Add raisins and chopped pecans to first mixture and pour into unbaked pie crust.

Bake 10 minutes in preheated hot oven (425° F.) Lower heat to moderate (350° F.) and bake 30 to 35 minutes longer. At this point filling may not seem quite firm, but it "sets" as it cools.

YIELD: One 9-inch pie

OLD-FASHIONED PUMPKIN PIE

1 cup sugar
1 tablespoon flour
½ teaspoon salt
1 teaspoon ground ginger
1 teaspoon ground cinnamon
½ teaspoon ground nutmeg
⅛ teaspoon ground black pepper
    (optional)
⅛ teaspoon ground cloves

3 large eggs
1½ cups mashed pumpkin
1 cup light cream *or* undiluted
    evaporated milk
9-inch, unbaked 1-crust pie shell
    (Never-Fail Pastry I*)

Mix together the first 8 ingredients. Beat in eggs. Stir in pumpkin and milk. Pour into a 9-inch unbaked pie shell. Bake in a preheated hot oven (400° F.) 50 minutes or until a knife inserted in the center comes out clean. Cool.

GINGER-PUMPKIN MERINGUE PIE

After removing the above pumpkin pie from the oven, spread top with 3 tablespoons of preserved ginger in syrup. Top with Meringue* for 9-inch pie. Bake in a preheated slow oven (325° F.) 15 minutes or until meringue has browned.

ORANGE-PUMPKIN MERINGUE PIE

In the above recipe for Ginger-Pumpkin Meringue Pie, replace preserved ginger in syrup with orange marmalade. Top with Meringue* for 9-inch pie and bake as directed above.

ANISE-PUMPKIN PIE

Omit the spices in the above recipe for Old-Fashioned Pumpkin Pie and add 1 teaspoon anise seed, crushed. Mix and bake as in above directions.

CARROT PIE

Omit pumpkin in the above recipe and add 1½ cups cooked sieved carrots.

SQUASH PIE

Omit pumpkin in the above recipe and add 1½ cups mashed, cooked, yellow winter squash.

SWEET POTATO PIE

Omit pumpkin in the above recipe and add 1½ cups cooked, mashed sweet potatoes. Reduce sugar to ¾ cup.

YIELD: One 9-inch pie

MOLASSES-PUMPKIN PIE

¾ cup sugar
1 tablespoon flour
½ teaspoon salt
1 teaspoon ground ginger
1 teaspoon ground cinnamon
¼ teaspoon ground cloves
____
¼ cup unsulphured molasses
2 cups mashed, cooked pumpkin
3 large eggs
____
1 cup undiluted evaporated milk *or* light cream
9-inch, unbaked 1-crust pie shell (Never-Fail Pastry I*)

Mix together the first 6 ingredients. Add the next 3 ingredients. Mix well. Stir in milk or cream. Pour mixture into a 9-inch unbaked pie shell. Bake in a preheated hot oven (400° F.) 40 minutes or until a knife inserted in the center comes out clean. Cool before serving.

YIELD: One 9-inch pie

UPPER CRUST PUMPKIN PIE

In the early days fat and white flour were so scarce that only the wealthy could afford to put both a lower and an upper crust on their pies. Therefore, this class of people became known as "the upper crust."

⅔ cup sugar
¼ teaspoon salt
1¾ teaspoons pumpkin pie spice
½ cup fine Almond Macaroon Crumbs*
1 teaspoon grated lemon rind
____
1 cup mashed, cooked pumpkin
3 large eggs
1 cup light cream
9-inch, unbaked pastry for 2-crust pie (Never-Fail Pastry III*)

Combine the first 5 ingredients in a mixing bowl. Stir in pumpkin and eggs. Mix well. Blend in cream. Turn into a 9-inch pie plate lined with unbaked pastry rolled to ⅛-inch thickness.

Top with remaining pastry rolled to ⅛-inch thickness.

Trim, turn under, and flute edge. Cut a vent in the top crust to allow for the escape of steam. Bake in a preheated hot oven (400° F.) 50 minutes. Cool before serving.

YIELD: One 9-inch pie

SPICED CHIFFON-PUMPKIN PIE

1 envelope unflavored gelatine
¼ cup water
¾ cup sugar
____
¼ teaspoon ground cardamom
¼ teaspoon ground mace
½ teaspoon ground ginger
½ teaspoon salt
____
1 cup mashed, cooked pumpkin

2 large eggs, separated
½ cup milk
9-inch, baked 1-crust pie shell
  (Never-Fail Pastry I*)
½ cup heavy cream, whipped
1 tablespoon sugar

Soften gelatine in cold water. Set aside to use later. Combine ½ cup of the sugar with the next 4 ingredients in the top of a double boiler. Blend in pumpkin and egg yolks. Mix well. Stir in milk. Stir and cook over hot water until mixture has thickened. Remove from heat and blend in gelatine. Chill over ice water until filling begins to thicken.

Beat egg whites until they stand in soft, stiff peaks. Gradually beat in the rest of the sugar. Quickly fold into the mixture. Turn into a *cold* baked pie shell. Chill until firm and ready to serve. Garnish with whipped cream, sweetened with the 1 tablespoon sugar.

SPICED SQUASH-CHIFFON PIE

Replace pumpkin in the above recipe with 1 cup mashed, cooked squash.

YIELD: One 9-inch pie

SHOO-FLY PIE

1¼ cups sifted all-purpose flour
½ cup sugar
½ teaspoon ground nutmeg
1 teaspoon ground cinnamon
¼ teaspoon salt
_____
½ cup (1 stick) soft butter *or*
  margarine
_____
¾ cup unsulphured molasses
¾ cup water
½ teaspoon soda
_____
9-inch, unbaked 1-crust pie shell
  (Never-Fail Pastry I*)

Combine first 5 ingredients. Add butter or margarine and cut it in with a pastry blender or 2 knives until the mixture resembles coarse crumbs. Set aside. Mix the next 3 ingredients and pour into an unbaked pie crust.

Sprinkle crumb mixture over the top. Bake in a preheated very hot oven (450° F.) 15 minutes. Reduce heat to 350° F. (moderate) and bake 35 to 40 minutes or until filling is firm. Serve warm or cold.

YIELD: One 9-inch pie

PRALINE SWEET POTATO PIE

9-inch, unbaked 1 crust pie shell
  (Never-Fail Pastry I*)
_____
⅓ cup sugar
⅓ cup light-brown sugar
¼ teaspoon salt
¾ teaspoon ground ginger
¾ teaspoon ground cinnamon
½ teaspoon ground nutmeg
1/16 teaspoon ground cloves
_____
1 cup mashed sweet potatoes (cooked fresh *or* canned)

2 large eggs, well beaten
¾ cup hot milk
½ cup light-brown sugar
¼ cup (½ stick) soft butter *or* margarine
¾ cup pecans, chopped medium fine
Heavy cream, whipped (optional)

Prepare pie shell and set aside. Combine the next 7 ingredients in a mixing bowl. Blend in sweet potatoes and eggs. Stir in hot milk. Pour into the unbaked pie shell. Bake 25 minutes in a preheated moderate oven (375° F.)

In the meantime, blend the ½ cup brown sugar with butter or margarine and pecans. Sprinkle over partially baked pie. Continue baking 30 minutes or until filling is firm in the center. Serve cold with whipped cream, if desired.

PRALINE PUMPKIN PIE
Replace the 1 cup mashed sweet potatoes in the above recipe with 1 cup mashed, cooked pumpkin.

YIELD: One 9-inch pie

FAVORITE COTTAGE CHEESE PIE

1 cup (8 ounces) creamy cottage cheese
3 large eggs, separated
_____
1 teaspoon grated lemon rind
½ teaspoon ground mace
1 teaspoon vanilla extract
2 tablespoons cornstarch
1 tablespoon butter *or* margarine, melted
_____
½ cup light cream *or* milk
¾ cup sugar
¼ teaspoon salt
9-inch, unbaked 1-crust pie shell (Never-Fail Pastry I*)

Force cottage cheese through a sieve. Beat in egg yolks. Add the next 5 ingredients. Stir in cream or milk and ½ cup of the sugar. Add salt to egg whites and beat them until they stand in soft, stiff peaks. Brush a little over the bottom of the unbaked pie crust. Gradually beat the remaining ¼ cup sugar into egg whites and fold into the cottage cheese mixture.

Turn into the unbaked pie crust. Bake in a preheated hot oven (400° F.) 12 minutes. Reduce heat to 350° F. (moderate) and bake 25 minutes or until a pointed knife inserted in the center comes out clean. Serve warm or cold.

YIELD: One 9-inch pie

LOUISIANA YAM PIE

1 cup light-brown sugar
½ teaspoon salt
½ teaspoon ground allspice
½ teaspoon ground ginger
½ teaspoon ground mace
_____
3 large eggs
1 cup mashed, cooked yams (sweet potatoes)

1½ cups top milk *or* light cream
9-inch, unbaked 1-crust pie shell
  (Never-Fail Pastry I*)
2 tablespoons preserved ginger syrup
⅓ cup sliced, preserved ginger
Meringue* for 9-inch pie

Combine the first 5 ingredients. Beat in eggs. Stir in sweet potatoes and milk. Turn mixture into a 9-inch pie plate, lined with unbaked pastry rolled to ⅛-inch thickness. Bake in a preheated hot oven (400° F.) 50 minutes or until a knife inserted in the center comes out clean.

Remove from the oven and while pie is hot, spread with ginger syrup. Top with sliced, preserved ginger. Cover with Meringue. Bake in a preheated slow oven (325° F.) 15 minutes. Cool.

YIELD: One 9-inch pie

PINEAPPLE-CHEESE PIE

1 tablespoon cornstarch
3 tablespoons sugar
1 cup (8-ounce can) crushed
  pineapple, undrained
½ teaspoon ground nutmeg
9-inch, unbaked 1-crust pie shell
  (Never-Fail Pastry I*)
1 package (3 ounces) cream cheese
½ cup sugar
2 large eggs
½ cup milk
½ teaspoon grated lemon rind
3 tablespoons chopped pecans

Mix cornstarch and the 3 tablespoons sugar in a saucepan. Stir in pineapple. Cook until mixture is clear and thickened, stirring frequently. Cool. Add nutmeg. Turn into an unbaked pastry shell.

Soften cream cheese. Gradually blend in sugar. Beat in eggs, 1 at a time. Stir in

milk and lemon rind. Spread over pineapple mixture. Sprinkle with chopped nuts. Bake in a preheated hot oven (400° F.) 10 minutes. Reduce heat to 325° F. (slow) and bake 50 minutes or until done. Cool before serving.

YIELD: One 9-inch pie

ITALIAN RICOTTA PIE
(TORTA DI RICOTTA)

3 cups (1½ pounds) Ricotta cheese
¼ cup sifted all-purpose flour
2 tablespoons grated orange rind
2 tablespoons grated lemon rind
1 tablespoon vanilla extract
1 teaspoon ground cinnamon
⅛ teaspoon salt
1 tablespoon finely chopped citron

4 large eggs
1 cup sugar
Ricotta Pie Pastry *(see below)*

Combine the first 8 ingredients and mix well. Beat eggs until foamy. Gradually beat in sugar with a rotary or an electric beater at medium speed, beating the mixture 2 minutes. Fold into cheese mixture. Roll half the Ricotta Pie Pastry to ⅛-inch thickness in a circle 1 inch larger than a 9-inch layer-cake pan. Fit it into the pan, leaving ½ inch of pastry hanging around the rim of pan. Fill with the cheese mixture.

Roll remaining pastry to ⅛-inch thickness and cut into strips ½ inch wide. Place over filling in crisscross fashion. Trim, turn under, and flute edges. Bake in a preheated moderate oven (350° F.) 1½ hours or until filling is firm and crust is brown. Serve cold.

RICOTTA PIE PASTRY

2 cups sifted all-purpose flour
3 tablespoons sugar
½ teaspoon salt
¾ cup shortening
2 large egg yolks, lightly beaten
1 to 2 tablespoons water

Sift together the first 3 ingredients. Add shortening and cut it in to crumb consistency with 2 knives or a pastry blender. Add egg yolks and only enough water to form a dough. Mix only until ingredients are blended.

YIELD: One 9-inch pie

LEMON SOUFFLE PIE

4 large eggs, separated
¾ cup sugar
½ teaspoon ground nutmeg *or* mace
¼ cup lemon juice
1 teaspoon grated lemon rind
1 teaspoon vanilla extract
1/16 teaspoon salt
9-inch, baked 1-crust pie shell
   (Never-Fail Pastry I*)

Mix, in the top of a double boiler, egg yolks, ¼ cup of the sugar, spice, and lemon juice. Stir and cook over hot water (NOT BOILING) until mixture has thick-

ened. Remove from heat and blend in lemon rind and vanilla extract.

Add salt to egg whites and beat them until they stand in soft, stiff peaks. Gradually beat in remaining ½ cup sugar. Fold into hot mixture. Turn into a baked 9-inch pie shell. Bake in a slow oven (325° F.) 30 minutes or until golden brown. Cool. Pie will settle a little on cooling.

YIELD: One 9-inch pie

LIME SOUFFLE PIE

Mace accentuates the lime flavor in this airy pie. It puffs up during baking, sits down slightly when cool.

½ cup sugar
1 tablespoon cornstarch
½ teaspoon ground mace
1 tablespoon water
4 large eggs, separated
⅓ cup lime juice
1½ teaspoons grated lime rind
½ teaspoon vanilla extract
¼ teaspoon salt
½ cup sugar
9-inch, baked 1-crust pie shell
   (Never-Fail Pastry I*)

Mix together first 6 ingredients in a saucepan or top of a double boiler. Stir and cook over low heat or hot water until custard is thick, about 10 minutes.

Remove from heat and stir in lime rind and vanilla extract. Add salt to egg whites and beat them until they stand in soft, stiff peaks into which gradually beat the remaining sugar. Fold into custard. Turn into the baked pastry shell. Bake in a preheated slow oven (325° F) 25 to 30 minutes. Cool before serving.

YIELD: One 9-inch pie

ORANGE CHIFFON PIE

3 large eggs, separated

2 tablespoons fresh lemon juice
⅓ cup fresh orange juice
2 teaspoons unflavored gelatine

1 cup sugar

¼ teaspoon ground nutmeg
½ teaspoon vanilla extract
1 teaspoon grated lemon peel
1 tablespoon grated orange peel

9-inch, baked 1-crust pie shell (Never-
   Fail Pastry I*) *or* Graham Cracker
   Poppy Seed Crust*
Grated orange peel (optional)

Beat egg yolks in top of a double boiler until they are very light and lemon-colored. Add next 3 ingredients and ½ cup of the sugar. Stir and cook over hot (NOT BOILING) water until thick. Cool. Stir in the next 4 ingredients. Beat egg whites until they stand in stiff, soft peaks. Gradually beat in the remaining ½ cup sugar. Fold into the custard. Turn into a *cold* baked 9-inch pastry shell. Garnish top with a sprinkling of grated fresh orange peel, if desired. Chill several hours or overnight.

YIELD: One 9-inch pie

LEMON CHIFFON PIE
(WITH POPPY SEED CRUST)

1 envelope unflavored gelatine
¼ cup water

1 cup sugar
½ teaspoon ground nutmeg
½ teaspoon salt
½ cup fresh lemon juice

4 large eggs, separated
1 teaspoon grated lemon rind
½ teaspoon vanilla extract
Graham Cracker Poppy Seed Crust* *or*
   9-inch, baked 1-crust pie shell (Never-
   Fail Pastry I*)

½ cup heavy cream, whipped
   (optional)

Soften gelatine in water. Combine the next 4 ingredients in the top of a double boiler. Beat egg yolks and add. Stir and cook over hot water (NOT BOILING) 10 minutes or until of custard consistency. Add gelatine, lemon rind, and vanilla extract. Mix well. Cool over ice water until mixture begins to thicken.

Beat egg whites until they stand in soft, stiff peaks. Fold into the mixture. Turn into a Graham Cracker Poppy Seed Crust or, if desired, turn into a *cold* baked 9-inch pastry shell. Chill until firm and ready to serve. If desired, garnish with whipped cream just before serving.

YIELD: One 9-inch pie

APPLE FLAN
We know the French flan as a pie or tart.

5 medium-size tart baking apples,
   such as Rome Beauty

½ cup sugar
½ cup water
1 teaspoon lemon juice
⅛ teaspoon salt

½ teaspoon ground nutmeg
¼ cup finely chopped, toasted,
   blanched almonds
½ cup heavy cream, whipped
8 baked tart shells, 3½ inches each
Meringue* for 9-inch pie

Peel and slice apples. Set aside. Mix next 4 ingredients in a saucepan. Bring to boiling point and boil 3 minutes. Add apples and nutmeg. Cook 8 minutes, or until apples are tender. Cool. Fold in almonds and whipped cream. Turn into baked tart shells. Top with Meringue. Bake in a preheated slow oven (300° F.) 20 minutes or until meringue has browned.

YIELD: 8 tarts

GLAZED BLUEBERRY TARTS

3 cups fresh blueberries
½ cup sugar
½ teaspoon ground cinnamon
1 tablespoon cornstarch
Dash salt
1 cup water
2 teaspoons fresh lemon juice
6 baked tart shells, 5 inches each
Heavy cream, whipped

Wash blueberries and drain well. Mix next 5 ingredients in a small saucepan. Stir and cook 4 to 5 minutes or until glaze mixture is clear and of medium thickness. Remove from heat and stir in lemon juice. Fill tart shells with blueberries, over which spoon the glaze. Chill until glaze is set and ready to serve. Garnish with whipped cream.

YIELD: 6 tarts

BLUEBERRY TART REGINA

Unbaked pie crust (Never-Fail Pastry III*)
1 envelope unflavored gelatine
¼ cup cold water
2 cups fresh blueberries
½ cup sugar
¾ teaspoon ground nutmeg
⅛ teaspoon salt
2 large eggs, separated
1¼ cups milk
¾ cup cream sherry wine
1 cup heavy cream

Roll unbaked pastry into a 10-inch circle ¼ inch thick. (This is extra thick.) Place over back of an 8-inch cake pan. Press pastry well around the edge and trim off excess dough. Prick top and sides well with a fork. Turn a larger pie plate over the pastry. (This makes a nicely shaped pastry shell.)

Bake in a preheated hot oven (425° F.) 10 minutes or until about half done. Remove the larger pie pan and bake pastry 5 more minutes or until golden. Cool on back of pan while preparing the filling.

Soften gelatine in cold water. Set aside to use later. Wash blueberries and pick out ½ cup of the largest to use as a garnish. Combine ⅓ cup of the sugar with nutmeg, salt, and egg yolks in the top of a double boiler. Add ¼ cup of the milk. Heat remaining milk and add to sugar and egg yolks. Stir and cook over hot water (NOT BOILING) until custard coats a metal spoon. Remove from heat and add softened gelatine. Slowly stir in sherry. Chill until custard begins to thicken. Whip ½ cup of the heavy cream and fold into the mixture. Beat egg whites until they stand in soft peaks. Gradually beat in remaining sugar. Fold into the mixture.

Remove crust from back of pan and place it on a serving plate. Fill with 2 alternating layers of each, blueberries and custard mixture, having blueberries on the bottom and custard mixture on the top. Chill several hours or overnight. One hour before serving, whip remaining cream and spread over surface of pie. Make cream rosettes around edge with remaining whipped cream forced through a decorators' tube. Garnish as desired with remaining blueberries. Serve cut in pie-shaped wedges.

YIELD: 6 to 8 servings

ITALIAN EASTER TARTS
(PASTIERA DI PASQUA)

6 tablespoons soft butter *or* margarine
½ cup sugar
2 cups sifted all-purpose flour
1/16 teaspoon salt
2 large egg yolks

Bake in a preheated very hot oven (450° F.) 10 minutes. Reduce heat to 325° F. (slow) and bake 50 minutes or until filling is firm and crust is brown. Cool before serving.

YIELD: 12 servings

PEACH TARTS

4 cups (2 pounds) sliced fresh
  peaches
¾ cup sugar
¼ teaspoon ground cinnamon
2 teaspoons fresh lemon juice

Water
1 tablespoon cornstarch
4 baked tart shells, 5 inches each
Heavy cream, whipped (optional)

Combine the first 4 ingredients and let peaches stand 20 to 30 minutes to form juice. Drain off juice into a measuring cup and finish filling it with enough water to make 1 cup. Turn into a 3-cup saucepan. Add cornstarch and mix well. Stir and cook until juice is clear and slightly thick. Cool.

Divide peaches equally among the baked tart shells. Spoon the cold sauce over each, being sure to cover each slice of peach. Chill until glaze has set. Garnish with whipped cream, if desired.

YIELD: 4 tarts

FRIED DRIED FRUIT PIES

(HALF MOONS)

1 pound dehydrated peaches, apples, apricots, or mixed dried fruits

½ cup sugar
⅛ teaspoon salt
¼ teaspoon ground cloves
½ teaspoon ground cinnamon
3 tablespoons butter or margarine

Short Biscuit Dough (see below)

3 to 4 tablespoons water
½ cup (1 stick) butter or margarine

1¾ cups sugar
½ teaspoon salt
2 teaspoons ground cinnamon
1 tablespoon vanilla extract

3 large eggs, beaten
2 pounds Ricotta cheese
1 tablespoon grated orange rind
1 teaspoon grated lemon rind
1 jar (8 ounces) mixed glacé fruit

Mix butter and sugar until fluffy. Add flour and salt and mix well. Blend in egg yolks. Add enough water to make a manageable dough. Knead until smooth on a lightly floured board. Chill dough 1 hour.

Reserve ¼ of the dough for top decoration. Roll remaining dough to ⅛-inch thickness and place in bottom and sides of a 13 x 9 x 2-inch baking pan. Set aside.

Combine remaining butter or margarine with next 4 ingredients and mix until fluffy. Add remaining ingredients and mix well. Turn into the pastry-lined baking pan. Roll remaining dough to ⅛-inch thickness. Cut into strips ½ inch wide. Place in lattice fashion across the filling.

Cook dehydrated fruit as directed on package. Remove from heat and mash to a pulp. Add next 5 ingredients. Mix well. Roll Biscuit Dough, half at a time, into a large circle between 1/16 and 1/8 inch thick. Using a saucer as a pattern, cut dough into 4 circles.

Place a heaping tablespoon of fruit on one side of each circle of dough, over which fold the other half of the circle. Seal edges and crimp them with a fork. Prick the top to allow for escape of steam.

Brown on both sides in a small amount of shortening in a heavy skillet or griddle. Bake in a preheated moderate oven (350° F.) 20 minutes. Serve hot or cold.

SHORT BISCUIT DOUGH
2 cups sifted all-purpose flour
3 teaspoons double-acting
    baking powder
1 teaspoon salt
_____
6 tablespoons shortening
About 1/2 cup milk

Sift together the first 3 ingredients. Add shortening and cut it in to crumb consistency. Stir in enough milk to make a soft dough. Knead about 20 seconds on a lightly floured board.

YIELD: 8 half-moon pies

LEMON BUTTER
5 large eggs, beaten
1½ cups sugar
¾ teaspoon ground mace
1½ tablespoons grated lemon rind
Dash of salt

Place all ingredients in the top of a double boiler. Stir and cook over hot water (NOT BOILING) until thickened, 20 to 25 minutes. Pour into a clean, hot jar. Store in the refrigerator. Serve in tart shells, as a filling for cake, or on toast.

YIELD: 1¾ cups

POULTRY

I believe surely that the entire gallinaceous race was created for the express purpose of filling our larders and enriching our banquets," philosophized Brillat-Savarin, "—from the quail to the turkey cock you can be certain of finding a delicate food and one that is flavorful, as good for the convalescent as for the sturdiest healthy man."

Ornithologists are sure that all species of domestic fowl are descendants of the wild jungle fowl of India and southeastern Asia. From there, different species of fowl have fluttered, or have been carried, to all parts of the world. Columbus brought poultry to the New World on his second voyage in 1493. We do not know which voyager first brought turkey from the New World to Europe.

Within a century after America was discovered, all kinds of interesting and delicious foods and spices were introduced to Europe from the West. These included corn, tomatoes, pineapples, avocados, allspice, capsicum— and the noble turkey.

However, other new foods were brought by the conquering Turks from the East. People became confused as to which came from where. Regarding the delicious big bird, for instance, should it be called *coq d'Inde* because America was once called "Western India," or should it be called *jesuit* because the Jesuit fathers brought it to France from Spanish America? Someone who could talk more persuasively than most must have insisted that the Turks had introduced this fowl. Therefore, to this day, we call our Thanksgiving bird a "turkey."

The best-known eating fowl is the chicken. One reason chicken is so popular is that its tender, bland-tasting meat can be seasoned in hundreds of ways. Almost any spice or herb may be used to give aroma to chicken. Another reason is that no religious taboos apply to chicken. Only strict vegetarians refuse it, as they do all meat or eggs.

Most people think that young chicken tastes best fried Southern style. Older birds are better stewed or roasted. (The traditional Thanksgiving turkey is always roasted and its seasonings, together with other delicacies, are placed in its stuffing.) Although chicken may be stewed in plain water, tastier results will be obtained if chicken stock or half water and half dry wine is used as the cooking liquor. Cream, preferably sour, enriches chicken stock if added at the end of the cooking period.

Other types of fowl may be prepared in manners similar to those used for chicken, the chief difference being in the manner of handling the fat. Since turkeys are active birds that develop more muscle than fat, their meat usually can stand a little extra butter or margarine in the cooking. On the other hand, the water fowl, such as duck or goose, have a layer of fat to keep them warm and to make their feathers waterproof. Therefore, they should be cooked in such a manner that the meat will not taste greasy.

TIMETABLE FOR ROASTING STUFFED POULTRY
(Chilled, but not frozen)

Kind of poultry	Ready-to-cook weight (pounds)	Cups of stuffing needed	Roasting time in a slow (325° F.) oven (hours)
Chicken			
Broiling or frying	1½ to 2½	1 to 2	1¼ to 2†
Roasting	2½ to 4½	2 to 5	2 to 3½†
Capons	4 to 8	5 to 7	3 to 5
Duckling	3 to 5	2 to 4	2½ to 3
Goose	4 to 8	3 to 6	2¾ to 3½
	8 to 14	6 to 10	3½ to 5
Turkey			
Very young	4 to 8	4 to 8	3 to 4½
Roasting (young	6 to 12	6 to 12	3½ to 5
adults, hen or	12 to 16	12 to 16	5 to 6
tom)	16 to 20	16 to 20	6 to 7½
	20 to 24	20 to 24	7½ to 9

†If whole chicken is roasted without stuffing, oven may be set at 400° F. and roasting time cut by ½ hour.

CHICKEN

BAKED CHICKEN
WITH GRAPES

3 (2 pounds each) ready-to-cook broiler
chickens
1½ cups chicken broth *or* 1½ chicken
bouillon cubes and 1½ cups boiling
water

2 tablespoons minced onion
1½ teaspoons salt
¾ teaspoon ground thyme
¼ teaspoon ground black pepper
⅛ teaspoon minced garlic

5 teaspoons cornstarch
5 teaspoons water
1 cup green seedless grapes
1 tablespoon dry sherry

Wash and split chickens. Place in a 15½
x 10½ x 2¼-inch baking dish. Add
enough chicken broth to half cover the
chicken. Combine next 5 ingredients.
Add to chicken.

Bake, uncovered, in a preheated moderate oven (350° F.) 1½ hours or until
chicken is tender. Remove chicken to a
serving dish. Thicken liquid in pan with
cornstarch mixed with the water. Add
grapes and sherry. Serve hot with gravy.

YIELD: 6 servings

CHICKEN BAKED
IN SOUR CREAM

2½-pound ready-to-cook chicken
1 cup sour cream
1 tablespoon fresh lemon juice
2 teaspoons salt

1 teaspoon celery salt
½ teaspoon ground black pepper
⅛ teaspoon garlic powder
2 teaspoons paprika

¾ cup flour
⅓ cup shortening

Wash and cut chicken into serving-size
pieces. Place in a refrigerator dish. Combine sour cream, lemon juice and 1 teaspoon of the salt with next 4 ingredients.
Pour over chicken, being sure each piece
is well coated. Cover and refrigerate
overnight.

Drain, if necessary, and dredge in flour
mixed with the remaining 1 teaspoon salt.
Melt shortening in a 12 x 8 x 2-inch pan,
into which place chicken in a single layer.
Bake, uncovered, in a preheated hot oven
(400° F.) 1 hour or until tender, turning
to brown both sides.

YIELD: 6 servings

CHICKEN BREASTS
VERONIQUE

3 breasts of chicken, split
2 teaspoons salt
½ teaspoon ground black pepper
3 tablespoons butter *or* margarine
2 teaspoons tarragon leaves
1 cup green seedless grapes
½ cup dry white wine
1 tablespoon flour
⅔ cup light cream
2 large egg yolks
6 slices toast

Rub chicken breasts with salt and black
pepper. Brown on all sides in butter or
margarine in a heavy skillet. Place chicken
in a baking pan, adding all the pan drippings. Sprinkle with tarragon. Add
grapes and wine.

Bake, uncovered, in a preheated slow
oven (325° F.) 40 minutes or until

chicken is tender. Remove chicken from baking pan and keep warm. Blend flour with a little of the cream, add remaining cream and egg yolks, beat well, and add to pan drippings. Add chicken and cook 5 minutes. DO NOT BOIL. Serve on toast. Garnish with clusters of green seedless grapes.

YIELD: 6 servings

CHICKEN WITH WINE
(COQ AU VIN)

3-pound ready-to-cook chicken
½ cup flour
½ teaspoon ground nutmeg
1 teaspoon salt
3 tablespoons butter *or* margarine
3 tablespoons cooking oil
½ cup chopped celery
½ cup chopped onion

1 cup chopped ham
1 bay leaf
½ teaspoon thyme leaves
¼ teaspoon instant minced garlic
2 teaspoons salt

Whole cloves
13 small white onions
12 small mushroom caps

¼ cup brandy
1¼ cups dry red wine
1½ tablespoons flour

Wash chicken and cut into serving-size pieces. Dredge in flour mixed with salt and nutmeg. Brown in butter or margarine and cooking oil, adding it as needed. Transfer chicken to a casserole.

Sauté celery and onion in pan drippings until golden. Stir in next 5 ingredients. Mix well and turn over chicken. Stick 4 cloves in 1 onion and add to casserole along with mushroom caps and the remaining whole onions. Heat brandy, pour over chicken, and ignite. Add 1 cup of the wine. Cover and cook in a preheated slow oven (325° F.) 1½ hours or until chicken is tender. Blend flour with the ¼ cup wine and add. Stir and cook until desired thickness.

YIELD: 6 servings

CHICKEN PARMESAN

2½-pound ready-to-cook chicken
1½ teaspoons salt
¼ teaspoon ground black pepper
¼ teaspoon crumbled rosemary leaves
¼ teaspoon instant minced garlic

2 to 3 tablespoons shortening
½ cup white wine, chicken stock, *or* water
1 tablespoon flour
2 tablespoons water
¼ cup grated Parmesan cheese

Cut chicken into quarters, wash, and wipe dry with paper towels. Combine the next 4 ingredients and rub on the surface of all sides of the chicken pieces. Heat shortening in a 10-inch skillet. Add chicken and cook over moderate heat, turning occasionally, until brown on all sides, about 25 minutes. Add wine, stock, or water.

AND HEZEKIAH HEARKENED
UNTO THEM AND SHOWED
THEM ALL THE HOUSE OF HIS
PRECIOUS THINGS, THE SILVER
AND THE GOLD, AND THE
SPICE

2 KINGS 20·13

Cover and simmer 30 minutes or until chicken is tender. Transfer chicken to a heat-proof platter or baking dish. Blend flour with water and stir into the pan drippings. Mix well and spoon over chicken. Sprinkle with Parmesan cheese. Bake in a preheated moderate oven (350° F.) 10 minutes. Serve hot with the gravy.

YIELD: 4 servings

SMOTHERED CHICKEN

3-pound ready-to-cook chicken

¾ cup flour
3 teaspoons salt
½ teaspoon ground black pepper
1¼ teaspoons poultry seasoning

About ⅓ cup shortening
About 3 cups hot water

Wash and cut chicken into serving-size pieces. Place next 4 ingredients in a paper bag. Add chicken, a few pieces at a time, or if desired, add all the chicken, and shake bag to coat pieces well with seasoned flour. Using a Dutch oven, brown chicken on all sides in shortening, adding it as needed.

Sprinkle all flour that is left in the bag over chicken. Add just enough hot water to barely cover chicken. Cover and bake in a preheated moderate oven (350° F.) 45 minutes or until chicken is tender.

YIELD: 6 servings

ROAST CHICKEN WITH LIVER-MATZO STUFFING

5- to 6-pound roasting chicken
⅓ cup chicken fat
1½ teaspoons paprika
3 teaspoons salt

1 cup chopped onion
½ pound chicken livers
3 tablespoons chopped parsley
⅓ cup diced celery

2 cups matzo farfel (small pieces of matzo)
1 cup hot water

2 large eggs, beaten
½ teaspoon ground ginger
¼ teaspoon ground black pepper

Wash and dry chicken. Blend 3 tablespoons of the chicken fat with paprika and 1 teaspoon of the salt. Rub inside of the chicken cavities with part of this mixture. Sauté next 4 ingredients in remaining chicken fat until livers are tender. Soften matzo farfel in hot water. Add to the liver mixture. Blend in remaining ingredients.

Spoon into the crop and body cavities of the chicken. Close openings with skewers or toothpicks and lace together with a strong thread. Rub skin of chicken with remaining fat and paprika mixture. Roast, uncovered, on a rack in a shallow pan in a preheated slow oven (325° F.) 3 to 3½ hours or until chicken is tender and appetizingly brown.

YIELD: 6 servings

ORIENTAL STUFFED CHICKEN

This is a real show-off chicken dish with a faintly exotic taste. It's slightly more complicated than the usual chicken concoction, but easily worth the effort.

⅔ cup uncooked rice
3 tablespoons butter *or* margarine
1¼ cups boiling water
½ cup sliced fresh mushrooms
2 tablespoons soy sauce
2½ teaspoons salt

1 cup diced celery
1 tablespoon instant minced onion
1 tablespoon parsley flakes
1 tablespoon grated orange rind
½ teaspoon ground ginger
⅛ teaspoon ground black pepper

4½- to 5-pound roasting chicken

¼ cup water
1 tablespoon honey
1 tablespoon cider vinegar
1 teaspoon soy sauce

Chicken Giblet Gravy*

Brown rice in 2 tablespoons of the butter or margarine. Add boiling water and cook 15 minutes or until rice is almost tender. Sauté mushrooms in remaining butter or margarine until they are limp. Add 1 tablespoon of the soy sauce and 1 teaspoon of the salt along with the next 6 ingredients.

Rub the body and neck cavities of the chicken with the remaining 1 tablespoon soy sauce. Fill with rice mixture. Close cavities with skewers. Lace tightly with strong cord. Rub skin of chicken with ½ teaspoon of the salt. Place chicken on a rack, breast-side up, in a shallow baking pan.

Cook in a preheated slow oven (325° F.) 20 minutes. Heat the remaining 1 teaspoon of salt with the next 4 ingredients. Brush over skin of chicken. Continue cooking 2½ to 3 hours or until chicken is tender, basting at 20 minute intervals. Serve with Chicken Giblet Gravy.

YIELD: 6 servings

*An asterisk after the name of a dish indicates that the recipe for this dish appears in the book. Consult the Index for the page number.

CHICKEN BROILED WITH CASHEW NUTS

Cashew nuts are native to Jamaica, B.W.I., and are widely used in a variety of dishes. They add crunchy richness and flavor to broiled chicken.

2½-pound ready-to-cook chicken
1½ teaspoons salt
½ teaspoon ground black pepper
½ teaspoon ground thyme
¼ cup (½ stick) butter *or* margarine
¼ cup chopped, toasted, salted
    cashew nuts
Paprika
4 slices fresh lime

Wash and cut chicken into quarters. Rub all sides with salt mixed with black pepper and thyme. Place chickens, skin-side down in a single layer, in a buttered 11¼ x 7½ x 1½-inch baking pan. Dot with butter or margarine. Place in a preheated broiler, having oven control set to 450° F. (very hot). Cook 30 minutes or until chicken is tender, turning to brown both sides. Sprinkle the skin side with cashew nuts 10 minutes before broiling time is up. Serve garnished with paprika and fresh lime slices.

YIELD: 4 servings

CHICKEN, MARYLAND STYLE

2½-pound ready-to-cook chicken

¾ cup flour
2 teaspoons salt
½ teaspoon celery salt
½ teaspoon ground black pepper

2 large eggs, beaten
¼ cup water
1 cup fine, dry bread crumbs
½ cup shortening
3 tablespoons hot water
Cream Gravy*

Wash chicken and cut into serving-size pieces. Measure next 4 ingredients into a paper or plastic bag. Shake to mix. Drop in chicken and shake well to coat each piece with the mixture. Then dip into eggs mixed with water and roll in bread crumbs. Heat shortening in a heavy 10-inch skillet. Add chicken and cook slowly, to prevent burning, until lightly browned.

Transfer chicken to a 10 x 6 x 2-inch baking pan. Stir the 3 tablespoons of hot water into fat in skillet and pour over chicken. Bake, uncovered, in a preheated moderate oven (350° F.) 30 to 40 minutes. Serve hot with rice and Cream Gravy.

YIELD: 6 servings

OVEN-FRIED SAVORY CHICKEN

This is almost as good as Southern Fried Chicken,* and you don't have to contend with spattering fat.

2½-pound ready-to-cook chicken
⅓ cup flour
_____
2 teaspoons salt
½ teaspoon ground black pepper
⅛ teaspoon garlic powder
¼ teaspoon onion powder
¾ teaspoon savory leaves
_____
1 large egg, beaten
1 tablespoon water
½ cup fine, dry bread crumbs
½ cup (1 stick) butter *or* margarine

Cut chicken into quarters and coat with flour mixed with the next 5 ingredients. Dip in egg blended with water and then coat with bread crumbs. Melt butter or margarine in a 10 x 6 x 2-inch baking pan in a hot oven (400° F.). Place chicken in pan, skin-side down. Bake

until chicken is tender, about 50 to 60 minutes, turning to brown both sides.

YIELD: 4 servings

SEATTLE FRIED CHICKEN

2½-pound ready-to-cook chicken
½ cup heavy cream
¾ cup flour
2½ teaspoons salt
½ teaspoon ground black pepper
¼ cup (½ stick) butter *or* margarine
¼ cup shortening
Cream Gravy*

Wash chicken and cut into serving-size pieces. Dip in cream and then into flour mixed with salt and black pepper. Melt butter or margarine and shortening in a heavy 10-inch skillet. Add chicken and cook over medium-low heat 50 to 60 minutes or until brown, turning to brown both sides. Serve hot with fluffy mashed potatoes or rice and Cream Gravy, made from pan drippings.

YIELD: 6 servings

OVEN-FRIED SESAME CHICKEN

2½-pound ready-to-cook chicken
2 tablespoons butter *or* margarine, melted
_____
¼ cup Toasted Sesame Seed*
3 teaspoons salt
½ teaspoon ground black pepper
¹⁄₁₆ teaspoon garlic powder
½ cup flour

Wash chicken, cut into serving-size pieces and wipe dry. Brush each piece with melted butter or margarine. Put remaining ingredients in a paper bag. Add chicken and shake well to coat every piece with the mixture. Place chicken in a foil-lined 15½ x 10 x 1-inch baking pan. Bake in a preheated hot oven (400° F.)

50 to 60 minutes or until browned, turning to brown both sides.

YIELD: 6 servings

SOUTHERN FRIED CHICKEN

2½-pound ready-to-cook frying chicken
2½ teaspoons salt
½ teaspoon ground black pepper
¾ cup flour
Shortening for frying

Wash and cut chicken into serving-size pieces. Rub 1 teaspoon of the salt into the skin. Mix remaining salt, black pepper, and flour. Dip the wet chicken pieces into the mixture, coating them well.

Melt sufficient shortening in a heavy skillet to provide a depth of ¼ inch. Add chicken and cook slowly 40 to 50 minutes or until tender, turning to brown evenly on both sides. Add more fat as the chicken cooks, if necessary. Drain on paper towels if chicken appears greasy. Serve with Cream Gravy made from the pan drippings *(see below)* and rice.

CURRIED FRIED CHICKEN
Add 1½ to 2 teaspoons curry powder to the flour in the above recipe. Fry as directed.

HERBED FRIED CHICKEN
Add ½ teaspoon ground thyme and ¼ teaspoon ground marjoram to the flour in the above recipe. Fry as directed.

ROSEMARY FRIED CHICKEN
Add ½ teaspoon crumbled rosemary leaves to the flour in the above recipe. Fry as directed.

TARRAGON FRIED CHICKEN
Add 1 teaspoon crumbled tarragon leaves

to the flour in the above recipe. Fry as directed.

ZESTY FRIED CHICKEN
Omit salt in the above recipe and add to the flour 2 teaspoons each of celery salt, garlic salt, and onion salt. Fry as directed.

CREAM GRAVY
Pour off fat left in the skillet. Return ¼ cup to the skillet and add ¼ cup of the seasoned flour left from coating the chicken, or additional flour if none is left. Stir to blend with the fat, scraping the browned bits from the bottom of the pan. Brown slightly.

Stir in 2½ cups milk or 1 cup light cream and 1½ cups stock or milk. Stir and cook until the mixture is of medium thickness. Season to taste with salt and ground black pepper. Serve with chicken.

YIELD: 6 servings

ANISE CHICKEN

3-pound ready-to-cook chicken
⅓ cup flour
¼ cup shortening
¼ cup onion flakes
3 tablespoons water
_____
1 cup chicken stock *or* 1 cup hot water and 1 chicken bouillon cube
2 teaspoons salt
¼ teaspoon anise seed
_____
1 tablespoon parsley flakes
⅛ teaspoon ground black pepper
_____
2 large egg yolks
1 tablespoon fresh lemon juice
⅓ cup water

Cut chicken into serving-size pieces, flour lightly, and brown on both sides in shortening, adding it as needed. Soften onion flakes in the 3 tablespoons water and add to chicken. Sauté 2 to 3 minutes. Add next 3 ingredients.

Cover and cook 30 minutes or until chicken is tender. Add parsley and black pepper 5 minutes before cooking time is up. Remove from heat. Mix next 3 ingredients and blend with the gravy. Heat ½ minute or until gravy is thick. Serve on rice.

YIELD: 6 servings

CHICKEN WITH RICE
(ARROZ CON POLLO)

2¾ teaspoons salt
1 teaspoon oregano leaves
½ teaspoon ground black pepper
¾ teaspoon garlic powder
1 teaspoon vinegar
2 teaspoons olive *or* salad oil

2½-pound ready-to-cook chicken
    thighs and breasts
3 tablespoons shortening

¼ cup chopped smoked ham
2 tablespoons chopped, lean, uncooked
    pork
¾ cup chopped green pepper

¼ cup onion flakes
3 tablespoons water

3 teaspoons capers
¼ cup chopped green olives
3¼ cups (1 pound, 13 ounces)
    canned tomatoes, chopped
1 tablespoon achote coloring
    (see below)
1½ cups long-grain rice
3 cups water *or* chicken broth

1 package (12 ounces) frozen peas
Pimiento

Blend first 6 ingredients. Rub chicken parts with mixture. Brown chicken on both sides in hot shortening. Reduce heat

to moderate and add the next 3 ingredients. Stir and cook 5 minutes. Add onion and the 3 tablespoons water. Stir and cook 5 minutes. Add the next 6 ingredients.

Turn into a 15½ x 10½ x 2¼-inch baking pan. Cover and bake in a moderate oven (350° F.) 1½ hours or until rice is tender and all liquid has been absorbed. Cook peas according to package directions. Add to the cooked mixture. Mix lightly with a fork. Garnish with pimiento.

TO MAKE ACHOTE COLORING
Wash ¼ cup achote seeds. Drain well. Place in a saucepan with ½ cup shortening. Heat to melt shortening. Remove from heat and let stand 10 minutes. Strain into a jar. Refrigerate and use as needed to color soups, stews, and rice dishes. (If achote seed is not available, replace it with 1 teaspoon crumbled saffron strands mixed with 1 tablespoon water.)

YIELD: 8 to 10 servings

CHICKEN, CHINESE STYLE
3-pound ready-to-cook chicken
About 2 tablespoons salad oil

½ cup boiling water
⅓ cup soy sauce
½ teaspoon ground ginger
1 teaspoon sugar
1 tablespoon fresh lemon juice
1 chopped green onion, tops and bulb

1 teaspoon cornstarch
1 tablespoon water

Wash chicken and cut into serving-size pieces. Pat dry with paper towels. Brown on all sides by cooking in oil over medium heat, adding more oil if necessary. Com-

bine next 6 ingredients and pour over chicken. Cover and cook slowly ½ hour or until chicken is tender, turning pieces occasionally.

Thicken sauce with cornstarch blended with the 1 tablespoon water. Stir and cook 1 minute. Serve pieces whole with gravy and rice or, if desired, cut meat off the bones into strips and serve over rice, Chinese style.

YIELD: 6 servings

CHICKEN KORMA

A korma *is one of the many forms of curry cooked in a spiced sauce which clings to the pieces of chicken. The moisture content of the onion flakes and water as given in this recipe approximates that of onions grown in India.*

3 pounds chicken breasts and legs
2¾ teaspoons salt
½ cup yogurt
½ cup water
¾ cup onion flakes
½ cup (1 stick) butter *or* margarine *or* peanut oil
7 whole cloves
8 whole black peppers
4 whole cardamom pods, cracked

1 cinnamon stick, 2 inches long
2 small bay leaves
1 teaspoon ground turmeric
¾ teaspoon garlic powder
1 tablespoon ground coriander
¾ teaspoon ground ginger
1 teaspoon ground cumin seed
½ teaspoon cayenne
½ cup tomato purée
1 cup water

Wash chicken, add salt and yogurt. Mix and let marinate 2 hours. Add water to onion flakes and let stand 8 minutes to absorb water. If butter or margarine is used, let it melt over low heat; remove and discard any foam that forms. Add onion to fat and cook 15 minutes, or until brown.

Tie cloves, whole black peppers, and cardamom pods in a cheesecloth bag and add along with next 3 ingredients. Cook 5 minutes, over low heat, stirring constantly or frequently enough to keep from scorching. Add chicken and continue cooking 30 minutes.

Add remaining ingredients. Cook 15 minutes or until sauce has thickened. If chicken is not brown enough, remove it from sauce and brown it in hot oil in another pan. Return chicken to sauce and serve with rice.

YIELD: 8 servings

CHICKEN, COSTA RICAN STYLE

4-pound fricassee chicken
4 cups water
2 teaspoons salt
1½ cups uncooked rice
3 tablespoons instant minced onion
½ cup diced celery
¼ cup diced green pepper

1 can (6 ounces) tomato paste
½ cup seedless raisins
½ cup sliced green olives
½ cup sliced ripe (black) olives
1 teaspoon paprika
½ teaspoon chili powder
¼ teaspoon ground black pepper

1 large ripe avocado
Pimiento, cut into strips

Place chicken, cut into serving-size pieces, water, and salt in a 6-quart saucepan. Cover and cook, slowly, 1¾ hours. Remove chicken from stock. Stir in next 4 ingredients. Cover and cook 25 minutes or until rice is tender. Add next 7 ingredients and chicken. Heat only until hot, about 10 minutes. Serve on a large platter, garnished with sliced avocado and pimiento strips.

YIELD: 10 servings

CHICKEN FRICASSEE WITH WINE
(FRICASE DE POLLO CON VINO)

4-pound ready-to-cook fricassee
  chicken

⅓ cup olive or salad oil
1¼ teaspoons salt
1 teaspoon celery salt
½ teaspoon garlic salt
1¼ teaspoons oregano leaves
¾ teaspoon ground white pepper

1 teaspoon instant minced onion
1 bay leaf
½ cup Spanish-type tomato sauce

½ cup dry sherry wine
1½ tablespoons flour

Wash chicken and cut into serving-size pieces. Combine the next 6 ingredients and rub 1 tablespoon over the skin of chicken. Brown chicken over moderate

heat on all sides in remaining seasoned oil. Add next 3 ingredients and ⅓ cup of the wine. Cover and cook 15 to 20 minutes or until chicken is tender. Blend flour with remaining wine, add, and continue cooking until sauce has thickened, about 2 minutes. Serve with rice.

YIELD: 6 servings

CHICKEN FRICASSEE, SOUTH TEXAS STYLE

4-pound fricassee chicken
2 cups boiling water
2 teaspoons salt

1 cup tomato juice
1 can (6 ounces) tomato paste
½ cup chopped ripe (black) olives
½ cup chopped green pepper

½ teaspoon oregano leaves
¼ teaspoon ground black pepper
1½ teaspoons chili powder

Wash chicken and cut into serving-size pieces. Cook until tender, about 1¾ hours, in water and salt in covered saucepan, over medium-low heat. Remove

chicken from pan. Measure the broth and add additional water, if necessary, to make 3 cups. Return chicken and stock to saucepan. Add the next 4 ingredients. Cover and cook slowly 25 minutes or until sauce has thickened. Add next 3 ingredients 10 minutes before cooking time is up. Serve hot over cooked rice or noodles.

YIELD: 6 servings

CHICKEN FRICASSEE WITH TOMATO DUMPLINGS

The tomato juice gives a rosy color and good flavor to these dumplings. A parsley garnish adds extra color.

5-pound ready-to-cook fricassee chicken
½ teaspoon whole allspice
1 teaspoon whole black pepper

1 tablespoon salt
1 rib celery, cut into pieces
3 cups boiling water

1 tablespoon instant minced onion
2 tablespoons flour
½ cup cold water
Tomato Dumplings *(see below)*

Cut chicken into serving-size pieces and place in a 6-quart saucepan. Tie allspice and black pepper in a cloth bag and add with the next 3 ingredients. Cover and cook slowly until chicken is very tender, about 2 hours. Add onion. Mix flour with cold water and add. Drop Tomato Dumpling mixture, in rounded tablespoon portions, over the chicken. Cover and cook *without lifting the lid* 15 minutes. Serve at once.

TOMATO DUMPLINGS
1 cup sifted all-purpose flour
½ teaspoon salt

1½ teaspoons double-acting baking powder
½ teaspoon powdered mustard
½ cup tomato juice

Sift flour with salt, baking powder, and mustard. Gradually stir in tomato juice. Cook over fricassee as directed.

YIELD: 6 servings

CHICKEN IN OLIVE SAUCE
(GALLINA EN SALSA DE ACEITUNAS)

4-pound ready-to-cook fricassee chicken
2 teaspoons salt
4 cups water
½ cup chicken fat
½ cup flour
5 cups chicken stock
2 thin slices bread, crumbled

½ cup finely chopped green pepper
1 dozen finely chopped green olives
2 dozen sliced green olives
1 cup (8 ounces) Spanish-type tomato sauce
⅓ cup seedless raisins
3 tablespoons instant minced onion
1 cinnamon stick, 1 inch long
2 teaspoons ground coriander
1½ teaspoons oregano leaves
½ teaspoon ground black pepper
½ teaspoon instant garlic
¼ teaspoon ground cumin seed
2 teaspoons wine vinegar *or* cider vinegar

Wash chicken and cut into serving-size pieces. Place, together with salt, and water, in a 6-quart saucepan. Cover and cook, slowly, 1¾ hours, or until chicken is tender. Remove chicken from stock. Skim fat from broth and save it for later use. Measure stock, adding water, if necessary, to make 5 cups.

Return chicken fat to saucepan and

blend in flour. Stir and cook until browned. Remove from heat and stir in stock and bread. Beat until smooth. Add remaining ingredients. Stir and cook until thickened. Add chicken. Cook, uncovered, 10 minutes, stirring frequently. Serve hot with rice or noodles.

YIELD: 8 servings

CHICKEN RIO GRANDE

3-pound ready-to-cook chicken

⅔ cup flour
4 teaspoons salt
½ teaspoon ground black pepper
½ teaspoon Italian seasoning
¼ teaspoon ground mace

¼ cup salad oil
2 tablespoons instant minced onion
2 teaspoons chili powder
¼ teaspoon instant minced garlic
1 cup chicken stock

Wash and cut chicken into serving-size pieces. Mix next 5 ingredients. Dredge chicken in seasoned flour and brown in hot oil. Add remaining ingredients. If you prefer a hot flavor, add a dash of red pepper to the chili powder. Cover and simmer 20 minutes or until chicken is tender. Serve hot with cooked rice.

YIELD: 6 servings

STEAMED (GEDAEMPHTE) CHICKEN

⅔ cup matzo meal
4 teaspoons salt
¼ teaspoon ground black pepper
1½ teaspoons marjoram leaves

3- to 4-pound ready-to-cook chicken
⅓ to ½ cup chicken fat or kosher shortening

2 tablespoons finely chopped parsley
⅔ cup diced onion
2 teaspoons paprika
1 cup water or chicken stock
2 to 3 medium-size carrots, peeled and quartered

Place the first 4 ingredients in a paper or plastic bag. Wash and cut chicken into serving-size pieces. Drop a few pieces of chicken at a time in the bag and shake well to coat with the mixture. Melt fat in a 9- or 10-inch skillet.

Add chicken, a few pieces at a time, and cook over moderate heat until browned on all sides, adding more fat as needed. As chicken browns, place the pieces in a saucepan or Dutch oven. Add remaining ingredients. Cover and simmer 1 hour.

YIELD: 6 servings

GINGERED CHICKEN
(POLLO EN JENGIBRE)

3-pound ready-to-cook chicken
3 teaspoons salt
1 teaspoon sugar
½ teaspoon ground ginger
½ cup olive or cooking oil

Wash chicken and cut into serving-size pieces. Combine salt, sugar, ginger, and 2 tablespoons of the oil. Rub on skin and cut surfaces of chicken. Brown chicken over moderate heat in oil in a 10-inch skillet. Cover and cook slowly until chicken is tender (approximately 50 minutes). Remove chicken.

To make gravy, pour fat out of skillet, return 3 tablespoons of it to the skillet and discard the remainder. Add 3 tablespoons flour and blend over low heat until smooth and bubbly. Add 1½ to 2 cups of water or chicken stock. Stir and heat gently until thickened (about 1 minute).

YIELD: 6 servings

PEPPERPOT CHICKEN

2½- to 3-pound ready-to-cook chicken
2 tablespoons soy sauce
⅓ cup flour
1 teaspoon salt
¾ teaspoon ground black pepper
3 tablespoons shortening

½ cup chopped onion
1 cup diced green pepper
¼ teaspoon ground ginger
¼ teaspoon garlic powder
1¼ cups hot water

Cut chicken into serving-size pieces. Turn in soy sauce and then in flour mixed with salt and black pepper. Brown over moderate heat on all sides in shortening. Add next 5 ingredients. Cover and cook 30 minutes or until chicken is tender. Serve hot over cooked rice.

YIELD: 6 servings

TARRAGON CHICKEN

This is our A-1 favorite way of preparing chicken. The tarragon and sour cream add marvelous flavor to the meat. Serve it on hot rice with a citrus and avocado salad. A company meal, "but it couldn't be easier!"

3-pound ready-to-cook chicken
2 teaspoons salt
1 small onion, peeled and sliced
2 tablespoons shortening
3 tablespoons flour
1 cup chicken stock
1 small bay leaf
1¼ teaspoons tarragon leaves
¼ teaspoon ground black pepper
1 cup sour cream

Wash chicken and cut into serving-size pieces. Season with salt. Brown chicken and onion in shortening in a Dutch oven or large heavy saucepan. Blend flour with a little of the chicken stock and add to chicken along with remaining stock and bay leaf.

Cover and simmer 25 minutes or until chicken is tender. Add tarragon and black pepper and continue cooking 5 more minutes. Stir in sour cream. Cook only until hot. After cream has been added, DO NOT BOIL. Serve with cooked noodles or rice.

YIELD: 6 servings

CHICKEN AND SHRIMP, ORIENTAL STYLE

¼ cup (½ stick) butter *or* margarine
2 cups sliced celery

1 cup sliced fresh mushrooms
⅓ cup sliced onions
1 cup peeled, deveined, uncooked shrimp

1 cup cooked, cold chicken, in julienne strips
1 teaspoon cornstarch
2 tablespoons soy sauce
½ cup cooked fresh peas
½ teaspoon salt
¼ teaspoon ground ginger
⅛ teaspoon ground black pepper

Melt butter or margarine in a 9- or 10-inch skillet. Add celery, cover, and cook over low heat 10 minutes. Add next 3 ingredients. Cover and cook over moderate heat until shrimp turns pink, stirring occasionally. Add chicken. Blend cornstarch with soy sauce and add along with peas and seasonings. Cook 2 minutes or until sauce has thickened and is transparent. Serve hot as the main dish.

YIELD: 6 servings

PAN-FRIED CHICKEN AND PORK, ORIENTAL STYLE

2 cups slivered, cooked chicken
2 cups slivered, leftover pork roast
⅓ cup soy sauce
3 tablespoons butter *or* margarine
½ pound sliced fresh mushrooms
½ head Chinese cabbage, sliced
1 cup bean sprouts, drained
¼ teaspoon ground black pepper
½ teaspoon ground ginger
1 teaspoon cornstarch

Slice chicken and pork in thin strips, ¼ to ⅜ inch thick, Chinese style. Soak in soy sauce 30 to 40 minutes. Remove chicken and pork from soy sauce and set aside. (Save sauce.) Melt butter or mar-garine in a 9-inch skillet. Add mushrooms, chicken, and pork. Sauté until mushrooms are limp. Add Chinese cabbage. Cook until barely wilted, about 5 minutes, stirring often. Add bean sprouts, black pepper, and ginger. Blend the soy sauce with cornstarch and pour over all. Heat thoroughly or until sauce is slightly thick.

YIELD: 6 servings

CURRIED CHICKEN PIE

3 cups cubed, cooked chicken
1 cup green peas
2 tablespoons diced pimiento
2 cans (10½ ounces each) condensed cream of mushroom soup
1 cup milk *or* chicken stock
2½ teaspoons curry powder

Unbaked pastry for 1-crust pie (Never-Fail Pastry I*)

Combine all ingredients except pastry in a 3-quart saucepan. Heat, DO NOT BOIL, and turn into a 2-quart casserole. Top with pastry, rolled ⅛ inch thick. Trim, turn under, and flute edge. Cut a gash in top of pastry to allow for the escape of steam. Bake in a preheated hot oven (425° F.) 30 minutes or until pastry has browned. Serve hot.

YIELD: 6 servings

CHICKEN CURRY

⅓ cup onion flakes
¼ teaspoon instant minced garlic
¼ cup water
¼ cup peanut oil *or* vegetable shortening

1 tablespoon ground coriander
1 teaspoon ground turmeric
1 teaspoon ground cumin

½ teaspoon ground ginger
½ teaspoon ground black pepper
¼ teaspoon ground red pepper
1 cinnamon stick, 2 inches long
___
3 pounds chicken cut up *or* chicken
  legs and breasts
3 teaspoons salt
¾ cup water
1 teaspoon lemon juice

Soften onion flakes and garlic in the ¼ cup water. Cook in hot oil or shortening until onions begin to change color. Add next 7 ingredients and cook 3 or 4 minutes. Cut chicken into serving-size pieces or use parts. Rub chicken well with 2 teaspoons of the salt. Add to spice mixture and fry 10 minutes, turning to cook on all sides. Add water and remaining salt.

Cover and cook 50 minutes, or until chicken is tender and the gravy begins to thicken. Remove the cover the last 5 minutes of cooking period. Add lemon juice just before serving. Serve over cooked rice.

YIELD: 6 servings

CURRIED BARBECUED CHICKEN

3 (2 to 2½ pounds each) ready-to-cook
  broiler chickens
1 cup hot water
5 teaspoons salt
⅓ cup (⅔ stick) butter *or* margarine,
  melted
1 teaspoon curry powder

Wash chickens and split in half lengthwise. Place over a very slow-burning charcoal fire. Cook 1½ to 2 hours, turning and basting with hot water mixed with salt as often as chickens look dry. Mix butter or margarine with curry powder and brush over chicken several times 10 minutes before cooking time is up. Serve hot.

CHILI BARBECUED CHICKEN

In the above recipe, replace curry powder with 1 teaspoon chili powder.

HERBED BARBECUED CHICKEN

In the above recipe, replace curry powder with ½ teaspoon rosemary leaves, ¾ teaspoon thyme leaves, or ¾ teaspoon marjoram leaves.

YIELD: 6 servings

CHICKEN PAPRIKASH WITH NOODLES

3-pound ready-to-cook chicken
½ cup chopped onion
¼ cup shortening
½ teaspoon ground black pepper
2 teaspoons salt
1 cup hot water
3 teaspoons paprika
¾ cup sour cream

Wash chicken and cut into serving-size pieces and set aside. Sauté onions in shortening 3 minutes or until limp and transparent. Rub black pepper and salt on the chicken, add to onion and shortening and brown, over moderate heat, on all sides. Add water, cover, and simmer 30 to 40 minutes or until chicken is tender. Stir in paprika 10 minutes before cooking time is up.

Remove chicken to a serving dish. Add sour cream to pan drippings. Mix well and heat thoroughly, but DO NOT BOIL. Pour over chicken. Serve with noodles cooked as directed on the package.

YIELD: 6 servings

CHICKEN LIVERS AND HAM WITH RICE
(MINUDOS DE GALLINA CON ARROZ)

½ pound chicken livers
1 cup chopped onion
¼ cup olive *or* salad oil

1 cup diced, cooked ham
2 cups diced, fresh tomatoes
2 tablespoons parsley flakes
4 teaspoons salt
½ teaspoon ground black pepper
2 tablespoons paprika
¼ teaspoon garlic powder
½ teaspoon crumbled saffron strands

1½ cups uncooked, long-grain rice
3 cups boiling water *or* chicken stock

Sauté liver and onions in oil until livers turn gray and onions are limp. Add the next 8 ingredients, stir, and cook until tomatoes are soft, 8 to 10 minutes. Blend in rice.

Pour in boiling water or stock. Boil over low heat 10 minutes, without stirring. Cover and bake in a preheated moderate oven (350° F.) 30 minutes or until rice is tender. Toss lightly before serving.

YIELD: 8 servings

TURKEY

HOW-TO-ROAST TURKEY I
(OVERNIGHT METHOD)

Close cavity openings of a stuffed turkey with skewers and lace tightly with a strong cord or sew with a strong string or thread. Fasten neck to back with skewers or toothpicks. Tie legs together and fasten string to tail, drawing the legs close to the body. Tie and cut string. Take tip end of wings and bend them back so they are held against the back of bird. (A string tied loosely around the middle of the bird holds the wings in place.)

Rub outside of skin with softened butter or margarine, using about 2 tablespoons, and sprinkle with salt. Place turkey on a rack or trivet, breast-side up, in a roasting pan or in a large baking pan about 3 inches deep. Cover fowl with heavy-duty foil. Tuck it down around sides of turkey but not over edges of pan. At bedtime, place turkey in a very slow oven (275° F.), no higher, being sure that your oven control is accurate. Cook

turkey, weighing up to 13 pounds, 30 minutes per pound or about 6 hours. Cook bird weighing more than this 7 to 8 hours. Set the alarm clock and go to bed.

When the alarm goes off, get up and turn off the oven heat, leaving the door closed. An hour before serving, remove turkey from oven and preheat the oven to slow (325° F.). Brush outside skin with pan drippings, using pastry brush. Return uncovered turkey to oven and cook 1 hour, brushing with pan drippings at 15 minute intervals. The bird will be beautifully browned in an hour.

HOW-TO-ROAST TURKEY II
(OPEN PAN METHOD)

Close cavity openings and prepare turkey for roasting as in Method I. Place turkey on a rack in an open pan, breast-side up. Brush skin with melted butter or margarine. Dip a clean white cloth (3 to 4 thicknesses of cheesecloth or a piece of clean old sheet large enough to completely cover fowl) into hot water mixed with butter or margarine, using 1 stick of butter to 1½ cups hot water. Wring cloth lightly and place over bird, covering it completely.

Bake in a preheated slow oven (325° F.); 12 to 16 pound fowl 5 to 6 hours; 16 to 20 pound bird 6 to 7½ hours, wetting the cloth in the hot butter water 5 to 6 times. If a thermometer is used, it should register 190° to 195° F. when turkey is done. If the breast and legs have a tendency to brown before the rest of the fowl, cover these parts with foil.

TO MAKE GRAVY

Skim off most of the fat from pan drippings. Stir in 1 tablespoon flour to each cup stock you plan to use. Gradually add stock and cook until gravy has thickened. Add salt and ground black pepper to taste. (Make stock by cooking neck and giblets in water to cover with 1 teaspoon salt and 1 small bay leaf.)

BARBECUED TURKEY ON A SPIT

"The turkey is the largest and, if not the most delicate, at least the most flavorful of our domestic birds," wrote French gastronomer, Brillat-Savarin, in the early nineteenth century. "It also enjoys the unique advantage of attracting to it every class of society." (Especially if prepared by this tasty method.)

5- to 6-pound ready-to-cook turkey
1 cup celery leaves

5 teaspoons salt
1 cup hot water

½ cup cider vinegar
⅓ cup fresh lemon juice
¼ cup tomato catsup

¼ cup water
1 tablespoon light-brown sugar
1 teaspoon salt
1½ teaspoons powdered mustard
1 teaspoon mixed pickling spice
1 teaspoon ground black pepper
¾ teaspoon cayenne
2 teaspoons instant minced onion
¼ teaspoon instant minced garlic

Wash turkey and wipe dry. Stuff body cavity with celery leaves. Close openings by stitching with thick cord or with skewers, pulling the skin over the neck opening and fastening it to the back. Insert spit lengthwise through the turkey, being sure to balance for even turning. Tie legs together, then tie legs and wings tightly against body and secure bird to spit, using strong string.

Make salt-water basting solution by combining salt and hot water in a small saucepan. Make sauce by combining remaining ingredients, bringing them to the boiling point and then setting aside. (The basting with salt water prevents the turkey from burning and permits the salt to penetrate the meat. This is applied before sauce in the cooking to avoid overcooking of sauce, whereby most of its flavors would be evaporated or burned out.) Roast turkey, adjusting temperature of coals and distance of turkey above them so that the turkey will cook in about 3 hours.

During most of the roasting time, baste whenever the turkey looks dry, using the salt water, applied with a brush or a swab made by tying a cloth to the end of a stick. During the last 30 to 40 minutes, baste with the spiced vinegar sauce. Serve hot.

YIELD: 8 servings

BRAISED TURKEY WITH MUSHROOMS

4- to 5-pound turkey
1 tablespoon salt
¼ teaspoon ground black pepper

2 to 3 tablespoons shortening

1 cup hot water
1 bay leaf
3 whole cloves
2 medium-size onions

¾ pound fresh mushrooms
3 tablespoons butter *or* margarine
3 tablespoons flour

Cut turkey into serving-size pieces, into which rub salt and black pepper. Brown in hot fat in heavy skillet or Dutch oven. Add next 4 ingredients. Cover and simmer 40 minutes or until tender. Wash mushrooms and slice stems and caps. Sauté in butter or margarine 5 minutes. Blend in flour. Drain off stock from turkey and add to mushrooms. Mix well. Cook until thickened. Pour over turkey and cook 5 minutes. Place turkey on a platter and pour sauce over it. Serve as a main dish with hot rice.

YIELD: 8 to 10 servings

TURKEY NEWBURG IN PATTY CASES

3 large egg yolks
1 cup light cream
½ teaspoon salt
⅛ teaspoon ground white pepper
½ teaspoon ground thyme

2 cups diced, cooked turkey
1 cup sliced mushrooms
3 tablespoons butter *or* margarine
¼ cup turkey stock *or* dry sherry
6 patty cases
Paprika

Combine the first 5 ingredients in the top of a double boiler. Stir and cook over hot water (NOT BOILING) until of custard consistency. Sauté turkey and mushrooms in butter or margarine 5 minutes or until thoroughly heated. Remove from heat and stir in stock or wine and sauce. Mix until blended. Serve at once in patty cases. Garnish with paprika.

YIELD: 6 servings

TURKEY BALLS IN MUSHROOM SAUCE

2 large eggs, beaten
3 cups finely ground, leftover cooked turkey
1 cup soft bread crumbs
¾ cup turkey stock
1 teaspoon instant minced onion
¼ teaspoon ground black pepper
¼ teaspoon ground allspice
¾ teaspoon powdered mustard

1 can (10½ ounces) condensed cream of mushroom soup
1 cup turkey stock

¼ teaspoon celery salt
⅛ teaspoon onion powder
¹⁄₁₆ teaspoon garlic powder
¹⁄₁₆ teaspoon ground black pepper

Combine the first 8 ingredients. Shape into sixteen 1½-inch balls. Place in a 12 x 8 x 2-inch baking pan. Combine remaining ingredients, heat to boiling point, and pour over turkey balls. Cook in a preheated moderate oven (350° F.) 50 minutes. Serve with rice, if desired.

YIELD: 8 servings

TURKEY HASH

½ cup chopped onion
½ cup diced green pepper
1 cup diced, uncooked potatoes, cut in julienne strips

2 tablespoons butter *or* margarine

2 cups diced, leftover cooked turkey
¼ cup turkey stock

1½ teaspoons salt
¼ teaspoon ground thyme
¼ teaspoon ground black pepper

Chopped parsley

Sauté first 3 ingredients in butter or margarine 10 minutes. Add next 5 ingredients. Mix well. Cook over low heat 10 minutes. Serve hot, sprinkled with parsley.

YIELD: 6 servings

HERBED TURKEY FONDUE

1 cup milk
1 cup turkey stock
2 tablespoons butter *or* margarine

1¾ cups soft bread crumbs
1¼ teaspoons salt
1 teaspoon ground thyme
¼ teaspoon ground black pepper
2 tablespoons lemon juice
2 cups diced, leftover turkey

5 large eggs, separated
Mushroom Sauce*

Heat together first 3 ingredients. Add next 6 ingredients. Beat egg yolks and gradually stir into the hot liquid. Stir and cook over low heat 5 minutes or until the mixture thickens. Remove from heat. Carefully fold in stiffly beaten egg whites. Turn into an ungreased 1½-quart casserole. Place in a pan of hot water. Bake in a preheated slow oven (325° F.) 1¼ hours, or until knife inserted in center comes out clean. Serve hot with Mushroom Sauce.

YIELD: 6 to 8 servings

DUCK and GOOSE

BAKED DUCKLING IN ORANGE JUICE

4-pound ready-to-cook duck
½ cup flour
3 tablespoons shortening

1 tablespoon instant minced onion
1½ teaspoons salt
¼ teaspoon ground ginger
1¼ cups fresh orange juice
1 teaspoon grated orange rind

1 tablespoon cornstarch
1 tablespoon water
Orange sections *or* slices
Fresh parsley (optional)

Remove and discard skin from duck and quarter. Dredge in flour. Brown on all sides in hot shortening. Place duck in a casserole. Add the next 5 ingredients. Cover and bake 1½ hours, or until duck is tender, in a preheated slow oven (325° F.). Remove duck to a serving dish and keep in a warm place while making the sauce.

Blend cornstarch with water and add to the liquid left in the casserole. Stir and cook 2 to 3 minutes or until sauce has thickened. Garnish with orange sections or slices and fresh parsley, if desired. Serve hot with white or wild rice.

YIELD: 4 servings

ROAST DUCK, CHINESE STYLE

4- to 5-pound ready-to-cook duck
Salt

2 tablespoons instant minced onion
2 tablespoons finely chopped celery
1½ teaspoons sugar
¼ teaspoon ground cinnamon
⅛ teaspoon anise seed
⅓ cup soy sauce

2 cups water

2 tablespoons honey
2 tablespoons cider vinegar
1½ tablespoons soy sauce
3½ teaspoons salt

1 teaspoon cornstarch
2 teaspoons water

Wash duck and remove and discard excess fat from body and neck cavities. Rub the inside lightly with salt. Combine the next 6 ingredients with 1 cup of the water. Bring to boiling point. Tie duck's neck tightly with a string so the sauce will not seep out while cooking. Pour hot sauce into duck cavity. Sew the opening tightly to prevent the sauce from bubbling out. Rub the outside of duck with a little of the sauce that will be left. Place duck on a rack, breast-side up, in a roasting pan. Cook in a preheated slow oven (325° F.) 20 minutes.

Then heat remaining 1 cup water with the next 4 ingredients and brush over skin of the bird. Continue cooking 1½ hours or until duck is done, basting at 20-minute intervals with the sauce. Remove from oven and drain sauce into a saucepan. Thicken with cornstarch mixed with the 2 teaspoons water. Cook until slightly thickened. Serve separately as gravy.

YIELD: 4 servings

CHRISTMAS DUCK, BRAZILIAN STYLE
(PATO DO NATAL)
4-pound ready-to-cook duck

1 cup dry white wine
3 tablespoons fresh lemon juice
1 tablespoon parsley flakes
1 teaspoon instant minced onion
¼ teaspoon instant minced garlic
_____
2½ teaspoons salt (or to taste)
Duck giblets
_____
1 tablespoon butter _or_ margarine, melted
½ teaspoon ground nutmeg
¼ teaspoon ground black pepper
_____
1 can (11 ounces) water-packed chestnuts

Wash duck and dry with paper towels. Combine next 5 ingredients with 1 teaspoon of the salt. Pour over duck. Marinate overnight in the refrigerator. Wash giblets and chop coarsely. Add next 3 ingredients and remaining salt. Chop chestnuts and add. Mix well and spoon into body and neck cavities of duck.

Close openings with skewers. Lace tightly with a string. Place duck on a rack in a shallow baking pan large enough to accommodate duck. Bake in a preheated moderate oven (325° F.) 2 hours or bake 2½ hours for a crisper brown skin.

YIELD: 4 servings

DUCK, HAWAIIAN STYLE
4- to 5-pound ready-to-cook-duck
1 cup Duck Broth (_see below_)
_____
1 cup fresh orange juice

1½ tablespoons cornstarch
1 teaspoon salt
1½ teaspoons curry powder
½ teaspoon ground ginger
2 teaspoons soy sauce
_____
1 cup fresh _or_ canned pineapple wedges
1 cup sliced scallions

Remove and discard excess fat from duck and cut duck into quarters. Place pieces, skin-side up, on a rack in a shallow roasting pan. Cover and cook _slowly_ 1 hour or until tender. Pour off fat. Mix duck broth with next 6 ingredients and heat to boiling point, stirring constantly. Add pineapple wedges. Place duck in a 13 x 9 x 2-inch baking dish, pour sauce over duck and continue cooking 1 hour or until duck is tender. Add scallions 15 minutes before cooking time is up.

DUCK BROTH
Place duck neck and giblets in a saucepan with 2 cups water, 1 teaspoon salt, and 4 whole black peppers. Cover and cook 1 hour or until tender. Strain off broth. Cool and allow fat to rise to top and skim it off.

YIELD: 4 servings

SPICED DUCK

3 cups duck *or* chicken stock
1 teaspoon salt
¼ teaspoon ground black pepper
1½ teaspoons ground coriander
1 tablespoon instant minced onion
¼ teaspoon instant minced garlic
½ teaspoon ground ginger
1/16 teaspoon cayenne

4-pound ready-to-cook duck
1 teaspoon sugar
1 tablespoon wine vinegar

Combine the first 8 ingredients in a large saucepan or Dutch oven. Wash and cut duck into quarters. Add to the first mixture. Cover and cook over medium-low heat 45 minutes or until duck is about half done. Stir in sugar and vinegar.

Continue cooking until gravy is almost absorbed and fat comes to the surface, about 15 minutes. Remove duck from pan. Skim off fat and put it in a 10-inch skillet. Heat and add duck and fry until duck is brown. Return duck to the saucepan and continue cooking 1 hour or until duck is tender. Serve on fluffy hot white or wild rice.

YIELD: 4 servings

DUCK VINDALOO

1 cup onion flakes
¼ teaspoon instant minced garlic
⅓ cup water
¼ cup peanut oil *or* vegetable
    shortening
7 teaspoons ground coriander
2 teaspoons ground turmeric
¾ teaspoon ground ginger
½ teaspoon ground cardamom
1 teaspoon ground cumin
1 teaspoon ground black pepper
1¼ teaspoons ground red pepper
    (or to taste)
1 teaspoon powdered mustard
3 tablespoons cider vinegar

4-pound ready-to-cook duck
3 teaspoons salt (or to taste)
1½ cups hot water

Soften onion flakes and garlic in the ⅓ cup water. Stir and cook over low heat in oil or shortening 2 minutes. Mix spices with vinegar to a smooth paste and add to cooked onion. Stir and cook 3 minutes. Cut duck into quarters. Trim off excess fat and rub duck well with 2 teaspoons of the salt.

Brown duck on all sides in the onion and spice mixture. Add remaining salt and 1 cup of the water, cover pan tightly and cook slowly 1½ hours or until duck is tender. Remove duck from pan. Pour off and discard excess fat from pan drippings. Add remaining ½ cup water and mix well. Heat to form gravy. Serve with hot cooked rice.

YIELD: 4 servings

DUCK WITH RICE

4-pound ready-to-cook duck
2 tablespoons butter *or* margarine
3 cups boiling water
1 tablespoon salt
¼ cup instant minced onion
2 teaspoons ground cumin seed
½ teaspoon ground marjoram
¼ teaspoon garlic powder
1/16 teaspoon ground red pepper
1 cup uncooked long-grain rice

Remove excess fat from duck and cut into 4 pieces. Brown over moderate heat in a Dutch oven or heavy deep skillet in butter or margarine. Add 1 cup of the water and salt. Cover and cook 1 hour or until duck is tender.

Skim off excess fat. Add spices, remaining water, and rice. Stir with a fork to blend spices and rice with the sauce. Cover and cook 20 minutes or until rice is tender. Serve hot.

YIELD: 4 servings

DUCK JAMBALAYA
(JAMBALAYA DE CANARD)
4-pound ready-to-cook duck
3½ teaspoons salt
¾ teaspoon ground black pepper
2 cups Giblet Stock (see below)
1 cup long-grain converted rice
Cold water to cover

⅓ cup instant chopped onion
¼ cup green pepper flakes
¼ teaspoon instant minced garlic

¼ cup water
½ pound sausage
1 medium-size bay leaf
½ teaspoon chili powder
½ teaspoon ground thyme
1 teaspoon parsley flakes
½ cup diced, cooked giblets
½ cup diced, cooked ham
1 cup canned tomatoes

Wash duck, cut into quarters, and trim off excess fat and bone. (Discard fat, but save bones to cook with giblets.) Mix 2 teaspoons of the salt with ½ teaspoon of the black pepper and rub into the duck. Brown 2 pieces of the duck at a time very slowly in a 4-quart saucepan (30 to 40 minutes).

After duck browns, place it on paper towels to absorb excess fat. Pour off and discard excess fat from saucepan and stir in 2 cups of the giblet stock. Add browned duck, cover, cook slowly 1½ hours or until tender. Soak rice, in cold water to cover, at least 30 minutes. Drain well. In the meantime, soften next 3 ingredients in the ¼ cup water and set aside.

Brown sausage, drain off and discard excess fat. Add rice and softened onion, green pepper, and garlic to sausage and stir and cook until rice is dry and sticks to bottom of pan. Remove duck from gravy and keep warm. Add rice to gravy along with remaining ingredients.

Cover and cook 15 minutes. Place duck over top of rice. Cover and cook 10 minutes. Serve rice, topped with a serving of duck.

GIBLET STOCK
Wash giblets and place in a saucepan with neck, bones, 1 quart cold water, ½ teaspoon salt, 8 whole black peppers, and 1 bay leaf. Cover and cook slowly 1 hour.

YIELD: 4 servings

DUCK AND RUTABAGA STEW
Duck and rutabaga are an excellent twosome because flavors are compatible and also because rutabaga absorbs a lot of the duck fat, making the rutabaga richer in flavor.

4-pound ready-to-cook duck
½ cup finely chopped onion
2 tablespoons shortening

½ cup finely chopped ham
3 cups hot water and 3 chicken bouillon cubes or 3 cups chicken stock
2 to 3 teaspoons salt
¼ teaspoon ground black pepper

2 cups diced rutabagas
12 small white onions
1 teaspoon thyme leaves
¼ teaspoon instant minced garlic
3½ tablespoons browned flour
1 cup hot water *or* chicken stock

Cut duck into serving-size pieces and set aside. Sauté onion in shortening in a Dutch oven or heavy saucepan large enough to cook stew. Add a few duck pieces at a time and brown over moderate heat on all sides. Add next 4 ingredients.

Cover and cook slowly 40 minutes or until almost tender. Stir in rutabagas and onion. Cover and cook 40 minutes or until duck is tender. Add thyme and garlic 10 minutes before cooking time is up. Brown flour in a dry skillet over medium heat and mix with water or stock. Add to stew and cook 3 minutes or until sauce has thickened. Serve hot.

YIELD: 6 servings

ROAST GOOSE WITH POTATO STUFFING

Because Elizabeth I of England and her court were eating roast goose on Michaelmas Day, September 29, 1588, when news arrived of the defeat of the Spanish Armada, the Queen decreed that roast goose should be served each Michaelmas Day to commemorate the victory. This recipe is of Jewish origin, with a very good stuffing.

¼ cup soft chicken *or* goose fat
2 teaspoons paprika
2½ tablespoons salt
12 medium (3 pounds) potatoes
½ teaspoon ground black pepper
1 cup chopped onion
⅓ cup chopped parsley
4 large eggs, beaten
1⅓ cups matzo meal

¼ cup hot chicken *or* goose fat
⅔ cup diced celery
8- to 10-pound ready-to-cook goose

Mix the ¼ cup chicken or goose fat with paprika and 2 teaspoons of the salt and rub a portion of it inside crop and body cavities of goose. Grate potatoes and mix remaining salt and next 7 ingredients. Spoon into the crop and body cavities. Close the openings with skewers and lace tightly with a string. Rub remaining fat and paprika mixture over the outside skin of goose.

Place on a rack, breast-side down, in a roasting pan. Cook in a preheated slow oven (325° F.) 3½ to 4 hours. When goose is ⅔ done, according to cooking time, turn breast up to finish cooking. To test for doneness, move drumstick up and down. The join should yield readily or twist out and the meat should feel very soft.

Siphon off fat with a poultry baster as it accumulates in roasting pan. Make gravy from pan drippings, using 1½ tablespoons flour to each cup water or stock. Add salt and black pepper to taste.

YIELD: 8 to 10 servings

RICE DISHES

THERE are few things tastier (or more basic) than light, freshly cooked, fluffy rice. The addition of certain spices in combination with other ingredients can elevate this simple foodstuff to heights of gourmet artistry.

SAFFRON RICE PILAF

¼ teaspoon powdered saffron
2 tablespoons boiling water

⅛ teaspoon garlic powder
¼ teaspoon ground white pepper
1 teaspoon salt
3 tablespoons olive *or* salad oil
2½ cups boiling chicken stock *or* 2½ cups boiling water and 3 chicken bouillon cubes

1 cup long-grain, uncooked rice
¼ cup seedless raisins

3 tablespoons shredded, blanched almonds

Dissolve saffron in the boiling water and place in a saucepan with next 5 ingredients. Bring to boiling point. Stir in rice and raisins. Bring to boiling point again. Turn into a 1-quart casserole. Cover and bake in a preheated moderate oven (350° F.) 45 minutes or until rice is tender. Stir in almonds 10 minutes before cooking time is up. Serve with chicken, lamb, shrimp, or crabmeat.

YIELD: 6 servings

TURMERIC RICE PILAF

2 tablespoons instant minced onion
2 tablespoons water
2 tablespoons butter *or* margarine
1 cup long-grain, uncooked rice
2 cups boiling chicken stock *or* 2 cups boiling water and 2 chicken bouillon cubes
_____
1 teaspoon salt
½ teaspoon turmeric
1 bay leaf
_____
1 tablespoon butter *or* margarine

Soften onion in water and sauté in butter or margarine 1 minute. Add rice and stir until grains are well coated with butter or margarine. Add chicken stock or bouillon cubes dissolved in boiling water and next 3 ingredients.

Turn into a 1-quart greased casserole, cover tightly, and bake in a preheated moderate oven (375° F.) 50 minutes or until rice is tender, adding additional stock if necessary. Toss together, with a fork, rice and remaining 1 tablespoon butter.

YIELD: 6 servings

PILAU

There are various spellings of pilao *or* pulao *or, farther west,* pilaf; *but it's always a flavorful rice dish which starts with rice which has been fried before it is cooked in water. Spices such as cinnamon, cardamom, bay leaves are added. In this recipe cloves, cinnamon and saffron season the rice which has been mixed with raisins and almonds.*

2 cups long-grain rice
4 cups cold water
¼ cup (½ stick) butter *or* margarine
2 whole cloves
1 cinnamon stick, 2 inches long
2 teaspoons salt
¼ teaspoon crumbled saffron
4 cups boiling water
½ cup seedless raisins
Almonds, blanched, toasted, and slivered

Soak rice in 4 cups cold water 30 minutes. Drain well. Stir and cook in butter or margarine 3 minutes or until rice begins to stick to pan. Remove from heat. Add cloves, cinnamon, and salt.

Mix saffron with boiling water and stir until water is well-colored. Pour over rice. Mix well. Cover and cook 15 minutes or until all water has been absorbed, lifting rice from bottom of the pan a couple of times with a fork (DO NOT STIR).

Add raisins and toss lightly with a fork. If raisins are dry, steam in a sieve over boiling water to moisten them. Serve hot with slivered almonds sprinkled over the top.

YIELD: 6 servings

PILAU

(WITH PEAS AND MUSHROOMS)

1 cup long-grain rice
1 cup water
2 tablespoons butter *or* margarine
2 cinnamon sticks, each 2 inches long
2 bay leaves
_____
5 whole cloves
5 whole cardamom seeds, crushed
¼ teaspoon whole black pepper
¼ teaspoon whole cumin seeds
_____
2 cups boiling chicken stock
1 teaspoon salt
1 teaspoon lemon juice
10-ounce package frozen peas
2½-ounce can white mushrooms, drained

Soak rice in water 30 minutes. Drain well. Stir and cook 4 to 5 minutes in butter or margarine along with cinnamon, bay leaves, and next 4 spices tied in a bag. Remove from heat when rice begins to stick to pan. Add chicken stock, salt, and lemon juice.

Cover and cook, without stirring, 15 minutes or until rice is tender and has absorbed all water. Remove spices. In the meantime, cook peas as directed on label, drain well, and add along with well-drained mushrooms. Toss very lightly, being careful not to break rice grains. Every grain should stand apart.

YIELD: 6 servings

CURRIED RICE

1 cup long-grain rice
2 cups water
2 tablespoons butter *or* margarine
2 teaspoons curry powder
2 cups boiling chicken stock *or* 2 cups water and 2 chicken bouillon cubes
¾ teaspoon salt (or to taste)
¼ teaspoon ground white pepper
¼ teaspoon instant minced garlic
1 tablespoon instant minced onion

Soak rice in water 30 minutes. Drain well. Sauté in butter or margarine along with curry powder until rice sticks to bottom of pan, stirring constantly. Stir in chicken stock or boiling water and bouillon cubes. Add salt, the amount depending upon salt in stock. Add pepper, garlic, and onion.

Cover and cook, without stirring, over medium heat 15 minutes. Turn off heat and leave, covered, until ready to serve. The rice will absorb all the moisture and every grain will stand apart. Serve hot with meat or poultry.

YIELD: 6 servings

SOUTH AFRICAN RAISIN RICE

1 cup converted, long-grain rice
2¼ cups boiling water

½ teaspoon grated lemon rind
1 cinnamon stick, 1 inch long
½ teaspoon ground turmeric
1 teaspoon salt

¾ cup seedless raisins
2 tablespoons butter *or* margarine
3 tablespoons sugar

Sprinkle rice into rapidly boiling water. Add the next 4 ingredients. Cover and boil slowly 20 minutes or until rice is tender. Add raisins, butter, and sugar. Toss lightly. Serve hot as an accompaniment to meat or poultry.

YIELD: 6 servings

PINK RICE

1 cup long-grain rice
2 cups water
2 tablespoons butter *or* margarine
2 cups chicken stock *or* 2 cups water and
2 chicken bouillon cubes
½ teaspoon salt
2 teaspoons paprika
¼ teaspoon ground white pepper

Soak rice in the 2 cups water 30 minutes. Drain and discard water. Sauté rice in butter or margarine until rice is dry and begins to stick to bottom of pan. Add chicken stock or water and bouillon cubes, salt, and paprika. Stir only until well blended.

Cover, bring to boiling point, and cook 12 to 15 minutes or until rice is almost tender. Remove from heat and let stand covered until ready to serve. Rice will absorb all the water and every grain will stand apart.

YIELD: 4 to 6 servings

SPICED RICE, KOREAN STYLE

3 tablespoons salad oil
2 cups long-grain rice
¼ pound ground chuck
¼ pound sliced mushrooms
⅓ cup onion flakes
⅓ cup water

3 tablespoons soy sauce
3 tablespoons Toasted Sesame Seed*
¼ to ½ teaspoon crushed red pepper

*An asterisk after the name of a dish indicates that the recipe for this dish appears in the book. Consult the Index for the page number.

2 teaspoons salt
2½ cups beef broth *or* 2 beef bouillon cubes and 2½ cups water

Heat 2 tablespoons of the oil in a saucepan large enough for cooking rice. Wash rice and add. Stir and cook 5 minutes or until rice is dry and begins to stick to the pan. Add beef and remaining oil and cook with rice until beef is no longer pink.

Soften onion in water and add along with mushrooms. Sauté until onions are limp and transparent. Stir in remaining ingredients. Cover, bring to boiling point over high heat. Reduce heat to slow and cook 20 minutes or until rice is tender.

YIELD: 8 servings

TURKISH PILAF

1 cup long-grain, uncooked rice
Water to cover
2 tablespoons chicken fat *or* butter

1 teaspoon salt
1 teaspoon ground black pepper
2¼ cups boiling chicken stock

2 tablespoons butter *or* margarine

Soak rice in water to cover 30 minutes. Drain. Sauté in hot chicken fat or butter until the rice is dry and begins to stick to the bottom of the pan. Add next 3 ingredients.

Cover and cook 20 minutes or until rice is tender and all the stock has been absorbed. Remove from heat. Add butter or margarine, cover, and let stand 5 minutes. Toss lightly to blend in butter, being careful not to mash rice grains.

YIELD: 6 servings

SALADS and
SALAD DRESSINGS

THE old herbalists had the highest regard for leafy greens. Parkinson declared "Lettices all cool a hot and fainting stomach," and Gerarde was sure "Lettuce cooleth the heate of the stomache, called the heart-burning, and helpeth it when it is troubled with choller." This kind of talk might never get Father to eat his salad, but it might help him sell it to your guests.

It is quite fitting to make a ceremony of the tossing of a delicious dinner salad, especially when the man of the house performs the ritual. It's great fun at buffet suppers, barbecues, and similar informal meals that are served indoors or out.

A visit to the antique shops may provide you with attractive accessories with which to enhance the scene: a spacious butter bowl, in which to mix the salad; pottery serving plates in a warm brown color to contrast colorfully with the salad greens; a tall pepper grinder and a salt mill; a mortar and pestle in which to crush and mix salad herbs; a pepper shaker, perhaps, with fine pouring holes in which to keep the powdered garlic, a salt shaker for the paprika; an old-fashioned castor set, if you can find it.

460

Beyond this fanfare, most important, of course, is the creation of the salad itself—which should look, smell, and taste good. To achieve this, you must develop an eye for artistic effects as well as keep your taste buds fresh.

It is best to choose an appropriate salad for a specific meal. If it is for dinner, with a main course featuring meat, fish, poultry, or some other protein food or hearty casserole dish, you may prefer a leafy green salad, whose dressing is well seasoned. A French-type dressing is usually best·on green salads, since it does not hide the rich bright greens.

Use salad dressing sparingly. Once tossed, each leaf should be lightly coated; there should not be much more than a tablespoonful of extra dressing left in the bottom of the bowl after the last spear of green has been eaten.

Wash salad greens well in advance of use so that the water may drain from the leaves. Jouncing your washed greens in one of those French wire salad baskets is an efficient way to dry them.

Tear, rather than cut, greens. For one thing, they look better. For another, cut edges bruise and turn brownish if greens are not used within an hour.

Use a sharp knife when cutting fruit. This prevents bruising and loss of juice. Cut fruit, meat, etc., in pieces large enough to identify the food.

Dip some fruits in citrus juice to prevent discoloration. This includes apples, bananas, peaches, and avocados. If citrus fruits are to be added to a fruit salad, wait to cut them until the last minute, as these lose their juice, and thin the dressing.

An interesting flavor is created by adding herbs such as chives, mint, basil, parsley, or tarragon to green salads. Toasted diced bread, dipped in garlic-flavored salad oil, is an interesting addition to green salads; so are crumbled Roquefort cheese; diced tart apple; pineapple chunks; bits of crisp bacon; Toasted Sesame Seed;* and capers, among a number of other things.

Meat, macaroni, and mild-flavored cooked vegetables, such as potatoes for potato salad, are all the more savory if allowed to stand in well-seasoned dressing for an hour or so. Do not, however, marinate leafy greens unless you prefer your salads to be what the French call *fatiguée*.

*An asterisk after the name of a dish indicates that the recipe for this dish appears in the book. Consult the Index for the page number.

BOSTON LETTUCE AND CURLY ENDIVE SALAD

1 medium-size head Boston lettuce
½ medium-size head curly endive
⅓ cup chopped fresh chives

1 teaspoon salt
¼ teaspoon ground black pepper
½ teaspoon tarragon leaves
½ teaspoon basil leaves
⅛ teaspoon finely minced garlic
¼ cup olive *or* salad oil
1 tablespoon lemon juice
1 tablespoon red wine vinegar

½ cup fried whole-wheat bread cubes
Onion rings

Wash, drain, and dry salad greens thoroughly. Tear into bite-size pieces and place in a salad bowl. Add chives. Mix next 8 ingredients and beat with a rotary beater. Just before serving, add dressing, bread cubes, and onion rings and toss lightly.

YIELD: 6 to 8 servings

ROMAINE SALAD CHIFFONADE

1 head romaine lettuce
1 tablespoon diced green *or* red pepper
1 tablespoon chopped sweet cucumber
    pickle

½ teaspoon basil leaves
½ teaspoon oregano leaves
¾ teaspoon salt
¼ teaspoon garlic powder
⅛ teaspoon coarsely ground black
    pepper
1 tablespoon fresh lemon juice
1 tablespoon wine vinegar
¼ cup salad *or* olive oil

1 large hard-cooked egg, sliced

Wash and dry romaine thoroughly. Tear into bite-size pieces and place in a salad bowl. Add green or red pepper and pickle. Mix the next 8 ingredients in a small bowl. Beat with a rotary beater. Pour over salad. Toss lightly, being sure to coat each piece of romaine with dressing. Garnish with sliced hard-cooked egg.

YIELD: 6 servings

TOSSED GREEN ARTICHOKE SALAD

Whether to serve the green dinner salad before, during, or after the main course is a matter of personal choice. Some gastronomers prefer it one way, some another. The first-century Roman poet, Martial, raised the point when he demanded:

Tell me why lettuce, which our grand-sires last did eat,

Is now of late become the first of all our meats?

½ head Chinese cabbage
    (celery cabbage)
1 head Boston lettuce
1 can (1 pound) artichoke hearts
1 cup fresh grapefruit sections
¼ cup salad *or* olive oil
2 tablespoons fresh lemon juice
½ teaspoon basil leaves
Salt to taste
Ground black pepper to taste

Wash and thoroughly dry Chinese cabbage and lettuce. Break into bite-size pieces. Place in a salad bowl. Top with drained artichoke hearts and grapefruit sections. Combine remaining ingredients, add, and toss lightly.

YIELD: 8 servings

ROQUEFORT CHEESE STUFFED LETTUCE SALAD

The United States is France's best market for its Roquefort cheese. Much of it (happily) goes into salad dressings.

1-pound head lettuce
2 packages (3 ounces each)
  cream cheese
⅓ cup Roquefort *or* Bleu cheese,
  crumbled
2 tablespoons milk
¼ teaspoon powdered mustard
Dash cayenne
1/16 teaspoon ground black pepper
Dash salt

Wash lettuce and drain well. Cut out the core and heart. (Save heart to use in other salads.) Blend together remaining ingredients. Pack in cavity of lettuce. Wrap in foil. Chill overnight or several hours. Cut in wedges and serve with mayonnaise or French dressing.

YIELD: 4 to 6 servings

SNAPPY CHEESE STUFFED LETTUCE SALAD

1-pound head lettuce
2 packages (3 ounces each)
  cream cheese
1½ packages (4½ ounces)
  Snappy cheese
Dash cayenne
⅛ teaspoon garlic powder
1/16 teaspoon ground white pepper
¾ teaspoon chili powder
1 tablespoon milk *or* sherry wine
Mayonnaise *or* French dressing

Wash lettuce and drain well. Cut out core and heart. (Save heart to use in other salads.) Blend together remaining ingredients. Pack in cavity of lettuce. Wrap in foil. Chill overnight or several hours. Cut in wedges and serve with mayonnaise or French dressing.

YIELD: 4 to 6 servings

LOW-CALORIE SALAD BOWL

Eat a large leaf of lettuce and you've picked up no more than 3 to 4 calories. And if you season a salad well, the oil can be kept to a minimum.

½ compact head lettuce
½ head curly endive

½ cup diced celery
½ cup diced green pepper
½ cup small white onion rings

½ teaspoon salt
½ teaspoon oregano leaves
½ teaspoon basil leaves

¼ teaspoon garlic powder
1 tablespoon fresh lemon juice
2 tablespoons salad *or* olive oil

1 cup grated carrots

Wash and thoroughly dry lettuce and endive. Tear into bite-size pieces and place in a salad bowl. Add next 3 ingredients.

Mix the next 6 ingredients in a small bowl. Beat with a rotary beater. Pour over salad greens. Toss lightly, being sure to coat each piece with the dressing. Sprinkle with grated carrots. Serve at once.

YIELD: 8 to 10 servings

AVOCADO SALAD WITH VINAIGRETTE DRESSING

½ medium-size head lettuce
2 medium-size avocados
Fresh lemon juice
Pimiento
Vinaigrette Salad Dressing*

Arrange lettuce on individual salad plates. Peel and slice avocados, dip in lemon juice, and place 3 to 4 slices on each plate. (When ripe enough to taste good, peeling can be pulled off as from a banana.) Garnish with pimiento cut into strips. Serve with Vinaigrette Salad Dressing.

YIELD: 6 servings

COLD ASPARAGUS WITH PARISIAN SAUCE

Cook asparagus until just barely fork-tender. Remove from heat, drain, and chill. Asparagus that has become discolored and mushy from overcooking isn't worthy of its Parisian Sauce. Chervil, incidentally, is one of the herbs widely used in French cookery, especially in salads.

2 packages (3 ounces each) cream cheese
    or creamy type French cheese
1 teaspoon salt
1½ teaspoons paprika
Dash ground white pepper
1 tablespoon fresh lemon juice
6 tablespoons salad *or* olive oil
1 teaspoon chervil leaves

2 pounds cold, cooked asparagus

Blend first 7 ingredients. Beat until sauce is fluffy. Serve over cold cooked asparagus.

YIELD: 6 servings

CAULIFLOWER SALAD, NEAPOLITAN STYLE

1 medium-size head cauliflower
1 inch boiling water
1 teaspoon salt

2 tablespoons olive *or* salad oil
1 cup wine vinegar
¾ teaspoon salt
½ teaspoon ground black pepper
¼ teaspoon basil leaves

6 anchovy fillets, diced
2 tablespoons capers
¼ cup chopped black olives
Curly endive

Wash cauliflower and break into flowerets. Place in a saucepan with 1-inch depth of boiling water and salt. Bring to boiling point, uncovered, and cook 5 minutes. Cover and cook 5 or 6 minutes or only until flowerets are crisp-tender. Drain and rinse in cold water. Place in a salad bowl. Combine next 5 ingredients. Mix well and pour over cauliflower. Add anchovies, capers, and olives. Toss lightly. Garnish with curly endive. Sprinkle with additional capers before serving.

YIELD: 6 servings

HERBED TOMATO SALAD

This is the sort of Italian-style flavor combination—tomatoes, oregano, and basil—that has made pizza such a great success.

6 firm, ripe tomatoes
⅛ teaspoon instant minced garlic
½ teaspoon salt
½ teaspoon sugar
½ teaspoon ground black pepper
½ teaspoon oregano leaves
½ teaspoon basil leaves
1 teaspoon cider vinegar
2 tablespoons olive *or* salad oil

Wash tomatoes. Do not peel. Cut into 1-inch cubes and toss lightly with remaining ingredients. Chill 30 minutes. Serve as a salad with or without lettuce.

YIELD: 6 to 8 servings

FAMILY-STYLE TOMATO SALAD

3 fresh, ripe tomatoes
¾ teaspoon salt (or to taste)
¼ teaspoon ground black pepper
⅛ teaspoon garlic powder
1¼ teaspoons oregano leaves
½ teaspoon sugar
3 tablespoons olive *or* salad oil
2 tablespoons red wine vinegar

Wash tomatoes and cut each into 4 slices. Combine remaining ingredients and sprinkle over tomatoes. Serve family style, as a vegetable or as a salad with lettuce and sliced, sweet red Spanish onion.

YIELD: 6 servings

FRESH ORANGE AND ONION SALAD

Sounds odd if you've never eaten it, but sliced oranges and paper-thin rings of

mild onion combine deliciously. A flavorful accompaniment for chicken, turkey, or ham, hot or cold.

¼ head curly endive
½ small head lettuce
½ head romaine
3 fresh oranges
½ cup mild, white onion rings
3 tablespoons fresh lemon juice
¼ cup salad oil
½ teaspoon garlic powder
¾ teaspoon salt
½ teaspoon powdered mustard
1 teaspoon sugar

Wash salad greens and dry thoroughly. Tear into bite-size pieces and place in a salad bowl. Peel oranges and cut into crosswise slices. Place as desired over the salad greens and top with onion rings. Combine remaining ingredients. Beat with a rotary beater. Add just before serving. Toss lightly.

YIELD: 8 to 10 servings

CHINESE BEAN SPROUT SALAD

¼ bunch water cress
2 large green peppers
1 large head lettuce
1 cup drained bean sprouts

¼ cup olive *or* salad oil
2 tablespoons cider vinegar
⅛ teaspoon garlic powder
¼ teaspoon ground black pepper
½ teaspoon sugar
¾ teaspoon ground ginger
1 teaspoon salt
2½ tablespoons soy sauce
1 tablespoon catsup
_____
1 large hard-cooked egg, chopped

Wash water cress, peppers, and lettuce and dry thoroughly. Cut water cress into 1-inch pieces and place in a salad bowl. Cut peppers into very thin slivers and add. Tear lettuce into bite-size pieces and add along with bean sprouts.

Mix the next 9 ingredients and add. Toss salad lightly, being sure to coat water cress and lettuce with dressing. Sprinkle chopped egg over the top.

YIELD: 10 servings

HUNGARIAN EGGPLANT SALAD
(TOROK PADLIZSAN-SALATA)

1 large (1¼-pound) eggplant
_____
½ cup finely chopped onion
2 teaspoons sugar
3 tablespoons fresh lemon juice
1½ teaspoons salt
¼ teaspoon ground black pepper
1 teaspoon crumbled basil leaves
⅛ teaspoon garlic powder
_____
1 tablespoon salad oil
2 ripe tomatoes, sliced
Fresh parsley

Wash eggplant and pierce holes in it with a fork. Place in a glass baking dish and bake in a preheated hot oven (400° F.) 1 hour or until tender. Cool slightly and peel. Chop fine. Add next 7 ingredients. Mix well. Cool. Just before serving, add oil and heap the mixture in center of serv-

ing plate. Garnish with sliced fresh tomatoes and parsley.

YIELD: 6 servings

GRAPE, APPLE, AND CABBAGE SALAD

1 cup diced, unpeeled apples
1 teaspoon lemon juice
1 cup seedless *or* seeded grapes
2 cups cabbage, shredded medium-fine
_____
3 tablespoons sour cream
¼ teaspoon ground anise
1 tablespoon honey
_____
½ teaspoon salt
⅛ teaspoon ground black pepper
Romaine lettuce

Mix apples with lemon juice to prevent discoloration. Add grapes and cabbage. Combine next 3 ingredients. Add to salad just before serving. Sprinkle with salt and black pepper. Toss lightly, but well. Serve on romaine lettuce.

YIELD: 6 servings

HAM SALAD

1½ teaspoons powdered mustard
2 tablespoons water
_____
3 cups diced, cooked ham
2 cups diced celery
¾ teaspoon salt
⅛ teaspoon ground black pepper
⅛ teaspoon onion powder
Dash garlic powder
_____
¼ cup mayonnaise
Head lettuce
Radish roses *or* large pimiento-stuffed olives

Mix mustard with water and let stand 10 minutes to develop flavor. Place the next 6 ingredients in a mixing bowl. Blend mustard with mayonnaise and add. Toss lightly. Serve on lettuce. Garnish with

THE
SPICE MILL

radish roses or large stuffed olives. Serve as a main-dish salad with sliced tomatoes and hot biscuits or corn bread squares.

YIELD: 6 servings

HAM AND FRESH ASPARAGUS SALAD

12 large *or* 18 small stalks fresh
asparagus, cooked

½ cup salad oil
1 teaspoon salt
⅛ teaspoon ground black pepper
¾ teaspoon powdered mustard
⅛ teaspoon garlic powder
1 teaspoon grated onion
2 tablespoons fresh lemon juice
2 tablespoons cider vinegar

6 slices ham
Head lettuce
Tomato wedges

Cool cooked asparagus and place in a refrigerator dish. Combine the next 8 ingredients and add. Marinate in refrigerator at least one hour. Just before serving, remove asparagus from the marinade, drain, and wrap each 2 (large) or 3 (small) stalks in a slice of ham. Serve on a salad plate with tomato wedges.

YIELD: 6 servings

CHICKEN, MUSHROOM, AND DEVILED EGG SALAD

1 tablespoon instant minced onion
1 tablespoon water

2 cups diced, cold chicken
1 can (4 ounces) sliced mushrooms
1 cup diced celery
1 teaspoon salt
½ teaspoon crumbled tarragon leaves
⅛ teaspoon ground black pepper
1 teaspoon fresh lemon juice
3 tablespoons mayonnaise

Head lettuce
6 Deviled Eggs*

Combine onion and water. Let stand 3 to 4 minutes. Mix with next 8 ingredients. Toss lightly. Place in a salad bowl lined with lettuce. Top with Deviled Eggs and serve as a main-dish salad.

YIELD: 6 servings

HERBED STUFFED EGGS WITH ASPARAGUS

6 large hard-cooked eggs

½ teaspoon salt
⅛ teaspoon ground oregano
⅛ teaspoon ground black pepper
¼ teaspoon garlic powder
2 tablespoons finely chopped celery
3 tablespoons finely chopped tomato
½ teaspoon fresh lemon juice

2 pounds fresh asparagus, cooked
3 tablespoons French dressing

Shell eggs and cut into halves crosswise. Remove yolks and mash with next 7 ingredients. Stuff the egg whites with this mixture. If stuffed ahead of serving time, put stuffed egg halves together, wrap in foil, and chill. Serve with cold, cooked, fresh asparagus marinated in French dressing.

YIELD: 6 servings

LAYERED TUNA-TOMATO SALAD

1 can (6 ounces) tuna fish

½ cup diced celery
¼ cup shredded sharp Cheddar cheese
¾ teaspoon salt
¼ teaspoon ground black pepper
¼ teaspoon garlic powder
3 tablespoons mayonnaise
½ teaspoon instant minced onion
½ teaspoon powdered mustard

6 medium-size, ripe tomatoes
Salad greens

Drain and discard oil from tuna fish. Break fish into flakes with a fork. Add the next 8 ingredients and mix lightly. Wash tomatoes and cut each into 3 crosswise slices. Put slices together with tuna fish filling in layer-cake fashion. Arrange on salad greens. Serve as a main-dish salad.

YIELD: 6 servings

TUNA AND KIDNEY BEAN SALAD

2 cups (1-pound can) red kidney beans, drained
1 can (7 ounces) chunk-type tuna fish, drained
6 anchovy fillets, quartered
1 cup sliced Pascal celery
2 tablespoons instant minced onion
¼ teaspoon instant minced garlic
¼ teaspoon ground black pepper
1½ teaspoons salt
1½ teaspoons basil leaves
1 teaspoon vinegar
¼ cup mayonnaise
Head lettuce
6 tomato wedges

Combine all ingredients except tomato and lettuce. Mix lightly to prevent breaking tuna chunks. Chill 1 hour. Serve on lettuce. Garnish with tomato wedges. Serve as a main-dish salad.

YIELD: 6 servings

MACARONI AND TUNA FISH SALAD

½ pound elbow macaroni, cooked
2 tablespoons instant minced onion
¼ cup French dressing
¼ teaspoon garlic powder
¼ teaspoon ground black pepper
2 teaspoons salt
1 teaspoon basil leaves
1 teaspoon fresh lemon juice
1 can (6 ounces) tuna fish, drained
1 cup diced celery
½ cup diced green pepper
¼ cup mayonnaise
Salad greens
Cherry tomatoes

Combine first 8 ingredients. Let stand at least 1 hour for flavors to blend. Add next 4 ingredients. Toss lightly. Chill and serve on salad greens. Garnish with cherry tomatoes.

YIELD: 10 to 12 servings

FAVORITE MACARONI SALAD

2 teaspoons celery salt
2 teaspoons onion salt
1 teaspoon garlic salt
4 cups boiling water
2 cups elbow macaroni
1 teaspoon cider vinegar
1 cup diced celery
½ cup cooked green peas
½ cup diced green pepper
¼ cup diced pimiento

2 large hard-cooked eggs, diced
¼ teaspoon ground black pepper
¼ cup mayonnaise
_____
Head lettuce
Paprika

Mix together first 3 ingredients. Add half of this mixture to the water in a saucepan. Bring to a boil, add macaroni, cover, and cook until macaroni is tender. Remove from heat, drain well, and chill.

Add remaining seasoning salts and the next 8 ingredients. Toss lightly. Serve on lettuce. Garnish with paprika.

YIELD: 8 servings

SHRIMP AND AVOCADO SALAD

3 medium-size avocados
3 tablespoons fresh lemon juice
_____
¼ teaspoon garlic powder
¼ teaspoon ground turmeric
¼ teaspoon ground poultry seasoning
⅛ teaspoon ground black pepper
¹⁄₁₆ teaspoon ground red pepper
1 teaspoon salt
1 tablespoon cider vinegar
1 tablespoon salad oil
_____
1½ cups cooked, deveined shrimp
1½ cups (2 medium) diced tomatoes
2 tablespoons mayonnaise
Water cress

Halve and pit avocados. Scoop out the halves to make the cavities ½ inch larger, saving the scooped-out portion for use in the filling. Brush lemon juice on the insides of the halves and on the reserved portion to prevent discoloration.

Combine remaining lemon juice with the next 8 ingredients in a bowl large enough to mix salad. Dice scooped-out avocado and add to seasonings along with shrimp, tomato, and mayonnaise. Mix lightly. Spoon into avocado halves. Garnish with water cress.

YIELD: 6 servings

CRABMEAT SALAD

¼ cup chili sauce
¼ cup mayonnaise
2 tablespoons instant minced onion
1 tablespoon fresh lemon juice
3 tablespoons tarragon vinegar
1 teaspoon salt
½ teaspoon powdered mustard
⅛ teaspoon ground black pepper
⅛ teaspoon instant minced garlic
_____
2 cups flaked, cooked crabmeat
4 large hard-cooked eggs, diced
1 medium-size green pepper, diced
½ cup diced celery
_____
Head lettuce
6 cherry tomatoes

Combine the first 9 ingredients. Add to next 4 ingredients and mix lightly. Serve on lettuce. Garnish portion with a cherry tomato. Serve as a main-dish salad.

YIELD: 6 servings

LOBSTER POTATO SALAD

½ teaspoon powdered mustard
2 tablespoons instant minced onion
2 tablespoons water
_____
2 cups cooked lobster *or* 2 cans,
    5 ounces each
1 cup cold, diced, cooked potatoes
2 tablespoons fresh lemon juice
1½ teaspoons salt (or to taste)
¼ teaspoon garlic powder
⅛ teaspoon ground black pepper
⅓ cup mayonnaise
_____
Head lettuce
Paprika

Soak mustard and instant minced onion in water 10 minutes. Combine with next 7 ingredients. Mix lightly. Serve on lettuce. Garnish with paprika.

YIELD: 6 servings

TOMATOES STUFFED WITH CURRIED POTATO SALAD

6 large, firm, fresh tomatoes
2½ cups Curried Potato Salad
 (see below)
Parsley
Salad greens

Wash tomatoes, cut a slice from the stem end of each and scoop out the inside. Sprinkle inside of tomatoes with salt and invert on a plate to drain. Spoon Curried Potato Salad into the tomato cups. Top each with a sprig of parsley. Serve on salad greens.

YIELD: 6 servings

CURRIED POTATO SALAD

1 tablespoon lemon juice
1 tablespoon cider vinegar
2 tablespoons salad oil

2½ teaspoons salt
¼ teaspoon ground black pepper
¼ teaspoon garlic powder
2 teaspoons curry powder

4 cups diced, cooked potatoes

1½ cups diced celery
⅔ cup diced green pepper
⅔ cup chopped onion
⅓ cup mayonnaise
Salad greens
Large hard-cooked eggs

Combine the first 7 ingredients. Pour over cooked potatoes. Cover and marinate 1 or more hours. (A longer time makes a better-flavored salad.)

Shortly before serving, add the next 4 ingredients. Mix lightly. Serve on lettuce and garnish with slices or wedges of hard-cooked eggs.

YIELD: 6 to 8 servings

DILLY POTATO SALAD

4 cups cold, diced, cooked potatoes
¼ cup salad oil
2 tablespoons fresh lemon juice
2 tablespoons instant minced onion
1½ teaspoons salt (or to taste)
½ teaspoon dill seed
¼ teaspoon ground black pepper
⅛ teaspoon garlic powder

2 tablespoons mayonnaise
2 tablespoons sour cream
Tomato wedges
Radishes

Combine the first 8 ingredients. Marinate 1 or more hours. Combine mayonnaise and sour cream and add. Toss lightly. Turn into a salad bowl. Garnish with tomato wedges and radishes.

YIELD: 6 servings

GERMAN HOT POTATO SALAD

1 cup chopped onion
¾ cup diced celery
⅓ cup bacon drippings

2 teaspoons salt
1 teaspoon sugar
⅛ teaspoon ground black pepper
⅔ cup water
½ cup cider vinegar

6 cups hot, diced, cooked potatoes
2 tablespoons mayonnaise
6 slices crisp bacon, crumbled
6 large pimiento-stuffed green olives

Sauté onions and celery in bacon drippings 5 minutes or until onions are limp. Add next 5 ingredients. Boil 2 minutes. Add potatoes, mayonnaise, and bacon. Toss lightly. Serve hot, garnished with stuffed green olives.

YIELD: 6 to 8 servings

POLISH POTATO AND APPLE SALAD

4 cups sliced, cold, cooked potatoes

1 small onion, diced
1 tablespoon minced parsley
1½ teaspoons salt
½ teaspoon chopped capers
¼ teaspoon ground dill seed
¼ teaspoon ground black pepper

1 tablespoon lemon juice
1 large egg, lightly beaten
2 large hard-cooked egg yolks, diced
½ cup sour cream

1 tart apple, diced
Salad greens

Slice potatoes ⅛ inch thick and put into a mixing bowl. Add the next 6 ingredients. Blend next 4 ingredients and add to potatoes along with diced apple. Mix lightly. Serve on salad greens.

YIELD: 6 to 8 servings

QUICK POTATO SALAD

4 cups hot, cooked, diced potatoes
1 large egg

2 tablespoons instant minced onion
2 tablespoons salad oil
1 tablespoon fresh lemon juice
1 tablespoon cider vinegar
2 teaspoons salt (or to taste)
¼ teaspoon ground black pepper
¼ teaspoon savory leaves
¼ teaspoon oregano leaves
⅛ teaspoon garlic powder
1 tablespoon boiling water

1 cup diced celery
½ cup diced green pepper
Lettuce

Place potatoes in a mixing bowl. Make a well in the center. Break egg into the well. Add the next 10 ingredients. Mix only until ingredients are blended. Add celery and green pepper and toss lightly. Serve on lettuce and garnish as desired.

YIELD: 6 servings

SOUR CREAM POTATO SALAD

½ teaspoon powdered mustard
2 teaspoons water

4 cups cold, diced, cooked potatoes
½ cup diced cucumber
1 tablespoon instant minced onion
2 teaspoons salt
½ teaspoon celery seed
½ teaspoon ground black pepper

4 large hard-cooked eggs
½ cup sour cream
¼ cup mayonnaise
1 tablespoon cider vinegar

Mix mustard with water and let stand 10 minutes. In the meantime, combine the next 6 ingredients with diced egg whites. Mash 3 of the egg yolks and blend with mustard and remaining ingredients. Add to potatoes and mix lightly. Serve on lettuce. Put remaining egg yolk through a sieve and sprinkle a little over each serving.

YIELD: 6 servings

SWEET-SOUR SPICED BEET RING

1½ cups (1 pound can) diced beets
Water
2 envelopes unflavored gelatine
1 tablespoon mixed pickling spice

1 tablespoon instant minced onion
⅛ teaspoon instant minced garlic
1 tablespoon sugar
1½ teaspoons salt
3 tablespoons cider vinegar

Salad greens
⅓ cup sour cream
⅓ cup mayonnaise
½ teaspoon instant minced onion

Drain beets and add water to juice to make 3 cups. Soften gelatine in 1 cup of the beet juice. Combine remaining beet juice and pickling spice and simmer 2 minutes. Strain out spices and pour hot juice over softened gelatine. Add next

5 ingredients. Chill until mixture begins to thicken. Fold in diced beets. Turn into an oiled 5-cup mold. Chill until firm and ready to serve. Just before serving, turn out onto a serving plate. Garnish with salad greens. Combine the last 3 ingredients and serve on salad.

YIELD: 6 to 8 servings

TURKEY SALAD MOLD

2 envelopes unflavored gelatine
½ cup water
2 cups hot turkey or chicken broth

½ teaspoon salt
½ teaspoon poultry seasoning
⅛ teaspoon ground black pepper
1 tablespoon fresh lemon juice

1 cup diced celery
1½ cups diced, cold, cooked turkey
½ cup mayonnaise

Soften gelatine in cold water and set aside. Mix hot turkey or chicken broth with next 4 ingredients. Chill until mixture begins to thicken. Stir in gelatine and remaining ingredients. Rinse a 5-cup mold in cold

water and fill with the turkey salad mixture. Chill until firm and ready to serve. Just before serving, turn out onto a serving plate and serve with cranberry sauce or jelly.

YIELD: 8 servings

ROQUEFORT CHEESE AND CUCUMBER SALAD MOLD

2 envelopes unflavored gelatine
½ cup cold water
—
1 cup hot water
¼ cup sugar
¼ teaspoon salt
¼ teaspoon powdered mustard
Dash garlic powder
¼ cup fresh lemon juice
—
1 cup (8 ounce package) creamy cottage cheese
½ cup crumbled Roquefort cheese
½ cup mayonnaise
1 large, unpeeled cucumber, sliced
Salad greens

Soften gelatine in cold water. Add next 6 ingredients. Chill until mixture is about as thick as fresh egg white. Beat cottage and Roquefort cheese together until well blended.

Add mayonnaise and mix well. Fold into gelatine mixture. Turn into an oiled 1-quart mold. Chill until ready to serve. To serve, unmold onto serving plate, around which arrange sliced cucumbers and salad greens.

YIELD: 8 servings

COLD HAM MOUSSE

Need an idea for a ladies' luncheon? Here is a good candidate, especially for summer.

2 envelopes unflavored gelatine
½ cup cold water

2 large egg yolks, beaten
Dash cayenne
½ teaspoon salt
½ teaspoon instant minced onion
½ teaspoon powdered mustard
1 cup milk
1 cup hot water
1 chicken bouillon cube
—
2 cups chopped cooked ham
1 teaspoon paprika
1 teaspoon cider vinegar
2 tablespoons chopped parsley
—
½ cup heavy cream, whipped
Water cress
Mayonnaise

Soften gelatine in cold water. Mix the next 8 ingredients in top of a double boiler. Stir and cook over hot water (NOT BOILING) 15 minutes or until mixture coats a metal spoon.

Stir in softened gelatine and next 4 ingredients. Chill over ice water until the mixture begins to thicken. Fold in whipped cream. Turn into a lightly oiled, 6-cup gelatine mold. Chill until firm and

next 4 ingredients. Mix well and chill until the mixture begins to thicken.

Fold in next 4 ingredients. Turn into an oiled 5-cup mold. Chill until firm and ready to serve. Unmold onto a serving plate. Garnish with salad greens and radishes.

CRABMEAT MOUSSE

In the above recipe, replace lobster with the same amount of crabmeat.

YIELD: 8 servings

SOUR CREAM-SALMON SALAD MOLD

1 envelope unflavored gelatine
¼ cup cold water

¼ cup boiling water
1½ teaspoons salt
1 tablespoon paprika

¾ cup sour cream
2 cans (7¾ ounces each) salmon

½ cup diced celery
2 tablespoons finely chopped pickle
1 tablespoon fresh lemon juice
⅛ teaspoon ground white pepper

½ cup thinly sliced cucumbers
Salad greens

Soften gelatine in cold water. Add next 3 ingredients. Let cool. Fold in sour cream. Drain and flake salmon and add to the mixture along with next 4 ingredients. Oil a 3-cup mold lightly. Pour in ⅓ of the mixture and cover with a layer of sliced cucumbers.

Repeat layers, until all the mixture and cucumbers are used, ending with a fish layer. Chill until firm. Unmold onto a serving plate. Garnish with salad greens. Serve as a main-dish salad.

YIELD: 6 servings

ready to serve. Unmold onto a serving plate. Garnish with water cress and top with mayonnaise.

YIELD: 8 servings

LOBSTER MOUSSE

2 envelopes unflavored gelatine
1 cup water
1 can (10½ ounces) condensed cream of tomato soup
1 package (4 ounces) cream cheese

½ teaspoon basil leaves
¼ teaspoon ground black pepper
1 tablespoon fresh lemon juice
2 teaspoons instant minced onion

1 cup mayonnaise
¼ cup chopped green olives
1 cup diced, cooked, fresh lobster *or* a 6½-ounce can lobster
1 cup diced celery

Salad greens
Radish roses

Soften gelatine in ½ cup of the water. Heat soup, to which add gelatine and cream cheese. Mix until smooth. (If any lumps remain, pass mixture through a sieve). Add remaining cold water and

SHRIMP PERFECTION ASPIC MOLD

1 envelope unflavored gelatine
¼ cup water
1 cup tomato juice

1 cup clam juice
1 tablespoon fresh lemon juice
1 teaspoon salt
½ teaspoon oregano leaves
¼ teaspoon ground black pepper
¼ teaspoon garlic powder
2 teaspoons instant minced onion

½ cup diced celery
½ cup diced green pepper
1 can (4½ ounces) peeled, deveined shrimp
Salad greens (optional)

Soften gelatine in cold water. Heat tomato juice and add to softened gelatine. Stir in next 7 ingredients. Chill until the mixture begins to thicken. Fold in celery, green pepper, and shrimp. Turn into an oiled 1-quart mold. Chill until firm and ready to serve. Unmold onto serving plate and garnish with salad greens if desired.

YIELD: 6 servings

SESAME SEED BANANA SALAD

6 medium-size, firm, ripe bananas
⅓ cup mayonnaise
3 tablespoons light cream or milk
Toasted Sesame Seed*

Peel bananas and cut each into crosswise pieces 1 inch long. Roll in mayonnaise that has been thinned with cream or milk. Arrange an equal number of banana chunks on each of 6 beds of lettuce on individual salad plates. Sprinkle with Toasted Sesame Seed.

YIELD: 6 servings

CHEESE-STUFFED PEAR SALAD

6 large, firm, ripe Bartlett pears
2 tablespoons fresh lemon juice
1½ cups (6 ounces) grated Cheddar cheese
¼ teaspoon garlic salt
⅛ teaspoon cayenne
Lettuce
French dressing

Wash, halve and core unpeeled pears. Brush cut surfaces with fresh lemon juice. Mix cheese with garlic salt and cayenne and pack into pear cavities. Wrap halves in foil or waxed paper. Chill several hours or overnight. Just before serving, cut in quarters and place on lettuce. Serve with French dressing.

YIELD: 6 servings

MINTED FRUIT SALAD MOLD

1 envelope unflavored gelatine
¼ cup water
2¾ cups mixed pineapple and grapefruit juice
2 teaspoons mixed pickling spice
1 teaspoon mint flakes
1 tablespoon sugar
1 tablespoon cider vinegar

1 cup pineapple tidbits, drained
1 cup sliced canned peaches, drained
¼ cup sliced maraschino cherries (optional)
Salad greens
Mayonnaise

Soften gelatine in water. Combine next 5 ingredients in a saucepan and boil 2 minutes. Strain out spices and pour hot juice over softened gelatine. Chill until mixture begins to thicken. Fold in fruit.

Turn into a lightly oiled, 1-quart mold. Chill until firm and ready to serve. Just before serving, turn out onto a serving plate. Garnish with salad greens. Serve with mayonnaise.

YIELD: 8 servings

CHEESE SALAD AND FRESH FRUIT MOLD

3 envelopes unflavored gelatine
1¼ cups cold water
1⅔ cups boiling water

2 cups grated Cheddar cheese
¾ cup mayonnaise
1 teaspoon powdered mustard
1 teaspoon salt
¹⁄₁₆ teaspoon cayenne

3 tablespoons chopped pimiento
3 tablespoons chopped, pimiento-stuffed olives
1 teaspoon fresh lemon juice

Soften gelatine in cold water. Add boiling water and stir to dissolve gelatine. Chill until mixture begins to thicken. Beat gelatine with an electric or rotary beater. Combine next 5 ingredients and mix well. Fold into the gelatine with pimiento, stuffed olives, and lemon juice. Turn into an oiled 1-quart mold. Chill until firm and ready to serve. Turn out onto a serving plate. Arrange assorted fresh fruit around the mold.

YIELD: 6 to 8 servings

SPICED PINEAPPLE AND BLUEBERRY MOLD

2 envelopes unflavored gelatine
½ cup cold pineapple juice

½ teaspoon whole cloves
½ teaspoon whole allspice
2 cinnamon sticks, each 2 inches long
3 cups pineapple juice

1 tablespoon fresh lemon juice

1 cup drained crushed pineapple
1 cup fresh blueberries

Soften gelatine in cold pineapple juice. Add spices to the 3 cups pineapple juice, bring to boiling point, and boil 5 minutes. Strain out spices and blend hot juice with softened gelatine. Cool and add lemon juice. Chill until the mixture begins to thicken.

Fold in crushed pineapple and blueberries. Rinse a 4-cup mold in cold water. Fill with pineapple mixture. Chill until firm and ready to serve. Unmold onto a serving plate. Garnish with salad greens and fresh blueberries. Serve with mayonnaise.

YIELD: 6 to 8 servings

SPICED BLACK CHERRY RING MOLD

(WITH CHICKEN SALAD)

Mixed pickling spice, we discovered, lends a subtle aroma to all kinds of cooked fruit mixtures. Use amount of spice called for and don't cook too long.

3½ cups (1 pound, 13 ounces) canned black cherries
Water
2 teaspoons mixed pickling spice
1 package (3 ounces) orange gelatine
⅓ cup fresh lemon juice

¾ cup chopped nuts
Salad greens
Chicken Salad *(see below)*

Drain and save cherries. Measure juice and add water to make 1¾ cups liquid. Pour into a 3-cup saucepan. Add mixed pickling spice; bring to boiling point and pour over gelatine through a sieve to strain out spices. Stir until gelatine is dissolved. Stir in lemon juice. Cool.

Chill until the mixture begins to thicken. Fold in cherries and nuts. Turn into an oiled 5-cup ring mold. Chill until firm and ready to serve. Just before serving, unmold gelatine onto a serving plate. Garnish with salad greens. Fill center with Chicken Salad.

CHICKEN SALAD

2 cups diced, cold, cooked chicken
1 cup sliced celery
2 teaspoons fresh lemon juice
¼ teaspoon instant minced onion
1 teaspoon salt
⅛ teaspoon ground black pepper
¼ cup mayonnaise

Combine all ingredients and mix lightly. Chill.

YIELD: 6 to 8 servings

SPICED FRUIT SALAD MOLD

1 envelope unflavored gelatine
¼ cup water
1¾ cups canned pineapple juice
1 tablespoon mixed pickling spice
¼ cup sugar
2 tablespoons lemon juice
1 cup green seedless grapes
1 cup fresh blueberries
Salad greens
⅓ cup mayonnaise
⅓ cup heavy cream, whipped

Soften gelatine in water. Set aside. Place pineapple juice and pickling spice in a saucepan. Bring to boiling point, cover, and cook 3 minutes. Strain out spices and pour over softened gelatine. Add sugar and lemon juice.

Chill until mixture begins to thicken. Fold in grapes and blueberries. Turn into an oiled 1-quart mold. Chill until firm and ready to serve. Just before serving, unmold onto a serving plate. Garnish with salad greens. Fold mayonnaise into whipped cream and serve on salad.

YIELD: 6 to 8 servings

PAPRIKA CHEESE APPLES

½ pound Cheddar cheese, grated
Whole cloves
Crisp young water cress leaves
Paprika

Shape grated cheese into 1-inch balls. Stick a whole clove (stem end first) in one end of each ball to simulate the bud end of an apple and insert another one (bud end first) in the opposite end to simulate the stem. Stick a small young water cress leaf in stem to simulate an apple leaf. Dust cheese apples lightly with paprika. Use to garnish salads, hors d'oeuvre trays, apple pie, or tarts.

YIELD: 30 one-inch apples

SALAD DRESSINGS

CLASSIC FRENCH DRESSING
1 clove garlic
2 teaspoons salt
1 teaspoon freshly-ground black pepper
1¼ cups olive oil
½ cup wine vinegar

Peel garlic and crush to a fine paste. Add remaining ingredients.

ROQUEFORT CHEESE DRESSING
Add ¼ cup crumbled Roquefort cheese to the above basic mixture.

MUSTARD DRESSING
Add 2 teaspoons powdered dry mustard to basic mixture.

EGG AND OLIVE DRESSING
Add 2 chopped, large hard-cooked eggs and 2 tablespoons chopped, pimiento-stuffed olives to the basic mixture.

ANCHOVY DRESSING
Add 1 teaspoon anchovy paste to basic mixture.

OREGANO DRESSING
Add 1 tablespoon oregano leaves to basic mixture.

YIELD: 2 cups

DELUXE FRENCH DRESSING
½ cup olive *or* salad oil
2¼ teaspoons salt
1 teaspoon powdered mustard
1 teaspoon paprika
½ teaspoon instant minced onion
¼ teaspoon instant minced garlic
¼ teaspoon coarsely ground
    black pepper
Dash cayenne
___
¼ cup chicken stock
3 tablespoons cider vinegar
2 tablespoons fresh lemon juice

Combine the first 8 ingredients and let stand 1 hour for flavors to blend. Add remaining ingredients. Beat with a rotary beater. Serve over vegetable, meat, seafood, egg, or poultry salads.

YIELD: 1 cup

ANISE FRENCH DRESSING
1 teaspoon anise seed
⅛ teaspoon instant minced garlic
1 teaspoon boiling water

1 cup salad oil
2 tablespoons fresh lemon juice
2 tablespoons wine vinegar
½ teaspoon salt
½ teaspoon sugar
⅛ teaspoon ground black pepper

Soak anise seeds and instant minced garlic 5 minutes in boiling water. Add to oil and let stand 1 hour. Add remaining ingredients. Beat with a rotary beater. Serve over salad greens or fruit salad.

YIELD: Approximately 1¼ cups

CARAWAY FRENCH DRESSING

1 tablespoon caraway seed
2 tablespoons water

1 cup olive or salad oil
⅓ cup vinegar
1 teaspoon salt
⅛ teaspoon ground black pepper
¼ teaspoon garlic powder
½ teaspoon onion powder

Place water and caraway seed in a saucepan and cook until all water is absorbed (approximately 5 minutes). Remove from heat. Combine remaining ingredients. Stir in caraway seed. Serve on crisp salad greens.

YIELD: About 1⅓ cups

CREAMY FRENCH DRESSING

1 teaspoon salt
1 teaspoon paprika
½ teaspoon powdered mustard
¼ teaspoon ground black pepper
½ teaspoon instant minced onion
⅛ teaspoon garlic powder
2 cups salad or olive oil
¼ cup catsup
½ cup cider vinegar
2 tablespoons fresh lemon juice
1 small egg white

Combine all ingredients. Beat until creamy with a rotary beater.

YIELD: Approximately 3 cups

HERBED FRENCH DRESSING

2 teaspoons salt
1 teaspoon powdered mustard
1¾ teaspoons paprika
¾ teaspoon garlic powder
¾ teaspoon crumbled basil leaves
⅛ teaspoon ground black pepper
1 teaspoon instant minced onion
½ cup olive or salad oil

3 tablespoons wine or cider vinegar
2 tablespoons fresh lemon juice
2 tablespoons pickle relish

Combine the first 8 ingredients. Let stand one or more hours. Add remaining ingredients and beat well. Serve over tossed green or cooked vegetable salads.

TARRAGON FRENCH DRESSING

Omit basil leaves in Herbed French Dressing; add ½ teaspoon tarragon leaves.

YIELD: ¾ cup

ONION FRENCH DRESSING

¾ cup salad oil
1 tablespoon instant minced onion
2 teaspoons salt
1 teaspoon paprika
½ teaspoon powdered mustard
½ teaspoon garlic powder
¼ teaspoon ground black pepper
1 teaspoon salt
¼ cup cider vinegar

Combine all ingredients and beat with a rotary beater.

YIELD: 1 cup

RASPBERRY FRENCH DRESSING

½ cup salad oil
2 tablespoons fresh lemon juice
2 tablespoons fresh raspberry juice
½ teaspoon salt
1/16 teaspoon ground white pepper
½ teaspoon dried tarragon leaves

Combine all ingredients. Beat well with a rotary beater. Serve over fruit salads.

YIELD: ¾ cup

HOMEMADE MAYONNAISE

2 large egg yolks *or* 1 large egg
¾ teaspoon salt (or to taste)
½ teaspoon powdered mustard
¼ teaspoon paprika
Dash cayenne

2 tablespoons fresh lemon juice
  or vinegar
1 cup salad oil
1 tablespoon boiling water

Place the first 5 ingredients in a mixing bowl and beat thoroughly with an electric or rotary beater. Add 1 tablespoon of the lemon juice or vinegar. Beat again. Gradually beat in oil, ½ teaspoon at a time, until ¼ cup is used.

Then add 1 to 2 tablespoons oil at a time until all oil is used, beating constantly. (Mayonnaise will curdle if oil is added too rapidly.) Add remaining lemon juice or vinegar as mixture thickens. Beat in boiling water.

TURMERIC MAYONNAISE

Add ½ teaspoon ground turmeric to ½ cup mayonnaise and use in poultry, fish, or egg salads or sandwich mixes.

ONION MAYONNAISE

Stir ¾ teaspoon instant minced onion into ½ cup mayonnaise. Let stand 10 minutes for onion to soften. Serve on meat, egg, or vegetable salads.

MUSTARD MAYONNAISE

Mix ½ teaspoon powdered mustard with 1 teaspoon water. Let stand 10 minutes to develop flavor. Stir into ½ cup mayonnaise. Serve on seafood, ham, or egg salads.

CURRY MAYONNAISE

Stir ½ teaspoon curry powder (or to taste) into ½ cup mayonnaise. This is especially good in potato, egg, or seafood salads.

HERBED MAYONNAISE
Mix ½ cup mayonnaise with ½ teaspoon poultry seasoning, 1 tablespoon capers, and ½ teaspoon instant minced onion. Serve with cold chicken, turkey, or veal salads or sandwiches.

YIELD: 1¾ cups

CAVIAR-SOUR CREAM DRESSING

This is Avanelle's very favorite, show-off salad dressing. The caviar runs up the cost but, served on Belgian endive, it makes a sensational salad. Avanelle adapted this dressing from a recipe given to her by a Russian woman in 1940— who said, very positively, that any "Russian Dressing" must include caviar.

½ cup mayonnaise
¼ cup sour cream
1-ounce jar black caviar
4 teaspoons catsup
¼ teaspoon onion juice
1 teaspoon fresh lemon juice
1/16 teaspoon salt

Combine all ingredients. Serve over Belgian endive or wedges of head lettuce. Garnish with strips of pimiento, if desired.

YIELD: 1 scant cup

COOKED SALAD DRESSING
2 tablespoons flour
1 tablespoon sugar
3 tablespoons salad oil
1½ teaspoons salt
1 cup water
2 large eggs, lightly beaten
¼ cup cider vinegar
Dash cayenne
1 teaspoon powdered mustard
2 teaspoons water

Combine the first 5 ingredients in the top of a double boiler. Stir and cook over direct medium heat until the consistency of medium white sauce. Mix together eggs and vinegar and gradually add to the mixture. (If added too fast dressing may curdle.)

Cook over hot (NOT BOILING) water until dressing is thick enough to mound. Stir in cayenne. Mix mustard with water and let stand 10 minutes. Stir into the mixture. Serve over meats, use in cole slaw, vegetable, meat, or seafood salad.

YIELD: 1½ cups

COOKED SOUR CREAM SALAD DRESSING
2 tablespoons flour
1 tablespoon sugar
1 teaspoon powdered mustard
¾ teaspoon salt
1/8 teaspoon ground white pepper
1/8 teaspoon garlic powder
½ cup cold water
1 large egg
2 large egg yolks
¼ cup cider vinegar

2 tablespoons butter *or* margarine
1 cup sour cream

Combine first 6 ingredients in top of double boiler. Blend in water. Let stand 10 minutes for mustard to develop full flavor. Beat eggs with vinegar and add. Stir and cook over hot water (NOT BOILING) until the mixture is smooth and thick. Remove from heat and add butter or margarine. Fold in sour cream. Cool and chill. Serve over vegetables, fish or meat salads.

YIELD: 2¼ cups

AVOCADO SALAD DRESSING

1 medium-size ripe avocado
1 tablespoon fresh lemon juice
¼ cup mayonnaise
½ teaspoon salt
½ teaspoon chili powder
1/16 teaspoon garlic powder
Dash cayenne

Peel avocado, cut in half, and remove seed. Mash with lemon juice to a smooth consistency or put into a blender and blend until a smooth purée is formed. (There should be 1 cup.) Add remaining ingredients and mix well. Serve over lettuce, seafood, or egg salad.

YIELD: 1¼ cups

CARAWAY SEED-COTTAGE CHEESE SALAD DRESSING

2 medium-size radishes
2 large hard-cooked egg yolks, mashed
⅓ cup creamy cottage cheese
1 tablespoon chopped green pepper
2 tablespoons fresh lemon juice
½ cup buttermilk
1 teaspoon salt
1 teaspoon caraway seed

½ teaspoon paprika
⅛ teaspoon garlic powder

Chop radishes very fine and blend with remaining ingredients. Serve on mixed salad greens or hearts of lettuce.

YIELD: 1¼ cups

CUCUMBER AND ALMOND SALAD DRESSING

¼ cup finely chopped unpeeled cucumbers
2 tablespoons slivered, toasted, blanched almonds
¾ cup salad oil
¼ cup fresh lemon juice
¾ teaspoon salt
¾ teaspoon ground dill seed
⅛ teaspoon ground black pepper
½ teaspoon powdered mustard
¼ teaspoon garlic powder

Combine all ingredients and mix well. Pour over vegetable, meat, or seafood salads. Toss lightly.

YIELD: 1 cup

GRAPEFRUIT SALAD DRESSING

1¼ teaspoons salt
1 teaspoon paprika
⅛ teaspoon ground white pepper
1 clove garlic, crushed
1 teaspoon chopped onion
1 tablespoon sugar
1 cup salad oil
¾ cup fresh grapefruit juice
3 tablespoons fresh lemon juice

Combine first 7 ingredients. Let stand 1 hour for flavors to blend. Beat in grapefruit and lemon juices. Serve over fruit salad or mild-flavored salad greens.

YIELD: 2 cups

PEAR SALAD DRESSING

1 large, firm, ripe, fresh pear
¼ cup fresh lemon juice
½ cup salad oil
2 teaspoons sugar
½ teaspoon powdered mustard
¼ teaspoon salt
⅛ teaspoon ground red pepper
2 teaspoons horseradish sauce

Peel and shred pear into the lemon juice. Add remaining ingredients. Mix thoroughly. Chill. Serve over fruit salad or head lettuce.

YIELD: 1⅔ cups

SOUR CREAM PAPRIKA DRESSING

¾ cup salad *or* olive oil
¾ teaspoon salt
⅛ teaspoon ground white pepper
½ teaspoon paprika
½ teaspoon instant minced onion
1/16 teaspoon instant minced garlic
¼ cup cider vinegar
1 cup sour cream
⅓ cup tomato catsup

Combine first 6 ingredients. Let stand at least one hour for flavors to blend. Gradually beat in vinegar with rotary or electric beater. Gradually stir in sour cream and tomato catsup. Beat until smooth. Serve as a salad dressing or, if desired, serve as a dip for raw vegetable sticks, crackers, or potato chips.

YIELD: 2⅓ cups

TOMATO SALAD DRESSING

1 cup diced, fresh tomatoes
½ teaspoon salt
¼ teaspoon ground black pepper
¼ teaspoon ground cumin seed
Dash garlic powder
3 tablespoons salad oil
2 teaspoons wine vinegar

Mash tomatoes and put them through a sieve. Add remaining ingredients. Beat with a rotary beater or blend in an electric blender ½ minute. Serve over tossed vegetable salads.

YIELD: 1 cup

VINAIGRETTE SALAD DRESSING

2 teaspoons salt
⅛ teaspoon ground black pepper
¾ teaspoon powdered mustard
½ teaspoon paprika
¼ teaspoon garlic powder
1 tablespoon finely chopped chives
½ cup olive *or* salad oil
2 tablespoons pickle relish
1 tablespoon finely chopped green pepper
3 tablespoons cider *or* wine vinegar
2 tablespoons fresh lemon juice

Combine the first 7 ingredients and marinate in the refrigerator 1 or more hours. Add remaining ingredients and beat thoroughly.

YIELD: 1 scant cup

SANDWICHES

"THE evil that men do lives after them; the good is oft interred with their bones." This does not, however, apply to the Fourth Earl of Sandwich, corrupt and unpopular eighteenth-century English politician and gambler. He is credited with having invented the sandwich, if by chance. In order to continue with his card game, to which he was addicted, and not have to pause to dine, he had ordered his servant to tuck a grease-dripping mutton chop between two slices of bread. This good of his survives, demonstrated by the seemingly limitless number of "sandwiches" we now consume annually.

Sandwiches taste best if the bread is fresh and sliced as thinly as possible. Chill an unsliced loaf of bread in the refrigerator for a few hours if you want to slice it thinly, but be sure to wrap it well in waxed paper so that it will not dry out.

Unless butter or margarine has been kept in a special unit in the refrigerator, let it stand at room temperature to soften.

Dainty sandwiches spread with flavored butter are ideal for party salads. Cream anchovy paste, horseradish, mustard, curry powder, etc., with softened butter before spreading over bread.

Season sandwich fillings generously. Bread is such a bland food, it tends to dull somewhat the effect of seasoning. Check your spice shelf for inspiration. Chicken salad, for example, becomes twice as tasty when a pinch of tarragon, rosemary, or curry powder is added. Grated or softened cheese

484

needs a little mustard, ginger, powdered sage, or caraway seed. Egg mixtures can be improved by herbs, curry or chili powder, garlic powder, mustard, or paprika. Toasted Sesame Seed* is delicious when added liberally to cream cheese. Use your imagination and consult the Spice Chart in the front of the book. It is advisable to first mix a small experimental batch, and taste. If it tastes right, do not belabor your creation. Often, a dash of garlic powder or fresh lemon juice will enliven a rather uninteresting sandwich filling.

*An asterisk after the name of a dish indicates that the recipe for this dish appears in the book. Consult the Index for the page number.

CURRIED CHICKEN SANDWICHES

2 cups diced chicken
½ cup diced celery
½ cup diced apples
⅓ cup seeded grapes, chopped
¼ cup mayonnaise
½ teaspoon salt
1½ teaspoons curry powder
2 teaspoons lemon juice
12 slices buttered bread

Combine first 8 ingredients. Spread on 6 slices of buttered bread. Top with remaining slices of buttered bread.

YIELD: 6 sandwiches

CURRIED EGG SANDWICH SPREAD

6 large hard-cooked eggs
⅓ cup finely chopped celery
¼ cup mayonnaise
1 teaspoon salt
2 teaspoons curry powder
⅛ teaspoon onion powder
¼ teaspoon ground black pepper
12 slices buttered bread

Chop eggs fine and blend with remaining ingredients. Spread between slices of buttered bread.

YIELD: 6 sandwiches

TURMERIC EGG SANDWICHES

6 large hard-cooked eggs
1 cup finely chopped celery
1 teaspoon salt
1 teaspoon ground turmeric
½ teaspoon powdered mustard
¼ teaspoon ground black pepper
⅓ cup mayonnaise
12 slices buttered bread

Chop hard-cooked eggs and combine with other ingredients. Spread between slices of buttered bread. Serve with tomato and cucumber salad.

YIELD: 6 sandwiches

GINGER CHEESE SANDWICH SPREAD

2 cups grated, sharp American cheese
6 tablespoons top milk or light cream

½ teaspoon ground ginger
½ teaspoon salt
⅛ teaspoon ground black pepper
6 slices crisp bacon, crumbled

Combine cheese and milk or cream. Mix well. Blend in remaining ingredients. Use as a spread for sandwiches, crackers, or for stuffing celery.

YIELD: 2 cups

CHEESE SOUFFLE SANDWICHES

12 slices white bread
Soft butter *or* margarine
6 slices American cheese
5 large eggs, lightly beaten
1½ cups milk
¾ teaspoon salt
¼ teaspoon ground black pepper
1 teaspoon paprika
⅛ teaspoon garlic powder
¾ teaspoon powdered mustard
½ teaspoon ground oregano

Remove crusts from bread and spread with butter or margarine. Place 6 slices in an oblong baking pan (16 x 10 x 1¾ inches). Place one slice of cheese over each of the bread slices. Cover with remaining bread slices.

Combine the remaining ingredients and pour over sandwiches. Chill in refrigerator 3 hours. Bake in a preheated slow oven (300° F.) 30 minutes. Increase heat to 325° F. and bake 15 minutes longer or until custard is set, puffy, and lightly browned. Serve at once.

YIELD: 6 sandwiches

POPPY SEED CHEESE DREAM

6 slices white bread
¼ pound grated Cheddar cheese
1 tablespoon hot water

1 tablespoon poppy seed
6 slices bacon, cut in half

Toast bread only on one side. Blend next 3 ingredients. Spread on toasted side of bread. Broil bacon until about half done. Arrange 2 halves on each piece of toast. Place under broiler, 4 inches from source of heat. Cook 5 minutes or until bacon is crisp and cheese has melted and browned.

YIELD: 6 servings

GRILLED CRABMEAT AND CHEESE SANDWICHES

6½-ounce can crabmeat
½ cup finely chopped celery
1 large hard-cooked egg, diced
¾ teaspoon salt
¾ teaspoon thyme leaves
Dash ground black pepper
1 teaspoon fresh lemon juice
2 tablespoons mayonnaise
6 slices buttered firm-textured bread
6 slices American cheese
Pimiento

Flake crabmeat and mix with next 7 ingredients. Spread butter or margarine on one side of bread. Top buttered side of each with crabmeat mixture and a slice of cheese. Broil to melt cheese. Garnish with a strip of pimiento.

YIELD: 6 sandwiches

GRILLED SHRIMP SANDWICHES

5-ounce can shrimp

½ cup finely chopped celery
1 teaspoon instant minced onion
½ teaspoon salt
½ teaspoon chili powder
¼ teaspoon garlic powder
¼ teaspoon ground black pepper
¼ cup mayonnaise

10 slices buttered bread
3 large eggs, lightly beaten
3 tablespoons milk
¼ teaspoon salt
Butter or margarine

Devein shrimp and chop finely. Add next 7 ingredients. Spread mixture on 5 of the buttered slices. Top with remaining slices. Press edges together. Mix eggs, milk, and salt. Dip each sandwich into egg mixture and brown in hot butter or margarine.

YIELD: 5 sandwiches

OPEN-FACED HAM AND TOMATO CHEESE PUFF SANDWICHES

6 slices firm-textured bread
Soft butter or margarine
6 slices boiled, baked, or spiced ham
2 large, squat tomatoes
Salt
Ground black pepper
2 large egg whites
¼ teaspoon salt

1 cup grated or finely shredded
  American cheese
½ teaspoon powdered mustard
½ teaspoon paprika
Dash cayenne

Spread one side of each slice of bread with softened butter or margarine. Cover with a slice of boiled, baked, or spiced ham. Wash tomatoes and dry. Cut into slices ½ inch thick and place one on each sandwich. Sprinkle with salt and ground black pepper to taste.

Combine egg whites and the ¼ teaspoon salt. Beat until very stiff. Fold in remaining ingredients. Spoon mixture over tomato on each sandwich. Arrange on baking sheet and place under broiler with temperature control set at 375° F. Broil 8 to 10 minutes or until cheese mixture is well-puffed and browned.

YIELD: 6 sandwiches

HOT OPEN-FACED CHICKEN SANDWICHES

1½ cups finely diced, cooked chicken
6 tablespoons soft butter or margarine

¼ cup heavy cream
1 tablespoon fresh lemon juice
½ teaspoon ground thyme
1 teaspoon salt
⅛ teaspoon ground black pepper

6 slices buttered toast
Grated Parmesan cheese
2 large hard-cooked eggs, sliced

Mix together chicken and 2 tablespoons butter or margarine. Stir in next 5 ingredients. Spread one side of each piece of buttered toast with a layer ¼ inch thick of chicken mixture. Sprinkle with grated Parmesan cheese. Place under

broiler to brown, about 2 minutes. Garnish with sliced hard-cooked egg.

YIELD: 6 sandwiches

HOT OPEN-FACED TURKEY SANDWICHES

6 slices buttered whole-wheat bread
Sliced cold, cooked turkey
6 slices Swiss cheese
6 slices crisp bacon
6 large hard-cooked eggs, sliced
Salt to taste
Ground pepper to taste
Herbed Mayonnaise*

Have all ingredients cold. Place on each slice of buttered bread, in the order listed, turkey, cheese, bacon, and 1 sliced, hard-cooked egg. Sprinkle lightly with salt and pepper. Top each with 2 tablespoons Herbed Mayonnaise. Brown under broiler. Serve piping hot.

YIELD: 6 servings

MOZZARELLA CHEESE SANDWICHES

12 thin slices white bread
1 teaspoon oregano leaves
⅓ cup (⅔ stick) soft butter *or* margarine
6 slices (⅛ pound) Mozzarella cheese
¼ teaspoon salt
1⁄16 teaspoon ground black pepper
1⁄16 teaspoon garlic powder
2 tablespoons Parmesan cheese
2 large eggs
Olive oil, butter, *or* margarine

Trim crusts from bread. Mix oregano with butter or margarine and spread on one side of each slice of bread. Cut 6 slices of Mozzarella cheese large enough to cover bread and place one on buttered side of each 6 slices.

Top with remaining bread slices, having buttered side next to cheese. Press edges together very firmly. Combine next 5 ingredients and beat well. Dip sandwiches into mixture. Fry on both sides until brown in hot olive oil, butter, or margarine.

YIELD: 6 sandwiches

OPEN-FACED DEVILED EGG SANDWICHES

6 large hard-cooked eggs

½ teaspoon salt
¼ teaspoon instant minced onion
½ teaspoon oregano
1⁄16 teaspoon ground black pepper
1 tablespoon fresh lemon juice
4 teaspoons salad *or* olive oil

6 slices buttered toast
Anchovy Béchamel Sauce*
Capers
Parsley flakes

Peel hard-cooked eggs. Cut in halves lengthwise. Scoop out the yolks and mash until smooth with next 6 ingredients. Pile into cavities of egg whites. Place two halves on each of 6 slices of buttered toast. Spoon Anchovy Béchamel Sauce over each and place under broiler until bubbly and slightly browned. Garnish with capers and parsley.

YIELD: 6 servings

TONGUE SANDWICHES WITH HOT MUSTARD SAUCE

1½ teaspoons powdered mustard
1 tablespoon water
1 tablespoon butter *or* margarine
1 tablespoon flour
1 cup tongue *or* beef broth

½ teaspoon instant minced onion
1⁄16 teaspoon garlic powder

¹⁄₁₆ teaspoon ground black pepper
Salt to taste

Sliced boiled tongue
Sliced bread

Mix mustard with water and let stand 10 minutes to develop flavor. Melt butter or margarine in saucepan. Remove from heat and blend in flour. Stir and cook ½ minute or until bubbly. Add moistened mustard and broth and cook until of medium thickness, stirring occasionally. Stir in next 4 ingredients. Place sliced tongue on bread slices. Spoon hot mustard sauce over sandwich.

YIELD: ⅔ cup sauce, enough for 5 or 6 sandwiches

CHILI AND FRANKFURTER HERO SANDWICHES

½ pound ground chuck
1 tablespoon butter *or* margarine

2 cans (15½ ounces each) red kidney beans, drained
1½ teaspoons salt
¼ teaspoon crushed red pepper
3 teaspoons chili powder
¼ cup tomato paste

12 frankfurters, split
6 Italian submarine rolls
Soft butter *or* margarine
Prepared mustard (optional)

Cook meat in butter or margarine until all the red disappears. Add next 5 ingredients. Stir and cook 2 minutes or until hot. Brown frankfurters. In the meantime, split rolls in half lengthwise. Spread with softened butter or margarine. Spoon meat and bean mixture between rolls. Top with cooked, split frankfurters. If desired, spread frankfurters with prepared mustard.

YIELD: 6 sandwiches

CURRIED LOBSTER FINGER ROLLS

4 small lobster tails
  (5 to 6 ounces each)
Boiling water
1 teaspoon salt

1 teaspoon curry powder
1 teaspoon lemon juice
½ cup mayonnaise

12 finger rolls

Place lobster tails in saucepan with enough boiling water to cover them and add 1 teaspoon salt. Bring to boiling point. Reduce heat to simmer and cook until tails turn pink, 5 to 7 minutes. DO NOT BOIL. Remove from water and cool.

Cut the membrane along each side of tails, between the meat and the shell, remove membrane and discard. Lift out meat and cut each in 3 lengthwise slices. Mix together next 3 ingredients.

Split finger rolls and spread each half generously with curry mayonnaise. Sprinkle lobster tails with salt and black pepper to taste and insert one piece between the 2 halves of each roll.

YIELD: 12 servings

HOT CHEESE AND EGG ROLLS

1 cup diced American cheese
5 large hard-cooked eggs, diced
½ cup finely chopped celery
1 tablespoon pickle relish
1 teaspoon instant minced onion
½ teaspoon salt
½ teaspoon poultry seasoning
⅛ teaspoon ground black pepper
3 tablespoons mayonnaise

Hamburger rolls

Combine the first 9 ingredients. Spread between split rolls. Wrap separately in foil. Place on a baking sheet and bake in a preheated moderate oven (350° F.) 30 minutes or until hot. Serve hot.

YIELD: 8 rolls

EGG AND HAM ROLLS

1 tablespoon butter *or* margarine
6 large eggs, beaten
⅓ cup milk
1 tablespoon parsley flakes
¼ teaspoon salt
⅛ teaspoon ground black pepper
12 thin slices baked *or* boiled ham
1 tablespoon butter *or* margarine

Melt butter or margarine in a 9- or 10-inch skillet. Combine eggs, milk, parsley flakes, salt, and black pepper. Pour into buttered skillet. Stir and cook over low heat until eggs are set.

Spread on slices of boiled or baked ham. Roll up as for a jelly roll. Heat in a buttered skillet only until ham is hot. Serve for breakfast, brunch, or supper.

YIELD: 6 servings

OPEN-FACED TOMATO AND ANCHOVY SANDWICHES

2 tablespoons (1 ounce) crumbled
    Roquefort *or* Bleu cheese
2 tablespoons mayonnaise
½ teaspoon powdered mustard
1 teaspoon finely chopped olives
1 teaspoon capers
1 teaspoon pickle relish *or*
    finely chopped cucumber pickle
1 teaspoon chopped parsley
———
3 large, squat tomatoes
9 slices firm-textured bread
Butter *or* margarine
Salt to taste
Ground black pepper to taste
18 anchovies

Combine first 7 ingredients. Set aside. Wash tomatoes and dry well. Cut into 3 crosswise slices ½ inch thick. Spread one side of each slice of bread with softened butter or margarine. Sprinkle salt and black pepper to taste over tomatoes and place a slice on each piece of bread.

Top each with 2 anchovies and about 1½ teaspoons cheese and mayonnaise mixture. Serve garnished with parsley sprigs or salad greens.

YIELD: 9 sandwiches

THREE-LAYER PARTY SANDWICH LOAF

1 unsliced loaf of bread
———
2 cups chopped ham
½ teaspoon ground cloves
1 teaspoon powdered mustard
1 teaspoon paprika
4 tablespoons mayonnaise
———
2 packages (3 ounces each)
    cream cheese
1 cup grated Cheddar cheese
½ cup sour cream
1 teaspoon oregano leaves
1 teaspoon parsley flakes
1 teaspoon instant minced green onions
———
Green food coloring
2 packages (3 ounces each)
    cream cheese
¼ cup milk
Radish roses

Trim crust from loaf of bread and slice bread in three horizontal lengthwise slices. Combine next 5 ingredients. Mix well and spread over bottom slice of bread and cover with a second slice.

Combine the next 6 ingredients. Add green food coloring, mixing until desired shade of green is reached. Spread mixture over second slice saving ½ cup for decoration. Cover with third slice of bread.

Soften additional cream cheese with milk and spread over top and sides of sandwich loaf. Chill 3 hours or until ready to serve.

This sandwich may be made the day before and frosted before serving. Place on serving platter and garnish with radish roses and remaining ½ cup green filling put through a pastry tube. Serve sliced.

YIELD: 12 slices

EVER-READY BUTTER SANDWICH SPREADS

If you must tax your imagination to create interesting sandwiches day after day, keep one or two seasoned butters on hand. Each of the following mixtures uses ½ cup (1 stick) butter or margarine. Let it soften at room temperature before mixing. Refrigerate until needed.

CURRIED MUSTARD BUTTER
For lamb, ham, pork, or poultry sandwiches. Blend ½ cup butter or margarine with 2 tablespoons prepared mustard and ¼ teaspoon curry powder.

CURRIED BUTTER
For chicken, turkey, or ham sandwiches. Blend ½ cup butter or margarine and ½ teaspoon curry powder.

CHILI BUTTER
For meat, fish, cheese, or egg sandwiches. Blend ½ cup butter or margarine with 1 teaspoon chili powder.

DEVILED HAM BUTTER
For American cheese or egg sandwiches. Blend ½ cup butter or margarine with ¼ cup deviled ham and ½ teaspoon horseradish.

SAUCES — Main Course and Dessert

A sauce is any liquid or semiliquid adjunct that complements a dish. It may be thin, medium, or thick; white, golden, or brown; bland, sweet, sour, or spicy. It gives glamour to ordinary foods and turns the best of them into gourmets' delights by improving, not disguising, their flavors.

Probably the simplest nonsweet sauce is drawn butter, which may be seasoned with salt, lemon juice, and herbs. Tartar Sauce,* commonly served with fish, is made with a mayonnaise base.

Most of the famous sauces are made from a *roux* base. A roux is concocted by melting butter, stirring in flour, and heating slowly while stirring. Sometimes chopped onion is heated with the butter and sometimes the flour is browned before adding. If the heating is just enough to cause the flour to swell, a "white roux" results. With longer heating, taking care not to burn, the color becomes darker and the roux is called "golden" or "brown." Then the liquid is added, and the mixture cooked slowly, with constant stirring, until it has thickened. Salt and other seasonings are added near the end of cooking. For a white sauce, the liquid is milk, light cream, or a mixture of milk or cream with veal, chicken, or fish stock. Beef stock (without milk) usually is used for the darker, heartier sauces. Béchamel Sauce* is made by simmering vegetables with chicken stock, straining and adding, together with cream, to a white roux, cooking and seasoning. Other roux-based sauces are made with tomatoes, cheese, or wine. A great variety of herbs and spices are

*An asterisk after the name of a dish indicates that the recipe for this dish appears in the book. Consult the Index for the page number.

suitable for use with them. (*Gravies* are sauces made with the fat and juice of the meat with which they are to be served.)

Another group of delicious thick sauces is made from butter, egg yolks, lemon juice or vinegar, and seasonings, but without flour. Hollandaise Sauce* uses lemon juice while Béarnaise Sauce* uses onion juice, tarragon, parsley, and tarragon vinegar.

The sweet dessert sauces are another division. They include the maple syrup served over pancakes, the crushed, sweetened strawberry topping for ice cream, and the soft custards and vanilla and chocolate sauces for puddings and plain cake. Their flavoring ingredients are the berries themselves, citrus juice or rind, vanilla and other extracts, chocolate, mint, ginger and other sweet spices, coffee and rum.

Good menu planning requires serving only one sauce with any course of a meal. Occasionally, an exception may be made by serving a heavy sauce, such as Hollandaise, over a vegetable, and another sauce over the meat.

MAIN-COURSE SAUCES

BASIC WHITE SAUCES

		Type		
Ingredient	*Measure*	*Thin*	*Medium*	*Thick*
Fat†	tablespoons	1	2	3 to 4
Flour	tablespoons	1	2	3 to 4
Liquid‡	cups	1	1	1
Salt	teaspoons	½	½	½
White pepper	teaspoons	$\frac{1}{16}$	$\frac{1}{16}$	$\frac{1}{16}$

†The fat may be butter, margarine, or chicken fat.

‡Although the liquid may be all milk, the sauce will be much better if you use half milk and half veal, chicken, or fish stock. Some cooks prefer to heat the liquid before adding.

Melt fat over low heat. Remove from heat, blend in flour. Return to heat, stir, and cook ½ minute or until mixture is bubbly. (This helps to take away the raw taste of the flour.) Remove from heat and add liquid. Mix well. Stir and cook until thickened. Add salt and pepper.

A *thin* sauce is used for cream soups; a *medium* sauce for gravies, creamed and scalloped dishes; and a *thick* sauce for croquettes and soufflés.

YIELD: About 1 cup

BROWN SAUCE

2 tablespoons butter, margarine,
   or other fat
3 tablespoons flour
1 cup beef stock
½ teaspoon salt
¹⁄₁₆ teaspoon white *or* black pepper

NOTE: Canned beef bouillon or 1 cup of hot water in which 1 beef bouillon cube or 2 teaspoons beef extract have been dissolved may be substituted for the beef stock, if desired.

Melt butter or other fat, stir in flour, and cook until browned, using low heat and stirring constantly to prevent scorching. Gradually add stock, heating and stirring until mixture boils and thickens, then cook about 3 minutes longer, stirring occasionally. Add seasonings.

Brown Sauce differs from White Sauce in the following 3 ways:
1) The butter-flour mixture is heated until it has browned.
2) Half again as much flour is used, since browning reduces the thickening power of the flour by converting its starch to dextrin.

3) Darker-colored and stronger-flavored ingredients, such as beef stock and black pepper, may be used.

YIELD: Approximately 1 cup

CELERY SAUCE

1 cup thinly sliced celery
2 tablespoons butter *or* margarine
1½ tablespoons flour
½ cup milk
½ cup chicken *or* beef stock
½ teaspoon instant minced onion
¾ teaspoon salt
1 teaspoon chopped parsley
¹⁄₁₆ teaspoon ground black papper

Sauté celery in butter or margarine. Remove from heat. Blend in flour. Stir and cook ½ minute or until bubbly. Remove from heat and stir in remaining ingredients. Stir and cook 2 to 3 minutes or until sauce is of medium thickness. Serve hot over fritters, croquettes, or cooked vegetables.

YIELD: 1¾ cups

CURRIED CREAM SAUCE

1 tablespoon finely chopped onion
2 teaspoons curry powder
2 tablespoons butter *or* margarine
3 tablespoons flour
2 cups chicken stock *or* 1 cup milk
   and 1 cup stock
½ teaspoon salt (or to taste)
¼ teaspoon sugar
¹⁄₁₆ teaspoon garlic powder
¹⁄₁₆ teaspoon ground black pepper

Sauté onion and curry powder in butter or margarine until onions are limp and tender, about 3 minutes. Remove from heat. Blend in flour and stir and cook ½ minute or until bubbly. Remove from heat and stir in stock or stock and milk.

Cook until of medium thickness. Blend in remaining ingredients. Serve over cooked asparagus, broccoli, or cauliflower.

YIELD: 2 cups

CHEDDAR CHEESE SAUCE

3 tablespoons butter *or* margarine
3 tablespoons flour
1½ cups milk
1 cup grated sharp Cheddar Cheese
1 teaspoon salt
¼ teaspoon ground black pepper
¼ teaspoon celery seed
¾ teaspoon powdered mustard
Dash cayenne

Melt butter or margarine in a saucepan. Remove from heat. Blend in flour and cook ½ minute or until bubbly. Remove from heat and gradually stir in milk. Stir and cook until mixture is of medium thickness. Add remaining ingredients and mix well. Heat only until cheese is melted.

YIELD: About 1½ cups

LEMON-CHEESE SAUCE

½ teaspoon powdered mustard
2 teaspoons water
¼ cup (½ stick) butter or margarine
2 tablespoons flour
1 cup milk
3 large egg yolks, lightly beaten
2 tablespoons fresh lemon juice
¾ cup grated sharp American cheese
⅛ teaspoon ground black pepper
½ teaspoon salt (or to taste)

Mix mustard with water and let stand 10 minutes. Melt butter or margarine in a 1-quart saucepan. Remove from heat. Blend in flour. Stir and cook ½ minute or until mixture is bubbly.

Remove from heat and add milk. Stir and cook until of medium thickness.

Blend egg yolk with lemon juice and blend with the sauce. Heat 1 minute. Stir in mustard and remaining ingredients. Serve over hard-cooked eggs and cooked vegetables.

YIELD: 1½ cups

MUSTARD-CHEESE SAUCE

1 tablespoon butter *or* margarine
1 tablespoon flour
1 cup milk
1 cup finely shredded, sharp
   American cheese
¼ teaspoon salt
½ teaspoon powdered mustard
1/16 teaspoon ground black pepper

Melt butter or margarine in a 3-cup saucepan. Remove from heat. Blend in flour. Stir and cook ½ minute or until mixture is bubbly. Remove from heat and add milk. Stir and cook until sauce begins to thicken.

Add remaining ingredients. Cook slowly until cheese has melted. Serve over Banana-Ham Rolls,* Deviled Eggs,* asparagus, broccoli, or cabbage wedges.

YIELD: 1 cup

BECHAMEL SAUCE

This creamy, all-purpose sauce was supposedly invented by Louis de Béchamel, Marquis de Nointel and Lord Steward of the Royal Household to Louis XIV of France.

½ teaspoon instant minced onion
2 carrot slices
½ bay leaf
½ teaspoon parsley flakes
6 whole black peppers
1 cup chicken stock
2 tablespoons butter *or* margarine
2 tablespoons flour

½ cup light cream *or* undiluted
   evaporated milk
½ teaspoon salt
¼ teaspoon ground black pepper
⅛ teaspoon ground thyme

Combine first 6 ingredients. Cover and
simmer 20 minutes. Strain. There should
be ½ cup of the liquid. If not, add water
to make ½ cup. Melt butter or margarine.
Remove from heat. Blend in flour. Stir
and cook ½ minute or until bubbly. Remove from heat and add stock, cream,
and seasonings. Stir and cook until of
medium thickness. Serve hot over cooked
vegetables, timbales, croquettes, mousse,
hard-cooked eggs, or fried chicken.

YIELD: 6 to 8 servings

ANCHOVY BECHAMEL SAUCE

2 carrot slices
¼ teaspoon instant minced onion
½ bay leaf
¼ teaspoon parsley flakes
6 whole black peppers
1 cup chicken stock *or* 1 chicken
   bouillon cube dissolved in
   1 cup hot water
___
2 tablespoons butter *or* margarine
2 tablespoons flour
½ cup light cream
1 teaspoon anchovy paste

Combine the first 6 ingredients in a
saucepan. Cover and simmer 10 minutes.
Strain. Melt butter or margarine in a
saucepan. Blend in flour. Remove from
heat and stir in stock and cream. Stir and
cook until of medium thickness. Add
anchovy paste. Serve over Deviled Eggs*
or with sliced or diced leftover veal.

YIELD: About 1 cup

EGG SAUCE

1 tablespoon butter *or* margarine
1 tablespoon flour
1 cup milk
___
½ teaspoon salt
1/16 teaspoon ground black pepper
1/16 teaspoon onion powder
___
2 large hard-cooked eggs, diced
2 teaspoons fresh lemon juice

Melt butter or margarine in saucepan.
Stir in flour. Add milk gradually along
with next 3 ingredients. Stir and cook
until slightly thickened. Add diced eggs
and lemon juice.

YIELD: Approximately 1½ cups

MUSHROOM SAUCE

¼ cup (½ stick) butter *or* margarine
1 teaspoon fresh lemon juice
1 cup sliced mushrooms, caps
   and stems
¼ cup flour
2 cups turkey stock
¼ cup heavy cream *or* milk
___
½ teaspoon salt (or to taste)
1/16 teaspoon ground black pepper
1/16 teaspoon garlic powder

Melt butter or margarine in a saucepan.
Add lemon juice and mushrooms. Sauté
until mushrooms are limp, about 3 minutes. Remove from heat and blend in
flour. Blend in turkey stock and cream
or milk. Stir and cook over medium heat
until of medium thickness. Add seasonings. Heat ½ minute longer. Serve hot
over turkey soufflé or similar dish.

YIELD: Approximately 2½ cups

TUNA FISH AND MUSHROOM SAUCE

Proceed as for Mushroom Sauce, adding

a 6-ounce can of tuna fish, drained, and 2 diced, hard-cooked eggs.

YIELD: Approximately 3 cups

POULETTE SAUCE

Poulette Sauce combines the flavor of chicken with the rich smoothness of cream. It's especially good on vegetables such as turnips, cabbage, parsnips, celery, zucchini and yellow summer squash; and on chicken, veal, and fish.

1½ tablespoons butter *or* margarine
1½ tablespoons flour
1 cup chicken stock
1 large egg yolk
⅓ cup heavy cream

½ teaspoon salt (or to taste)
⅛ teaspoon ground white pepper
¼ teaspoon paprika
1 teaspoon fresh lemon juice

Melt butter or margarine in a 3-cup saucepan. Remove from heat. Blend in flour. Stir and cook ½ minute or until mixture is bubbly. Remove from heat and add stock. Stir and cook until the sauce begins to thicken.

Mix egg yolk with cream and add to the sauce. Cook until of medium thickness, stirring constantly. Add remaining ingredients. Serve hot over cooked vegetables.

YIELD: 1¼ cups

SWEDISH LEMON SAUCE

(FOR FISH)

3 tablespoons butter *or* margarine
3 tablespoons flour
1¼ cups fish stock, strained
½ cup heavy cream

1 teaspoon salt
¼ teaspoon ground white pepper
3 tablespoons fresh lemon juice

Melt butter or margarine in a 3-cup saucepan. Remove from heat. Blend in flour. Stir and cook ½ minute or until mixture is bubbly. Remove from heat and add stock and cream. Stir and cook until of medium thickness. Add remaining ingredients. Serve over fish.

YIELD: 2 cups

VELOUTE SAUCE

It was the statesman Talleyrand who quipped, "France has 3 religions and 300 sauces; England has 3 sauces and 300 religions." Velouté is one of the basic French sauces that can be varied to make it suitable for vegetables, chicken, baked or broiled fish, croquettes, etc. When served with fish, fish stock is usually used in place of chicken stock.

2 tablespoons butter *or* margarine
3 tablespoons flour
1 cup chicken stock *or* 1 chicken bouillon cube and 1 cup hot water

½ teaspoon salt
⅛ teaspoon ground white pepper
⅛ teaspoon garlic powder
⅓ cup heavy cream

Melt butter or margarine in a 3-cup saucepan. Remove from heat. Blend in flour. Stir and cook ½ minute or until mixture is bubbly. Remove from heat and add stock. Stir and cook until of medium thickness. Add remaining ingredients. Cook ½ minute. Serve over cooked vegetables such as cabbage wedges, asparagus, cauliflower; and over chicken, seafood, or croquettes.

ALLEMANDE SAUCE

Proceed as for Velouté Sauce, using 2 tablespoons flour rather than 3 tablespoons flour. Blend 1 egg yolk with the cream and add.

DILL VELOUTE SAUCE

In the above recipe add 1½ teaspoons dill seed (or to taste) to the butter and proceed as directed.

CARAWAY VELOUTE SAUCE

In the above recipe add 1½ teaspoons caraway seed (or to taste) to the butter and proceed as directed.

YIELD: 1¼ cups

BLACK PEPPER BUTTER

1 teaspoon ground black pepper
½ teaspoon parsley flakes
¼ teaspoon onion powder
1/16 teaspoon garlic powder

2 teaspoons fresh lemon juice
⅓ cup (⅔ stick) soft butter or margarine

Add spices and lemon juice to butter or margarine. Serve on broiled steak, lamb chops, or chicken.

YIELD: ⅓ cup

BROWNED BUTTER-SESAME SAUCE

Brown ¼ cup (½ stick) butter or margarine in a small saucepan until golden. Add 2 tablespoons Toasted Sesame Seed.* Serve over vegetables or fish.

YIELD: ⅓ cup

LEMON-SESAME SAUCE

Melt 2 tablespoons butter or margarine in a small saucepan. Add 2 tablespoons Toasted Sesame Seed* and 1 tablespoon fresh lemon juice. Serve over vegetables or fish.

YIELD: ¼ cup

HERBED CAPER BUTTER

(FOR VEGETABLES)
¼ cup (½ stick) butter or margarine
⅛ teaspoon ground black pepper
½ teaspoon oregano leaves
2 teaspoons capers

Combine all ingredients in a small saucepan. (Chop capers if they are large.)

MOREOVER THE LORD SPAKE
UNTO MOSES SAYING:
TAKE THOU ALSO UNTO THEE
PRINCIPAL SPICES, OF PURE
MYRRH FIVE HUNDRED SHEKELS
AND OF SWEET CINNAMON
HALF SO MUCH

EXODUS 30·23

Heat until butter is melted. Serve over cooked vegetables such as broccoli, Brussels sprouts, cabbage, cauliflower, or snap beans.

YIELD: ¼ cup

LEMON-PARSLEY BUTTER

⅔ cup (1⅓ sticks) butter *or* margarine
⅓ cup chopped parsley
2 teaspoons salt
½ teaspoon ground black pepper
¼ teaspoon paprika
2 tablespoons fresh lemon juice

Soften butter or margarine and blend with remaining ingredients. Store in a covered jar in refrigerator to use over cooked vegetable and fish dishes.

YIELD: ¾ cup

PAPRIKA-BROWNED BUTTER SAUCE

¼ cup (½ stick) butter *or* margarine
2 tablespoons fresh lemon juice
2 teaspoons paprika
¼ teaspoon onion salt
⅛ teaspoon celery salt
⅛ teaspoon ground black pepper

Heat butter or margarine in a small saucepan until golden brown. Blend in remaining ingredients. Serve over hot cooked vegetables or broiled fish.

YIELD: ¼ cup sauce

BARBECUE SAUCE

(FOR FISH)

1 teaspoon powdered mustard
1 tablespoon water

2 tablespoons fresh lemon juice
3 tablespoons cider vinegar
1 teaspoon salt
½ teaspoon garlic salt
½ teaspoon paprika
½ teaspoon ground black pepper
¼ teaspoon cayenne

Mix mustard with water and let stand 10 minutes for flavor to develop. Combine with remaining ingredients. Heat only to boiling point. Use as a barbecue sauce for fish.

YIELD: Scant ½ cup

BARBECUE STEAK SAUCE

½ cup soy sauce
1 tablespoon light-brown sugar
2 tablespoons salad oil
¼ teaspoon ground allspice
½ teaspoon coarsely ground
    black pepper
1/16 teaspoon cayenne
2 pieces whole ginger, each 1 inch long

Combine all ingredients. Heat to boiling point. Cool. Pour over steak and marinate 2 hours before cooking. Baste with sauce while cooking as often as steak looks dry. This sauce keeps well. Keep a bottle on hand for basting meat.

YIELD: ⅔ cup

CHICKEN BARBECUE SAUCE

1 cup (8-ounce can) tomato juice
¼ cup salad oil
¼ cup cider vinegar
1 tablespoon instant minced onion
1½ teaspoons salt (or to taste)

1 teaspoon basil leaves
½ teaspoon thyme leaves
¼ teaspoon cayenne
¼ teaspoon ground black pepper
¼ teaspoon garlic powder

Combine all ingredients. Heat to boiling point and cook 1 minute. Use for barbecuing chicken either over the grill or in the broiler.

YIELD: 1¼ cups

GREEN PEPPER BARBECUE SAUCE

1 teaspoon powdered mustard
1 tablespoon water
1½ teaspoons chili powder
1 teaspoon salt
⅛ teaspoon cayenne
2 tablespoons light-brown sugar
1 tablespoon instant minced onion
2 tablespoons chili sauce
½ cup diced green pepper
2 tablespoons salad oil
2 slices lemon
½ cup cider vinegar

Combine all ingredients in a saucepan. Cook 3 minutes. Use for basting spareribs, pork chops, and chicken. To cook meat, place on a rack in a baking pan. Bake in a preheated moderate oven (350° F.) 45 minutes to 1 hour or until meat is tender, basting with the sauce at 15 minute intervals.

YIELD: 1 cup

HOT BARBECUE SAUCE

This was the pet sauce of a distinguished barbecue chef from Rome, Georgia. While his cookery was "by gosh and by golly," the results were inevitably superb. His recipe, had it ever appeared in writing, would have read something like this:

1 teaspoon powdered mustard
¼ cup water
_____
½ cup cider vinegar
¼ cup tomato catsup
¼ cup lemon juice
1 tablespoon light-brown sugar
1 teaspoon salt
1 teaspoon red pepper
½ teaspoon ground black pepper
½ teaspoon onion powder
⅛ teaspoon garlic powder
2 tablespoons cooking oil, butter, *or* margarine

Combine mustard and water and let stand 10 minutes for flavor to develop. Add remaining ingredients and heat to boiling point. Use to barbecue chicken, pork, beef, or lamb. Store leftover sauce in a covered jar in the refrigerator.

YIELD: 1½ cups

SOUTHERN BARBECUE SAUCE

1 teaspoon powdered mustard
1 tablespoon water
_____
1 cup cider vinegar
1 teaspoon ground black pepper
1 teaspoon cayenne
¼ teaspoon ground ginger
¼ teaspoon instant minced garlic
¼ cup catsup
_____
¼ cup salad oil

Mix mustard with water and let stand 10 minutes to develop flavor. Blend with the next 6 ingredients. Bring to boiling point and boil ½ minute. Stir in oil. Use to baste poultry and all kinds of meat. Store leftover sauce in a covered jar in the refrigerator for future use.

YIELD: 1⅓ cups

SOUTHWESTERN BARBECUE SAUCE

1 cup (8-ounce can) Spanish-type
  tomato sauce
½ cup water
⅓ cup cider vinegar
2 tablespoons lemon juice
2 tablespoons sugar
1 teaspoon ground black pepper
2½ teaspoons salt
½ teaspoon garlic salt
1 teaspoon chili powder
¼ teaspoon cayenne
1 tablespoon instant minced onion

1 teaspoon powdered mustard
1 tablespoon water

Combine the first 11 ingredients. Simmer 5 minutes. Blend mustard with the 1 tablespoon water and let stand 10 minutes. Add and mix well. Use to barbecue beef or pork.

YIELD: 2 cups

THICK BARBECUE SAUCE

(FOR PORK, VEAL, OR CHICKEN)

1 teaspoon powdered mustard
1 tablespoon water

1 cup tomato catsup
⅓ cup cider vinegar
½ cup water
2 tablespoons light-brown sugar
1 tablespoon instant minced onion
2 tablespoons fresh lemon juice
½ teaspoon salt
½ teaspoon ground black pepper
¼ teaspoon garlic salt
¼ teaspoon cayenne

Mix mustard with the 1 tablespoon water. Let stand 10 minutes for flavor to develop. Combine with remaining ingredients. Cover and cook 5 minutes. Use to barbecue pork, veal, or chicken.

YIELD: 1¾ cups

TOMATO BARBECUE SAUCE

4 teaspoons powdered mustard
¼ cup water
2 quarts (4 pounds) diced,
  fresh tomatoes
½ cup chopped onion
2 cloves garlic, chopped

1 cup fresh lemon juice
1 cup cider vinegar
¼ cup light-brown sugar
1 tablespoon salt
4 teaspoons paprika
2 teaspoons cayenne
2 tablespoons bottled red-hot sauce

Mix mustard and water and let stand until ready to use. Cook tomatoes, onion, and garlic in a covered saucepan 25 minutes. Rub the mixture through a sieve. Discard pulp. Add mustard and remaining ingredients. Bring to boiling point.

Pour into hot ½-pint jars. Adjust lids. Process in a boiling water bath (212° F.) 10 minutes, counting the time after water reaches boiling point. Store for future use. To use, heat to boiling point with 1 tablespoon butter or margarine to each ½ pint of sauce. Use for barbecuing all meats or poultry.

YIELD: 6 jars, ½ pint each

HOLLANDAISE SAUCE

¾ cup (1½ sticks) butter *or* margarine
3 large egg yolks
1½ tablespoons lemon juice
Dash salt
Dash cayenne

Divide butter into 3 parts and place one part in the top of a double boiler along with egg yolks and lemon juice. Cook and beat with a wire whisk over hot water (NOT BOILING) until butter melts. Add the second piece of butter and continue beating and cooking, never allowing the water in the bottom of the boiler to boil.

When butter has melted, add the last piece. Beat and cook until sauce has thickened. Add salt and cayenne. Serve over cooked vegetables, fish, or shellfish. If sauce has a tendency to curdle, place pan in ice water and beat vigorously.

MUSTARD HOLLANDAISE SAUCE

Mix 1½ teaspoons powdered mustard with 1 tablespoon water and let stand 10 minutes. Stir into Hollandaise Sauce. Serve over vegetables, fish, shellfish, eggs, chicken and cheese dishes.

BEARNAISE SAUCE

Add to the above Hollandaise Sauce 1 teaspoon onion juice, ¼ teaspoon tarragon leaves, ¼ teaspoon parsley flakes, and 1 tablespoon tarragon vinegar. Serve on broiled steak, fish, or eggs.

CURRY HOLLANDAISE SAUCE

Add to the above Hollandaise Sauce ¾ to 1 teaspoon curry powder. Serve on eggs, seafood, fish, or broccoli.

GRAPE HOLLANDAISE SAUCE

Add 1 cup seedless or seeded grapes, cut in half, to above Hollandaise Sauce. Serve over broiled fish steaks.

YIELD: 1 cup

SAUCE SUPREME

3 large egg yolks
¼ cup milk
¼ cup (½ stick) butter *or* margarine
2 teaspoons fresh lemon juice
$\frac{1}{16}$ teaspoon ground nutmeg
$\frac{1}{16}$ teaspoon ground black pepper
Dash salt
—
⅓ cup heavy cream, whipped

Place first 7 ingredients in top of double boiler. Mix well. Cook over hot water (NOT BOILING) until sauce has thickened, stirring constantly. Remove from heat and fold in whipped cream. Serve over cooked vegetables, fish, or shellfish.

YIELD: 1 cup

REMOULADE SAUCE

A favorite in the Cajun country of Louisiana. Creole prepared mustard is available in Louisiana, Texas, and other southern states. Dijon prepared mustard is available in most other sections of the country. Both are hot and spicy.

3 tablespoons white vinegar
2 tablespoons prepared Creole *or* Dijon mustard
1½ teaspoons instant minced onion
4 teaspoons horseradish sauce
1 teaspoon parsley flakes
1½ teaspoons salt
¼ teaspoon garlic salt
¼ teaspoon ground black pepper
⅛ teaspoon cayenne
2 tablespoons finely chopped celery
⅔ cup olive *or* salad oil

Combine all ingredients except oil. Add oil, a little at a time, beating well after each addition. Serve as a cocktail sauce for shrimp, lobster, or crabmeat.

YIELD: 1 cup

LEMON-MAYONNAISE SAUCE

2 tablespoons fresh lemon juice
1/16 teaspoon ground white pepper
½ cup mayonnaise

Combine all ingredients in the top of a double boiler. Stir and cook *only* until hot. Serve over fish.

YIELD: ⅔ cup

LEMON SAUCE
(FOR FRESH VEGETABLES)

½ cup mayonnaise
2 tablespoons fresh lemon juice
¼ teaspoon paprika

Combine all ingredients in the top of a double boiler. Heat over hot water, stirring constantly. Serve over hot, cooked fresh vegetables such as asparagus, broccoli, Brussels sprouts, cabbage, and snap beans.

YIELD: ½ cup

HOT TARTAR SAUCE

1 tablespoon butter *or* margarine
1 tablespoon flour
½ cup milk
⅓ cup mayonnaise
1½ teaspoons pickle relish
1½ teaspoons finely chopped green olives
½ teaspoon parsley flakes
½ teaspoon salt
½ teaspoon instant minced onion
½ teaspoon cider vinegar
¼ teaspoon tarragon leaves
1/16 teaspoon ground black pepper

Melt butter or margarine in a 3-cup saucepan. Remove from heat. Blend in flour. Stir and cook ½ minute or until mixture is bubbly. Remove from heat and add milk. Stir and cook until of medium thickness. Add remaining ingredients and heat only until hot. Serve over fish, cauliflower, or cabbage.

YIELD: ¾ cup

TARTAR SAUCE

1 cup mayonnaise
1 tablespoon chopped capers
1 tablespoon chopped green olives
1 tablespoon chopped mixed sweet pickles
1 tablespoon chopped parsley
½ teaspoon paprika

Combine all ingredients and mix well.

YIELD: 1¼ cups

RED CABBAGE SAUCE

(FOR FRIED OYSTERS)

1 cup very finely chopped red cabbage
½ cup mayonnaise
¼ cup light cream
1 teaspoon salt
¼ teaspoon ground black pepper
½ teaspoon paprika
Dash cayenne
1 teaspoon sweet relish

Combine all ingredients. Serve as a sauce for fried oysters.

YIELD: 1¼ cups

TARRAGON DRESSING

Tarragon speaks French. While it has a delicate flavor, this is an herb which must be used with discretion.

½ cup mayonnaise
½ teaspoon tarragon leaves
2 teaspoons fresh lemon juice

Combine all ingredients. Serve over chilled, cooked vegetables, seafood, chicken or fruit salad, or tomatoes.

YIELD: 6 servings

CHILI COCKTAIL SAUCE

½ cup catsup
½ teaspoon salt
¾ teaspoon chili powder
⅛ teaspoon ground cayenne
⅛ teaspoon garlic powder
2 teaspoons horseradish sauce
4 teaspoons lime *or* lemon juice

Combine all ingredients. Chill. Serve with shrimp, crabmeat, or lobster as the appetizer course.

YIELD: About ¾ cup

CHILI TOMATO SAUCE

2 tablespoons butter *or* margarine
1½ tablespoons flour
2 cups canned tomatoes
1 beef bouillon cube
2 tablespoons instant minced onion
½ teaspoon instant minced garlic
¾ teaspoon salt
¾ teaspoon chili powder
¼ teaspoon ground black pepper
⅛ teaspoon ground cumin seed

Melt butter or margarine in a saucepan. Blend in flour. Push tomatoes through a sieve and add along with remaining ingredients. Stir and cook until of medium thickness. Serve over meat croquettes, soufflés, fish, or frankfurters.

YIELD: 1½ cups

HERBED TOMATO SAUCE

3 tablespoons salad oil
½ cup finely chopped green pepper
¼ cup finely chopped celery
1 cup (8-ounce can) Spanish-type tomato sauce
2 tablespoons instant minced onion
1 teaspoon sugar
1 teaspoon salt (or to taste)
½ teaspoon basil leaves

⅛ teaspoon ground black pepper
1 teaspoon parsley flakes

Heat oil in a 1-quart saucepan. Add remaining ingredients. Cook 15 minutes or until sauce has thickened. Serve over Grilled Salisbury Steak.*

YIELD: Approximately 1 cup

MUSHROOM GIBLET GRAVY

3 medium-size mushrooms, sliced
3 tablespoons turkey fat, butter,
  or margarine
3 tablespoons flour

3 cups turkey stock
1 teaspoon salt (or to taste)
½ teaspoon instant minced onion
⅟₁₆ teaspoon ground black pepper
⅟₁₆ teaspoon garlic powder
1½ cups chopped giblets
½ teaspoon Kitchen Bouquet

2 large hard-cooked eggs, chopped

Sauté mushrooms in turkey fat, butter, or margarine. Remove from heat. Blend in flour. Stir and cook ½ minute or until bubbly. Remove from heat and add the next 7 ingredients. Stir and cook until of medium thickness. Add eggs. Serve over turkey and stuffing.

YIELD: 4 cups

ITALIAN TOMATO SAUCE I

4 cups (2 cans, 1 pound each)
  tomatoes
2 tablespoons olive oil
½ teaspoon garlic powder
1 teaspoon basil leaves
1 teaspoon oregano leaves
2 teaspoons parsley flakes
2 teaspoons salt
¼ teaspoon ground black pepper

Combine all ingredients in a saucepan. Cook slowly 30 minutes or until of medium thickness. Serve over beefsteak or spaghetti.

YIELD: 2 cups

ITALIAN TOMATO SAUCE II

¼ cup olive *or* salad oil
½ cup diced onion
½ cup finely diced green pepper
⅓ cup finely diced celery

3 tablespoons chopped parsley
2 cups finely diced fresh tomatoes
1 teaspoon salt
1 teaspoon sugar
⅛ teaspoon ground black pepper
1 teaspoon basil leaves

Heat oil in a saucepan. Add onion, green pepper, and celery, and cook until limp and transparent. Stir in remaining ingredients. Cook 10 minutes or until of medium thickness. Serve over cooked hot vegetables, croquettes, fish, soufflés, and cheese dishes.

YIELD: 6 servings

SAVORY TOMATO SAUCE

1½ tablespoons butter *or* margarine
1½ tablespoons flour

½ cup Spanish-type tomato sauce
¾ cup beef broth *or* consommé
2 teaspoons finely chopped green pepper
2 teaspoons instant minced onion
¼ teaspoon basil leaves
1/16 teaspoon garlic powder
⅛ teaspoon salt

Melt butter or margarine. Remove from heat. Blend in flour and cook until mixture is bubbly. Add remaining ingredients. Stir and cook 3 to 4 minutes.

YIELD: 1 cup

TOMATO AND BACON SAUCE

1 can (10½ ounces) cream of
    tomato soup
⅓ cup water
1 beef bouillon cube
⅛ teaspoon ground black pepper
⅛ teaspoon garlic powder
½ teaspoon instant minced onion
Salt to taste
4 slices crisp bacon, crumbled

Combine all ingredients and heat thoroughly. Serve over Hamburger Puffs.*

YIELD: 1¼ cups

TOMATO GRAVY

¼ cup chopped onion
¼ cup chopped green pepper
3 tablespoons butter *or* margarine
3 tablespoons flour

½ cup water
1¼ cups tomato purée
1 teaspoon sugar
1 teaspoon salt
⅛ teaspoon powdered mustard

Dash cayenne
1/16 teaspoon ground black pepper

Sauté onion and green pepper in butter or margarine. Remove from heat. Blend in flour and cook until bubbly. Add remaining ingredients. Mix well. Stir and cook until of medium thickness.

YIELD: 1½ cups

CHICKEN GIBLET GRAVY

Chicken giblets (neck, gizzard,
    liver, and heart)
3 cups water
1 teaspoon salt
2½ teaspoons flour

1 teaspoon instant minced onion
⅛ teaspoon ground ginger
⅛ teaspoon garlic powder
1/16 teaspoon ground black pepper
½ teaspoon soy sauce (optional)

Wash giblets and place in a saucepan with 2 cups of the water. Cook until giblets are tender, about 1 hour. Remove giblets from stock and dice. Blend flour with remaining 1 cup water and add to stock. Add remaining ingredients. Stir and cook 2 minutes or until gravy has thickened.

YIELD: 2 cups

CURRIED GRAPE SAUCE

(FOR HAM, TONGUE, OR POULTRY)

2 tablespoons chopped onion
2 teaspoons curry powder
2 tablespoons butter *or* margarine
3 tablespoons flour
2 cups chicken, ham, *or* tongue stock

½ teaspoon salt (or to taste)
¼ teaspoon sugar
⅛ teaspoon ground black pepper
Dash garlic powder
½ teaspoon lemon juice

1 cup green seedless grapes *or*
seeded grapes

Sauté onion and curry powder in butter or margarine until onions are limp and transparent. Remove from heat. Blend in flour. Stir and cook ½ minute or until bubbly. Remove from heat and stir in stock. Add seasonings and lemon juice. Stir and cook until sauce is of medium thickness. Add grapes 1 minute before cooking time is up. Serve hot over cooked ham, tongue, shrimp, or poultry.

YIELD: 3 cups

COTTAGE CHEESE TOPPING

1 cup (8-ounce package) creamy
cottage cheese
1 tablespoon chopped chives
¼ teaspoon salt
½ teaspoon paprika
⅛ teaspoon ground black pepper

Combine all ingredients. Serve over hot new potatoes.

YIELD: 1 cup

SESAME SEED TOPPING

(FOR CASSEROLE DISHES)

2 tablespoons sesame seed
1 cup soft bread crumbs
3 tablespoons butter *or* margarine

Combine all ingredients in a saucepan. Stir and cook over low heat until butter or margarine has melted. Sprinkle over casserole dishes made of poultry, seafood, meat, eggs, cheese, or vegetables. Bake as specified in the recipe for casserole dishes.

YIELD: Topping for a 10-inch casserole

VINAIGRETTE SAUCE

½ cup French dressing (oil and
vinegar type)
1 tablespoon parsley flakes
1 tablespoon chopped green pepper
2 tablespoons chopped pickle
1 teaspoon chopped chives
½ teaspoon paprika

Combine all ingredients. Beat well with a rotary beater. Serve over hot, cooked snap beans or other vegetables.

YIELD: ⅔ cup

MUSTARD-HORSERADISH SAUCE

1 teaspoon water
½ teaspoon powdered mustard
¼ cup prepared horseradish

Combine water and mustard. Let stand 10 minutes for flavor of mustard to develop. Add horseradish. Mix well. Serve with ham, pork, roast beef, and tongue.

YIELD: ¼ cup

DESSERT SAUCES

OLD ENGLISH HARD SAUCE

1 teaspoon vanilla extract
½ teaspoon grated orange rind
¼ teaspoon ground nutmeg
⅓ cup (⅔ stick) soft butter *or* margarine

About 2¼ cups sifted confectioners' sugar
1 tablespoon milk
2 tablespoons unsulphured molasses

Combine the first 4 ingredients. Gradually add remaining ingredients. Serve over warm puddings.

YIELD: 1⅔ cups

BRANDY HARD SAUCE

⅔ cup (1⅓ sticks) butter *or* margarine
¼ teaspoon ground nutmeg
2 cups sifted confectioners' sugar
2 tablespoons brandy
Ground nutmeg

Mix butter or margarine with the ¼ teaspoon nutmeg. Add sugar alternately with brandy. Mix until fluffy. Serve over plum puddings or warm fruit desserts. Garnish with additional nutmeg.

YIELD: 1½ cups

SPICED HARD SAUCE

½ teaspoon grated orange rind
⅛ teaspoon ground nutmeg

¼ teaspoon ground ginger
⅓ cup (⅔ stick) soft butter *or* margarine

2¼ cups sifted confectioners' sugar
1 tablespoon milk
1 tablespoon lemon juice

Combine the first 4 ingredients. Gradually add remaining ingredients. Serve over hot puddings.

YIELD: 1⅔ cups

CREAM AND BRANDY SAUCE

Whip ½ cup heavy cream until stiff. Fold in ¼ cup brandy. Serve over coconut pudding, gingerbread, or cake.

YIELD: Approximately 1 cup

VANILLA SAUCE

½ cup sugar
⅛ teaspoon salt
1 tablespoon cornstarch
1 cup water
2 tablespoons butter *or* margarine
½ teaspoon vanilla extract

Combine sugar, salt, and cornstarch in a 2-cup saucepan. Add water. Mix well. Stir and cook 5 minutes or until sauce is clear and it begins to thicken. Remove from heat and add butter or margarine and vanilla extract. Serve over Pineapple Cottage Pudding* or similar dessert.

YIELD: 1⅓ cups

EGGNOG SAUCE

2 tablespoons sugar
1 tablespoon flour
⅛ teaspoon salt

1 large egg, separated
1¼ cups milk
¼ teaspoon ground nutmeg
1 tablespoon rum
1 tablespoon sugar

Mix the first 3 ingredients in the top of a double boiler. Add the egg yolk and beat well. Then add the milk slowly, stirring constantly. Cook over rapidly boiling water 5 minutes, stirring occasionally. Remove from heat. Cool.

Add nutmeg and rum. Beat egg white until foamy; add 1 tablespoon sugar gradually, beating constantly until the mixture stands in soft peaks. Fold into sauce.

YIELD: About 2 cups

BUTTERSCOTCH SAUCE

½ cup light-brown sugar
⅔ cup light corn syrup
3 tablespoons butter *or* margarine
¹⁄₁₆ teaspoon salt

⅔ cup light cream
1½ teaspoons vanilla extract

Mix the first 4 ingredients in a 3-cup saucepan. Bring to boiling point and cook 3 minutes. Add cream and bring to a quick boil. Remove from heat. Cool and stir in vanilla extract. Stir before serving. Spoon over cakes, puddings, or ice cream.

YIELD: 2 cups

CARAMEL SAUCE

2 cups light-brown sugar
1 cup light cream *or* undiluted evaporated milk
2 tablespoons butter *or* margarine
1 teaspoon vanilla extract

Combine brown sugar and cream or evaporated milk in a saucepan. Stir and cook over medium low heat until boiling point is reached. Add butter or margarine. Continue cooking (WITHOUT STIRRING) 10 minutes or until mixture is smooth and syrupy. Remove from heat and add vanilla extract. Serve warm or cold over Molded Coconut Pudding* or similar pudding.

YIELD: 1½ cups

GINGER SAUCE

½ cup sugar
2 teaspoons cornstarch
½ teaspoon ground ginger
⅛ teaspoon salt

1 cup hot water
1 tablespoon butter *or* margarine
1 teaspoon fresh lemon juice

Blend the first 4 ingredients in a sauce-pan. Gradually stir in hot water. Cook until mixture is clear and slightly thickened. Stir in butter and lemon juice. Serve over Baked Pears.*

YIELD: 1 cup

SPICED CHOCOLATE SAUCE

2 squares (2 ounces)
    unsweetened chocolate
1 tablespoon butter *or* margarine

1 cup sugar
½ teaspoon cornstarch
⅛ teaspoon salt
¼ teaspoon ground cloves
¼ teaspoon ground cinnamon

¾ cup boiling water
¾ teaspoon vanilla extract

Melt chocolate and butter or margarine over hot water. Combine next 5 ingredients and blend with melted chocolate. Stir in boiling water. Boil 3 minutes. Cool. Stir in vanilla extract. Serve over ice cream or cake.

YIELD: 1¼ cups

FOAMY SAUCE

½ cup (1 stick) butter *or* margarine
¼ teaspoon ground mace
1 cup sifted confectioners' sugar

1 large egg, beaten
1 teaspoon vanilla extract
½ teaspoon grated lemon rind

½ cup heavy cream, whipped

Mix butter or margarine until fluffy. Blend in mace and sugar. Gradually beat in next 3 ingredients. Stir and cook over boiling water 2 to 3 minutes. Remove from heat and cool. Fold in whipped cream.

YIELD: Approximately 1 cup

FOAMY NUTMEG SAUCE

¼ cup (½ stick) butter *or* margarine
1 cup sifted confectioners' sugar

1 large egg yolk
¼ cup fresh orange juice
¼ teaspoon grated lemon rind
¼ teaspoon ground nutmeg

⅓ cup heavy cream, whipped

Stir butter or margarine until fluffy. Gradually blend in confectioners' sugar. Beat in next 4 ingredients. Fold in whipped cream. Serve over puddings or cakes.

YIELD: 1½ cups

BRANDIED FOAMY SAUCE

1⅓ cups sifted confectioners' sugar
½ cup (1 stick) soft butter *or*
    margarine
Dash salt
1 large egg, separated
2 tablespoons brandy
½ cup heavy cream, whipped
Ground nutmeg

Gradually add sugar to butter or margarine. Beat salt into egg yolk and add. Stir and cook over hot water 6 to 7 minutes or until mixture is light and fluffy. Add brandy.

Beat egg white until it stands in soft, stiff peaks. Fold into the sauce along with whipped cream. Garnish with nutmeg. Serve over hot steamed puddings, plain cake, or other desserts.

SPICED FOAMY SAUCE

Omit brandy in the above recipe and add ⅛ teaspoon each of ground ginger and ground nutmeg and 1 teaspoon vanilla extract.

YIELD: 2 cups

LEMON SAUCE

½ cup sugar
¹⁄₁₆ teaspoon salt
¹⁄₁₆ teaspoon ground cloves
1 tablespoon cornstarch

¼ cup cold water
¾ cup boiling water

3 tablespoons fresh lemon juice
1 teaspoon grated lemon rind
2 tablespoons butter *or* margarine
½ teaspoon vanilla extract

Combine first 4 ingredients in a 3-cup saucepan. Blend in cold water and then add boiling water. Stir and cook over moderate heat until sauce is clear and has begun to thicken, about 5 minutes. Add remaining ingredients. Serve over puddings, gingerbread, or plain cake.

YIELD: 1¼ cups

GOLDEN LEMON SAUCE

½ cup sugar
1 tablespoon cornstarch
½ teaspoon salt

¼ cup cold water

¾ cup boiling water
1 large egg yolk
3 tablespoons fresh lemon juice
1 teaspoon grated lemon rind
2 tablespoons butter *or* margarine

Combine first 3 ingredients in a saucepan. Add cold water and mix well. Gradually stir in boiling water. Stir and cook over medium heat 10 to 12 minutes or until clear and of medium thickness.

Blend egg yolk with lemon juice and gradually stir into the mixture. Cook 1 minute, stirring constantly. Stir in lemon rind and butter or margarine. Serve warm over Apple Turnovers.*

YIELD: 1⅓ cups

DATE AND NUT SAUCE

1 tablespoon cornstarch
½ cup sugar
1 cup water
⅛ teaspoon salt

2 tablespoons fresh lemon juice

¾ teaspoon grated lemon rind
1 tablespoon butter *or* margarine
¼ cup chopped nuts
¼ cup chopped dates

Combine the first 4 ingredients in a small saucepan. Gradually add fresh lemon juice. Stir and cook until thickened and transparent. Add remaining ingredients. Serve over Spicy Apple Squares.*

YIELD: 1½ cups

BANANA TOPPING

1 large egg white
1 large ripe banana
2 tablespoons sugar
⅛ teaspoon salt
½ teaspoon ground nutmeg
1 teaspoon fresh lemon juice
¼ teaspoon grated lemon rind

Place all ingredients in a small mixing bowl. Beat with a rotary or electric egg beater until light and fluffy. Serve as a topping for cakes and puddings.

YIELD: 1⅔ cups

PEACH ICE CREAM SAUCE

4 peaches (1 cup mashed pulp)
¹⁄₁₆ teaspoon salt
½ cup sugar
¼ teaspoon ground allspice

Peel, slice, and mash peaches. Measure pulp into a saucepan. Add salt, sugar, and allspice. Cover and cook 3 minutes over low heat. Uncover and continue to cook until sauce is thick, about 3 to 4 minutes. Cool. Serve over ice cream or plain cake.

YIELD: ¾ cup sauce

BLUEBERRY SAUCE

4 teaspoons cornstarch
½ cup sugar

1 cup water
¼ teaspoon ground cinnamon
1 teaspoon lemon juice
1 cup fresh blueberries

1 tablespoon butter *or* margarine

Blend cornstarch with sugar. Add next 4 ingredients. Stir and cook over low heat until sauce has thickened and is transparent. Add butter or margarine. Serve warm over Blueberry Curls* or plain cake.

YIELD: 1⅓ cups

SPICED-PINEAPPLE SAUCE

2 tablespoons sugar
2 tablespoons cornstarch
⅛ teaspoon salt
¼ teaspoon ground nutmeg

1 can (20 ounces) crushed pineapple
1 tablespoon butter *or* margarine

½ teaspoon grated lemon rind
1½ teaspoons vanilla extract

Combine first 4 ingredients in a saucepan. Blend in crushed pineapple. Stir and cook over medium heat until of desired thickness. Add butter or margarine. Stir in grated lemon rind and vanilla extract. Serve over cake squares.

YIELD: 2 cups

RICH ORANGE SAUCE

½ cup sugar
1½ tablespoons cornstarch
¼ teaspoon salt
½ teaspoon ground mace

½ cup hot water
½ cup fresh orange juice
2 tablespoons fresh lemon juice
1 large egg yolk

½ teaspoon grated orange rind
½ teaspoon grated lemon rind
3 tablespoons butter *or* margarine
Orange sections

Combine first 4 ingredients in a small saucepan. Stir in hot water and cook until thickened, stirring constantly. Mix fruit juices with egg yolk and blend with cooked mixture. Cook until slightly thickened, stirring constantly. Stir in remaining ingredients. Serve over squares of gingerbread, cake, or cottage pudding. Garnish with orange sections.

YIELD: 1½ cups

SOUFFLES

A soufflé is a glamorous, fluffy baked dish which can be made either sweet and light for use as a dessert, or hearty for use as a main dish.

It is created by adding beaten egg yolks and whites to a sauce base and baking for a long time at a low temperature. The air in the beaten eggs expands with the heat and makes the soufflé rise.

A soufflé differs from an omelet in that its sauce base, usually thickened with flour, is as important an ingredient as are the eggs, the latter being added principally to serve as leavening.

The simplest dessert soufflé is made from a white sauce with sugar, flavoring and, of course, eggs. The heartier soufflés are made without sugar, but with stock; solid pieces of meat, poultry, fish, or vegetables; or with grated cheese. Those of puréed vegetables or fruits tend to be delicate, but rather unstable.

The two most important phases of making a soufflé, besides selecting and making the base, are the handling of the egg whites and the baking.

The egg yolks should be well beaten, then mixed into the base. Immediately before baking, the egg whites (at least as many whites as yolks, though more would do no harm) should be beaten until fairly stiff, but with slightly rounded peaks, and then folded in. Mixing, though it must be thorough enough to disperse the egg white to all parts of the base, must somehow at the same time avoid allowing the air to be expelled. It is wise to first blend in about ¾ of the egg white until it is thoroughly dispersed and then to quickly fold in the remainder.

Select a baking dish or casserole having straight sides and not too wide a diameter. If the dish is not deep enough to hold the raised soufflé, its sides

513

may be extended by fitting it with a collar of foil or brown paper tied on with string. Grease only the bottom of the dish. The sides should be ungreased so that the soufflé will stick to them and not fall back after rising.

Preheat the oven, but bake at a low temperature, since protein foods should be cooked at a low temperature to keep them tender and digestible. Unless otherwise specified, use an oven temperature of 325° F., and place the dish in a pan of hot water.

AVANELLE'S CHEESE SOUFFLE

This soufflé may be held in a very low oven (250° F.) 30 to 40 minutes.

¼ cup (½ stick) butter *or* margarine
4 tablespoons flour
¼ teaspoon salt
1 cup milk
1 cup (¼ pound) shredded
　　Cheddar cheese
3 large eggs, separated

1 teaspoon powdered mustard
2 teaspoons water
Dash cayenne
¼ teaspoon ground black pepper
¼ teaspoon cream of tartar

Melt butter or margarine in a saucepan. Remove from heat. Blend in flour and salt. Stir and cook ½ minute or until bubbly. Remove from heat. Stir in milk and cook until of medium thickness, stirring constantly. Add cheese and mix until blended. Beat egg yolks until thick and lemon-colored, into which blend a little of the hot sauce. Then stir into remaining hot sauce.

Soak mustard in water 10 minutes and add along with cayenne and black pepper. Beat egg whites until foamy, add cream of tartar, and beat until they stand in soft, stiff peaks. Fold into the mixture. Turn into a 1½-quart casserole, having only the bottom buttered. Place in a pan of hot water. Bake in a preheated slow oven (325° F.) 1¼ hours or until well puffed and brown. Serve immediately.

YIELD: 4 to 6 servings

LIL'S CHEESE SOUFFLE

¼ cup (½ stick) butter *or* margarine
4 tablespoons flour
1½ cups milk
½- to ¾-pound sharp American
　　cheese, shredded
1 teaspoon salt

6 large eggs, separated
½ teaspoon powdered mustard
1 teaspoon water
¼ teaspoon ground ginger
1 teaspoon Italian seasoning

Melt butter or margarine in top of a double boiler over boiling water. Remove from heat and blend in flour. Add milk gradually, stirring until smooth. Return to the boiling water and cook until smooth and thick, stirring constantly. Add cheese and salt and cook over hot water, NOT BOILING, until cheese is melted.

Beat egg yolks, into which beat a little of the hot mixture. Then add to the remaining hot sauce, stirring until well blended. Mix mustard with water and let stand 10 minutes and add to the sauce along with ginger and Italian seasoning. Beat egg whites until they stand in soft, stiff peaks. Fold into the mixture. Turn into a 2-quart casserole, having only the bottom buttered. Place in a pan of hot water. Bake in a preheated slow oven (325° F.) 1 hour or until firm.

YIELD: 5 servings

MUSHROOM SOUFFLE

2 cups (½ pound) finely chopped
   fresh mushrooms
6 tablespoons butter or margarine
¼ cup all-purpose flour
1 cup milk

1¾ teaspoons salt
⅛ teaspoon ground black pepper
¼ teaspoon ground thyme
1 teaspoon instant minced onion

4 large eggs, separated

Cheddar Cheese Sauce*
Parsley

Cook mushrooms slowly in 2 tablespoons of the butter or margarine 5 minutes or

until tender, stirring frequently. Melt remaining butter or margarine in a saucepan. Remove from heat and blend in flour. Stir and cook ½ minute or until bubbly. Remove from heat and stir in milk. Cook over medium heat 3 minutes or until thickened, stirring constantly.

Add mushrooms and the next 4 ingredients. Beat egg yolks until light and lemon-colored and add. Beat egg whites until they stand in soft, stiff peaks and carefully fold into the mixture. Turn into a 1½-quart casserole having only the bottom buttered. Place in a pan of hot water. Bake in a preheated slow oven (325° F.) 1½ hours or until nicely browned and center is firm to the touch. Serve at once with Cheddar Cheese Sauce. Garnish with parsley.

YIELD: 8 servings

TUNA FISH SOUFFLE

1 cup finely chopped celery
¼ cup quick-cooking tapioca
1 cup boiling water

1 teaspoon salt
¼ teaspoon ground nutmeg
1/16 teaspoon ground black pepper
1 cup light cream or top milk

4 large eggs, separated
6½-ounce can tuna fish
2 teaspoons fresh lemon juice
Egg Sauce*

*An asterisk after the name of a dish indicates that the recipe for this dish appears in the book. Consult the Index for the page number.

Cook celery and tapioca in boiling water 3 minutes or until tapioca is transparent, stirring frequently. Add next 4 ingredients. Beat egg yolks well and add along with tuna fish and lemon juice. Beat egg whites until they stand in soft, stiff peaks. Fold into the mixture.

Turn into a 1½-quart casserole having only the bottom buttered. Place in a pan of hot water. Bake in a preheated slow oven (325° F.) 1½ hours or until a knife inserted in the center comes out clean. Serve hot with Egg Sauce.

YIELD: 6 servings

ROSEMARY TURKEY SOUFFLE

3 tablespoons butter *or* margarine
3 tablespoons flour
½ cup milk *or* light cream
½ cup turkey stock
4 large eggs, separated

½ teaspoon salt
¼ teaspoon rosemary leaves
¹⁄₁₆ teaspoon ground black pepper
2 cups chopped leftover turkey
1 teaspoon fresh lemon juice

Mushroom Sauce*

Melt butter or margarine in a saucepan. Remove from heat. Blend in flour. Stir and cook ½ minute or until bubbly. Remove from heat and stir in milk or cream and turkey stock. Stir and cook over low heat until of medium thickness and of smooth consistency. Beat egg yolks and add. Blend in next 5 ingredients.

Beat egg whites until they stand in stiff, soft peaks. Carefully fold into the mixture. Turn into a 1-quart soufflé dish or casserole, having only the bottom buttered. Place in a pan of hot water. Bake in a preheated slow oven (325° F.) 1½ hours

or until a knife inserted in center comes out clean. Serve with Mushroom Sauce.

YIELD: 6 servings

BANANA SOUFFLE

3 firm ripe bananas
1½ tablespoons fresh lemon juice

⅓ cup sugar
1 tablespoon cornstarch
⅛ teaspoon salt
½ teaspoon ground nutmeg
¼ teaspoon grated lemon rind

¾ cup milk
3 large eggs, separated
2 tablespoons butter *or* margarine
1½ teaspoons vanilla extract
Heavy cream, whipped
Sugar

Peel and slice bananas and dip in lemon juice. Mix together in a saucepan the next 5 ingredients. Add milk and mix well. Stir and cook over medium heat until thickened. Add a little of the hot mixture to beaten egg yolks. Then mix it with remaining hot mixture. Stir in butter or margarine and sliced bananas.

Beat egg whites until they stand in soft, stiff peaks. Fold into the cream mixture along with vanilla extract.

Turn into a 1½-quart soufflé dish having only the bottom buttered. Place in a pan of hot water. Bake in a preheated slow oven (325° F.) about 1½ hours or until firm. Serve as dessert with whipped cream sweetened to taste with sugar.

YIELD: 6 servings

CHOCOLATE SOUFFLE

3 tablespoons butter *or* margarine

¼ cup all-purpose flour
½ teaspoon ground cinnamon
¼ teaspoon salt

1 cup scalded milk
2 squares (2 ounces) unsweetened chocolate
3 large eggs, separated
⅓ cup sugar
1½ teaspoons vanilla extract
Heavy cream, whipped
Sugar

Melt butter or margarine in a saucepan. Remove from heat. Blend in next 3 ingredients. Stir and cook ½ minute or until bubbly. Remove from heat and gradually stir in milk and chocolate. Stir and cook over low heat or hot water until thickened. Beat egg yolks with ½ of the sugar and add to cooked mixture. Add vanilla extract. Cool.

Beat egg whites until they stand in soft, stiff peaks, into which beat in remaining sugar. Fold into custard. Turn into a 1-quart casserole, having only the bottom buttered. Place in a pan of hot water. Bake in a preheated slow oven (325° F.) 1 hour or until firm. Serve at once with whipped cream sweetened to taste with sugar.

YIELD: 6 servings

BAKED LEMON SPONGE

¾ cup sugar
¼ cup all-purpose flour
½ teaspoon ground mace
1/16 teaspoon salt

2 large eggs, separated
1 cup milk
2 tablespoons melted butter *or* margarine
2 teaspoons grated lemon rind
¼ cup lemon juice

Sift together the first 4 ingredients. Set aside. Beat egg yolks with milk and add to dry mixture. Stir in butter, lemon rind, and juice. Beat egg whites until they stand in soft, stiff peaks, into which gradually beat remaining ¼ cup sugar. Gently fold into the mixture.

Turn into a 1-quart casserole or in six 6-ounce custard cups, having only the bottom buttered. Place in a pan of hot water. Bake in a preheated slow oven (325° F.) 50 to 60 minutes or until a knife inserted in the center comes out clean. Cool.

YIELD: 6 servings

LEMON-ORANGE SOUFFLE

¼ cup (½ stick) butter *or* margarine

⅓ cup all-purpose flour
¼ teaspoon salt
¼ teaspoon ground cardamom

1 cup strained orange juice
3 tablespoons lemon juice
4 large eggs, separated

2 tablespoons grated lemon rind
1 tablespoon grated orange rind
1 teaspoon vanilla extract

6 tablespoons sugar
Confectioners' sugar
Foamy Sauce*

Melt butter or margarine in a saucepan. Remove from heat. Blend in next 3 ingredients. Stir and cook ½ minute or until bubbly. Remove from heat and stir in orange and lemon juices. Stir and cook over low heat or hot water until very thick. Remove from heat and beat in egg yolks, one at a time. Stir in next 3 ingredients.

Beat egg whites until they stand in soft, stiff peaks, into which gradually beat sugar. Fold into the custard. Turn into a 1½-quart casserole having only the bottom buttered. Sprinkle top with confectioners' sugar. Place in a pan of hot water and bake in a preheated slow oven (325° F.) 1 hour and 40 minutes. Remove from oven and serve at once with Foamy Sauce.

YIELD: 8 servings

SPICED SOUFFLE

3 tablespoons butter *or* margarine
3 tablespoons flour
¾ cup milk
3 large eggs, separated
⅓ cup sugar

½ teaspoon ground mace
1½ teaspoons vanilla extract
¼ teaspoon salt
Confectioners' sugar
Vanilla Whipped Cream *(see below)*

Melt butter or margarine in a saucepan. Remove from heat. Blend in flour. Add milk and mix well. Stir and cook over moderate heat until of medium thickness. Remove from heat. Beat egg yolks until thick and lemon-colored. Beat in next 3 ingredients. Stir into cooked mixture.

Add salt to egg whites and beat until they stand in soft, stiff peaks. Fold into the mixture. Turn into a soufflé dish having only the bottom buttered. Place in pan of hot water and bake in a preheated slow oven (325° F.) 2 hours or until firm in center. Serve at once from baking dish. Top with Vanilla Whipped Cream.

VANILLA WHIPPED CREAM
Whip ⅓ cup heavy cream. Mix with 2 teaspoons sugar and ½ teaspoon vanilla extract.

YIELD: 6 servings

SOUPS and
SOUP ACCOMPANIMENTS

S OUP," declared the French gastronomer, Grimod de la Reyniere, "is
to a dinner what a portico or a peristyle is to a building . . . not only
the first part of it, but it must be made in such a manner as to set the tone
of the whole banquet, in the same way as the overture of an opera makes
known the subject of the work." He was speaking as a Frenchman, of course,
where the *pot au feu* is traditional, and grand dinners have included not one
soup, but two one clear, one thick.

The many hundreds of soups can be distinguished as those made
with stock or with milk—cream soups, bisques, etc.

Clear soups, such as consommé or bouillon, should be sharply seasoned
to stimulate the appetite at the beginning of a dinner. Generally, they will be
served hot—really hot—in heated plates. Or, in hot weather, they can be
chilled until ice-cold and jellied, then served with a wedge of lemon and a
parsley garnish. The thicker soups—chowders, beef and vegetable combinations—are satisfying as a main course at either lunch or supper. They are
most appetizing as between-meal or midnight snacks, too.

519

Canned soups in variety may be spiced to suit your taste. Stir a dash of allspice into a chicken noodle soup, for instance, or add a few grains of nutmeg or a thread of saffron to a cream of chicken soup. Add just a little basil to tomato soup; savory ("the bean herb") to a bean-and-bacon soup; curry powder to a cream of pea soup. Marjoram is delightful in almost any soup, while a pinch of oregano improves the deliciousness of cream of mushroom soup. These suggestions are offered as a sort of stimulant, to set you thinking of all the exciting possibilities that exist on your spice shelf—when you open a can of soup.

VEGETABLE-BEEF SOUP

2 pounds beef soup meat
2 pounds beef bones
2 quarts cold water
2 tablespoons salt
___
1 tablespoon mixed pickling spice
1 cup sliced fresh carrots
1 cup sliced celery
2 cups fresh snap beans, in 1-inch lengths
¾ cup fresh corn, cut from the cob
3½ cups canned (1 pound, 13 ounces) tomatoes
2 tablespoons parsley flakes
¼ cup onion flakes

Place first 4 ingredients in a 6-quart saucepan. Tie pickling spice in a bag and add. Cover, bring to boiling point, reduce heat, and simmer 3 hours. Remove spice bag and soup bones.

Trim off all meat that may be on the bones; discard bones. Cut soup meat into small pieces and return to soup kettle. Stir in remaining ingredients. Cover and cook slowly until vegetables are tender, about ½ hour. If desired, freeze leftover soup for future use.

YIELD: About 1 gallon

NEW ENGLAND CLEAR VEGETABLE SOUP

2 pounds soup meat
4 pounds soup bones
2 quarts cold water
4 teaspoons salt
3 large onions, quartered
___
2½ cups strained canned tomatoes
1 cup shredded uncooked carrots
¼ cup shredded uncooked potatoes
¼ cup shredded uncooked turnips
¼ cup finely chopped onion
1 teaspoon sugar
1 teaspoon celery salt
¾ teaspoon savory
½ teaspoon basil leaves
⅛ teaspoon ground black pepper
¼ teaspoon ground ginger
¼ teaspoon garlic powder

Place the first 5 ingredients in an 8-quart saucepan. Cover and simmer 3 hours. Remove soup meat, bones, and onions. (Save meat for use in sandwiches or casserole dish). Strain stock. Add remaining ingredients. Bring to boiling point and boil 5 minutes or until vegetables are tender. Serve hot.

YIELD: 2 quarts

SAN JUAN MEAT BROTH

1 pound brisket of beef

2 pounds beef soup bones
4 cups cold water
½ teaspoon whole black pepper
1 tablespoon salt

⅓ cup (2 ounces) diced ham
2 medium-size carrots, sliced
¾ cup coarsely chopped green pepper
¼ cup onion flakes
½ teaspoon instant minced garlic
2 bay leaves
2 medium-size tomatoes, diccd

2 tablespoons parsley flakes
Croutons

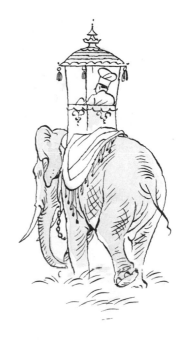

Cut meat into small pieces and place in a 4-quart saucepan. Add next 4 ingredients. Let stand ½ hour. Add next 7 ingredients. Bring to boiling point, reduce heat, and simmer 2 hours. Strain. Add parsley flakes and serve with croutons.

YIELD: 1 quart

MULLIGATAWNY SOUP

Mulligatawny *means "pepper water" in southern India. It is a highly seasoned clear consommé served with rice and dry curries. There are numerous versions of this recipe, some of them even flavored with a pinch of asafetida. But that one is just a touch too exotic for Western taste buds, so we have not included it.*

7 or 8 pounds bony chicken parts
1 quart water
½ cup diced carrot
½ cup chopped celery
½ cup chopped mushroom stems
2 tablespoons parsley flakes
2 tablespoons instant minced onion

¼ cup instant minced onion
¼ cup water
2 tablespoons butter *or* margarine

4 teaspoons flour
1 tablespoon curry powder
4 teaspoons salt

½ cup heavy cream
¾ cup cooked rice

Cook together the first 7 ingredients until chicken is tender. Remove chicken from stock. Mix ¼ cup instant minced onion and ¼ cup water and let stand 3 or 4 minutes. Brown in butter or margarine. Stir in next 3 ingredients.

Add chicken stock gradually and cook 7 to 8 minutes. Rub through a fine sieve. Stir in heavy cream. Heat thoroughly, but do not boil. Add 2 tablespoons hot rice and a little of the chicken picked from the bones to each serving of soup.

YIELD: 6 servings

SCOTCH SOUP
(COCK-A-LEEKIE)

Cock-a-leekie is a very good Scotch soup made, as the name implies, with chicken and plenty of leeks. This is a very hearty soup.

3- to 4-pound stewing chicken
¼ cup (½ stick) butter *or* margarine
8 cups water
4 teaspoons salt (or to taste)
3 cups finely chopped leeks, tops and bulbs
¾ cup finely diced carrots
1¼ cups finely diced celery
⅓ cup chopped parsley
¾ to 1 teaspoon thyme leaves
¼ teaspoon ground black pepper
¼ teaspoon garlic powder

Disjoint chicken, wash, and wipe dry. Fry on all sides over medium-low heat in butter or margarine. Add water and salt. Cover and simmer 1½ to 2 hours or until meat falls from bones.

Lift chicken from pot and remove meat from the bones. Skim excess fat from stock. Return meat to pot. Add remaining ingredients. Cover and cook 12 to 20 minutes or until vegetables are tender. Serve hot.

YIELD: 2¼ quarts

COSTA RICAN CORN SOUP
(SOPA DE MAIZE)

4 cups rich strained chicken stock
2 cups canned tomatoes
1 teaspoon salt (or to taste)
1 cup fresh corn, cut from the cob, *or* frozen *or* canned whole kernel corn
—————
½ teaspoon oregano leaves
¼ teaspoon garlic powder
⅛ teaspoon ground black pepper
—————
Lime slices

Combine the first 4 ingredients and bring to boiling point. Cook gently 5 minutes. Add next 3 ingredients. Cook 3 minutes. Serve hot with a thin slice of lime floating over the top. Serve tortillas or crackers, if desired.

YIELD: 1½ quarts

MEXICAN CORN SOUP
(SOPA DE ELOTE)

Sopa de Elote is the Mexican name. (Elote means corn-on-the-cob.) Chicken necks and backs are always bargain-priced, so start this wonderfully good soup by simmering about 4 pounds of chicken backs 1½ hours in 2½ quarts of water and use it for the stock.

6 ears fresh corn
2 quarts chicken *or* beef stock
½ cup minced onion
2 tablespoons butter *or* margarine
⅓ cup tomato purée
2½ teaspoons salt
¼ teaspoon ground black pepper

1 teaspoon sugar
1 teaspoon fresh lemon juice

3 cups beef stock *or* 3 beef bouillon
  cubes and 3 cups water
½ teaspoon fennel seed
6 tablespoons sour cream
Chopped parsley

Combine first 5 ingredients and 1 cup of the beef stock. Cover and cook 15 minutes or until vegetables are tender. Put through a coarse sieve. Add remaining stock and fennel seed. Heat. Serve hot, each serving topped with a tablespoon of sour cream and a sprinkling of chopped parsley.

YIELD: 1½ quarts

MUSHROOM SOUP, HUNGARIAN STYLE

4 cups (¾ pound) coarsely chopped, fresh mushrooms
2 tablespoons bacon drippings

2 teaspoons instant minced onion
¼ teaspoon instant minced garlic
2 teaspoons salt
1 teaspoon paprika
¼ cup all-purpose flour
½ teaspoon chervil leaves

1½ quarts rich chicken stock
1 large egg, lightly beaten
½ cup sour cream

Sauté mushrooms in bacon drippings until mushrooms are tender, about 10 minutes. Stir in next 6 ingredients. Add stock, mix well, and cook until soup is hot and slightly thickened. Blend egg with sour cream and place in soup tureen. Pour in hot soup, stirring constantly. Serve hot.

YIELD: 2½ quarts

½ cup heavy cream
⅛ teaspoon garlic powder
Dash cayenne
½ teaspoon ground cumin seeds
½ teaspoon sugar

Remove husks from corn and boil 3 of the ears in boiling water to cover 10 minutes or until tender. Remove from water and cool. Then, cut kernels off the cob and save for later use. Cut the kernels from the uncooked corn by first running a sharp knife down each row of kernels, cutting them in half. Then cut a thin layer from the entire cob of each ear. Scrape cobs with the bowl of a tablespoon. Add to the stock.

Sauté onions in butter or margarine until limp and transparent. Add to uncooked corn and stock along with tomato purée, cooked corn kernels, salt, and black pepper. Cover and cook slowly 20 minutes or until raw corn is cooked. Add remaining ingredients and cook only until hot.

YIELD: 2½ quarts

BEET SOUP

2 cups shredded fresh beets
1 cup shredded beet leaves
½ teaspoon salt

HOT CUCUMBER SOUP

⅔ cup sliced leeks

4 cups diced, unpeeled cucumbers
1 cup finely diced uncooked potatoes
¼ cup chopped parsley
4 cups chicken broth
1½ teaspoons salt
½ teaspoon powdered mustard
½ teaspoon savory leaves

¼ teaspoon ground white pepper
⅔ cup heavy cream

Wash leeks well and slice. Place in a saucepan with next 7 ingredients. Cover and cook until tender. Strain through a sieve, being sure to push as much of the vegetable through as possible. Heat. Just before serving, add white pepper and cream. Serve hot.

YIELD: 2 quarts

FISH SOUP
(COURT BOUILLON AU POISSON)

3 pound ready-to-cook whole fish (cod fish, haddock, *or* other white-meat fish)

7 cups water
2 tablespoons salt
1 bay leaf
12 whole black peppers
½ teaspoon instant minced garlic

2 teaspoons salt
¼ teaspoon ground black pepper
1 teaspoon oregano leaves
½ teaspoon sugar
¼ teaspoon instant minced garlic
1 teaspoon cider vinegar
1 tablespoon olive *or* salad oil

½ cup (1 stick) butter *or* margarine
1 can (1¾ pounds) tomatoes
2 tablespoons olive *or* salad oil
1 tablespoon cider vinegar
⅓ cup onion flakes

1 teaspoon parsley flakes
Croutons

Remove heads and tails from fish and place them in a 4-quart saucepan. Reserve fish for later use. Add the next 5 ingredients. Cover, bring to boiling point, reduce heat, and simmer 1 hour (DO NOT BOIL). In the meantime, combine the next 7 ingredients. Cut fish into slices ½ inch thick. Rub both sides with spice mixture. Marinate until stock has cooked.

Strain stock and add next 5 ingredients. Cover and simmer 30 minutes. Add fish and parsley flakes. Simmer 12 to 15 minutes or until fish is flaky. Serve hot with croutons. Cool and freeze leftover soup for future use.

YIELD: 4 quarts

GOULASH
(MAIN-DISH SOUP)

A goulash is a hearty and flavorful meat and vegetable stew-soup, the favorite dish of the Hungarian peasant and herdsman. Do not spare the paprika when making goulash, and if you love a distinct nip of seasoning, dash in a mere pinch of red pepper.

2 pounds beef stew meat
1⅓ cups chopped onion
2 tablespoons shortening
2 tablespoons paprika

2 cups diced green pepper
2 cups diced fresh tomatoes
8 cups boiling water
1 ham bone
3 teaspoons salt

½ pound German *or* Hungarian-type sausage
3 cups diced potatoes
½ teaspoon ground black pepper

Cut stew meat into ½-inch pieces. Brown along with onion in shortening in a large saucepan. Stir in paprika and cook 2 minutes. Add next 5 ingredients. Cover and simmer 2 hours or until meat is tender.

Cut sausage into pieces ½ inch thick and add along with potatoes. Cover and cook 15 to 20 minutes or until potatoes are tender. Stir in black pepper. Serve hot. Leftover soup may be frozen.

YIELD: 1 gallon

CREME VICHYSSOISE

This is one of those rich, high-calorie, elegant concoctions that are so hard to resist. The recipe was created by the late chef Louis Diat of the old Ritz-Carlton at Madison Avenue and 46th Street, New York City. It was named for his home town in France.

1½ cups minced leeks, using only the white portion
2 tablespoons butter *or* margarine
3 cups rich chicken stock *or* 4 chicken bouillon cubes and 3 cups boiling water

2 tablespoons instant minced onion
1 teaspoon parsley flakes
¼ cup chopped celery
2 cups thinly sliced potatoes
½ cup thinly sliced carrots

1 cup heavy cream
1 teaspoon salt (or to taste)
¼ teaspoon ground white pepper
2 tablespoons chopped fresh chives

Sauté leeks in butter or margarine until transparent but not browned. Add chicken stock or bouillon cubes dissolved in boiling water. Add next 5 ingredients. Cover and simmer until vegetables are tender. Push mixture through a fine sieve. Stir in heavy cream, salt, and pepper. Cool and chill. Serve, in bowls, as the first course. Garnish with chopped chives.

CURRIED VICHYSSOISE
Add 1 teaspoon curry powder (or to taste) to the above recipe. Chill and serve with ¼ small apple diced into each bowl.

YIELD: 2 quarts

GREEN PEPPER SOUP

3 tablespoons instant minced onion
3 tablespoons water
2 tablespoons butter *or* margarine
¾ cup finely chopped green pepper

3 cups chicken stock
¼ teaspoon oregano leaves
½ teaspoon basil leaves

1½ tablespoons butter *or* margarine
1½ tablespoons flour
1½ cups milk
¾ teaspoon salt (or to taste)
Green pepper (optional)

Soften instant minced onion in water. Sauté in butter or margarine along with green pepper. Add next 3 ingredients and simmer (DO NOT BOIL) 10 minutes. Put the mixture through a coarse sieve or blend to a purée in an electric blender. Set aside.

Melt butter or margarine in a saucepan. Blend in flour. Stir and cook over low heat until roux is bubbly. Remove from heat and stir in milk. Stir and cook until the sauce is smooth and slightly thickened. Add green pepper purée. Serve hot or chilled, garnished with a little finely chopped green pepper, if desired.

YIELD: 1 quart

GREEN PEPPER AND TOMATO SOUP

3 cups diced green peppers
1 quart diced fresh tomatoes
½ cup chopped onion
2 tablespoons chopped parsley
½ cup water

2 tablespoons butter *or* margarine
2½ tablespoons flour
2 teaspoons salt
¼ teaspoon ground black pepper
¼ teaspoon garlic powder
1 teaspoon sugar
½ teaspoon basil leaves
¼ teaspoon crumbled oregano
½ cup heavy cream (optional)

Cook first 5 ingredients in a covered saucepan until vegetables are very tender, about 20 minutes. Push mixture through a medium sieve. Melt butter or margarine in a saucepan. Blend in flour. Gradually stir in strained mixture. Add seasonings and bring to boiling point. Serve hot or cold. Stir in heavy cream just before serving, if desired.

YIELD: 1 quart

KALE AND BACON SOUP

¼ cup onion flakes
¼ teaspoon instant minced garlic
3 tablespoons water
½ cup chopped green pepper
3 tablespoons bacon fat
1 pound fresh kale, washed

1 teaspoon sugar
1½ teaspoons salt
¼ teaspoon ground black pepper
1 teaspoon oregano leaves

2 cups milk
1 cup beef stock *or* 2 bouillon cubes and 1 cup hot water
3 slices crisp bacon, crumbled

Soften onion and garlic in the 3 tablespoons water. Sauté, along with green pepper, in bacon fat until soft. Add kale and the next 4 ingredients. Cover and steam 20 minutes over low heat. Chop and put through a coarse sieve or use a blender. Add milk and beef stock or bouillon cubes and hot water. Cook only until hot. Serve at once with ½ slice bacon crumbled over each serving.

YIELD: 1½ quarts

CHILI POTATO SOUP

2 strips bacon
⅔ cup chopped onion
3 cups diced potatoes
2 cups boiling water
1½ teaspoons salt
2½ cups milk
1 to 1½ teaspoons chili powder
¼ teaspoon oregano leaves
1/16 teaspoon garlic powder
1/16 teaspoon ground black pepper
Grated Parmesan cheese

Fry bacon until crisp in soup kettle. Remove bacon. Add onions to hot bacon fat and sauté until limp. Add potatoes, boiling water, and salt. Cover. Cook until potatoes are soft. Then mash and add milk and seasonings. Heat thoroughly. Serve with grated cheese sprinkled over the top.

YIELD: 2 quarts

CURRIED POTATO SOUP

2 tablespoons butter *or* margarine
⅔ cup finely chopped onion
3 teaspoons curry powder

3 cups diced potatoes
2 cups boiling water
1¾ teaspoons salt
—————
2½ cups milk

Melt butter or margarine in a saucepan. Add onion and curry powder and cook until onions are limp. Add next 3 ingredients. Cover and cook until potatoes are soft. Mash and add milk. Heat thoroughly.

YIELD: 1½ quarts

JAMAICA PUMPKIN SOUP

1 cup mashed, cooked pumpkin
2½ cups chicken broth
1 tablespoon flour
1 teaspoon salt
⅛ teaspoon ground ginger
⅛ teaspoon ground nutmeg
1 cup top milk *or* evaporated milk
1 teaspoon instant minced onion
2 large eggs, beaten
Chopped parsley *or* chives

Combine pumpkin and chicken stock in a saucepan or double boiler. Mix flour with salt and spices. Add ¼ cup of the milk and mix to a smooth paste. Add milk and eggs. Stir into the pumpkin mixture. Cook 5 minutes over low heat or hot water, stirring constantly. Serve garnished with chopped parsley or chives.

YIELD: 1¼ quarts

NEW ENGLAND CLAM BISQUE

This recipe was given to us by Mrs. George Farnham, Manager of the Mystic (Connecticut) Seaport Galley. It's as flavorful as clam chowder, but less hearty. A perfect first course for a seafood dinner. Ask for "chowder" clams at your fish market.

1 pint fresh "chowder" clams
¼ cup (½ stick) butter *or* margarine
3 tablespoons flour
1⅔ cups milk
⅔ cup light cream
¾ teaspoon salt
1 teaspoon onion salt
¼ teaspoon ground nutmeg
⅛ teaspoon ground white pepper
1/16 teaspoon garlic powder
Parsley

Remove necks from clams and put them through the food chopper, using coarse blade. Add clams and clam juice and cook below boiling point 5 minutes or until tender. Melt butter or margarine in a saucepan. Remove from heat and blend in flour. Stir in milk and cream. Cook until of medium thickness (DO NOT BOIL). Add clams and seasonings and serve immediately, garnishing with parsley. If bisque thickens on standing, thin to desired thickness with a little hot water.

YIELD: 1¼ quarts

OYSTER STEW

24 fresh oysters *or* a 12-ounce package
    frozen oysters with liquid

2¼ cups milk
2 tablespoons butter *or* margarine
¾ teaspoon ground black pepper
¼ teaspoon thyme leaves
½ teaspoon salt (or to taste)
¹⁄₁₆ teaspoon onion powder

Paprika

Heat oysters in the liquid *only* until edges
curl. (If frozen oysters are used, defrost
them before cooking.) Add next 6 ingredients and heat only until mixture is
hot. DO NOT BOIL OR OVERCOOK. Serve
hot, garnished with a dash of paprika.

YIELD: 1 quart

CORN AND SEAFOOD CHOWDER

2½ cups water
1½ teaspoons salt
8 whole black peppers
4 whole cloves
1 small bay leaf

4 frozen lobster tails
    (2 packages, 10 ounces each), thawed
6 fresh "chowder" clams
½ cup chopped onion
¼ teaspoon instant minced garlic
2 tablespoons butter *or* margarine
1½ cups diced potatoes
½ of 12-ounce package frozen fish fillets,
    thawed
2 cups fresh corn, cut from the cob
1 cup light cream *or* undiluted
    evaporated milk
¼ teaspoon ground thyme

Place first 5 ingredients in a large saucepan. Bring to boiling point, adding lobster tails and clams. Cover and cook over
low heat 12 to 15 minutes or until lobster
turns pink and clam shells open. Drain
off liquid and reserve it. Remove lobster
and clams from shells and set aside.

Sauté onion and garlic in butter or
margarine. Add strained lobster and clam
stock to onion. Add potatoes. Cover and
cook 15 minutes or until potatoes are
tender. Add fish and cook 5 minutes.
Add lobsters, clams, corn, cream or milk,
and thyme. Cover and cook slowly 5
minutes (DO NOT BOIL).

YIELD: 1½ quarts

PUERTO RICAN SHRIMP CHOWDER (ASOPAO BASICO)

1 cup long-grain rice
1 cup water

½ cup diced ham
1 strip bacon
1 cup chopped green peppers

1 cup diced, fresh tomatoes
12 green olives, chopped
1 tablespoon capers
½ cup Spanish-type tomato sauce
1½ teaspoons salt

3 cups boiling water
1 teaspoon oregano leaves
2 tablespoons ground coriander
1 pound fresh shrimp, peeled and
    deveined

Soak rice in water 30 minutes. In the
meantime, stir and cook the next 3 ingredients together in a 10-inch heavy
saucepan or Dutch oven. Add the next
5 ingredients. Stir and cook 10 minutes.
Drain rice and add. Stir in boiling water
and herbs.

Cover, bring to boiling point, reduce
heat, and cook 15 minutes or until rice
is almost tender. Peel and devein shrimp,
add, mix lightly with a fork. Cover and

cook 5 minutes or until shrimp turns pink. Serve hot in soup bowls as the main dish.

YIELD: 2 quarts

MINESTRONE ALLA MILANESE

A minestrone must, by definition, be a thick soup. This is the best known of Italy's minestras.

¼ pound bacon
½ cup diced onion
1 clove garlic, quartered
3 pints beef stock

½ cup sliced carrots
½ cup diced celery
1 cup fresh snap beans
½ cup diced potatoes

1 cup sliced zucchini squash
1 cup shredded cabbage
3 medium (1 pound) fresh tomatoes, peeled and diced
¼ cup chopped parsley
1 tablespoon salt
1 teaspoon basil leaves

½ teaspoon ground black pepper
Grated Parmesan cheese

Cook bacon until crisp. Remove bacon and add onion and garlic to the drippings. Cook until they are golden. Add stock and bring to boiling point. Add next 4 ingredients, cover, and simmer 45 minutes. Add next 6 ingredients, cover, and cook 20 minutes or until vegetables are tender. Crumble bacon and add along with black pepper. Serve with grated Parmesan cheese sprinkled over the top.

YIELD: 1¼ quarts

CHILI TOMATO AND SPLIT PEA SOUP

1 can (10½ ounces) cream of tomato soup

1 can (10½ ounces) split pea soup
2 cans (10½ ounces each) water
½ teaspoon salt
⅛ teaspoon ground black pepper
2 teaspoons chili powder

Combine all ingredients. Heat and serve for lunch or supper.

YIELD: 1¼ quarts

QUICK VEGETABLE SOUP WITH CHILI MEAT BALLS

1 can (10½ ounces) beef broth
1 can (10½ ounces) vegetable soup
2 tablespoons instant minced onion
⅓ cup grated carrots
½ cup any leftover cooked vegetables (peas, beans, corn, okra, etc.)
1 cup canned *or* cooked tomatoes
⅓ cup packaged, precooked rice
1½ teaspoons salt

Chili Meat Balls *(see below)*

Combine first 8 ingredients. Heat to boiling, add Chili Meat Balls, simmer 10 minutes. Serve at once.

CHILI MEAT BALLS
1 pound ground beef
2 tablespoons instant minced onion
1½ teaspoons salt
⅛ teaspoon garlic powder
2 teaspoons chili powder
¼ cup fine, dry bread crumbs
¼ cup tomato juice

1 to 2 tablespoons shortening.

Combine first 7 ingredients. Shape into sixteen 1-inch balls. Brown on all sides in hot shortening. Add to soup as directed.

YIELD: 1¼ quarts

TOMATO AND PEA SOUP

1 can (10½ ounces) tomato soup
1 can (10½ ounces) split pea soup
2 cans (10½ ounces each) water
½ teaspoon salt
¾ teaspoon oregano leaves
½ teaspoon chili powder
⅛ teaspoon garlic powder
¼ teaspoon instant minced onion
Fresh lemon slices

Place all ingredients except lemon slices in saucepan. Heat. Serve hot. Float a slice of lemon on each serving.

YIELD: 1¼ quarts

SAVORY VEGETABLE-BEEF BROTH

2¼ cups rich beef broth *or* 2 cans beef broth, 10½ ounces each
2 cups tomato juice
½ cup diced celery
¼ cup shredded carrots
1 tablespoon instant minced onion
½ teaspoon salt (or to taste)
¾ teaspoon oregano leaves
⅛ teaspoon ground black pepper
1/16 teaspoon garlic powder

Combine the first 6 ingredients in a 1½-quart saucepan. Cook over low heat 15 to 20 minutes or until vegetables are tender. Add remaining ingredients 5 minutes before cooking time is up. Serve hot.

YIELD: 1 quart

CHILI CROUTONS

3 slices firm-textured bread
3 tablespoons butter *or* margarine, melted
¾ teaspoon chili powder

Trim crusts from bread and cut into ½-inch squares. Combine butter or margarine and chili powder, add bread, and mix until all butter is absorbed. Place on a cooky sheet and brown in a preheated moderate oven (350° F.) 10 to 12 minutes. Serve over soup, salads, or over cooked vegetables.

CURRIED CROUTONS

In the above recipe, replace chili powder with ¾ teaspoon curry powder.

YIELD: Sufficient for 6 servings of soup

TOASTED PAPRIKA CHEESE CRACKERS

¼ cup (½ stick) soft butter *or* margarine
¼ cup grated American cheese
¼ teaspoon salt
¼ teaspoon powdered mustard
Dash cayenne

Sesame seed crackers
Paprika

Blend the first 5 ingredients. Spread on sesame seed crackers. Sprinkle with paprika. Toast under the broiler until cheese is melted and bubbly.

YIELD: Approximately 2 dozen crackers

CURRIED POPCORN

⅓ cup unpopped popcorn
⅓ cup (⅔ stick) butter *or* margarine, melted
1 teaspoon salt
1 teaspoon curry powder

Pop corn in a covered skillet or saucepan over low heat or in a wire popper over red coals in the fireplace. Turn into a large bowl. Mix butter or margarine, salt, and curry powder and pour over popped corn. Mix well.

YIELD: About 1 quart

STUFFINGS

MAKING a good stuffing is among those things that must be done right the very first time—like parachute jumping. There are hundreds of ways to make stuffings—thus called in most areas of the country, though the names "dressings" and "fillings" are also used. Stuffings can be moist or dry, as desired, but they should never be soggy. Most of us prefer to bake the stuffing in the bird, but some good cooks bake an empty bird and prepare the stuffing—which should, in that case, be called "dressing"—in a separate bowl, in the same oven.

Bread, corn bread, rice, and potatoes may be used for the starchy ingredients, and sausage, oysters, nutmeats, chestnuts, fruit, or mushrooms to add interesting flavor and texture. Butter, margarine, chicken fat, broth, wine, and certain fruit and vegetable juices may be used to moisten the mixture.

There are a few basic rules that apply to all stuffings. Make the stuffing at your leisure—preferably the night before—and store in the refrigerator, but do not fill the bird until just before cooking time. Pack or spoon stuffing in loosely. Stuffing swells and overstuffing gives a soggy, compact texture. A time-honored rule is to allow a cup of stuffing for each pound of bird. Should there be extra stuffing, bake it separately in a small casserole, baste once or twice with giblet stock, and cover with foil.

BEAN AND SAUSAGE STUFFING

3 cups (2 cans, 1 pound each) kidney beans, drained
9 cups toasted bread crumbs *or* small cubes (croutons)
1½ cups finely chopped celery
⅓ cup instant minced onion
12 (1 pound) sausage links
⅓ cup (⅔ stick) butter *or* margarine, melted
3 teaspoons salt (or to taste)
1½ teaspoons poultry seasoning
3 to 4 teaspoons chili powder (or to taste)

Combine the first 4 ingredients. Cut sausage links into ½-inch slices and brown. Add to bread and bean mixture, discarding fat. Stir in remaining ingredients. Spoon into crop and body cavities of a 12- to 15-pound turkey. Close openings with skewers and lace tightly with a string.

YIELD: Stuffing for 12- to 15-pound turkey

CHESTNUT-SAUSAGE DRY STUFFING

1 pound sausage meat
1 cup chopped onion
1 cup sliced celery
½ cup chopped parsley
15 cups toasted bread cubes (croutons)
2 teaspoons salt
1 teaspoon crumbled thyme leaves
1 teaspoon marjoram leaves
2 teaspoons ground sage
½ teaspoon ground black pepper
½ cup diced green olives
1 pound (2½ cups) chopped chestnuts, roasted
¼ cup (½ stick) butter *or* margarine, melted
½ cup water *or* turkey stock

NOTE: Roast chestnuts *after* they have been chopped.

Brown sausage lightly in skillet along with onion and celery. Drain off all excess fat. Add remaining ingredients. Mix well. Spoon mixture into the crop and body cavities of a 15- to 18-pound turkey.

YIELD: Stuffing for 15- to 18-pound turkey

CORN BREAD STUFFING

½ cup instant minced onion
½ cup water
⅓ cup finely chopped celery
7 cups toasted corn bread crumbs
4 cups toasted bread cubes (croutons)
5 teaspoons poultry seasoning
2 teaspoons salt
½ teaspoon ground black pepper
1 cup (2 sticks) butter *or* margarine, melted
1 cup turkey stock

Soften onion in the ½ cup water and mix with remaining ingredients. Spoon into the crop and body cavity of a 12- to 15-pound ready-to-cook turkey. Close openings with skewers and lace tightly with a string.

YIELD: Stuffing for a 12- to 15-pound turkey

ITALIAN HAM AND OLIVE STUFFING

4 cups cooked rice
4 cups toasted bread cubes (croutons)
4 large eggs, lightly beaten
1 cup diced, leftover cooked ham
1 cup diced celery
1 cup chopped onion
⅔ cup chopped green olives
½ cup chopped parsley
1 teaspoon salt
1 teaspoon ground sage

1 teaspoon ground marjoram
½ teaspoon ground black pepper
¼ teaspoon garlic powder

Combine all ingredients. Rub the inside of crop and body cavities of a 12- to 15-pound turkey with ¾ teaspoon salt. Fill with stuffing mixture. Close openings with skewers and lace tightly with string.

YIELD: Stuffing for a 12- to 15-pound turkey

HERBED LIVERWURST STUFFING

½ pound liverwurst
⅓ cup instant minced onion
½ cup chopped celery
3 tablespoons parsley flakes
2½ teaspoons salt
2 teaspoons poultry seasoning
½ teaspoon ground black pepper
8 cups toasted bread cubes (croutons)
⅔ cup (1⅓ sticks) butter *or* margarine, melted
½ cup turkey stock *or* 1 chicken bouillon cube and ½ cup hot water

Put liverwurst through a food chopper, using a coarse blade. Mix with remaining ingredients. Spoon into the crop and body cavities of a 10- to 12-pound ready-to-cook turkey. Close openings with skewers and lace tightly with a string.

YIELD: Stuffing for a 10- to 12-pound turkey

MUSHROOM STUFFING

12 cups toasted bread cubes (croutons)
1½ cups chopped onion
½ cup chopped parsley
¾ cup chopped celery
2 teaspoons poultry seasoning
¼ teaspoon ground black pepper
2 teaspoons salt

½ pound mushrooms
½ cup (1 stick) butter *or* margarine
2 teaspoons fresh lemon juice

Combine the first 7 ingredients. Wash mushrooms, slice both caps and stems, and sauté them in butter or margarine and lemon juice until mushrooms are tender. Mix with bread cubes. Spoon lightly into crop and body cavities of a 12- to 15-pound ready-to-cook turkey. Close opening with skewers and lace tightly with a strong cord.

YIELD: Stuffing for a 12- to 15-pound turkey

DRY SAGE STUFFING

9 cups toasted soft bread crumbs *or* toasted bread cubes (croutons)
1½ teaspoons salt
3 teaspoons ground sage
½ teaspoon ground black pepper
½ cup turkey stock *or* 1 chicken bouillon cube and ½ cup hot water
⅓ cup instant minced onion
1 cup (2 sticks) butter *or* margarine, melted

Toast bread crumbs or cubes. Mix with remaining ingredients. Spoon into the crop and body cavities of a 10- to 12-pound ready-to-cook turkey. Close openings with skewers and lace tightly with string.

YIELD: Stuffing for 10- to 12-pound turkey

SESAME SEED RICE STUFFING

⅔ cup chopped celery
⅓ cup (⅔ stick) butter *or* margarine
¼ teaspoon ground black pepper
2 teaspoons salt
1 teaspoon poultry seasoning
2 tablespoons onion flakes
2 tablespoons parsley flakes
⅓ cup Toasted Sesame Seed*
4 cups cooked rice

Sauté celery in 1 tablespoon of the butter or margarine. Melt remaining butter and add to celery along with rest of the ingredients. Mix well. Fill crop and body cavities of a 10- to 12-pound ready-to-cook turkey.

YIELD: Stuffing for a 10- to 12-pound turkey

SWEET POTATO-SAUSAGE STUFFING

2 cups mashed sweet potatoes
6 cups toasted bread cubes (croutons)
1 cup chopped celery
⅔ cup chopped onion
8 sausage links
2½ teaspoons salt
½ teaspoon ground black pepper
2 teaspoons poultry seasoning
¼ cup (½ stick) butter *or* margarine, melted

Combine first 4 ingredients. Cut sausage links into 1-inch pieces, brown, and add to the mixture. Add seasonings and melted butter or margarine. Mix well and spoon lightly into the crop and body cavities of a 10- to 12-pound ready-to-cook turkey. Close openings with skewers and lace tightly with strong cord. Make *half* of this recipe if you wish to stuff a 5- to

*An asterisk after the name of a dish indicates that the recipe for this dish appears in the book. Consult the Index for the page number.

6-pound ready-to-cook chicken or capon.

YIELD: Stuffing for a 10- to 12-pound turkey; ½ recipe is stuffing for a 5- to 6-pound chicken or capon

HERBED LIVER STUFFING

⅓ cup (⅔ stick) butter *or* margarine *or* chicken fat
1 teaspoon paprika
3 teaspoons salt
½ cup chopped onion
½ pound chicken livers
½ cup diced celery
5 cups day-old bread cubes
2 large eggs, beaten
¼ teaspoon garlic powder
¼ teaspoon ground black pepper
1 teaspoon poultry seasoning

Mix 3 tablespoons butter, margarine, or chicken fat with paprika and 1 teaspoon of the salt. Rub the crop and body cavities with a portion of the mixture. Sauté onion, chicken livers and celery in remaining fat, butter or margarine until livers are tender. Add to bread cubes along with remaining salt and next 4 ingredients. Mix well.

Spoon into the crop and body cavities of a 5- to 6-pound ready-to-cook chicken or small turkey. Close openings with skewers and lace tightly with a string. Rub remaining paprika-butter mixture over the skin of the bird.

YIELD: Stuffing for a 5- to 6-pound chicken or small turkey

ITALIAN SALAMI STUFFING

½ cup toasted, fresh bread crumbs or toasted bread cubes (croutons)
3 slices salami, diced
½ cup finely chopped celery
¼ cup grated Romano cheese
1 cup unseasoned mashed potatoes

1 tablespoon parsley flakes
½ teaspoon ground sage
¼ teaspoon ground black pepper
¼ cup chicken *or* turkey stock

Toast bread crumbs or cubes in a moderate oven (350° F.). Mix with remaining ingredients. Spoon into the crop and body cavities of a 5-pound ready-to-cook chicken or turkey. Close openings with skewers and lace tightly with a string.

YIELD: Stuffing for a 5-pound chicken or turkey

SAGE CORN BREAD STUFFING

½ cup chopped onion
½ cup (1 stick) butter *or* margarine

1 cup chopped celery
¼ cup chopped parsley
1½ teaspoons salt
1 teaspoon ground sage
3 cups toasted bread cubes (croutons)
2 cups day-old corn bread crumbs
½ cup chicken stock *or* hot water

Sauté onion in butter or margarine until limp and transparent. Add remaining ingredients and mix well. Spoon into the crop and body cavities of a 5- to 6-pound ready-to-cook capon or turkey. Close openings with skewers and lace tightly with a string.

YIELD: Stuffing for a 5- to 6-pound capon or turkey

RAISIN, NUT, AND APPLE CIDER STUFFING

12 cups toasted bread cubes (croutons)
¾ cup onion flakes
¼ cup parsley flakes
1½ teaspoons poultry seasoning
3 teaspoons celery seed
3 teaspoons salt
½ teaspoon ground black pepper

1½ cups seedless raisins
½ cup chopped nuts
½ cup (1 stick) butter *or* margarine, melted
1 cup apple cider

Combine the first 9 ingredients. Mix well. Stir in butter or margarine and cider. Spoon into crop and body cavities of a 10-pound ready-to-cook goose. Close opening with skewers and lace tightly with a string. Make *one-third* of this recipe if you wish to stuff a ready-to-cook duck.

YIELD: Stuffing for a 10-pound goose; ⅓ recipe is stuffing for a duck

POTATO DRESSING

4 cups hot, fluffy mashed potatoes
1½ cups fine, dry bread crumbs
⅔ cup bacon fat
½ cup finely chopped onion
½ cup chopped celery
2 teaspoons salt
½ teaspoon ground black pepper
½ teaspoon ground sage
1 large egg, beaten

Combine all ingredients. Turn into a greased 8 x 8 x 2-inch pan. Bake in a preheated moderate oven (350° F.) 30 minutes or until browned. Serve with pork, beef, lamb, or fowl.

YIELD: 6 to 8 servings

VEGETABLES

IF you are accustomed to being complimented on how expertly you cook vegetables, then be pleased, indeed, at having passed a cookery test which so many cooks fail. If, however, the vegetables you serve leave much to be desired, both in appearance and flavor, you might value a brief review of the principles of this culinary art.

In boiling vegetables, the secret is to cook them immediately before serving, using the smallest amount of water and the least possible cooking time. Most of the water should be absorbed by the vegetable, little or none being lost by draining at the end of the cooking period.

Start all vegetables in boiling salted water. Let the water boil vigorously for two minutes or so to drive off the free oxygen. This trick, it has been discovered, lessens considerably the Vitamin C loss during cooking. The amount of water required depends on how quickly the vegetable cooks—from ¼- to 1-inch depth in the pan is usually sufficient for vegetables such as potatoes, carrots, lima beans, etc.

In "hard water," where white vegetables are likely to cook to an off-white color due to minerals in the water, a teaspoonful of fresh lemon juice or white vinegar in the cooking water keeps vegetables white. (The addition of 1 tablespoonful of milk in the cooking water achieves the same result.)

Alkaline water will give red vegetables, such as beets and red cabbage, a bluish tone. The answer here is also to add a bit of lemon juice or vinegar to the cooking water.

Yellow vegetables are easy to cook, since they are neither affected by

536

the chemical content of the cooking water nor by the cooking techniques used. But do not drown them, especially a mild vegetable like the carrot, which can be so delicious when cooked properly.

Green vegetables are the real problem—which is why we mention them last. Incorrect cooking transforms their color to an unattractive brownish green. This is caused by a gas, otherwise harmless, which is released when the vegetables begin cooking. This gas, if trapped in proximity with the vegetable in a tightly covered saucepan, fades that fresh natural green color. The remedy is as simple as the ailment: Cook green vegetables uncovered for several minutes prior to covering the saucepan. Or, lift the lid three or four times during the first part of the cooking time to release any accumulated gas.

Spinach is an exception. Because spinach is cooked with no more than the water that clings to the leaves after washing, and because it is done in a minute or two, spinach may be covered. This very brief contact with the gaseous steam does not fade the green color of the spinach.

Do not use soda. Even though it keeps vegetables green, it destroys some of the vitamins and flavor. This regrettable cookery suggestion has been with us since about the fourth century, A.D., when it appeared in *Roman Cookery* by Apicius.

Strong-flavored vegetables, such as onions, turnips, and members of the cabbage family, should be cooked in one of the following ways: 1. Leave whole or cut into a few large pieces and cook in an uncovered pan in a moderate amount of water. This method produces a mild flavor, but loses some of the nutrients. 2. Cook in less water—about 1 inch—with cover on during the last half of the cooking or leave the cover on during the entire cooking period, but lift the lid three or four times to let gases escape. 3. Cut vegetables into small pieces and cook in a covered saucepan in a small amount of water until just tender. By this method, vegetables cook so quickly that no objectionable flavors develop.

SUGGESTIONS FOR SPICING VEGETABLES

Each vegetable can be enhanced by certain compatible spices and herbs. Black and white pepper, onion and garlic products, and parsley give pleasing flavor to almost any vegetable. They are therefore omitted from the following chart, which lists those aromatic seasonings especially suited to the individual vegetable.

ARTICHOKE   Basil, chervil, oregano, ginger, curry powder
ASPARAGUS   Almost all herbs, sesame and poppy seed; curry powder, nutmeg
BEANS, LIMA   Savory, thyme, dill, nutmeg
BEANS, SNAP   Sesame and poppy seed, dill, basil, nutmeg, mustard

BEETS   Celery seed, dill, caraway, cloves, allspice, cinnamon

BROCCOLI   Dill, marjoram, celery seed, basil, caraway seed, mustard, curry powder

BRUSSELS SPROUTS   Season as you would broccoli

CABBAGE   Season as you would broccoli

CAULIFLOWER   Season as you would broccoli

CARROTS   Allspice, cloves, cinnamon, ginger, basil, curry powder

CELERY   Almost all herbs, but especially basil, thyme, rosemary, tarragon

COLLARD   Season as you would broccoli

CORN   Curry powder, chili powder, nutmeg, oregano

EGGPLANT   Almost all herbs, curry and chili powder, Toasted Sesame Seed*

KALE   Marjoram, oregano, tarragon, mustard, nutmeg

MUSHROOMS   Almost any herb, but especially oregano and thyme, curry powder, nutmeg

MUSTARD GREENS   Season as you would kale

ONIONS   All herbs, celery seed, chili and curry powder, mustard, nutmeg

PARSNIPS   Allspice, cinnamon, ginger, nutmeg, curry and chili powder, rosemary, cumin

PEAS, GREEN   Basil, mint, thyme, nutmeg

PEPPERS, GREEN   Chili powder, oregano, mustard, celery seed

POTATOES   All herbs, especially dill and basil, caraway and celery seeds, nutmeg

SPINACH   Most herbs, especially basil, nutmeg, curry powder

SQUASH, SUMMER   Almost all herbs, curry and chili powder, cumin seeds

*An asterisk after the name of a dish indicates that the recipe for this dish appears in the book. Consult the Index for the page number.

SQUASH, WINTER   The sweet spices, such as cinnamon, cloves, cardamom, Toasted Sesame Seed*

SWEET POTATOES   Season as you would winter squash

SWISS CHARD   Season as you would beets

TOMATOES   Almost every herb, but especially basil and oregano, cinnamon or cloves (very lightly)

TURNIP GREENS   Season as you would kale

TURNIPS, RUTABAGAS   Sage, basil, thyme, dill, nutmeg, mace, ginger

ARTICHOKES, ITALIAN STYLE

4 medium-size artichokes

¼ cup olive oil
¼ cup chopped onion
1 clove garlic, minced
½ teaspoon salt
⅛ teaspoon ground black pepper
1 teaspoon oregano leaves
1 tablespoon chopped parsley

Wash artichokes, cut off stems and pull off tough outer leaves. Cut off and discard the top third of each. Stand artichokes in upright position in a saucepan just big enough to fit them snugly or tie each with a string to hold them in shape. Add boiling water to cover and cook 20 to 30 minutes, or only until partially tender. Remove from water and drain, reserving cooking water.

Place remaining ingredients in a saucepan and sauté until lightly browned. Remove and discard the fuzzy choke from the artichokes with a teaspoon and place artichokes in an upright position in a deep, round close-fitting saucepan. Pour in reserved cooking water, not over the artichokes, but around them.

Pour the sautéed onion sauce over the artichokes, allowing some to fall into the centers. Cover and simmer 30 to 40 minutes or until tender. Serve hot with some of the liquid, in a little cup, with each serving.

YIELD: 4 servings

HOW TO COOK FRESH ASPARAGUS

Cut or break off each stalk as far down as it snaps easily. Remove scales with a knife. Then wash thoroughly, using a brush.

UPRIGHT METHOD

Tie 5 or 6 stalks of asparagus in a bundle with a string. Stand upright in the bottom part of a double boiler. Cover with the top part of the double boiler, inverted. Boil 15 to 20 minutes or until *just* crisp-tender. Lift out by catching tines of fork in string. Place on platter. Cut strings. The boiling water cooks the stalks while the rising steam cooks the tender heads. By this method the whole stalk is uniformly cooked.

SKILLET OR LARGE BOTTOM SAUCEPAN METHOD

Place asparagus in 2 layers in a 9- or 10-inch skillet or saucepan. Sprinkle with 1 teaspoon salt. Pour on boiling water to a depth of 1 inch. Bring to boiling point and cook, uncovered, 5 minutes. Cover. Boil 10 minutes or until the lower part of stalk is just crisp-tender. Lift out with a pancake turner, tongs, or 2 forks. Serve with butter, margarine, or one of the following sauces.

Browned Butter-Sesame Sauce*
Hollandaise Sauce*
Lemon Sauce*
Lemon Mayonnaise Sauce*
Mustard Cheese Sauce*
Sauce Supreme*
Vinaigrette Sauce*

YIELD: Allow 2½ pounds for 6 servings

ASPARAGUS AND PEAS, FRENCH STYLE

1½ pounds fresh asparagus
1 cup shelled fresh peas
½ inch boiling water
½ teaspoon salt
1/16 teaspoon ground black pepper
¼ teaspoon basil leaves
1 teaspoon chopped fresh parsley
1 tablespoon butter *or* margarine

Wash asparagus and cut the green tender portion into crosswise slices ¼ inch thick. Leave tips whole. Place in a saucepan with fresh peas and salt. Add boiling water to a depth of ½ inch. Bring to boiling point and boil 5 minutes uncovered. Cover and cook an additional 3 minutes or until tender. Drain, if necessary, and toss lightly with remaining ingredients. Serve hot.

YIELD: 6 servings

BAKED ASPARAGUS CHEESE PUDDING

1½ pounds fresh asparagus
3 slices bread
1 cup shredded, sharp
   American cheese

2 large eggs, lightly beaten
2 cups milk
1 teaspoon salt

½ teaspoon ground black pepper
½ teaspoon celery salt
¼ teaspoon garlic powder
1 tablespoon butter *or* margarine

Wash asparagus and cut 2-inch tips from 8 of the stalks. Wrap tips in foil and bake until tender while pudding is baking. Save to garnish the top. Cut remaining asparagus into 1-inch pieces. Cut bread into 1-inch squares and toast. Arrange alternate layers of toasted bread squares, asparagus, and cheese in a 10 x 6 x 2-inch baking dish. Combine remaining ingredients and pour into the casserole. Bake in a preheated slow oven (325° F.) 1 hour or until egg mixture is firm. Arrange baked asparagus tips over the top for garnish. Serve hot.

YIELD: 8 servings

ASPARAGUS AND SHRIMP

2 pounds fresh asparagus
½ inch boiling water
1 teaspoon salt
8 large peeled, deveined, uncooked
   shrimp
2 tablespoons salad *or* olive oil

1 teaspoon sugar
1½ to 2 teaspoons ground ginger
2 tablespoons soy sauce
2 tablespoons asparagus cooking water

Wash asparagus and cut or break off stalks as far down as they snap easily. Remove scales with a knife and wash thoroughly. Cut stalks into 1-inch pieces. Place in a saucepan with boiling water and ½ teaspoon of the salt. Cover. Bring to boiling point and boil 3 minutes.

Drain and save water to use later. Cut shrimp into ½-inch pieces and sauté in hot oil until they turn pink. Add asparagus, remaining salt, and rest of the ingredients. Cover and cook 10 minutes or

until shrimp are tender. Serve hot with rice, if desired.

YIELD: 4 servings

FRENCH FRIED ASPARAGUS

2 pounds fresh asparagus, cooked
1 large egg, lightly beaten
2 tablespoons water
½ cup fine, dry bread crumbs
1 teaspoon salt
¼ teaspoon ground black pepper
½ teaspoon paprika
½ cup grated Parmesan cheese

Drain freshly cooked asparagus and set aside. Combine egg and water and set aside. Mix remaining ingredients. Dip asparagus into bread crumb mixture, then in egg, and in crumbs again. Chill one hour so the crumbs will cling to asparagus while frying. Fry in deep fat heated to 375° F. 4 to 5 minutes or until brown. Drain on absorbent paper and serve hot, at once.

YIELD: 6 servings

ASPARAGUS, ORIENTAL STYLE

Don't overcook asparagus. Remember the comparative attributed to the Roman Emperor Augustus: "Quicker than you can cook asparagus."

2 pounds fresh asparagus
2 tablespoons salad oil, butter, *or* margarine
½ teaspoon salt
¼ teaspoon ground ginger
3 tablespoons water
1 teaspoon cornstarch
1 tablespoon soy sauce

Wash asparagus, remove scales from stalks, wash again, and drain well. Cut asparagus in very thin diagonal crosswise slices, leaving 1½-inch tips. Heat oil, butter, or margarine in a 9-inch skillet. Add asparagus, salt, ginger, and water.

Cover and cook 6 minutes over low heat until asparagus is crisp-tender. Blend cornstarch with soy sauce and add. Stir and cook, uncovered, 2 minutes or until sauce has slightly thickened.

YIELD: 6 servings

ASPARAGUS TIMBALES

Asparagus Timbales are ideal for a spring-time luncheon or Sunday brunch. As with all custardy things, bake at a low temperature.

13½ ounce jar asparagus spears, well drained
3 large eggs, well beaten
1¾ cups warm milk
½ teaspoon salt
¾ teaspoon onion salt
⅛ teaspoon ground white pepper
¼ teaspoon ground nutmeg
1 teaspoon fresh lemon juice

Broiled sausages
Curried Cream Sauce* (optional)

Butter four 6-ounce custard cups very well. Cut asparagus spears to fit around sides and bottoms of cups so that the tips meet in the bottom center. Save ends to use in salads. Combine the next 7 ingredients and mix well. Carefully pour custard mixture into cups so as not to disturb asparagus.

Place in a pan of hot water and bake in a preheated slow oven (325° F.) 1¼ hours or until a knife inserted into center comes out clean. Gently loosen custard from around sides and turn out on individual plates. Garnish with sausages and serve with Curried Cream Sauce, if desired.

YIELD: 4 servings

HOW TO COOK FRESH SNAP BEANS

Wash and remove tips from fresh snap beans. Leave whole, cut into 1-inch pieces, or French style (long strips). Place in a saucepan with ½ to 1 teaspoon salt and ½- to 1-inch boiling water. Bring to boiling point and cook, uncovered, 5 minutes. Cover and cook 10 to 12 minutes or only until beans are crisp-tender. Cook whole beans 2 to 3 minutes longer. Drain if necessary and add salt and black pepper to taste. Toss lightly with butter, margarine, or bacon fat, using 2 tablespoons to each one pound beans.

YIELD: Allow 1 pound beans for each 5 to 6 servings

CURRIED SNAP BEANS

The aromatic spice blend known as curry powder goes well with many vegetables. Add it to taste, or about 1 teaspoonful per pound of vegetable.

2 tablespoons butter *or* margarine
2 tablespoons minced onion
2 teaspoons curry powder
1½ pounds cooked, fresh snap beans *or* 2 packages cooked frozen snap beans
½ teaspoon salt

Heat butter or margarine in a heavy skillet. Add onions and cook only until limp. Blend in curry powder. Cook 2 to 3 minutes over low heat. Pour over cooked snap beans cooked with the ½ teaspoon salt. Serve hot.

YIELD: 6 servings

SNAP OR WAX BEANS, ITALIAN STYLE

Basil is one of the most delightful herbs for snap or wax beans. Use it, too, with such bland vegetables as zucchini and summer squash and new potatoes.

1½ pounds wax beans
¼ cup olive oil
1 clove garlic, crushed
1 tablespoon chopped onion
¾ cup diced green pepper
_____
¼ cup boiling water
1 teaspoon salt
1 teaspoon basil leaves
_____
½ cup grated Parmesan cheese
Green pepper rings

Wash beans and cut off tips. Leave whole or cut into 1-inch lengths. Heat oil and garlic in a saucepan. Add onion and green pepper and cook 2 to 3 minutes. Stir in beans and next 3 ingredients.

Cover and cook 15 minutes or until beans are tender. (Cooking time depends upon the age of beans.) Watch beans closely to avoid burning. Stir in ¼ cup of the cheese. Turn into a serving dish and sprinkle with remaining cheese. Garnish with green pepper rings. Serve hot.

YIELD: 8 servings

SNAP BEANS, ORIENTAL STYLE

¾ pound fresh snap beans
1 clove garlic
¼ teaspoon ground ginger
2 tablespoons butter *or* margarine
2 small white onions, peeled and sliced
1½ tablespoons soy sauce
___
¾ cup chicken stock
¾ teaspoon salt
1 cup slivered, cooked, leftover pork, ham, *or* chicken
⅛ teaspoon ground black pepper

Wash beans, remove tips, cut French style and set aside. Chop garlic fine, mix with ginger, and brown in 1 tablespoon of the butter or margarine. Separate onions into rings and add to garlic along with beans and soy sauce. Mix well. Stir in remaining ingredients.

Cover and cook over gentle heat 10 minutes or only until beans are crisp-tender. Turn into a serving dish. Dot with remaining tablespoon butter or margarine. Serve at once as the main dish.

YIELD: 5 servings

SOFRITO SNAP BEANS

In Puerto Rican cookery sofrito is the very basic sauce in which other foods are cooked. Snap beans, for instance, are delicious in a sauce that calls for bacon, ham, flavorful vegetables and spices. Use this same mixture with shredded cabbage, zucchini, broccoli, etc.

1 tablespoon instant minced onion
⅛ teaspoon instant minced garlic
1 tablespoon water
1 slice bacon, diced
2 tablespoons finely chopped ham
2 tablespoons finely chopped green peppers
2 tablespoons finely chopped tomatoes
1 pound fresh snap beans
___
1 tablespoon chopped olives
¼ teaspoon chopped capers
½ teaspoon oregano leaves
1 teaspoon salt
⅛ teaspoon ground black pepper
¼ cup water

Soften instant minced onion and garlic in the 1 tablespoon water. Fry bacon and ham together until bacon is crisp. Then add softened minced onion and garlic, green pepper and tomato. Stir and cook over low heat 5 minutes. In the meantime, wash beans, cut off tips and cut French style. Add to the fried mixture along with remaining ingredients. Cover and cook over low heat 15 minutes or until beans are tender.

YIELD: 6 servings

SNAP BEANS WITH NUTMEG BUTTER

3 tablespoons butter *or* margarine
¼ teaspoon ground nutmeg
⅛ teaspoon ground black pepper
1 pound fresh snap beans *or* 2 packages (10 ounces each) frozen snap beans, cooked

⅛ teaspoon ground black pepper
½ teaspoon salt (or to taste)
Pimiento strips

Cook beans as directed on package, until not quite done. Drain. Heat oil in a skillet. Add garlic powder and beans. Sauté 2 to 3 minutes. Add the next 4 ingredients. Cook only until hot. Serve hot garnished with pimiento strips.

YIELD: 6 servings

Melt butter or margarine. Add nutmeg and black pepper. Pour over cooked snap beans. Mix lightly. Serve hot.

YIELD: 6 servings

SNAP BEANS WITH POPPY SEED BUTTER

1 tablespoon poppy seed
2 tablespoons butter *or* margarine

1 tablespoon fresh lemon juice
⅛ teaspoon ground black pepper
½ teaspoon sugar
¼ teaspoon salt

1 pound snap beans, cooked

Cook poppy seed with butter or margarine until butter is golden. Add next 4 ingredients and pour over hot cooked beans. Mix lightly. Serve hot.

YIELD: 6 servings

BEANS WITH TOMATOES, SPANISH STYLE

2 packages (10 ounces each) frozen
    whole snap beans
1 tablespoon olive oil
¼₆ teaspoon garlic powder

3 tablespoons Spanish-style
    tomato sauce
1 teaspoon paprika

ITALIAN BEANS AND RICE

1 cup dried navy *or* pea beans
3 cups water
3 tablespoons onion flakes
¼ teaspoon instant minced garlic
2 tablespoons water
1 tablespoon finely chopped salt pork
2 tablespoons butter *or* margarine
2 tablespoons olive *or* salad oil

1 cup canned tomatoes
2 teaspoons salt
1 tablespoon sugar
1 teaspoon sage leaves

2 cups long-grain rice
4 cups beef *or* chicken broth
1 tablespoon parsley flakes
3 tablespoons grated Parmesan cheese

Wash beans and soak overnight in the 3 cups water. Soften onion flakes and garlic in the 2 tablespoons water. Sauté softened onions and garlic until lightly browned in salt pork and half the butter or margarine and oil in a 4-quart saucepan.

Add the soaked beans, along with next 4 ingredients. Cover and simmer 1 hour. Wash rice and add along with broth. Cover and simmer 30 minutes or until rice is tender and has absorbed most of the broth. Add remaining butter, parsley flakes, and cheese. Mix lightly and serve hot.

YIELD: 10 servings

BEAN AND TOMATO AU GRATIN

2 cups (1 pound) dried navy beans
5 cups boiling water
1½ cups grated sharp Cheddar cheese

1 can (6 ounces) tomato paste
½ cup chopped onion
⅓ cup unsulphured molasses
4 teaspoons salt
1 teaspoon powdered mustard
¼ teaspoon ground black pepper

4 strips bacon

Wash beans. Add boiling water and boil 2 minutes in a covered saucepan. Remove from heat and soak 1 hour. Cook, covered, 1 hour or until beans are tender. Drain off water and reserve 1 cup, adding more water if necessary. Pour half the beans into a 2-quart casserole. Sprinkle with half the cheese. Add remaining beans.

Mix the reserved 1 cup bean liquid with next 6 ingredients and pour over beans. Top with remaining cheese. Cover and bake in a preheated slow oven (325° F.) 2 hours. Remove cover and arrange bacon strips over the top. Bake, uncovered, 20 minutes or until bacon is crisp and beans are brown.

YIELD: 8 to 10 servings

BARBECUED BAKED BEANS

2 cups (1 pound) dried navy *or* pea beans
6 cups tomato juice
¼ pound salt pork

¼ cup light-brown sugar
1 teaspoon chili powder
1 teaspoon powdered mustard
½ teaspoon ground black pepper
1 tablespoon Worcestershire sauce
¾ cup chopped onion

3 teaspoons salt
1 tablespoon cider vinegar

Wash beans and soak overnight in 5 cups of the tomato juice. Cover and cook over low heat 1½ hours or until beans are tender (DO NOT BOIL). Turn beans into a 2-quart bean pot. Wash and score pork (cut in slashes ½ inch apart just to the rind) and press into top of beans.

Mix remaining 1 cup tomato juice with next 6 ingredients. Pour over beans. Cover and cook in a preheated slow oven (300° F.) 2 hours. Remove cover and stir in salt and vinegar. Lift pork to top of beans. Bake, uncovered, 30 to 40 minutes or until beans are brown.

YIELD: 10 servings

BAKED BEANS WITH SPARERIBS

2 cups (1 pound) dried beans (any kind)
5 cups boiling water
2 pounds spareribs

½ cup chopped onion
¼ cup unsulphured molasses
1 tablespoon Worcestershire sauce
1 teaspoon powdered mustard
¼ teaspoon instant minced garlic

4 teaspoons salt
¼ teaspoon ground black pepper

Wash beans. Add boiling water and boil 2 minutes in a covered saucepan. Remove from heat and soak 1 hour. Cut spareribs in serving-size pieces, add to beans, cover and cook 1 hour or until beans are tender. Drain off water and reserve 1 cup, adding more water to make 1 cup if necessary.

Turn beans and spareribs into a 2-quart casserole. Combine the reserved 1 cup liquid with the next 5 ingredients and pour over beans. Cover and bake in a preheated slow oven (325° F.) 1½ hours. Remove cover and stir in salt and black pepper. Bake, uncovered, 1 hour longer or until beans have browned.

YIELD: 10 servings

SPICED BAKED BEANS

When humorist Don Marquis promised, "There will be no beans in the Almost Perfect State," he can't have meant beans seasoned as well as these.

2 cups (1 pound) dried navy *or* pea beans
5 cups water
3 teaspoons salt

⅓ cup onion flakes
¼ teaspoon instant minced garlic
¼ teaspoon ground ginger
½ teaspoon ground cinnamon
¾ teaspoon ground black pepper
1 teaspoon powdered mustard
¼ cup unsulphured molasses
¼ cup catsup

¼ pound salt pork

Wash beans. Add water, cover, bring to boiling point, and boil 2 minutes. Remove from heat and let stand 1 hour. (This takes the place of long soaking in cold water.) Add salt and cook 1 hour or until beans are barely tender. Drain off water, measure, and add additional water to make 3 cups. Mix with the next 8 ingredients.

Cut pork in half; score each piece and place one half in bottom of a 2-quart bean pot. Add beans and top with remaining pork. Add seasoned liquid. Cover and bake 2 hours in a preheated slow oven (325° F.). Remove cover and bake 30 minutes, or until beans are browned.

"OLD-FASHIONED" BAKED BEANS

Proceed as for Spiced Baked Beans, but simmer beans until about half done (when skins break). Bake in a slow oven (300° F.) 6 to 8 hours.

YIELD: 6 to 8 servings

BAKED KIDNEY BEANS, ENGLISH STYLE

2 cans (20 ounces each) red kidney beans, drained
1 teaspoon salt
¾ teaspoon powdered mustard
¼ teaspoon ground black pepper
½ teaspoon onion powder
½ cup diced green pepper

3-ounce package Snappy cheese
¼ cup tomato juice
6 strips bacon

Cook the first 6 ingredients together 5 minutes. Cut cheese into ½-inch pieces and add to beans along with tomato juice. Turn into a 10 x 6 x 2-inch baking dish. Fry bacon until about half done and arrange over beans.

Place under broiler, 4 inches from the source of heat, 4 to 5 minutes, or until browned. Serve a strip of bacon with each serving.

YIELD: 6 servings

MUSTARD BAKED LIMA BEANS

2 cups dried lima beans
5 cups cold water

4 teaspoons salt
3 tablespoons light-brown sugar
¼ cup chopped onion
1½ teaspoons powdered mustard
¼ teaspoon ground black pepper
1 cup canned tomatoes

4 strips bacon

Wash beans. Add water and soak overnight or about 12 hours. Cover and cook slowly, in same water in which beans were soaked, 1 hour or until beans are tender. Drain. Save 2 cups bean liquid, adding more water if necessary to make 2 cups and mix with next 6 ingredients.

Pour beans and liquid mixture into a 2-quart bean pot or casserole. Cover. Bake in a preheated slow oven (325° F.) 2 hours. Remove cover and place bacon strips over the top. Bake, uncovered, 30 minutes or until bacon is crisp.

YIELD: 8 servings

PICKLED NAVY BEANS

1 pound (2 cups) dried navy beans
7 cups water
½ cup onion flakes
½ teaspoon instant minced garlic
⅓ cup water
½ cup olive oil

¼ cup cider vinegar
8 whole black peppers
1 bay leaf
1 tablespoon salt

Wash beans, changing water 3 to 4 times. Place in a saucepan with water. Bring to a full boil and boil 2 minutes. Remove from heat. Let stand 1 hour. Do not drain. Cover and cook 2 hours or until beans are tender. Drain and cool. Turn into a bowl.

Soften onion flakes and instant minced

garlic in water. Cook in hot olive oil 1 minute. Add remaining ingredients. Pour over beans. Let stand overnight or several hours before serving.

YIELD: 8 to 10 servings

SPICED BEETS AND EGGS

2 cans (1 pound each) sliced beets

1¼ cups cider vinegar
3 tablespoons sugar
1 teaspoon salt
¼ teaspoon ground black pepper

1 tablespoon mixed pickling spice
3 large hard-cooked eggs

Drain beets and place in mixing bowl. Heat together for 5 minutes the next 4 ingredients and pickling spice (tied in a cheesecloth bag). Remove bag and pour mixture over beets. Add whole hardcooked eggs. Refrigerate for several hours, turning eggs occasionally to color uniformly. Slice eggs just before serving.

YIELD: 6 servings

HERBED FRESH BEETS

2 pounds (about 12) fresh beets
1 teaspoon salt
Boiling water to cover
3 tablespoons butter *or* margarine
2 teaspoons fresh lemon juice
½ teaspoon salt
⅛ teaspoon ground black pepper
½ teaspoon crumbled marjoram leaves
Onion rings

Cut off tops of beets, leaving 1 inch of stem attached. Do not cut root ends. Wash thoroughly. Place in a saucepan with 1 teaspoon salt and boiling water to cover. Cover and cook 25 to 35 minutes until beets are tender. (Cooking time depends upon size and age of beets.) Meanwhile, melt butter or margarine and blend in lemon juice and seasonings. Peel and slice beets. Add lemon butter and mix lightly. Garnish with onion rings.

YIELD: 6 servings

BEET PANCAKES

1 cup finely chopped cooked fresh
  beets
2 tablespoons cornstarch
4 large egg yolks, beaten
3 tablespoons heavy cream *or* undiluted
  evaporated milk
½ teaspoon sugar
1 teaspoon salt
½ teaspoon ground nutmeg

Combine all ingredients in a mixing bowl. Mix well and bake in pancake fashion on a hot buttered griddle or heavy skillet. Serve with fruit marmalade or preserves.

YIELD: 12 pancakes

HOW TO COOK FRESH BROCCOLI

Broccoli is a strong-flavored green vegetable which develops an even stronger flavor (as well as a brown color) if over-cooked. This is due to the action of acids and heat on certain of the flavoring materials and pigments.

Wash broccoli and trim off bits of stem end if they are tough. Do not remove the stem since the whole stalk is edible. Make lengthwise gashes in the stems, almost to the flowerets, if they are more than ½ inch in diameter, or cut through the flowerets, making two pieces.

SAUCEPAN METHOD

Place broccoli, loose, in a saucepan with 1 inch boiling water and ½ teaspoon salt. Cook, uncovered, 5 minutes after boiling point is reached. Cover and cook 10 to 15 minutes or only until crisp-tender. Or if desired, leave cover on during the entire cooking period, but lift cover 3 to 4 times to permit gases to escape with the steam. Cook only until crisp-tender.

UPRIGHT METHOD

Tie broccoli in bunches. Stand upright in the bottom part of a double boiler, containing about 2 inches boiling water and 1 teaspoon salt. Bring to boiling point. Cover with the inverted top of the double boiler and cook 15 to 20 minutes. Since the top of the double boiler does not fit tightly, a little longer cooking time is required.

Serve broccoli with any of the following sauces:

Béchamel Sauce*
Browned Butter-Sesame Sauce*
Béarnaise Sauce*
Curry Mayonnaise*
Hollandaise*
Herbed Caper Butter*
Italian Tomato Sauce*
Mustard-Cheese Sauce*
Vinaigrette Sauce*

YIELD: Allow 2 pounds broccoli for 6
    servings

FRESH BROCCOLI ON TOAST WITH EGG SAUCE

1½ pounds (1 bunch) fresh tender broccoli
1 cup boiling chicken broth *or* 1 cup boiling water and 1 chicken bouillon cube
6 slices toast
2 cups Medium White Sauce*
2 large hard-cooked eggs
2 teaspoons Toasted Sesame Seed* (optional)

Wash broccoli and trim off the tough portion of the stems. Place in a saucepan with boiling chicken broth. Cover. Bring to boiling point and boil 15 minutes or only until crisp-tender, lifting the cover 2 or 3 times to retain the bright green color of the broccoli and to give milder flavor. Drain. Place on toast.

Combine White Sauce with one chopped, hard-cooked egg. Spoon over broccoli. Sprinkle with Toasted Sesame Seed, if desired. Slice the remaining hard-cooked egg and place a slice on each serving.

YIELD: 6 servings

FRENCH FRIED BRUSSELS SPROUTS

1 quart Brussels sprouts
1 inch boiling water
1 teaspoon salt
About ½ cup fine, dry bread crumbs
½ teaspoon salt
⅛ teaspoon ground nutmeg
¼ teaspoon ground black pepper
1 large egg, beaten
1 tablespoon milk *or* water
Shortening *or* oil for frying
Seasoned salt

Wash and trim Brussels sprouts. Soak 20 minutes in 1 quart cold water and 1 tea-spoon salt. Drain. Place in a saucepan with 1 inch boiling water and ½ teaspoon salt. Bring to boiling point and cook, uncovered, 5 minutes. Drain.

Mix bread crumbs with remaining ½ teaspoon salt, nutmeg, and black pepper into which roll Brussels sprouts. Then dip in egg beaten with milk or water and roll in bread crumbs again.

Fry until browned on all sides in ¾ inch hot fat. Drain on paper towels and sprinkle with seasoned salt. Serve hot as a vegetable or as a hot hors d'oeuvre.

YIELD: 5 servings

HERBED CREAMED BRUSSELS SPROUTS

2 (10-ounce) packages frozen Brussels sprouts
3 tablespoons butter *or* margarine
3 tablespoons flour
1½ cups milk
½ teaspoon salt
⅛ teaspoon ground black pepper
¼ teaspoon ground marjoram
¼ teaspoon ground thyme
Parsley

Cook Brussels sprouts according to directions on the package. Drain. In the meantime, melt butter or margarine in a

saucepan. Blend in flour. Remove from heat. Gradually stir in milk. Add remaining ingredients. Return to heat. Stir and cook until of medium thickness. Pour over drained, cooked Brussels sprouts. Garnish with parsley.

YIELD: 6 to 8 servings

COOKED CABBAGE, AUSTRIAN STYLE

A cabbage-eater will stop at nothing when he gets a yen for this venerable vegetable. There's a legend about this: One Christmas Eve, in Germany, a peasant was seized with a longing for cabbage. Having none himself, he slipped into his neighbor's garden to cut some. Just as he finished filling his basket, the Christ Child rode past on his white horse and said, "Because thou hast stolen on the holy night, thou shalt immediately sit in the moon with thy basket of cabbage." The culprit was promptly wooshed up to the moon, where he sits to this day.

Here's a good and simple way to cook that cabbage, no matter how you've come by it.

9 cups shredded cabbage
¼ cup bacon fat
2 teaspoons salt

2 teaspoons paprika
2 tablespoons finely chopped onion
1 cup sour cream

Sauté cabbage in bacon fat 5 minutes. Add salt, paprika, and onion. Turn into a 1-quart baking dish and pour sour cream over the top. Bake in a preheated moderate oven (350° F.) 30 minutes. Serve hot.

YIELD: 4 to 6 servings

STUFFED CABBAGE LEAVES, HUNGARIAN STYLE

12 large cabbage leaves
Boiling water to cover
1 teaspoon salt
12-ounce can luncheon meat *or* 2 cups ground, cooked ham
3 slices bread
_____
1 large egg, beaten
⅔ cup finely chopped onion
2 teaspoons paprika
¾ teaspoon salt
¼ teaspoon ground black pepper
⅛ teaspoon ground dill seed
_____
1 tablespoon bacon fat *or* shortening
⅓ cup water
1 teaspoon flour
1 tablespoon water
½ cup sour cream
Salt to taste
¹⁄₁₆ teaspoon ground black pepper

Wash and cut off about 1 inch from the base of cabbage leaves. Place cabbage in a saucepan with boiling water to cover and the 1 teaspoon salt. Cover and cook 3 minutes or until leaves have wilted. Remove cabbage from water and drain. Set aside. Put luncheon meat through the food chopper, using the medium blade.

Dip bread in water, squeeze dry, and add to meat. Blend in next 6 ingredients.

Lay cabbage leaves flat and place a tablespoon of the mixture in the center of each. Fold leaves over stuffing and fasten ends with toothpicks. Heat bacon fat or shortening in a 9-inch skillet. Add cabbage rolls and brown on all sides. Add the ⅓ cup water. Cover and simmer 20 minutes.

Remove rolls to serving dish. Mix flour with the tablespoon water and add. Cook ½ minute. Add sour cream and heat, but DO NOT BOIL. Season with salt to taste and the 1/16 teaspoon ground black pepper. Serve with sauce spooned over cabbage rolls.

YIELD: 6 servings

TUNA-STUFFED CABBAGE LEAVES

6 large cabbage leaves
Boiling water to cover
½ teaspoon salt
2 cans (6 ounces each) tuna fish

1½ cups soft bread crumbs
3 tablespoons finely chopped onion
1 teaspoon salt
¼ teaspoon ground thyme
¼ teaspoon ground black pepper
¼ cup (½ stick) butter *or* margarine, melted
2 tablespoons cabbage stock

½ cup finely chopped celery
½ cup finely shredded carrots
½ cup diced fresh tomato
⅓ cup finely chopped onion
¼ cup finely chopped green pepper
1 teaspoon salt
1 cup water

Wash and cut off about 1 inch from the base of the cabbage leaves. Place cabbage in a saucepan with boiling water to cover and the ½ teaspoon salt. Cover and cook 3 minutes or until leaves have wilted. Remove cabbage from water and drain. Set aside. Flake tuna fish and mix with the next 7 ingredients. Lay cabbage leaves flat and top each with an equal amount of the mixture, using it all. Fold leaves over the stuffing and fasten ends with toothpicks.

Place in a shallow baking dish. In the meantime, combine remaining ingredients in a saucepan. Bring to boiling point and cook 2 minutes. Pour over stuffed cabbage leaves. Cover and bake in a preheated moderate oven (350° F.) 30 to 40 minutes, basting with the sauce 3 times. Serve with sauce spooned over each.

YIELD: 6 servings

CABBAGE PIE

"When we can't think of anything else to eat, we have cabbage pie," said the Fort Valley, Georgia, woman who gave us this recipe. Oddly enough, it ends up tasting not unlike oysters!

7 cups medium-shredded cabbage
16 soda crackers
2 cups milk
¼ cup (½ stick) butter *or* margarine
2 teaspoons salt
½ teaspoon ground black pepper
½ teaspoon celery seed

Fill a 1½-quart casserole with alternating layers of cabbage and coarsely crumbled soda crackers, having 3 layers of each with cabbage as bottom layer and crackers as the top layer. Heat milk with remaining ingredients and pour over cabbage. Bake in a preheated moderate oven (350° F.) 40 minutes or until lightly browned over the top.

YIELD: 6 to 8 servings

HOT COLE SLAW

1 medium-size head cabbage
Boiling water
2 teaspoons salt
¼ teaspoon ground black pepper
1 teaspoon dill seed
½ teaspoon sugar
½ cup sour cream
2 tablespoons wine vinegar

Shred cabbage and immerse in boiling water to cover for 1 minute. Drain well. Remove to another bowl. Combine remaining ingredients and add to cabbage. Toss and serve.

YIELD: 6 servings

RED CABBAGE, DUTCH STYLE

½ cup chopped onion
2 tablespoons butter *or* margarine
3 cups shredded red cabbage
1 cup diced apples
3 whole cloves
1¼ teaspoons salt
⅛ teaspoon ground black pepper
1 teaspoon wine vinegar
¼ cup stock

Sauté onion in butter or margarine until limp and transparent. Add remaining ingredients. Cover and cook 10 minutes.

YIELD: 4 servings

CARROT, SWEET POTATO, AND APPLE TZIMMES

While there are numerous varieties of Tzimmes—depending on the national origin of the cook—this vegetable and dried fruit mixture, with or without meat is a Jewish holiday favorite. No Rosh Hashonah menu would be complete without it, for the golden color and rich sweetness wish all the guests a sweet and blessed New Year. Make it the day before since the flavor improves upon standing.

5 medium-size fresh carrots
3 medium (about 1 pound) sweet potatoes
1 teaspoon salt
1 inch boiling water
———
½ teaspoon salt
¼ teaspoon ground ginger
⅛ teaspoon ground black pepper
———
3 tart cooking apples
⅓ cup strained honey
2 tablespoons chicken fat

Wash, peel, and slice carrots and sweet potatoes. Place in a saucepan with the 1 teaspoon salt and 1 inch boiling water. Cover and cook 25 minutes or until vegetables are tender. Remove from heat and drain if necessary. Mash until fluffy and free from lumps. Add the next 3 ingredients.

In the meantime, pare and slice apples thinly. Grease a 1-quart casserole with chicken fat and fill with alternate layers of mashed carrot, potatoes, and sliced apples, having the vegetable mixture as bottom and top layers.

Dribble honey and chicken fat over each layer. Bake in a preheated moderate oven (350° F.) 45 minutes or until top begins to brown. Remove from oven. This dish is very tasty when freshly baked. However, it is even better the second day.

YIELD: 6 servings

CURRIED CARROTS WITH PINEAPPLE

3 cups coarsely shredded fresh carrots
1½ cups firm, fresh pineapple wedges
3 tablespoons light-brown sugar
3 tablespoons butter *or* margarine
3 tablespoons hot water
¼ teaspoon salt (or to taste)
½ teaspoon curry powder (or to taste)

Combine all ingredients in a 1-quart saucepan. Cover and cook 5 to 7 minutes or until pineapple and carrots are tender. Serve hot with pork, duck, chicken, or turkey.

YIELD: 6 servings

DEVILED FRESH CARROTS

12 young tender carrots
½ cup (1 stick) butter *or* margarine

2 tablespoons light-brown sugar
¾ teaspoon salt
1 teaspoon powdered mustard
⅛ teaspoon ground black pepper
Dash cayenne

Wash carrots, peel and cut each in lengthwise halves. Sauté in butter or margarine 5 minutes. Add remaining ingredients. Cover and cook 10 minutes or until carrots are tender. Serve hot.

YIELD: 6 servings

GINGERED CARROTS

1 pound fresh carrots
2 teaspoons fresh lemon juice
¾ teaspoon salt
½ teaspoon ground ginger
¹⁄₁₆ teaspoon ground black pepper
2 tablespoons butter *or* margarine

Pare carrots and cut into crosswise pieces ½ inch thick. Place in a buttered 1-quart baking dish. Combine lemon juice and seasonings and sprinkle over carrots. Dot with butter or margarine. Cover. Bake in a preheated hot oven (400° F.) 30 minutes or until tender.

YIELD: 5 servings

LYONNAISE CARROTS

"The Carrot," wrote sixteenth-century herbalist, J. Gerarde, "serveth for love matters; and Orpheus, as Pliny writeth, said that the use thereof winneth love...." If nothing more, a dish of Carrots Lyonnaise may get you a pat on the head and a few kind words.

2 tablespoons butter *or* margarine
¼ cup chopped onion
3 cups very thinly sliced fresh carrots
¼ teaspoon crumbled thyme leaves
1 teaspoon sugar
¼ teaspoon salt
Dash ground black pepper

Melt butter or margarine in saucepan. Add remaining ingredients. Cover. Simmer 5 to 8 minutes or until carrots are tender, turning occasionally. Serve hot.

YIELD: 4 servings

MAPLE-FLAVORED CARROTS

Carrots are such a marvelous source of Vitamin A that they should be served regularly. Here is one good way to prepare them.

18 small, young, tender carrots
1 inch boiling water
½ teaspoon salt
1 teaspoon sugar
¼ cup maple-flavored syrup
¼ cup (½ stick) butter *or* margarine
1 teaspoon powdered mustard
⅛ teaspoon ground white pepper

Wash carrots and peel. Place in a saucepan with 1 inch boiling water, salt, and sugar. Cover and cook 10 minutes or until crisp-tender. Remove carrots to a dish and keep warm.

Cook the carrot water until it is reduced to about ½ cup. Add maple-flavored syrup, butter or margarine, and mustard. Cook until a heavy syrup is formed, about 7 minutes. Add white pepper and carrots. Cook until carrots are glazed. Serve hot.

YIELD: 6 servings

CARROTS VINAIGRETTE

12 medium-size fresh carrots
1 inch boiling water
2 teaspoons salt
3 whole allspice
Vinaigrette Salad Dressing*

Wash, pare, and cut carrots into lengthwise quarters. Cut each quarter in half, crosswise. Place carrots, boiling water, salt, and allspice in a saucepan. Cover and cook 10 minutes or until crisp-tender. Drain well. Add Vinaigrette Salad Dressing to cover carrots. Cover and refrigerate about 1 hour. Serve as a cold vegetable.

YIELD: 6 servings

CARROTS WITH CARAWAY SEED

14 small, young carrots
1 inch boiling water
1 teaspoon salt
1 tablespoon butter *or* margarine
1 tablespoon flour
1 teaspoon caraway seed
1/16 teaspoon ground black pepper
1 tablespoon chopped parsley

Wash, scrape, and dice carrots. Place carrots, water, and salt in a saucepan. Cover, bring to boiling point, and cook 10 minutes or until carrots are crisp-tender. Drain water into measuring cup and save. Melt butter or margarine in a saucepan. Blend in flour and caraway seed. Stir and cook until lightly browned. Remove from heat and gradually stir in carrot water, adding more water to make 1 cup if necessary. Cook until slightly thickened. Stir in carrots, black pepper, and parsley. Serve at once.

YIELD: 6 servings

CARROTS NEWBURG

An unusual vegetable dish that teams well with chicken, seafood, or a main-dish soufflé. The ginger accents the flavor.

4 cups diced, fresh carrots
1 inch boiling water
1 teaspoon salt
½ teaspoon sugar

2 tablespoons butter *or* margarine

2 tablespoons flour
¼ teaspoon ground ginger
⅛ teaspoon ground black pepper
¼ teaspoon salt

¾ cup chicken stock
¼ cup heavy cream
½ teaspoon chopped parsley
¾ teaspoon minced onion
2 teaspoons minced green pepper

Place the first 4 ingredients in a saucepan. Cover, bring to boiling point, and cook 10 to 12 minutes or only until carrots are crisp-tender. Melt butter or margarine in a saucepan. Blend in next 4 ingredients. Stir and cook only until bubbly. Remove from heat and stir in remaining ingredients. Cook 5 minutes or until of medium thickness, stirring constantly. Add carrots. Serve hot.

YIELD: 6 servings

CAULIFLOWER AND TUNA CASSEROLE

4 cups sliced, fresh cauliflower
½ cup boiling water
1 teaspoon salt
2 tablespoons butter *or* margarine
2 tablespoons flour
1⅓ cups milk

⅛ teaspoon garlic powder
⅛ teaspoon thyme leaves
⅛ teaspoon ground black pepper
7-ounce can tuna fish, drained

1 tablespoon butter *or* margarine, melted
½ cup soft bread crumbs

Place cauliflower, water, and salt in a saucepan. Bring to boiling point, uncovered, and cook 5 minutes. Cover and cook 3 minutes or until partly done. Drain and set aside. Melt butter or margarine

in a saucepan. Blend in flour. Stir and cook until bubbly. Remove from heat and add milk. Stir and cook over moderate heat until of medium thickness.

Remove from heat and add the next 4 ingredients. Arrange cauliflower and tuna fish mixture in alternate layers in a buttered 1-quart casserole. Combine butter or margarine and bread crumbs and sprinkle over the top. Bake in a preheated moderate oven (350° F.) 35 minutes or until golden brown.

CAULIFLOWER AND HAM CASSEROLE

Omit tuna fish in the above recipe and add 2 cups diced, cooked ham or a 12-ounce can luncheon meat, diced.

YIELD: 6 servings

FRESH CAULIFLOWER WITH CAPER-CHEESE SAUCE

"Don't cook 'til you see the whites of their eyes!" should be the motto of the homemaker when preparing cauliflower for family and guests. It should be cooked just before serving, and then only long enough for it to become crisp-tender. Overcooking spoils both the flavor and texture of this attractive vegetable.

1 large head cauliflower
1 teaspoon salt
Boiling water
3 tablespoons butter *or* margarine
3 tablespoons flour
1½ cups milk *or* milk and vegetable
  stock
_____
1 teaspoon salt
⅛ teaspoon ground black pepper
½ teaspoon powdered mustard
_____
1 cup shredded sharp Cheddar cheese
2 tablespoons capers

Wash cauliflower and remove outer leaves, leaving tender inner leaves attached. Place whole cauliflower head in a saucepan with 1 teaspoon salt and boiling water to cover. Bring to boiling point and cook, uncovered, 5 minutes. Cover and cook 20 minutes or until cauliflower is crisp-tender, turning head once to cook uniformly. Melt butter or margarine in a saucepan. Blend in flour. Stir and cook until bubbly.

Remove from heat and add milk and next 3 ingredients. Stir and cook until sauce is of medium thickness. Remove from heat and add cheese and capers. Place cauliflower head in a serving dish. Pour some of the sauce over the top, letting it dribble down the sides. Serve remaining sauce in a separate bowl.

YIELD: 6 servings

CURRIED CELERY

2 cups sliced celery
½ teaspoon salt
½ inch boiling water
_____
1 medium-size baking apple
⅓ cup sliced onion
1½ tablespoons butter *or* margarine
1 tablespoon flour
1 teaspoon curry powder
½ teaspoon salt
⅛ teaspoon ground black pepper

Place the first 3 ingredients in a saucepan. Cover, bring to boiling point, and cook 5 minutes or until celery is crisp-tender. Sauté apples and onions in butter or margarine. Push apples and onions to one side of the skillet and stir in flour and curry powder. Cook ½ minute or until bubbly.

Drain celery, if necessary, and add. Blend with apples, onions, and curry butter, being careful not to break apples. Cook slowly 2 minutes. Add salt and black pepper. Serve hot as a vegetable with poultry, pork, or lamb.

YIELD: 5 servings

INDIAN CHICK PEAS

½ cup onion flakes
⅓ cup water
¼ cup (½ stick) butter *or* margarine
1 teaspoon ground cumin seed
¼ teaspoon ground red pepper
2 teaspoons salt
2½ cups (about 2 medium) diced,
  fresh tomatoes
2 cans (1 pound each) chick peas
2 tablespoons flaked coconut
4 teaspoons fresh lemon juice

Soften onion in water. Sauté in butter or margarine until onions begin to brown. Add spices and cook 2 minutes. Stir in salt and tomatoes. Cook 2 minutes. Add peas and cook 5 minutes. Add lemon juice and coconut just before serving.

YIELD: 6 servings

HERBED COLLARD GREENS

2 pounds fresh collard (turnip *or*
  mustard) greens
3 slices salt pork, cut ½ inch thick
½ cup boiling water
¼ teaspoon salt
⅛ teaspoon ground black pepper
½ teaspoon oregano leaves

Wash young greens carefully 4 or 5 times. Cut off root ends and coarse stems. Place in a saucepan. Brown salt pork in a skillet and add to collards. Pour in boiling water. (Omit water if greens are very young.) Add salt, black pepper, and oregano. Cover and cook until collards are tender, 20 to 30 minutes. (The cooking time will be less if the collard greens are very young.) Chop greens 2 or 3 times before eating. Serve at once.

YIELD: About 6 servings

COLLARD GREENS, ITALIAN STYLE

2 pounds fresh collard greens
1 cup diced, fresh tomatoes *or* tomato juice
3 tablespoons olive *or* salad oil
1 whole medium-size onion
¾ teaspoon salt
⅛ teaspoon ground black pepper
¼ teaspoon ground marjoram
¼ cup grated Parmesan cheese

Wash collard greens thoroughly and cut off tough ends. Heat tomatoes in olive or salad oil in a saucepan large enough for cooking collards. Add onion and collard greens. Cover and cook slowly 10 minutes. Remove and discard onion. Add salt. Cover and cook 20 minutes or until collards are tender. Add black pepper and marjoram 5 minutes before cooking time is up. Mix well and serve hot, sprinkled with grated Parmesan cheese.

YIELD: 6 servings

SPICED COLLARD GREENS

2 pounds fresh collard greens
¼ pound salt pork
½ cup boiling water

½ teaspoon mixed pickling spice
1 teaspoon sugar
1¾ teaspoons salt

¼ teaspoon ground black pepper
1 tablespoon chopped onion

Wash collard greens in water 4 or 5 times and slice coarsely. Set aside. Cut pork into slices ⅛ inch thick. Fry until about half done in saucepan large enough for cooking collards. Add hot water and collards. Cover and cook 35 minutes or until collards are tender. Tie spice in a cheesecloth bag and add along with remaining ingredients, 10 minutes before cooking time is up. Remove spice bag. Serve collards hot, each serving topped with a small piece of the salt pork.

YIELD: 6 to 8 servings

CORN AND ZUCCHINI SQUASH

Latin Americans love corn, tomatoes, and zucchini seasoned with a little ground cumin. A good accompaniment for chicken.

2 tablespoons bacon fat
2 cups corn, cut from the cob
2 cups diced, fresh tomatoes
2 cups sliced zucchini squash
1½ teaspoons salt
½ teaspoon sugar
½ teaspoon ground cumin seed
⅛ teaspoon ground black pepper

Heat bacon fat in a 9- or 10-inch skillet or saucepan. Add vegetables and seasonings. Cover and cook 10 minutes or until vegetables are tender. Serve hot.

YIELD: 6 to 8 servings

CORN PUDDING

2 cups corn, cut from the cob
2 teaspoons sugar
¼ teaspoon ground nutmeg
1½ teaspoons salt
⅛ teaspoon ground black pepper

3 large eggs, lightly beaten
2 tablespoons butter *or* margarine
2 cups milk

Combine the first 5 ingredients in a mixing bowl. Add eggs and mix well. Add butter or margarine to milk and heat only until butter is melted. Blend with the corn and egg mixture. Turn into a buttered 1-quart casserole. Place in a pan of hot water. Bake in a preheated slow oven (325° F.) 1 hour or until a knife inserted in the center comes out clean.

YIELD: 6 servings

CORN RAREBIT WITH BACON

2 ears fresh corn
3 tablespoons bacon fat

3 tablespoons flour
¾ teaspoon salt (or to taste)
¼ teaspoon powdered mustard
⅛ teaspoon ground black pepper

1 cup thin cream *or* top milk
½ cup shredded sharp Cheddar cheese
6 slices toast
12 slices crisp bacon

Remove husks and silks from corn. Split kernels lengthwise with a sharp knife. Cut

a thin layer of corn from the cob. Repeat, cutting 2 more layers. Then scrape cob with bowl of a tablespoon to extract all the milk. (The spoon prevents corn from spattering.) There should be 1½ cups.

Place bacon fat in a saucepan. Blend in next 4 ingredients. Add cream or top milk and corn. Stir and cook 4 minutes or until of medium thickness. Add cheese. Heat only until cheese is melted. Serve on toast, topped with crisp bacon for lunch or supper.

YIELD: 6 servings

CORN, SOUTHWESTERN STYLE

½ clove garlic, crushed
½ cup sliced onions
½ cup chopped green pepper
¼ cup (½ stick) butter *or* margarine
3 cups corn, cut from the cob
1 cup diced fresh tomatoes
½ cup boiling water
2 teaspoons salt
1 teaspoon chili powder
⅛ teaspoon ground black pepper

Sauté garlic, onions, and green pepper in butter or margarine for 5 minutes or until onions are limp and transparent. Add remaining ingredients and cook, covered, 8 to 10 minutes or until vegetables are tender, stirring occasionally. Serve at once.

YIELD: 6 servings

DILLY CUCUMBER PUDDING

This dish is especially good with fish.

3 large eggs, separated
1 cup milk

2 cups finely shredded cucumbers,
  well drained
1½ teaspoons salt
1 teaspoon instant minced onion
1 teaspoon sugar
½ teaspoon ground white pepper
¼ teaspoon ground dill seed
⅛ teaspoon instant minced garlic

2 tablespoons flour
1 teaspoon double-acting baking
  powder

Beat egg yolks until light and lemon-colored. Add next 8 ingredients. Sift flour with baking powder and blend with the mixture. Beat egg whites until they stand in soft, stiff peaks. Fold in carefully. Turn into a 1-quart baking dish having only the bottom buttered. Place in a pan of hot water and bake in a preheated moderate oven (325° F.) until firm, 1 hour.

YIELD: 6 servings

FRIED CUCUMBERS

2 large cucumbers
Cold water to cover
1 teaspoon salt
Fine, dry bread crumbs
1 large egg, well beaten
1 tablespoon milk
Chopped parsley
Celery salt

Peel and cut cucumbers in lengthwise slices, about ⅛ inch thick. Soak in cold water to cover and the 1 teaspoon salt for 1 hour. Drain and pat dry on a clean towel. Dip cucumber slices in bread crumbs. Then dip in beaten egg mixed with milk. Dip in bread crumbs again.

Fry in deep fat, preheated to 365° F., until well browned. Drain on paper towels or brown paper. Sprinkle with chopped parsley and celery salt.

YIELD: 6 to 8 servings

EGGPLANT A LA RUSSE

1 medium-size (1 pound) eggplant
1 cup flour
1 teaspoon salt
¼ teaspoon ground black pepper
6 tablespoons salad *or* olive oil
¼ cup (½ stick) butter *or* margarine
2 tablespoons flour
2 cups sour cream
¼ teaspoon garlic powder
¼ cup grated Parmesan cheese

Wash eggplant and cut into crosswise slices 1 inch thick and remove peel from each. Dip in flour mixed with salt and black pepper. Heat 3 tablespoons of the salad oil in a 9- or 10-inch skillet. Add eggplant and sauté until golden, adding more oil as needed. Place in a 16 x 10 x 2 inch baking dish or in 6 individual casseroles. Set aside.

Melt butter or margarine in a saucepan. Blend in the 2 tablespoons flour. Stir and cook until bubbly. Add sour cream and garlic powder. Heat sauce and spread over eggplant, being sure each slice is entirely covered. Sprinkle with Parmesan cheese. Broil 7 minutes or until browned.

YIELD: 8 servings

EGGPLANT AND TOMATO CASSEROLE

Eggplant and tomatoes combine appetizingly in this hearty casserole. If desired, add sliced or diced leftover meats or fish to make this a complete meal-in-one.

1 eggplant (1¼ pounds)
½ cup shortening
1 large green pepper, sliced
1 large onion, sliced
1½ teaspoons salt
¼ teaspoon ground black pepper
½ teaspoon ground basil
4 large fresh tomatoes
½ cup soft bread crumbs
½ cup grated, sharp American cheese

Peel eggplant and cut into crosswise slices about ¼ inch thick. Sauté in 6 tablespoons of the shortening, adding the shortening as needed. Set aside. Sauté peppers and onions in the remaining shortening. Place in a 2-quart casserole alternating with layers of eggplant, beginning and ending with eggplant, sprinkling each layer with a mixture of seasonings. Slice tomatoes and arrange over the top. Combine bread crumbs with cheese and sprinkle over tomatoes. Bake in a preheated moderate oven (350° F.) 45 minutes or until browned over the top.

YIELD: 6 servings

SPICED EGGPLANT AND POTATOES

Eggplant is said to have originated in India. This dish—bhujiya—is authentically Indian. And like so many Indian dishes, it owes its intriguing flavor to the use of numerous spices.

5 tablespoons salad oil

2 cups diced, peeled, uncooked eggplant
1¼ cups diced, uncooked potatoes
2 tablespoons chopped onion
¾ teaspoon salt
¾ teaspoon powdered mustard
¾ teaspoon ground turmeric

⅛ teaspoon ground ginger
⅛ teaspoon cayenne

½ cup boiling water

Heat oil in a 10-inch skillet. Add the next 8 ingredients. Cook until vegetables have browned, stirring frequently. Add water. Cover and cook 10 to 15 minutes or until all water has evaporated and vegetables are tender. Serve hot.

YIELD: 6 servings

HERBED EGGPLANT CASSEROLE

12 slices eggplant, peeled
½ teaspoon salt

2 cups diced tomatoes
½ cup chopped green pepper
⅓ cup chopped onion
⅓ cup sliced celery
¼ cup sliced, pimiento-stuffed olives
1½ teaspoons salt
¼ teaspoon ground black pepper
¼ teaspoon crumbled rosemary leaves

¾ cup soft bread crumbs
2 tablespoons butter *or* margarine,
  melted
1 cup shredded, sharp Cheddar cheese

Sprinkle eggplant with the ½ teaspoon salt. Place in a buttered 2-quart casserole. Combine next 8 ingredients and pour over eggplant. Cover and bake in a preheated hot oven (400° F.) 30 minutes. Mix bread crumbs with butter or margarine and cheese. Sprinkle over the top. Bake, uncovered, 10 minutes or until crumbs are brown.

YIELD: 6 servings

FRIED SLICED EGGPLANT

1 medium-size eggplant (1 pound)

⅔ cup fine, dry bread crumbs
⅓ cup grated Parmesan cheese
2 teaspoons salt
½ teaspoon celery salt
¼ teaspoon ground black pepper

2 large eggs
2 tablespoons milk
Flour
About ½ cup cooking oil *or*
  shortening
Celery salt (optional)

Wash eggplant and cut into crosswise slices ½ inch thick. Remove peel. Combine the next 5 ingredients and set aside. Beat together eggs and milk and set aside. Dip eggplant into flour, then into eggs and milk and in seasoned bread crumbs. Fry in a 10-inch skillet in hot cooking oil or shortening, turning to brown both sides. Drain on paper towel. Sprinkle with celery salt, if desired. Serve hot.

EGGPLANT FINGERS
Cut eggplant slices into strips ½ inch

wide. Crumb and fry as in above directions.

YIELD: 6 to 8 servings

PICKLED EGGPLANT
(CAPONATA)

2 large (1 pound, 4 ounces each)
  eggplants
4 cups water
2¼ cups cider vinegar
1 cup cauliflowerets
1 cup diced celery
2 tablespoons sugar
3 tablespoons onion flakes
1 tablespoon oregano leaves

5 small bay leaves
½ cup pine nuts (pinola) *or* sliced,
  blanched almonds
5 tablespoons capers
½ cup cider vinegar
1¼ teaspoons salt
¼ teaspoon ground black pepper

¾ cup olive *or* salad oil

Wash eggplant, dry thoroughly, and cut into 1-inch cubes. Place water and vinegar in a saucepan. Bring to boiling point and add eggplant, cauliflower, and celery. Cover and cook 5 minutes or until vegetables are tender. Drain and cool.

Add sugar, onion, half the oregano and next 6 ingredients. Cover and chill 2 hours. Remove from refrigerator and drain off all the liquid, pressing with a saucer. Add remaining oregano and oil. Cover and chill 3 to 4 days.

YIELD: 2 quarts

ITALIAN HERBED ESCAROLE

2 pounds escarole
2 cloves garlic, split
¼ cup olive oil

½ teaspoon oregano leaves
1½ teaspoons salt
¼ teaspoon ground black pepper

Wash escarole and trim off all damaged outside leaves. Separate the leaves and cut them into quarters. Brown garlic in hot oil and then remove it. Add escarole and oregano. Cover and cook 10 to 15 minutes or until leaves are tender. (The cooking time will be less if the greens are very young.) Season with salt and black pepper. Serve hot as a vegetable.

YIELD: 5 to 6 servings

HERBED KALE

2 pounds fresh kale

2 tablespoons chopped onion
¾ teaspoon salt
½ teaspoon ground marjoram
½ teaspoon sugar
⅛ teaspoon ground black pepper

2 tablespoons bacon fat

Wash kale and cut off all tough stems. Place in a saucepan with next 5 ingredients. Cover and cook 20 minutes or un-
til tender. Add bacon fat, mix well, and serve.

YIELD: 6 servings

SAVORY KALE

1½ pounds fresh kale

2 tablespoons bacon fat
¼ cup boiling water
½ teaspoon salt

1/16 teaspoon ground black pepper
¼ teaspoon ground nutmeg

Wash kale and cut off all tough stems. Place in a saucepan with the next 3 in-
gredients. Cover and cook 20 minutes or only until leaves are tender. Add black pepper and nutmeg. Mix lightly. Serve hot immediately.

YIELD: 6 servings

LEEKS WITH VINAIGRETTE SALAD DRESSING

6 medium-size leeks
½ inch boiling water
¾ teaspoon salt
¾ cup finely chopped onion
½ cup Vinaigrette Salad Dressing*

Wash leeks thoroughly. Remove most of the green tops and save them for soup or salad. Place leeks in a saucepan with boiling water and salt. Bring to boiling point and cook, uncovered, 5 minutes. Cover and cook 10 minutes or until leeks are tender. Place leeks on a platter, sprinkle with chopped onion. Chill. Serve with Vinaigrette Salad Dressing.

YIELD: 6 servings

HERBED MUSHROOM CREPES

*This is a super-duper mushroom concoc-
tion—the kind of thing you might like to*

serve for a midnight supper. Both the crêpes and the filling can be made several hours ahead of time, then filled, rolled, and baked at the last minute.

2 large eggs
2 large egg yolks
1¾ cups milk

1 cup sifted all-purpose flour
1 teaspoon sugar
¼ teaspoon salt

2 tablespoons butter *or* margarine, melted
Herbed Mushroom Filling *(see below)*

Beat eggs and egg yolks in a mixing bowl. Stir in milk. Sift together the next 3 ingredients and gradually add to eggs, mixing well. Stir in butter or margarine. Beat batter until smooth. Let stand 1 hour before using. Heat a 5- or 6-inch skillet. Rub bottom with butter or margarine before cooking each crêpe to prevent sticking. Pour 2 tablespoons batter in pan for each crêpe or just enough to barely cover bottom of pan. Rotate pan quickly to spread batter uniformly over the surface. Cook on one side 1 to 2 minutes or only until browned underneath. Turn to cook the other side. Place crêpes as they are cooked on a clean towel. Fill with Herbed Mushroom Filling, roll and heat as directed below.

HERBED MUSHROOM FILLING

¼ pound fresh mushrooms
¼ cup chopped onion
¼ teaspoon instant minced garlic
1 tablespoon olive *or* salad oil
2 medium-size fresh tomatoes

1¼ teaspoons salt
½ teaspoon sugar
⅛ teaspoon ground black pepper
⅛ teaspoon ground marjoram

⅔ cup grated Parmesan cheese
3 tablespoons butter *or* margarine

Wash and slice mushrooms, stems and caps. Sauté with onion and garlic in oil 10 minutes. Peel and dice tomato and add. Stir in next 4 ingredients. Cook, uncovered, until liquid has evaporated. Place a heaping tablespoon on each crêpe. Roll and place in a buttered 12 x 8 x 2-inch baking pan, sprinkle each layer with grated Parmesan cheese. Dot with butter or margarine. Bake in a preheated hot oven (400° F.) 15 minutes or until hot.

YIELD: 18 crêpes

MUSHROOM PAPRIKASH

1 pound fresh mushrooms
2 tablespoons butter *or* margarine
1 teaspoon fresh lemon juice

2 tablespoons instant minced onion
1 teaspoon flour
½ teaspoon salt
1½ teaspoons paprika
Dash cayenne

⅓ cup sour cream

Wash and slice caps and stems of mushrooms. Sauté in butter or margarine and lemon juice 5 to 6 minutes or until mushrooms are tender. Combine the next 5 ingredients and add. Stir and cook 1 minute. Add sour cream. Heat, but DO NOT BOIL. Serve hot.

YIELD: 6 servings

MUSHROOM SAUTE

Cultivated mushrooms require only a gentle washing in cold water and a quick trimming of the cut ends of the stems to be ready for use. Cook over low to moderate heat. Don't overcook: it makes them tough and tasteless.

1½ pounds fresh mushrooms
3 tablespoons butter *or* margarine
2 tablespoons fresh lemon juice

1 teaspoon salt (or to taste)
⅛ teaspoon ground black pepper
¼ teaspoon ground ginger
2 tablespoons fine, dry bread crumbs

Wash and slice mushrooms, leaving stems attached. Melt butter or margarine in a 9-inch skillet. Add mushrooms and lemon juice and cook over medium heat until mushrooms are tender, stirring frequently. Blend in remaining ingredients. Heat 1 minute. Serve hot as a vegetable.

YIELD: 6 to 8 servings

FRENCH FRIED MUSHROOMS

20 medium-size fresh mushrooms
¾ teaspoon salt
¼ teaspoon celery salt
¹⁄₁₆ teaspoon ground black pepper
¼ cup all-purpose flour
2 large eggs, beaten
¾ cup fine, dry bread crumbs
Onion salt

Wash mushrooms and dry well, leaving stems attached. Slice mushrooms ⅓ inch thick. Sprinkle with salt mixed with celery salt. Blend black pepper with flour, into which roll mushroom slices. Then dip in beaten egg and roll in bread crumbs. Fry until golden in deep fat preheated to 370° F. Drain on paper towels. Serve with steak, fish, or lamb, pork or veal chops.

YIELD: 6 servings

HERBED MUSHROOMS

1½ pounds fresh mushrooms
3 tablespoons butter *or* margarine
1 tablespoon fresh lemon juice
1½ teaspoons crumbled marjoram
   leaves
¾ teaspoon salt (or to taste)
⅛ teaspoon ground black pepper
1 teaspoon cornstarch
2 teaspoons water
Chopped parsley

Wash and slice mushrooms, leaving stems attached. Melt butter or margarine in a 9-inch skillet. Add lemon juice, marjoram, and mushrooms. Cook over medium heat 10 to 15 minutes or until mushrooms are tender, stirring frequently. Stir in salt and black pepper. Mix cornstarch with water and blend with the pan juices. Cook ½ minute or until juices have thickened. Serve hot garnished with chopped parsley.

YIELD: 6 servings

MUSHROOMS IN SOUR CREAM ON TOAST

4 cups sliced mushrooms (1 pound)
½ cup sliced onion
2 teaspoons caraway seed
2 teaspoons fresh lemon juice
⅓ cup (⅔ stick) butter *or* margarine

1 teaspoon salt
⅛ teaspoon ground white pepper
¼ cup all-purpose flour

½ cup milk
1 cup sour cream
½ cup chopped fresh parsley
6 slices toast
Paprika

Sauté first 4 ingredients in butter or margarine until mushrooms are tender and onion is limp. Stir in next 3 ingredients. Add milk, mix well, and cook 1 minute or until thickened. Add sour cream. Mix well. Heat, but DO NOT BOIL. Just before serving, add parsley. Serve over toast. Garnish with paprika.

YIELD: 6 servings

PAPRIKA MUSHROOMS OVER CROUTONS

1 cup sliced onion
4 cups sliced, fresh mushrooms
  (1 pound)
3 tablespoons butter *or* margarine

1 teaspoon salt
1 tablespoon paprika
¹⁄₁₆ teaspoon cayenne
⅛ teaspoon ground black pepper
1 tablespoon parsley flakes

1 cup sour cream
Croutons (toasted bread cubes)

Sauté onions and mushrooms in butter or margarine until they are tender and limp. Add next 5 ingredients. Cook slowly 2 minutes. Stir in sour cream. Heat but DO NOT BOIL. Serve hot over croutons.

YIELD: 6 servings

STUFFED MUSHROOMS WITH BEARNAISE SAUCE

12 large fresh mushrooms
1 teaspoon fresh lemon juice
1 teaspoon salt
½ pound chicken livers

1 teaspoon salt
¼ teaspoon ground black pepper
½ teaspoon paprika
⅛ teaspoon ground thyme

2 tablespoons butter *or* margarine
½ cup Béarnaise Sauce*

Remove stems from mushrooms and save them for use in sauces and stuffings. Wash caps and place in a saucepan with ½ inch boiling water, lemon juice, and 1 teaspoon salt. Cover, bring to boiling point, and cook 2 minutes. Combine chicken livers with next 4 ingredients. Sauté in butter or margarine until livers lose their rosy color.

Place a piece of chicken liver in each mushroom cap. Bake in a preheated moderate oven (350° F.) 5 to 8 minutes or until hot. Serve hot topped with Béarnaise Sauce.

YIELD: 6 servings, 2 caps each

ONION AND CHEESE PIE

3 tablespoons butter *or* margarine
3 large onions, thinly sliced

3 large eggs, lightly beaten
1 teaspoon salt
⅛ teaspoon ground white pepper
1½ teaspoons celery salt
1 teaspoon parsley flakes
⅔ cup finely shredded Cheddar cheese
1½ cups scalded top milk

9-inch unbaked pie crust (Never-Fail Pastry I*)
Onion rings
Mushroom Sauce*

Melt butter or margarine in a 1½-quart saucepan. Add onions and sauté until they are limp and transparent, about 10 minutes, stirring frequently. Add the next 7 ingredients. Mix well. Turn into an *unbaked* pie shell.

Bake in a preheated hot oven (425° F.) 10 minutes. Reduce heat to 325° F. (slow) and bake 30 to 40 minutes or until pie is firm in the center. Garnish with onion rings. Serve as the main dish, with Mushroom Sauce, for lunch or supper.

YIELD: 6 servings

CURRIED ONIONS AND PEAS

1 pound small white onions
1 inch boiling water
1 teaspoon salt
1 pound green peas (1 cup shelled)
3 tablespoons butter *or* margarine
1 teaspoon curry powder
¼ teaspoon salt
⅛ teaspoon ground white pepper

Peel onions and place in a saucepan with boiling water and salt. Bring to boiling point and cook, uncovered, 5 minutes. Cover and cook 15 to 20 minutes or until onions are tender. Add peas 5 minutes before cooking time is up.

Drain vegetables. Melt butter or margarine and blend in remaining ingredients. Pour over vegetables and mix lightly until onions are glazed with curry butter.

YIELD: 6 servings

SAVORY ONION FRITTERS

1 cup sifted all-purpose flour
1 teaspoon double-acting baking powder
½ teaspoon salt
½ teaspoon ground allspice
½ teaspoon ground turmeric
1 teaspoon sugar

1 large egg, well beaten
⅔ cup water
¾ pound (3 medium-size) onions
¾ teaspoon salt

Sift together the first 6 ingredients. Blend egg with water and add. Beat to make a smooth batter. Peel onions, wash, and cut into crosswise slices ¼-inch thick. Add the ¾ teaspoon salt. Mix well.

Dip onions into batter and fry in deep fat preheated to 360° F. until browned and they float to the top of fat. Drain on paper towels. Serve hot.

YIELD: 6 servings

BAKED WHOLE ONIONS

6 large, unpeeled Bermuda onions
3 tablespoons butter *or* margarine
¼ teaspoon salt
⅛ teaspoon ground black pepper
¼ teaspoon ground savory, thyme, *or* marjoram

Onions may be baked in their skins. Wipe unpeeled onions with a damp cloth. Bake in a preheated moderate oven (350° F.) 1

to 1¼ hours or until onions are tender when pierced with a pointed knife. Remove from oven and peel off skins. Blend butter with remaining ingredients. Serve over hot onions.

YIELD: 6 servings

GRILLED SLICED ONIONS

Large onions
Melted butter *or* margarine
Garlic *or* celery salt
Ground black pepper
Salt

Peel onions. Slice ½ inch thick. Top each slice with ½ pat of butter or margarine. Wrap slices separately in aluminum foil. Cook on the grill until tender, turning to cook both sides, or if desired, cook in the embers. Sprinkle with garlic or celery salt, ground black pepper, and salt.

YIELD: Allow 2 large slices per serving

OKRA FRITTERS

1 cup sifted all-purpose flour
1½ teaspoons double-acting
    baking powder
2 teaspoons salt
¼ teaspoon ground black pepper
¼ teaspoon ground nutmeg

2 large eggs, well beaten
⅓ cup milk
2 tablespoons butter *or* margarine,
    melted
2 cups sliced fresh okra

Sift together the first 5 ingredients. Combine eggs and milk and stir into flour mixture. Add butter or margarine and okra and mix well. Drop batter from a tablespoon into deep fat preheated to 350° F. Cook 3 to 5 minutes or until golden brown. Drain on paper towels. Serve hot.

YIELD: 25 fritters

PARSNIP CAKES

2 cups mashed, cooked parsnips
1½ teaspoons salt
¼ teaspoon ground black pepper
1 teaspoon sugar
1 teaspoon paprika
1 teaspoon fresh lemon juice
1 large egg
½ cup fine, dry bread crumbs
Flour
Bacon drippings

Combine first 8 ingredients. Mix well. Shape into 2½-inch patties ½ inch thick. Dip in flour. Sauté in bacon drippings, turning to brown both sides. Serve hot.

YIELD: 4 to 5 servings

PARSNIP PUDDING
FLAMBE

6 large (2 pounds) fresh parsnips
1 inch boiling water
1 teaspoon salt
1 tablespoon butter *or* margarine
1 tablespoon flour
1½ teaspoons salt
¼ teaspoon ground cumin
¼ teaspoon ground coriander
½ teaspoon sugar

½ cup milk
1 tablespoon grated orange rind
2 large eggs, beaten
1 tablespoon butter *or* margarine, melted
Orange sections
⅓ cup Cointreau

Pare and dice parsnips. Place in a saucepan with boiling water and salt. Cover and cook until parsnips are tender (20 to 25 minutes). Melt butter or margarine. Blend in next 5 ingredients. Add milk. Stir and cook until the sauce begins to thicken. Remove from heat. Add orange rind. Drain parsnips, mash, and add to sauce along with eggs. Turn into a buttered 1-quart casserole. Brush top with 1 tablespoon melted butter or margarine.

Bake in a preheated moderate oven (350° F.) 40 minutes. Remove from oven. Cut orange slices in half and heat with Cointreau in a small saucepan until the mixture comes to a boil. Just before bringing to table, remove orange slices and arrange over top of the pudding. Pour hot Cointreau over top, igniting with a match as you pour. Serve flaming.

YIELD: 6 servings

FRIED ROSEMARY PARSNIPS

4 (1 pound) parsnips
½ inch boiling water
1 teaspoon salt
2 large eggs, beaten
1 cup fine, dry bread crumbs
½ teaspoon salt
1 teaspoon crumbled rosemary leaves
¼ cup shortening

Wash, pare, and slice parsnips ⅛ inch thick, lengthwise. Add parsnips to a saucepan containing ½ inch boiling water and the 1 teaspoon salt. Cover. Cook about 12 minutes or until tender. (For a milder flavor, lift the cover 3 to 4 times to permit the acids to escape with the steam).

Carefully remove parsnips from the pan. Dip into beaten eggs and then in bread crumbs mixed with the ½ teaspoon salt and rosemary. Brown on both sides in hot shortening.

YIELD: 6 servings

GLAZED MUSTARD PARSNIPS

8 boiled parsnips
2 tablespoons butter *or* margarine
2 tablespoons light-brown sugar
½ teaspoon powdered mustard

Quarter parsnips and place them in a buttered 1-quart casserole. Dot with butter or margarine. Mix sugar with mustard and sprinkle over the top. Bake in a preheated hot oven (400° F.) 20 minutes or until parsnips are glazed and browned.

YIELD: 4 servings

SPICED BUTTERS FOR PARSNIPS

The Roman Emperor Tiberius was a great parsnip eater and it is reported that he sent his messengers as far north as the Rhine to gather them. Parsnips can be spiced in many different ways, all good.

For 6 portions of hot cooked parsnips, mix 2 tablespoons melted butter or margarine with any one of the spices listed below and toss lightly:

¼ teaspoon ground allspice
⅛ teaspoon ground cinnamon
⅛ teaspoon ground nutmeg
¼ teaspoon ground ginger
¼ teaspoon curry powder
¼ teaspoon crumbled basil

½ teaspoon basil leaves
½ inch boiling water

⅛ teaspoon ground black pepper
2 tablespoons butter *or* margarine

Shell peas and place in a saucepan with next 4 ingredients. Bring to boiling point and cook, uncovered, 5 minutes. Cover and cook 5 minutes or until peas are barely tender. (Cooking time will be less for young, small peas.) Drain if necessary and season with black pepper and butter or margarine.

YIELD: 6 servings

GREEN PEAS WITH MINT BUTTER

2 tablespoons butter *or* margarine
1½ tablespoons mint flakes
1 package frozen peas, cooked
Pimiento strips

Melt butter or margarine. Add dried mint flakes and let stand for 15 minutes. Pour over hot, cooked peas. Garnish with pimiento strips. Serve with roast lamb.

YIELD: 4 servings

CORN-STUFFED GREEN PEPPERS

6 medium-size green peppers
3 cups corn, cut from the cob
1 cup diced fresh tomato
1½ teaspoons instant minced onion
1¼ teaspoons salt
¼ teaspoon ground black pepper
⅛ teaspoon garlic powder
1 teaspoon chili powder
3 tablespoons flour
2 tablespoons butter *or* margarine, melted

Slice tops from green peppers. Carefully remove seeds and membranes. Parboil in

⅛ teaspoon crumbled rosemary leaves
⅛ teaspoon ground thyme

SPICED GLAZED PARSNIPS

6 medium-size parsnips
Boiling water to cover
2 tablespoons butter *or* margarine

¼ cup light-brown sugar
⅛ teaspoon salt
¼ teaspoon ground cloves
3 tablespoons fresh orange juice

Wash parsnips and cook them in their skins in boiling water to cover, 30 minutes or until they are tender. Lift out of water and cool until they can be handled. Remove skins and cut parsnips in half lengthwise. Set aside. Melt butter or margarine in a skillet. Blend in next 4 ingredients. Heat. Add parsnips and cook slowly until they are hot and glazed.

YIELD: 6 servings

HERBED FRESH PEAS

3 pounds fresh green peas

1 teaspoon salt
1 teaspoon sugar

covered saucepan for 5 minutes in boiling water to cover and ½ teaspoon salt. Drain. Combine remaining ingredients and spoon into drained green peppers. Place in a baking pan and bake in a preheated moderate oven (375° F.) 35 minutes or until done.

YIELD: 6 servings

FRENCH FRIED GREEN PEPPERS

2 large green peppers
6 tablespoons fine, dry bread crumbs

1½ teaspoons salt
¼ teaspoon oregano leaves
⅛ teaspoon ground black pepper
⅓ cup grated Parmesan cheese

1 large egg
2 tablespoons water

Wash green peppers. Cut off tops, remove seeds, and core. Cut into rings ⅛ inch thick and then cut each ring in half or thirds, depending upon the size. Dip in crumbs mixed with next 4 ingredients, then in egg beaten with water, and then in crumbs again. Chill about 1 hour. Fry in ½ inch hot fat (375° F.) Drain on absorbent paper. Serve with steak, chops, or as a hot cocktail or tea savory.

YIELD: 4 servings

POTATO AND ONION PANCAKES

1½ cups fluffy, mashed potatoes
1 tablespoon instant minced onion
1¼ teaspoons salt
¼ teaspoon ground black pepper
¼ teaspoon thyme leaves
1/16 teaspoon instant minced garlic
¼ cup sifted all-purpose flour
1 large egg, beaten

¾ cup milk
About 1 tablespoon butter *or* margarine
Crisp bacon (optional)
Applesauce (optional)

Combine the first 8 ingredients with ¼ cup of the milk. Mix well. Blend in remaining milk. Drop batter from the tip of a tablespoon onto a lightly buttered griddle. Cook over medium heat, turning to brown both sides. Serve with bacon and applesauce, if desired.

YIELD: Eight 4-inch pancakes

PAPRIKA POTATO APPLES

Here's a good and simple potato dish to keep in mind when planning company meals. Potato "apples" are particularly attractive set around the roast as a garnish.

1 can (1 pound) small, whole potatoes
Whole cloves
½ teaspoon salt
⅛ teaspoon ground black pepper
2 tablespoons butter *or* margarine
Paprika

Open can of potatoes and drain. Insert a whole clove in opposite ends of each potato and place in a baking pan. Mix salt and pepper and sprinkle over the top. Dot with butter or margarine and sprinkle with paprika. Bake in a preheated moderate oven (350° F.) 20 minutes or until potatoes are hot. Sprinkle with ad-

ditional paprika. Place on platter around roast, fish, or baked ham.

YIELD: 6 servings

HERBED POTATO PUFFS

2 cups hot, mashed potatoes
2 large egg yolks
¼ cup milk
1 tablespoon butter *or* margarine, melted
1 teaspoon salt
⅛ teaspoon ground white pepper
⅛ teaspoon paprika
½ teaspoon celery seed

Combine all ingredients and mix well. Arrange in mounds with a tablespoon or squeeze mixture through a pastry bag onto a buttered cooky sheet. Bake in a preheated hot oven (450° F.) 10 minutes or until potatoes are flecked with brown. Serve hot.

YIELD: 8 servings

POTATOES AND CHICK PEAS, INDIAN STYLE

3 tablespoons salad oil *or* shortening
¾ cup chopped onion
¾ teaspoon ground turmeric

¾ teaspoon salt
1 teaspoon ground ginger
1 teaspoon ground coriander
½ teaspoon cayenne

1 can (1 pound, 4 ounces) chick peas
1½ cups cooked, diced potatoes *or* 1 can (8½ ounces) white potatoes

Heat shortening or oil in a saucepan. Add onion and turmeric and sauté until onions are brown, stirring frequently. Add next 4 ingredients. Stir and cook 2 minutes. Stir in undrained chick peas and potatoes. Cover and cook 10 minutes or until the sauce has thickened and vegetables are hot. Serve as a vegetable or meat substitute.

YIELD: 6 servings

BROILED CHILI POTATOES

4 medium-size potatoes
1½ teaspoons salt
¼ teaspoon ground black pepper
3 tablespoons butter *or* margarine
Chili powder

Peel and slice potatoes ⅛ inch thick. Place in a 9-inch round cake pan and sprinkle with a mixture of the salt and black pepper. Dot with butter or margarine. Place under broiler preheated to 350° F. (moderate). Cook 30 to 35 minutes or until potatoes have browned and puffed. Sprinkle with chili powder to taste and serve hot.

YIELD: 6 servings

HERBED CREAMED POTATOES

3 cups (6 medium-size) diced, cooked potatoes
1 cup commercial sour cream
2 tablespoons onion flakes
1 tablespoon parsley flakes

1½ teaspoons salt
½ teaspoon ground white pepper
———
Paprika

Place all ingredients except paprika in a saucepan. Heat slowly about 5 minutes or until cream begins to bubble over potatoes. Serve at once garnished with paprika.

YIELD: 4 servings

POTATOES LORETTE

1 pound (about 3 to 4 medium)
    potatoes
1 inch boiling water
½ teaspoon salt
———
1 tablespoon butter *or* margarine
1 teaspoon salt
⅛ teaspoon ground black pepper
⅛ teaspoon ground nutmeg
———
3 large eggs
1 large egg yolk
½ cup water
1 tablespoon butter *or* margarine
¼ teaspoon salt
½ cup sifted all-purpose flour

Peel, dice, and cook potatoes 12 to 15 minutes or until tender, in boiling water and the ½ teaspoon salt in a covered saucepan. Drain well and mash until potatoes are smooth. Evaporate excess moisture from potatoes by shaking pan over low heat. Stir in the next 4 ingredients. Beat 1 egg with the 1 egg yolk and add to potatoes. Beat until fluffy.

Heat the ½ cup water with remaining 1 tablespoon butter or margarine and salt to boiling point. Stir in all the flour at one time. Mix until well blended and the mixture leaves the sides of the pan. Remove from heat and beat in 2 remaining eggs, 1 at a time. Continue beating until mixture is smooth and leaves sides of pan.

Blend with potatoes. Drop mixture from a teaspoon into deep fat preheated to 375° F. Fry until puffed and browned. Drain on paper towels. Serve as the potato dish for dinner.

YIELD: 2 dozen balls

SEASONED MASHED POTATOES

Prepare 2 envelopes instant potatoes according to directions on the package. Add ¼ teaspoon each onion and garlic salt and mash until fluffy.

YIELD: 6 to 8 servings

NEW POTATOES GRUYERE

18 small, new potatoes
1 teaspoon salt
½ inch boiling water
½ teaspoon basil leaves
⅛ teaspoon ground black pepper
⅔ cup Gruyère cheese
¼ cup light *or* heavy cream

Wash and scrape potatoes. Place in a saucepan with salt and ½ inch boiling water. Cover and cook 20 minutes or until potatoes are tender. Drain. Add remaining ingredients. Heat only until cheese is *almost* melted. Serve at once.

YIELD: 6 servings

SAVORY NEW POTATOES

12 (2½ pounds) medium-size
    new potatoes
2 cups chicken *or* beef stock *or* 2 cups
    boiling water and 2 beef bouillon cubes
2 tablespoons flour
½ cup light cream
⅛ teaspoon ground black pepper
¼ teaspoon ground nutmeg
Salt to taste

Wash and scrape potatoes and place in a saucepan with stock or bouillon cubes and boiling water. Cover, bring to boiling point, and cook 25 minutes or until tender. Drain. Blend flour with cream and add to potatoes along with remaining ingredients. Mix lightly to prevent breaking potatoes. Cook 1 minute. Serve hot.

YIELD: 6 servings

NEW POTATOES WITH CARAWAY VELOUTE SAUCE

2 pounds new potatoes
1 teaspoon salt
1 inch boiling water
Caraway Velouté Sauce*

Wash and scrape potatoes. Place in a saucepan with salt and boiling water. Cover and cook 20 to 25 minutes or until potatoes are tender. Drain off water if necessary. Turn into a serving dish. Dress with Caraway Velouté Sauce. Serve hot.

NEW POTATOES WITH DILL VELOUTE SAUCE

In the above potato recipe, replace Caraway Velouté Sauce with Dill Velouté Sauce.*

YIELD: 6 servings

POPPY SEED POTATOES

1 can (1 pound, 4 ounces)
  sliced potatoes
2 tablespoons butter *or* margarine
2 teaspoons poppy seed
¼ teaspoon salt
⅛ teaspoon ground black pepper

Drain water from potatoes and place potatoes in 9-inch skillet. Melt butter or margarine and add seasonings. Pour over potatoes. Cook over medium-low heat

until potatoes are hot and browned, turning carefully to prevent breaking.

YIELD: 4 servings

GINGERED BAKED PUMPKIN

Since botanists themselves aren't quite certain whether to classify a pumpkin as a winter squash or vice versa, either vegetable may be used.

2 pounds fresh pumpkin *or*
  winter squash

¼ cup (½ stick) butter *or* margarine,
  melted
¼ cup light-brown sugar
2 tablespoons chopped preserved ginger
⅛ teaspoon salt
⅛ teaspoon ground white pepper

3 tablespoons hot water

Remove and discard seeds and fiber from pumpkin or winter squash. Peel and cut pumpkin into 1½ squares. Score each square. Combine next 5 ingredients and mix with pumpkin. Turn into a buttered 8 x 8 x 2-inch baking pan. Pour in hot water. Cover and bake in a preheated moderate oven (350° F.) 45 minutes. Remove cover and bake 15 minutes or until pumpkin is tender, basting frequently with pan liquid.

YIELD: 6 servings

MASHED PUMPKIN

1 small whole pumpkin
  (about 5 pounds)
Boiling water to cover
3 tablespoons butter *or* margarine
¼ cup sugar
¼ teaspoon salt
⅛ teaspoon ground black pepper
¼ teaspoon ground ginger
¼ teaspoon ground allspice
¼ teaspoon ground mace

Wash pumpkin, leave whole, and cook in enough boiling water to cover, about 1 hour. Remove from water, cut in half, and remove and discard seeds and fibers. Scoop out pulp. Mash well or put through a sieve. There should be about 4½ cups. Stir in remaining ingredients. Serve hot as a vegetable.

YIELD: 6 servings

SPICED PUMPKIN CASSEROLE

4 cups cooked, mashed, fresh pumpkin
¼ cup light-brown sugar
½ teaspoon salt
⅛ teaspoon ground black pepper
¼ teaspoon ground nutmeg
½ teaspoon ground ginger
¼ teaspoon ground cinnamon
1 teaspoon grated lemon rind
1 teaspoon grated orange rind
¼ cup (½ stick) butter *or* margarine, melted

Combine all ingredients. Turn into a buttered 1-quart casserole. Bake in a preheated moderate oven (350° F.) 1 hour or until hot and the top is lightly flecked with brown. Serve as a vegetable.

YIELD: 6 servings

SPICED GLAZED BAKED PUMPKIN

2 pounds fresh pumpkin
¼ cup (½ stick) butter *or* margarine, melted
¼ cup sugar
½ teaspoon ground ginger
⅛ teaspoon salt
⅛ teaspoon ground black pepper
3 tablespoons orange marmalade
1 tablespoon hot water

Cut pumpkin in half, remove and discard seeds and fibers. Peel pumpkin and cut into 1½-inch squares. Score each square. Combine the next 6 ingredients and mix with pumpkin. Turn into a buttered 8 x 8 x 2-inch pan. Add hot water.

Cover and bake in a preheated moderate oven (350° F.) 45 minutes. Remove cover and bake 30 minutes or until pumpkin is tender, basting frequently with liquid in the pan. Serve as a vegetable.

YIELD: 6 servings

GOLDEN RUTABAGA BALLS

2 cups mashed, cooked rutabagas
1 cup mashed, cooked potatoes
1 large egg
1 teaspoon salt
1 teaspoon sugar
¼ teaspoon ground nutmeg
⅛ teaspoon ground black pepper
1 large egg, beaten
1 tablespoon milk
½ cup fine, dry bread crumbs

Combine the first 7 ingredients. Mix well. Chill until mixture can be shaped. Roll into 1-inch balls. Mix beaten egg with milk, into which dip balls. Roll in bread crumbs. Fry until golden in deep fat preheated to 350° F. Drain on paper towels. Serve with poultry or meat. Or sprinkle lightly with celery salt and serve on toothpicks as an appetizer.

YIELD: 2½ dozen balls

RUTABAGA CASSEROLE

7 cups (2½ pounds) rutabagas, peeled and sliced
1 inch boiling water
1 teaspoon salt
½ teaspoon sugar

3 tablespoons flour
3 tablespoons bacon drippings
1½ cups beef stock or 2 beef bouillon cubes and 1½ cups boiling water
¼ teaspoon sage
⅛ teaspoon ground black pepper
1 cup soft bread crumbs
2 tablespoons butter or margarine, melted

Place the first 4 ingredients in a saucepan. Bring to boiling point and cook, uncovered, 5 minutes. Cover and cook 15 to 20 minutes or until rutabagas are about half done. Drain and turn into a buttered 1½-quart casserole. Blend flour with bacon drippings. Stir in beef stock or bouillon cubes and water.

Stir and cook until of medium thickness. Add sage and black pepper. Pour over rutabagas. Mix bread crumbs with melted butter or margarine and sprinkle over the top. Bake in a preheated moderate oven (350° F.) 30 minutes or until crumbs are brown.

YIELD: 6 servings

RUTABAGA PUDDING

3 cups mashed rutabagas
2 tablespoons milk
¼ cup (½ stick) butter or margarine

1 teaspoon salt
½ teaspoon sugar
¼ teaspoon ground nutmeg
⅛ teaspoon ground black pepper

Put mashed rutabagas through a sieve. Add milk, 2 tablespoons butter or margarine, and seasonings. Mix well. Turn into a buttered 9-inch pie plate. Make indentations over the top with the tip of a tablespoon.

Melt remaining 2 tablespoons butter or margarine and pour over the surface. Bake in a preheated moderate oven (375° F.) 40 to 50 minutes or until top is well flecked with brown.

YIELD: 6 servings

RUTABAGA PUFFS

1 cup cooked, mashed rutabagas
½ cup cooked, mashed potatoes

½ cup sifted all-purpose flour
2 teaspoons double-acting baking powder
1¼ teaspoons salt
¼ teaspoon ground black pepper
⅛ teaspoon ground ginger

2 large eggs, beaten

Combine rutabagas and potatoes. Sift together the next 5 ingredients and add. Beat in eggs. Drop a rounded tablespoon of the mixture at a time into ½ inch hot fat. Cook until golden, turning to brown both sides. Serve hot.

YIELD: 12 puffs or 6 servings

SPICED BUTTERS FOR RUTABAGAS or TURNIPS

For 6 portions of diced cooked rutabagas or turnips, melt 2 tablespoons butter or margarine. Add any one of the following spices or herbs listed below:

¼ teaspoon crumbled basil leaves
¼ teaspoon chili powder
⅛ teaspoon ground cinnamon
⅛ teaspoon ground mustard
⅛ teaspoon ground nutmeg
1 teaspoon caraway seed

Add to vegetable and mix lightly.

DILLED RUTABAGAS WITH BACON

1½ quarts (3 pounds) peeled, diced
    rutabagas
2 teaspoons sugar
1½ teaspoons salt
½ teaspoon dill seed

1 inch boiling water
⅓ cup sour cream
⅛ teaspoon ground black pepper
2 teaspoons fresh lemon juice
6 slices bacon

Place the first 4 ingredients in a 2½-quart saucepan. Add 1 inch boiling water. Cover, bring to boiling point, and cook 10 minutes. Drain and discard water. Mix vegetable lightly with sour cream, black pepper, and lemon juice. Turn into a 1½-quart casserole. Cover.

Bake 20 minutes or until rutabagas are tender. Cook bacon until about half done. Arrange the half-cooked slices over the top of casserole. Place under broiler to brown and crisp. Serve hot. Especially good with pork.

YIELD: 6 servings

SPINACH CHEESE PUFFS

These are well worth the effort of getting out the deep fat pot! Serve as a fritter with any kind of meat or fish.

1 cup cooked, well-drained, fresh spinach
2 large eggs, beaten

1¼ cups fine, dry bread crumbs
2 tablespoons fresh lemon juice
2 teaspoons instant minced onion
1 teaspoon salt
¼ teaspoon nutmeg
⅛ teaspoon ground black pepper
¾ cup grated American cheese

1 large egg, beaten
1 tablespoon milk
⅓ cup fine, dry bread crumbs

Put spinach through a sieve or chop very fine. Blend in next 8 ingredients. Shape into 1½-inch puffs. Mix remaining egg with milk into which dip each spinach puff. Then roll them in the remaining bread crumbs. Fry in deep fat (375° F.) until brown and crisp. Drain on paper towels. Serve hot.

YIELD: 12 puffs

SAVORY FRESH SPINACH

2 pounds young, tender, fresh spinach
2 tablespoons butter *or* margarine
⅓ cup chopped onion

½ teaspoon crumbled oregano leaves
½ teaspoon sugar
1¼ teaspoons salt
⅛ teaspoon garlic powder
⅛ teaspoon ground black pepper
1 teaspoon fresh lemon juice

3 tablespoons grated Cheddar *or*
    Parmesan cheese
Onion rings

Wash spinach and place in a saucepan with only the water that clings to the leaves. Cover and cook *only* until spinach is wilted and tender, about 5 minutes. Remove from heat and cut crisscross with 2 knives. Drain if necessary.

Heat butter or margarine in a saucepan. Add onion and sauté until limp, about 3 minutes. Add seasonings and lemon juice. Pour over spinach. Toss lightly. Turn into a serving dish. Sprinkle with grated cheese. Garnish with onion rings as desired.

YIELD: 5 servings

MASHED HUBBARD SQUASH

3 pounds Hubbard squash
Boiling water to cover

3 tablespoons butter *or* margarine
¼ teaspoon salt
¼ teaspoon ground cinnamon
¼ teaspoon ground ginger
¼ teaspoon ground allspice
¹⁄₁₆ teaspoon ground black pepper
3 tablespoons maple *or* cane sugar syrup

Wash squash, leave whole, and place in a large saucepan with boiling water to cover. Cover and cook 30 to 40 minutes or until tender. Remove from water and drain well. Cut squash in half, remove seeds and stringy portion. Scoop out the squash and place in a mixing bowl. Mash and add remaining ingredients. Mix well. Serve hot as a vegetable. This dish is especially good with poultry, pork, ham, or veal.

YIELD: 6 servings

SQUASH PUFFS

3 cups cooked yellow winter squash
¼ cup milk
3 tablespoons flour
1 tablespoon light-brown sugar
½ teaspoon salt
½ teaspoon ground nutmeg
⅛ teaspoon ground black pepper
2 tablespoons sherry
2 large eggs, beaten

Combine all ingredients and mix well.

Turn into a buttered 1-quart casserole. Bake in a preheated moderate oven (350° F.) 35 minutes or until top is well-flecked with brown. Serve with turkey, pork, or ham.

YIELD: 6 servings

ZUCCHINI, MEDITERRANEAN STYLE

4 medium (1½ pounds) fresh tomatoes
2 tablespoons instant minced onion
½ cup finely diced celery

½ teaspoon basil leaves
⅓ cup olive oil

1 tablespoon capers
1½ teaspoons salt
¼ teaspoon ground black pepper

¹⁄₁₆ teaspoon garlic powder
8 medium-small (2¼ pounds), unpeeled zucchini squash
Flour
3 large hard-cooked eggs
¼ cup finely chopped fresh parsley

Combine first 3 ingredients. Cover and cook slowly 20 minutes or until vegetables are soft. Put through a food mill or sieve. Add basil and olive oil. Cook 10 minutes or until thickened. Stir in next 3 ingredients. Keep warm while preparing squash. Wash zucchini, cut, unpeeled, into lengthwise slices ¼ inch thick. Sprinkle with flour. Cook slowly in olive oil until lightly browned on both sides. Remove to serving platter. Spoon the tomato sauce over the top. Chop hard-cooked eggs finely, mix with parsley, and sprinkle over the top.

YIELD: 8 servings

BANANA AND SWEET POTATO PUFF

When Columbus found sweet potatoes on his first trip to the New World, he reported that they looked like yams and tasted like chestnuts. Twenty years later a Spaniard, Oviedo, compared their sweet and delicate flavor favorably with marzipan candy. Some of the herbalists of the day classed sweet potatoes among the aphrodisiacs. Those who worried about appearances ate the batata Hispanorum *on the sly.*

3 cups cold, cooked, mashed
    sweet potatoes
3 bananas, mashed
1 tablespoon fresh lemon juice
3 tablespoons butter *or* margarine
⅓ cup light-brown sugar
½ teaspoon ground mace
¼ teaspoon salt
⅛ teaspoon ground black pepper
⅓ cup light cream *or* undiluted
    evaporated milk
3 large eggs, beaten

The sweet potatoes must be cold to prevent discoloring the bananas. Combine

all ingredients. Mix well. Turn into a buttered 1-quart casserole. Place in a pan of hot water. Bake in a preheated moderate oven (350° F.) 1 hour or until mixture is puffed and browned. Serve with poultry, ham, or pork.

YIELD: 6 servings

SWEET POTATO AND HAM PATTIES

3 cups mashed, cooked, fresh sweet
    potatoes (about 1¾ pounds)
2 cups finely chopped cooked ham
3 tablespoons butter *or* margarine
¾ teaspoon salt
⅛ teaspoon ground black pepper
¼ teaspoon powdered mustard
1 tablespoon sugar
1¾ cups crushed corn flakes
Shortening for frying

Combine mashed sweet potatoes with next 6 ingredients and 1 cup of the corn flakes.

Shape into twelve 3-inch patties. Coat on all sides with remaining corn flakes. Fry on both sides in a small amount of shortening over low heat. Serve at once as luncheon main dish.

YIELD: 12 patties

SWEET POTATO PUDDING

2 cups mashed, cooked sweet potatoes
¾ cup hot milk
3 tablespoons butter *or* margarine
¼ teaspoon salt
¼ teaspoon ground allspice
¼ teaspoon ground cardamom seed
2 tablespoons sugar

1 large egg, separated
2 tablespoons sugar

Combine the first 7 ingredients. Beat egg yolk into potato mixture. Beat egg white until it stands in soft, stiff peaks, into which gradually beat in the remaining 2 tablespoons sugar. Carefully fold into the mixture.

Turn into a 1-quart casserole having only the bottom buttered. Bake in a preheated moderate oven (350° F.) 1 hour or until pudding is firm in the center. Serve with pork, ham, or poultry.

YIELD: 6 servings

SPICED SWEET POTATO PUFFS

3 cups hot, mashed, fresh
  sweet potatoes
½ teaspoon ground allspice
¾ teaspoon ground nutmeg
⅛ teaspoon ground black pepper
½ teaspoon salt
3 tablespoons butter *or* margarine
3 tablespoons milk

6 teaspoons maple *or* cane sugar syrup
6 marshmallows

Combine the first 7 ingredients. Form into 6 mounds with a large serving spoon or an ice-cream scoop. Place on a buttered cooky sheet. Dribble 1 teaspoon of syrup over each and top with a marshmallow. Bake in a preheated moderate oven (375° F.) 45 minutes.

YIELD: 6 servings

SWEET POTATOES RHUMBA

4 cups hot, boiled, riced sweet potatoes
¼ cup (½ stick) butter *or* margarine
⅓ to ½ cup heavy cream
½ teaspoon ground nutmeg
½ teaspoon salt
¼ cup sugar
2 tablespoons rum

1 tablespoon butter *or* margarine,
  melted
1 tablespoon grated orange rind

Combine the first 7 ingredients, adding only enough cream to make the mixture light and fluffy. Turn into a buttered 1-quart casserole. Brush top with melted butter or margarine. Sprinkle with grated orange rind. Bake in a preheated hot oven (400° F.) 30 to 40 minutes or until top is brown.

YIELD: 8 servings

SHERRIED SWEET POTATOES

4 cups mashed, cooked sweet potatoes
½ cup sugar
¼ cup (½ stick) butter *or* margarine
½ teaspoon salt
½ teaspoon ground ginger
½ teaspoon ground nutmeg
¼ cup cooking sherry *or* dry
  sherry wine
½ cup milk

Combine all ingredients. Beat until fluffy. Turn into a buttered 1-quart casserole. Bake in a preheated moderate oven (375° F.) 45 minutes or until top is flecked with brown. Serve hot with meat or poultry.

YIELD: 6 servings

SPICED FRIED SWEET POTATOES

2 medium-size (1½ pounds)
    sweet potatoes
Butter *or* margarine
2 tablespoons sugar
¼ teaspoon ground cinnamon

Peel sweet potatoes and cut them into slices ¼ inch thick. Fry in butter or margarine over medium-low heat until soft and brown, turning to brown both sides. Mix sugar with cinnamon and sprinkle over potatoes. Serve hot for breakfast, lunch, or supper.

YIELD: 4 servings

BAKED STUFFED TOMATOES, ITALIAN STYLE

6 medium-size fresh tomatoes
1½ teaspoons salt
1 tablespoon butter *or* margarine
2 teaspoons flour
⅔ cup milk
1 large egg yolk
½ teaspoon salt
Dash ground nutmeg
¹⁄₁₆ teaspoon ground black pepper
½ teaspoon basil leaves
1½ cups diced cooked potatoes
¾ cup diced Mozzarella cheese
1 tablespoon chopped parsley
⅓ cup fine, dry bread crumbs

Wash tomatoes, cut a slice from stem end of each, and scoop out the inside, leaving shells intact. Sprinkle inside of tomatoes with salt and invert on a plate to drain. Melt butter or margarine in a saucepan. Blend in flour.

Remove from heat and add milk. Stir and cook until mixture has thickened slightly. Mix egg yolk with a little of the sauce and then add it to remaining sauce. Add seasonings. Stir and cook ½ minute. Blend with potatoes and cheese.

Spoon mixture into tomato cups. Sprinkle with parsley and bread crumbs. Place in a close-fitting baking pan. Bake in a preheated moderate oven (350° F.) 30 minutes. Serve hot.

YIELD: 6 servings

BAKED STUFFED TOMATOES WITH BREAD CUBES

6 large firm tomatoes
1 teaspoon salt
2 cups ½-inch bread cubes

3 tablespoons salad oil

1 cup diced Cheddar cheese
1½ teaspoons basil leaves
1 tablespoon parsley flakes
1 teaspoon salt
¾ teaspoon ground black pepper
½ teaspoon sugar
¼ teaspoon instant minced garlic

6 tablespoons tomato liquid

Wash tomatoes and cut a slice from the top of each. Scoop out tomato centers. Sprinkle inside of tomato cups with salt and invert on a plate to drain. (Save pulp and juice to use later.) Brown bread cubes in hot oil. Mix with the next 7 ingredients. Spoon into tomato cups.

Mash the tomato centers to extract the juice, strain, and pour 1 tablespoon over each serving. Place in a close-fitting dish. Pour ¼ cup hot water in baking dish. Bake in a preheated moderate oven (375° F.) 15 minutes or until done. Serve hot.

YIELD: 6 servings

BROILED TOMATOES ON TOASTED BREAD ROUNDS

3 large, fresh tomatoes
2 tablespoons fresh lemon juice
1 teaspoon salt
⅛ teaspoon ground black pepper
3 teaspoons butter or margarine

½ cup grated Cheddar cheese
½ cup soft bread crumbs
¼ teaspoon basil leaves
¼ cup (½ stick) butter or margarine, melted

6 rounds hot buttered toast
6 anchovy fillets (optional)

Wash tomatoes, cut each in half, and place on a baking sheet, cut-side up.

Sprinkle with lemon juice, salt and black pepper. Place ½ teaspoon butter or margarine on each half.

Mix next 4 ingredients and sprinkle over the tops. Place under broiler to brown, 2 to 3 minutes. Serve on rounds of buttered toast. Garnish with anchovy fillets, if desired.

YIELD: 6 servings

CHILI STUFFED TOMATOES

6 medium-size fresh tomatoes
Salt

1 cup diced cooked beef or ham
½ cup diced celery
1 cup cold, canned kidney beans, drained
1 teaspoon salt (or to taste)
4 to 5 teaspoons chili powder
¼ teaspoon ground black pepper
3 tablespoons mayonnaise

Head lettuce
2 large hard-cooked eggs

Wash tomatoes and cut a slice from the stem end of each. Scoop out the inside, leaving the shells intact. (Save centers for later use.) Sprinkle inside of tomato shells with salt and invert on a plate to drain.

Dice tomato centers and combine with next 7 ingredients. Mix lightly. Spoon into tomato cups. Serve on lettuce, garnished with sliced hard-cooked eggs.

YIELD: 6 servings

TOMATOES STUFFED WITH POTATOES AND CHEESE

6 large, firm, ripe tomatoes
½ teaspoon salt
Dash ground black pepper

1½ cups diced, cooked potatoes
¾ cup diced Mozzarella cheese
1½ teaspoons salt
¾ teaspoon basil leaves
⅛ teaspoon ground black pepper
3 large egg yolks

3 tablespoons butter *or* margarine
3 tablespoons grated Parmesan cheese

Wash tomatoes and cut a slice from the stem end of each. Scoop out some of the tomato pulp, leaving a ½-inch shell, being careful not to cut through the bud end. Sprinkle inside of each tomato with about 1/16 teaspoon salt and a dash of black pepper.

Combine the next 6 ingredients and cook in butter or margarine, being careful not to overcook, since Mozzarella cheese becomes stringy if cooked too much. Spoon into tomato cavities. Sprinkle each with Parmesan cheese. Place in a close-fitting pan. Bake, uncovered, in a preheated moderate oven (350° F.) 40 minutes. Serve hot.

YIELD: 6 servings

TURNIPS AND PORK, CHINESE STYLE

1½ tablespoons cornstarch
1 tablespoon soy sauce
¼ teaspoon ground black pepper
2 teaspoons salt
⅛ teaspoon ground ginger

1 pound lean, fresh pork
4 cups turnip strips
Boiling water
2 tablespoons salad oil *or* shortening
1 teaspoon sugar
Dash cayenne

Combine the first 5 ingredients. (This mixture is thick, but do not add water or more soy sauce.) Trim and discard fat from pork and cut lean pork into strips or 1-inch cubes. There should be 1 pound lean meat after fat is removed. Add to soy sauce mixture. Mix well and marinate 1 hour.

Cut turnips into 2 x 1 x ½-inch strips and place, with ¾ teaspoon of the salt and 1 inch boiling water, in a saucepan. Cook, uncovered, 5 minutes. Cover and cook 20 minutes or until turnips are tender. Drain off water, if necessary. Heat oil or shortening in a 9- or 10-inch skillet. Add pork and cook 20 to 25 minutes or until it is well done and browned. Add turnips and remaining ingredients. Cover and simmer 5 minutes. Serve hot as the main dish.

YIELD: 6 servings

TURNIPS GLACES AU JUS

6 (2 pounds) white turnips,
    2½-inch diameter
Boiling water to cover

2 bouillon cubes
2 cups boiling water
½ teaspoon salt
½ teaspoon sugar
⅛ teaspoon ground nutmeg
⅛ teaspoon ground white pepper

2 tablespoons flour
2 tablespoons butter *or* margarine

Wash and peel turnips. Cut them in crosswise slices ¼ inch thick. Parboil in boiling water to cover 5 minutes or until about half done. Drain off water. Add next 6 ingredients. Cover and cook 30 minutes or until turnips are tender.

Mix flour with butter to form a roux and add to the turnips. Tilt the saucepan to mix roux with pan liquid, stirring only until blended. Cook ½ minute or until sauce has thickened. Serve hot.

YIELD: 6 servings

TURNIPS WITH POPPY SEED BUTTER

2 tablespoons butter *or* margarine
3 teaspoons poppy seed
¼ teaspoon salt
¼ teaspoon ground black pepper
4 cups (1½ pounds) diced, cooked, hot turnips

Combine butter or margarine and poppy seed in a small saucepan. Stir and cook until butter is golden. Add salt and black pepper. Pour over hot turnips. Toss lightly. Serve hot.

YIELD: 6 servings

MARINATING TECHNIQUES

LETTING food stand for some length of time in an appropriate marinade is an artful way to accomplish two purposes: tenderize the food and give it new, exquisite flavor. Some recipes include the use of a marinade only for its flavor contribution. Others use it for both purposes.

Marinades first began as simple brines for preserving fish (which accounts for the name *marinade* stemming from the same root as the word *maritime*). What a long way these savory concoctions have come since then!

As interpreted today, a marinade consists of a cooking oil, an acid (vinegar and/or lemon juice and/or wine), and spices. As the food stands or *marinates* in the mixture, the acid, assisted by the oil, carries with it the savory flavors of the spices; the acid also has a tenderizing action.

Because of the tenderizing effect of a marinade, its use is most often associated with the preparation of the less expensive, tougher cuts of meat. However, its flavor-enhancing effect is so great that it also should be used to develop the full flavor potential of meats, and other foods, which do not require tenderizing. For example, while the naturally tender lamb is chosen for making shish kebab, it must be marinated in order to achieve the provocative flavor that characterizes this dish. Likewise poultry, seafood, and vegetable salads are at their best only after their ingredients have been skill-fully treated with a carefully selected marinade.

Offhand, it would seem to be the simplest thing in the world to pour a little of this and that over meat and let it "soak" for x number of hours. Actually, there is much science and art connected with the proper selection and preparation of a suitable marinade. There is an almost unlimited number of them, some better for use with certain foods and some better for others. A complete discussion of the subject is beyond the scope of this book. However, a few generalities are given below. The various recipes for marinated dishes recommend suitable marinades.

The kind and amount of spices and the length of time to marinate depends upon the food. For example, beef and lamb can take a marinade containing an appreciable amount of pepper and some of the more potent herbs such as bay leaves and thyme, or strong-charactered spices like cloves and caraway seed. For highly seasoned specialty dishes such as Sauerbraten,* a well-rounded blend of especially strong spices should be used.

For best results, choose a container about the same size as the meat portion to be marinated in order to cover the meat with the least amount of marinade. Place a weight on the meat, if necessary, to hold it down beneath the liquid. Turning occasionally also helps.

A cut of meat with long, narrow dimensions is a better choice for marinating than a shorter, broader piece. With long, slender-shaped pieces more surface is exposed to the marinade and the marinade has less distance to penetrate to the center of the piece. The larger the pieces, the longer the marinating will take. For an 8- to 10-pound roast, marinate overnight. For small cubes of meat, a few hours is sufficient. For preparing the highly seasoned Sauerbraten, as long as 2 days may be required to marinate the meat.

For vegetables, the emphasis shifts to herbs such as basil, tarragon, marjoram, parsley flakes, and so on. For fish, the marinade is again more herbed than spicy, though seeds such as dill, celery, or fennel add interesting variety.

Most marinades include the flavors of onion and garlic. Here the modern cook can take advantage of the various forms of dehydrated products. Since the liquid in the marinade reconstitutes them, no advance preparation is needed.

Wine is not normally used in vegetable marinades. Either wine or vinegar (or both) is suited to marinades for meats, poultry, and seafood. Lemon juice is useful in any marinade. If the food is to stand 24 hours or more, it is advisable to reduce the amount of vinegar, since it tends to build up in strength.

*An asterisk after the name of a dish indicates that the recipe for this dish appears in the book. Consult the Index for the page number.

There are two major classes of marinades: "cooked" marinades and "uncooked" or "light" types of marinades. Cooked marinades are made by cooking the spices, usually whole, and then cooling before adding the food. They are used with large cuts of meat and for shortening the time necessary to marinate a food. In the uncooked or light marinades, the ingredients are combined without heating. They use the ground spices, except that whole leaf herbs such as bay leaves, thyme, marjoram, and the like release their flavors so readily that they may be added without pulverizing.

The use of whole spices has two advantages. First, they are easy to remove if the marinade is to be used later on in a sauce for the meat. Second, the fact that they give up their flavors more slowly means that there is a steady, more even spicing of the marinade when long marinating times are used, thereby benefiting the meat flavoring. An unheated liquid would not extract enough flavor from such spices as whole black peppers, cloves, or mustard seeds in their whole natural form. Heating initiates the release of the spice flavor and from there on the spices continue to give up their flavor to the cold marinade as long as they are left in it.

WEIGHTS AND MEASURES; TABLES OF EQUIVALENTS

COMMONLY USED EQUIVALENT MEASURES

$\frac{1}{16}$ teaspoon	= ½ of ⅛ teaspoon
⅛ teaspoon	= ½ of ¼ teaspoon
3 teaspoons	= 1 tablespoon
1½ teaspoons	= ½ tablespoon
1 teaspoon	= ⅓ tablespoon
2 tablespoons	= ⅛ cup
4 tablespoons	= ¼ cup
5 tablespoons + 1 teaspoon	= ⅓ cup
8 tablespoons	= ½ cup
10 tablespoons + 2 teaspoons	= ⅔ cup
12 tablespoons	= ¾ cup
16 tablespoons	= 1 cup
2 cups	= 1 pint†
2 pints	= 1 quart†
4 quarts	= 1 gallon
32 ounces (liquid measure)	= 1 quart
16 ounces (avoirdupois weight)	= 1 pound

†Whether measuring liquids or solids, all references in this book to "pints" or "quarts" refer to U.S. Liquid Measure.

LIQUID MEASURES

These measures are used for all liquids and for small quantities of certain solids such as sugar, flour, and shortening. Most recipes call for these ingredients to be measured in teaspoons, tablespoons, and cups. These terms refer to the standard measuring tools made especially for this purpose and readily available in most American shops. The ordinary spoons and cups used for serving and eating vary greatly in capacity and should not be used for measuring purposes. Users living in other countries where these standard measures are not readily available may calibrate available measures with water, filling from a glass cylinder graduated in milliliters, obtainable from any chemical laboratory supply house. The equivalent capacities in milliliters are given in the following table. The spoons made of aluminum and the cups made of aluminum or glass usually are more reliable than are those made of plastic. Larger quantities of liquids are measured in graduated 1-pint and 1-quart measuring pitchers.

All measurements must be level. When measuring solids, such as sugar, the measure should first be overfilled and then leveled off flush with the top by means of a spatula or other straight edge. Flour should be sifted and then lightly spooned into the measuring cup without packing or compressing. Solid shortening may be measured by placing water in the measuring vessel and then adding shortening until the water rises to the proper level (i.e., to measure 1 cup of shortening, place 1 cup of water in a 2-cup measure and then add shortening until the water level rises to the top. Take care to shake out all water before adding to the mix). Liquids may be measured in transparent graduated vessels, filling to the proper line.

CONVERSION FACTORS
Liquid Measure Equivalents[1]

Common Measure	Fluid Ounces[2] (fl. oz.) (U.S.)	Milliliters[3] (ml.) (approx.)
1 teaspoon	⅙	5
1 tablespoon	½	15
1 cup	8	237
1 pint[4]	16	473
1 quart[4]	32	946
1 gallon[4]	128	3785

[1]In this book, the above measures are used for both liquids and solids.

[2]The British fluid ounce is approximately 4 per cent smaller than the U.S. fluid ounce. There are 40 British fluid ounces in a British quart, but only 32 U.S. ounces in a U.S. quart.

[3]1000 milliliters (ml.) = 1 liter = 35.20 fl. oz. (Brit.) = 33.815 fl. oz. (U.S.).

[4]The British Imperial pint, quart, and gallon each is approximately 20 per cent (⅕) larger than the corresponding U.S. measure. One British Imperial gallon of water at 62° F. weighs 10.00 pounds or 4.536 kilograms, while one U.S. gallon of water at 60° F. weighs 8.337 pounds or 3.782 kilograms. (One liter of water at 4° C. weighs 1 kilogram.)

Weight Equivalents

Avoirdupois		Grams (Metric)
1 ounce	=	28.35
1 pound	=	453.6
2.2046 pounds	=	1000.0 (1 kilogram)

Temperature Equivalents

Degrees Fahrenheit ° F.	Degrees Centigrade ° C.	Example or Common Term
Oven Temperatures		
225	107	Baking hard meringue
250 to 275	121 to 135	Very slow oven
300 to 325	149 to 163	Slow oven
350 to 375	177 to 191	Moderate oven
400 to 425	204 to 218	Hot oven
450 to 475	232 to 246	Very hot oven
Miscellaneous		
80 to 85	26.7 to 29.4	Yeast dough rises
98.6	37	Body temperature (lukewarm)
Reference Points		
32	0	Water freezes
212	100	Water boils

To Calculate Other Points

$$\tfrac{5}{9} \, (° F. - 32) = ° C.$$
$$\tfrac{9}{5} \, (° C.) + 32 = ° F.$$

Example (a): Given 140° F. To find corresponding ° C.
Solution: $140 - 32 = 108$. $108 \times \tfrac{5}{9} = \tfrac{540}{9} = 60$ (° C.).

Example (b): Given 60° C. To find corresponding ° F.
Solution: $\tfrac{9}{5} \, (60) = \tfrac{540}{5} = 108$. $108 + 32 = 140$ (° F.)

WEIGHTS AND MEASURES OF COMMON INGREDIENTS
(Given in Alphabetical Order)

Food and description	Measure	Weight	Comments
Almonds	1 cup	5½ oz.	
Apples, pared, diced	1 cup	3⅓ oz.	1 lb. as purchased makes 3 cups diced or sliced
Apricots, dried	1 cup	5⅓ oz.	1 lb. as purchased makes 5 cups cooked
Asparagus, fresh	16 to 20 stalks	1 lb.	
Bananas	3 medium	1 lb.	
Beans, snap *or* wax, cut in 1-inch pieces	3 cups	1 lb.	
Beets, cooked, diced	1 cup	½ lb.	
Bran, dry	1 cup	2 oz.	
Bread crumbs, fine, dry	1 cup	3¼ oz.	5 cups per lb.
Bread crumbs, soft, large	1 cup	1½ oz.	10 cups per lb.
Brussels sprouts	1 quart	1 lb.	
Butter *or* margarine	1 cup	½ lb.	1 stick butter weighs 4 oz.; measures ½ cup
Cabbage, raw, shredded	1 quart	1 lb.	
Carrots, diced *or* shredded	2½ cups	1 lb.	
Cheese, American, grated	1 cup	4 oz.	
Cheese, cottage	1 cup	½ lb.	
Cherries, candied, whole	1 cup	7 oz.	
Chocolate, bitter	1 square	1 oz.	
Citron, dried, sliced	1 cup	6½ oz.	
Cocoa	1 cup	4 oz.	
Coconut, shredded	1 cup	2¼ oz.	
Corn, cut from the cob	1 cup		4 med. ears
Corn meal	1 cup	5 oz.	
Cornstarch	1 cup	4½ oz.	
Cracker crumbs, fine	1 cup	2½ oz.	
Cranberries, uncooked	1 cup	4 oz.	
Cream, heavy *or* light	1 cup	½ lb.	Heavy cream doubles in bulk if whipped
Dates, dried, pitted, cut	1 cup	6 oz.	
Eggs, minus shell, whole, yolk *or* white	1 cup	8⅔ oz.	Large eggs, 8 to a pound, measure 5 whole per cup; 12 yolks per cup; 8 or 9 whites per cup
Fats, cooking, hydrogenated	1 cup	6⅔ oz.	
Fats, cooking, lard	1 cup	½ lb.	
Fats, liquid	1 cup	½ lb.	
Flour, cake	1 cup	3⅓ oz.	
Flour, wheat, sifted all-purpose	1 cup	4 oz.	

WEIGHTS AND MEASURES OF COMMON INGREDIENTS (Continued)
(Given in Alphabetical Order)

Food and description	Measure	Weight	Comments
Flour, whole-wheat	1 cup	7 oz.	
Ginger, crystallized, diced	1 cup	6 oz.	
Honey	1 cup	12 oz.	
Lard (*see* Fats)			
Lemons	1 medium	4 oz.	Yields about 2⅔ tbsps. juice
Macaroni, dry, 1-inch pieces	1 cup	4 oz.	After cooking measures generous 2 cups
Margarine (*see* Butter)			
Meat, ground, raw	1 cup	½ lb.	
Milk, sweet *or* sour, skimmed, buttermilk	1 cup	8⅔ oz.	
Molasses	1 cup	11½ oz.	
Mushrooms, raw, medium	35 to 45	1 lb.	
Noodles, dry, 1-inch pieces	1 cup	2⅔ oz.	1 lb. after cooking measures 9 cups
Oils (*see* Fats, liquid)			
Oranges, whole	1 medium	½ lb.	Should yield about ⅓ cup juice
Peaches, whole	1 medium	4 oz.	
Peanuts, shelled	1 cup	5 oz.	
Pears, whole	1 medium	4 oz.	
Pecans, halved	1 cup	3¾ oz.	Allow 3 lbs. pecans in shell to yield 1 lb. meats
Potatoes, white	3 medium	1 lb.	2½ cups peeled and diced
Raisins, seeded	1 cup	5 oz.	
Raisins, seedless	1 cup	5¾ oz.	
Rice, uncooked	1 cup	7 oz.	1 lb. after cooking measures 8 cups
Spaghetti, dry, 2-inch pieces	1 cup	3⅓ oz.	1 lb. after cooking measures 10 cups
Sugar, brown (firmly packed)	1 cup	7 oz.	
Sugar, confectioners'	1 cup	4½ oz.	
Sugar, granulated	1 cup	7 oz.	
Syrup, corn	1 cup	11½ oz.	
Syrup, maple	1 cup	11 oz.	
Tapioca, quick-cooking	3 tbsp.	1 oz.	
Walnuts, shelled halves	1 cup	3½ oz.	

MENUS FOR
SPECIAL OCCASIONS

"To roast some beef, to carve a joint with neatness,
To boil up sauces, and to blow the fire,
Is anybody's task; he who does this
Is but a seasoner and broth-maker.
A cook is quite another thing. His mind
Must comprehend all facts and circumstances;
Where is the place, and what the time of supper;
Who are the guests, and who the entertainer;
What fish he ought to buy, and where to buy it."
—DIONYSIUS

TEEN AGE PARTY
Tomato Juice
Onion Sour Cream Dip*
Celery   Carrot Sticks
Radishes   Assorted Crackers
Chili-Size*
Lettuce   Sliced Tomatoes   Cole Slaw
Ice Cream with Chocolate Sauce*
Assorted Cupcakes*
Cola Beverages
Milk

TEEN AGE BUFFET
Chili Potato Soup*
Italian Bread Sticks*
Puerto Rican Pizza*
Grape, Cabbage, and Apple Salad*
Cole Slaw
Lazy Daisy Chocolate Cake*
Assorted Fruit Tray
Hot Spiced Fruit Punch*
Cola Beverages

SUNDAY SUPPER (I)
Herbed Stuffed Egg with Asparagus*
Sliced Tomatoes and Cucumbers
Grilled Shrimp Sandwich*
Ham Sandwich
Five Spice Gingerbread*
Lemon Sauce*
Coffee   Tea   Milk

SUNDAY SUPPER (II)
Tomato and Pea Soup*
Carrot Sticks   Chili Croutons*
Cheese Stuffed Pear Salad*
Quick Poppy Seed Crescents*
Grated Fresh Apple Snow*
Oatmeal Crispies*
Coffee   Tea   Milk

BUFFET SUPPER
Cocktails
Sour Cream Clam Dip*
Crabmeat Bouchées
Assorted Vegetable Nibblers
Arroz con Pollo*
Tossed Lettuce, Avocado,
and Pink Grapefruit Salad
Caraway Seed French Bread
Pumpkin Flan* or Molded
Coconut Pudding*
Ginger Wafers*
Coffee

BUFFET LUNCHEON
Gaspacho
Crabmeat Fondue*
Fresh Asparagus with
Mustard Hollandaise Sauce
Sesame Seed Sally Lunn Bread*   Butter
Frozen Creamy Lemon Pie*
Iced Tea   Iced or Hot Coffee

BUFFET SUPPER
Cocktails
Chopped Chicken Livers on Crackers*
Bleu Cheese-Onion Dip
Carrot Sticks   Cauliflowerets
Apple Slices
Veal Paprikash*
Rice
Fresh Asparagus and Peas,
French Style*
Romaine Salad Chiffonade
Quick Poppy Seed Crescents*
Orange Trifle*
Assorted Fresh Fruit and Cheese Tray
Coffee

COMPANY DINNER
Fresh Fruit Cocktail
Marinated Short Ribs of Beef*
Savory New Potatoes*
Brussels Sprouts Almondine
Belgian Endive   Caviar Dressing*
Onion French Bread*
Bay-Roc Coconut Pudding*
Cream and Brandy Sauce*
Coffee

COMPANY LUNCHEON
Honeydew Melon
Chicken, Chinese Style*
Rice
Snap Beans with Almond Browned Butter
Avocado and Orange Salad*
Anise French Dressing*
Hot Parker House Rolls   Butter
Ginger Ice Cream*
Anise Cookies*
Coffee

AFTER-THE-GAME SUPPER
Green Goddess Avocado Dip*
Relish Tray (Assorted Vegetable
Sticks, Olives, and Pickles)
Chili Con Carne Cheese Balls*
Mixed Vegetable Salad with
Creamy French Dressing*
Garlic French Bread*
Apple Pie*
Assorted Cheese Tray with Crackers
Coffee   Spiced Rum Cider*
Mints   Salted Nuts

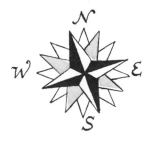

BUFFET SUPPER
Rosemary Gin Pineappleade*
Chili Pecan Rolls*
Beaten Biscuit Ham Puffs*
Oven Company Stew*
Pickled Navy Beans*
Fresh Orange and Onion Salad*
Herbed Italian Bread*
Old-Fashioned Devil's Food Cake*
Lemon Cream*
Coffee

BRIDAL SHOWER BUFFET
Reception Punch*
Chicken Salad*
Spiced Fruit Salad Mold*
Sour Cream Dressing
Cheese Stuffed Celery
Quick Poppy Seed Crescents*
Butter Balls   Strawberry Jam
Molded Ice Cream Wedding Bells
Wedding Ring Cake*
Coffee   Tea

COMPANY BREAKFAST
Fresh Fruit in Season
Sausage
Apple Pancakes*
Butter   Maple Syrup
Coffee

BRUNCH
Gingered Cantaloupe *or*
Honeydew Melon*
Canadian Bacon
Swiss Eggs*
Cinnamon Pinwheel Biscuits*
Butter
Spiced Peach and Pineapple Marmalade*
Coffee

BACKYARD BARBECUE

Herbed Beef Kebabs*
Frankfurter Rolls
Corn on the Cob
Assorted Corn Butters*
Hearty Vegetable Salad*
Sliced Tomatoes   Cucumber Slices
Green Onions
Two-Crust Blueberry Pie*
Assorted Fresh Fruit in Season
Coffee   Iced Tea

PICNIC

Curried Fried Chicken*
Sour Cream Potato Salad*
Cajun Stuffed Eggs*
Tomato Wedges   Carrot Sticks
Celery
Buttered Rolls
Coconut-Pineapple Cake*
Assorted Fresh Fruit
Rhubarb Punch*   Coffee

THANKSGIVING DINNER

(NEW ENGLAND)

New England Clam Bisque*
Toasted Paprika Crackers
Roast Turkey*
Oyster Stuffing*   Giblet Gravy*
Seasoned Mashed Potatoes*
Snap Beans with Nutmeg Butter*
Rutabaga or Turnip Pudding*
Spiced Cranberry Catsup*
Sliced Cucumber and Onion Pickle*
Poached Apple Wedges*
Parker House Rolls
Mince Pie
Molasses Pumpkin Pie*
Fresh Fruit Bowl   Nuts
Coffee   Apple Cider

THANKSGIVING DINNER

(SOUTHERN)

Shrimp Cocktail*
Celery Hearts   Olives   Radishes
Roast Turkey*
Corn Bread Stuffing*   Giblet Gravy*
Rice   Buttered Peas
Sherried Sweet Potatoes*
Apple, Cabbage, and Pineapple Salad
Corn Pudding*
Tart Cranberry-Orange Sauce*
Spiced Fresh Peaches*
Hot Rolls or Biscuits
Old-Fashioned Pumpkin Pie*
Spiced Georgia Pecan Pie*
Fresh Fruit and Nut Tray
Coffee

THANKSGIVING or COMPANY DINNER

Fresh Grapefruit with Crème de Menthe
Baked Cornish Hens with
Sweet Potato-Sausage Stuffing*
Wild Rice
Cranberry and Apple Relish*
Mushroom Sauté*
Herbed Creamed Brussels Sprouts*
Clover Leaf Rolls   Butter
Assorted Fresh Vegetable
Sticks with Olives
Spiced Chiffon Pumpkin Pie*
Coffee

THANKSGIVING SUPPER
Apple Cider*
Caraway *or* Herbed Cheese Pot*
Crackers
Cold Turkey Sandwiches with
Horseradish-Cranberry Sauce
Anise Fruit Compote*
Orange-Coconut Cookies*
Coffee

HALLOWE'EN BUFFET
Spiced Glazed Ham*
Mustard Baked Lima Beans*
Tossed Green Salad
Sliced Tomatoes
Praline Pumpkin Pie*
Apple Cider
Coffee

HALLOWE'EN REFRESHMENTS
Assorted Party Sandwiches*
Doughnuts
Pumpkin Spice Cake*
Hallowe'en Candies
Spiced Cashew Nuts*
Hot Spiced Orange Tea*
Coffee

GRADUATION BUFFET
Lemon Beer Punch*
Tarragon Chicken*
Turkish Pilaf*
Fresh Asparagus and Peas, French Style*
Celery Hearts   Carrot Curls
Cucumber Slices
Olives   Ginger Pears*   Radishes
Onion French Bread*
Vanilla Ice Cream
Diploma Roll*
(Cinnamon-Chocolate Sponge Roll)
Iced Tea   Coffee

NEW YEAR'S EVE SUPPER
Cheese Soufflé Sandwich*
Cold Sliced Ham
Cold Sliced Turkey
Cranberry Stuffed Pears*
Brown and Serve Poppy Seed Rolls*
Frozen Plum Pudding*
Christmas Cookies*
Fruit Cake*
Coffee

CHRISTMAS DINNER
(SOUTHERN)
Clear Tomato Soup with Sippets
Assorted Raw Vegetable Tray with
Olives and Cucumber Pickles
Roast Turkey*
Chestnut-Sausage Stuffing*
Rice   Giblet Gravy*
Spiced Sweet Potato Puffs*
String Beans with Poppy Seed Butter*
Herbed Fresh Beets*
Tressa's Watermelon Rind Pickles*
Molded Cranberry Salad*
Hot Cinnamon Yeast Rolls*
Ambrosia
Assorted Christmas Cakes*
Fresh Fruit and Nut Tray
Coffee

EGGNOG PARTY (I)
Assorted Canapés*
Christmas Cookies*   Fruit Cake*
Southern Eggnog*   Coffee
Christmas Candies
Spiced Cashew Nuts

EGGNOG PARTY (II)
Southern Eggnog*
Christmas Cookies*   Fruit Cake*
Coffee
Mints   Salted Nuts

CHRISTMAS or COMPANY DINNER

Spiced Cranberry Juice*

Carrot Curls   Cucumber Sticks

Radishes   Celery Hearts

Spiced Jelly Baked Ham*

Curried Grape Sauce*

Potatoes au Gratin

Herbed Fresh Peas*

Herbed Fresh Mushrooms*

Spiced Fresh Pear Pickles*

My Best Mustard Pickle*

Hot Rolls   Onion Corn Sticks*

Steamed Holiday Pudding*

Brandy Hard Sauce*

Coffee

CHRISTMAS DINNER

New England Clear Vegetable Soup*

Croutons

Stuffed Roast Suckling Pig*

Suckling Pig Gravy*

Herbed Potato Puffs*

Gingered Carrots*

Spiced Apple Wedges*

Broccoli with Browned

Butter Sesame Sauce*

Jellied Cranberry Sauce

Celery   Turnip Sticks   Radishes

Stollen*   Corn Muffins

Baked Indian Pudding

with Whipped Cream*

Fresh Fruit Tray   Assorted Nuts

Coffee

INDEX